Financial Accounting
An Introduction

Visit the *Financial Accounting: An Introduction*, Second Edition, Companion Website at **www.pearsoned.co.uk/benedict** to find valuable **student** learning material including:

- Detailed worked solutions for over 800 multiple choice questions featured within the book.

Financial Accounting
An Introduction

Second Edition

Augustine Benedict

Formerly London South Bank University,
now London College of Accountancy

Barry Elliott

Formerly Brighton University

Financial Times
Prentice Hall
is an imprint of

Harlow, England • London • New York • Boston • San Francisco • Toronto • Sydney • Singapore • Hong Kong
Tokyo • Seoul • Taipei • New Delhi • Cape Town • Madrid • Mexico City • Amsterdam • Munich • Paris • Milan

Pearson Education Limited

Edinburgh Gate
Harlow
Essex CM20 2JE
England

and Associated Companies throughout the world

Visit us on the World Wide Web at:
www.pearsoned.co.uk

First published 2008
Second edition published 2011

ISBN: 978-0-273-73765-0

British Library Cataloguing-in-Publication Data
A catalogue record for this book is available from the British Library

Library of Congress Cataloging-in-Publication Data
Benedict, Augustine.
Financial accounting : an introduction / Augustine Benedict, Barry Elliott. — 2nd ed.
p. cm.
Rev. ed. of: Financial accounting : an introduction. 2008.
Includes bibliographical references and index.
ISBN 978-0-273-73765-0
1. Accounting. 2. Financial statements. I. Elliott, Barry. II. Title.
HF5636.B46 2011
657–dc22
2010036352

10 9 8 7 6 5 4 3
15 14 13 12

Typeset in 9/12pt Stone Serif by 35
Printed and bound by Ashford Colour Press, Gosport

Contents in brief

Supporting resources

Visit **www.pearsoned.co.uk/benedict** to find valuable online resources:

Companion Website for students:

- Detailed worked solutions for over 800 multiple choice questions featured within the book.

For instructors:

- Downloadable PowerPoint slides for use in lessons and lectures.
- Detailed solutions to test questions from the text, designed for use as overhead slides.
- Customisable multiple choice questions, ideal for testing and revision.

Also: The Companion Website provides the following features:

- Search tool to help locate specific items of content.
- Online help and support to assist with website usage and troubleshooting.

For more information, please contact your local Pearson Education sales representative or visit **www.pearsoned.co.uk/benedict**.

Contents in detail

Acknowledgements

Author acknowledgements

We are indebted to Matthew Smith, Robin Lupton, and Georgina Clark-Mazo of Pearson Education for their active support in keeping us largely to schedule and the attractively produced and presented text.

We are grateful for the support and tolerance shown by our wives, Doris and Diana, throughout this project.

Publisher acknowledgements

We are grateful to the following for permission to reproduce copyright material:

The Association of Accounting Technicians for questions from AAT examination papers; the Association of Chartered Certified Accountants (ACCA) for questions from ACCA and CAT (Certified Accounting Technician) examination papers; Edexcel for a question from an Edexcel examination paper; the University of Oxford; the Chartered Institute of Management Accountants (CIMA) for questions from CIMA examination papers; the Institute of Chartered Secretaries and Administrators (ICSA) for a question from an ICSA examination paper; the Northern Ireland Council for the Curriculum, Examinations and Assessment for a question from a CCEA examination paper; the Welsh Joint Education Committee (WJEC) for questions from a WJEC examination paper.

In some instances we have been unable to trace the owners of copyright material and we would appreciate any information that would enable us to do so.

Guided tour

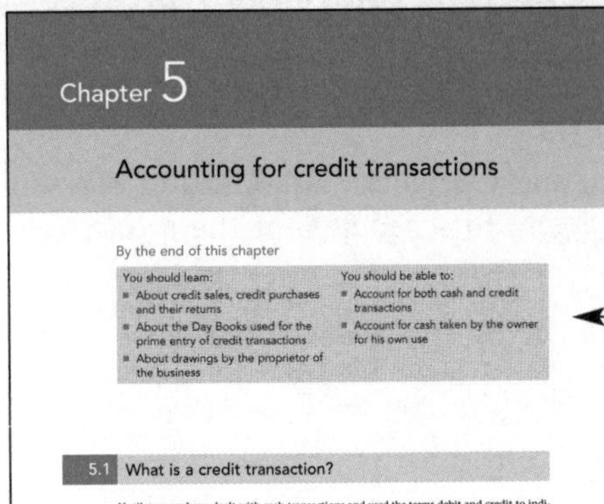

Chapter 5

Accounting for credit transactions

By the end of this chapter

You should learn:	You should be able to:
■ About credit sales, credit purchases and their returns ■ About the Day Books used for the prime entry of credit transactions ■ About drawings by the proprietor of the business	■ Account for both cash and credit transactions ■ Account for cash taken by the owner for his own use

5.1 What is a credit transaction?

Until now we have dealt with cash transactions and used the terms debit and credit to indicate the left and right side of a ledger account. We now use the term credit giving it its everyday meaning, i.e. getting something without having to pay for it immediately. In a business the word credit is used also with the same meaning. The word is derived from the Latin word *credere* which means trust. In business then, a *credit sale* is a sale accepting on trust the customer's willingness and ability to pay later. This is not blind trust, of course, and routine steps are taken to establish the extent to which a particular customer may be trusted. These steps include:

- checking on *creditworthiness* by obtaining references,
- setting a *credit limit* by advising the customer of the maximum amount (say £3,000) that could be bought before payment is required, and
- agreeing a *credit period*, i.e. the length of time (say 30 days) allowed before payment is required.

Just as a business can sell on credit, it can also buy goods from its suppliers on credit. These are referred to as *credit purchases* and the supplier would take similar credit check steps before agreeing to supply goods.

Chapter objectives outline what you will learn from reading the chapter, and the new skills you can acquire.

Activities within each chapter give you the chance to check your learning and test your understanding. Suggested answers to activities can be found at the end of the chapter.

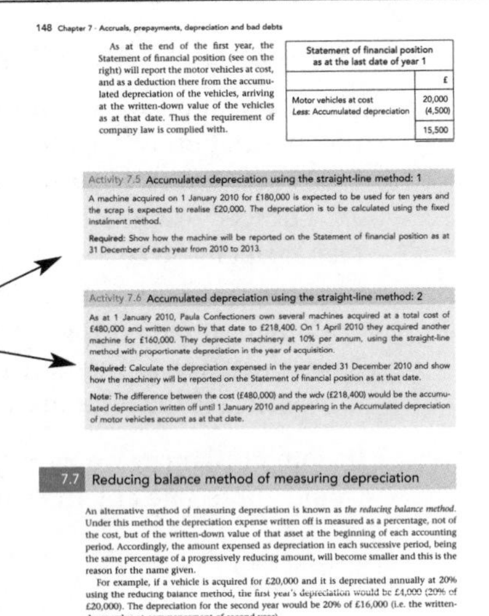

148 Chapter 7 · Accruals, prepayments, depreciation and bad debts

As at the end of the first year, the Statement of financial position (see on the right) will report the motor vehicles at cost, and as a deduction there from the accumulated depreciation of the vehicles, arriving at the written-down value of the vehicles as at that date. Thus the requirement of company law is complied with.

Statement of financial position as at the last date of year 1	
	£
Motor vehicles at cost	20,000
Less: Accumulated depreciation	(4,500)
	15,500

Activity 7.5 **Accumulated depreciation using the straight-line method: 1**

A machine acquired on 1 January 2010 for £180,000 is expected to be used for ten years and the scrap is expected to realise £20,000. The depreciation is to be calculated using the fixed instalment method.

Required: Show how the machine will be reported on the Statement of financial position as at 31 December of each year from 2010 to 2013.

Activity 7.6 **Accumulated depreciation using the straight-line method: 2**

As at 1 January 2010, Paula Confectioners own several machines acquired at a total cost of £480,000 and written down by that date to £218,400. On 1 April 2010 they acquired another machine for £160,000. They depreciate machinery at 10% per annum, using the straight-line method with proportionate depreciation in the year of acquisition.

Required: Calculate the depreciation expensed in the year ended 31 December 2010 and show how the machinery will be reported on the Statement of financial position as at that date.

Note: The difference between the cost (£480,000) and the wdv (£218,400) would be the accumulated depreciation written off until 1 January 2010 and appearing in the Accumulated depreciation of motor vehicles account as at that date.

7.7 Reducing balance method of measuring depreciation

An alternative method of measuring depreciation is known as *the reducing balance method*. Under this method the depreciation expense written off is measured as a percentage, not of the cost, but of the written-down value of that asset at the beginning of each accounting period. Accordingly, the amount expensed as depreciation in each successive period, being the same percentage of a progressively reducing amount, will become smaller and this is the reason for the name given.

For example, if a vehicle is acquired for £20,000 and it is depreciated annually at 20% using the reducing balance method, the first year's depreciation would be £4,000 (20% of £20,000). The depreciation for the second year would be 20% of £16,000 (i.e. the written-down value at commencement of second year).

References 239

Summary

- Most businesses of any significant size in the UK are limited liability companies.
- Operating as a limited company brings many advantages as well as some disadvantages.
- Limited companies can be of two types – public (plc) and private (Ltd) – the latter suffer from some restrictions but enjoy some concessions. Some of the public companies may be listed.
- Limited companies raise finance by issuing shares and loan notes (debentures).
- At any point of time the Share capital account reports the so far called-up value (until that point) of the number of shares in issue.
- If amount received on issue of shares is more than the par value, the excess must be stated as Share premium, which may be used only for a bonus issue or to write off expenses on issuing the same shares.
- Financial statements must be prepared both for internal use and for publication.
- Financial statements prepared for publication should be in the prescribed format.
- Additional disclosures are required of items such as directors' remuneration.
- Tax expense in an accounting period could include, in addition to current tax, adjustment for any under-provision or over-provision in previous year as well as deferred tax.
- Correction of prior period errors and impact of changes in accounting policy on performance in prior periods are shown in the Statement of changes in equity as adjustments from retained earnings brought forward.
- Ordinary dividends paid or declared are reported in the Statement of changes in equity, whereas final dividend proposed is only reported as a note.
- Dividends to preference shares are always included in the Statement of income, ordinarily after tax, but before tax in the event the preference shares are redeemable.
- The Statement of comprehensive income is a Statement of income with additional information included for drawing attention to the total comprehensive income recognised in the accounting period.
- A Statement of changes in equity needs to be published. It may be prepared either in the short format (tracing changes in the Retained earnings only) or in an extended format (tracing changes that have taken place during the year in the Share capital account as well in every one of the reserves).

References

1. Companies Act 2006, section 7 & 8, effective from 1 October 2009, London, The Stationery Office.
2. *The Combined Code on Corporate Governance*, 2006, London, Financial Reporting Council.
3. Companies Act 2006, section 762, London, The Stationery Office.
4. Companies Act 2006, section 59, 271 & 336, London, The Stationery Office.
5. *Henry v Great Northern Railway Company* (1857), 1 De G and J 606.
6. Companies Act 2006, section 542, London, The Stationery Office.
7. The Gedge Committee Report, 1954, Gedge Committee, Cmd 9112, London, HMSO, http://www.bopcris.ac.uk/bopall/ref9192.html.
8. Companies Act 2006, section 610, London, The Stationery Office.
9. IAS 12 *Income Taxes*, issued in 1979, amended in December 2003, London, International Accounting Standards Board.

Chapter summaries are bullet-pointed lists of the key concepts in the chapter – ideal for revision and for testing yourself.

References are provided at the end of the chapter to help you take your learning further.

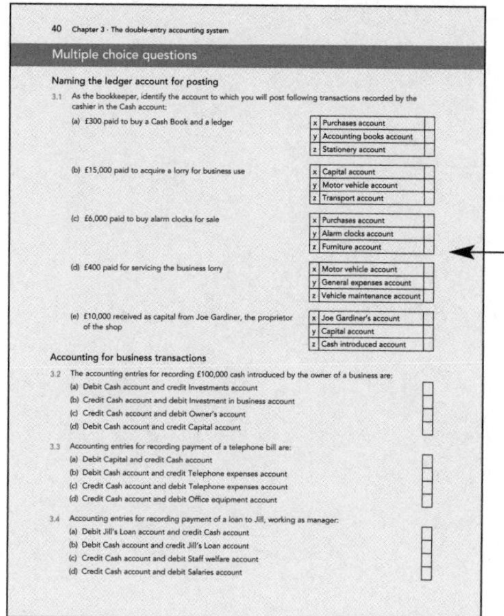

40 Chapter 3 · The double-entry accounting system

Multiple choice questions

Naming the ledger account for posting

3.1 As the bookkeeper, identify the account to which you will post following transactions recorded by the cashier in the Cash account:

(a) £300 paid to buy a Cash Book and a ledger

x	Purchases account	
y	Accounting books account	
z	Stationery account	

(b) £15,000 paid to acquire a lorry for business use

x	Capital account	
y	Motor vehicle account	
z	Transport account	

(c) £6,000 paid to buy alarm clocks for sale

x	Purchases account	
y	Alarm clocks account	
z	Furniture account	

(d) £400 paid for servicing the business lorry

x	Motor vehicle account	
y	General expenses account	
z	Vehicle maintenance account	

(e) £10,000 received as capital from Joe Gardiner, the proprietor of the shop

x	Joe Gardiner's account	
y	Capital account	
z	Cash introduced account	

Accounting for business transactions

3.2 The accounting entries for recording £100,000 cash introduced by the owner of a business are:
(a) Debit Cash account and credit Investments account
(b) Credit Cash account and debit Investment in business account
(c) Credit Cash account and debit Owner's account
(d) Debit Cash account and credit Capital account

3.3 Accounting entries for recording payment of a telephone bill are:
(a) Debit Capital and credit Cash account
(b) Debit Cash account and credit Telephone expenses account
(c) Credit Cash account and debit Telephone expenses account
(d) Credit Cash account and debit Office equipment account

3.4 Accounting entries for recording payment of a loan to Jill, working as manager:
(a) Debit Jill's Loan account and credit Cash account
(b) Debit Cash account and credit Jill's Loan account
(c) Credit Cash account and debit Staff welfare account
(d) Credit Cash account and debit Salaries account

Multiple choice questions: An extensive selection of questions, ranging from the general to the specific, are found in the majority of chapters. A set of suggested answers to these Activity questions is provided at the end of the chapter and detailed solutions are available on the Companion Website. These are also provided as an Instructor Resource in a format suitable for revision or test purposes.

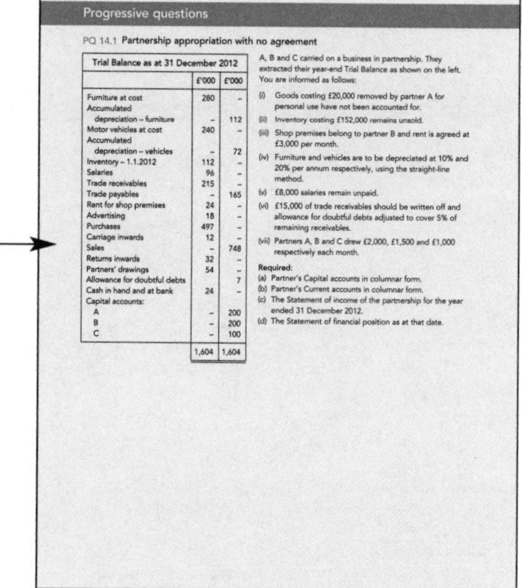

438 Chapter 14 · Accounting for partnerships

Progressive questions

PQ 14.1 **Partnership appropriation with no agreement**

Trial Balance as at 31 December 2012		
	£'000	£'000
Furniture at cost	280	–
Accumulated depreciation – furniture	–	112
Motor vehicles at cost	240	–
Accumulated depreciation – vehicles	–	72
Inventory – 1.1.2012	112	–
Salaries	96	–
Trade receivables	215	–
Trade payables	–	165
Rent for shop premises	24	–
Advertising	18	–
Purchases	497	–
Carriage inwards	12	–
Sales	–	748
Returns inwards	32	–
Partners' drawings	54	–
Allowance for doubtful debts		7
Cash in hand and at bank	24	–
Capital accounts:		
A	–	200
B	–	200
C	–	100
	1,604	1,604

A, B and C carried on a business in partnership. They extracted their year-end Trial Balance as shown on the left. You are informed as follows:

(i) Goods costing £20,000 removed by partner A for personal use have not been accounted for.
(ii) Inventory costing £152,000 remains unsold.
(iii) Shop premises belong to partner B and rent is agreed at £3,000 per month.
(iv) Furniture and vehicles are to be depreciated at 10% and 20% per annum respectively, using the straight-line method.
(v) £8,000 salaries remain unpaid.
(vi) £15,000 of trade receivables should be written off and allowance for doubtful debts adjusted to cover 5% of remaining receivables.
(vii) Partners A, B and C drew £2,000, £1,500 and £1,000 respectively each month.

Required:
(a) Partner's Capital accounts in columnar form.
(b) Partner's Current accounts in columnar form.
(c) The Statement of income of the partnership for the year ended 31 December 2012.
(d) The Statement of financial position as at that date.

Progressive questions at the end of each chapter provide a range of more advanced exercises, similar to exam questions. Suggested answers for all Progressive questions are provided at the end of the book.

352 Chapter 12 · Accounting ratios and interpretation of financial statements

Test questions

Test 12.1 **A comprehensive question on ratio analysis**

The financial statements for the current year (2011) and the preceding one are summarised below:

Statements of financial position as at 30 September		
2010		2011
£		£
	Non-current assets:	
70,000	Premises	150,000
65,000	Plant and equipment	162,000
135,000		312,000
	Current assets:	
51,200	Inventory	85,300
29,700	Trade receivables	55,700
15,600	Cash and bank	3,500
96,500		144,500
231,500		456,500
£		£
100,000	Share capital £1 each	120,000
25,000	Share premium account	30,000
36,000	Retained earnings	50,600
161,000		200,600
	Non-current liability	
–	7% Loan notes	100,000
	Current liabilities:	
52,300	Trade payables	131,100
18,200	Taxation	24,800
231,500		456,500

Statement of income for year to 30 September		
2010		2011
£		£
386,400	Sales	764,200
29,600	Inventory on 1.10.	51,200
310,720	Purchases	682,400
(31,200)	Inventory on 30.9.	(85,300)
(309,120)	Cost of sales	(648,300)
77,280	Gross profit	115,900
(43,400)	Admin. expenses	(37,650)
(14,680)	Distribution cost	(24,650)
–	Interest	(7,000)
19,200	Profit before tax	46,600
(4,600)	Taxation	(20,000)
14,600		26,600

You are required to comment on:
(a) the profitability
(b) the liquidity
(c) the operational performance and
(d) the capital structure of Burstow Ltd, supporting your answer with pertinent accounting ratios.

Test 12.2 **Working capital cycle (ACCA 1.1)**

(a) Explain the meaning of the term 'working capital cycle' for a trading company.
(b) Calculate the working capital cycle in days from the information provided on the right.
(c) State one advantage to a business of keeping its working capital cycle as short as possible.

	£'000	£'000
Sales (all on credit)		1,000
Less:		
Opening inventory	100	
Purchases	800	
Closing inventory	(200)	(700)
Gross profit		300
Receivables at year end		250
Payables at year end		150

Test questions are provided at the end of chapters. Detailed solutions to all Test questions are provided in Word format as an Instructor Resource.

Part A

THE FINANCIAL ACCOUNTING SYSTEM

Chapter 1

The need for accounting

By the end of this chapter

You should learn:

- What financial accounting is
- Why a business keeps accounting records and prepares financial statements

You should be able to:

- Prepare a statement of financial position for a sequence of transactions and a statement of income
- Identify who needs accounting information
- Appreciate the need for International Financial Reporting Standards

1.1 What is financial accounting?

Financial accounting involves two related functions – the recording of transactions and the preparation of financial statements. A *transaction* is any activity involving money. Running, dancing and taking a bath are all activities. Such activities become a transaction in accounting terms only if there is a payment involved.

1.1.1 Recording of transactions

A business engages in numerous transactions, such as when it buys and sells goods and pays rent and salaries. The transactions are recorded in books of account and this recording is referred to as *bookkeeping*. The name came from the fact that, before the use of computer accounting packages, the records were kept manually in books. Nowadays, even the smallest business might be using a computer accounting package, but the accounting principles and procedures that we explain in this text will apply to all recording of transactions – whether the recording is done manually in a book or using a computer package.

1.1.2 The preparation of financial statements

At regular intervals the information recorded in books of account is summarised and presented in reports, referred to as *financial statements*. One of the financial statements is a

Statement of financial position which is also known as a balance sheet – this shows the resources that a business controls, how it obtained those resources and how it has used them. Another financial statement is the *Statement of income* which shows how much has been earned – in accounting we refer to earnings as *income or revenue*, and the costs incurred to earn this income as *expenses*.

1.2 The Statement of financial position

A Statement of financial position consists of two separate parts.

- The first identifies the resources controlled by the business, for example the business premises, office equipment, goods for sale and cash – these are known as *assets*.
- The second identifies the source of the funds that were used to acquire the assets – these would normally have been provided by the owner of the business and others such as the bank and suppliers. Funds provided by the owner are known as *capital* and those provided by others are known as *liabilities*.

1.3 The impact of transactions on the Statement of financial position

We will prepare a succession of Statements of financial position tracing the effect on it of each of six transactions.

Transaction one: Noel commences in business introducing £200,000 as his capital. A Statement of financial position drawn at this point (see on the right) reports on its first section as asset cash amounting to £200,000 and reports on its second section the source of that asset as Capital. Observe that the total of the first part (£200,000) is the same as the total of the second.

Statement of financial position as at xxxx	
Assets:	£
Cash	200,000
	200,000
Capital:	£
Capital	200,000
	200,000

Transaction two: the business pays £125,000 to acquire shop premises. This transaction reduces one asset (cash) and replaces it by another (premises). There are now two assets listed on the first part but its total remains the same as that of the second.

Statement of financial position as at xxxx	
Assets:	£
Premises	125,000
Cash	75,000
	200,000
Capital:	£
Capital	200,000
	200,000

Transaction three: the business obtains a bank loan of £100,000. The loan increases the cash held by the business so that the total of its assets increases to £300,000. These resources held by the business have come from two sources – one is capital provided by the owner and the other an amount obtained from the bank as a loan which we refer to as liability. The total of the resources held by the business (£300,000) remains the same as the total of the items listed on the second part as capital and liability.

Statement of financial position as at xxxxx	
Assets:	£
Premises	125,000
Cash	175,000
	300,000
Capital and liability:	£
Capital	200,000
Bank loan	100,000
	300,000

Transaction four: the business pays £90,000 to buy goods for sale. These goods are referred to as *inventory* and they are listed on the first part as another asset. But the cash held by the business is reduced, by the amount paid, so that the total of the resources available to the business (assets) remains £300,000. The sources of these assets listed on the second part also add up to the same amount.

Statement of financial position as at xxxxx	
Assets:	£
Premises	125,000
Inventory	90,000
Cash (175 – 90)	85,000
	300,000
Capital and liability:	£
Capital	200,000
Bank loan	100,000
	300,000

Transaction five: the business sells for £80,000 some of the goods for which it had paid £50,000. The sale increases cash by £80,000, but the inventory decreases by only £50,000. As a result the total of the assets increases to £330,000 i.e. an improvement of £30,000. Such improvement is referred to as *profit*. Sale is the way a business earns and such earning is referred to as *income*. The earning has been at a cost (i.e. giving away inventory which cost £50). Costs suffered in the earning process are referred to as *expense*. The amount by which income (£80,000) exceeds expense (£50,000) is the *profit*.

The Statement of financial position lists the assets on the first part, amounting in all to £330,000, and lists the sources on the second part as capital, profit and the loan from the bank.

Statement of financial position as at xxxxx	
Assets:	£
Premises	125,000
Inventory (90 – 50)	40,000
Cash (85 + 80)	165,000
	330,000
Capital and liability:	£
Capital	200,000
Profit	30,000
Bank loan	100,000
	330,000

Transaction six: the business pays £18,000 to its staff as salary. The payment reduces the cash so that the total of the assets held by the business is now reduced to £312,000. Salary is another expense incurred in the earning process and needs to be offset from the income identifying the profit as £12,000 (i.e. £30,000 – £18,000). Thus the total of sources listed on the second part of the Statement of financial position remains the same as the total of its assets listed on the first part.

Statement of financial position as at xxxx	
Assets:	£
Premises	125,000
Inventory (90 – 50)	40,000
Cash (85 + 80 – 18)	147,000
	312,000
Capital and liability:	£
Capital	200,000
Profit (30 – 18)	12,000
Bank loan	100,000
	312,000

With these six transactions we have illustrated one of the key features of a Statement of financial position – that is that the total of the assets will always equal the total of the capital and liabilities.

In real life a business prepares a Statement of financial position only on the last day of an *accounting period* – this can be at the end of a month, quarter, half-year or, as is common, a year.

1.4 The Statement of income

The Statement of income is a report stating the earnings of a business within an accounting period and comparing them with its expenses to identify whether it made a profit during the period (if income is more than the expenses) or a loss (if otherwise). Assuming that Noel's business had only six transactions in the accounting period, its Statement of income would appear as shown on the right. The amount by which sales exceeds the cost of what was sold is referred to as *gross profit*. All other expenses are deducted from gross profit to identify the *net profit* in the period.

Statement of income for year ended xxx	£
Sales	80,000
Cost of goods sold	(50,000)
Gross profit	30,000
Expenses	(18,000)
Net profit	12,000

Activity 1.1 The resources of a business and their sources

Let us assume that a business commenced by Albert had only a single transaction each day, as listed below:

Day one: Albert introduced £100,000 in cash as his capital
Day two: the business borrowed £200,000 from a bank
Day three: the business paid £180,000 for items of furniture
Day four: the business paid £90,000 to buy goods for sale
Day five: the business sold for £75,000 goods it had bought for £50,000
Day six: the business paid £2,000 as salary and £3,000 as other expenses
Day seven: the business paid £65,000 to buy more goods for sale
Day eight: the business repaid £30,000 of the bank loan

Required: identify the resources used and their sources on each of the eight days.

1.5 Why does a business need to keep accounting records?

There are many reasons, and the main ones depend on whether the business is operated by a sole trader, a partnership or a company.

A *sole trader* refers to a situation where a single person owns a business. It is usual for tradesmen such as electricians and plumbers to carry on their business as sole traders. With the growth of the Internet, there are many who carry on web-based businesses as sole traders. To identify why these sole traders need to keep accounting records let us focus on the needs of a coffee shop proprietor – let us call her Mary Latte. Like many sole traders, Mary may have the following reasons for keeping accounting records:

1. To prevent cash and other assets such as property, vehicles and inventory from being stolen or improperly used.
2. To monitor the cash available to the business, checking whether there is enough to pay bills on time.
3. To keep checking whether the business is doing well – that is whether there is sufficient reason for continuing to carry on with the business.
4. To satisfy the tax inspectors.

There are, of course, many more reasons. For instance, if Mary's Coffee Shop buys milk from The Jersey Farm on an agreement to pay at monthly intervals, Mary needs accounting records so that she knows how much to pay The Jersey Farm.

Activity 1.2 Further reasons why a business keeps accounting records

Stated above are some reasons why a business carried on by a sole trader would keep accounting records of its transactions. Can you identify two more reasons?

A *partnership* is a business owned by more than one person. If, for example, Mary and her sister Anne owned the Coffee Shop this would be known as a partnership. In addition to the reasons listed above, accounting records are essential for partners to be confident that they are each receiving their fair share of any profit. Maintaining accurate accounts is essential also to avoid disputes and possible litigation. Many professions carry on business as partnerships, e.g. solicitors, doctors, chiropodists and auditors.

A *limited company* is a business carried on by an entity that has been legally registered as a limited liability company. If Mary and her sister decide to operate their business as a limited company, they have to choose an appropriate name – say Mary's Coffee Shop Limited – and apply to the Registrar of Companies for registration, submitting certain legally required documents. Upon registration, Mary and Anne (who own the company) would be known as shareholders and would provide the money (referred to as *share capital*) for the company to operate. Either one (or both of them) will have to take responsibility for managing the business and that one (or both) will be known as the *director*(s). A significant advantage of running the business as a company is that, should the business fail and is not in a position to pay what it owes in full, the shareholders do not forfeit any more than the amount they agreed to contribute as capital to the company.

When a business is run as a company, company law requires that (a) proper accounting records are maintained and (b) financial reports are made to the owners as well as others. This is because of many reasons, including the following:

1. **Protection of those to whom a company owes money**: let us assume that Mary's Coffee Shop is operated as a company, with Mary and Anne as the only shareholders, that each of them contributed £100,000 as share capital, and that the Coffee Shop obtained a loan of £400,000 from a bank. If the Coffee Shop fails and all of its assets are lost, Mary and Anne will not be expected to bring in any more capital to settle the bank loan. Such a situation places the interests of the bank and others to whom the company owes money (referred to as *creditors*) in jeopardy. It becomes important, therefore, that parties to whom a company owes money should have access to full and accurate financial reports from a company.
2. **Protection of shareholders**: in most companies shareholders are many but the directors who manage the company are few and may not even be shareholders. In such a situation there is a risk that the directors may make decisions that benefit themselves rather than the shareholders, for example paying themselves excessive salaries and bonuses. The government has recognised that risk and seeks to control it by insisting on transparency – i.e. requiring that shareholders should be provided with sufficient information. If the shareholders have sufficient information they are able to see for themselves how well the directors are managing the company.

Activity 1.3 Types of business organisations

Business may be carried on either as a sole proprietorship, partnership or as a limited company. Identify the type of organisation of each of the following businesses:

(a) PriceWaterhouseCoopers, a firm of chartered accountants.

(b) Marks and Spencer plc, a department store.

(c) Sally's, a stationers shop.

1.6 Why those outside the business need accounting information

We have seen that accounting information is essential for the owners of the business. The investment in the business is theirs and they are interested both in safeguarding their investment and watching to see how that investment performs. There are others outside the business who are also interested in receiving accounting information from a business – these include the following user groups:

1. Banks and others to whom the business owes money – because they need to assess the ability of the business to pay what is due to them; this group also includes suppliers who allow the business a period of credit.
2. Employees of the business – because they are interested in whether they are being paid fairly and also want to assess whether the business will survive and continue to provide employment and pension benefits.
3. The government and its agencies – for collecting appropriate taxes and for regulating the activities of the business in the interest of the whole community.
4. The public – both as customers interested in the continuation of the goods and services that the business supplies and as potential investors.

These diverse groups of users with an interest in financial statements have been identified in the *Framework for the Preparation and Presentation of Financial Statements*,[1] which has recognised that the information needs of each of these groups are not necessarily the same. For example, the main focus of those who invest in a business is on its financial performance, i.e. how well the business performs because on that will depend how much return they get on their investment. This is known as *profitability*.

The main focus of those to whom the business owes money is on whether the business remains in a position to pay back what is owed to them. The ability of a business to meet their bills as and when they fall due is known as *liquidity*.

In an ideal world a business would prepare different financial statements to meet the needs of each user group. In real life this would be too costly and time-consuming and so there has to be compromise. The compromise adopted by the accounting profession is to accept that there is a sufficient overlap in the information requirements of the different user groups to make the financial statements prepared for the investors reasonably suitable for the other groups. The argument is that, to varying degrees, all groups have an interest in the financial performance (i.e. whether the business is making profit or incurring loss) and the financial position (i.e. whether it has sufficient assets to meet all its liabilities).

Activity 1.4 External information users and their information needs

(a) Do you agree with the assertion that the main focus of an investor is profit?

(b) Would an investor have any interest in liquidity?

(c) Would a person to whom the business owes money be interested in profitability?

1.7 Why managers within a business need accounting information

Those responsible for managing a business from day to day require accounting information to:

1. Ensure that business resources (including cash) are protected and applied in the best manner possible.
2. Plan the business activities within the resources available.
3. Establish targets such as how much they hope to earn and the amount of expense they are likely to incur.
4. Control costs, a task which is essential for survival in a competitive market – for example the owner of Mary's Coffee Shop may lose customers if her costs and therefore her prices were higher than those of her competitors.
5. Establish business strategies, e.g. whether to buy or rent the business premises; whether to invest in a faster coffee-making machine; whether to diversify and sell soup as well as coffee; and whether to maintain the competitive advantage by, say, choosing between lowering the price and improving the quality.

Managers make decisions on a day-to-day basis and for this they require accounting information tailored to meet specific needs. For example they may need to:

- use information on past performance in order to estimate likely future performance, e.g. in deciding how best to advertise they will need information on how successful different forms of advertising have been in the past;
- analyse and evaluate the outcome of decisions already made so that the successful aspects may be exploited and unsuccessful ones mitigated;
- predict the likely outcomes of alternative courses of action.

In contrast with all other groups who require accounting information, managers are at an advantage because they are able to obtain accounting information which is:

- comprehensive – being more detailed than that which is usually provided to other users;
- timely – being available as and when needed;
- relevant – being specific to their particular needs.

The production and application of accounting information to satisfy the needs of managers is the role of a *management accountant* and this major branch of accounting is known as *management accounting*. Accounting to satisfy the needs of the other groups who are external to the business is known as *financial accounting*. This book focuses on financial accounting.

1.8 Maintaining confidence in the accuracy of accounting information

Investors, lenders and suppliers do not have access to the records of the business. They make their decisions based on information provided by the business in financial statements. It is essential, if they are to continue to be prepared to invest and make credit available, that they should have confidence that the accounting information provided to them in financial statements is (i) free from material errors, (ii) treats similar transactions in the same way, and (iii) complies with statutory requirements.

1.8.1 Free from material errors

It would be too expensive to require all information to be 100 per cent accurate – this would require every detail to be checked and double-checked. Instead the emphasis is on the information being free from material errors, i.e. errors which if they had been known about at the time would have caused someone to have come to a different decision. For example, if the bank were proposing to grant an overdraft of £100,000 it would not affect their decision if they were made aware that the cashier had misappropriated £2,000 over the last two years – it would be quite different if the business fails to disclose, for instance, that it owes someone a substantial amount, such as say £200,000.

What checks are there that information is free from material error?

In the case of sole proprietors and small partnerships there is an assumption that the owners are so close to the business that they know what is happening. In the case of the larger limited liability companies where the owners do not manage the business there is a statutory requirement for the records and financial statements to be audited by an independent qualified auditor.

1.8.2 Similar transactions treated in the same way by all companies

It is important that managers and directors are not allowed to manipulate the way in which information is reported in the financial statements to tell a favourable but unfair story. To ensure that transactions are recorded correctly and reported in such a way as to convey a *true and fair view* companies are required to comply with the requirements of International Financial Reporting Standards.

The International Accounting Standards Board (IASB)

Internationally, there has been a growing trend towards the globalisation of trade and the movement of investments across national boundaries. This has meant that there is a need for all countries to apply the same accounting treatments for recording and reporting transactions. To achieve this an International Accounting Standards Committee (IASC) was set up in June 1973. In 2001, the work of this committee was taken over by an International Accounting Standards Board (IASB). The pronouncements issued by the IASC are known as International Accounting Standards (IASs) and those of the IASB as International Financial Reporting Standards (IFRSs). The aim of these standards is to ensure that financial information reported in any country is both transparent and comparable.

The Accounting Standards Board (UK)

Many countries (including the UK) make their own national accounting standards. In 1970 the *Accounting Standards Committee* was formed in the UK with responsibility for developing Accounting Standards. The Standards which were issued are known as *Statements of Standard Accounting Practice* (SSAPs). Since 1990 this responsibility has been taken over by the *Accounting Standards Board* (ASB) and the Standards which the ASB issues are known as *Financial Reporting Standards* (FRSs).

1.8.3 Complying with statutory requirements

Each country has its own statutory requirements. For example, in the UK the Companies Act 2006 includes requirements for companies to keep accounting records, publish financial statements and, when it is necessary, to appoint auditors to check these records and financial statements.

1.9 Accounting terminology

Transaction – a business activity involving money

Assets – resources available to a business

Liabilities – amounts owed by a business

Capital – amount invested in a business by its owner

Income **or** ***revenue*** – what the business earns from the sale of goods or provision of services

Expenses – what it cost the business to earn the income

Gross profit – the difference between sales revenue and cost of what was sold

Net profit – gross profit less all expenses

Statement of financial position – a list of resources (assets) and of sources of these assets (capital and liabilities)

Statement of income – report of income and expenses

Inventory – goods available for sale

Summary

- Financial accounting records business transactions.
- Bookkeeping is the process of recording transactions and analysing them in a systematic manner.
- The bookkeeping process is the same whether the recording is made manually or by computer.
- The preparation of financial statements is one of the accounting functions.
- Two of the financial statements are a Statement of financial position (balance sheet) and a Statement of income.
- Information in financial statements needs to be free from material error because they are relied on by the owners of a business and other interested parties for making decisions.
- Material errors are errors which if they had been known about at the time would have caused someone to have come to a different decision.
- The IASB (and ASB in the UK) issue Accounting Standards as part of their continuous effort to ensure that financial statements are comparable.

Reference

1. *Framework for the Preparation and Presentation of Financial Statements* (1989), London, International Accounting Standards Board.

Suggested answers to activities

1.1 The resources of a business and their sources

	Day one	Day two	Day three	Day four	Day five	Day six	Day seven	Day eight
Resources:								
Furniture	–	–	£180,000	£180,000	£180,000	£180,000	£180,000	£180,000
Inventory	–	–	–	£90,000	£40,000[d]	£40,000	£105,000[i]	£105,000
Cash	£100,000	£300,000[a]	£120,000[b]	£30,000[c]	£105,000[e]	£100,000[g]	£35,000[j]	£5,000[k]
	£100,000	£300,000	£300,000	£300,000	£325,000	£320,000	£320,000	£290,000
Sources:								
Capital	£100,000	£100,000	£100,000	£100,000	£100,000	£100,000	£100,000	£100,000
Profit	–	–	–	–	£25,000[f]	£20,000[h]	£20,000	£20,000
Bank loan	–	£200,000	£200,000	£200,000	£200,000	£200,000	£200,000	£170,000[l]
	£100,000	£300,000	£300,000	£300,000	£325,000	£320,000	£320,000	£290,000

(a) 100,000 + 200,000 = 300,000
(b) 300,000 – 180,000 = 120,000
(c) 120,000 – 90,000 = 30,000
(d) 90,000 – 50,000 = 40,000
(e) 30,000 + 75,000 = 105,000
(f) 75,000 – 50,000 = 25,000
(g) 105,000 – 2,000 – 3,000 = 100,000
(h) 25,000 – 2,000 – 3,000 = 20,000
(i) 40,000 + 65,000 = 105,000
(j) 100,000 – 65,000 = 35,000
(k) 35,000 – 30,000 = 5,000
(l) 200,000 – 30,000 = 170,000

1.2 Further reasons why a business will keep accounting records

1. If the business sells goods to customers, permitting them to settle for the goods say by the end of each month, it has to keep track of how much each customer owes.
2. If a business seeks a loan from a bank it has to convince the bank of its ability to continue in business and to repay the loan on the agreed date. This means that the bank needs to be confident that the business will be profitable and have sufficient cash to make the repayment.

1.3 Types of business organisations

(a) PriceWaterhouseCoopers is a partnership.
(b) Marks and Spencer plc is a limited company.
(c) Sally's Stationers shop is a sole proprietorship.

1.4 External information users and their information needs

(a) Although the main aim of making an investment is usually to earn profit, a prudent business person aims more at the stability that arises from keeping customers satisfied rather than maximising profit.
(b) Even one focused on profitability should be mindful of the importance of liquidity because if a business suffers from inadequacy of cash it may miss opportunities of making profit.
(c) Those to whom the business owes money would be aware of the importance of profitability because losses will erode the liquidity of the business.

Multiple choice questions

1.1 Only transactions need to be accounted for. Which of the following are transactions?

(i) Choosing a name for the business
(ii) Bringing £10,000 in to the business as the capital
(iii) Buying goods for sale
(iv) Selecting a suitable person to conduct the business

a	i & ii	
b	ii & iii	
c	i, ii & iii	
d	i & iv	

1.2 Which of the following would be the most frequently occurring daily transaction in a retail shop?

(a) Paying salary to the sales assistant
(b) Sale of goods
(c) Payment of rent for the shop premises
(d) Payment for advertising the goods available for sale

1.3 Which of the following are valid reasons for maintaining books of accounts?

(i) To know whether the business has sufficient money to pay its bills
(ii) To protect the business resources such as cash, goods for sale, furniture
(iii) To monitor whether carrying on the business is worthwhile
(iv) To satisfy the tax inspector

a	i & ii	
b	i, ii & iii	
c	ii & iii	
d	i, ii, iii & iv	

1.4 Who, among the following, deserve to receive financial statements from a business on a regular basis?

(i) The owner, partners or shareholders who invested capital in the business
(ii) A rival business competing for share of the market
(iii) Those from whom the business would like to borrow
(iv) Those who work for the business as employees

a	i, ii & iv	
b	i, ii & iii	
c	i & iv	
d	i, ii, iii & iv	

1.5 As the owner of a business you should receive financial statements regularly so that you could monitor:

(i) Profitability – whether the business earns sufficient return on your investment.
(ii) Liquidity – whether the business is able to pay its bills as they fall due
(iii) Whether you have become richer than your neighbour
(iv) Whether business resources are not stolen or wrongly used

a	i, ii & iv	
b	i, ii & iii	
c	i, iii & iv	
d	i, ii, iii	

1.6 Which of the following statements is incorrect? The Accounting Standards are authoritative statements:

(a) intended to enhance the reliability of the financial statements
(b) are, like law, enacted by Parliament and issued by the government of each country
(c) in compliance with which financial statements have to be prepared
(d) are issued in the UK by the Accounting Standards Board

Answers to multiple choice questions
1.1: b 1.2: b 1.3: d 1.4: c 1.5: a 1.6: b

Progressive questions

PQ 1.1 The effect of transactions on the Statement of financial position (1)

A new business entered into the following transactions:

1. Cash of £300,000 was introduced as capital.
2. Shop premises were acquired for £100,000 paid in cash.
3. A loan of £50,000 was obtained from the bank.
4. £75,000 was paid in cash to acquire inventory for resale.
5. (a) Inventory costing £30,000 was sold.
   (b) This inventory was sold for £75,000 cash.
6. Employees were paid £8,000 as salary.

Required: Show the effect of each transaction on the Statement of financial position and prepare a Statement of income to explain the increase in the capital.

PQ 1.2 The effect of transactions on the Statement of financial position (2)

A new business entered into the following transactions:

1. Cash of £480,000 was introduced as capital.
2. Vehicles were acquired for £160,000 paid in cash.
3. £120,000 was paid in cash to acquire inventory for resale.
4. (a) Inventory costing £48,000 was sold.
   (b) This inventory was sold for £120,000 cash.
5. A loan of £80,000 was obtained from the bank.
6. Employees were paid £13,000 in cash.

Required: Show the effect of each transaction on the Statement of financial position and prepare a Statement of income to explain the increase in the capital.

Chapter 2

Accounting for cash

By the end of this chapter

You should learn:	You should be able to:
■ The importance of controlling cash	■ Write up the Cash account
■ The usual methods of controlling cash	■ Write up the Bank account

2.1 Why cash should be controlled

We have learnt that any activity involving money is referred to, among accountants, as a *transaction*. Any transaction which involves an immediate receipt or payment of cash is known as a *cash transaction*. Let us start by assuming that cash means notes and coins.

There are numerous businesses (such as those of window cleaners, hairdressers, taxi services) which are carried on strictly on a cash basis.

Cash is the lifeblood of any business. It is arguably the most important of all the resources used within a business, and the owners and managers need to be aware at all times of their cash position. There are two reasons for this – a commercial one and a security one.

Commercial reason

Just as we need to know in our personal life that we have sufficient cash to pay the rent and feed ourselves, so in our business life we need to know that there is sufficient cash to pay suppliers and staff on time – if not supplies may be cut off and staff leave.

Security reason

Cash is vulnerable and the secret is to avoid putting temptation in anyone's way. There is the risk that it could be stolen or used to pay for non-business items, for example a garage employee may use business cash to buy new tyres for his own car. Stealing cash from a business or applying it other than for a legitimate business purpose is referred to as *misappropriation*.

Misappropriation is often carried out by the staff. It frequently involves small amounts, sometimes over long periods, but it can also involve quite large amounts. It is particularly difficult to control if it is carried out by a senior figure, as in the case of Christopher Woodhead. Woodhead had set up a number of companies providing external textured coatings for houses and withdrew large cash sums from these businesses on the pretext that he was paying suppliers in cash or was making cash refunds to clients: in reality he was using the money to meet his personal needs. Following a prosecution by the Serious Fraud Office (www.sfo.gov.uk) he was convicted on 27 July 2004 and ordered to pay back £428,000. Misappropriation of funds can affect businesses of all sizes, from major companies such as Enron down to the local restaurant.

How serious is the risk?

A survey conducted for Bank of Scotland Business Banking in 2006 found that the cash flow of nearly a quarter of UK small businesses (900,000 businesses) was under threat from losses due to staff theft or fraud. The moral of this is that it is the responsibility of every business to take active steps to control its cash – it is negligent not to do so.

2.2 How is cash controlled?

There is no single solution. There are the steps taken by management, for example noticing if a member of staff has a change in lifestyle (holidays, new car, expensive clothing) or in the day-to-day operation of the business comparing cash takings on the days they work with takings on their day off.

In this chapter, however, we are concentrating on the procedures within the financial accounting system and explain the steps taken within that system to control cash. These include:

Daily routines

- There needs to be written and reliable evidence to support every amount received and paid. Such evidence is known as a *voucher*:
  - (i) The voucher evidencing cash sales is often the till roll from a cash register.
  - (ii) The voucher evidencing a payment is usually a *receipt* issued by the person to whom the payment has been made. It should be possible to see from the receipt the reason for the payment and, if it is a substantial payment, it would be normal for it to be authorised by a responsible employee.
- Every amount received and paid is recorded in a *Cash account*, with a cross-reference to the corresponding voucher that provides evidence of and an explanation for the transaction.
- To avoid holding excessive amounts of cash, amounts surplus to the immediate requirements of the business are placed in a bank and movements in and out of the bank are recorded in a *Bank account*.
- The Cash account and the Bank account are written up in a *Cash Book*.

Random routines

- Physical checks are made from time to time to confirm that the difference between the total received and the total paid is actually held.

2.3 The Cash account

The person having custody and control of cash in a business is usually known as the *cashier*. It is the cashier's responsibility to (i) receive and pay cash, (ii) keep vouchers as evidence of every amount received and paid, and (iii) record every amount received and paid in a *Cash account*. One way of writing up the Cash account would be to record every amount received and, as deductions, to record every amount paid out, so that, at any point, the cashier would be aware of the amount in his custody. This method, however, would be prone to error and delay the recording function. An alternative way, the one which is commonly in use, is to divide a page into two equal halves, by drawing a double line vertically down the centre, so that amounts received could be recorded on the first half of the page and the amounts paid on the second half. By adding together all amounts received, say in a day, and deducting from the total the sum of all amounts paid, the cashier identifies the amount that should remain in his custody by the end of the day.

The cashier could improve the format of the Cash account by including on each side further columns in which he could state the date of the transaction, a cross-reference to the corresponding voucher and particulars of that transaction. A Cash account so formatted would appear as follows:

Cash account

Date	Voucher	Particulars	F	Amount	Date	Voucher	Particulars	F	Amount
2010				£	2010				£
1.1	RV1	Capital		500	1.1	PV1	Purchases		280
1.1	RV2	Sales		140	1.1	PV2	Rent		100
1.1	RV3	Sales		320	1.1	PV3	Wages		80
1.1	RV4	Sales		210	1.1	PV4	Purchases		175
									635
					1.1	–	Balance c/d		535
				1,170					1,170
2.1	–	Balance b/d		535					

Note that:

1. The column identified as F (for *folio* or page) will be explained in Chapter 3.
2. Vouchers with the prefix RV (standing for receipt voucher) can take a number of different forms. In a retail shop, for example, it might be a copy of an itemised *cash sales memo* or simply an entry on a till roll. These vouchers should be numbered so that a manager can check that none has been omitted and the cash misappropriated.
3. Vouchers with the prefix PV are obtained from the people to whom payment has been made. It is good practice to sequentially number each voucher as received so that it is possible to check the sequence in the Cash Book to confirm that (i) none has been omitted and (ii) no payments have been made without a supporting voucher.

4. Each receipt and payment is recorded in chronological order (i.e. in the order in which they took place). Notice that the second payment for purchases occurred after the payment of wages.
5. Deducting the total of all payments (£635) from the sum of all amounts received during the day (£1,170), the balance of cash that should remain in hand by the end of the day is arrived at as £535.
6. The total of all amounts paid (£635) together with the amount of cash remaining in hand (£535) equals the total of amounts recorded as receipts (£1,170).
7. If the actual amount of cash in hand, ascertained by doing a physical cash count, is found to be £535, then it is presumed that the Cash account has been written up correctly. This process of establishing the correctness of the Cash account is known as *balancing the Cash Book.*
8. The balance of £535 is carried down (c/d) from 1 January to be stated as the balance brought down (b/d) on 2 January. When the Cash account is written up with transactions on 2 January, the balance brought forward from the previous day (£535) plus all amounts received on 2 January should equal the sum of all amounts paid out on 2 January and the balance carried down to 3 January.

Activity 2.1 Writing up a Cash account

Angela Knight commenced business on 1 January as a dealer in laptop computers of a standard make and model. She introduced £10,000 in cash as her capital. Her transactions in the first week of business have been listed below in the date sequence:

Date	Transaction	£	Date	Transaction	£
1.1	Paid for cabinets for storage	1,500	5.1	Paid for five more laptops	4,000
1.1	Paid for five laptops	4,000	6.1	Sold three laptops for	3,600
3.1	Paid for advertising	350	6.1	Paid for a Ford saloon car	7,500
3.1	Paid as rent	200	6.1	Sold a laptop computer for	1,200
4.1	Paid for writing material	140	7.1	Sold two more laptops for	2,400
4.1	Sold three laptops for	3,600	7.1	Paid again for advertising	240
5.1	Received as a loan from Joe	5,000	7.1	Sold one more laptop for	1,200

Required:

(a) Write up the Cash account recording the transactions and carry down the balance in hand at the end of the week.

(b) How could Angela satisfy herself that the Cash account has been correctly written up?

(c) Angela started with a cash balance of £10,000, and ends the week with only £9,070. Does it mean that her business is performing poorly?

(d) Explain what could possibly have happened if, on doing a cash count at close of business for the day, it is found that the actual cash in hand is only £4,070.

2.4 Possible misappropriation of cash

We have already mentioned the risk of misappropriation and some of the general steps taken to combat it. Here we look at methods of misappropriation involving vouchers and the record in the Cash account.

In a business where all transactions are in cash, the most common method is for an employee or the owner to omit to record a sale and to keep the cash. If the business normally issues a pre-numbered sales receipt, to avoid accounting for a cash sale it would be necessary either to avoid giving the customer a receipt or to give the receipt from a separate receipt book which is not part of the pre-numbered set.

There might also be alterations made to a voucher, reducing the amount say on RV2 from £140 to £40 (misappropriating the difference) or increasing the amount on PV1 from £280 to £380 pocketing the difference, or increasing the wages amount from £80 to £160 on the pretext that there was another temporary member of staff.

It is of course perfectly normal and legitimate for an owner to take cash out of a business for personal use. An amount so taken for own use is referred to as *drawings* and would be entered as a payment in the Cash account. This is quite different from taking cash without recording it coming into the business or recording as a business expense an amount taken for personal use.

Activity 2.2 Reliance on vouchers to control cash

Richard owns a newsagents shop. One day a week he employs a relief manager. He wants to be confident that all amounts received from sales are being fully recorded and every amount paid out is for a legitimate purpose. What advice would you give him?

2.5 Writing up a Bank account

We made the assumption in our illustrations so far that cash meant only notes and coins and that the only record required was a Cash account. In practice, of course, it is the norm for businesses to deposit the bulk of their cash in a bank and to make payments by writing out cheques instructing the bank to make the payment out of the amount deposited with it.

The transactions that involve the bank are recorded by the cashier in a Bank account. For this purpose the cashier would format a Bank account as follows:

Bank account

Date	Voucher	Particulars	F	Amount	Date	Chq no	Voucher	Particulars	F	Amount
2010				£	2010					£

Amounts deposited in the bank are recorded as a payment in the Cash account and a receipt in the Bank account. Every payment made by writing out a cheque is recorded as a payment in the Bank account. As cheques issued by a business are sequentially numbered, by recording the cheque numbers in a separate column on the payment side of the Bank account and checking that there is no break in the sequence of cheque numbers recorded, it is possible to confirm that each cheque issued by the business has been recorded. Cheques received from customers, however, come from different cheque books, so that it is not possible to carry out a similar sequence check.

Activity 2.3 Writing up a Cash account and a Bank account

Angela started her second week with a cash balance of £9,070. She deposited £3,000 of this into a bank account which she opened that day. The second week transactions (stated in the date sequence in which they took place) were as follows:

Date	Transaction
8.1	Paid £2,400 for three more laptops by cheque number 0001
8.1	Sold two laptops at £1,200 each
8.1	Paid £80 in cash for additional writing material
9.1	Paid £150 for advertising by cheque number 0002
10.1	Sold a laptop for £1,200
10.1	Deposited £4,000 in the bank
11.1	Paid £3,200 for four more laptops by cheque number 0003
14.1	Deposited in the bank all cash held in hand only leaving a balance of £500 in hand

Required: Write up the Cash account and the Bank account and calculate the end of week balance for each.

2.6 A two-column Cash Book

Instead of writing up a Bank account separately from a Cash account, businesses find it convenient to write up both accounts on the same page (in accounting a page is referred to as a *folio*), formatting the folio as follows:

Cash Book (two-column)

Date	V	Particulars	F	Cash	Bank	Date	V	Chq no	Particulars	F	Cash	Bank
2010				£	£	2010					£	£

A Cash Book where the Cash account and the Bank account are both written up on the same folio is known as a *two-column Cash Book*.

Activity 2.4 Writing up a two-column Cash Book

Using the information in Activity 2.3 above, write up the Cash Book in two-column format.

2.7 Accounting terminology

Cashier – the person who holds the cash and writes up the Cash Book

Purchases – goods bought for resale

Sales – goods sold to customers

Motor vehicles – lorries, vans and cars bought for use in a business

Furniture – tables, chairs, cabinets etc. bought for use by a business

Stationery – items such as copy paper, pen, ruler

Acquisition – buying of items for use rather than sale (e.g. a delivery van)

Disposal – selling of items acquired for use rather than sale

Capital – the amounts invested in a business by its owner

Drawings – any amount the owner takes from the business for personal use

Folio – a page in a book of account

Casting – adding together the amounts written on a folio (e.g. adding up total receipts)

Summary

- Cash needs to be controlled for commercial as well as security reasons.
- Cash transactions are recorded in a Cash account written up in a Cash Book.
- Every amount received and paid out should be suported by vouchers.
- Cash surplus to immediate needs is, for safety, placed in a Bank account.
- Amounts deposited in a bank and paid out from the bank are recorded in a Bank account.
- A two-column Cash Book records the Cash account and Bank account side by side.

Suggested answers to activities

2.1 Writing up a Cash account

(a)

Cash account

Date	Voucher	Particulars	F	Amount	Date	Voucher	Particulars	F	Amount
2010				£	2010				£
1.1	Rec.001	Capital		10,000	1.1	PV001	Furniture		1,500
4.1	RV001	Sales		3,600	1.1	PV002	Purchases		4,000
5.1	Rec.002	Joe's loan		5,000	3.1	PV003	Advertising		350
6.1	RV002	Sales		3,600	3.1	PV004	Rent		200
6.1	RV003	Sales		1,200	4.1	PV005	Stationery		140
7.1	RV004	Sales		2,400	5.1	PV006	Purchases		4,000
7.1	RV005	Sales		1,200	6.1	PV007	Motor vehicles		7,500
					7.1	PV008	Advertising		240
									17,930
					7.1		Balance c/d		9,070
				27,000					27,000
7.1		Balance b/d		9,070					

(b) By balancing the Cash account (i.e. checking whether the results of a physical count of the cash in hand reveals a balance of £9,070, the same as shown in the Cash account) Angela would satisfy herself on the accuracy of the Cash account.

(c) Cash in hand is only one of the resources (assets) available to a business. Although the cash balance of £9,070 is lower than what she had at commencement, Angela has several other resources she did not have at commencement. For example she has furniture and a motor vehicle. At the same time she owes Joe £5,000. Whether her business has done well or not cannot be ascertained from the cash balance alone.

(d) If the actual balance in hand is £4,070 (or any amount other than £9,070) the reason could be:

(i) Errors in recording:
- One (or more) amount(s) received has been recorded at more than the actual amount received.
- One (or more) payment(s) has not been recorded.
- One (or more) payment(s) has been recorded at less than the actual amount paid.
- There could be arithmetical mistake(s) in adding or ascertaining the balance.

(ii) Errors in handling the cash: mistakes may be made in counting the cash received or paying out incorrect change.

(iii) Misappropriation: cash could have been stolen.

2.2 Reliance on vouchers to control cash

(a) Richard should insist on:

- a Cash account being maintained;
- every receipt and payment being recorded and cross-referenced to a voucher;
- all vouchers being retained.

(b) Control over cash receipts. However, control over cash receipts is difficult given that the vouchers supporting amounts received are produced internally by the relief manager. This means that we cannot be certain that all cash takings (sales proceeds) are being fully recorded. For example, some customers may not have been issued with vouchers. All that Richard can do is to:

1. Insist that every customer is issued a voucher – a prominent notice requesting each customer to insist on receiving a voucher could help.
2. Arrange that such vouchers are prepared from pre-printed pads printed under strict security arrangements and that each cash sales memo is sequentially numbered. Greater reliance may be placed on mechanically produced vouchers such as till rolls in cash registers, provided adequate safeguards are instituted.
3. Undertake other control checks. For example, if Richard usually fixes his sale price at 20% above cost, he could periodically check whether the sales amount to 120% of the cost of what was sold.

(c) Control over cash payments. As regards payments Richard should:

1. insist that every payment voucher, as received from third parties, is sequentially numbered and filed in the sequence they were received;
2. inspect every payment voucher to identify the reason for the payment and whether it is legitimate and to verify whether it bears the initials of the person who authorised the payment;
3. periodically check that all vouchers have been accounted for by tracing their number sequence – if the number sequence is broken, revealing that a voucher is missed out, an adequate explanation is required.

(d) Control over cash in hand. Richard should insist on balancing the Cash Book every day – i.e checking that the balance carried down in the Cash account is exactly the same as the amount of cash in hand.

(e) Remove temptation. Amounts in excess of what is required for immediate use should be placed in a Bank account and payments by cheque (rather than cash) should be encouraged.

2.3 Writing up a Cash account and a Bank account

Cash account

Date	Voucher	Particulars	F	Amount	Date	Voucher	Particulars	F	Amount
2010				£	2010				£
8.1	–	Balance b/d		9,070	8.1	PV9	Bank		3,000
8.1	RV7	Sales		2,400	8.1	PV10	Stationery		80
10.1	RV8	Sales		1,200	10.1	PV13	Bank		4,000
					14.1	PV14	Bank		5,090
									12,170
					14.1	–	Balance c/d		500
				12,670					12,670
14.1		Balance b/d		500					

Bank account

Date	Voucher	Particulars	F	Amount	Date	Chq no	Voucher	Particulars	F	Amount
2010				£	2010					£
8.1	PV9	Cash		3,000	8.1	0001	PV11	Purchases		2,400
10.1	PV13	Cash		4,000	9.1	0002	PV12	Advertising		150
14.1	PV14	Cash		5,090	11.1	0003	PV15	Purchases		3,200
										5,750
					14.1			Balance c/d		6,340
				12,090						12,090
14.1		Balance b/d		6,340						

The payment voucher for bank deposits (in support of both payments recorded in the Cash account and the corresponding receipt recorded in the Bank account) is the bank paying-in slip authenticated by the bank teller.

2.4 Writing up a two-column Cash Book

Cash Book (two-column)

Date	V	Particulars	F	Cash	Bank	Date	V	Chq no	Particulars	F	Cash	Bank
2010				£	£	2010					£	£
8.1	–	Balance b/f		9,070	–	8.1	PV9	–	Bank		3,000	–
8.1	PV9	Cash		–	3,000	8.1	PV10	–	Stationery		80	–
8.1	RV7	Sales		2,400	–	8.1	PV11	001	Purchases		–	2,400
10.1	RV8	Sales		1,200	–	9.1	PV12	002	Advertising		–	150
10.1	PV13	Cash		–	4,000	10.1	PV13	–	Bank		4,000	–
14.1	PV14	Cash		–	5,090	11.1	PV14	–	Bank		5,090	–
						14.1	PV15	003	Purchases		–	3,200
											12,170	5,750
						14.1			Balance c/d		500	6,340
				12,670	12,090						12,670	12,090
14.1		Balance b/d		500	6,340							

Multiple choice questions

2.1 A business accounts only for transactions. Which of the following is *not* a transaction?

(a) The owner introduces £100,000 as capital

(b) The business enquires about buying some land

(c) £75,000 was paid to buy land and building

(d) £600 was paid for advertising

2.2 In a retail shop, selling confectionery, which of the following transactions may be expected to occur most frequently on a daily basis:

(a) Payment of rent

(b) Sale of confectionery

(c) Receiving money as capital from the owner

(d) Payment of salary to staff

2.3 Which of the following statements is incorrect? Business entities systematically record their receipts and payments in a Cash account and balance it on a daily basis in order to:

(a) protect cash from being stolen

(b) identify whether the business has made a profit or loss

(c) maintain an accurate chronological record of transactions

(d) continuously assess whether they have enough cash to meet their commitment

2.4 Which of the following statements is incorrect? To keep proper control of the cash held by a business:

(a) Every receipt and payment of cash should be recorded as soon as it happens

(b) Every entry in the Cash account should be substantiated by an appropriate voucher

(c) The Cash Book entries should be in pencil so that any mistakes can be corrected

(d) Difference between amounts received and paid should agree with amount in hand

2.5 If a business commenced the day with £3,400 in hand, receives and pays out £42,800 and £44,200 respectively during the day, the cash in hand at the end of the day would be:

(a) £1,400

(b) £2,000

(c) £4,800

(d) £46,200

2.6 If a business commenced the day with £14,200, paid out £58,900 during the day and has £22,900 by the end of the day, it should have received during the day:

(a) £1,400

(b) £21,800

(c) £50,200

(d) £67,600

2.7 The Cash account of a confectioner records the sales as £216,480 and the purchases as £196,475 in the first year of business. Sales are always made at cost plus 20% and no confectionery remains unsold at the year-end. The owner suspects that part of the amount received from sales has been misappropriated by the manager who has now resigned. What is the extent of suspected misappropriation?

a	£19,290	
b	£20,005	
c	£23,291	

2.8 You, as the cashier, check the accuracy of your Cash account by ascertaining whether the cash in hand matches the amount stated as the balance in the Cash account.
Tick the appropriate grid to identify the amount by which the cash physically in your hand will differ from the Cash account balance if the only mistake is each of the following:

(a) £4,620 paid for purchasing goods for sale is recorded on the payment side of the Cash account as £462

x	£462 more	
y	£4,158 less	
z	£4,158 more	

(b) £460 received from sales is not recorded at all in the Cash account

x	£460 less	
y	Same	
z	£460 more	

(c) £620 paid for stationery was recorded on the payment side of the Cash account as £260

x	£620 more	
y	£360 more	
z	£360 less	

(d) £106 paid for staff tea was not recorded at all in the Cash account

x	£106 more	
y	£106 less	
z	Same	

(e) £1,200 paid for office furniture was recorded on the payment side of the Cash account but stated as purchases

x	£1,200 less	
y	£1,200 more	
z	Same	

(f) £165 paid for advertising was recorded on the receipt side of the Cash account

x	£165 less	
y	£330 less	
z	£330 more	

2.9 Tick one of the grids on the right to state whether each of the following transactions will increase, reduce or make no change to the total cash a business has both in hand and at bank:

(a) Deposited £2,800 from the day's collection into its bank account
(b) Received a cheque for £5,000 from a customer
(c) Paid £6,000 as rent by cheque
(d) Wrote out a cheque for £500 to withdraw money for office use
(e) The bank deducts £15 from account as bank charges

Increase	Reduce	Same
x	y	z

Answers to multiple choice questions
2.1: b 2.2: b 2.3: b 2.4: c 2.5: b 2.6: d 2.7: a 2.8a: y 2.8b: z 2.8c: z 2.8d: y 2.8e: z 2.8f: y 2.9a: z 2.9b: x 2.9c: y 2.9d: z 2.9e: y

Progressive questions

PQ 2.1 Control over cash

(a) Identify six types of business which operate on a cash basis.
(b) Why is it important that a business should write up a Cash account?
(c) In addition to writing up a Cash account, what further controls do you think are necessary for a business to safeguard its cash?

PQ 2.2 Sorting out the side

As the cashier in a retail shop you maintain a Cash account which has two sides. Assuming all amounts received are identified by you as 'in' and all payments are identified as 'out', state the side on which you will record each of the following transactions:

(a) £56 paid for postage
(b) £15 received on sale of goods held for sale
(c) £65 paid for staff refreshments
(d) £500 received as loan from Dave, a friend of the owner
(e) £1,000 paid as rent for the shop premises
(f) Two ten-pound notes given to a customer as change for a £20 note

In	Out	None
x	y	z

PQ 2.3 Writing up the Cash account

Arnold commenced business on 1.1.2010 and has made the following transactions:

Date	Transaction	£	Date	Transaction	£
1.1	Started business	15,000	4.1	Bought stationery for cash	60
2.1	Made purchases for cash	300	5.1	Acquired second-hand vehicle	1,500
2.1	Paid rent in cash	1,500	6.1	Paid motor vehicle expenses	225
2.1	Bought stationery for cash	90	6.1	Took cash for living expenses	450
2.1	Received cash from sales	450	7.1	Received cash from sales	250
3.1	Made purchases for cash	150	7.1	Paid motor vehicle expenses	40

Required: Show how these transactions would be recorded in the Cash account.

PQ 2.4 Writing up the Cash account and Bank account

On 1st April 2010 Bennett started in business selling toys with a capital of £12,000 which he deposited immediately in a Bank account. The following transactions took place during the first week of business:

Date	Transaction	£	Date	Transaction	£
1.4	Paid 6 months' rent by cheque no 01	3,000	4.4	Paid electricity by cheque no 06	270
1.4	Paid for shop fittings by cheque no 02	1,200	4.4	Received from sales	2,500
1.4	Bought toys by cheque no 03	2,400	4.4	Paid for advertising by cheque no 07	124
2.4	Paid for advertising by cheque no 04	240	5.4	Paid telephone bill by cheque no 08	115
2.4	Received from sales	1,200	5.4	Received from sales	3,400
3.4	Received from sales	1,800	5.4	Bennet took cash for personal use	250
3.4	Paid cash for shop cleaning	140	5.4	Paid weekly wages in cash	300
3.4	Bought toys by cheque no 05	1,800	5.4	Deposited into the Bank account	7,800

Required: Record these transactions in a Cash account and Bank account maintained separately.

PQ 2.5 Two-column Cash Book

On the basis of the transactions reported in respect of PQ 2.4 you are required to record these transactions in the Cash account and the Bank account, in a two-column Cash Book.

PQ 2.6 Balancing the Cash account

(a) What is the procedure usually adopted by a cashier to satisfy himself that the Cash account has been written up correctly?

(b) Would the balancing of the Cash account provide conclusive proof that it is a full and accurate record of all cash transactions that have taken place?

(c) At close of business on 17 October 2010 the cash in hand totalled £11,560.25. However, the balance carried down in the Cash account was £12,780.50. List four possible reasons for this discrepancy.

Test questions

2.1 Writing up the Cash account

Faisal Ahmed commenced business on 7 November 2010 selling flat panel computer monitors. He brought in £15,000 in cash as his capital. He has a supplier from whom he purchases the monitors at £180 each. He sells the monitors at £250 each. His receipts and payments during the first week of trading were as stated below:

Date	Transaction	£
7.11	Paid rent for the month	1,000
8.11	Acquired office equipment	3,000
9.11	Bought office stationery	45
9.11	Acquired a van	2,500
9.11	Paid road tax and insurance	185
10.11	Purchased 28 monitors	?
11.11	Paid for local press advertising	200
11.11	Sold 16 monitors	?
11.11	Paid staff wages	550

Required: Write up the Cash account for the week, carrying down the balance at the end of the first week.

2.2 Writing up the Cash account and Bank account (week 2)

Faisal Ahmed, referred to in the previous question, continued with his business selling flat panel computer monitors. He had a cash balance of £6,480 brought forward from the previous week. He opened a bank account on 14 November with a deposit of £5,000. His instruction to his cashier was to bank all shop takings daily, leaving a cash float of only £500 in hand. Apart from bank deposits made on a daily basis the business transactions in the second week were as stated below:

Date	Transaction	£
14.11	Sold 12 monitors @ £250 each	?
14.11	Received a loan from Olga	2,000
14.11	Paid in cash for office cleaning	175
15.11	Paid for 20 monitors @ £180 each by cheque no 001	?
15.11	Motor car expenses paid in cash	225
15.11	Sold 9 monitors @ £250 each	?
15.11	Paid for advertising by cheque no 002	340
16.11	Sold 14 monitors @ £250 each	?
16.11	Paid for stationery in cash	120
16.11	Paid for 12 monitors @ £180 each by cheque no 003	?
17.11	Paid for electricity by cheque no 004	180
17.11	Paid for office cleaning in cash	175
17.11	Sold 12 monitors @ £250 each	?
18.11	Paid for advertising by cheque no 005	340
18.11	Sold 8 monitors @ £250 each	?
18.11	Faisal took cash out for his own use	600
18.11	Paid staff wages in cash	550
18.11	Paid vehicle running expenses by cheque no 006	240

Required: Write up the two-column Cash Book.

Chapter 3

The double-entry accounting system

By the end of this chapter

You should learn:	You should be able to:
■ The need to analyse entries in the Cash account ■ The double-entry system of accounting	■ Post transactions recorded in the Cash account to the ledgers ■ Prepare a Trial Balance

3.1 Why do we need to analyse cash transactions?

In Chapter 2 we learned how to control cash and how to record cash transactions in a chronological order (i.e. date sequence) in a Cash account. Whilst the Cash account provides us with a record of all receipts and payments, these have not been analysed so that we can quickly see, for example, the total amounts paid out for any particular purpose.

This means that to find out how much has been paid for say purchases, we would have to list and add up each payment to get to the total purchase figure. Receipts would need to be treated in a similar fashion if we wanted to know how much came from sales and other sources.

In accounting, we say that we are analysing the payments according to their nature and the receipts according to their source.

3.2 Methods of analysing receipts and payments

In a small business it might be appropriate to carry out this analysis in the Cash account itself at the time the cash entry is made. If the business decides to do this then an extra column is required for each type of income and expense. The number will vary from business to business depending on the expenses the management want separately identified. In our example, we have two types of receipt and four types of expense as shown below:

Analysis – receipts | Cash account | *Analysis – payments*

Capital	Sales		£		£	Furniture	Purchases	Advertising	Stationery
10,000	–	Capital	10,000	Purchases	4,680	–	4,680	–	–
–	4,200	Sales	4,200	Furniture	1,800	1,800	–	–	–
–	1,800	Sales	1,800	Advertising	240	–	–	240	–
–	2,450	Sales	2,450	Purchases	2,850	–	2,850	–	–
–	1,260	Sales	1,260	Stationery	95	–	–	–	95
				Purchases	1,450	–	1,450	–	–
				Advertising	225	–	–	225	–
10,000	9,710				11,340	1,800	8,980	465	95
				Balance	8,370				
			19,710		19,710				

How do we know that the analysis is accurate?

This can be checked by adding up the columns and cross-casting totals. For example, by cross-casting the receipts analysis subtotals we can check that the capital £10,000 plus the sales £9,710 does equal the total amount received of £19,710. Similarly, we can check that the sum of the four analysis columns (£1,800 + £8,980 + £465 + £95) equals the total payments of £11,340. This method of analysis is useful in a small business but it is impractical when there is a large variety of transactions – it needs too many columns.

How do we analyse cash transactions in larger businesses?

The traditional method used to overcome this problem is to use a separate page (rather than a separate column on one sheet) for analysing each type of payment and receipt. For example, each payment for a particular purpose – say purchases – is copied from the Cash account onto one page that only records purchases. In accounting this copying is referred to as *posting* and the page to which the posting is made is referred to as an *account.*

The page to which every payment for purchases has been posted is called a *Purchases account* and there would be an account also for each of the other types of receipts and payments, i.e. *Capital account, Sales account, Furniture account, Advertising account* and *Stationery account.*

The pages are collated and together are referred to as a *ledger* – this is simply an accounting term for what is essentially a book. When we refer to books of account, accounting staff know that this is a reference to *ledgers.*

How do we know the analysis is accurate?

For a small business we have seen that the analysed Cash Book provides the facility to cross-cast the receipts analysis and agree with the total receipts and to cross-cast the payments analysis and agree with the total payments. When we record each type of receipt and payment on separate pages we still need to carry out a similar check, i.e. verify whether the total of the various individual pages in which payments have been analysed agrees with the total payments made; and similarly for receipts.

3.3 Checking the correctness of the analysis

The method traditionally adopted for checking the correctness of the analysis is to:

1. format each account in the same way as the Cash account – i.e. by dividing the page into two halves, drawing a vertical line down the centre;
2. require that an amount recorded in the Cash account on one side (say left) should be posted to the opposite side (say right) of the account written up for analysis.

The result is that a pair of entries – i.e. an entry in the Cash account and a matching corresponding entry (for analysis) in an appropriate account – record every transaction. If the two entries are made on opposite sides of the two accounts and if the sum of all entries on one side of all accounts equals the sum of all entries on the opposite side of all accounts, one could assume that every entry has been posted for analysis.

For convenience each of the two sides in every account is given a name: the left side of every account is known as the *debit* (abbreviated as Dr) and the right side as *credit* (abbreviated as Cr). Remember that debit and credit are no more than the name given to the left side and right side respectively of every account. Care must be taken not to attribute any other meaning to these two words.

3.4 The double-entry system of accounting

The system of recording every transaction by making two matching entries, one a debit and the other a credit, is known as the *double-entry system of accounting*.

The system requires that:

1. For every receipt recorded by the cashier on the debit side of the Cash account, an equal amount is posted to the credit side of an appropriate account such as a Capital account for cash brought in by the owner and a Sales account for cash received from sales.
2. For every payment recorded by the cashier on the credit side of the Cash account, an equal amount is posted to the debit side of an appropriate account such as Furniture account, Purchases account, Wages account and Stationery account.
3. The posting of the entries made by the cashier is usually done by the bookkeeper or in larger companies by *ledger clerks*, and the accounts providing the analysis are written up in one or more books known as the *ledger*.

3.5 Recording transactions on the double-entry system

The double-entry system of accounting operates as follows:

- In a cash-based business, the cashier records amounts received on the debit (left) side of the Cash account and amounts paid on the credit (right) side.
- The second entry is made on the opposite side in an account written up in the ledger to analyse each transaction.

Each of these accounts is formatted like the Cash account with a debit side and a credit side. An amount debited by the cashier (e.g. receipt of £10,000 as capital) is credited in the corresponding (capital) account. Similarly, an amount credited by the cashier (e.g. payment for furniture) is debited in an appropriate account (furniture account). Thus two entries are made to record every transaction. The first entry (referred to as the *prime entry*) for recording every cash-based transaction is made in the Cash Book. The second entry (referred to as the *double-entry*) is made when the same amount is posted to an appropriate account in the ledger. This method of recording transactions using a pair of entries is known as the *double-entry system of accounting*.

The pair of entries to account for a payment of £3,000 made to acquire furniture will appear as follows:

Dr Cash account Cr

	£		£
		Furniture a/c	3,000

Dr Furniture account Cr

	£		
Cash a/c	3,000		

Cross-referencing each double-entry: Note that when the cashier credits £3,000 in the Cash account he states against that amount the name of the account in which the debit entry should be made. Similarly, when £3,000 is posted to the opposite (debit) side in the Furniture account, in that account is stated the name of the account where the first (prime) entry is. In addition, having done the posting, the person who does the posting (bookkeeper) states in the Cash account, in a column built in for the purpose, the folio (page) of the ledger account in which he has made the second entry and also states in the Furniture account the folio of the Cash Book in which the prime entry can be found. This is for the purpose of cross-referencing the pair of entries.

Activity 3.1 Introduction to debit and credit

The double-entry system of accounting requires a debit entry and a matching credit entry for recording every transaction. In respect of each of the transactions stated below state the account to be debited and the one to be credited:

Transactions	Debit entry	Credit entry
1. £100,000 received as capital from owner		
2. £30,000 paid to acquire a vehicle for business use		
3. £24,000 paid to purchase goods for sale		
4. £36,000 received from sales		
5. £10,000 paid as a loan to Robert, a salesman		
6. £2,400 paid for advertising		

3.6 Illustration of how the double-entry system operates

We will now illustrate the double-entry system using the Cash account of Angela's computer business (see Chapter 2) which is as follows:

Cash account

Date	Voucher	Particulars	F	Amount	Date	Voucher	Particulars	F	Amount
2010				£	2010				£
1.1	Rec.001	Capital		10,000	1.1	PV001	Furniture		1,500
2.1	RV001	Sales		3,600	1.1	PV002	Purchases		4,000
2.1	Rec.002	Joe's loan		5,000	3.1	PV003	Advertising		350
3.1	RV002	Sales		3,600	3.1	PV004	Rent		200
6.1	RV003	Sales		1,200	4.1	PV005	Stationery		140
7.1	RV004	Sales		2,400	5.1	PV006	Purchases		4,000
7.1	RV005	Sales		1,200	6.1	PV007	Motor vehicles		7,500
					7.1	PV008	Advertising		240
									17,930
					7.1		Balance c/d		9,070
				27,000					27,000
7.1		Balance b/d		9,070					

Every entry recording the receipts (on the debit side of the Cash account) is posted to the credit of the appropriate accounts, which would then appear as follows:

Capital account

Date	Particulars	F	Amount	Date	Particulars	F	Amount
				2010			£
				1.1	Cash a/c		10,000

Joe's Loan account

Date	Particulars	F	Amount	Date	Particulars	F	Amount
				2010			£
				2.1	Cash a/c		5,000

Sales account

Date	Particulars	F	Amount	Date	Particulars	F	Amount
				2010			£
				2.1	Cash a/c		3,600
				3.1	Cash a/c		3,600
				6.1	Cash a/c		1,200
				7.1	Cash a/c		2,400
				7.1	Cash a/c		1,200
							12,000

Observe that the total of the credit balances (i.e. the balance appearing on the credit side) of the three accounts shown above (£10,000 + £5,000 + £12,000) equals the £27,000 recorded as the total of the receipts on the debit side of the Cash account. This proves that every receipt has been posted (i.e. included in the analysis).

Similarly, every amount from the credit side of the Cash account is posted to the debit side of the appropriate account in the ledger as follows:

Furniture account

Date	Particulars	F	Amount	Date	Particulars	F	Amount
2010			£				
1.1	Cash a/c		1,500				

Purchases account

Date	Particulars	F	Amount	Date	Particulars	F	Amount
2010			£				
1.1	Cash a/c		4,000				
5.1	Cash a/c		4,000				
			8,000				

Advertising account

Date	Particulars	F	Amount	Date	Particulars	F	Amount
2010			£				
3.1	Cash a/c		350				
7.1	Cash a/c		240				
			590				

Rent account

Date	Particulars	F	Amount	Date	Particulars	F	Amount
2010			£				
3.1	Cash a/c		200				

Stationery account

Date	Particulars	F	Amount	Date	Particulars	F	Amount
2010			£				
4.1	Cash a/c		140				

Motor vehicles account

Date	Particulars	F	Amount	Date	Particulars	F	Amount
2010			£				
6.1	Cash a/c		7,500				

Observe that the total of the debit balances in the six accounts written up for analysing payments (£1,500 + £8,000 + £590 + £200 + £140 + £7,500) equals the £17,930 recorded as the total of the payments on the credit side of the Cash account. This proves that all payments have been analysed, i.e. posted.

3.7 Balancing each ledger account

Just as we balanced the Cash account in order to see the amount of cash in hand at the end of the period, so we may need to balance the ledger account if it has amounts posted to both its debit and credit sides.

For example, upon receiving the loan, Joe's Loan account would have a balance of £5,000 on its credit side. If £1,000 is repaid to him, this amount is credited in the Cash account and posted to the debit side of Joe's Loan account. Joe's Loan account would have an amount stated on both the debit and credit side and would appear as follows:

Joe's Loan account

Date	Particulars	F	Amount	Date	Particulars	F	Amount
2010			£	2010			£
7.1	Cash a/c		1,000	2.1	Cash a/c		5,000
7.1	Balance c/d		4,000				
			5,000				5,000
				8.1	Balance b/d		4,000

The amount on the credit side of Joe's Loan account (£5,000) is £4,000 more than the amount on its debit side. That difference is carried down to the credit side so as to show that £4,000 is still payable to Joe. Thus Joe's Loan account has a credit balance of £4,000.

Activity 3.2 Columns on each side of a ledger account

Each ledger account is formatted like the Cash account, divided into two sides – a debit side and a credit side. However, whereas each side of the Cash account has five columns, each side of a ledger account has only four. Identify the column not drawn into the ledger account and explain why that column is not required.

Activity 3.3 Posting the ledger

Remember that every cash transaction is:

1. recorded in the Cash Book, the receipts being entered on the debit side and the payments on the credit side;
2. posted to a ledger account, ensuring that the second entry is on the side opposite the one in the Cash Book.

Required: State the side (debit or credit) of the named ledger account in which the following transactions of a business will be posted:

Transactions	Account	Side
1. Amount received from owner as capital	Capital	
2. Amount paid to acquire a car for the business	Motor vehicle	
3. Amount paid to purchase goods for sale	Purchases	
4. Amounts received from the sale of the goods	Sales	
5. Amount paid to the landlord as rent	Rent	
6. Amount paid to buy staff refreshments	Staff welfare	
7. Amount received as a loan from John Kitchener	John's loan	
8. Amount paid as staff salary	Salaries	
9. Amount paid to buy a Cash Book and a Ledger	Stationery	

3.8 The Trial Balance

If every transaction is accounted for in compliance with the rule of double-entry, i.e. by making a debit entry and a matching credit entry in two different accounts, the total of the debit balances in all the accounts should equal the total of the credit balance in all the accounts. Whether this is so can be established by listing out the balances in every account, including the Cash account, as shown on the right. Such a list is known as a *Trial Balance*.

Trial Balance as at 7 January 2010		
	Debit	Credit
	£	£
Cash account	9,070	–
Capital account	–	10,000
Joe's Loan account	–	5,000
Sales account	–	12,000
Furniture account	1,500	–
Purchases account	8,000	–
Advertising account	590	–
Rent account	200	–
Stationery account	140	–
Motor vehicles account	7,500	–
	27,000	27,000

Observe that in the Trial Balance extracted from the books recording Angela's transactions, on 7 January 2010, the total of debit balances in all the accounts is £27,000 and this is the same as the total of all the credit balances. Hence we could reasonably infer that:

(a) all transactions accounted for by the cashier have been posted; and

(b) every transaction has been accounted for by a matching pair of debit and credit entries.

The Trial Balance is no more than a mere list serving a limited purpose – namely that of establishing whether every debit entry has been matched by a credit entry, complying with the rules of the double-entry system of accounting. Any failure to comply with rules of double-entry will be flagged up by a failure of the Trial Balance to balance.

For example, if the second payment of £240 for advertising is not posted, the Advertising account balance would have been reported as £350 on the Trial Balance. This would result in the debit column total of £26,760 failing to be equal to the credit column total of £27,000.

Activity 3.4 Preparing a Trial Balance

On 31 December 2010, the last day of the accounting period, Bernard's Retail Stores reports the balances in all the accounts as follows:

Motor vehicles a/c	Debit	£8,200	Joe's Loan a/c	Credit	£3,500
Stationery a/c	Debit	£145	Rent a/c	Debit	£400
Capital a/c	Credit	£5,000	Salaries a/c	Debit	£800
Cash a/c	Debit	£538	Advertising a/c	Debit	£528
Purchases a/c	Debit	£4,215	Vehicle maintenance a/c	Debit	£412
Sales a/c	Credit	£6,948	Interest on Loan a/c	Debit	£210

Required: Prepare a Trial Balance as at 31 December 2010.

3.9 More about the Trial Balance

Note the following relating to the Trial Balance:

1. A Trial Balance is prepared to provide confirmation that every transaction has been accounted for, in accordance with the rules of double-entry, by a pair of debit and credit entries.
2. It may be prepared at any time whenever there is need for assurance that every debit is matched by a credit. Many businesses prepare such a Trial Balance at the end of each month.
3. It does not provide conclusive proof that there is nothing wrong with the business's accounting records. This is because the Trial Balance will still balance, despite errors having occurred such as the following:
   - A transaction is completely omitted, e.g. not recorded in either the Cash account or the ledger account.
   - A transaction is wrongly recorded in the Cash Book, e.g. a sale of £600 being recorded as £60 in the Cash account and posted to the credit of the Sales account as £60.
   - A transaction is posted to the correct side of the wrong account, e.g. a payment of £240 for stationery posted to the debit of the Advertising account.

Activity 3.5 Trial Balance and accounting errors

Identify the impact of each of the following accounting errors on the Trial Balance:

(a) £1,200 paid as rent has been entered in the Cash account but has not been posted;

(b) £150 received from sales has not been entered in the Cash account;

(c) £645 paid for stationery has been posted to the Advertising account as £465;

(d) £140 paid for office furniture has been debited to the Purchases account;

(e) £180 paid for servicing a vehicle has been posted to the Motor Vehicles account;

(f) £500 given as a loan to an employee has been posted to the Salaries account.

Summary

- The receipts and payments recorded in the Cash account need to be analysed.
- To obtain the analysis each transaction is posted to another account opened in the ledger.
- Every account in the ledger is formatted with a debit side and a credit side.
- The double-entry system of accounting requires a matching debit and credit entry for recording each transaction.
- A Trial Balance is prepared to establish that all transactions recorded in the Cash account have been posted and that postings have been in compliance with the rules of double-entry accounting.
- A Trial Balance might balance even though the accounting entries may be incorrect.

Suggested answers to activities

3.1 Introduction to debit and credit

Transactions	Debit entry	Credit entry
1. £100,000 received as capital from the owner	Cash account	Capital account
2. Bought a vehicle for £30,000	Motor vehicles account	Cash account
3. £24,000 paid to purchase goods for sale	Purchases account	Cash account
4. £36,000 received from sales	Cash account	Sales account
5. £10,000 paid as loan to Robert, a salesman	Robert loan account	Cash account
6. £2,400 paid for advertising	Advertising account	Cash account

3.2 Columns on each side of a ledger account

The column drawn on each side of the Cash account but not in any ledger account is the one for recording the voucher reference. This is because a transaction needs to be substantiated with a supporting voucher only when it is recorded for the first time and that would be in a book of prime entry, i.e. the Cash Book.

3.3 Posting the ledger

Transactions	Account	Side
1. Amount received from the owner as capital	Capital	Credit
2. Amount paid to acquire a car for the business	Motor vehicles	Debit
3. Amount paid to purchase goods for sale	Purchases	Debit
4. Amounts received by selling the goods	Sales	Credit
5. Amount paid to the landlord as rent	Rent	Debit
6. Amount paid to buy staff refreshments	Staff welfare	Debit
7. Amount received as a loan from John Kitchener	John's Loan	Credit
8. Amount paid as staff salary	Salaries	Debit
9. Amount paid to buy a Cash Book and a ledger	Stationery	Debit

3.4 Preparing a Trial Balance

Trial Balance as at 31 December 2010		
	Dr	Cr
	£	£
Motor vehicles a/c	8,200	–
Stationery a/c	145	–
Capital a/c	–	5,000
Cash a/c	538	–
Purchases a/c	4,215	–
Sale a/c	–	6,948
Joe's Loan a/c	–	3,500
Rent a/c	400	–
Salaries a/c	800	–
Advertising a/c	528	–
Vehicle maint a/c	412	–
Interest a/c	210	–
	15,448	15,448

3.5 Trial Balance and accounting errors

(a) The debit side will fall short by £1,200 because the payment has not been posted.

(b) No impact – because neither a debit nor a credit entry has been made.

(c) Debit side will be short by £180 because the credit is £645 whereas the debit is only £465.

(d), (e) and (f) No impact on the Trial Balance because every credit matches with a corresponding debit, although the posting is to a wrong account.

Multiple choice questions

Naming the ledger account for posting

3.1 As the bookkeeper, identify the account to which you will post following transactions recorded by the cashier in the Cash account:

(a) £300 paid to buy a Cash Book and a ledger

x	Purchases account	
y	Accounting books account	
z	Stationery account	

(b) £15,000 paid to acquire a lorry for business use

x	Capital account	
y	Motor vehicle account	
z	Transport account	

(c) £6,000 paid to buy alarm clocks for sale

x	Purchases account	
y	Alarm clocks account	
z	Furniture account	

(d) £400 paid for servicing the business lorry

x	Motor vehicle account	
y	General expenses account	
z	Vehicle maintenance account	

(e) £10,000 received as capital from Joe Gardiner, the proprietor of the shop

x	Joe Gardiner's account	
y	Capital account	
z	Cash introduced account	

Accounting for business transactions

3.2 The accounting entries for recording £100,000 cash introduced by the owner of a business are:

(a) Debit Cash account and credit Investments account ☐
(b) Credit Cash account and debit Investment in business account ☐
(c) Credit Cash account and debit Owner's account ☐
(d) Debit Cash account and credit Capital account ☐

3.3 Accounting entries for recording payment of a telephone bill are:

(a) Debit Capital and credit Cash account ☐
(b) Debit Cash account and credit Telephone expenses account ☐
(c) Credit Cash account and debit Telephone expenses account ☐
(d) Credit Cash account and debit Office equipment account ☐

3.4 Accounting entries for recording payment of a loan to Jill, working as manager:

(a) Debit Jill's Loan account and credit Cash account ☐
(b) Debit Cash account and credit Jill's Loan account ☐
(c) Credit Cash account and debit Staff welfare account ☐
(d) Credit Cash account and debit Salaries account ☐

3.5 Accounting entries for repayment of a loan received from Richard, the owner's friend:

(a) Debit Cash account and credit Richard's Loan account
(b) Debit Cash account and credit Capital account
(c) Credit Cash account and debit Richard's Loan account
(d) Credit Cash account and debit Capital account

3.6 As the bookkeeper, to which side of the appropriate ledger account will you post the following transactions already recorded in the Cash account:

	DEBIT (x)	CREDIT (y)
(a) Payment of rent for business premises		
(b) Receipt of capital from the proprietor		
(c) Amounts received on sale of goods		
(d) Payment for a vehicle		
(e) Payments for purchasing goods for sale		
(f) Payment of telephone bills		
(g) Receipt of an amount as loan		
(h) Repayment of part of the loan		

The Trial Balance

3.7 Which of the following statements is correct:

(a) A Trial Balance is a list of all entries made in the books of account
(b) A Trial Balance is a list of balances in all ledger accounts
(c) A Trial Balance is a list of balances in the Cash account and all ledger accounts
(d) A Trial Balance is another ledger account

3.8 Which of the following statements is correct:

(a) A Trial Balance will always balance
(b) A Trial Balance reports the profit or loss made by a business
(c) A Trial Balance reports the financial position of a business
(d) A Trial Balance reveals whether the double-entry principle has been complied with

3.9 The total of the debit balances listed in a Trial Balance will not be equal to that of credits:

(a) If an amount entered in the prime entry book is not posted
(b) If an amount paid for purchases is posted to the Stationery account
(c) If a transaction has not been entered in the book of prime entry
(d) If an amount drawn by the owner is posted to the debit of the Capital account

3.10 Which of the following errors will a Trial Balance fail to reveal?

(a) Payment of £240 for stationery being posted as £420
(b) Payment of £2,800 for goods to be sold being posted to the Stationery account
(c) £7,500 received from sales being posted to the Sales account as £5,700
(d) Sales account total being added as £36,400 instead of £39,400

3.11 Which of the following errors would have caused a difference in the Trial Balance?

(a) Posting payment of £21,000 for stationery as £12,000 to the Stationery account

(b) Not recording in the Cash account £15,000 paid for purchasing goods for sale

(c) Posting to the Motor vehicles account £600 paid for servicing vehicles

(d) Recording a sale of £30,000 as £3,000 in the Cash Book

3.12 A trader, who commenced business in the year, extracted his Trial Balance on the last day of the first month as shown on the right. It failed to balance. Which of the following would explain the failure:

Trial Balance	Debit	Credit
Capital account	–	£50,000
Motor vehicles account	£20,000	–
Purchases account	£112,000	–
Sales account	–	£186,000
Salaries account	–	£34,000
Other expenses account	£22,000	–
Cash account	£48,000	–
	£202,000	£270,000

(a) The Trial Balance fails to include one or more of account balances

(b) Salaries, an expenditure, has been stated in error as a credit balance

(c) The Trial Balance has been added wrongly

(d) A payment has been posted wrongly to the credit side of an account instead of debit

3.13 Assuming that each of the errors stated below is the only accounting error, identify by placing a tick in the appropriate box the amount by which the Trial Balance will fail to balance.

(a) £360 received on sales is not posted

x	Excess credit of £360	
y	Excess debit of £360	
z	Excess debit of £720	

(b) £1,800 paid for purchases is posted as £180

x	Trial Balance will balance	
y	Excess credit of £1,620	
z	Excess credit of £1,800	

(c) £145 paid for servicing the vehicle was posted to the Motor vehicles account

x	Excess debit of £145	
y	Excess credit of £145	
z	Trial balance will balance	

(d) £500 paid as a loan to John, a salesman, has been posted to the credit of John's Loan account

x	Excess credit of £1,000	
y	Excess credit of £500	
z	Excess debit of £1,000	

(e) £160 received on sales is not recorded at all by the cashier

x	Excess debit of £160	
y	Excess credit of £160	
z	Trial Balance will balance	

(f) £260 paid for stationery was posted to the Stationery account as £620

x	Excess credit of £360	
y	Excess debit of £260	
z	Excess debit of £360	

(g) The debit side of the Cash account is overcast by £200 (casting means adding)

x	Trial balance will balance	
y	Excess debit of £200	
z	Excess credit of £200	

Answers to multiple choice questions

3.1a: z 3.1b: y 3.1c: x 3.1d: z 3.1e: y 3.2: d 3.3: c 3.4: a 3.5: c 3.6a: x 3.6b: y 3.6c: y 3.6d: x 3.6e: x 3.6f: x 3.6g: y 3.6h: x 3.7: c 3.8: d 3.9: a 3.10: b 3.11: a 3.12: b 3.13a: y 3.13b: y 3.13c: z 3.13d: x 3.13e: z 3.13f: z 3.13g: y

Progressive questions

PQ 3.1 The double-entry system of accounting

(a) What is the double-entry system of accounting?

(b) Why does the double-entry system of accounting require that every transaction should be accounted for by a matching pair of accounting entries – one a debit and the other a credit?

PQ 3.2 The Cash account entry and the ledger account entry

Guy Smith commenced business as a dealer in CCTV cameras. His transactions on the first day of business were as follows:

Transactions	Account – Debit	Account – Credit
1. Received in cash as capital from Guy Smith		
2. Paid £2,400 for two tables and six chairs		
3. Paid £1,200 to buy CCTV cameras for sale		
4. Paid £215 for advertising the CCTV cameras		
5. Received £600 from the sale of some CCTV cameras		
6. Received £8,000 as a loan from Jerry Baxter		
7. Paid £500 as rent for shop premises		
8. Paid £48 to buy a Cash Book and a ledger		
9. Paid £12,500 to buy a vehicle for office use		
10. Paid £45 for fuel		
11. Paid back £2,000 to Jerry Baxter		
12. Paid £210 to repair the car		

Required: How should these transactions be accounted for?

PQ 3.3 Identify the account and the side to which the entry is made

Philip McDonald commenced business as a dealer in cellphones. How should the following transactions of his business be accounted for?

Transactions	Cash account side	Ledger account Name	Ledger account Side
1. Commenced business bringing £25,000 in cash			
2. Paid £800 for four chairs and two desks for the office			
3. Paid £225 for a press notice announcing start of business			
4. Paid cash to buy 18 cellphones at £30 each			
5. Paid £45 for office files, a Cash Book and ledger			
6. Paid £2,400 to buy a second-hand vehicle for business use			
7. Paid £540 for a steel cabinet for the office files			
8. Paid £800 to make the vehicle roadworthy			
9. Paid £225 for insuring the vehicle			
10. Paid £85 to buy fuel for the vehicle			
11. Paid £24 to buy envelopes and postage stamps			
12. Paid £2,400 as school fees for Philip's son			
13. Sold ten cellphones at £50 each			
14. Paid £125 for servicing the vehicle			
15. Paid £90 to settle the office telephone bill			

PQ 3.4 Posting from the Cash account

Arnold commenced business on 3 January 2010. His receipts and payments have been recorded in a Cash account as shown on the right.

Required: Post each transaction to the appropriate account in the ledger and extract a Trial Balance as at 9 January 2010.

Cash account

2010		£	2010		£
3.1	Capital	15,000	4.1	Purchases	300
4.1	Sales	450	4.1	Rent	1,500
9.1	Sales	250	4.1	Stationery	90
			5.1	Purchases	150
			6.1	Stationery	60
			7.1	Motor vehicles	1,500
			8.1	Motor vehicle maint	225
			8.1	Drawings	450
			9.1	Motor vehicle maint	40
					4,315
			9.1	Balance c/d	11,385
		15,700			15,700

PQ 3.5 Posting from the Cash account and the Bank account

Bennett, a wholesale dealer in toys, commenced business on 1 April 2010 with a capital of £12,000 which he deposited immediately in a Bank account. His transactions in the first week have already been entered in the Cash account and Bank account and appear as follows:

Cash account

		£			£
2.4	Sales	1,200	3.4	Cleaning	140
3.4	Sales	1,800	5.4	Drawings	250
4.4	Sales	2,500	5.4	Wages	300
5.4	Sales	3,400	5.4	Bank	7,800
					8,490
			5.4	Balance	410
		8,900			8,900
6.4	Bal.	410			

Bank account

		£		Chq		£
1.4	Capital	12,000	1.4	1	Rent	3,000
5.4	Cash	7,800	1.4	2	Furniture	1,200
			1.4	3	Purchases	2,400
			2.4	4	Advertising	240
			3.4	5	Purchases	1,800
			4.4	6	Electricity	270
			4.4	7	Advertising	124
			5.4	8	Telephone	115
						9,149
			5.4	–	Balance c/d	10,651
		19,800				19,800
5.4	Balance	10,651				

Required: Post these transactions to appropriate ledger accounts and extract a Trial Balance as at 5 April 2010.

PQ 3.6 A ledger account and its balance

Listed below are the names of some ledger accounts. State whether you would expect to find a debit balance or a credit balance in each.

Name of ledger account	Side
Capital account	
Purchases account	
Stationery account	
Office equipment account	
Advertising account	
Sales account	
Rent account	

Name of ledger account	Side
Loan due to the business	
Loan owed to a Mr Rich account	
Staff welfare account	
Motor vehicle account	
Motor vehicle maintenance account	
Building upkeep account	
Staff salaries account	

PQ 3.7 Preparation of a Trial Balance when one balance is omitted

The list of account balances, stated below, has been extracted from the books of a newsagent 'First with the News' as at the year-end on 31 March 2010. The only balance not included in the list is the one in the Capital account.

Accounts	£
Cash account	2,500
Purchases account	170,500
Sales account	295,900
Rent account	18,000
Audit fees account	1,200
Motor vehicles account	60,000
Loan to Cashier account	5,000
Machinery account	7,000

Accounts	£
Furniture account	24,000
Bank loan account	3,000
Stationery account	400
Salaries account	21,600
Advertising account	4,200
Sales commission account	9,200
Telephone expense account	300

Required: Prepare the Trial Balance for First with the News as at 31 March 2010 assuming that the Trial Balance is in balance when the Capital account is included.

PQ 3.8 Posting from the Cash account

Faisal Ahmed commenced business on 7 November 2010 selling flat panel computer monitors. He buys them for £180 each and sells them at £250 each. The Cash account shown below records his receipts and payments in the first week of business. As the bookkeeper you are required to post these transactions to appropriate ledger accounts and check on the accuracy of your posting by extracting a Trial Balance as at 11 November 2010.

Cash account

2010		£	2010		£
7.11	Capital	15,000	7.11	Rent	1,000
10.11	Sales	4,000	8.11	Office equipment	3,000
11.11	Sales	3,000	9.11	Stationery	45
			9.11	Motor vehicle	2,500
			9.11	Motor vehicle maint	185
			10.11	Purchases	5,040
			11.11	Advertising	200
			11.11	Wages	550
					12,520
			11.11	Balance c/d	9,480
		22,000			22,000
12.11	Balance	9,480			

PQ 3.9 Accounting under the double-entry system

Mike Burton commenced trading on 3 January 2010 with a capital in cash of £10,000. His transactions during the first week were as follows:

Date	Transaction	Date	Transaction
3.1	Deposited £9,500 in a Bank account	5.1	Paid £50 in cash for office cleaning
3.1	Paid £800 by cheque no 01 for furniture	5.1	Paid £2,240 by cheque no 06 for purchases
3.1	Paid £1,800 by cheque no 02 for purchases	5.1	Sold goods for £1,850
3.1	Paid £40 in cash for office cleaning	5.1	Paid £420 by cheque no 07 for advertising
3.1	Paid £240 by cheque no 03 for advertising	5.1	Deposited £5,840 in the Bank account
3.1	Sold goods for £2,100	6.1	Paid £40 in cash for office cleaning
4.1	Paid £1,450 by cheque no 04 for purchases	6.1	Sold goods for £1,250
4.1	Received £1,000 as a loan from Sylvia	6.1	Paid £1,800 by cheque no 08 for purchases
4.1	Sold goods for £1,840	7.1	Sold goods for £2,480
4.1	Paid £1,600 by cheque no 05 for furniture	7.1	Paid £280 by cheque no 09 for advertising

Required:

(a) Record these transactions in the Cash account and in the Bank account, drawn as a two-column Cash Book and post them to appropriate ledger accounts.

(b) Prepare a Trial Balance of Mike Burton's business as at 7 January 2010.

(c) State whether the balancing of the Trial Balance should convince Mike that his accounts provide a full and accurate record of the transactions of his week's trading.

Test questions

Test 3.1 Prime entry to Trial Balance

Zaidi commenced business on 4 January 2010 introducing £20,000 as his capital. Stated below is a summary of his transactions during the week to 8 January:

Paid for furniture	£24,000	Paid as rent for shop premises	£800
Paid to buy goods for sale	£54,600	Received from sale of goods	£62,500
Received as loan from Rizwi	£5,000	Paid for a car for business use	£4,000
Paid as staff salary	£3,000	Paid for gas and electricity	£240
Paid for advertising his goods	£400	Paid for a Cash Book and ledger	£300

Required:

(a) Record these transactions in a Cash account, carrying down the balance as at 8 January.

(b) Post each transaction to the appropriate account in the ledger.

(c) Extract a Trial Balance as at close of business on 8 January 2010.

Test 3.2 Withholding the balance in the Capital account

Joe Cameron extracted the following balances from his books of account on 31.12.2010:

Stationery a/c	£320	Postage a/c	£125	Bank a/c	£7,675
Salaries a/c	£12,800	Cash a/c	£1,465	Motor vehicles a/c	£18,000
Electricity a/c	£960	Furniture a/c	£12,000	Delivery expenses a/c	£1,250
Sales a/c	£94,500	Loan from Peter	£3,000	Office equipment a/c	£4,600
Heating a/c	£2,650	Purchases a/c	£68,400	Sales commission a/c	£2,555

Required: Assuming that the only balance he did not extract is the one from the Capital account, set out these balances in the form of a Trial Balance as at 31.12.2010.

Test 3.3 An incorrectly prepared Trial Balance

When Alan Rayan failed the finals of his Business Administration degree, he opened a shop near the university selling second-hand books. The bookkeeper who maintained his ledger resigned shortly after the year-end. Alan felt that he had sufficient knowledge to extract a Trial Balance from his books of account and is surprised when the Trial Balance (see on the right) failed to balance.

Required:

(a) Explain to Alan why his Trial Balance fails to balance.

(b) Re-draft the Trial Balance as at 31 December 2010.

Trial Balance as at 31.12.2010

	Dr	Cr
	£'000	£'000
Furniture a/c	–	120
Telephone expenses a/c	10	–
Cash and bank	23	–
Sales a/c	299	–
Rent a/c	12	–
Purchases a/c	–	148
Advertising a/c	14	–
Stationery a/c	6	–
Staff salary a/c	–	46
Capital a/c	80	–
	444	314

Chapter 4

The Statement of financial position and Statement of income

By the end of this chapter

You should learn:

- How accounts are classified
- How a credit and a debit balance indicates a class
- How, according to the class, each account is included in either the Statement of income or the Statement of financial position
- The accounting equation

You should be able to:

- Prepare a Statement of income
- Prepare a Statement of financial position
- Prepare an accounting equation

4.1 Five classes of accounts

We have seen that in a cash-based business every transaction is recorded in a Cash Book, either in a Cash account or a Bank account and then posted to an appropriate ledger account for the purpose of analysing where the cash has come from and how it has been spent. We will learn in this chapter that payments are classified as *assets* or *expenses* and receipts as *income, liability or capital.*

4.2 Identifying assets from expenses

4.2.1 Assets

We know that our personal assets include a television, a vehicle and probably a house. We refer to them as our assets because we own them and we expect to benefit from them for a number of years. On the other hand we would regard as an expense (rather than as asset) the amount we paid for a lunch or for a seat at the football match. Such payments do give us satisfaction (otherwise we would not have made them), but the satisfaction derived does not last long.

A business too draws similar distinction between assets and expenses, but with two important differences. These are:

- First, for a business, ownership is not a prerequisite. What is important is whether it is in control of that item. When a business pays £100,000 for leasing shop premises, for say ten years, it regards the lease (though not owned) as an asset, because the premises would be within its control and it could use the premises for generating income during the ten years.
- Secondly, a business identifies an item as an asset when it is assured that economic benefits from it will continue for more than a year, i.e. beyond the current accounting period.

Accordingly, a business regards as assets only those resources that are within its control and from which it expects to receive future economic benefit – these will be reported in the *Statement of financial position*. Applying these criteria many items, such as pemises, machinery, vehicles and office equipment, are identified as assets of a business.

4.2.2 Expenses

An accounting period is normally of one year's duration. A payment that results in an item which produces economic benefits after the end of the accounting period is classified as an asset. If there is no economic benefit after the end of the accounting period, then the payment is classified as an expense. Examples of expenses include payments for advertising, salary, electricity and postage. In this chapter we assume that each of these expense classifications will cease to provide economic benefits beyond the end of the accounting period – in later chapters we will see the accounting treatment where there is still some benefit expected.

Activity 4.1 Identifying assets from expenses in a business

Jeremy opened a vehicle repair garage with a capital of £10,000. He made the following payments on the first day:

(a) Paid £1,000 as rent for the premises.

(b) Paid £3,000 for furniture.

(c) Paid £4,200 for buying a crankshaft and other tools.

(d) Paid £180 to advertise his services.

(e) Paid £20 on staff lunch.

Required: identify whether each payment is for an asset or is an expense.

4.3 Identifying income from liabilities and capital

4.3.1 Income

In everyday terms, income is seen as the amount we earn. When we receive our salary or a grant we regard it as our income because there would be no need to pay it back. The income earned by a business depends on the nature of its activity, for example a trader's income is from sales, a school's income is from tuition fees and a money lender's income is the interest receivable on the loans that have been made.

4.3.2 Liabilities

Whereas *income* is an amount earned, a *liability* is an amount owed. Unlike a salary, if we receive a bank loan there is an obligation to repay it and we would regard it as a liability. The same applies in a business and whatever it owes is classified as a liability. The main liabilities in a business often include bank loans, amount remaining unpaid to a supplier from whom it made its purchases and, in the case of a limited company, amounts of unpaid income tax.

Definition of a liability

For accounting purposes, i.e. for inclusion in the Statement of financial position, a business identifies as a liability any obligation to pay (transfer economic benefit), provided three conditions are met. These are that:

(a) it should be a present obligation, i.e. the obligation to pay should have already arisen;

(b) the obligation should be certain or at least probable, i.e. there should be no realistic expectation that it could be avoided; and

(c) it should be possible to reliably estimate the amount payable.

4.3.3 Capital

It would be convenient to say that whatever a business receives would either be an income or a liability. We have seen, for example, that an amount received from sales is not repayable and is income, whereas an amount received as a loan is repayable and is, therefore, a liability. The question that arises is whether capital can be classified as a liability. To decide we have to consider whether capital satisfies the three conditions needed for recognition as a liability.

(a) It should be a present obligation, i.e. the obligation to pay should have already arisen. This condition is not satisfied because there is no present obligation to pay back the capital. It is only if the business is to be closed that this obligation arises.

(b) The obligation should be certain or at least probable, i.e. there should be no realistic expectation that it could be avoided; and this condition again would only be satisfied on the eventuality of a closure of the business.

(c) It should be possible to reliably estimate the amount payable. This condition is not satisfied because the capital could be eroded by the business incurring losses. For example, if the capital received from the owner is £10,000 and the first year's operation results in a loss of £3,000, the amount owed to the owner would only be the remaining £7,000. If the business had to cease and sell off its assets this amount could be even less. It is not, therefore, possible to reliably estimate the amount that would be payable if the business were to cease trading. There is a risk that either could happen – losses might be incurred on trading and on any forced sale of the assets and there might be an unforeseen increase in the liabilities such as the warranty claims against Toyota for fitting faulty accelerators on their cars. Therefore, even if the business is to close down the amount repayable to the owners is uncertain.

In the circumstances we classify capital as *equity*, i.e. the remaining interest in assets after all of the liabilities have been paid.

4.4 Accounting treatment of payments

We know that every payment is recorded by the cashier on the credit side of the Cash (or Bank) account and posted to the debit of an appropriate account. We should now learn that payments are for one of three reasons as follows:

1. To acquire an asset.
2. To meet an expense.
3. To settle a liability.

4.4.1 A payment to acquire an asset

Posted to the debit of an appropriately named asset account. It might be appropriate to post similar items to a single asset classification to avoid a proliferation of ledger accounts. For example, payments made for the purchase of a bus, car or van may all be posted to the debit of a Motor vehicle account and, similarly, payments made to buy shelves, tables or chairs may be posted to the debit of a Furniture account. The level of detail needed will vary from business to business. Note that an asset account will always have a debit balance.

4.4.2 A payment for an expense

Posted to the debit side of the appropriate account with the name of each account identifying the nature of the expense, e.g. Salaries account, Rent account, Telephone account. This means that every expense account too would have a debit balance.

4.4.3 A payment to settle a liability

Posted to the account recording the liability; for example, a loan repayment would be made to the Loan account. As we will learn in the next paragraph a liability account always reports a credit balance. When repayment of that liability is debited to the liability account, the credit balance in that account is reduced or eliminated, depending on whether it is in part or full settlement.

Activity 4.2 Accounting for payments

Thelma Splash is the owner of Waterways4U, a business hiring out kayaks. The following payments made by the business have been all credited in the Bank account. Thelma wishes to know whether each payment would increase or decrease an asset, expense or a liability.

Reason for the payment	Amount	Asset	Expense	Liability
Paid for a Bedford van	£18,000			
Paid as staff salary	£7,200			
Paid to part settle a loan from Omar	£5,000			
Paid to buy ten kayaks	£15,000			
Paid as rent	£6,000			
Paid to buy desktop computers for office use	£1,500			

Activity 4.3 How each payment affects account balances

Upon recording and posting the transactions until 9 March 2010, the balances in the ledger include those stated on the right. The following transactions took place on 10 March:

Motor vehicles account	£12,000
Loan from Ibrahim account	£10,000
Furniture & fittings account	£18,400
Rent account	£4,000

Paid £8,000 for shop fittings.
Paid £3,000 as part settlement of amount owed to Ibrahim.
Paid £2,000 as rent on shop premises for the month of March.
Paid £18,000 to buy a Toyota Sedan vehicle for use of office staff.

Required: what would be the balances remaining in the four accounts named above, identifying whether it would be a debit or a credit balance, after the four payments have been posted to these accounts?

4.5 Accounting treatment of receipts

Every amount received by a business and recorded by the cashier as a debit in the Cash (or Bank) account would be one of the following:

1. an income earned by the business,
2. a liability owed by the business or capital contributed by the owner, or
3. conversion of an asset (disposal) or an expense into cash.

4.5.1 Income

Amounts earned are posted to the credit of an account named in accordance with the nature of the earning. For example, in the case of a trader, sales revenue is credited to the Sales account. Similarly, a school would post the fees it receives to the credit of a School fees account. This means that every account reporting an income would always report a credit balance.

4.5.2 Liabilities and capital

Cash received as a loan, recorded as a debit in the Cash account, is credited to an account opened in the name of the party to whom the amount is owed. For example, £5,000 received as a loan from Henry would be recorded on the debit side of the Cash account and posted to the credit of Henry's Loan account. Amounts contributed as capital by the owner are accounted for identically. This means that every liability account (until it is settled) as well as the Capital account will always have a credit balance.

4.5.3 Conversion into cash of assets and expenses

Amounts received from disposal of an asset, recorded as a debit in the Cash (Bank) account, would be posted to the appropriate asset account, reducing the debit balance in that account. However, we need to draw a distinction between two situations:

(a) ***Accounting treatment where the amount receivable from an asset is fixed***: the amount receivable is a fixed amount, for example, in the case of a loan. Let us assume that the business had made a staff loan of £10,000 repayable in five equal instalments. When the repayment of £2,000 is received back from the employee it will be posted to the credit of the Staff Loan account which will be reduced to £8,000.

(b) ***Accounting treatment where the amount receivable from an asset is uncertain***: we have seen that with a loan the total amount that will be received is certain. This would not be true when selling assets such as a vehicle. For example, a vehicle acquired for £10,000 may be sold for a higher or lower amount. This would give rise to a gain or loss on disposal which would be reported in the Statement of income. Accounting for gains and losses on disposal are dealt with in detail in Chapter 8.

An interesting question that arises is how can an expense be converted into cash? This is not a common occurrence. One example is where a business recovers from its staff the cost of any private telephone calls that may have been made or amounts disallowed on an expenses claim.

We should by now be clear that any account reporting capital, a liability or a source of income will always have its balance stated on the credit side. It follows, therefore, that the opposite is true – any account with a credit balance would be reporting either capital, a liability or an income.

A debit entry made in any of these accounts would reduce the balance in it, e.g. a cash payment of £1,000 made to a supplier who is owed £5,000 would be debited to the supplier's (liability) account, reducing to £4,000 the amount owed to that supplier.

Activity 4.4 How amounts received affect account balances

Transactions had been recorded and posting was up to date as at 17 May 2010. Four of the ledger balances are shown on the right. The following amounts were received on 18 May:

Capital account	£12,000
Loan given to Stella	£10,000
Telephone account	£18,400
Sales account	£4,000

Received from sales £1,500.
Received £3,000 as additional capital from the owner.
Received £2,000 from Stella as part repayment of her loan.
Received £300 from a salesman for private calls made using the office phone.

Required:
(a) What balances remain in the four accounts after the four payments have been posted?
(b) State whether each balance is a debit or credit balance.

4.6 How the class of an account is identified

A Cash account will always report a debit balance and be reported in the Statement of financial position as an asset. A Bank account too would usually be an asset reporting a debit balance. If, however, by arrangement with the bank, *overdraft* facilities have been obtained then it would have a credit balance because it would then be reporting a liability.

Thus all accounts written up in the books of a business would belong to one of five classes – namely an asset, a liability, capital, an expense or income. Irrespective of the name by which an account is identified, the following will always apply:

- If it has a debit balance it should be reporting an asset or an expense.
- If it has a credit balance it should be reporting a liability, capital or income.

Activity 4.5 The class of an account identified by its balance

State in Column A the side on which each of the accounts listed below would have its balance, and in column B whether you would classify each of the named accounts as an asset account, liability account, capital account, expense account or income account.

Name of account	Column A (debit side or credit side)	Column B (classify the account)
1. Capital account		
2. Motor vehicles account		
3. Purchases account		
4. Sales account		
5. Rent account		
6. Cash account		
7. Bank account (overdraft)		
8. Staff welfare account		
9. Telephone expenses a/c		
10. Loan from John account		
11. Salaries account		
12. Stationery account		

Note: The Purchases account is regarded as an expense on the assumption that all goods purchased have been sold by the year-end. Admittedly this assumption is unrealistic for most businesses and we will see in Chapter 6 how to account when not all of the goods purchased have been sold by the end of the period.

Activity 4.6 Classifying the accounts

In Chapter 3 we accounted for Angela's transactions during the first week of her business and extracted a Trial Balance showing the balances in all her accounts at close of business on that day, as shown on the right.

Required:
Classify each of the accounts.

Trial Balance as at 7 January 2010			
	Debit	Credit	Classify
	£	£	
Cash a/c	9,070	–	
Capital a/c	–	10,000	
Joe's Loan a/c	–	5,000	
Sales a/c	–	12,000	
Furniture a/c	1,500	–	
Purchases a/c	8,000	–	
Advertising a/c	590	–	
Rent a/c	200	–	
Stationery a/c	140	–	
Motor vehicles a/c	7,500	–	
	27,000	27,000	

4.7 Statement of income

The performance of a business in each accounting period is measured by identifying whether it made a profit or a loss in that period. If the income earned in the period is more than the expenses it incurred, the business would have made a profit; otherwise it would have made a loss.

To identify the profit or loss in each accounting period, the balances recorded in the income accounts need to be matched with the balances recorded in all its expense accounts. This matching is achieved by transferring the balances to a Statement of income as follows:

- Income accounts will each be debited and the Statement of income credited.
- Expense accounts will each be credited and the Statement of income debited.

For purposes of illustration let us refer to Angela's transactions as reported in Activity 4.6 and consider how well she has done in that accounting period, by taking four steps as follows:

Step one: transfer the balance from the income account

At the end of the period (of seven days) her Sales account reports a credit balance of £12,000. This is transferred to the Statement of income by debiting the Sales Account with £12,000 (leaving no balance in that account) and crediting the Statement of income. The accounts concerned will then appear as follows:

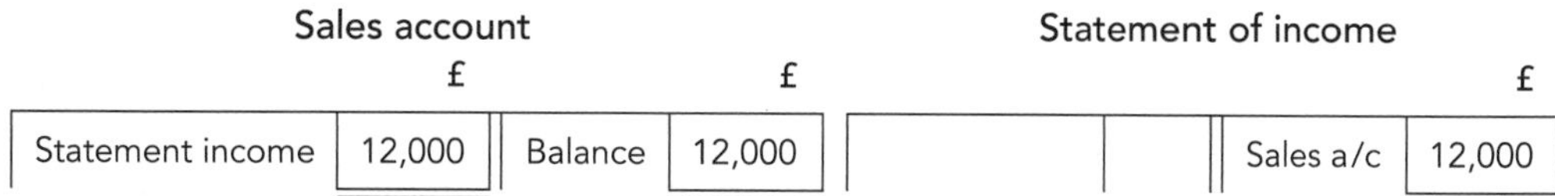

Sales account

	£		£
Statement income	12,000	Balance	12,000

Statement of income

			£
		Sales a/c	12,000

Step two: Transfer the cost of goods sold

Purchases account

	£		£
Balance b/f	8,000	Statement of income	8,000
	8,000		8,000

Statement of income

	£		£
Purchases a/c	8,000	Sales a/c	12,000
Gross profit c/d	4,000		
	12,000		12,000
		Gross profit b/d	4,000

Next we transfer the balance in the Purchases account (assuming that all computers bought by Angela have been sold out) to the Statement of income.

This enables us to compare the sales income with the cost of the computers sold (see on left), identifying the difference of £4,000 as the *gross profit* made by Angela in an accounting period of seven days.

Step three: transfer the balances in all other expense accounts

All remaining expense accounts are closed by transferring the balances in each of them to the Statement of income, a pair of accounting entries being needed to make each transfer. The amount by which gross profit (£4,000) exceeds the total of all other expenses (£930) is referred to as *net profit* and for the accounting period net profit is identified as £3,070. If the expenses were more than the gross profit a *net loss* would have resulted.

Statement of income – seven days to 7 January 2010

	£		£
Purchases a/c	8,000	Sales a/c	12,000
Gross profit c/d	4,000		
	12,000		12,000
Advertising a/c	590		4,000
Rent a/c	200		
Stationery a/c	140		
	930		
Net profit c/d	3,070		
	4,000		4,000
		Net profit b/d	3,070

Step four: transfer the net profit to the owner

The net profit is then transferred, by another pair of entries (debiting Statement of income and crediting the Capital account), to the Capital account. The transfer to the Capital account is made because, having invested the capital in the business and taken the business risks, Angela (as the sole owner) is entitled to the profit the business earns. The Statement of income shown below is how it was traditionally prepared. When prepared in this format it was known as the *Trading and Profit and loss account.*

The first section identifying the gross profit is known as the Trading account, and the lower section identifying the profit or loss for the period as the Profit and loss account. Its lowest portion showing the transfer of the profit to the owner is referred to as the appropriation section of the Profit and Loss account.

Statement of income – for seven days to 7 January 2010			
	£		£
Purchases a/c	8,000	Sales a/c	12,000
Gross profit c/d	4,000		
	12,000		12,000
Advertising a/c	590	Gross profit b/d	4,000
Rent a/c	200		
Stationery a/c	140		
	930		
Net profit c/d	3,070		
	4,000		4,000
Capital a/c	3,070	Net profit b/d	3,070
	3,070		3,070

The current practice is to present the Statement of income in a vertical format (as a statement rather than as an account) so that it would be meaningful even to those not familiar with the language of accounting.

Note that although each amount stated in the Statement of income has been transferred from a ledger account, for the sake of clarity, income and expenses are reported in the Statement of income without using the word *account* or its abbreviation *a/c*.

Statement of income xxxx		
		£
Sales		12,000
Purchases		(8,000)
Gross profit		4,000
Advertising	590	
Rent	200	
Stationery	140	(930)
Net profit		3,070

4.8 The Statement of financial position

A *Statement of financial position (Balance Sheet)* is a list, usually prepared on the last day of each accounting period, of all the balances remaining in any account, after closing all income accounts and expense accounts by transfer to the Statement of income. We know that there are in all five classes of account – income, expenses, assets, liabilities and capital. When income and expense accounts have been closed, what remain would be the accounts reporting assets, liabilities and capital.

In Angela's business the only ledger accounts that still remain open are the Capital account, the Furniture account, the Motor vehicles account, the Cash account and the Loan account. A statement of financial position of her business prepared as at 7 January, taking care to list the assets separately from capital and liabilities, appears below. The Statement of financial position lists only the balances remaining in various asset and liability accounts on the day it is prepared. As an exception, bearing in mind that Angela is the owner of the business, we have included more particulars – the capital she started with, the profit earned in the accounting period of seven days, and what her capital is on the day of reporting.

Although the Statement of financial position lists the balances in various ledger accounts, the word account is avoided for the sake of clarity.

Statement of financial position as at 7 January 2010	
	£
Assets:	
Furniture	1,500
Motor vehicle	7,500
Cash	9,070
	18,070

Capital and liabilities:	£
Capital – on 1 January	10,000
Add: Profit until 7 Junuary	3,070
Capital on 7 January	13,070
Joe's loan	5,000
	18,070

4.9 Statement of financial position compared with Trial Balance

A Statement of financial position, just like a Trial Balance, lists balances in all the accounts remaining open at the point it is prepared. But there are three important points of difference:

1. A Trial Balance may be extracted at any time to check the accuracy of the postings made under the double-entry system; whereas the Statement of financial position is generally only prepared to show the position of a business on the last day of its accounting period.
2. A Trial Balance lists the balances in all five classes of accounts. The Statement of financial position reports only the balances in the asset accounts, Capital account and liability accounts. This is because it is prepared *after* the income and expense accounts have been all closed by transferring their balances to the Statement of income.
3. In a Trial Balance the account balances may appear in any sequence, whereas in a Statement of financial position it is usual to list the assets and liabilities in a set order.

4.10 The set order of items in a Statement of financial position

The UK and the International Accounting Standards make the following requirements on the set order in which assets, liabilities and capital should be reported in a Statement of financial position:

1. The assets should be listed in the reverse order of their *liquidity*. Accountants use the word liquidity to refer to the time it would take to convert an asset to cash. Cash and bank balances are regarded as the most liquid assets and are stated last when listing the assets. Other assets are listed according to the reverse sequence in which they are likely to be converted to cash. For example, it is unlikely that a business would dispose of its premises unless in desperate circumstances. Therefore business premises are usually reported as the first item.
2. When reporting assets *current assets* should be reported separately from *non-current assets*. Current assets are defined as:

   (a) cash and bank balance; and

   (b) those assets which are likely to be converted to cash (e.g. inventory and amounts receivable from trade customers) and those which are likely to be used up (e.g. rent paid in advance and stationery remaining unused) in the following accounting period.

   Assets other than those identified as current assets are identified as *non-current assets* – this includes assets like premises, machinery, furniture and motor vehicles.
3. Liabilities should be listed in the reverse order in which the business expects to discharge them.

   Any liability (e.g. amounts owed to suppliers and expenses like rent remaining unpaid) which are expected to be discharged within the following accounting period are reported last and are identified as *current liabilities*. Others, for example loans, are listed as *non-current liabilities*. *Capital* which will not be paid back until the business ceases is reported first on the liability side of the Statement of financial position.

   The Statement of financial position of Angela's business as at 7 January 2010, prepared with the required headings identifying current and non-current assets as well as current and non-current liabilities, would appear as shown on the next page.

Statement of financial position as at 7 January 2010	
	£
Non-current assets:	
Furniture	1,500
Motor vehicle	7,500
Current assets:	
Cash	9,070
Total assets	18,070

Capital:	£
Capital as at 1.1.2010	10,000
Add: Profit in seven days	3,070
Capital as at 7.1.2010	13,070
Non-current liabilities:	
Joe's Loan	5,000
	18,070

Activity 4.7 Preparing Statements of income and financial position

Bernard's Retail extracted a Trial Balance from their books of accounts on 31 December 2010, the last day of its accounting period, as shown on the right. You are informed that:

(a) All goods purchased have been sold by the the year-end.

(b) No expenses remain unpaid.

(c) Ignore depreciation.

Required:

(i) The Statement of income for the year ended 31 December 2010.

(ii) The Statement of financial position as at 31 December 2010.

Trial Balance as at 31 December 2010		
	Debit	Credit
	£	£
Motor vehicles a/c	8,200	–
Stationery a/c	145	–
Capital a/c	–	5,000
Cash a/c	628	–
Purchases a/c	4,125	–
Sales a/c	–	6,948
Joe's Loan a/c	–	3,500
Rent a/c	400	–
Salaries a/c	800	–
Advertising a/c	528	–
Vehicle maintenance a/c	412	–
Interest a/c	210	–
	15,448	15,448

4.11 The elements of financial statements

We have classified all the accounts recording the transactions of any business into five classes. IASB identifies these five classes as *elements of financial statements*. This is because income and expenses are the elements that constitute the Statement of income; while assets, liabilities and equity are the elements that constitute the Statement of financial position.

4.12 Accounting equation

In Angela's Statement of financial position (see p. 61) the total of the assets (£18,070) equals the sum of the capital and liabilities. This equality is known as the *accounting equation*. The equality is achieved if the transactions have all been accounted for correctly in compliance with the rules of double-entry.

The accounting equation is stated as follows:

Capital + (Income – Expenses) + Liabilities = Total assets

We could describe this accounting equation in narrative form as: the amount that the owner started with *plus* the amount by which it has grown *plus* any monies owed by the business should *equal* the total assets existing as at the end of the period.

Thus, in the case of Angela's business the position as at the end of the accounting period is:

Capital + (Income – Expenses) + Liabilities = Total assets

£10,000 + (£12,000 – £8,930) + £5,000 = £18,070

Expressed as above the accounting equation identifies that the total assets of the business have been financed by Angela (£10,000 given as capital and the £3,070 profit she leaves in the business) and by a loan of £5,000.

Depending on where the emphasis is to be laid, it is possible to switch the accounting equation around. For example, if Angela wishes to highlight how much of the business assets are hers the accounting equation may be restated as:

Capital = Assets – Liabilities

Angela's capital of £13,070 = total assets (£18,070) less liabilities (£5,000). That portion of the total assets (£13,070) which is financed by the owner of a business is also referred to as the *net assets*. This is the amount the business owes to the owner. This is referred to also as the *owners' equity*.

Activity 4.8 An exercise illustrating the accounting equation

The following information relates to four different businesses – A to D.

	Capital	+ Income	– Expense	+ Liability	= Assets
A	£40,000	£24,000	£15,000	0	
B	£50,000	£36,000	£21,000	£25,000	
C	£80,000	£54,000	£62,000	0	
D	£90,000	£74,500	£98,000	£20,000	

Required: On the basis of the information provided in respect of each, calculate what the total assets of each business would be.

The accounting equation is also helpful when one of the items is missing as seen in the following Activity:

Activity 4.9 Use the accounting equation to calculate the missing figure

Fill the blank grid with the appropriate values, bearing in mind that the assets of a business less its liabilities would be the amount of the owner's capital.

Business	Assets	Liabilities	Capital
A	£280,000	£50,000	?
B	£428,000	?	£375,000
C	?	£54,000	£424,600

4.13 Accounting errors

If the financial statements are to report a true and fair view of the performance as well as position of a business (a) the accounting records should fully and correctly record all transactions that took place within an accounting period, and (b) the financial statements must be correctly prepared, properly and fully reporting the information in the accounting records. Any error either in the records or in the preparation of financial statements would affect the information communicated in the financial statements.

We will consider the accounting errors on the basis of the accounting stage at which they arise, noting whether they are likely to be flagged up and how each would affect the information conveyed by the financial statements.

(a) Errors at the prime entry stage

Any error made by the cashier will be drawn to attention when balancing the Cash Book, because the amount held in hand would be different from the balance in the Cash account. Except where the error is an arithmetical one, the Trial Balance would balance despite such errors, because the wrong amount recorded in the Cash Book would have been faithfully posted. Following are some of the errors the cashier could make:

1. ***An error of omission***: this is where a transaction (an amount received or paid) is not recorded at all. If, for example, an amount received from sales is not recorded at all (by the cashier) the Trial Balance would still balance (because the bookkeeper would not post what is not recorded); but, provided the amount is not misappropriated, such errors would be flagged up when balancing the Cash Book. An error of not recording a sale would result in profit as well as the position of the business being understated.
2. ***An error of duplication***: an example of an error of duplication arising at the stage of prime entry is where a payment (say for purchases) is entered twice by the cashier. The Trial Balance would balance despite such an error because there would be a debit to

match the wrong credit. Here again, unless misappropriation is involved, attention would be drawn to the error when balancing the Cash Book. Unless detected and remedied such errors affect the information conveyed in financial statements.

3. ***An entry error***: where the amount recorded in the Cash Book is not the amount actually received or paid. Even where this is not deliberate, errors of the following type are common:
   (a) *Omission of a zero*: where a payment of £3,600 is recorded in the Cash Book as £360.
   (b) *Transposition of figures*: where a payment of £3,600 is entered as £6,300.
4. ***Arithmetical error*** when adding up the receipts or payments or when striking the balance. Attention will be drawn to such an error both when balancing the Cash Book and by a failure of the Trial Balance to balance.

(b) Errors at the posting stage

1. ***Double-entry error***: this expression covers three types of errors.
   - The first is where an amount recorded in the Cash account is not posted at all.
   - The second is where the amount posted is different from the amount recorded in the Cash Book. For example, the person doing the posting may be guilty of an omission of a zero or transposition of figures.
   - The third is where the rule of double-entry (that every credit must be matched by a debit) is not complied with when posting.

   Any double-entry error will be flagged up when the Trial Balance fails to balance. However, care needs to be taken because there might be a *compensating error* where the Trial Balance continues to balance, because the effect of one or more errors may have been cancelled by other errors.
2. ***Error of commission***: this is where the correct amount is posted though to an incorrect account, but the class of that incorrect account is the same as that of the correct one, e.g. posting to the Stationery account instead of the Purchases account where both are expense accounts. Note that in the example we have referred to, as a result of the error the net profit will be unchanged but the gross profit will be higher than it should be.
3. ***Error of principle***: this is where the correct amount is posted to an incorrect account but the incorrect account is of a different class – e.g. posting the cost of fuel to the Motor vehicles account – i.e. posting to an asset account instead of an expense. In such a case the reported net profit as well as assets will be higher than it should be. This is a serious error and yet, despite the error, the Trial Balance will balance.

4.14 More accounting terminology

Revenue items – refers to all income accounts and expense accounts

Revenue expenditure – refers to expenses

Capital expenditure – refers to payments to acquire assets

Current assets – includes cash and balance at the bank and any assets expected to be converted into cash or used up within one year after the end of the accounting period

Non-current assets – assets other than current assets

Current liabilities – any liability intended to be repaid within one year

Non-current liabilities – any liability other than current liability

Summary

- All accounts, the Cash account, Bank account and all of the other accounts in the ledgers belong to one of five classes or elements.
- The class of an account can be identified on the basis of whether it has a debit balance or credit balance. An account with a debit balance records an asset or an expense; an account with a credit balance records the capital, a liability or an income.
- Each payment recorded as a credit in the Cash account is posted as a debit to increase an asset or expense account or to reduce a liability account.
- Each receipt recorded as a debit in the Cash account is posted as a credit to increase the balance in a capital, liability or income account or to reduce the balance in an asset or expense account.
- On completion of each accounting period the balances in the income accounts and expense accounts are transferred to a Statement of income with the difference between them representing either a profit or loss. This statement is also known as a Statement of financial performance or, in the UK, as a Trading and Profit and Loss account.
- On completion of the Statement of income, the balances in the remaining accounts are listed in a Statement of financial position – also known as a Balance Sheet.
- The Statement of financial position, stating the assets, capital and liabilities in a set order, reports the financial position of the business on the last day of the accounting period.
- The accounting equation is represented by the formula

  Capital + (Income – Expenses) + Liabilities = Total assets

- The accounting equation can be presented in other forms such as:

  Capital = Total assets – (Income – Expenses) – Liabilities

  Capital + (Income – Expenses) = Total assets – Liabilities

Suggested answers to activities

4.1 Identifying assets from expenses

(a), (d) and (e) are expenses; (b) and (c) are assets.

4.2 Accounting for payments

Reason for the payment	Amount	Asset	Expense	Liability
Paid for a Bedford van	£18,000	Increase		
Paid as staff salary	£7,200		Increase	
Paid to part settle a loan from Omar	£5,000			Decrease
Paid to buy ten kayaks	£15,000	Increase		
Paid as rent	£6,000		Increase	
Paid to buy desktop computers	£1,500	Increase		

4.3 How each payment affects account balances

Name of account	Side of the balance	Amount
Motor vehicles account	Debit balance	£30,000
Loan from Ibrahim account	Credit balance	£7,000
Furniture and fittings account	Debit balance	£26,400
Rent account	Debit balance	£6,000

4.4 How amounts received affect account balances

Name of account	Side of the balance	Amount
Capital account	Credit balance	£15,000
Loan to Stella account	Debit balance	£8,000
Telephone account	Debit balance	£18,100
Sales account	Credit balance	£5,500

4.5 The class of an account identified by its balance

Name of account	Column A (debit side or credit side)	Column B (classify of account)
1. Capital account	Credit balance	Equity
2. Motor vehicles account	Debit balance	Asset
3. Purchases account	Debit balance	Expense
4. Sales account	Credit balance	Income
5. Rent account	Debit balance	Expense
6. Cash account	Debit balance	Asset
7. Bank account (overdraft)	Credit balance	Liability
8. Staff welfare account	Debit balance	Expense
9. Telephone expenses a/c	Debit balance	Expense
10. Loan from John account	Credit balance	Liability
11. Salaries account	Debit balance	Expense
12. Stationery account	Debit balance	Expense

4.6 Classifying the accounts

Trial Balance as at 7 January 2010			
	Debit	Credit	Classify
	£	£	
Cash a/c	9,070	–	Asset
Capital a/c	–	10,000	Equity
Joe's Loan a/c	–	5,000	Liability
Sales a/c	–	12,000	Income
Furniture a/c	1,500	–	Asset
Purchases a/c	8,000	–	Expense
Advertising a/c	590	–	Expense
Rent a/c	200	–	Expense
Stationery a/c	140	–	Expense
Motor vehicles a/c	7,500	–	Asset
	27,000	27,000	

4.7 Preparing Statements of income and financial position

Statement of income for the year ended 31 Decemaber 2010		
	£	£
Sales		6,948
Cost of goods sold		(4,125)
Gross profit		2,823
Stationery	145	
Rent	400	
Salaries	800	
Advertising	528	
Vehicle maintenance	412	
Interest	210	(2,495)
Net profit		328

Statement of financial position as at 31 Decemaber 2010		
		£
Non-current assets:		
Motor vehicle		8,200
Current assets:		
Cash		628
Total assets		8,828
	£	£
Capital a/c	5,000	
Add: Profit for the year	328	5,328
Non-current liabilities:		
Joe's Loan a/c		3,500
		8,828

4.8 Exercise illustrating the accounting equation

(a) £49,000 (b) £90,000 (c) £72,000 (d) £86,500

4.9 Using the accounting equation to calculate the missing figure

Business	Assets	Liabilities	Capital
A	£280,000	£50,000	*£230,000*
B	£428,000	*£53,000*	£375,000
C	*£478,600*	£54,000	£424,600

Multiple choice questions

Classification of accounts

4.1 To which class of account would the bookkeeper post each of the payments listed below?

(a) Payment for paper for the office photocopier
(b) Payment of rent for office premises
(c) Repayment of part of a loan borrowed from a friend
(d) Payment of salaries for office staff
(e) Payment to repair office vehicle
(f) Payment for goods bought for sale
(g) Payment for furniture acquired for office use

Asset	Expense	Liability
x	y	z

4.2 To which class of account would you post each of following amounts received?

(a) Receipt from sale of goods
(b) Receipt of capital from the owner of the business
(c) Recovery of part of a loan given to a salesman
(d) Receipt of dividend from shares held in a company
(e) Recovery from an employee of cost of a private call

Capital	Income	Asset	Expense
w	x	y	z

Definitions and identification

4.3 Which of the following would you say is the essential quality of an asset?

(a) The business should own it
(b) It should be possible to see, feel and use it
(c) It should bring economic benefit to business even after current accounting period
(d) It should be possible to sell it

4.4 Which of the following is an asset?

(a) Capital
(b) Cash
(c) Sales
(d) Salaries

4.5 Which of the following accounts reports an asset?

(a) Bank loan account
(b) Bank account
(c) Sales account
(d) Capital account

4.6 Which of the following statements describes a liability?

(a) Amount by which expenses exceed income of a business
(b) Amounts which have to be repaid within the accounting period
(c) Amounts owed
(d) Amounts payable within one year after the end of the accounting period

4.7 Which of the following is a liability?

(a) Bank loan
(b) Stationery
(c) Land and buildings
(d) Sales

4.8 Which of the following is not an expense of an estate agent?

(a) Rent for business premises
(b) Commission earned by the business
(c) Staff salary
(d) Advertising

4.9 The balance in the Capital account represents:

(a) The total of all assets of the business
(b) Cash and any other assets introduced by the owner at commencement of business
(c) The amount of cash introduced by the owner at the commencement of business
(d) Total assets of the business minus its liabilities at any point of time

4.10 What is an accounting period?

(a) A calendar year
(b) Twelve months ending exactly on the anniversary of commencing business
(c) A period of one year
(d) Any regular period, usually of 12 months' duration, selected by a business for reporting accounting information

The class of account and its balance

4.11 Which of the following accounts will have a credit balance?

(a) Motor vehicle account ☐
(b) Sales account ☐
(c) Cash account ☐
(d) Salaries account ☐

4.12 Which of the following accounts will have a debit balance?

(a) Sales account ☐
(b) Furniture account ☐
(c) Capital account ☐
(d) Commission earned account ☐

4.13 Which pair of accounts stated below will have balances on opposite sides?

(a) Sales account and Capital account ☐
(b) Furniture account and Cash asccount ☐
(c) Capital account and Purchases account ☐
(d) Stationery account and Salaries account ☐

The accounting equation

4.14 Birdland paid cash to purchase bird cages for re-sale. Which of the following is correct?

(a) Total assets of the business would increase ☐
(b) Owner's capital will decrease ☐
(c) There will be no effect on the total assets of the business ☐
(d) Total assets of the business will decrease ☐

4.15 The owner of Birdland paid in additional capital amounting to £50,000 in cash.
As a result of this:

(a) The assets and capital will decrease ☐
(b) The liabilities and capital will increase ☐
(c) The assets will increase and liabilities will decrease ☐
(d) The assets and capital will increase ☐

4.16 If the effect of a transaction is that it reduced both the assets and the liabilities of a business by £100,000, which of the following is that transaction likely to be:

(a) Discharge of a loan ☐
(b) Disposal of an asset ☐
(c) Introduction of additional capital by the owner ☐
(d) Sale of goods ☐

4.17 Which of the following transactions would cause £50,000 increase in both total assets and total liabilities of a business:

(a) Acquisition of a computer for office use for £50,000 on delayed payment terms

(b) Payment of £50,000 in part settlement of a loan obtained by the business

(c) Payment of staff salary of £50,000

(d) Collection in full of a debt of £50,000 due to the business

4.18 The owner of a business transferred her private car into the business for use by her staff.

The effect of this transaction would be:

(a) Decrease owner's capital and increase assets

(b) Increase owner's capital and increase assets

(c) Decrease assets and decrease liabilities

(d) Increase assets and increase liabilities

4.19 Will the total assets increase, decrease or remain unchanged by each of the following transactions?

	Increase	Decrease	No change
	x	y	z
(a) Additional cash introduced as capital by the owner			
(b) Salary paid to staff			
(c) Loan received from a friend			
(d) Payment of cash to acquire a vehicle for business use			
(e) Cash removed by the owner for personal use			
(f) Part of the loan repaid to the friend			
(g) Interest paid to the lender			

4.20 Which of the following is known as the accounting equation?

(a) Liabilities = assets + owner's capital

(b) Assets = liabilities – owner's capital

(c) Assets – liabilities = owner's capital

(d) Owner's capital = assets + liabilities

4.21 How would you define the 'net assets' of a business?

(a) Total assets – owner's capital

(b) Total assets + liabilities

(c) Total assets – liabilities

(d) Owner's capital + liabilities

4.22 If, as at the year-end, the total assets of a business were £189,000 and business liabilities were £126,000, what would be the owner's capital as at that date?

(a) £63,000

(b) £126,000

(c) £189,000

(d) £315,000

4.23 If the net assets of a business totalled £540,000 and its liabilities totalled £316,800, its total assets on that date would amount to:

(a) £223,200
(b) £540,000
(c) £633,600
(d) £856,800

4.24 If net assets of a business totalled £200,000 and its total assets on that date amounted to £325,000, its liabilities would amount to:

(a) £125,000
(b) £200,000
(c) £525,000
(d) Not sufficient information to calculate

Rahim's first day in business

4.25 Rahim started a mobile car wash service – The Visit and Shine. As capital he introduced £2,000. The effect of bringing that amount on the accounting equation would be:

(a) Liabilities and assets are both decreased
(b) Assets are increased and the owner's equity decreased
(c) The owner's equity and assets are both increased
(d) The owner's equity is increased and liabilities are decreased

4.26 Rahim received £40 when he carried out his first car wash job. The effect of this transaction on the accounting equation is:

(a) Liabilities and assets are both increased by £40
(b) Liabilities and assets are both decreased by £40
(c) The owner's equity and the assets are both increased by £40
(d) The owner' equity and the assets are both decreased by £40

4.27 Which of the following would be an appropriate description of £40 received by Rahim for his first car wash job?

(a) Revenue expenditure of £40
(b) Capital expenditure of £40
(c) A capital receipt of £40
(d) A revenue receipt of £40

4.28 Which of the following would be an appropriate description of £9 Rahim paid to advertise his services:

(a) Revenue expenditure of £9
(b) Capital expenditure of £9
(c) A capital receipt of £9
(d) A revenue receipt of £9

The effect of accounting entries on ledger balances

4.29 The effect of a credit entry on the balance in a ledger account is

(a) Increase the balance in an asset account ☐
(b) Decrease the balance in a liability account ☐
(c) Increase the balance in asset and expenditure and decrease the balance in others ☐
(d) Increase the balance in capital, income and liability accounts and decrease the balance in an asset or expense account ☐

4.30 Which of the following statements is incorrect? According to the rules of double-entry:

(a) A debit entry increases the balance in assets and expenses accounts ☐
(b) A credit entry increases the balance in income, liability and capital accounts ☐
(c) A debit entry increases the balance in the capital account ☐
(d) A debit entry decreases or eliminates balances in income and liability accounts ☐

Finding the balance in each account

4.31 Place a tick in the appropriate grid to identify the balance that would be brought down in each of the following named accounts, in the books of Rizwy Mohamed:

(a) In the Cash account: if Rizwy commenced business with a capital in cash of £10,000 and paid £6,000 for a vehicle, £400 as rent and £1,200 for purchases

x	Credit £2,400	
y	Debit £2,400	
z	No balance	

(b) In Nizar Loan account: if Rizwy gave Nizar a loan of £3,000 and has already received back from Nizar two instalments of £300 each

x	Credit £2,400	
y	Debit £2,700	
z	Debit £2,400	

(c) In Bank Loan account: if Rizwy obtained a bank loan of £20,000 and has repaid to the bank six instalments of £200 each

x	Credit £18,800	
y	Debi: £21,200	
z	Debit £18,800	

(d) In Office equipment account: if Rizwy paid £3,000 each for three computers and then returned one because it is not suitable for the intended purpose, recovering the amount paid for it

x	Credit £6,000	
y	Debit £6,000	
z	Debit £9,000	

(e) In Telephone account: if Rizwy paid £460 to settle the month's telephone bill and then received £80 from his salesmen for personal calls taken by them

x	Debit £540	
y	Debit £380	
z	Credit £380	

Types of accounting errors

4.32 What type of accounting error has occurred when a payment of £1,570 for advertising was entered in the Cash account as £5,170?

(a) Error of principle
(b) Error of omission
(c) Entry error
(d) Error of duplication

4.33 What type of accounting error has occurred when payment for office stationery is posted to the Purchases account?

(a) Error of duplication
(b) Double-entry error
(c) Entry of principle
(d) Error of commission

4.34 What type of accounting error has occurred when the cost of redecorating office premises is posted to the Land and buildings account?

(a) Entry error
(b) Error of duplication
(c) Error of principle
(d) Double-entry error

4.35 What type of accounting error has occurred when the same payment of £32 for office cleaning is recorded twice in the Cash account?

(a) Error of principle
(b) Entry error
(c) Entry of principle
(d) Error of duplication

4.36 What type of accounting error has occurred when £,4500 paid for purchases is not posted?

(a) Double-entry error
(b) Error of principle
(c) Error of commission
(d) Compensating error

Preparation of Statement of income and Statement of financial position

4.37 Every business prepares its annual financial statements using the balance/balances in

(a) all accounts in the ledger and the balance in the Cash account
(b) in the Cash Book
(c) the Trial Balance
(d) all accounts in the ledger

4.38 The list of balances in all the accounts remaining after the income and expense accounts have been closed by transfer of their balances to the Statement of income is called:

(a) The List of balances

(b) The Trial Balance

(c) The Statement of financial position

(d) Statement of affairs

4.39 Which of the following statements is correct: A Statement of financial position reports:

(a) how well off a business is as at that date

(b) the wealth of the one owning the business

(c) the assets and liabilities as stated in the accounting records of a business

(d) the balances in all the ledger accounts

Answers to multiple choice questions

4.1a: y 4.1b: y 4.1c: z 4.1d: y 4.1e: y 4.1f: y 4.1g: x 4.2a: x 4.2b: w 4.2c: y 4.2d: x 4.2e: z 4.3: c 4.4: b 4.5: b 4.6: c 4.7: a 4.8: b 4.9: d 4.10: d 4.11: b 4.12: b 4.13: c 4.14: c 4.15: d 4.16: a 4.17: a 4.18: b 4.19a: x 4.19b: y 4.19c: x 4.19d: z 4.19e: y 4.19f: y 4.19g: y 4.20: c 4.21: c 4.22: a 4.23: d 4.24: a 4.25: c 4.26: c 4.27: d 4.28: a 4.29: d 4.30: c 4.31a: y 4.31b: z 4.31c: x 4.31d: y 4.31e: y 4.32: c 4.33: d 4.34: c 4.35: d 4.36: a 4.37: a 4.38: c 4.39: c

Progressive questions

PQ 4.1 Effect of an entry on an account

Identify whether you need to make a debit entry or credit entry in each of the five accounts stated below to increase and decrease the balance in that account.

The account name	To increase	To decrease
Capital account		
Staff salary account		
Motor vehicles account		
Sales account		
Loan from Sally account		

PQ 4.2 Preparation of a Trial Balance and identification of class

Stated below is a list of account balances extracted from the books of a trader on the last day of his accounting period.

List of balances as at 30 June 2010	
	£
Cash a/c	8,476
Capital a/c	5,000
Furniture a/c	330
Purchases a/c	8,400
Sales a/c	12,600
Loan from Jim a/c	1,200
Advertising a/c	355
Stationery a/c	55
Staff welfare a/c	40
Office equipment a/c	300
Telephone a/c	49
Salaries a/c	780
Postage a/c	15

Trial Balance as at 30 June 2010			Class of account
	Debit	Credit	
Cash a/c			
Capital a/c			
Furniture a/c			
Purchases a/c			
Sales a/c			
Jim's Loan a/c			
Advertising a/c			
Stationery a/c			
Staff welfare a/c			
Office equipment a/c			
Telephone a/c			
Salaries a/c			
Postage a/c			

Required:

(a) Set out the account balances in the form of a Trial Balance and identify the class of each account (assuming that all goods purchased have been sold).

(b) Prepare the Statement of income for the year ended 30 June 2010 and set out the Statement of financial position as at 30 June 2010, assuming that there are no unsold goods or expenses remaining unpaid and ignoring the need to depreciate non-current assets.

PQ 4.3 Sorting out the side of the balance in an account

In a retail shop owned by Daisy Hall, all transactions were correctly recorded in the Cash Book and posted strictly in compliance with the rules of double-entry accounting to appropriate ledger accounts. The balances in all the accounts, as at the year-end – 31.3.2010 – are listed on the right.

(a) Set out these balances in the form of a Trial Balance, stating the debit balances in one column and credit balances in another and then checking whether the total of each column is identical to that of the other.

(b) Assuming that all goods bought for sale have been sold, identify the class to which each account belongs; and

(c) prepare the Statement of income for the year ended 31 March 2010 and the Statement of financial position as at that date.

Capital account	£50,000
Salaries account	£12,160
Furniture account	£24,500
Loan from Penny Hall	£10,000
Motor Vehicles account	£36,000
Telephone account	£3,440
Sales account	£269,600
Advertising account	£11,220
Staff welfare account	£3,230
Cash account	£18,450
Purchases account	£208,600
Rent account	£12,000

PQ 4.4 Trial Balance extracted wrongly

Bernard owns a retail outlet. His qualified bookkeeper who maintained his accounting records has resigned by the year-end. Bernard was so confident that he had sufficient knowledge of double-entry accounting that he extracted the year-end Trial Balance, as shown on the right.

He is surprised that his Trial Balance fails to balance. He seeks your help to:

(a) identify the reasons why the Trial Balance is not balancing; and

(b) prepare the correct Trial Balance as at 31 December 2010.

(c) Assuming that all goods purchased have been sold and that no expenses remain unpaid and ignoring depreciation, prepare the financial statements of Bernard's Retail.

Trial Balance as at 31 December 2010

	Debit	Credit
	£	£
Motor vehicles a/c	7,200	–
Stationery a/c	–	145
Capital a/c	–	4,000
Cash a/c	–	538
Purchases a/c	4,215	–
Sales a/c	–	6,948
Joe's Loan a/c	–	3,500
Rent a/c	400	–
Salaries a/c	–	800
Advertising a/c	–	528
Vehicle maintenance a/c	–	412
Interest on loan a/c	210	–
	12,025	16,871

PQ 4.5 When a business operates at a loss

On 31 March 2010, the last day of his accounting period, Jim Barrymore, a retailer, extracted the following balances from all accounts in his books:

Sales account	£86,000
Purchases account	£62,500
Cash account	£1,495
Interest on loan	£900
Salaries account	£14,250
Rent account	£3,000

Stationery account	£240
Motor vehicles account	£12,000
Vehicle maintenance a/c	£1,075
Bank loan	£5,000
Postage account	£105
Staff welfare account	£325

Advertising account	£4,200
Office expenses account	£165
Furniture account	£8,000
Bank account	£7,245
Capital account	£25,000
Audit fees account	£500

Required:

(a) Set out the above balances in the form of a Trial Balance.

(b) Assuming that he holds no unsold goods and no expenses remain unpaid by the year-end, prepare his Statement of income for the year ended 31 March 2010 and his Statement of financial position as at that date.

PQ 4.6 Preparing the financial statements

Peter Roger, who owns and operates a retail outlet, has extracted the year-end Trial Balance from the books of his business as shown on the right. He explains that all amounts stated have been rounded off to the nearest thousand pounds sterling as £'000 and that he has reported as a single amount the cash in hand as well as the balance at bank. He informs you further that:

(i) he has no unsold goods remaining in hand by the year-end;

(ii) he has no expenses remaining unpaid; and

(iii) he does not wish to depreciate furniture.

Required:
Prepare the Statement of income for the year ended 31 December 2010 and the Statement of financial position as at that date.

Trial Balance as at 31 December 2010		
	Debit	Credit
	£'000	£'000
Furniture a/c	120	–
Telephone a/c	10	–
Cash & bank a/c	23	–
Sales a/c	–	299
Rent a/c	12	–
Purchases a/c	148	–
Advertising a/c	14	–
Stationeries a/c	6	–
Staff salaries a/c	46	–
Capital a/c	–	80
	379	379

Test questions

Test 4.1 Preparing the financial statements

Faisal Ahamed carries on a business selling flat panel computer monitors. He buys each monitor at £180 and sells each at £250. His transactions during the first week of business, ending 12 November 2010, have been accounted for and the accuracy of accounting verified by preparing a Trial Balance set out on the right. He has paid his expenses in full and does not wish to depreciate any of his non-current assets.

Required: Prepare, for Faisal's business:
(a) the Statement of income for the week ending 12 November 2010, and
(b) the Statement of financial position as at that date.

Trial Balance as at 12 November 2010		
	Debit	Credit
	£	£
Cash a/c	9,480	–
Capital a/c	–	15,000
Rent a/c	1,000	–
Office equipment a/c	3,000	–
Motor vehicles a/c	2,500	–
Motor vehicle maint a/c	185	–
Purchases a/c	5,040	–
Advertising a/c	200	–
Wages a/c	550	–
Sales a/c	–	7,000
Stationery a/c	45	–
	22,000	22,000

Test 4.2 Preparing the Statements of income and financial position

On completion of one week of trading Mike Burton extracted a Trial Balance from his books of account as shown on the right. He informs you that:

(a) all goods bought for sale have been sold;

(b) all expenses have been paid for; and

(c) he does not want to depreciate the furniture.

Required:

(a) The Statement of income for the week ending 7 January 2010, and

(b) the Statement of financial position as at that date.

Trial Balance as at 7 January 2010

	Debit	Credit
	£	£
Capital a/c	–	10,000
Cash a/c	5,050	–
Bank a/c	4,710	–
Furniture a/c	2,400	–
Purchases a/c	7,290	–
Sales a/c	–	9,520
Office cleaning a/c	130	–
Advertising a/c	940	–
Sylvia Loan a/c	–	1,000
	20,520	20,520

Test 4.3 Preparing the financial statements

The year-end Trial Balance extracted from the books of a business owned by Joe Cameron is shown on the right. You are informed as follows:

(a) All goods purchased for sale have been sold by the year-end.

(b) All expenses relating to the year have been paid in full.

(c) Ignore depreciation of non-current assets.

Required:

Prepare for the business the Statement of income for the year ended 31 December 2010 and the Statement of financial position as at that date.

Trial Balance as at 31 December 2010

	Debit	Credit
	£	£
Stationery a/c	320	–
Salaries a/c	12,800	–
Electricity a/c	960	–
Sales a/c	–	94,800
Heating a/c	2,650	–
Postage a/c	125	–
Cash a/c	1,465	–
Furniture a/c	12,000	–
Peter's Loan a/c	–	3,000
Purchases a/c	68,400	–
Bank a/c	7,675	–
Motor vehicle a/c	18,000	–
Delivery expenses a/c	1,250	–
Office equipment a/c	4,600	–
Sales commission a/c	2,555	–
Capital a/c	–	35,000
	132,800	132,800

Chapter 5

Accounting for credit transactions

By the end of this chapter

You should learn:

- About credit sales, credit purchases and their returns
- About the Day Books used for the prime entry of credit transactions
- About drawings by the proprietor of the business

You should be able to:

- Account for both cash and credit transactions
- Account for cash taken by the owner for his own use

5.1 What is a credit transaction?

Until now we have dealt with cash transactions and used the terms debit and credit to indicate the left and right side of a ledger account. We now use the term credit giving it its everyday meaning, i.e. getting something without having to pay for it immediately. In a business the word credit is used also with the same meaning. The word is derived from the Latin word *credere* which means trust. In business then, a *credit sale* is a sale accepting on trust the customer's willingness and ability to pay later. This is not blind trust, of course, and routine steps are taken to establish the extent to which a particular customer may be trusted. These steps include:

- checking on *creditworthiness* by obtaining references,
- setting a *credit limit* by advising the customer of the maximum amount (say £3,000) that could be bought before payment is required, and
- agreeing a *credit period*, i.e. the length of time (say 30 days) allowed before payment is required.

Just as a business can sell on credit, it can also buy goods from its suppliers on credit. These are referred to as *credit purchases* and the supplier would take similar credit check steps before agreeing to supply goods.

5.2 Accounting for credit sales

5.2.1 How credit sales are accounted for

Cash sales are accounted for when the cash received from sales and debited in the Cash account is posted to the credit of the Sales account. The credit sales too are accounted for as a credit in the Sales account but, because the cash has not been received at the time of the sale, the debit is not in the Cash account. Instead it is an account opened in the name of the customer buying the goods where it is held until the amount is received from the customer.

Let us assume that there is a cash sale for £6,000 and, in addition, a credit sale to a customer, Henry, for £4,000. The cash sale is accounted for when the amount of £6,000 received and recorded as a debit in the Cash account is posted to credit the Sales account. For a credit sale, the accounting entries are to credit the Sales account with £4,000 making a total of £10,000 and to debit an account in Henry's name with £4,000. Henry is then referred to as a *debtor* – a name that recognises that there is a debit balance in his account. In accounting, a debtor arising from a trading transaction is referred to as a *trade debtor* or, using the terminology in the international accounting standards, as a *trade receivable*.

Henry's account is classified as an asset on the basis that there is a future economic benefit expected from the account, i.e. when we receive the £4,000 he owes. If the amount due from Henry remains unpaid at the end of the accounting period, the balance in Henry's account will be reported under Current assets in the Statement of financial position.

5.2.2 Vouchers for credit sales

The voucher supporting a credit sale is a copy of the *invoice*, the original of which is issued to the customer as evidence of the transaction.

5.2.3 The prime entry and double-entry when accounting for credit sales

Prime entry means nothing more than the first recording of a transaction in books of account. The prime entry for a credit sale is made in a *Sales Day Book* (illustrated on the right) in which the date, the invoice number, the customer's name and the amount are entered. However, the entry made in the Sales Day Book is not regarded as one of the pair of entries needed to account on the double-entry basis. The Sales Day Book is referred to as *a subsidiary book of account* because all it does is to provide the information necessary for making the double-entries. The information is the basis for debiting the individual amount of each invoice in the account opened for each customer, e.g. debit Jill West with £400, and crediting the total of the four invoices (£1,160) in the Sales account. Observe that because the credit sales of the day have been listed in the Day Book, the four different credit sales are accounted for by four debit entries but only a single credit entry – making five entries instead of eight entries that would

Sales Day Book				
Date	Voucher	Customer's name	F	Amount
2010				£
1.1	Inv712	Jill West	?	400
1.1	Inv713	Peter May	?	250
1.1	Inv714	S Kumar	?	325
1.1	Inv715	M Nizar	?	185
		Sales a/c	?	1,160

have been needed if each credit sale were accounted for separately. Imagine if there were a thousand different credit sales in a day, only one thousand and one entries would be needed to account for them rather than two thousand entries. The sum of the four different debit entries is the same as the single credit entry posted to the Sales account which means that the Trial Balance would balance.

The folio column in the Sales Day Book is filled in by the person responsible for posting the information recorded in the Sales Day Book. After the debit entry is made in the customer's account, e.g. £400 in Jill's account, in order to be able to trace back to the invoice in the event of a query, there is a cross-reference between the Day Book and the ledger account. The cross-reference is achieved by entering the Day Book folio in Jill's ledger account and the ledger folio of Jill's account in the Day Book. Similar cross-referencing is done when the total is posted to the credit of the Sales account. Accountants refer to this as creating an audit trail back to the prime entry.

Activity 5.1 The need for a Sales Day Book

(a) What are the advantages of recording the invoices for credit sales first in a Sales Day Book?

(b) Bearing in mind that the double-entry system requires a pair of entries for recording each transaction, would you regard the entry made for credit sales in the Sales Day Book to be one of the pair?

(c) Why is it important that the copies of the sales invoices issued to customers should be filed in their sequential number order?

The Sales Day Book is used when accounts are written up manually. If the accounting function is computerised, the same information is required on the daily credit sales for posting to the ledger accounts. A hard copy printout of this information may be known by different names such as *daily credit sales* and *daily sales listing*. The important thing to remember is that computerising the information does not reduce the need for the same amount of detail and the same entries in the ledgers.

Activity 5.2 Accounting for credit sales

As at 31 May 2010	Debit	Credit
	£	£
Non-current assets	7,400	–
Cash and bank	780	–
Capital a/c	–	15,000
Purchases a/c	8,550	–
Joe Lunt's Loan a/c	–	3,000
Expenses a/c	1,270	–
	18,000	18,000

Shown on the left is the Trial Balance extracted from the books of a shop owned by Jane Grey. No entries have yet been made to record the credit sales shown on the right.

Customer	Amount
Jill Collins	£1,850
Peter May	£2,210
Ivor Sands	£4,180
Mary Ladd	£3,490

Required:

(a) Prepare a Trial Balance after accounting for the credit sales.

(b) Prepare the shop's Statements of income and financial position.

5.3 Accounting for sales returns

There are a number of situations in which customers may return goods and expect to have their debt cancelled. This could happen, for example, if goods are damaged or fail to meet with the customer's specification. Mail order companies have a marketing policy to accept returns and make a refund, subject of course to the items still being in good condition.

If a business agrees to cancel a trade debt, a *credit note* is prepared, the first copy sent to the customer and the carbon copy retained as the voucher supporting the prime entry. The prime entry is made in another subsidiary book of account known as the *Sales Returns Day Book* (illustrated below) in which the date, the credit note number, the name of the customer and the amount are listed. The Sales Returns Day Book, like the Sales Day Book, merely provides the information for the accounting for sales returns on the double-entry basis in the ledger. In the ledger, the amount stated in each credit note is credited to the respective customer's account (e.g. £50 credited to Jill's account) and the total of all returns (£90) debited to the Sales account, so that net of the returns the Sales account would report £1,070 (£1,160 – £90). Accounting for sales returns in this way is logically correct because the return cancels the sale and should, therefore, reverse the entries that recorded the sale.

Sales Returns Day Book

Date	Voucher	Customer's name	F	Amount
2010				£
1.1	CN21	Jill West	?	50
1.1	CN22	Mohamed Nizar	?	15
1.1	CN23	S Kumar	?	25
		Sales returns a/c	?	90

However, in practice, the managers prefer the amount of sales returns to be recorded in a separate account, a Sales returns account, rather than in the Sales account itself. The reason for this is that it would flag up a warning signal if the amount of returns appears to be increasing or is unusually high. It provides an opportunity to look for reasons and take prompt action. For example, they would want to check whether returns were because the customers were unhappy with the quality of the goods supplied; or because of mistakes made by the dispatch department sending out the wrong goods; or because goods were being damaged in delivery and, if so, whether a claim can be made against the delivery company.

The current practice, therefore, is to account for sales returns as shown below:

Sales returns account

Jill West a/c	£50		

Jill West account

Sales a/c	£400	Sales returns a/c	£50
		Balance c/d	£350
	400		400
Balance b/d	350		

Let us assume that May was a particularly quiet month and there was only one sale, that made to Jill for £400, and one return for £50. In the Statement of income, if prepared for that month, the balance in the Sales returns account will be reported as a deduction from the balance in the Sales account (see on the right), identifying the sales income for that month as £350. Note that it is common to refer to Sales returns also as *Return inwards*.

Statement of income for the period ended 31 May 2010	
	£
Sales	400
Less: Sales returns	(50)
Net sales	350

5.4 Accounting for credit purchases

5.4.1 Accounting for credit purchases

A cash purchase is accounted for when the payment made for the purchase, recorded as a credit in the Cash account, is posted to the debit of the Purchases account. A credit purchase too is accounted for as a debit in the Purchases account so that it may report the total expense and, because there is no immediate payment, as a credit in an account opened in the name of the supplier – say City Traders Ltd. The City Traders would be referred to as a *creditor* – because there is a credit balance in the account maintained for them, or in international accounting language as a *payable*, and their account would be reporting a liability.

5.4.2 Vouchers for credit purchases

The voucher for purchases made on credit terms are the invoices received from the suppliers. The numbers printed on these invoices, being issued by different suppliers, would have no relationship to each other. It is necessary, therefore, to give a sequential number to each invoice as received, after each is checked for whether:

- the goods they relate to were ones that were ordered,
- the goods have been received and were in good condition, and
- the price charged for them is as agreed.

5.4.3 The prime entry for credit purchases

The supplier's invoices, once approved, are first entered in a **Purchases Day Book** (see on the right) stating in separate columns the date when the invoice was approved, the sequential number assigned to each invoice, the name of the supplier and the amount payable. The Purchases Day Book is again only a subsidiary book of account intended to convey the information on credit purchases, so that they may be accounted, on double-entry basis, in the ledger.

Purchases Day Book				
Date	Voucher	Supplier's name	F	Amount
2010				£
1.1	Inv34	City Traders Ltd	?	800
1.1	Inv35	Peter May & Sons	?	1,200
1.1	Inv36	London Suppliers plc	?	745
1.1	Inv37	Brown & Co. Ltd	?	1,525
		Purchases a/c	?	4,270

5.4.4 The double-entry accounting for credit purchases

On the basis of the information recorded in the Purchases Day Book the double-entry accounting for credit purchases is done when the amount of each invoice is credited to the account opened in the name of each supplier (e.g. £800 in City Traders' account) and the total (£4,270) debited to the Purchases account. As in the case of the credit sales, the folio column in the Purchases Day Book is filled in by the person doing the posting. Again, as in the case of credit sales, the sum of the several credits would equal the single debit so that the Trial Balance would balance.

Activity 5.3 Writing up the Purchases Day Book

Betty commenced trading as a greengrocer on 1 July 2010 with £5,000 cash as capital. On the first day she paid £4,750 for non-current assets and £810 for expenses and received £3,150 from cash sales. However, her purchases, listed on the right, were all on credit. Suppliers have allowed her one month's credit.

Suppliers	
Dave Mini Market	£600
Stella Grocers	£550
Maniam & Co.	£420

Required:

(a) Identify the books of prime entry recording each of Betty's transactions.

(b) Extract a Trial Balance at close of business on the first day.

(c) Assuming that all goods purchased have been sold on the same day, prepare a Statement of income and a Statement of financial position.

5.5 Accounting for purchase returns

Should a need arise to return goods to the supplier a *debit note* is prepared and sent back to the supplier with the goods requesting the liability to be cancelled. If the supplier agrees to cancel the debt he would confirm that position by sending a credit note to the business.

Purchases Returns Day Book				
Date	Voucher	Supplier	F	Amount
2010				£
1.1	DN07	City Traders Ltd	?	45
1.1	DN08	London Suppliers plc	?	30
		Purchases Returns a/c	?	75

The copies of the debit notes sent along with goods returned to suppliers are entered in a Purchases Returns Day Book (see above) which is again a subsidiary book of account for providing the information on purchases returns. On the basis of this information the purchases returns are accounted for in the ledgers on the double-entry basis, by debiting the account of the supplier with the amount on the debit note and crediting the total (£75) in a Purchases returns account.

Just as for the sales returns, the management of a business prefers to record the amount of purchase returns in a separate account, named Purchases returns account, rather than in the Purchases account. A separate account allows them to monitor the level of the returns because indiscriminate returns could well antagonise suppliers. Purchases returns are also referred to as *returns outwards*.

As in the case of Sales returns, on the Statement of income the balance in the Purchases returns account is shown as a deduction from the balance in the Purchases account.

Activity 5.4 Books of prime entry and subsidiary books of account

(a) Name the five books of prime entry that we have discussed so far.

(b) Explain, with reason, which among these books of prime entry you would regard as subsidiary books of account, i.e. not part of the double-entry system.

Activity 5.5 Prime entry for credit purchases and returns

The following information appears in Rob Reid's Purchases Day Book and Purchases Returns Day Book for May 2010.

Purchases Day Book		
Date	Suppliers	£
4.5	Brown & Co.	1,850
7.5	White Bros	2,160
9.5	Black & sons	725
14.5	Brown & Co.	3,125
19.5	Greys Ltd	1,285
27.5	Brown & Co.	1,945

Purchases Returns Day Book	
Suppliers	£
Brown & Co.	415
Greys Ltd	160
Brown & Co.	145

You are informed that as at 1 May 2010 Rob Reid owed his supplier Brown and Co. £1,450; and that Rob's Cash account records two payments in May to Brown & Co. of £2,885 and £3,125.

Required: On the basis of the information provided write up the account of Brown & Co. in the books of Rob Reid, bringing down the balance in that account as at 31 May.

5.6 Trade discount

A trader is usually allowed a discount – a reduction in price – when he buys goods that he intends to resell. For example, a product with a retail price of £100 may be invoiced by the wholesaler to the retailer at £90, allowing 10% discount. This is known as *trade discount* and it is the discounted price (£90) that is recorded in the Purchases Day Book and posted to the credit of the Supplier's account and a debit to the Purchases account. The discount is stated on the invoice but it is not recorded in any of the books of account of either the wholesaler who allows it or the retailer who receives it. The expression trade discount, though referring originally to reduction in price permitted to fellow traders, is used also to include reductions permitted to anyone – be they staff or friends. However, it should not be confused with *Cash discount* which we will learn of in Chapter 15.

5.7 Day Books with analysis columns

We have seen that Day Books serve as books of prime entry for credit transactions, providing the information for making the entries in the ledgers. They can also provide additional information for management. For example, in the case of sales, a sales analysis can be obtained by including additional columns in the Sales Day Book.

For example, a trader dealing in three lines of designer clothing for men, women and children may wish to monitor the performance of each line and may wish the sale to each customer to be analysed accordingly. In a manual system this is achieved by including analysis columns in the Sales Day Book as shown below:

Sales Day Book					Analysis by line of business		
Date	V	Customer	F	Amount	Menswear	Ladieswear	Childrenswear
2010				£	£	£	£
1.8	A426	Paul Russel & Co.	DL1	76,500	21,400	38,500	16,600
1.8	A427	Allen Stern Bros	DL8	28,856	4,815	19,566	4,475
1.8	A428	Simon de Silva	DL6	54,258	11,965	36,245	6,048
1.8	A429	Tony Martin Ltd	DL9	34,658	5,450	21,256	7,952
1.8	A430	S Tarrimo plc	DL2	16,250	5,600	7,250	3,400
		Sales a/c	NL2	210,522	49,230	122,817	38,475

It is now common in major retail shops for much of this analysis to be obtained at the till through barcode readings, e.g. retailers such as Tesco need to know immediately which lines are selling better and which lines require restocking.

5.8 Drawings by the owner of a business

As we have seen, the amount received as capital from the owner is posted from the Cash account to the credit of the Capital account. Therefore, it would appear logical that when any cash is paid back to the owner for personal use, the payment should be posted from the Cash account to the debit of the Capital account. This would have been acceptable but for the fact that the credit balance recorded in the Capital account is not normally regarded as available for the proprietor's withdrawal at will.

In theory, amounts withdrawn for personal needs during the period should be restricted to the profits earned in that period. The thinking is that debiting the Capital account may well send out a wrong message, i.e. that the owner is free to keep on drawing until the limit of the balance in the Capital account is reached. To do this would reduce the assets available to run the business – indeed, the cash received from the proprietor might already be tied up in non-current assets and goods held for sale. It is to guard against conveying such an impression that amounts withdrawn for personal use, known as *drawings*, are posted from the Cash account to the debit of a *Drawings account*.

Let us assume that the capital received from the proprietor is £100,000 and his drawings in the year amounted to £5,000. The cash drawn by the proprietor is posted from the Cash account to the debit, not of the Capital account, but of a Drawings account.

Capital account

		Cash a/c	£100,000

Drawings account

Cash a/c	£5,000		

When financial statements are prepared at the end of an accounting period, the profit for the period is credited to the Capital account and the debit balance in the Drawings account is transferred to the Capital account. If drawings are less than the profit for the year, capital will have increased and if drawings are more, capital will have decreased.

For example, if the capital at the commencement of the accounting period was £100,000, the profit for the period was £30,000 and the proprietor drew £2,000 per month, then the Capital account by the end of the period will appear as shown below on the left and the information reported on the Statement of financial position as on the right:

Capital account

Drawings	£24,000	Balance b/f	£100,000
Balance c/d	£106,000	Profit	£30,000
	£130,000		£130,000
		Balance b/d	£106,000

Statement of financial position

Capital on 1.1		£100,000
Profit for the year	£30,000	
Less: Drawings	(£24,000)	£6,000
		£106,000

Activity 5.6 Accounting for proprietor's drawings

Dave Logan commenced the year 2010 with a Capital account balance of £32,500. His net profit for the year ended 31 December 2010 amounted to £11,240, while his drawings were £400 per month for living expenses and £1,500 in August for his holiday expenses.

Required: Calculate the balance in Dave's Capital account as at 31 December 2010.

Activity 5.7 Impact of profit and drawings on the proprietor's capital

Summarised below are particulars relating to four sole traders. Fill in the grids remaining blank.

	Capital 1.1.2010	Profit (Loss)	Drawings	Capital 31.12.2010
Albert	£120,000	£26,800	£18,400	
Benjamin	£90,000	£18,500	£39,500	
Cader	£320,000		£24,000	£412,500
Dawood	£175,500	£29,500		£112,600

5.9 Types of ledgers

We have learnt that all accounts, other than the Cash account and the Bank account, are written up in a ledger. As the number of ledger accounts increased to the level where a single ledger was impractical, more ledgers were needed.

To begin with the accounts of customers (Receivables) and suppliers (Payables) were written up in a *Personal ledger* and other accounts in an *Impersonal ledger*. As the number of accounts in the Personal ledger increased it became necessary to have one ledger for writing up the accounts of customers and another for accounts of suppliers. The one in which the customers' accounts are written up is known by various names, e.g. *Debtors' ledger, Trade receivables ledger, Sales ledger* and *Sold ledger*. The one in which the suppliers' accounts are written up is also known by various names, e.g. *Creditors' ledger, Trade payables ledger, Purchases ledger* and *Bought ledger*.

In many businesses all the impersonal accounts are written up in the Nominal ledger. In others, the accounts recording income and expenses are written up in a *Nominal ledger*, e.g. the Sales account and Wages account; while all other impersonal accounts are written up in a ledger referred to usually as the *General ledger*, e.g. the Office furniture account and the Capital account.

Summary

- Credit transactions do not involve the immediate receipt or payment of cash.
- Sales Day Book, Purchases Day Book, Sales Returns Day Book and Purchases Returns Day Book are written up to provide the prime entry for credit transactions and these are all subsidiary books.
- Computerised accounting systems require the same information as that illustrated in the manually written up Day Books.
- There are, in most businesses, more than one ledger. The customers' accounts are written up in the Sales ledger, the suppliers' accounts in a Purchases ledger, income and expense accounts in a Nominal ledger and all other accounts in a General ledger.

Suggested answers to activities

5.1 The need for a Sales Day Book

(a) The advantage of recording credit sales first in a Sales Day Book is that it provides a means for easy access to vouchers because the sales invoices would be recorded in the Sales Day Book in the chronological sequence in which sales took place.

(b) The entry made in the Sales Day Book is only a prime entry and is not part of the pair of entries required under the double-entry rules. For example, a credit sale of £3,000 to Joe Peter is accounted for by a debit to Joe's account and a credit (included within a larger amount) to the Sales account. The Sales Day Book is, therefore, a subsidiary book of account which will not feature, for example, on a Trial Balance.

(c) If sales invoices are filed in their sequential number order, checking that the sequence of numbers is unbroken provides confirmation that every sale made has been accounted for.

5.2 Accounting for credit sales

Trial Balance as at 31 May 2010

	£	£
Non-current asset	7,400	–
Cash and bank	780	–
Capital	–	15,000
Purchases	8,550	–
Joe's Loan	–	3,000
Expenses	1,270	–
Sales	–	11,730
Jill Collin	1,850	–
Peter May	2,210	–
Ivor Sands	4,180	–
Mary Ladd	3,490	–
	29,730	29,730

Statement of income for the month ended 31 May 2010

	£
Sales	11,730
Purchases	(8,550)
Gross profit	3,180
Expenses	(1,270)
Net profit	1,910

Statement of financial position as at 31 May 2010

	£	£
Non-current asset		7,400
Current assets:		
Trade receivables:		
Jill Collin	1,850	
Peter May	2,210	
Ivor Sands	4,180	
Mary Ladd	3,490	
	11,730	
Cash and bank	780	12,510
		19,910

		£
Capital	15,000	
Profit	1,910	16,910
Joe's Loan		3,000
		19,910

5.3 Writing up the Purchases Day Book

(a) The prime entry for credit purchases would be in the Purchases Day Book. All others would be in the Cash Book.

Trial Balance as at 1 July 2010

	£	£
Non-current asset	4,750	–
Cash and bank	2,590	–
Capital	–	5,000
Purchases	1,570	–
Expenses	810	–
Sales	–	3,150
Dave Mini Market	–	600
Stella Groceries	–	550
Mariam and Co.	–	420
	9,720	9,720

Statement of income for first day – 1.7.2010

	£
Sales	3,150
Purchases	(1,570)
Gross profit	1,580
Expenses	(810)
Net profit	770

Statement of financial position as at 1 July 2010

	£	£
Non-current asset		4,750
Current asset:		
Cash and bank		2,590
		7,340

	£	£
Capital	5,000	
Profit for the day	770	5,770
Current liabilities:		
Trade payables:		
Dave Mini Market	600	
Stella Groceries	550	
Mariam and Co.	420	1,570
		7,340

5.4 Books of prime entry and subsidiary books of account

The books of prime entry are:

- The Cash Book
- Purchases Day Book
- Purchases Returns Day Book
- Sales Day Book
- Sales Returns Day Book.

Other than the Cash Book the four remaining prime entry books are subsidiary books of account.

5.5 Prime entry for credit purchases and returns

Brown and Co. account

		£			£
?	Cash account	2,885	1.5	Balance b/f	1,450
11.5	Purchases Returns Day Book	415	4.5	Purchases Day Book	1,850
?	Cash account	3,125	14.5	Purchases Day Book	3,125
29.5	Purchases Returns Day Book	145	27.5	Purchases Day Book	1,945
31.5	Balance c/d	1,800			
		8,370			8,370
			1.6	Balance b/d	1,800

5.6 Accounting for proprietor's drawings

Capital account balance: £32,500 + £11,240 – (£4,800 + £1,500) = £37,440

5.7 Impact of profit and drawings on proprietor's capital

	Capital 1.1.2010	Profit (Loss)	Drawings	Capital 31.12.2010
Albert	£120,000	£26,800	£18,400	£128,400
Benjamin	£90,000	£18,500	£39,500	£69,000
Cader	£320,000	£116,500	£24,000	£412,500
Dawood	£175,500	£29,500	£92,400	£112,600

Multiple choice questions

Accounting for credit transactions

5.1 Which of the following is not a subsidiary book of accounts?

(a) Purchases Day Book
(b) Cash Book
(c) Sales Day Book
(d) Purchases Returns Day Book

5.2 The Sales Day Book is:

(a) a book of prime entry in which credit sales are first recorded
(b) a book of prime entry for recording all sales
(c) a book of prime entry in which cash sales are first recorded
(d) a summary of sales of both goods held for sale and those acquired for use in business

5.3 A credit note issued to a customer:

(a) informs the customer of amounts his account is to be debited with
(b) communicates to a customer the discount he is entitled to if he pays promptly
(c) informs the customer of the amount his account is to be credited with
(d) reminds a customer of the offer of credit and the credit terms

5.4 In order to obtain the total of the Return Inwards for the Statement of income, the total from the Day Book is posted to:

(a) the credit of the Sales account
(b) the credit of the Purchases returns account
(c) the debit of the Purchases account
(d) the debit of the Sales returns account

5.5 The Return Inwards account would be found in:

(a) the Sales ledger
(b) the Nominal ledger
(c) the Purchases ledger
(d) the General ledger

5.6 The accounts you would find in a Sales ledger are those of:

(a) Income and expenses
(b) Non-current assets
(c) Trade payables
(d) Trade receivables

5.7 Which of the following accounting entries are correct?

	Debit	Credit
(a) Goods purchased on credit for sale	Cash account	Sales a/c
(b) Credit sale to Paul	Paul's account	Sales a/c
(c) £400 paid to Peter for goods purchased on credit	Peter's account	Cash a/c
(d) £900 received from customer John for goods sold	Cash account	John's a/c

a	All	
b	a, b	
c	b, c, d	
d	c, d	

5.8 Which of the following accounting entries are correct?

		Double entry	
Transaction	Prime entry	Debit	Credit
(a) Credit sale	Sales Day Book	Customer	Sales
(b) Goods returned by customer	Purchases Returns Day Book	Sales	Customer
(c) Cash purchases	Purchases Day Book	Purchases	Cash
(d) Goods returned to supplier	Sales Returns Day Book	Supplier	Cash

a	All	
b	a	
c	a, b, c	
d	a, b	

5.9 Assuming that the total of the following prime entry books are posted at periodical intervals to the appropriate nominal account, which of the following accounting entries are correct:

Prime entry book	Account	Side
(a) Purchases Day Book	Purchases account	Debit
(b) Sales Returns Day Book	Sales returns account	Debit
(c) Sales Day Book	Sales account	Credit
(d) Returns Outwards Day Book	Purchases returns account	Credit

a	All	
b	a, b	
c	a, c, d	
d	b, c, d	

The class of account and the side of its balance

5.10 Which of the following accounts will have a balance on the debit side?

(a) Sales account
(b) Sales returns account
(c) Capital account
(d) Bank loan account

5.11 Which of the following accounts will have a balance on the credit side?

(a) Carriage inwards account
(b) Carriage outwards account
(c) Purchases returns account
(d) Motor vehicles account

5.12 Which of the following pairs of accounts will have their balances on the same side?

(a) Sales account and Sales returns account
(b) Purchases account and Purchases returns account
(c) Capital account and Drawings account
(d) Carriage inwards account and Carriage outwards account

Impact on the Trial Balance

5.13 What would be the impact on the Trial Balance of each of the following errors?

(a) A copy of sales invoice for £4,000 is not recorded in the Sales Day Book

x	Excess credit £4,000	
y	Excess debit £4,000	
z	No impact	

(b) A supplier's invoice for £2,500 is posted to the debit of the Trade payables account

x	Excess debit £2,500	
y	Excess debit £5,000	
z	Excess credit £2,500	

(c) The daily total of the Sales Day Book is stated as £345,000 instead of £315,000 (i.e. overcast by £30,000)

x	No impact	
y	Excess credit £30,000	
z	Excess debit £30,000	

(d) A purchase invoice is recorded in the Purchases Day Book as £18,500, without taking account of 10% of that amount offered as trade discount

x	Excess debit £1,850	
y	No impact	
z	Excess credit £1,850	

(e) A sales invoice for £21,000 has been posted to the customer's account as £12,000

x	Excess debit £12,000	
y	Excess credit £12,000	
z	Excess credit £9,000	

(f) A credit note for £2,400 received from a supplier has been posted to the credit to the supplier's account

x	Excess credit £4,800	
y	Excess debit £2,400	
z	Excess credit £2,400	

(g) The year-end balance in a Trade receivables account has been carried down as £14,800, instead of £18,400

x	Excess debit £3,600	
y	Excess credit £3,600	
z	No impact	

(h) The total of the Returns Outwards Day Book, amounting to £9,800, has been posted to the debit of the Purchases returns account

x	No impact	
y	Excess debit £9,800	
z	Excess debit £19,600	

Types of accounting error

5.14 Which of the following would be an error of principle?

(a) Credit purchase of furniture for office use is entered in the Purchases Day Book

(b) A sale of £21,400 has been entered in the Sales Day Book as £24,100

(c) A supplier's credit note is not entered in the Returns Outwards Day Book

(d) A credit note issued to a customer has not been posted

5.15 What type of accounting error has occurred when an amount received from Guy Smith is posted to George Smith?

(a) Error of duplication

(b) Double-entry error

(c) Error of principle

(d) Error of commission

5.16 What type of accounting error has occurred when a sale entered in the Sales Day Book has not been posted?

(a) Entry error

(b) Error of duplication

(c) Error of principle

(d) Double-entry error

5.17 A supplier's invoice for £1,500 less 10% trade discount has been entered in the Purchases Day Book as £1,500 instead of £1,350. What type of error would this be?

(a) Error of principle

(b) Entry error

(c) Error of principle

(d) Error of commission

Accounting terminology

5.18 The gross profit is the amount by which:

(a) The income earned in an accounting period exceeds expenses incurred in that period

(b) The sales in an accounting period exceed the cost of goods sold in that period

(c) The sales in an accounting period exceed the purchases in the same period

(d) The profit made within an accounting period before deducting taxes

5.19 Which of the following statements is incorrect?

(a) The gross profit less all expenses of operating a business is the net profit

(b) The amount a business owes its proprietor decreases by the drawings he makes in the year

(c) The amount a business owes its proprietor decreases by the net profit it makes in the year

(d) Sales minus the cost of goods sold minus all expenses incurred equals net profit

5.20 The entry to transfer a balance from the Sales account to the Statement of income is known as:

(a) A closing entry

(b) A double-entry

(c) An unnecessary entry

(d) A prime entry

5.21 The Statement of financial position of a business is intended to report:

(a) the value at which the business may be sold
(b) the earning power of the business
(c) the assets, liabilities and capital of the business to the extent accounted for
(d) how well the business has done until then

5.22 The net worth of a business, as reported on its Statement of financial position, is:

(a) its non-current assets plus current assets
(b) its total assets minus its liabilities
(c) the capital plus its liabilities
(d) the current assets minus the liabilities

5.23 The expression 'non-current asset' means:

(a) Assets such as land and buildings fixed to the ground
(b) Assets other than those that cannot be seen or touched
(c) Assets transferred to the business by its owner rather than ones acquired by the business
(d) Assets intended to be used continuously in the operations of a business

5.24 Which of the following would you find reported on a Statement of financial position?

(a) Motor vehicle maintenance expense
(b) Sales for the year
(c) Drawings by the proprietor
(d) Advertising expenses

5.25 Which of the following should *not* be reported in a Statement of financial position as a non-current asset?

(a) Bank balance
(b) Motor vehicles
(c) Land and buildings
(d) Office equipment

5.26 Which of the following best describes 'current assets'?

(a) Assets which are readily convertible into cash on demand
(b) Assets specifically set aside to discharge liabilities maturing within the next accounting period
(c) Assets expected to be converted to cash within the next accounting period
(d) Assets expected to be converted to cash or be used up within the next accounting period

5.27 Which of the following best describes 'capital' in a business?

(a) Cash and other assets the proprietor brings in when he commences a business
(b) Total of non-current and current assets of a business
(c) Assets introduced at commencement plus any profit the business makes
(d) Assets minus liabilities of the business on any date

5.28 A credit note would be issued by a business:

(a) As evidence of goods sold on credit
(b) As reference for creditworthiness of a long-standing customer
(c) As evidence of amount received as deposit in respect of a sale
(d) For cancelling fully or partly amounts receivable from customers

5.29 In which of the following ledgers would you find the account of a supplier?

(a) Sales ledger
(b) Purchases ledger
(c) Nominal ledger
(d) Impersonal ledger

Calculation of net worth

5.30 Bill Carmen commenced business introducing a vehicle worth £24,000, furniture valued at £8,000 and £5,000 in cash along with a bank loan of £2,500. His Capital account balance at commencement of business is:

a	£37,000	
b	£24,000	
c	£32,000	
d	£34,500	

5.31 In a Statement of financial position the 'drawings' by the proprietor should be shown:

(a) As an addition to the Capital account balance
(b) As a deduction from the Capital account balance
(c) Along with Trade receivable balances
(d) Along with Trade payable balances

5.32 Joe Smith's Capital on 1 January 2011 was £74,200. What would be his capital by 31 December 2011, if during the year ending on that date:

	w		x		y		z	
(a) Net profit was £18,200 and drawings none	£56,000		£74,200		£92,400		£110,600	
(b) Net profit was £22,600 and drawings £5,000	£46,600		£56,600		£91,800		£101,800	
(c) Net loss was £15,400 and drawings none	£58,800		£74,200		£89,600		£105,000	
(d) Net loss was £18,200 and drawings £6,000	£50,000		£62,000		£86,400		£98,400	

Answers to multiple choice questions

5.1: b 5.2: a 5.3: c 5.4: d 5.5: b 5.6: d 5.7: c 5.8: b 5.9: a 5.10: b 5.11: c 5.12: d 5.13a: z 5.13b: y 5.13c: y 5.13d: y 5.13e: z 5.13f: x 5.13g: y 5.13h: z 5.14: a 5.15: d 5.16: d 5.17: b 5.18: b 5.19: c 5.20: a 5.21: c 5.22: b 5.23: d 5.24: c 5.25: a 5.26: d 5.27: d 5.28: d 5.29: b 5.30: d 5.31: b 5.32a: y 5.32b: y 5.32c: w 5.32d: w

Progressive questions

PQ 5.1 Writing up the Sales Day Book

Jim Keith started trading with a capital in cash of £20,000 on 1 January 2010. On the first day of business he paid £8,000 for furniture, £800 for expenses and £4,600 to purchase goods for sale. His cash sales were £2,800 and credit sales as stated on the right. By the end of the day he holds no unsold goods. Ignore depreciation.

John Lyon	£450
Duncan Brown	£725
Liza Lester	£975
Ron Dyer	£845

Required:

(a) Record the transactions in appropriate books of prime entry.
(b) Post the transactions.
(c) Extract a Trial Balance at close of business on 1 January 2010.
(d) Prepare the Statement of income for the day and the Statement of financial position at close of business on that day.

PQ 5.2 Books of prime entry

A retail trader makes the prime entry for all his cash transactions in the Cash Book (CB) and other transactions in one of the four special books of prime entry as follows:

Purchases Day Book (PDB) Purchases Returns Day Book (PRDB)
Sales Day Book (SDB) Sales Returns Day Book (SRDB)

	CB	PDB	PRDB	SDB	SRDB	None
(a) Paid £650 to purchase goods for sale						
(b) Purchased goods for £7,200 from Selma Ltd						
(c) Paid £15,000 for a vehicle for business use						
(d) Received £20,000 as a loan from Jim Mitchie						
(e) Cash sales £450						
(f) Repaid £30 on return of cash sale						
(g) Returned to Selma Ltd goods purchased for £600						
(h) Repaid £500 to Jim Mitchie						
(i) Sold to Dave Prichard goods for £9,000						
(j) Dave Prichard returned goods sold to him for £450						
(k) Acquired on credit office furniture for £1,500 from City Traders						

Required: Identify (placing a tick in the appropriate column of the grid) the book of prime entry in which each of the transactions will be entered.

PQ 5.3 The ledgers

The main books of account maintained by Lovelace and Co consists of a Cash Book (CB) and four ledgers as follows: Nominal ledger (NL), General ledger (GL), Receivables ledger (RL) and Payables ledger (PL).

Names of accounts	CB	NL	GL	RL	PL
(a) Electricity account					
(b) Plant and machinery account					
(c) Timothy Ltd, a customer					
(d) Sales account					
(e) Salaries and wages account					
(f) Wren plc, a supplier					
(g) Cash account					
(h) Capital account					
(i) Bad debts account (an expense)					
(j) Depreciation account (an expense)					

Required: Identify (by ticking the appropriate space on the grid) the ledger in which you would find each of the accounts named above.

PQ 5.4 Prime entry for sales and returns inwards

Stated on the right are the credit sales and customer returns of Joe Prentice, a wholesaler, in January 2010. He requests you to:

(a) Record them in an appropriate books of prime entry.

(b) Post them correctly to the ledger accounts (he is agreeable to your posting monthly totals to nominal accounts).

(c) Show how the accounts reporting these transactions will appear on the Trial Balance extracted from Joe's books on 31 January.

Date	Voucher	Customer	Sales	Returns
2.1	Inv484	S. Ally	£14,500	–
4.1	Inv485	Peter Gill	£6,800	–
7.1	Inv486	Jane Butt	£11,200	–
9.1	CN14	Peter Gill	–	£1,400
11.1	Inv487	S. Ally	£6,200	–
12.1	Inv488	Bob Smith	£3,600	–
14.1	CN15	S. Ally	–	£2,200
16.1	Inv489	Sally John	£5,400	–
19.1	CN16	Bob Smith	–	£400
22.1	Inv490	Jane Butt	£3,200	–
25.1	Inv491	S. Ally	£2,600	–
29.1	Inv492	Peter Gill	£2,900	–

PQ 5.5 Prime entry, posting and extraction of a Trial Balance

Hilda Prentice commenced a wholesale business on 1 April 2010 introducing cash of £10,000 as her capital. The following transactions took place within the first week:

Date	Transaction
4.4	Paid £4,000 for furniture
4.4	Paid £300 as rent for the week
4.4	Purchased goods for sale on credit from City Stores for £1,480 and Global Ltd for £2,175
5.4	Paid £280 for advertising

5.4 Sold goods on credit to Hugh Soft for £1,150, Mary Bold for £825 and Shelly Gray for £855

Date	Transaction
5.4	Cash sales £845
6.4	Received back goods sold to Mary Bold for £85 and to Shelly Gray for £30
6.4	Paid for advertising £120
7.4	Purchased goods for sale on credit from Global Ltd for £1,645 and from City Stores for £2,185
7.4	Sold goods on credit to Mary Bold for £1,865 and to Hugh Soft for £1,775
7.4	Returned to City Stores goods purchased for £140
7.4	Paid Global Ltd £2,175
8.4	Received £745 from Mary Bold
8.4	Received back goods sold to Hugh Soft for £210 and to Mary Bold for £145
8.4	Cash sales £565
8.4	Hilda took £200 in cash to meet her household expenses
8.4	Returned to Global Ltd goods purchased for £210
8.4	Sold goods on credit to Shelly Gray for £1,565 and to Hugh Soft for £825

Required:
(a) Set out the prime entry recording every transaction reported above.
(b) Post to appropriate ledger accounts.
(c) Extract a Trial Balance as at 8 April 2010.

PQ 5.6 How returns and drawings are treated in financial statements

The year-end Trial Balance of a business owned by Guy Maurice appears as shown on the right. Guy assures you that:

(i) goods purchased have been all sold;

(ii) no expenses remain unpaid; and

(iii) he does not wish to depreciate furniture.

Required: Prepare the Statement of income for the year ended 30 June 2010 and the Statement of financial position on the last day of the accounting period, with an explanation of how you have reported the returns accounts and drawings in the financial statements.

Trial Balance as at 30 June 2010

	Debit	Credit
	£	£
Cash a/c	6,510	–
Capital a/c	–	10,000
Drawings a/c	200	–
Furniture a/c	4,000	–
Rent a/c	300	–
Advertising a/c	400	–
Purchases a/c	7,485	–
Purchases returns a/c	–	350
Sales a/c	–	10,270
Sales returns a/c	470	–
City Stores a/c	–	3,525
Global Ltd a/c	–	3,610
Hugh Soft a/c	3,540	–
Mary Bold a/c	2,460	–
Shelly Gray a/c	2,390	–
	27,755	27,755

PQ 5.7 Books of account of a continuing business

Statement of financial position as at 8 April 2010		
	£	£
Non-current assets:		
Furniture		4,000
Current assets:		
Trade receivables:		
Hugh Soft	3,540	
Mary Bold	2,460	
Shelly Gray	2,390	
Cash account	6,510	14,900
		18,900
	£	£
Capital account	10,000	
Profit	1,965	
Drawings	(200)	11,765
Current liabilities		
Trade payable		
City Stores	3,525	
Global Ltd	3,610	7,135
		18,900

Shown on the left is the Statement of financial position of a business owned by Hilda Baker and listed below are the transactions during the next week:

Date	Transaction
11.4	Deposited £5,500 in a bank
11.4	Paid £3,610 to Global Ltd by cheque no 01
11.4	Purchased on credit from Global Ltd for £3,250
11.4	Received a cheque for £2,390 from Shelly Gray
11.4	Sold goods to Hugh Soft for £1,825 and to Shelly Gray for £1,550.
12.4	Purchased goods for £1,200 from City Stores
12.4	Sold goods to Mary Bold for £1,285
12.4	Paid £275 for advertising by cheque no 02
13.4	Purchased from Global Ltd for £2,140 and from City Stores for £1,835
13.4	Sold goods to Shelly Gray for £1,125 and to Mary Bold for £975
14.4	Sold goods to Hugh Soft for £725
14.4	Paid £300 as the week's rent by cheque no 03
14.4	Sold goods to Shelly Gray for £845
15.4	Hilda took £250 in cash for personal expenses
15.4	Sold goods to Hugh Soft for £835
15.4	Sold goods to Shelly Gray for £945
15.4	Paid £225 for advertising by cheque no 04

Note: assume that cheques received from customers are immediately deposited in a bank.

Required:

(a) Set out the prime entry recording every transaction reported above.
(b) Post to appropriate accounts.
(c) Extract a Trial Balance as at 15 April 2010.
(d) Prepare Statements of income and financial position.

Test questions

Test 5.1 Recording transactions prior to preparing financial statements

Grace Bert commenced business on 1 January 2010 with a capital in cash of £10,000. Her transactions in the first month were as follows:

Date	Transaction
1.1	Purchased goods for sale from City Stores for £8,200
1.1	Purchased more goods for sale for £3,800
2.1	Sold goods for £1,200
2.1	Sold goods to Sally Jones for £4,200
2.1	Acquired a motor vehicle for £6,000

Date	Transaction
4.1	Paid £300 for office stationery
4.1	Returned to City Stores goods purchased from them for £1,200
5.1	Sold goods to Jim Mitchie for £7,200
6.1	Received £5,000 as a long-term, interest-free, loan from Zoe Budd
7.1	Paid £250 for advertising
7.1	Jim Mitchie returned goods sold to him for £1,500
9.1	Sold goods for £1,500
9.1	Sold goods to S.M. Patel for £3,600
10.1	Purchased goods for sale for £2,400
11.1	Received £3,000 from Jim Mitchie
11.1	Purchased goods for £4,600 from VC Ltd
14.1	Sold goods for £1,400
14.1	Sold goods to Bob Cameron for £1,600
14.1	Paid £150 for stationery
17.1	Grace Bert took £500 for household expenses
19.1	Sold goods to S.M. Patel for £4,200
19.1	Purchased goods from City Stores for £3,800
19.1	Paid £150 for advertising
22.1	Paid £90 for vehicle fuel and oil
22.1	Sold goods to Jim Mitchie for £5,200
24.1	Paid £1,800 as staff salaries
24.1	Purchased goods for £5,400 from Latiff Bros
27.1	Sold goods for £1,800
27.1	Sold goods to R. Rajan for £3,400
27.1	Purchased goods from City Stores for £2,600
27.1	Paid £1,000 as rent
29.1	Rajan returned goods sold to him for £900

If a transaction identifies the other party assume it to be on credit terms. There are no unsold goods in hand at the month-end and ignore depreciation.

Required:

(a) Record the transactions in appropriate books of prime entry.
(b) Post them to the Nominal ledger, Receivables ledger and Payables ledger, as appropriate.
(c) Extract a Trial Balance from the books of Grace Bert as at 31.1.2010.
(d) Prepare the Statement of income for the month ended 31.1.2010 and a Statement of financial position as at that date.

Test 5.2 Again recording transactions prior to preparing financial statements

Note: If a transaction names the other party to it, assume that it is on credit terms.

Jacob commenced business as a wholesaler. His transactions during the first week were:

Date	Transaction
1.1	Commenced business with a capital in cash of £15,000
	Paid £4,000 to acquire shop furniture and fittings
	Purchased goods for sale from Larry Bros for £7,500
	Paid £300 for advertising
2.1	Returned to Larry Bros goods purchased for £250
	Sold goods to Essex plc for £4,500
	Paid £150 for stationery
	Purchased goods for £4,500 from Wembley Traders
	Sold goods to Nord plc for £6,000
3.1	Essex Ltd returned goods sold to them for £400
	Sold goods to Westmore Ltd for £5,600
	Purchased goods for £3,000 from Larry Bros
	Received £4,100 from Essex Ltd
	Westmore Ltd returned goods sold to them for £400
	Paid the whole amount due to Larry Bros on this date
4.1	Purchased goods for £5,250 from Larry Bros
	Sold goods for £3,000 to Southey Ltd
	Returned to Larry Bros goods purchased for £250
	Paid £200 for advertising
	Purchased goods for £4,000 from Wembley Traders
	Paid £1,000 as rent
5.1	Southey Ltd returned goods sold to them for £150
	Sold goods for £8,600 to Essex plc
	Westmore Ltd returned goods sold to them for £300
	Sold goods to Nord plc for £5,800
	Received £6,000 from Nord plc
	Paid £4,500 to Wembley Traders
	Paid £1,800 as salaries

Required:

(a) Record the transactions in appropriate books of prime entry, post the transactions, assuming that Day Books' totals are posted to the nominal accounts only at the end of each week.

(b) Extract a Trial Balance as at 5 January.

(c) Prepare the financial statements of Jacob's business for the five days to 5 January.

Test 5.3 From prime entry to the Statement of financial position

Jane Butt, who commenced a wholesale store on 1.8.2010, has summarised her transactions during the first week of business as follows:

Cash receipts

Date	Particulars	Amount
1.8	Capital	£10,000
1.8	Sales	£526
2.8	Sales	£412
3.8	Paul Russell	£1,236
3.8	Sales	£168
4.8	Allen Stern	£1,214
4.8	Sales	£320
5.8	Allen Stern	£1,425
5.8	Sales	£460

Cash payments

Date	Particulars	Amount
1.8	Furniture	£8,000
1.8	Salaries	£140
2.8	Drawings	£165
2.8	Rent	£1,000
2.8	Salaries	£140
3.8	Chris Meall	£515
3.8	Drawings	£120
3.8	Advertising	£165
3.8	Salaries	£140
3.8	Stationery	£36
4.8	Salaries	£140
4.8	Drawings	£90
5.8	Stella Naylor	£415
5.8	Salaries	£140

Purchases on credit

Date	Supplier	Purchases	Returns
1.8	Stella Naylor	£1,460	–
1.8	Chris Meall	£580	–
2.8	Luke Perera	£345	–
3.8	Chris Meall	–	£65
3.8	Stella Naylor	£795	–
4.8	Chris Meall	–	£70
4.8	Luke Perera	£1,225	–
4.8	Stella Naylor	–	£45
4.8	Chris Meall	£1,565	–

Sales on credit

Date	Customer	Sales	Returns
1.8	Paul Russell	£765	–
1.8	Allen Stern	£650	–
1.8	Simon de Silva	£425	–
2.8	Tony Martin	£468	–
2.8	Allen Stern	£684	–
2.8	Paul Russell	£526	–
3.8	S Tarrimo	£722	–
3.8	Allen Stern	–	£120
3.8	Allen Stern	£900	–
3.8	Simon de Silva	£544	–
3.8	Paul Russell	–	£55
4.8	Allen Stern	£525	–
4.8	S Tarrimo	–	£30
4.8	Tony Martin	£488	–
4.8	Simon de Silva	–	£75
5.8	Paul Russell	£265	–
5.8	S Tarrimo	£186	–
5.8	Allen Stern	£342	–

Note: Jane has paid all her expenses by the weekend and holds no unsold goods.

Required:

(a) Record Jane's transactions in the appropriate books of prime entry.
(b) Post the transactions to the Nominal ledger, Receivables ledger and Payables ledger.
(c) Extract a Trial Balance as at 5 August 2010.
(d) Prepare the Statement of income for the five days to 5 August 2010 and the Statement of financial position as at that date.

Note: ignore depreciation of furniture.

Test 5.4 Preparation of financial statements from information in a Trial Balance

Set out on the right is the year-end Trial Balance extracted from the books of a shop owned by Bruce Willis.
You are informed as follows:

(a) All goods purchased have been sold by the year-end.

(b) All expenses for the period have been fully paid up.

(c) Furniture is not to be depreciated.

(d) Mathew, Sahib and Charles are customers of the shop while Natwell Bros and South and Son are suppliers.

(e) Loan from Richard is interest free and is not repayable until June 2014.

Required: Prepare the Statement of income for the year ended 30 June 2010 and the Statement of financial position as at that date.

Trial Balance as at 30 June 2010		
	£	£
Furniture account	4,000	–
Sales account	–	26,500
Cash account	320	–
Bank overdraft	–	850
Stationery account	180	–
Mathew account	7,200	–
Sahib account	5,800	–
Charles smith	4,500	–
Purchases a/c	23,500	–
Return outwards a/c	–	450
Return inwards a/c	1,450	–
Salaries a/c	1,200	–
Rent account	600	–
Loan from Richard	–	2,000
Advertising account	950	–
Netwell Bros a/c	–	3,400
South and Son a/c	–	9,200
Drawings account	270	–
Capital account	–	10,000
	52,400	52,400

Chapter 6

Inventories, profit margin and gross profit ratio

By the end of this chapter

You should learn:	You should be able to:
■ Accounting for inventory ■ The cost of goods sold ■ The profit margin and the gross profit ratio	■ Account for goods remaining unsold at the end of each period ■ Match sales income with the cost of goods sold ■ Calculate the profit margin and gross profit ratio

6.1 Reporting unsold purchases as an asset

It is unrealistic to assume, as we have until now, that all goods purchased for sale would be sold by the end of each accounting period. The reality is that some remain unsold and are accounted for as an asset, referred to as *inventory*. Inventory is an asset because it is within the control of the business and is expected to generate future economic benefit when it is sold in the next accounting period.

To illustrate, let us assume that in 2010 Joe Blunt, a trader, purchased ten computers at £1,000 each and sold only seven of them at £1,500 each by the year-end. His Sales account would report an income of £10,500 (£1,500 × 7) while his Purchases account would report £10,000, being the cost of all ten computers.

In order to calculate the gross profit, we need to match the income from sales with the cost of the goods sold, i.e. the cost of seven computers. We do this at the end of the year by transferring the cost of the three unsold computers (£3,000) out of the Purchases account to an asset account called Inventory and then transferring the remaining balance of £7,000 in the Purchases account to the Statement of income as the Cost of goods sold. Thus gross profit is identified as £3,500, which we know is correct because we made a profit of £500 on each of seven computers sold in the period.

The ledger accounts will appear as follows:

Purchases account

	£		£
Balance	10,000	Inventory a/c	3,000
		Statement of income	7,000

Inventory account

	£		
Purchases a/c	3,000		

Statement of income	
	£
Sales	10,500
Cost of goods sold	(7,000)
Gross profit	3,500

The Statement of income, prepared in vertical format, will appear as shown on the left. The Inventory account, with its debit balance of £3,000, reports an asset which will be reported as a current asset in the Statement of financial position because it is expected to be converted into cash (i.e. sold) during the next accounting period.

Activity 6.1 Accounting for inventory

The year-end Trial Balance extracted from the books of a trader includes the account balances listed on the right. The cost of inventory remaining unsold by the year-end is identified as £8,250. Prepare the Statement of income in the vertical format, identifying the gross profit in the year ended 31.12.2010.

Trial Balance as at 31.12.2010		
	£	£
Sales	–	54,800
Purchases	42,400	–
Returns inwards	3,940	–
Returns outwards	–	1,850

6.2 Goods lost or disposed of otherwise than by sale

We ned to remember that gross profit is the profit on goods actually sold and it is identified by matching the sales (income) with the cost of those goods that had in fact been sold. If, therefore, any of the goods intended for sale have been physically lost or used for other purposes (say donated to a charity or distributed free as part of a sales promotion exercise), their cost needs to be removed from the Purchases account and transferred to appropriately named expense accounts. The balance in the Purchases account would then only be the cost of goods actually sold.

Let us assume that at 31 December 2010 Joe Blunt finds that one of the three unsold computers has been lost. We know that the sales were £10,500, the cost of goods sold £7,000 and the gross profit was £3,500. This position remains unchanged by the loss of one computer. To arrive at the amount of £7,000 as the cost of goods sold, it is necessary to make two transfers out of the Purchases account as follows:

1. transfer the cost of goods remaining in hand (£2,000) to an Inventory account, i.e. credit the Purchases account and debit the Inventory account; and
2. transfer the cost of goods lost (£1,000) to an expense account that may be named Loss of goods account, i.e. credit the Purchases account and debit the Loss of goods account.

The transfers leave £7,000 in the Purchases account which, when matched with sales, would result in the correct figure for gross profit. It is *after* the gross profit has been calculated that the balance in the Loss of goods account is deducted, along with all other expenses, from the gross profit to identify the net profit.

Activity 6.2 Accounting for inventory disposal other than by way of sale

An extract from the year-end Trial Balance of a trader is shown on the right. During the year goods costing £250 have been donated to a charity and the cost of inventory remaining unsold at the year-end was £8,000.

Required: Identify the gross profit and net profit of the business for the year ended 2010.

Trial Balance as at 31 December 2010		
	£	£
Sales	–	54,800
Purchases	42,400	–
Returns inwards	3,940	–
Returns outwards	–	1,850
Expenses	11,480	–

6.3 Accounting for closing and opening inventory

The inventory remaining unsold at the period-end is usually referred to as the *closing inventory*. What we now have to learn is that in the following accounting period the same inventory is referred to as *opening inventory* and would then be reported an *expense*. This is rather intriguing and needs to be illustrated. Let us assume that in addition to the three computers remaining in hand Joe Blunt purchased fifteen more at £1,000 each in 2011, and then consider two alternative situations where (a) all the computers were sold and (b) only some of the computers were sold:

Situation (a): let us assume that all eighteen computers were sold in 2011. In this situation, the cost of goods sold (the expense to be matched with the income) is obtained from two different accounts, i.e. £3,000 in the Opening inventory account and £15,000 in the Purchases account. These accounts are closed at the end of the year by transferring their balances to the Statement of income.

Situation (b): Alternatively let us assume that only thirteen computers were sold in 2011. If Joe is, somehow, certain that the thirteen sold consisted of three left over from 2010 and the remainder purchased in 2011, then the accounting entries would be as follows:

1. Transfer to the Statement of account the whole of the balance of £3,000 from the Opening inventory account as well as £10,000 from the Purchases account, making up the total of £13,000 which is the cost of computers sold.
2. Transfer the remaining balance of £5,000 from the Purchases account to a Closing inventory account.

Remember that the above entries are justified only if Joe is certain that the thirteen computers sold were all of those purchased in 2010 and ten purchased in 2011. Normally there cannot be such a certainty. Therefore, in real life the accounting entries usually made are as follows:

1. Transfer to the Statement of income all of the balances both in the opening Inventory account (£3,000) and in the Purchases account (£15,000).
2. Transfer back from the Statement of income to the Closing inventory account £5,000, the cost of computers remaining unsold by the end of 2011.

The Statement of income (see on the right) would thus match sales with the cost of goods sold.

Statement of income year ended 31 December 2011		
	£	£
Sales (13 @ £1,500)		19,500
Opening inventory	3,000	
Purchases	15,000	
	18,000	
Closing inventory	(5,000)	(13,000)
Gross profit		6,500

6.4 Goods removed for personal use by the proprietor

Some of the goods purchased for sale by the business may well be removed by the proprietor for personal use, e.g. the owner of a shop selling televison sets may take a set home. It would then be necessary to charge the proprietor with the *cost* of the goods removed, by transferring the cost from the Purchases account to the Drawings account.

To illustrate let us continue with Joe Blunt's computer shop. Let us recall that in 2011 Joe had an opening inventory of three computers and purchased fifteen more in 2011 – all at a cost of £1,000 each – and sold thirteen at £1,500 each. The new development is that Joe took one computer for personal use, so that only four unsold computers were remaining in hand. Unless Joe is certain on whether the computer he removed was one purchased in 2010 or 2011, the accounting entries recording the removal can only be as they were with regard to the closing inventory. Accounting entries for goods taken by the owner are made at the time the Statement of income is prepared, as seen on the right.

Statement of income year ended 31 December 2011		
	£	£
Sales (13 @ £1,500)		19,500
	3,000	
Opening inventory	15,000	
Purchases	18,000	
Drawings	(1,000)	
Closing inventory	(4,000)	(13,000)
Gross profit		6,500

Activity 6.3 Accounting for opening and closing inventory

An extract from the year-end Trial Balance is shown on the right. Goods costing £4,200 have been issued free for a sales promotion while goods costing £500 have been lost. The cost of inventory remaining unsold at 31.12.2010 was £39,580.

Required: Prepare the Statement of income for the year ended 31.12.2010.

Trial Balance as at 31 December 2010		
	£	£
Sales	–	214,800
Purchases	164,560	–
Inventory – 1.1.2010	29,420	–
Returns inwards	1,120	–
Expenses	42,840	–

Notes: *(1)* The inventory appearing in the Trial Balance is the Opening inventory, which would have been reported as Closing inventory at close of the previous year. *(2)* The information provided on closing inventory, lost goods, donated goods and goods taken by the proprietor is for the purpose of calculating the Cost of goods sold so that an accurate gross profit figure is reported.

6.5 Expenses to be included within the cost of sales

So far we have identified the cost of sales of an item as the price paid to buy that item. This is not always so and the cost might also include certain expenses that have been incurred to:

(a) bring the item to the place (location) from where it is sold; and

(b) bring the item to the condition in which it is sold.

6.5.1 Expenses to bring goods to the location of sale

Accountants refer to the cost of transporting the goods as *carriage*. The expense of transporting the goods to the place of business is referred to as *carriage inwards* and is regarded as part of the cost of sales. Hence, if a computer sold for £1,500 was purchased for £1,000 and £25 was paid for carriage inwards, the total cost of sales would be £1,025 and the gross profit reduced to £475 (£1,500 – £1000 – £25). Similar expenses might arise on imported goods. For example, a dealer who imported goods will include in his cost of sales not only the price paid to the overseas supplier but also all other expenses incurred in bringing the goods to the location from which they are sold such as insurance, import duty and freight.

On the other hand, the cost of delivering the goods to the customer is referred to as the *carriage outwards* and it is treated as a selling expense, which is deducted *after* gross profit is calculated.

6.5.2 Expenses on bringing goods to a saleable condition

Any expense incurred on bringing the goods sold to the *condition* in which they are sold is also included as part of cost of sales. For example, a dealer in second-hand vehicles will include within his cost of sales not only the purchase price of the vehicle but also all other expenses, such as the cost of new tyres, repairs and respraying. If the dealer also uses non-current assets such as a paint-baking equipment when respraying, there would also be an amount included for the depreciation of that equipment.

Activity 6.4 The cost of goods sold

Rebeca imports dolls from Taiwan and hand-paints them before selling them in the UK. The cost of dolls she held on 1 January 2010 was £42,500, and on 31 December 2010 was £107,300. Her sales in 2010 were £394,500, and her expenses for the year are listed on the right.

She informs you that:

(a) 75% of wages had been paid to those directly engaged in hand-painting dolls; and

(b) in October 2010 dolls costing £12,800 were gifted to charity.

Wages	£28,800
Advertising	£29,450
Purchase of dolls	£184,250
Materials for improving dolls	£11,820
Rent	£12,000
Import duty	£27,540
Freight and insurance	£16,950
Telephone and postage	£5,825
Carriage outwards	£7,650
Packing for delivery	£7,845

Required: Identify the gross profit and net profit of Rebeca's business for the year ended 31 December 2010.

6.6 Finding the quantity of closing inventory

Those dealing in items of high value and those individually identifiable by say a serial number or description, e.g. a motor car, computer, valuable item of jewellery, would be in a position to keep track of the quantity sold and to identify not only what should remain unsold at year-end but also the cost of these items. To illustrate let us assume that the only transactions of Mervin Hume, a trader selling yachts, were as follows:

Date of purchase	The item purchased	Serial number	Cost price (£)	Date of sale	Sale price (£)	Profit (£)
3.1.2010	Yacht	SK100	100,000	30.10.2010	189,000	89,000
14.3.2010	Yacht	PV300	58,000	28.9.2010	69,000	11,000
26.7.2010	Yacht	XR251	102,000	–	–	–

The performance for the year and the position of the business as at the end of the year will be reported as shown below.

Statement of income for the year to 31 December 2010		
	£	£
Sales		258,000
Cost of sales:		
SK100	100,000	
PV300	58,000	(158,000)
Gross profit		100,000

Statement of financial position as at 31 December 2010	
	£
Inventory (XR251)	102,000

More commonly, however, inventories consist of many different small-value items that have been bought at different times during the year and at varying prices. For example, the inventory held by a general store could range from perishable foodstuffs such as milk and bread to non-perishables such as canned foods to household products such as toiletries and cleaners with each of the items stocked in a variety of brand names, sizes and packaging and prices. In these circumstances the store would find it difficult, or at least not cost-effective, to:

1. identify the specific units that remain unsold at end of each accounting period; and
2. identify the actual cost of the specific items sold and remaining in closing inventory.

Let us consider how these two tasks are commonly dealt with.

6.7 Identification of goods remaining unsold

To obtain a valuation of the closing inventory we need to know the quantities and the prices to be used for the valuation. There are two methods for determining the quantities, namely, through a perpetual inventory system or a system that relies on a physical count of inventory at the year-end.

1. **Perpetual inventory:** this is a system used by large businesses such as the supermarkets where the inventory is updated by computer in real time. The inventory is updated when goods are brought into the store and updated at the point of each sale when the barcode is read.
2. **Physical count at the year-end:** it is not cost-effective for many businesses to invest in computer facilities to maintain a perpetual inventory. In their case, the common method of identifying the quantities in closing inventory is by physically counting and listing each item. The count might take place at the year-end date or, more commonly, a convenient day close to it such as the following weekend when the firm is closed or the business is slower.

6.8 Controls needed when doing a physical count of inventory

We know that closing inventory is deducted from purchases to arrive at the cost of goods sold. Any error with the inventory count, therefore, has a direct impact on the gross profit figure which is increased or decreased £ for £ by the amount of the error. This means that there needs to be proper controls over the actual counting process and the valuation process. Some of these controls are as follows:

1. Identify every location where inventory is held.
2. Make sure that the personnel involved in counting have sufficient knowledge and experience to recognise the inventory being counted and to assess their condition.
3. The quantities counted should be recorded on pre-numbered inventory sheets.
4. Items have to be valued as follows.
   - The initial value should preferably be the actual cost or, where that is not possible, on the basis of assuming a cost flow (see paragraph 6.10).
   - This initial value should be reduced if it appears that an item could not be sold for a higher amount than its cost. For example, its sales value might be reduced below cost because it is obsolete, shop-soiled, out of date, damaged etc.

Closing inventory is then the sum of the quantities times their cost (or a figure below cost if expected to be sold for less than cost).

6.9 When physical count results may need adjustment

The quantities on the business premises might have been counted accurately but still not represent the actual quantities that need to be included in the closing inventory that is reported in the financial statements. Adjustments might need to be made for reasons such as:

1. Items, although belonging to the business, may not have been included when the inventory was counted. This may happen, for example, when items were out with customers (on approval or sale or return basis) or with third parties like agents or consignees. Such items should be added to the results of the count.
2. Items for which a sales invoice was issued and posted to the Sales account may, for some reason, still have remained on the premises and been included in the count. The cost of these items should be deducted from the results of the inventory count.
3. Items of expense stock (such as stationery or packing material) may have been incorrectly included within the count, being wrongly treated as inventory for sale. The cost of these items will need to be dealt with separately. Instead of reducing the cost of goods sold the expense on stationery, which is deducted from the gross profit, will need to be reduced.
4. Further adjustments may be needed to the results of the inventory count if, as is usual, the inventory count had taken place on a date other than the last day of the accounting period. There would then be a need to adjust the count results for purchases and sales that occurred between the end of the year and the date of the count.

Activity 6.5 Where the results of inventory count may need adjustment

Dave Supermarket store their inventory at five sites and the inventory count conducted on each of these sites at close of business on the last day of the accounting period identified the cost of unsold inventory as £348,500. However, the following information has become available:

(a) Listed on the inventory sheets were packing materials costing £1,200.

(b) Goods costing £12,500, included within the count, have been invoiced to customers and accounted for as sales, although the delivery has been delayed and the goods are still in the warehouse.

(c) Goods costing £14,800, accounted for as purchases, remain in a bonded warehouse of HM Revenue and Customs.

Required: Identify the amount at which the supermarket should account for its closing inventory.

Activity 6.6 Where the inventory count is delayed after year-end

A trader's year ended on 31 December 2010. The cost of inventory in hand, ascertained on the basis of a count taken on 5 January 2011, was £348,400. During the five days to 5 January 2011 purchases and sales were £20,000 and £24,000 respectively. The sales were made at cost plus 25%.

Required: Identify the cost of inventory as at 31 December 2010.

6.10 Valuing the closing inventory

The cost of units remaining unsold is easily identifiable for high-value items as we found in the case of yachts that Mervin sells. But in other cases, the best that can be done is to attach a cost to items remaining unsold by assuming, sometimes arbitrarily, what is called a cost flow.

To illustrate the alternative cost-flow assumptions that can be used to attach costs to year-end inventory, let us use the case of Samuel, a builder's merchant, and assume that his purchases and sales of sand in 2010 were as follows:

Purchases				Sales			
Date 2010	Quantity in tonnes	Unit cost per tonne (£)	Total cost (£)	Date 2010	Quantity in tonnes	Unit price per tonne (£)	Total sale (£)
1.1	100	10	1,000	4.2	90	30	2,700
17.4	400	20	8,000	26.5	310	35	10,850
28.6	1,200	25	30,000	14.9	450	40	18,000
11.10	100	35	3,500	5.11	200	40	8,000
	1,800		42,500		1,050		39,550

Comparing the quantities purchased and sold (1,800 – 1,050) we can identify that 750 tonnes of sand remain unsold by the year-end. The problem is how we can establish the cost at which these particular 750 tonnes were purchased? That would be an almost impossible task and we have to make a choice from among alternative assumptions which include the following three:

1. The assumption that the units were sold in the sequence in which they were bought. This is known as *first in first out* (FIFO). If we make this assumption then the 750 units would have been those that were purchased last and would, therefore, be valued at the latest prices.
2. The assumption that goods were moved out in the reverse order of their arrival. This is the most likely scenario in Samuel's business because he would have piled up the sand as it arrived and with every sale he would be taking out sand from the top of the pile. This is known as *last in first out* (LIFO). On the basis of this assumption the tonnes of sand remaining unsold would be valued at the earliest prices.
3. The assumption that the appropriate price for valuing the closing inventory is the average price paid in the year. In practice, there are two methods for calculating the average price. There is the *simple average cost* which does not take into account the quantity purchased at each price and *weighted average cost* which takes into account the quantity purchased at each price.

There is no single correct assumption and, as we will soon learn, each assumption results in a different closing inventory figure which, in turn, means a different gross profit figure and a different current asset value in the Statement of financial position.

It is for this reason that the Accounting Standard[1] requires that the assumption made for identifying the cost of closing inventory should be disclosed as part of the financial statements. For example, the Annual Report of Tesco plc for year ended 28 February 2009 states:

> Inventories comprise goods held for re-sale . . . and are valued at . . . cost . . . using the weighted average cost basis.[2]

whereas the J Sainsbury 2009 Annual Report states:

> Inventories are valued at the lower of cost and net realisable value. Inventories at warehouses are valued on a first-in, first-out basis. Inventories at retail outlets are valued at calculated average cost prices. Cost includes all direct expenditure and other appropriate attributable costs incurred in bringing inventories to their present location and condition.[3]

6.10.1 First in first out (FIFO)

FIFO assumes that the inventory is sold in the sequence in which it was purchased with the result that the unit price of items remaining unsold is presumed to be the most recently invoiced price. FIFO is by far the commonest cost-flow assumption adopted in the UK and many other countries. This is not so in e.g. Germany, Italy, South Africa and some countries of South America. This assumption would accord with the actual situation obtaining, particularly in businesses where inventory rotation is important such as those dealing in perishables (like fruits, vegetables and eggs) and date-marked processed food. These businesses need to ensure that early purchases are sold before their expiry dates.

Continuing with the Samuel example, the FIFO valuation of the 750 tonnes of sand would apply the latest prices which were paid on 28 June and 11 October and the cost of 750 tonnes would be calculated as follows:

Cost of closing inventory			
Tonnes	Bought on	Unit cost (£)	Cost (£)
650	28.6.10	25	16,250
100	11.10.10	35	3,500
750			19,750

Statement of income – year ended 31.12.2010		
	£'000	£'000
Sales		39,550
Purchases	42,500	
Less: Inventory	(19,750)	(22,750)
Gross profit		16,800

The advantages of using FIFO include the following:

- The assumed sequence of inventory movement may reasonably reflect reality.
- The Statement of financial position will report inventory at values which, being the latest paid, may approximate those currently prevailing on that date.
- The method is acceptable to the tax authorities.

The disadvantages of using FIFO include the following:

- The expense (cost of goods sold) charged to the Statement of income is based on outdated prices and, if prices are rising, the cost charged against sales revenue will not reflect the cost of replacing the item sold.
- If the whole of the profit calculated on this assumption were to be distributed there would be insufficient funds retained to replace the same number of items sold.

6.10.2 Last in first out (LIFO)

LIFO assumes that the goods move out in the reverse order of their arrival. Hence, the items remaining unsold are presumed to be the ones which arrived the earliest and their cost assumed to be the earliest price paid. This method is used in the USA but has been discouraged in the UK because, in the context of rising prices, the prices at which unsold inventory is reported under LIFO would not reflect their current cost. However, as we have already seen, the LIFO assumption of the sequence of inventory movements might well apply to a business such as Samuel's. If Samuel opts to make this assumption he would value the closing inventory as follows:

Cost of closing inventory			
Tonnes	Bought on	Unit cost (£)	Cost (£)
100	1.1.10	10	1,000
400	17.4.10	20	8,000
250	28.6.10	25	6,250
750			15,250

Statement of income – year ended 31.12.2010		
	£'000	£'000
Sales		39,550
Purchases	42,500	
Less: Inventory	(15,250)	(27,250)
Gross profit		12,300

The main advantage of LIFO is:

Profit reported on this assumption is more accurate because the costs at which goods are matched with sales revenue will be closer to those on the date of the sales.

The disadvantages of using LIFO are as follows:

1. When the unit price increases, the value of inventory in the Statement of financial position becomes ever further removed from contemporary market prices.
2. The assumption is often not in keeping with the sequence of inventory movements in real life.
3. To attach earliest paid prices to closing inventory it becomes necessary to maintain detailed records of prices paid many years earlier.

Company law[4] requires accounts to be prepared in accordance with Accounting Standards[1] which do not permit the use of this method. It is also not acceptable to the UK tax authorities.

6.10.3 Average cost (AVCO)

AVCO is not based on a cost-flow assumption. This method makes no assumption regarding the sequence in which the goods move. Instead, it values the unsold units at the average of the prices paid. It is a compromise between FIFO and LIFO and shares to a lesser extent the advantages and disadvantages of both.

Simple average cost

If Samuel opts for simple average cost he will value 750 tonnes remaining unsold at the average of the four different prices he paid in the year, without taking into account the quantities purchased at each of these prices. The average would be £22.50 per tonne ((£10 + £20 + £25 + £35)/4). The closing inventory of 750 tonnes @ £22.50 would amount to £16,875.

Weighted average cost

If Samuel opts for the weighted average cost, having weighted the price paid with the quantity purchased at each price (see box), he would identify the weighted average cost as £23.61 (i.e. £42,500/1,800 tonnes). The cost of the closing inventory would then be identified as 750 @ £23.61 = £17,708.

Date	Tonnes	Unit cost	Total cost
1.1	100	£10	£1,000
17.4	400	£20	£8,000
28.6	1,200	£25	£30,000
11.1	100	£35	£3,500
	1,800		£42,500

Under each of these AVCO methods Samuel's performance will be reported as follows:

Using simple average cost:

Statement of income – year ended 31.12.2010		
	£'000	£'000
Sales		39,550
Purchases	42,500	
Less: Inventory	(16,875)	(25,625)
Gross profit		13,925

Using weighted average cost:

Statement of income – year ended 31.12.2010		
	£'000	£'000
Sales		39,550
Purchases	42,500	
Less: Inventory	(17,708)	(24,792)
Gross profit		14,758

Activity 6.7 Finding the cost of closing inventory

At the beginning of an accounting period Charlotte's inventory consisted of 12 ladies' garments each of which cost £45. During the current accounting period her purchases are listed on the right, in the sequence in which they were made. During the current year she sold 55 garments at £90 each.

Units	Unit price
30	£50
40	£60

Required: Report her performance in the current period and her position as at the end of the period, valuing the unsold inventory using:

(a) FIFO
(b) LIFO
(c) Simple average cost
(d) Weighted average cost.

6.11 Goods with customers on a sale or return basis

As a sales promotion technique it is possible that a business may have delivered some goods to customers allowing them a specified time to decide whether they wish to retain the goods or return them. So long as customers make up their mind before the end of the accounting period there would be no accounting problem – those that have been retained will have been accounted for as sales and those returned would have been included within closing inventory.

However, it is possible that goods with customers in respect of which the returnable period had not expired by the year-end may have been wrongly accounted for as sales, i.e. the Sales account credited and the customer's account debited. To correct such a mistake before financial statements are prepared, two steps become necessary as follows:

1. the Sales account and Trade receivable (customer) account entries need to be reversed; and
2. the *cost* of these goods, although still held by the customers, should be included within the closing inventory.

Activity 6.8 Goods with customers on approval basis

Henry, dealing in hover lawnmowers, provides you with an extract from his accounts as stated on the right. You are informed that:

Opening inventory	£960
Purchases	£6,720
Sales	£8,100
Receivables	£2,700
Expenses	£590

(i) Henry buys each unit at £240 and sells at £300.

(ii) He has five units in hand at the year-end.

(iii) Three units still with customers are within their returnable period, but have been accounted for as sold.

Required:

(a) Explain the adjustment that would need to be made to the balances to record the reversal of the entries made for the goods that remain out on approval.

(b) Prepare the Statement of income for the accounting period.

6.12 Valuing closing inventory at net realisable value

An asset should never be reported on the Statement of financial position at a value in excess of the future economic benefit expected from it. Accordingly, it is a requirement of IAS 2, *Inventories*,[1] that inventory should be reported as an asset at the lower of cost or *net realisable value* (NRV). Net realisable value is the price at which the item is expected to be sold less any expenses that need to be incurred (a) to bring the item to a condition in which it can be sold and (b) to make the sale.

To illustrate, let us assume that Robert, who deals in laptop computers buying them at £1,000 each and selling at £1,500 each, has six laptops remaining unsold, as stated on the right. Assuming that the six remaining unsold can be sold at prices higher than cost he would have prepared his Statement of income as shown at the top of the next page.

	Laptops
Opening inventory	4
Purchases	12
Sales	(10)
Closing inventory	6

On the other hand, if we assume that one of the six laptops remaining unsold was dropped and damaged, a decision needs to be made on whether the damaged laptop can be sold. If not, the cost of that laptop would need to be transferred from the closing inventory to the Loss of goods account. This would not change the

Sales (10 units @ £1,500)		£15,000
Opening inventory	£4,000	
Purchases	£12,000	
Closing inventory	(£6,000)	
Cost of ten laptops sold		(£10,000)
Gross profit (10 units @ £500)		£5,000

gross profit, but Inventory reported on the Statement of financial position would be only £5,000, because the loss from the damaged laptop would be deducted as an expense from gross profit.

On the other hand, if the expectation is that the damaged laptop can be sold for £900 but only after repairing it at a cost of £150, then its net realisable value (NRV) would be only £750. The laptop should then be reported as an asset, not at its cost (£1,000), but at its lower NRV of £750. This means that the closing inventory would be reported as an asset at £5,750, i.e. £5,000 cost of five laptops in good condition and £750 NRV of the damaged one.

In order to identify the gross profit at £5,000, the cost of goods sold needs to be maintained at £10,000 and this could be done only if the closing inventory removed from the total of opening inventory and purchases remains £6,000 (see on the right). Thereafter, £250 is removed from the closing Inventory account to be reported as an expense (shown as a deduction from gross profit). The accounting entries would be:

Sales (10 units @ £1,500)		£15,000
Opening inventory	£4,000	
Purchases	£12,000	
Closing inventory	(£6,000)	
Cost of ten laptops sold		(£10,000)
Gross profit		£5,000
Loss on damaged laptop		(£250)

1. Debit the Inventory account and credit the Statement of income with £6,000 being the cost of six laptops remaining unsold.
2. Debit the Loss on damaged laptop account and credit the Inventory account with £250 so that the loss is deducted from gross profit and the inventory is reported as £5,750.

Activity 6.9 Value of closing inventory where items have NRV lower than cost

Shown on the right is an extract from the year-end Trial Balance of a dealer in office coolers.

The cost of closing inventory is ascertained at £298,000. This amount includes, at £54,000, the cost of two units used as display models. These two units, if reconditioned at a cost of £500 each, may be sold for £15,000 each. Sales commission of 10% is payable on the sale of reconditioned units.

Trial Balance as at 30 June 2011		
	£'000	£'000
Inventory as at 1.7.2010	214	–
Sales	–	980
Purchases	648	–
Carriage inwards	21	–
Other expenses	224	–
Carriage outwards	38	–
Sales commission at 5%	49	–

Required: Show the Statement of income for the year ended 30 June 2011 and state the amount at which Inventory will be reported on the Statement of financial position.

Note that when carrying out a comparison of cost with net realisable value it is not acceptable for this to be done for the inventory taken as a whole. The comparison should be done either individually for each item in the inventory or for groups of fungible (interchangeable) items of inventory. The aim of this requirement, known as the *non-aggregation rule*,[3] is to avoid an anticipated loss on some items remaining unsold being offset against a gain expected on other items.

Activity 6.10 Comparison of cost with NRV of fungible groups

The year-end inventory of Reyney's Electronics consists of the following items:

Model of television	Units in hand	Unit cost	Unit sale price
PYE 28″ Colour	320 sets	£380	£450
SATCHI 28″ Colour	106 sets	£320	£375
GODWIN 25″ Colour	85 sets	£175	£160
SELKIRK 15″ Colour	64 sets	£190	£150

Required: State the value at which the inventory should be reported in the year-end Statement of financial position.

6.13 The requirements of IAS 2

6.13.1 With regard to cost-flow assumptions

IAS 2 *Inventories*[1] requires that:

1. Unless items of inventory are interchangeable (i.e. one item is no different from another – company law refers to this as 'fungible') inventory shall be valued at the specific cost at which each item was purchased. Attaching costs to items of inventory on the basis of a cost-flow assumption is permitted only when the items involved are interchangeable. In a general store selling toothpaste, different varieties of toothpaste would not be interchangeable because those preferring Sensodyne would not buy Colgate. But Colgate tubes of a specific size and packing would be interchangeable. In such a circumstance, costs may be attached to Colgate tubes remaining in inventory on the basis of one of the cost-flow assumptions.
2. If the items in inventory are interchangeable and, therefore, use of a cost-flow assumption is permitted, the only approved assumptions are either FIFO or weighted average cost.
3. The cost-flow assumption chosen by a business should be applied to all inventories of similar nature in that business.

6.13.2 With regard to what constitutes the cost

The cost of inventories should include:

1. **All costs of purchase.** In addition to the invoiced price, this includes import duty, transport, handling and other costs directly attributable to purchase, and after deducting trade discounts and rebates.
2. **The costs of conversion.** A business engaged in manufacturing activity (i.e. purchasing items and converting them prior to sale) would include, in the cost of what it holds for sale, the cost of direct labour involved in such conversion process and also production overheads (such as factory rent, power and wages paid for supervision).
3. Other costs provided these are incurred to bring the inventory to its present location and condition.

6.13.3 With regard to comparison of cost with NRV

1. In keeping with the principle that an asset should not be reported at more than the future economic benefit expected from it, IAS 2 requires that Inventory should be reported at the lower of cost or net realisable value.

   However, there is one circumstance in which there is no need to write down the inventory to its lower NRV, and that is if the inventory involved is intended to be incorporated into a product which itself can be sold at or above its cost. For example, Sahid, a manufacturer of travel bags, purchased combination locks to be fitted on to the bags at £5 each and then finds that the locks cannot be sold for more than £3 each. If he has no intention of selling these locks because the locks are intended to be fitted on to the bags, and as long as the bags can be sold at prices higher than the cost of producing them, Sahid does not have to write down the locks to their net realisable value.
2. Comparison of cost with NRV should be done for each item of inventory individually, or for groups of similar items.

6.14 Profit margin and gross profit percentage

It is important to understand the difference between profit margin and gross profit percentage.

6.14.1 The profit margin

Usually profit is the main motivation for operating a business. A business makes its (gross) profit by effecting its sales at a price higher than the price it paid. The targeted profit is often set by adding to the cost price a percentage known as the *profit margin*. For example, if Richard purchased a computer for £1,000 and added a profit margin of 25% (25% of £1,000 = £250) he would fix his selling price as £1,250. Thus the expression profit margin traces how the profit is related to the purchase price. Richard's profit margin is one-fourth (i.e. 25%) of cost.

6.14.2 The gross profit percentage

When Richard sells a computer for £1,250 he earns a gross profit of £250 (£1,250 – £1,000). Hence Richard's gross profit percentage is £250/£1,250 × 100 = 20% (i.e. one-fifth). Thus the expression *gross profit ratio* or *percentage* traces how gross profit is related to the sale price.

6.14.3 Relationship between profit margin and gross profit percentage

It is useful to observe that there is a definite pattern in how the profit margin of a business corresponds with the gross profit ratio of the same business. We observed that Richard's profit margin was one-fourth of cost and his gross profit ratio one-fifth of sales.

Similarly, if X buys an item for £30 and adds a profit margin of a third of cost, selling it for £40, X would report his profit margin at one-third of cost and his gross profit ratio as one-fourth of sale price.

If Y buys an item for £50 and adds a fifth of that amount as profit, to sell the item for £60, he would report his profit margin as one-fifth of cost and his gross profit ratio as one-sixth of sale price. Again if Z buys an item for £70 and adds two-sevenths of that amount as profit, selling the item for £90, he would report his profit margin as two-sevenths and his gross profit ratio as two-ninths of the sale price.

Thus there is a clear pattern of how the profit margin of a business corresponds with the gross profit ratio of the same business.

Study the table on the right to understand how the two are related. That understanding will be useful in situations such as in Activity 6.11.

If profit margin is		gross profit ratio is
1/2 of cost price	=	1/3 of sale price
1/3 of cost price	=	1/4 of sale price
1/4 of cost price	=	1/5 of sale price
1/5 of cost price	=	1/6 of sale price
2/10 of cost price	=	2/12 of sale price
3/10 of cost price	=	3/13 of sale price
6/10 of cost price	=	6/16 of sale price

Activity 6.11 A furniture dealer estimates closing inventory

Sally sells second-hand furniture at a price set always at 20% above cost. The year-end Trial Balance of her business appears as stated on the right. She did not take a year-end inventory but reports that she has taken for her own use inventory costing £7,000 and has given free to her old school's library furniture costing £15,000.

	£'000	£'000
Inventory – 1.10.2010	228	–
Staff salary	34	–
Sales	–	900
Rent	48	–
Purchases	688	–
Non-current assets	180	–
Cash and bank	12	–
Capital	–	300
Drawings	10	–
	1,200	1,200

Required:

(a) Prepare a Statement of income for the year ended 30 September 2011, and

(b) a Statement of financial position as at that date.

Summary

- Goods purchased for resale that remain unsold at the year-end are treated as an asset named inventory and reported as a Current asset in the Statement of financial position.
- The Cost of goods sold is calculated by adding the inventory brought forward from the previous period to the purchases made in the current period and deducting the closing inventory and the cost of goods disposed of otherwise than by sale.
- All expenses incurred in bringing goods to a location from which they are sold and to a condition ready for sale are included as part of the Cost of goods sold.
- It is common for many businesses to ascertain their unsold goods at the year-end by counting the physical inventory; when this does not take place on the last day of the period appropriate adjustments are required.
- In the absence of precise information allowing a business to identify the specific cost of the unsold item, it has, provided the goods are interchangeable, to make a cost-flow assumption. The assumptions permitted in the UK are FIFO and weighted average cost.
- Inventory, when reported as an asset, should be stated at cost or lower net realisable value.
- Profit margin relates profit to cost of goods sold; whereas the gross profit percentage relates profit to sales and there is a clear relationship between them.

References

1. IAS 2 *Inventories*, revised 2003, effective 1.1.2005, London, International Accounting Standards Board.
2. http://www.investis.com/tesco/TESCO_Report_final.pdf.
3. http://www.j-sainsbury.co.uk/files/reports/ar2009_report.pdf.
4. Companies Act (2006) Sections 395 and 403, London, The Stationery Office.

Suggested answers to activities

6.1 Accounting for inventory

Statement of income	£	£
Sales		54,800
Less: Returns inwards		(3,940)
		50,860
Purchases	42,400	
Less: Returns outwards	(1,850)	
	40,550	
Less: Closing inventory	(8,250)	
Cost of goods sold		(32,300)
Gross profit for the year		18,560

6.2 Inventory disposal

Statement of income	£	£
Sales		54,800
Less: Returns inwards		(3,940)
		50,860
Purchases	42,400	
Less: Returns outwards	(1,850)	
	40,550	
Less: Charity issue	(250)	
Closing inventory	(8,000)	
Cost of goods sold		(32,300)
Gross profit for the year		18,560
Expenses	11,840	
Charity	250	(12,090)
Net profit for the year		6,470

6.3 Accounting for opening and closing inventories

Statement of income year ended 31.12.2010	£	£
Sales		214,800
Less: Returns		(1,120)
		213,680
Inventory 1.1.2010	29,420	
Purchases	164,560	
Sales promotion	(4,200)	
Loss of goods	(500)	
Inventory 31.12.2010	(39,580)	
Cost of goods sold		(149,700)
Gross profit		63,980
Expenses	42,840	
Sales promotion	4,200	
Loss of goods	500	(47,540)
Net profit		16,440

6.4 The cost of goods sold

Statement of income	£	£
Sales		394,500
Less:		
Inventory – 1.1.2010	42,500	
Purchases	184,250	
Freight and insurance	16,950	
Import duty	27,540	
Improvement material	11,820	
Salaries and wages –75%	21,600	
Inventory – 31.12.2010	(107,300)	
Goods to charity	(12,800)	
Cost of goods sold		(184,560)
Gross profit		209,940
Salaries and wages	7,200	
Rent	12,000	
Telephone/post	5,825	
Advertising	29,450	
Carriage outwards	7,650	
Packing	7,845	
Charity	12,800	(82,770)
Net profit		127,170

6.5 Where results of inventory count . . .

Inventory count results	£348,500
Less: Packing material	(£1,200)
Less: Goods already sold	(£12,500)
Add: Goods in warehouse	£14,800
Inventory to be accounted	£349,600

6.6 Where inventory count is delayed

Results of inventory count		£348,400
Less: Purchases after year-end		(£20,000)
Add: Sales after year-end	£24,000	
Less: Profit*	(£4,800)	£19,200
Inventory to be accounted		£347,600

* As we will learn in paragraph 6.12 of this chapter, if the profit margin is 25% of cost, assuming cost to be £100, the sale price will be £125. Hence on a sale of £24,000 the profit included would be calculated as: £24,000 × 25/125 = £4,800.

6.7 Finding the cost of closing inventory

	FIFO		LIFO		Simple average		Weighted average	
	£	£	£	£	£	£	£	£
Sales		4,950		4,950		4,950		4,950
Inventory	540		540		540		540	
Purchases	3,900		3,900		3,900		3,900	
Closing inventory	(1,620)		(1,290)		(1,395)		(1,462)	
Cost of goods sold		(2,820)		(3,150)		(3,045)		(2,978)
Gross profit		2,130		1,800		1,905		1,972

6.8 Goods with customers on approval basis

The sales should be reduced by £900 as it currently includes an amount that could be returned. The receivables also need to be reduced by £900 as the person holding the goods has not agreed to actually buy them and would be unwilling to pay until deciding to do so. The following journal entry is the normal format used by accountants to record the bookkeeping entries that would be made, and we will be explaining journal entries in Chapter 16.

Journal:		Dr	Cr
Sales a/c	Dr	900	–
To Receivables		–	900
Being sales remaining on approval			

Statement of income for the year ended . . .		
	£	£
Sales		7,200
Opening inventory	960	
Purchases	6,720	
Closing inventory	(1,920)	(5,760)
Gross profit		1,440
Expenses		(590)
Profit for the year		850

Inventory: 5 in own custody plus 3 with customers = 8 × £240 = £1,920.

6.9 Value of closing inventory where items have NRV lower than cost

	£'000	£'000
Sales		980
Inventory – 1.7	214	
Purchases	648	
Carriage inwards	21	
Inventory 30.6	(298)	(585)
Gross profit		395
Other expenses	224	
Carriage outwards	38	
Sales commission	49	
Loss – shop-soiled[a]	4	(315)
Net profit		80

Sale price of damaged goods (15,000 × 2)	£30,000
Less: reconditioning expenses (500 × 2)	(£1,000)
Less: sales commission @ 10% of 30,000	(£3,000)
Net realisable value	£26,000

Closing inventory at cost		£298,000
Less: Shop-soiled goods at cost	30,000	
Shop-soiled goods at NRV	(26,000)	
Loss by shop-soiling[a]		(£4,000)
		£294,000

6.10 Comparison of cost with NRV of fungible groups

Valuation of inventory at cost or lower net realisable value						
Model	Units	Unit cost	Unit sale price	Total at cost	Total at sale price	Lower of cost or NRV
PYE 28"	320	£380	£450	£121,600	£144,000	£121,600
SATCHI 25"	106	£320	£375	£33,920	£39,750	£33,920
GODWIN 25"	85	£175	£160	£14,875	£13,600	£13,600
SELKIRK 25"	64	£190	£150	£12,160	£9,600	£9,600
TOTAL				£182,555	£206,950	£178,720

6.11 A furniture dealer estimates closing inventory

Statement of income for the year ended 30.9.2011		
	£'000	£'000
Sales		900
Inventory – 1.10.2010	228	
Purchases	688	
Drawings	(7)	
Gift to school	(15)	
Inventory – 30.9.2011	(144)	
Cost of sales		(750)
Gross profit		150
Gift to school	15	
Rent	48	
Staff salary	34	(97)
Net profit		53

Statement of financial position as at 30 September 2011	
	£'000
Non-current assets	180
Inventory	144
Cash and bank	12
	336
	£'000
Capital	300
Profit for the year	53
Less: Drawings	(10)
Furniture taken	(7)
	336

As the profit margin is a fifth of cost, the gross profit percentage is a sixth of sales resulting in a gross profit of £150,000. This means that the cost of goods sold was (£900,000 – £150,000) = £750,000. The cost of closing inventory is arrived at by removing the cost of goods sold (£750,000) from the cost of opening inventory plus purchases less the cost of goods taken away for own use by the proprietor and the cost of furniture gifted to the school library.

Multiple choice questions

Inventory and cost of sales

6.1 A trader reports opening inventory at £122,800, purchases in the year at £824,700 and closing inventory at £154,200. During the year goods costing £24,800 were lost, others costing £12,500 had been removed for own use by the proprietor and some costing £10,000 gifted to charity. What is the cost of sales?

a	£758,500	
b	£746,000	
c	£770,800	
d	£783,300	

6.2 Which of the following expenses would you regard as part of the cost of goods sold?

(a) Advertising the goods for sale

(b) Insurance and freight on importing goods for sale

(c) Packing the goods for delivery to customers

(d) Insurance of goods in the warehouse against fire and theft

6.3 If carriage inwards amounting to £57,800 is included as part of carriage outwards the impact of the error would be:

(a) Gross profit as well as net profit will be understated

(b) Gross profit will be overstated but net profit unaffected

(c) Gross profit as well as net profit will be overstated

(d) Gross profit as well as net profit will not be affected

6.4 How would you account for the goods removed for own use by the proprietor?

(a) Credit Sales account and debit Drawings account with the sale price of the goods

(b) Credit Purchases account and debit Drawings account with the cost price of the goods

(c) Credit 'Opening' inventory account and debit Drawings account with cost price of the goods

(d) Credit Statement of income and debit Drawings account with the cost price of the goods

6.5 If closing inventory is accounted for as £240,000 instead of £180,000:

(a) Gross profit and net profit would both be understated

(b) Gross profit will be exaggerated and net profit understated

(c) Gross profit will be overstated but net profit correctly reported

(d) Gross profit as well as net profit will be overstated

6.6 Which of the following will result from a failure to account for goods removed by the proprietor for own use:

(a) Both net profit and the Capital account balance at year-end will be understated

(b) It would not make any difference to the net profit for the year or the Capital account balance

(a) Net profit will remain the same but the closing balance in the Capital account will be overstated

(d) Net profit will be understated but the closing balance in the Capital account will not change

6.7 If goods lost are not accounted for:

(a) Gross profit as well as net profit will be overstated ☐
(b) Gross profit and net profit will be understated ☐
(c) Gross profit will be understated but net profit will be correctly reported ☐
(d) Gross profit will be overstated but net profit will be correctly stated ☐

6.8 Which of the following is incorrect? The cost of sales is:

(a) Opening inventory + purchases – closing inventory ☐
(b) Opening inventory + purchases + carriage inwards – closing inventory ☐
(c) Opening inventory + purchases + carriage outwards – closing inventory ☐
(d) Sales – return inwards – gross profit ☐

6.9 Having reported its financial performance in the year a business finds that goods costing £74,500 removed by the owner have not been accounted for. The effect of correcting this error would be:

(a) No change in gross profit and net profit ☐
(b) Gross profit increases by £74,500 and net profit increases by the same amount ☐
(c) Gross profit increases by £74,500; but no change in net profit ☐
(d) Gross profit as well as net profit decrease by £74,500 ☐

6.10 On the basis of the information provided on the right a business reported the gross profit for the period as £34,000 and net profit as £14,000. Since then it has been discovered that closing inventory is in fact £280,000. The effect of correcting this error is:

Opening inventory	£354,000
Purchases	£712,000
Sales	£900,000
Closing inventory	£200,000

(a) Gross profit as well as net profit remain unchanged ☐
(b) Gross profit decreases by £80,000 and net profit remains unchanged ☐
(c) Gross profit increases by £80,000 and net profit remains unchanged ☐
(d) Gross profit as well as net profit increase by £80,000 ☐

6.11 Which of the following statements is incorrect?

(a) Carriage inwards is included in the Statement of income as part of cost of sales ☐
(b) Carriage outwards is shown in the Statement of income as a deduction from gross profit ☐
(c) Gross profit is the difference between purchases and sales ☐
(d) Net profit is gross profit less all expenses other than those included in the Cost of sales ☐

6.12 A retailer of designer menswear reports as stated on the right. The closing inventory includes £30,000 being the cost of 200 pairs of trousers damaged in storage. If repaired at a cost of £40 a pair, the trousers may be sold for £100 a pair. The gross profit for the year and the inventory value in the year-end Statement of financial position would be:

Opening inventory	£184,800
Purchases	£752,400
Sales	£858,600
Closing inventory	£248,200

(a) Gross profit £101,000 and Inventory value £248,200 ☐
(b) Gross profit £151,600 and Inventory value £230,200 ☐
(c) Gross profit £83,000 and Inventory value £230,200 ☐
(d) Gross profit £83,000 and Inventory value £248,200 ☐

6.13 The year-end Trial Balance of a trader includes the balances stated on the right. 75% of carriage is for delivering goods to customers. The cost of closing inventory has been ascertained to be £185,000. However, it includes £36,000 as the cost of shop-soiled goods. If cleaned at a cost of £1,800 these goods could be sold for £15,000. Ascertain the trader's gross profit for the year and the value at which closing inventory should be reported on the year-end Statement of financial position.

Opening inventory	£128,000
Purchases	£594,000
Sales	£790,000
Carriage	£84,000

(a) Gross profit £209,200 and Inventory value £162,200

(b) Gross profit £139,200 and Inventory value £162,200

(c) Gross profit £162,000 and Inventory value £185,000

(d) Gross profit £139,200 and Inventory value £198,200

Delayed physical inventory

6.14 A wholesale merchant effects his sales at cost plus 20%. His accounting period ended on 31 March 2011 but he was able to ascertain the cost of his unsold goods as £482,800 when he conducted a physical inventory on 5 April. Assuming that the remainder of information is as stated in each of the following alternative circumstances, ascertain the cost of 'closing' inventory as at 31 March:

(a) Purchases and sales, during the five days since 31 March, were £78,400 and £58,800 respectively. The cost of packing material at £4,500 and £800, being the cost of stationery remaining unused, has been included in the inventory along with £124, the cost of spark plugs acquired for vehicle maintenance

w	£457,776	
x	£458,576	
y	£507,024	
z	£447,976	

(b) During the five days since 31 March purchases were £84,200 though goods costing £5,400 did not arrive till 7 April. Sales were £95,700, but goods invoiced for £4,500 were delivered to customers after 6 April

w	£480,000	
x	£489,800	
y	£485,600	
z	£487,500	

(c) Purchases and sales during the five days since 31 March were £79,400 and £105,300 respectively. An inventory sheet total has been carried forward from one page to another as £342,800 instead of £324,800. 48 units of an item were stated as £300 each whereas the real cost of these items was £300 per dozen

w	£443,250	
x	£477,500	
y	£459,950	
z	£522,350	

(d) Purchases and sales during the five days since 31 March were £82,400 and £97,200 respectively. As at 31 March goods invoiced to customers at £37,350 were with customers, on approval. A third of these goods were returned by the customers on 4 April

w	£460,650	
x	£502,150	
y	£504,950	
z	£512,525	

Identifying the cost of inventory

6.15 Which of the following statements would be contrary to what is stated in IAS 2 *Inventories*?

(a) Inventory should be reported at cost or lower realisable value

(b) Unless the items in inventory are interchangeable cost-flow assumptions cannot be used

(c) LIFO cost-flow assumption cannot be used even when items in inventory are interchangeable

(d) Cost of the inventory may include an appropriate portion of office expenses

6.16 Roger, dealing in second-hand pianos of different makes and models, uses the FIFO cost-flow assumption to ascertain the cost of unsold inventory. This would be wrong because:

(a) This is not the practice used by others in the trade

(b) Cost-flow assumptions may be used only when the items in the inventory are interchangeable

(c) The profit for the accounting period will be overstated

(d) It is not possible to sell each piano in the sequence in which they were purchased

6.17 If a supermarket uses LIFO cost-flow assumption to ascertain the cost of closing inventory which of the following reasons would an auditor have for disapproving of this?

(i) Use of LIFO is not permitted by IAS (2) *Inventories*

(ii) In times of rising prices LIFO understates inventory

(iii) Other supermarkets do not use LIFO cost-flow assumption

(iv) In times of rising prices LIFO understates profit

a	i, ii, iii	
b	ii, iii, iv	
c	i, iii, iv	
d	i, ii, iv	

6.18 Which among the following expenses may be included as part of the cost of closing inventory?

(i) Factory staff salary	(ii) Machinery depreciation	(iii) Sales commission	(iv) Raw materials used
(v) Accounting expenses	(vi) Office rent	(vii) Stationery	
(viii) Interest paid	(ix) Sales commission	(x) Direct labour	
(xi) Factory rent	(xii) Advertising	(xiii) Postage	
(xiv) Bad debts	(xv) Import duty	(xvi) Discount allowed	

a	i, ii, iii, ix, xiii	
b	i, ii, iv, x, xi, xv	
c	ii, vii, xi, x, xi	
d	i, iv, vi, x, xi, xv	

6.19 Sophie deals in DVD players of the same make and model. At the commencement of the year on 1 January she held 40 units purchased for £30 each. She sells each unit for £60. Her sales in the year amounted to £12,000. Her purchases during the year are stated on the left. Ascertain the cost of closing inventory on each cost-flow assumption stated on the right.

March	90 units @ £40
May	80 units @ £45
July	30 units @ £50

	FIFO	Weighted average	
a	£1,950	£1,650	
b	£2,000	£2,400	
c	£1,950	£2,400	
d	£2,000	£1,650	

Profit margin and gross profit percentage

6.20 Stated on the right is information in respect of a wholesale merchant. The cost of closing inventory has been ascertained as £198,600. What is his:

(a) Profit margin (as a percentage)

(b) Gross profit percentage

Opening inventory	£142,400
Purchases	£596,200
Sales	£675,000

x		y		z	
20%		25%		50%	
20%		25%		50%	

6.21 A trader reports his sales in 2010 as £548,700. What would be his gross profit in each of the following independent circumstances:

(a) His gross profit percentage is 25%

(b) He effects his sales at cost plus 25%

(c) He effects his sales at cost plus 20%

(d) He effects his sales at cost plus 40%

x	y	z
£182,900	£137,175	£109,740
£182,900	£137,175	£109,740
£91,450	£109,740	£137,175
£365,800	£219,480	£156,771

6.22 A retail trader fixes his sale price by adding 25% to the cost of every item purchased. He provides you with the information relating to 2010 as stated on the right.

Opening inventory		£284,400
Purchases		£842,800
Sales		£985,500

	x	y	z
(a) His closing inventory should be?	£305,950	£388,075	£338,800
(b) If his closing inventory was only £250,000 the cost of goods lost is?	£55,950	£138,075	£88,800

6.23 A retail trader fixes his sale price by adding a third to the cost of every item purchased. He provides you with the information relating to 2010 as stated on the right. He suspects his sales staff of misappropriating cash takings. Estimate the misappropriation.

Opening inventory	£152,800
Purchases	£746,200
Sales	£985,800
Closing inventory	£68,300

(a) £91,350
(b) £121,800
(c) £1,107,600

General

6.24 Which of the following would be the transaction which decreases both the assets and the liabilities?

(a) A vehicle was acquired paying £32,000
(b) A loan of £25,000 was settled
(c) Goods were purchased for sale from Orlando Ltd for £12,800
(d) Received a cheque for £5,850 from a credit customer

6.25 Which of the following would not be classified in a Statement of financial position as current assets?

(a) Trade receivables
(b) 'Opening' inventory
(c) 'Closing' inventory
(d) Bank balance

6.26 Which of the following is not a current asset?

(a) Trade receivables
(b) Trade payables
(c) Bank balance
(d) Motor vehicles

6.27 On its Statement of financial position a business would report as a current liability the amounts:

(a) It intends to repay within one year of the date of the Statement of financial position
(b) It intends to pay immediately after the date of the Statement
(c) It intends to pay as early as possible but not later than a month after the date of the Statement
(d) It hopes to repay one day

6.28 The accounting entries for stationery remaining unused at the year-end are:

(a) Debit Inventory account and credit Stationery account

(b) Debit Stationery inventory account and credit Stationery account

(c) Debit Stationery account and credit Cash account

(d) Debit Capital account and credit Stationery account

6.29 If the daily total of the Sales Day Book has been stated as £112,400 instead of £122,400 the effect would be:

(a) Trial Balance will not be disturbed

(b) The credit side of the Trial Balance will exceed the debit side by £10,000

(c) The debit side of the Trial Balance will exceed the credit side by £10,000

(d) The debit side of the Trial Balance will exceed the credit side by £20,000

6.30 An extract of the year-end Trial Balance is shown on the right. The Inventory figure appearing therein is the stock remaining unsold by the year-end. What has happened then to the opening inventory?

	Debit	Credit
Cost of sales	£348,694	–
Sales	–	£542,965
Inventory	£74,850	–

(a) There has been no stock left over at the end of the previous year

(b) It has been included within the amount of cost of goods sold

(c) It has been removed by the shop's owner for personal use

(d) It has been stolen

6.31 Which of the following is *not* acceptable as an explanation for a fall in gross profit ratio?

(a) Reduction in profit margin as a sales promotion strategy

(b) Error in ascertaining the amount and cost of closing inventory

(c) Failure to account for goods removed by proprietor or disposed of otherwise than by sale

(d) Shifting from LIFO to FIFO in times of rising prices

6.32 In relation to reporting inventory on the Statement of financial position which of the following statements is incorrect?

(a) Comparison of cost with NRV should be done for each item or groups of fungible items

(b) The NRV is found by deducting from sale price expected trade discount and cash discount

(c) An item of inventory need not be written down to lower NRV if it is not intended for sale

(d) The requirement to report inventory at lower NRV is to ensure that an asset is not reported on the Statement of financial position at an amount higher than the future economic benefit expected to flow from it.

6.33 Which of the following pairs of accounts will never appear together in the same Trial Balance?

(a) Opening inventory account and Closing inventory account

(b) Sales account and Return inwards account

(c) Cash account and Bank account

(d) Purchases account and Returns outwards account

6.34 In the system of accounting as used in the UK which of the following is not recorded in an account?

(a) Loss of goods bought for sale ☐

(b) Goods removed by the owner for own use ☐

(c) Cash discount ☐

(d) Trade discount ☐

6.35 IAS 2 *Inventories* requires year-end inventory to be reported at the lower of cost or net realisable value. Which of the following defines net realisable value?

(a) The price at which the unsold inventory could be sold ☐

(b) The price at which the unsold inventory was purchased ☐

(c) The price at which unsold inventory could be sold less expenses of selling them ☐

(d) The price at which unsold inventory could be sold plus expenses of selling them ☐

Answers to multiple choice questions

6.1: b 6.2: b 6.3: b 6.4: d 6.5: d 6.6: d 6.7: c 6.8: c 6.9: b 6.10: d 6.11: c 6.12: b 6.13: a 6.14a: z 6.14b: w 6.14c: y 6.14d: x 6.15: a 6.16: b 6.17: d 6.18: b 6.19: a 6.20a: y 6.20b: x 6.21a: y 6.21b: z 6.21c: x 6.21d: z 6.22a: z 6.22b: z 6.23: b 6.24: b 6.25: b 6.26: b 6.27: a 6.28: b 6.29: c 6.30: b 6.31: d 6.32: b 6.33: a 6.34: d 6.35: c

Progressive questions

PQ 6.1 The effect of ignoring closing inventory

On completion of his first year of business as a dealer in fashion-wear, Bernard prepared his financial statements as shown on the right. The only mistake he has made is that he has failed to take into account the unsold fashion-wear costing £112,000 remaining in hand on 31 December 2010.

Required: Re-draft his financial statements correctly.

Statement of income year ended 31.12.2010	£'000
Sales	640
Purchases	(516)
Gross profit	124
Expenses	(94)
Profit	30

Statement of financial position as at 31.12.2010	£'000
Non-current assets	240
Loan to staff	15
Cash and bank	75
	330
	£'000
Capital	300
Profit	30
	330

PQ 6.2 Consistent profit margin as a check on accounting

Jerry Noel retails computer software, fixing his selling price consistently at cost plus a third. The account balances recording his transactions during the year to 31 December 2010 are stated on the right. His physical count as at the year-end reveals the cost of inventory held as £546,000.

Inventory – 1.1.2010	£324
Purchases	£4,620
Sales	£5,840
Return inwards	£124
Return outwards	£76

Required:

(a) Explain whether Jerry has any reason to be unhappy with the year-end inventory valuation.

(b) Identify the reasons which may have caused the results of inventory taken at year-end to be different from what the figure should have been as at 31.12.2010.

PQ 6.3 A purchase invoice yet to be accounted for

Chris Day, a retailer, extracted the year-end Trial Balance as shown on the right. He informs you that

(a) All expenses have been fully paid.

(b) Included within other expenses is an amount of £11,400 paid for carriage inwards.

(c) Although the goods have been received, the purchase invoice for £22,500 was received and entered in the Purchases Day Book only after the Trial Balance had been prepared.

(d) The cost of inventory, as at 31 December 2010, including goods referred to in (c) above, was £242,600.

(e) Goods costing £450 removed by Chris for his personal use have not been accounted for.

Required: Prepare the Statement of income for the year ended 31 December 2010 and the Statement of financial position as at that date. Ignore depreciation.

Trial Balance as at 31 December 2010		
	£	£
Non-current assets	180,000	–
Sales	–	563,200
Drawings	18,000	–
Inventory – 31.12.2009	146,800	–
Trade receivables	98,500	–
Trade payables	–	64,200
Staff salary	24,800	–
Other expenses	29,400	–
Cash and bank	11,700	–
Purchases	418,200	–
Capital	–	300,000
	927,400	927,400

PQ 6.4 Identifying the inventory included in a Trial Balance

The year-end Trial Balance of Barlow Garments is set out on the right. You are informed as follows:

(a) All expenses in the year have been paid in full.

(b) Goods costing £54,000 issued free for sales promotion, and others costing £12,000 taken by Mr Barlow for personal use, have not been accounted for.

(c) On the basis of a physical inventory conducted on 31 December 2010 the cost of unsold goods has been identified as £592,000.

(d) Ignore depreciation.

Required:

(a) Make the accounting entries necessary for finding the cost of goods sold and then extract another Trial Balance at that point.

(b) Proceed to identify the gross profit and at that point extract another Trial Balance.

(c) Prepare a Statement of income for the year ended 31 December 2010, starting with gross profit, and a Statement of financial position as at that date.

(d) When not identified with a date next to it, how would you know whether inventory stated in a Trial Balance is opening inventory or closing inventory?

Trial Balance as at 31 December 2010		
	£'000	£'000
Non-current assets	910	–
Inventory – 31.12.2009	412	–
Purchases	3,248	–
Sales	–	4,845
Drawings	148	–
Carriage inwards	112	–
Salaries and wages	288	–
Rent	150	–
Returns inwards	125	–
Returns outwards	–	96
Trade receivables	495	–
Trade payables	–	326
Other expenses	165	–
Cash and bank	14	
Capital	–	800
	6,067	6,067

PQ 6.5 The need to revise the value of closing inventory

Refer to the information stated in respect of Barlow Garments in PQ (6.4) above. When ascertaining the cost of closing inventory at £592,000, the following errors have been made:

(i) The inventory includes 400 party frocks at their cost of £40 each. These frocks have a defect. It would cost £3 per frock to remedy the defect and thereafter each of them can be sold for only £28.

(ii) The inventory includes 480 casual shirts at £100 each; whereas these shirts cost £100 per dozen.

Required: Prepare a revised Statement of income for the year ended 31 December 2010 and the Statement of financial position as at that date, making appropriate corrections of the errors identified.

PQ 6.6 Possible reasons for a fall in gross profit ratio

The City Emporium sells many different products. Though their turnover (sales) for the year was marginally better than that of the previous year, the gross profit ratio was significantly lower. Identify reasons which may have caused this.

PQ 6.7 Identifying inventory on basis of GP ratio (GCSE Edexcel, London)

The sixth formers at the Broadway School run a tuck shop business. They began trading on 1 December 20X6 and sell two types of chocolate bar, Break and Brunch. Their starting capital was a £200 loan from the School Fund. Transactions are for cash only. Each Break costs the sixth form 16p and each Brunch costs 12p. 25% is added to the cost to determine the selling price. Transactions during December are summarised below:

December 6: Bought five boxes of Break, each containing 48 bars, and three boxes of Brunch, each containing 36 bars.

December 20: The month's sales amounted to 200 Breaks and 90 Brunches.

Required:

(a) Record the transactions in the Cash, Purchases and Sales accounts.

(b) On December 20 (the final day of term) a physical inventory-taking showed 34 Breaks and 15 Brunches in stock. Calculate the value of closing inventory and prepare a Statement of income to report the gross profit/loss for the month of December 20X6.

(c) Explain the number of each item that should have been in stock.

PQ 6.8 A trader takes inventory after the year-end date

Hanson Stores finalises its accounts on 31 March 2011, but was unable to do a physical inventory count until 6 April 2011. Inventory was then physically counted and entered on inventory sheets. Every item on the inventory sheets was then priced at cost. The total value of inventory on hand, at cost price, was determined as £216,400. You have ascertained as follows:

(i) Adjustments required for movements between the year-end and the date of the inventory:

Between 1.4.2011 and the time the inventory was taken, purchases amounted to £48,400, sales to £74,100 and sales returns to £2,100. The figure of sales referred to includes goods invoiced at £6,000 but which were not delivered to customers until 8.4.2011 which was after the time inventory was taken. Hanson Stores fixes the sales price to achieve a profit margin of 50% on cost.

(ii) Adjustments required for errors in taking inventory:

- A subtotal of £156,500 has been carried forward from one inventory sheet to the next as £165,500.
- Inventory sheets include packing material costing £1,600 and unused stationery costing £2,800.

(iii) Adjustment required for inventory held by third parties at the time of the inventory was taken: certain goods costing £164,400 included within purchases in the year to 31.3.2011 were not cleared from the bonded warehouse until the second week of April 2011.

(iv) Adjustment required for inventory held by customers:

Inventory with customers on sale or return basis on 31 March 2011 had been pro forma invoiced to them (as usual at cost plus 50%) for £5,400. A third of these goods had been returned by 6 April and the rest retained by customers. (A pro forma invoice is a sample invoice – no sale is recognised until the customer confirms retention of goods or passing of return deadline.)

(v) Adjustment required for items expected to be sold at or below cost:

Included in the Inventory sheets at cost of £14,400 are certain shop-soiled items which are expected to be sold at only £12,000 and subject to the payment of sales commission of 5%.

Required: Determine the value of inventory to be included in the Statement of income for the year ended 31 March 2011 and the Statement of financial position as at 31 March 2011.

PQ 6.9 A manufacturer's inventory taken after the year-end

Furniture Mart manufactures and retails household and office furniture and accounts for sales at the point the furniture is ready for delivery. It prepares accounts annually up to 30 June. On the basis of an inventory conducted on 5 July 2011, Furniture Mart ascertained that the cost of its unsold goods in hand on that date was £865,200. You are provided with the following information:

(i) On the inventory sheets 1,200 sets of furniture rollers have been valued at £20 per set whereas they cost £20 per dozen.

(ii) Sales during the first five days of July amounted to £144,000, though a third of these were not delivered to the customer until 6 July. Sales are effected at cost plus a third.

(iii) Purchases during the five days to 5 July amounted to £200,000, but only 25% of this was delivered by the time of the inventory.

(iv) Wood, for which £75,000 was paid on 18 June 2011 and accounted for as purchases in the year, was not received at Furniture Mart until 6 July.

(v) Included in the inventory sheet at its cost of £15,000 are brass cabinet hinges, the market value of which has since gone down by 20%. These hinges were intended for making cabinets – a line which has been discontinued.

(vi) Four hundred office shelves, included in the inventory sheets at cost of £300 each, are no longer in fashion and cannot be retailed at more than £225 a shelf.

(vii) A dining room suite, made to a customer's order at an agreed price of £6,000, has been included in the inventory sheets at its cost of £4,800. To abide by the recent change in legislation, the suite cannot be delivered to the customer until it is re-upholstered in non-inflammable material and that is expected to cost £1,500.

Required: Determine the inventory to be reported on the Statement of financial position as at 30 June 2011.

PQ 6.10 Physical count taken after the year-end (ACCA)

After stock taking for the year ended 31 May 2011 had taken place the closing inventory of Cobden Ltd was aggregated to a figure of £87,612. During the course of the audit that followed the undernoted facts were discovered:

(i) Some goods stored outside had been included at their normal cost price of £570. They had, however, deteriorated and would require an estimated £120 to be spent to restore them to their original condition, after which they can be sold for £800.

(ii) Some goods had been damaged and were now unsaleable. They could, however, be sold for £110 as spares after repairs estimated at £40 had been carried out. They had originally cost £200.

(iii) One stock sheet had been over-added by £126 and another under-added by £72.

(iv) Cobden Ltd had received goods costing £2,010 during the last week of May 2011, but because the invoices did not arrive until June 2011 they have not been included in the inventory.

(v) A stock-sheet total of £1,234 had been transferred to the summary sheet as £1,243.

(vi) Invoices totalling £638 arrived during the last week of May 2011 (and were included in purchases and in creditors) but, because of transport delays, the goods did not arrive until June 2011.

(vii) Portable generators on hire from another company at a charge of £347 were included at this figure in the inventory.

(viii) Free samples sent to Cobden by various suppliers had been included in the inventory at the catalogue price of £63.

(ix) Goods costing £418 sent to customers on sale or return basis had been included in the inventory at their selling price of £602.

(x) Goods sent on sale or return basis to Cobden had been included in the inventory at the amount payable (£267) if retained. No decision to retain has been made.

Required: Ascertain the inventory to be included in the Statement of financial position as at 31 May 2011.

PQ 6.11 Using GP ratio to identify misappropriation (CIMA)

DEX Stores sells three different types of product. The business is made up of three different departments each having its own manager who is responsible for buying/selling a particular type of product. The owner determines the pricing policy and fixes the sale price.

	Department A	Department B	Department C
Prices are fixed at cost plus →	40%	25%	100%
The takings during April 20X5 were →	£18,725	£11,750	£147,000
The opening stock on 1 April 20X5 at cost was →	£4,200	£7,800	£22,500
Inventory at cost on 3 May 20X5 →	£3,700	£8,100	£21,600

Transactions that occurred between end of April and 3 May 20X5:

	Department A	Department B	Department C
Sales	£420	£250	£1,500
Purchases	–	£1,500	–
Returns inwards	–	–	£300
Returns outwards	£270	–	£800
Purchases during April 20X5 amounted to →	£14,200	£8,400	£74,000

The owner has recently become concerned that the gross profit shown by the accounts does not reconcile with these percentages profit mark-ups and suspects that some of the stock may be stolen.

Required:
Calculate (a) the value of stock on 30 April 20X5 (b) the extent to which the owner's suspicions are justified.

PQ 6.12 Delayed inventory count

Hendon Traders, with a year-end of 31 December 2010, were able to identify the cost of unsold inventory as £412,850 on 6 January 2011. The following information is provided:

(a) Sales within the six days to 6 January, at cost plus 25%, were £128,400. £42,000 of these goods had, however, been returned by 6 January.

(b) Purchases within the same six days were accounted for in the book of prime entry at £74,800. £800 of these goods did not arrive until 7 January. Further invoices for £12,400, received after 6 January, were for goods that had been delivered before that date.

(c) Goods invoiced to customers at £40,000 (at cost plus 25%), though in the hands of customers, were within the returnable period permitted to them of two weeks. The delivery, as well as the invoicing of these goods, had taken place prior to 31 December 2010.

(d) One of the sheets in which inventory was listed has stated the total as £94,800 instead of £84,800 and on another sheet the cost of 48 items has been stated at £15 each whereas they actually cost £15 per dozen.

(e) The inventory sheets include packing material acquired at a cost of £3,000 and spare parts for machine maintenance acquired at a cost of £4,000.

(f) Inventory includes 18 items at their cost of £900 each. These items, however, were shop-soiled and are expected to be sold for £400 each after their condition has been restored at a cost of £50 each.

Required: Identify the cost of inventory to be reported on the Statement of financial position as at 31 December 2010.

PQ 6.13 Cost-flow assumption – FIFO, LIFO and AVCO

Mathew Eagle buys and sells wetsuits. Inventory is counted on the last day of each month. He sells each suit for £50. On 1 January 2010 he held in inventory 50 suits, each of which cost £30. The first quarter's transactions are stated on the right.

Required:

(a) Calculate the cost of inventory on 31 January and 31 March, using each of the following cost-flow assumptions:
   (i) FIFO
   (ii) LIFO
   (iii) Weighted average cost.

(b) Identify two of the above three cost-flow assumptions approved for use in the UK and explain why the third assumption is not approved.

(c) On the basis of each of the cost-flow assumptions that may be used in the UK, identify the gross profit ratio for the three months to 31 March 2010.

Date	Purchases	Sales
Jan 08	–	30
Jan 10	100 at £30.00 each	–
Jan 12	–	30
Jan 15	–	50
Jan 21	120 at £30.50 each	–
Jan 23	–	30
Jan 28	–	60
Feb 01	–	20
Feb 05	–	30
Feb 14	150 at £31.00 each	–
Feb 20	–	40
Feb 23	–	60
Mar 01	–	30
Mar 04	120 at £31.50 each	–
Mar 10	–	50
Mar 14	–	30
Mar 19	–	40
Mar 23	100 at £32.00 each	–
Mar 27	–	60
Mar 30	–	60

Test questions

Test 6.1 An easy question

The year-end Trial Balance of a general store owned by Dolly Stress has been extracted as shown on the right. You have been informed as follows:

(a) On the basis of a physical count the cost of inventory held on 30 June 2011 is established as £715,000.

(b) The following have not been accounted for:

Goods costing £3,000 taken home by Dolly
Goods costing £12,000 have gone missing.

(c) All expenses have been paid in full.

(d) Ignore depreciation of non-current assets.

Required:

(a) The Statement of income for the year ended 30 June 2011; and

(b) the Statement of financial position as at that date.

Trial Balance as at 30 June 2011		
	£'000	£'000
Non-current assets	820	–
Inventory on 30 June 2010	594	–
Purchases	7,215	–
Sales	–	9,950
Returns inwards	124	–
Carriage inwards	219	–
Salaries and wages	1,245	–
Rent	600	–
Drawings	30	–
Returns outwards	–	55
Trade receivables	124	–
Trade payables	–	295
Other expenses	298	–
Cash and bank	31	–
Capital	–	1,000
	11,300	11,300

Test 6.2 A more difficult question

Carol Fox, the owner of a shop selling solar panels, has extracted the year-end Trial Balance from the books of account as stated on the right. She provides the following additional information:

(a) Certain panels, invoiced to customers at £12,000 and accounted for as sold, are still on approval and could be returned any time until 5 April. These panels have been invoiced at cost plus 20%.

(b) Cost of unsold panels, excluding those held by customers on approval basis, is £392,000 as at the year-end.

(c) Panels costing £24,000 taken by Carol for own use have yet to be accounted for.

(d) £74,000 incurred as carriage inwards is included within the amount reported as Transport.

Assume that all expenses have been paid in full and ignore depreciation.

Required: Prepare the Statement of income for the year ended 31 March 2011 and the Statement of financial position as at that date.

Trial Balance as at 31 March 2011		
	£'000	£'000
Receivables and payables	742	498
Salaries	594	–
Sales	–	8,480
Returns inwards	345	–
Rent	90	–
Drawings	45	–
Purchases	5,245	–
Inventory as at 31.3.2010	418	–
Advertising	128	–
Transport	432	–
Non-current assets	2,450	–
Capital	–	1,800
Other expenses	292	–
Cash and bank	19	–
Bank overdraft	–	22
	10,800	10,800

Test 6.3 Inventory counted after the year-end date

The financial year of Ladybird Ltd ends on 31 December. In order to avoid interference with trading, the inventory count for the year ended 31 December 2010 was carried out on 8 January 2011 when the inventory on the company's premises, at cost, amounted to £117,567. The following further information is available:

(i) Selling prices in 2010 yielded a gross profit of 25% on sales. On and after 1 January 2011, they were determined by adding 20% to the cost of goods sold.

(ii) Sales in the month of December 2010 not dispatched until early in 2011 amounted to £2,800. These goods were all dispatched during the period 1–8 January with the exception of goods sold for £80, which were not dispatched until 10 January 2011.

(iii) Sales for the period 1–8 January 2011 amounted to £19,590 of which goods sold for £2,700 were not dispatched until after 9 January.

(iv) Purchases for the period 1–8 January 2011 amounted to £14,685, and all the goods were received within the same period.

(v) Goods purchased on 31 December 2010 for £150 and entered in the books on that date were not received until 10 January 2011.

Required: Ascertain the amount at which the inventory should be included in the financial statements for the year ended 31 December 2010.

Test 6.4 Cost-flow assumptions to find the cost of inventory

Unicombs deal in personal computers of a standard make and model. During the year ended 31.12.2011 they made their purchases at different prices; but they retailed them consistently at £1,200 per unit until 1.10.2011 when they increased the sale price by 10%. An inventory of 320 units was reported in their Statement of financial position on 31.12.2010 at £128,000. Particulars of their purchases and sales in the year ended 31 December 2011 are as follows:

Purchases		
Date	Units	Unit cost (£)
16.2.2011	600	725
7.4.2011	800	850
11.7.2011	1,200	957
5.10.2011	1,000	1,050

Sales in 2011	
Month of sale	Units
Jan to March	620
April to June	860
July to Sept	920
October to Dec	810

Required:

(a) Determine the cost of inventory held on 31.12.2011 on each of the following alternative cost-flow assumptions: (i) FIFO, (ii) LIFO, (iii) simple average cost, (iv) weighted average cost.

(b) Trace the effect of each of the above cost-flow assumptions on the company's performance and position.

Chapter 7

Accruals, prepayments, depreciation and bad debts

By the end of this chapter

You should learn:

- Basic year-end adjustments

You should be able to:

- Adjust expenses for accruals and prepayments
- Adjust for deferred income
- Measure and account for the depreciation of non-current assets
- Measure and account for allowances for bad and doubtful debts

7.1 The accruals concept

IASB[1] requires that if financial statements are to achieve their objective they should be prepared on the basis of the accruals concept. The essence of the accruals concept is that income and expenses should be recognised and accounted for as they occur in each accounting period and not as cash is received or paid. Let us consider each in turn:

- Income should be accounted for in each period at the full amount earned in that period, even if a part of that amount is still to be received by the end of that period. For illustration let us assume that during an accounting period a trader's cash sales are £1,000, credit sales are £4,000 of which £3,600 has been received as cash by the period-end. The accruals concept requires that the income for the period should be accounted for as £5,000 – including the £400 that has been earned but not yet received.
- Expenses should be accounted for at the full amount incurred in that period even if a part of it remains unpaid by the end of the period. For example, if a trader agrees to pay rent for his shop premises at £300 a month, in an accounting period of 12 months' duration, the expense he incurs is £3,600 and that is the amount at which the trader should account for the expense even if he delays the payment of say the last month's rent until after the period-end.

Unless financial statements are prepared in compliance with the accruals concept a business would be in a position to report a better profit by merely delaying paying for its expenses until the next accounting period.

Activity 7.1 The need for the accruals basis of accounting

Upon completing her first year of business as a hairdresser, Sally Potter reports a net profit of £1,740 as shown on the right. However, she has not taken into account three months' rent as well as £500 salary to her assistant that remain unpaid as at the year-end.

Earnings from hairdressing	£18,500
Rent (£1,000 per month)	(£9,000)
Assistant's salary	(£5,500)
Advertising	(£1,800)
Telephone	(£460)
Net profit	£1,740

Required:
(a) Prepare a revised Statement of income complying with the accruals concept and
(b) explain why unpaid expenses cannot be ignored.

7.2 Accounting for accrued expenses

To report the correct amount of profit in an accounting period, the whole of the income earned in that period needs to be matched with the whole of the expense incurred in the earning process, irrespective of whether the expense has been paid for by the end of that period. To illustrate, let us assume that having agreed to pay rent at £1,000 per month, only eight months' rent had been paid by the end of the year, so that the Rent account would report a balance of £8,000 posted to it from the Cash Book.

In order to account for the full expense incurred in the year, an additional £4,000 needs to be debited to the Rent account and credited to a liability account which may be named *Rent payable account* or *Rent accrued account*. The ledger accounts would then appear as follows:

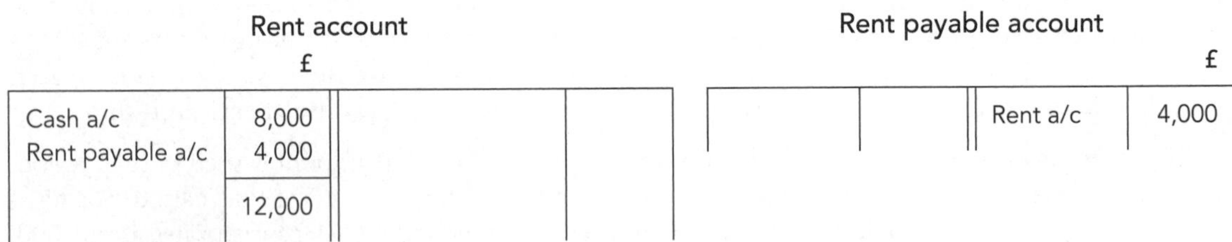

Rent account

	£		
Cash a/c	8,000		
Rent payable a/c	4,000		
	12,000		

Rent payable account

			£
		Rent a/c	4,000

Instead of opening a separate ledger account to record the liability relating to each type of expense, there are two common practices which are to (a) show the liability as a credit balance in the expense account, and (b) to open a composite account as illustrated below.

(a) Rather than opening a separate liability account, it is common practice to carry down the unpaid portion as a credit balance in the expense account (see the Rent account at the top of the next page). If this is done the current liability will appear as a credit balance in the expense account instead of appearing as a credit balance in a separately named account.

Rent account

	£		£
Cash a/c	8,000	Statement of income	12,000
Balance c/d	4,000		
	12,000		12,000
		Balance b/d	4,000

(b) Other businesses prefer to report the unpaid portion of all expenses in a single composite liability account named *Accrued expenses account.*

The £12,000 in the Rent account, reporting the whole of the expense for the period, is transferred to the Statement of income, while the credit balance of £4,000 in the Rent payable account is shown, together with all other accrued expenses, as a current liability in the Statement of financial position.

7.3 Accounting for prepaid expenses

In order to calculate the correct profit earned in an accounting period it is necessary to match the income earned in the accounting period with the expense relating to that period. If an amount paid and debited to an expense account is expected to bring economic benefit in the following period, an appropriate proportion of the payment should be recognised as an asset at the year-end. The asset is referred to as a *prepayment* and is included among the current assets stated in a Statement of financial position. The effect of the adjustment is to reduce the amount charged as an expense in the Statement of income.

For illustration, let us assume that a business entered into a rental agreement on 1 January 2010 to pay £2,000 per month and that by the year-end it had actually paid an amount of £30,000. Because only £24,000 of the balance in the Rent account is the expense for the year, the excess of £6,000 would be an asset representing the right of the business to continue occupation of the premises for a further three months after 31 December 2010. Accordingly £6,000 is transferred from the Rent account to a Prepaid rent account. The rent account and prepaid rent account would appear as shown.

Rent account

	£		£
Cash a/c	30,000	Prepaid rent a/c	6,000
		Income statement	24,000
	30,000		30,000

Prepaid rent account

	£		
Rent a/c	6,000		

Again, rather than opening a new account to report the prepayment, some businesses prefer to carry down the prepaid amount as a debit balance in the expense account. The prepaid rent is reported in the Statement of financial position under current assets.

Activity 7.2 Accounting for expenses accrued and prepaid

Expenses listed in the year-end Trial Balance on 31 December 2010 include those on the right. In addition, salary and advertising amounting to £24,500 and £8,400 respectively remain unpaid at the year-end; while rates have been paid for five quarters at £1,200 each.

Salaries	£128,600
Advertising	£21,800
Rates	£6,000

Required: Identify the amounts at which each expense should be stated in the Statement of income and any related asset or liability to be shown in the Statement of financial position.

7.4 Accounting for deferred income

We have seen that expenses incurred but not paid are included in the Statement of income and reported as current liabilities in the Statement of financial position. Similarly, any income received but not earned in the period is described as *deferred income* and is reported in the Statement of financial position as a liability, provided it is expected to qualify for treatment as income in a future accounting period.

To illustrate, let us assume that, having agreed upon a rent of £2,000 per month, a landlord has actually received £30,000 by the year-end. In the landlord's books the Rent account would report a credit balance of £30,000 posted to it from the Cash Book. Since only £24,000 of this amount would have been earned in that accounting period and should be regarded as income for the period, the balance of £6,000, representing the rental income that will be earned in the three months after the period-end, should be removed from the income account (by a debit entry) and posted to the credit of a deferred income account which may be named *Rent received in advance account*. The accounts will then appear as follows:

Rent receivable account (income)

	£		£
Rent received in advance	6,000	Cash a/c	30,000

Rent received in advance account (liability)

			£
		Rent receivable a/c	6,000

The balance remaining in the Rent receivable account, after removing the amount deferred, is transferred to the Statement of income, while the balance in the account reporting the deferred income is included in the Statement of financial position under current liabilities.

Activity 7.3 Is deferred income a liability?

In the case of the landlord referred to above it has been suggested that the rent received in advance for next year should be treated as a liability. The landlord challenges this treatment, pointing out that a liability is an obligation to pay, whereas he has no intention to repay the rent even if the tenant should leave the premises by the year-end.

What then is the justification for transferring the unearned portion of rental income to a liability account?

7.5 Depreciation and the straight-line method of measurement

7.5.1 How is depreciation measured?

Non-current assets, with the exception of land, will not last for ever no matter how well they are looked after. Accountants refer to this as an asset having a *finite economic life*, i.e. the number of years that a business can use an asset to generate profit. During those years it is necessary to estimate how much of the cost of the asset should be matched with the income that it generates. If it is an asset like a lease of the premises, we know the amount that it costs each year. However, for other assets we need to estimate:

(a) how much of the total cost is to be regarded as an expense over the period of that asset's use (this is known as the *depreciable cost* of the asset); and

(b) how much of the depreciable cost should be regarded as an expense in each year of its use (this is known as the *depreciation*).

(a) ***Identifying the depreciable cost:*** let us assume that a motor vehicle is acquired for £20,000. It is expected to be in use for four years, i.e. has an economic life of four years, and is expected to be disposed of after that for £2,000 being its estimated *scrap value*. This means that the four years' use of the vehicle costs (£20,000 – £2,000) = £18,000 which is referred to in accounting as the depreciable cost of the asset.

(b) ***Identifying the depreciation:*** the portion of depreciable cost treated as an expense in each accounting period is referred to as depreciation and we need to find a systematic way of calculating it. The most common way is to charge an equal amount of the depreciable cost as the depreciation expense – a method known as the *straight-line* or *fixed instalment method*. There are other methods (described in 7.7 below) but we will at this point illustrate accounting when the straight-line method is used.

Given that the depreciable cost of the vehicle is £18,000 and its economic life four years, the annual depreciation charge would be £4,500, i.e. one-fourth of £18,000.

Activity 7.4 Measurement of depreciation

(a) What is depreciation?

(b) What information do you require to determine the amount of the cost of an asset to be regarded as depreciation in an accounting period?

(c) If a vehicle costing £30,000 is expected to be used for four years and to be sold as scrap for £6,000 at the end of the four years, how much depreciation will be expensed in its first year of use, applying the straight-line method for the measurement?

(d) John acquired a car for £20,000 and uses it to provide a taxi service. He reports his profit in the first year as £21,800 without depreciating his vehicle. Why do you think he should depreciate his vehicle?

7.5.2 What information is there about depreciation in the financial statements?

The amount of depreciation charged as an expense in any year is affected by the management's choice of the method chosen for measuring it and their estimate of how long that asset could be used economically. For this reason companies are required to disclose both the method used for measuring depreciation and their estimates of the economic life of each major class of non-current asset. This is a requirement of company law[2] as well as Accounting Standards.[3]

For example, though Tesco and Sainsburys have both chosen the straight-line method for measuring depreciation, their estimates of economic life of each class of asset differ (see box on the right) and accordingly the amount of depreciation recognised as expense in each accounting period would differ.

	Buildings	Plant, equipment
Tesco	40 years	3 to 10 years
Sainsburys	50 years	3 to 15 years

In these circumstances the profit reported by a company is not directly comparable unless the company discloses, as the named supermarkets have done, both the method used for measuring depreciation and their estimates of the economic life of each major class of non-current asset.

7.5.3 How much depreciation should be charged if an asset is not used for a full year?

We need to consider this question when an asset is (a) bought during an accounting period and (b) when it is physically available but not used for part of an accounting period.

(a) When an asset is used for less than a whole year, it is depreciated for the nearest number of months of use. For example, if a vehicle, depreciated at 20% per annum using the straight-line method, is acquired for £20,000 three months prior to the end of the accounting period, depreciation is calculated as £20,000 × 20% × 3/12 months = £1,000. This is referred to as *time apportioning the depreciation.*

In practice, a business may choose to avoid apportioning in this way and adopt a policy of accounting for depreciation for the whole year in the year of acquisition and, to compensate for this, not to depreciate that asset in the year of disposal. For study and examination purposes, the question should preferably state which approach to take in answering the question.

(b) When an asset is acquired but not used immediately, the depreciation charge starts from the date of acquisition. For example, assuming that a building was acquired and ready for use from 1 March but was not occupied until 1 May, the depreciation charge to 31 December would be calculated for the ten months it could have been used, although it was used only for eight in that accounting period. This is a requirement of IAS 16[3] *Property, Plant and Equipment.*

7.6 Accounting for depreciation

There are two approaches to accounting for depreciation in the ledger accounts. These are to (a) reduce the asset account and (b) open an accumulated depreciation account.

(a) ***Reduce the asset account:*** the amount of depreciation expense to be charged in an accounting period may be accounted for by transferring that amount from the asset account (say Motor vehicles account) to the depreciation account. When a depreciation of £4,500 is so accounted for the two accounts will appear as shown below:

Motor vehicles account

	£		£
Balance b/f	20,000	Depreciation a/c	4,500
		Balance c/d	15,500
	20,000		20,000
Balance b/d	15,500		

Depreciation of motor vehicles account

	£		£
Motor vehicles	4,500	Statement of income	4,500
	4,500		4,500

When financial statements are prepared the balance in the depreciation account, being an expense, is transferred to the Statement of income. The balance in the Motor vehicle account, reporting the value to which the asset has been written down (this is referred to as the *written-down value* – abbreviated as wdv), is included among the non-current assets stated on the Statement of financial position. This process of accounting for depreciation, when repeated over the next three years, will write down the asset to its estimated scrap value of £2,000.

(b) ***Open an accumulated depreciation account:*** there is a company law[2] requirement that, rather than reporting the wdv, the Statement of financial position should show the cost of each class of non-current assets and also show separately the accumulated amount that has been written off as depreciation up to the date of the Statement. To achieve this, the amount of depreciation in each accounting period is accounted for by debiting the depreciation account (expense) and crediting (not the asset account) but a separate account which is named Accumulated depreciation account – a name appropriate to it because in it the amounts written off as depreciation in each accounting period are accumulated. At the end of the first year the three accounts involved would appear as shown below. The depreciation account, with the debit balance, records the expense, whilst the one with the credit balance holds the credit entry which would otherwise have been made in the Motor vehicle account.

Motor vehicles account

	£		
Bank a/c	20,000		

Accumulated depreciation of motor vehicles account

			£
		Depreciation	4,500

Depreciation of motor vehicles account

	£		£
Accumulated depreciation a/c	4,500		

As at the end of the first year, the Statement of financial position (see on the right) will report the motor vehicles at cost, and as a deduction there from the accumulated depreciation of the vehicles, arriving at the written-down value of the vehicles as at that date. Thus the requirement of company law is complied with.

Statement of financial position as at the last date of year 1	
	£
Motor vehicles at cost	20,000
Less: Accumulated depreciation	(4,500)
	15,500

Activity 7.5 Accumulated depreciation using the straight-line method: 1

A machine acquired on 1 January 2010 for £180,000 is expected to be used for ten years and the scrap is expected to realise £20,000. The depreciation is to be calculated using the fixed instalment method.

Required: Show how the machine will be reported on the Statement of financial position as at 31 December of each year from 2010 to 2013.

Activity 7.6 Accumulated depreciation using the straight-line method: 2

As at 1 January 2010, Paula Confectioners own several machines acquired at a total cost of £480,000 and written down by that date to £218,400. On 1 April 2010 they acquired another machine for £160,000. They depreciate machinery at 10% per annum, using the straight-line method with proportionate depreciation in the year of acquisition.

Required: Calculate the depreciation expensed in the year ended 31 December 2010 and show how the machinery will be reported on the Statement of financial position as at that date.

Note: The difference between the cost (£480,000) and the wdv (£218,400) would be the accumulated depreciation written off until 1 January 2010 and appearing in the Accumulated depreciation of motor vehicles account as at that date.

7.7 Reducing balance method of measuring depreciation

An alternative method of measuring depreciation is known as *the reducing balance method*. Under this method the depreciation expense written off is measured as a percentage, not of the cost, but of the written-down value of that asset at the beginning of each accounting period. Accordingly, the amount expensed as depreciation in each successive period, being the same percentage of a progressively reducing amount, will become smaller and this is the reason for the name given.

For example, if a vehicle is acquired for £20,000 and it is depreciated annually at 20% using the reducing balance method, the first year's depreciation would be £4,000 (20% of £20,000). The depreciation for the second year would be 20% of £16,000 (i.e. the written-down value at commencement of second year).

Activity 7.7 The accumulated depreciation using the reducing balance method

A machine acquired on 1 January 2010 for £300,000 is to be depreciated at 20% per annum using the reducing balance method.

Required: Show amount of the depreciation in each of the first four years and how the machine would be reported in the Statement of financial position at the end of each year.

Note the following two points with regard to the reducing balance method of depreciating non-current assets:

1. Since the amount written off in each period is the same percentage of a progressively reducing amount, the percentage used has to be almost double that used in the straight-line method.
2. Whereas when using the straight-line method the asset is written down to nil (or a scrap if one is anticipated), the reducing balance method will never completely eliminate the asset from the books of account because in every successive year only a percentage of whatever balance is remaining in the asset account is written off as depreciation.

Activity 7.8 Accounting for depreciation using the reducing balance method

As at 1 January 2010, Kite Metalwork owns machinery acquired for £720,000 and written down to £384,800 by that date. The business acquired another machine on 1 August 2010 for £120,000. Depreciation is calculated at 25% per year using the reducing balance method, with proportionate depreciation in the year of acquisition.

Required: Show the entries in the asset account and the Accumulated depreciation account for the year ended 31 December 2010.

7.8 Sum of the years' digits method of measuring depreciation

This method attaches weights to each year of the asset's economic life. The weight depends on the asset's economic life remaining at the commencement of each year. For example, if an asset acquired on 1.1.2010 is expected to have an economic life of four years, the weights attached to each of these four years 2010, 2011, 2012 and 2013 would be 4 : 3 : 2 : 1 respectively and the sum of these weights (referred to as digits) would be 10. Accordingly the depreciation written off in 2010 would be four-tenths of the asset's depreciable cost.

To illustrate, let us assume that an asset costing £20,000 and having no scrap value has a four-year life:

Year	Remaining life	Depreciation in the year	Depreciation (£)
2010	4 years	4/10 × (Cost – Scrap value)	8,000
2011	3 years	3/10 × (Cost – Scrap value)	6,000
2012	2 years	2/10 × (Cost – Scrap value)	4,000
2013	1 year	1/10 × (Cost – Scrap value)	2,000
	10 years	Sum of the years' digits	

This is a method that provides for accelerated depreciation with £8,000 depreciation in the first year; whereas if the straight-line method had been used in identical circumstances, the depreciation would have been £5,000 (£20,000/4).

7.9 Bad debts and allowance for doubtful debts

Amounts due from customers may be reported as assets in the Statement of financial position only if there is a reasonable assurance that the amounts are recoverable. At the end of each accounting period the trade receivable balances are, therefore, reviewed to see if there is a reasonable expectation that each of the customers will pay in full. The results of this review could fall into one of three categories:

1. Yes there is reasonable expectation that they would – then show the amounts as asset.
2. No there is no reasonable expectation; then reclassify as a bad debt and treat the amount as an expense.
3. Although there is no expectation there is still some hope; then reclassify as a doubtful debt and treat a proportion of the debt as an expense.

Let us now consider how the second and third categories are accounted for.

7.9.1 Accounting for bad debts

Having recorded an amount receivable as an asset, if it is decided that it is not recoverable, then it ceases to be an asset and has to be reclassified as an expense. The accounting entries needed to record this situation are a credit in the account recording the asset and a debit in an expense account named *Bad debts*. Assuming that the debt in question is one due from Jim Gee, the accounts involved will appear as:

Jim Gee's account

	£		£
Balance b/f	18,000	Bad debts a/c	18,000

Bad debts account

	£		
Jim Gee's a/c	18,000		

The above entries close Jim Gee's account and show the loss as a debit balance in a Bad debts account, which at the end of the accounting period will be transferred to the Statement of income.

7.9.2 Accounting for doubtful debts – specific allowance

The situation is not always so clear-cut that a receivable can be definitely regarded as irrecoverable and immediately treated as a loss. In real life there could be receivables that are probably irrecoverable but where it would be premature to close the customer's account, as we have done with Jim Gee, until all efforts have been made to obtain payment, e.g. making a personal telephone request, sending a solicitor's letter, applying to the court for an order.

Whilst these steps are being taken the Receivable account should remain open but it should be recognised that there might be a loss and it would be prudent to take this loss into account when preparing the Statement of income to identify profit or loss for the period. The way such possible loss is recognised in accounting is to create an *allowance for doubtful debts*. In the same way as we avoided having to credit the Motor vehicles account when we depreciated the asset, we avoid crediting the Receivable account when recording that debt as not recoverable. The credit entry is made in an account which is named 'Allowance for doubtful debts'.

Illustrating the opening of an Allowance for doubtful debts account

Let us assume that the amount receivable from Jim Gee might not be recoverable. This possibility is recognised and the anticipated loss accounted for with a debit in the Bad debts account and a credit, not in Gee's account, but in an Allowance for doubtful debts account (as shown below). When financial statements are prepared at the period-end the balance in the Bad debts account, being an expense, is transferred to the Statement of income; while the balance in the Allowance for doubtful debts account is shown on the Statement of financial position as a deduction from Trade receivable (see below).

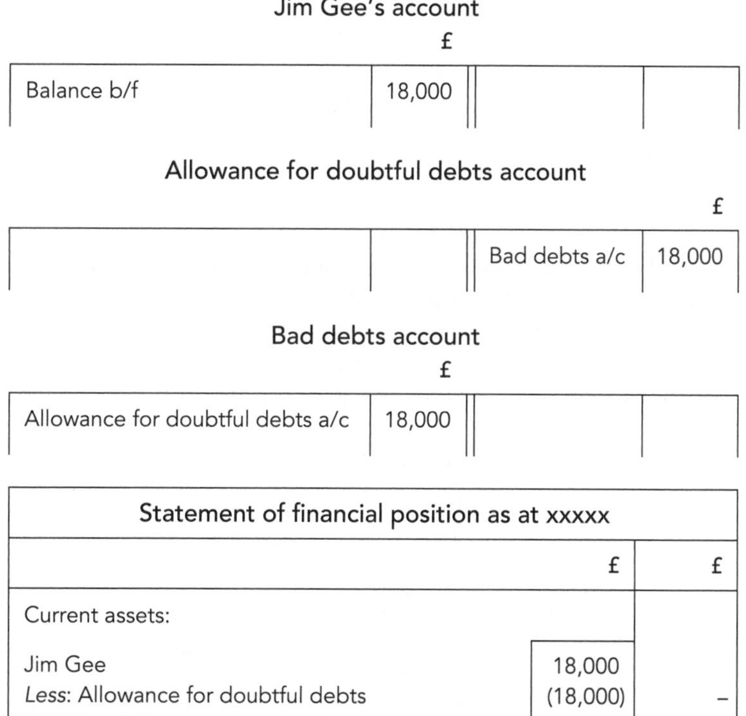

Jim Gee's account

	£		
Balance b/f	18,000		

Allowance for doubtful debts account

			£
		Bad debts a/c	18,000

Bad debts account

	£		
Allowance for doubtful debts a/c	18,000		

Statement of financial position as at xxxxx		
	£	£
Current assets:		
Jim Gee	18,000	
Less: Allowance for doubtful debts	(18,000)	–

What if the customer pays in full after the Allowance for doubtful debts has been opened?

If, after setting up the Allowance account in one accounting period, contrary to expectation Jim Gee pays what he owes in the next, the balance in the Allowance account, being no longer needed, is treated as an income in the next period and transferred to the Statement of income.

What if the debtor is actually unable to pay?

If the situation turns out to be as bad as expected, and it is decided that it is no longer worth pursuing Jim, both the Receivable account and the Allowance account are closed by transferring the credit balance in the Allowance account to Jim's account.

Jim Gee's account

	£		£
Balance b/f	18,000	Allowance for doubtful debts	18,000

Allowance for doubtful debts account

	£		£
Jim Gee's a/c	18,000	Bad debts a/c	18,000

Identifying a particular customer (Jim Gee) and setting up an Allowance account in respect of the amount due from him is known as a *specific allowance for doubtful debt.*

7.9.3 Accounting for doubtful debts – general allowance

A business may not always be able to identify the specific debts that are likely to become irrecoverable but may be able to make a good estimate based on past experience, e.g. past experience might indicate that say 5% of trade receivables might become bad. It is common practice to base the estimate of the allowance required on an *age analysis* of debtors outstanding. For example, experience might indicate that no allowance is required to be made in respect of debts that are less than 30 days old (particularly if that is the agreed credit period), but that an allowance of 2% should be made on trade receivables outstanding for 30 to 60 days and 5% on those outstanding for more than 60 days. Such an allowance is referred to as a *general allowance.*

To illustrate, let us assume that Fresh Fish Supplies allows its customers 30 days' credit. As at the year-end on 31 December 2010 the amounts of trade receivable, the agreed dates by which these amounts are receivable and, based on past experience, the Allowance for doubtful debts likely to be needed are tabulated below.

Amount receivable	Payment due by	% allowance needed
£70,000	31.1.2011	–
£35,000	31.12.2010	2%
£10,000	30.11.2010	5%
£115,000		

The amount to be reported in the Statement of income for the year ended 31 December 2010 as bad debts would be 2% of £35,000 plus 5% of £10,000 = £1,200. On the Statement of financial position as at 31 December 2010 the trade receivable net of the Allowance for doubtful debts will appear as shown on the right.

Statement of financial position as at 31 December 2010

	£
Current assets:	
Trade receivables	115,000
Allowance for doubtful debts	(1,200)
	113,800

Activity 7.9 Accounting for doubtful debts

Trade receivables reported in the books of J&B Watersports as at 31 December 2010 amounted to £208,500. An analysis of the number of days debts had been outstanding showed the position as stated on the right: after undertaking a review of all trade receivables it was decided that a debt of £3,600 outstanding for more than 60 days was definitely not recoverable and past experience indicated that an allowance should be made of 2% of amounts outstanding for between 31 and 60 and 5% of amounts outstanding for more than 60 days.

Days outstanding	£
Within 30 days	124,500
Between 31 and 60 days	62,400
Beyond 60 days	21,600

Required: Calculate the amount to be written off as bad debts in the Statement of income and show how trade receivables will be reported in the Statement of financial position as at 31 December 2010.

How is the Allowance for doubtful debts treated in subsequent years?

The same procedure is adopted, on completion of each accounting period, to estimate the amount that should appear as the balance on the Allowance for doubtful debts account and an adjusting debit or credit is made to the amount of expense (Bad debts account) to be included in the Statement of income.

1. *If the allowance needs to be increased:* let us assume that having accounted for an allowance of £1,200 at the end of 2010, Fresh Fish Supplies finds in 2011 that it needs to write off a debt of £2,000 and as at 31 December 2011 it estimates Allowance for doubtful debt necessary is £1,500. The relevant accounts will appear as follows:

Bad debts account

	£		£
Receivables	2,000		
Allowance for doubtful debt	300	Statement of income	2,300
	2,300		2,300

Allowance for doubtful debts account

	£		£
		Balance b/f	1,200
Balance c/d	1,500	Bad debts a/c	300
	1,500		1,500
		Balance b/d	1,500

Thus the amount to be included as expense in the Statement of income for 2011 would be the bad debt of £2,000 written off in that year, increased by the amount of £300 to adjust the balance in the Allowance for doubtful debts account from £1,200 to £1,500.

2. *If the Allowance needs to be decreased:* on the other hand, if the Allowance for doubtful debts necessary as at 31 December 2011 is only £1,000, the amount included as bad debt (expense) in the Statement of income in 2011 would be the debt of £2,000 written off in that year reduced by £200 excess released from the Allowance account.

Activity 7.10 Adjusting the allowance for doubtful debts

The year-end Trial Balance reports trade receivables at £438,000 and the allowance for doubtful debts at £12,500. It is decided that a debt of £18,000 should be written off and the allowance adjusted to cover 5% of outstanding debts.

Required: Set out the Trade receivables account and the Allowance for doubtful debts account, indicating the expense written off in the Statement of income and the asset reported in the Statement of financial position.

Summary

- Results of the operations in each accounting period are determined on the basis of the accruals concept, i.e. income is accounted for when it is earned (even if yet to be received) and expenses are accounted for when a commitment is made (even if part remains unpaid at the end of the accounting period).
- Any income received but yet to be earned by the end of the accounting period is regarded as deferred income and treated as if it were a liability at the end of the accounting period.
- Expenses in an accounting period include:
  - depreciation which is an appropriate portion of the depreciable cost of non-current assets;
  - bad debts which are trade receivables not expected to be recovered;
  - an allowance for doubtful debts which are trade debts which may not be recovered.
- The straight-line, reducing balance and sum of the years' digits are methods that may be used for measuring depreciation.

References

1. *Framework for the Preparation and Presentation of Financial Statements*, commonly referred to as the IASB Framework, was published by the International Accounting Standards Committee Board in April 1989.
2. Companies Act (2006) London, The Stationery Office.
3. IAS 16 *Property, Plant and Equipment*, revised 2003, effective 1.1.2005, London, International Accounting Standards Board.

Suggested answers to activities

7.1 The need for the accruals basis of accounting

For correctly reporting the performance in an accounting period the expenses need to be accounted on an accruals basis, i.e. not at the amount paid in that period but at the amount incurred. If unpaid expenses are ignored, as Sally did, the results will be as follows:

(a) Expenses are understated; hence performance overstated, reporting in her case a profit instead of loss.

(b) Liabilities are not reported in the Statement of financial position.

Statement of income year ended xxxx	
	£
Earnings from hairdressing	18,500
Rent	(12,000)
Staff salary	(6,000)
Advertising	(1,800)
Telephone	(460)
Net loss for the year	(1,760)

7.2 Accounting for expenses accrued and prepaid

In the Statement of income:

Salaries: 128,600 + 24,500 = £153,100

Advertising: 21,800 + 8,400 = £30,200

Rates: 6,000 – 1,200 = £4,800

In the Statement of financial position:

As current asset:

Prepaid rates £1,200

As current liabilities:
Salary accrued: £24,500
Advertising accrued: £8,400

7.3 Is deferred income a liability?

Irrespective of the landlord's intentions, the rent relating to the period after the year-end should be regarded as unearned and therefore accounted for as deferred income. Such deferred income is treated as if it were a liability because, although not falling within the definition of a liability (as present obligation to transfer economic benefit), there is no other place in which it could be included within the Statement of financial position.

7.4 Measurement of depreciation

(a) Depreciation is the amount of the depreciable cost (i.e. the cost less the amount of scrap) of a non-current asset, allocated to each accounting period in a systematic and appropriate manner.

(b) Information needed to determine depreciation:

(i) the cost of the asset;
(ii) estimated scrap value at the end of its life;
(iii) estimated useful economic life.

(c)

Cost of vehicle	£30,000
Scrap value	(£6,000)
Depreciable cost	£24,000

Depreciation : 24,000/4 years = £6,000

(d) Why John should depreciate his vehicle:

- Unless an appropriate portion of the asset's cost is matched with the income generated by the asset the profit will be overstated.

- Continuing to report the vehicle in the Statement of financial position year after year at the amount at which it was acquired will not fairly reflect the resource available to the entity at each point.
- Depreciating the vehicle reduces the amount of profit which John would feel entitled to draw out of the business. Hence corresponding resources are automatically retained within the business so that it becomes possible to replace the asset at the end of its useful life, except where inflation spoils the situation.

7.5 The Accumulated depreciation account

Statement of financial position as at 31 December				
	2010	2011	2012	2013
	£'000	£'000	£'000	£'000
Machine at cost	180	180	180	180
Less: Accumulated depreciation account	(16)	(32)	(48)	(64)
Written-down value	164	148	132	116

7.6 Accounting for depreciation using the straight-line method

Depreciation expense:

10% of £480,000	£48,000
10% of £160,000 × 9/12 months	£12,000
	£60,000

Statement of financial position as at 31 December 2010:

Machinery at cost (480,000 + 160,000)	£640,000
Accumulated depreciation (261,600[a] + 60,000)	(£321,600)
Written-down value	£318,400

Note: (a) Accumulated depreciation on 1.1.2010 = 480,000 – 218,400 = £261,600.

7.7 The accumulated depreciation using the reducing balance method

1.1.2010: Cost	£300,000
2010 Depreciation	(£60,000)
1.1.2011: WDV	£240,000
2011 Depreciation	(£48,000)
1.1.2012: WDV	£192,000
2012 Depreciation	(£38,400)
1.1.2013: WDV	£153,600
2013 Depreciation	(£30,720)

Statement of financial position as at 31 December				
	2010	2011	2012	2013
	£	£	£	£
Machinery at cost	300,000	300,000	300,000	300,000
Accumulation depreciation	(60,000)	(108,000)	(146,400)	(177,120)
Written-down value	240,000	192,000	153,600	122,880

Note: Each year's depreciation is calculated at 20% of the written down value at commencement of that year.

7.8 Accounting for depreciation using the reducing balance method

Accumulated depreciation on 1.1.2010: 720,000 – 384,800 = £335,200.

Depreciation in 2010:

25% of (£720,000 – £335,200)	£96,200
25% of (£120,000 × 5/12 months)	£12,500
	£108,700

Machinery account

		£			
1.1	Balance b/f	720,000			
1.8	Cash a/c	120,000			
		840,000			

Accumulated depreciation on Machinery account

					£
			1.1	Balance b/f	335,200
			31.12	Depreciation	108,700
					443,900

7.9 Allowance for doubtful debts

Statement of income	£
Written off	3,600
2% of 62,400	1,248
5% of 21,600 – 3,600	900
	5,748

Statement of financial position as at 31.12.2010	£
Trade receivables (208,500 – 3,600)	204,900
Less: Allowance for doubtful debts	(2,148)
	202,752

7.10 Adjusting the Allowance for doubtful debts

Trade receivables account

	£		£
Balance b/f	438,000	Bad debts	18,000
		Balance c/d	420,000
	438,000		438,000
Balance b/d	420,000		

Allowance for Doubtful debts account

	£		£
Bad debts	18,000	Balance b/f	12,500
Balance c/d	21,000[a]	Income statement	26,500
	39,000		39,000
		Balance b/d	21,000

Bad debt expense in the Statement of income:	£26,500

Statement of financial position	
Trade receivables	£420,000
Less: Allowance for doubtful debts	(£21,000)
	£399,000

Note:
(a) The balance c/d in the Allowance account is calculated at 5% of receivables (£420,000) = £21,000.

Multiple choice questions

Accruals and prepayments

7.1 Which of the following is correct? Where accounting records are maintained on accrual basis:

(a) Income should be accounted for only when received

(b) Expenses should be accounted for only when payment has been made

(c) Income should be accounted on an accruals basis and expenses on a payments basis

(d) Income and expenditure relating to the accounting period should be fully accounted for even if income is still to be received and expenses have yet to be paid

7.2 An accrued expense amounting to £18,000 was overlooked when ascertaining the profit for the year. The effect of this error is that:

(a) Net profit is overstated and liability understated

(b) Net profit as well as liability are overstated

(c) Net profit is not affected but liability is understated

(d) Net profit as well as liability are understated

7.3 Expenses relevant to the accounting period which remain unpaid by the period-end should be:

(a) Ignored until they are paid for in the next period

(b) Included with expenses for the period and shown as a liability at the period-end

(c) Deducted from the amount already paid and shown as a liability at the period-end

(d) Included with expenses for the period and shown as an asset at the period-end

7.4 Staff salary remaining unpaid as at the year-end should be accounted for as:

(a) Debit Staff salary account and credit Cash account

(b) Debit Staff salary account and credit Salary accrued account

(c) Debit Salary accrued account and credit Staff salary account

(d) Debit Prepaid salary account and credit Staff salary account

7.5 As at 1 January 2010 salary outstanding was £128,400. During the year ended 31 December 2010 £598,800 was paid as salary and as at 31 December 2010 salary amounting to £142,900 remained unpaid. What is the salary expense to be written off in the Statement of income for the year ended 31 December 2010?

a	£584,300	
b	£598,800	
c	£613,300	
d	£741,700	

7.6 Rent prepaid as at the commencement of the year was £8,000. Having agreed to pay rent at £4,000 per month, the business was able to pay during the year only £28,000. The position by year-end is:

(a) Rent accrued £20,000

(b) Rent prepaid £12,000

(c) Rent accrued £12,000

(d) Rent prepaid £4,000

7.7 Rent paid for eight months up to 28 February 2010 amounts to £32,000. Since then rent has been increased by 20%. The rent written off as expense in the Statement of income for the year ended 30 June 2010 and stated as accrued (liability) as at that date would be

	Expense	Accrued	
a	£48,000	£16,000	
b	£51,200	£19,200	
c	£38,400	£6,400	
d	£57,600	£25,600	

7.8 Having agreed on a monthly rent of £4,000 for business premises, three months' rent was in arrears as at 1 January 2010, though £44,000 was paid as rent during the year to 31 December 2010. What will appear as rent accrued on the Statement of financial position as at 31 December 2010?

a	£8,000	
b	£12,000	
c	£16,000	
d	£24,000	

7.9 Camilus pays rent regularly quarterly in advance on 1 March, 1 June, 1 September and 1 December. Annual rent, agreed at £180,000, has been increased to £240,000 from 1 July 2010. An additional £10,000 was paid on 1 July 2010. The amount to be expensed in the year to 31.12.2010 and reported as Prepaid as at that date would be:

	Expense	Prepaid	
a	£240,000	£60,000	
b	£180,000	£70,000	
c	£210,000	£55,000	
d	£210,000	£40,000	

7.10 Romulus pays rent regularly quarterly in arrears on 31 March, 30 June, 30 September and 31 December. Annual rent, agreed at £240,000, was increased to £300,000 from 1 July 2010. The amount to be expensed in the year to 31 August 2011 and reported as accrued as at that date would be:

	Expense	Accrued	
a	£200,000	£60,000	
b	£240,000	£50,000	
c	£300,000	£50,000	
d	£290,000	£60,000	

7.11 The year-end Trial Balance as at 31 March 2011 reports a debit balance of £9,800 in the Insurance account. This figure includes £6,000 paid on 1 January 2011 as insurance for the year ended 31 December 2011. Ascertain the amount to be written off as insurance in the year ended 31 March 2011.

a	£5,300	
b	£6,000	
c	£9,800	
d	£15,800	

7.12 A Transporter's Trial Balance at year-end on 31 December 2010 reports the balance in the Motor vehicle maintenance account as £216,500. This amount includes £27,000 paid on 1 August 2010 for servicing the fleet of vehicles over three years from that date. The amounts to be expensed in 2010 and reported as prepaid as at the year-end are:

	Expense	Prepayment	
a	£216,500	£27,000	
b	£189,500	£27,000	
c	£193,250	£23,250	
d	£239,750	£23,250	

7.13 If an accrual as at year-end of £1,500 was treated as a prepayment, the net profit for the year would be:

(a) understated by £1,500

(b) overstated by £1,500

(c) overstated by £3,000

(d) understated by £3,000

7.14 A loan of £30,000 at 6% interest per year was given to a member of staff in the previous year. No interest has been received during the year. The accounting entries for accruing interest income are:

(a) Debit Cash account and credit Interest earning account ☐
(b) Debit Staff loan account and credit Interest earnings account ☐
(c) Debit Interest receivable account and credit Interest earnings account ☐
(d) Debit Interest receivable account and credit Staff loan account ☐

7.15 A retailer paid £75,000 as rent and treated the whole amount as expenditure for the year, overlooking the fact that the amount was for a five-year period commencing from the beginning of that year. The effect of this error would be:

(a) Net profit and current liabilities will be understated by £75,000 ☐
(b) Net profit and current assets are understated by £75,000 ☐
(c) Net profit and current assets are understated by £60,000 ☐
(d) Net profit and current assets are overstated by £60,000 ☐

7.16 After reporting the profit for the year it is found that £13,200 of stationery reported as an asset by the year-end has in fact been fully used up. The effect of the correction of this error would be:

(a) The gross profit as well as net profit would both increase by £13,200 ☐
(b) The gross profit and net profit would both decrease by £13,200 ☐
(c) The gross profit would decrease by £13,200 but net profit would remain unchanged ☐
(d) The gross profit will remain unchanged but net profit will decrease by £13,200 ☐

Deferred income

7.17 A business earns income by renting out properties. During the year ended 31 December 2010 it received £38,400 as rent. This amount includes £5,400 received as advance for 2011. During 2011 it received £34,500 as rent and a third of this amount relates to 2010. The financial statements for the year ended 31 December 2010 should report:

	Rental income	Rent in arrears	
a	£38,400	None	☐
b	£49,900	£11,500	☐
c	£44,500	£11,500	☐
d	£49,900	£11,500	☐

7.18 A business sublets three apartments in its office premises, each at £500 per month. During the year ended 30 June 2011 it received £18,500 as rent. This includes rent received in advance on one apartment for six months to 31 December 2011. As at 30 June 2011:

	Current asset	Deferred income	
a	£18,500	None	☐
b	£2,500	£3,000	☐
c	None	None	☐
d	£3,000	£2,500	☐

7.19 In addition to the information stated as 7.18 above, you are informed that as at 30 June 2010 rent in arrears was £2,500 and rent received in advance £1,500. Identify the related current asset and deferred income as at 30 June 2011:

	Current asset	Deferred income	
a	£3,500	£3,000	☐
b	£2,500	£3,000	☐
c	£3,000	£2,500	☐
d	£500	None	☐

7.20 Stated below on the left is information relating to rental income of a business.

As at 31 December	2010	2011
Rent received in advance	£4,500	£6,000
Rent in arrears	£18,000	£24,000

During the year to 31 December 2011 £74,500 was received as rent. The rental income for the year ended 31 December 2011 would be:

a	£43,000	
b	£70,000	
c	£79,000	
d	£106,000	

7.21 A part of office premises has been sublet. The rent agreed at £9,000 per year, until 31 March 2011, has been increased to £12,000 per year since then. Rent is regularly received half yearly in advance on 1 October and 1 April. Items in the financial statements for the year ended 31.12.2011 will be:

	Income	Deferred income	
a	£11,250	£3,000	
b	£10,500	–	
c	£12,000	£2,250	
d	£9,000	£3,000	

Depreciation – the concept and accounting

7.22 The most compelling reason for accounting for depreciation is:

(a) To write down the non-current assets to what they are worth at the end of the period

(b) To build up resources for the purpose of replacing the non-current assets

(c) To match a portion of the depreciable cost of the asset against the income generated by it

(d) Because that is a requirement of company law

7.23 Which of the following describes the balance in the Accumulated depreciation account?

(a) A liability account

(b) Depreciation expense written off in an accounting period

(c) The cumulative sum of all depreciation expenses from the date of asset's acquisition to date

(d) None of the above

7.24 Accumulated depreciation should be shown on the statement of financial position:

(a) As a current liability

(b) As a deduction from current assets

(c) As part of owner's equity

(d) As a deduction from the cost of corresponding non-current assets

7.25 What do you understand when one refers to the 'net book value' of a non-current asset?

(a) The cost of the asset

(b) The cost less accumulated depreciation up to the date of reporting

(c) The cost of the asset less amount expensed as depreciation in the current period

(d) The current worth of the asset

7.26 Which of the following would you include within the cost of sales?

(a) Depreciation of vehicles

(b) Depreciation of furniture

(c) Depreciation of office equipment

(d) Depreciation of machinery used in the production effort

7.27 A wholesale dealer who uses his fleet of vehicles for delivering his goods to customers reports his net profit for the year without accounting for depreciation of his vehicles. The effect is:

(a) Gross profit as well as net profit is overstated
(b) Gross profit is not affected but net profit is overstated
(c) Gross profit as well as net profit is understated
(d) Gross profit is not affected but net profit is understated

7.28 Joe Pickard, a shoemaker, reports his profit without accounting for depreciation of machinery. As a result:

(a) Gross profit as well as net profit is overstated
(b) Gross profit is not affected but net profit is overstated
(c) Gross profit as well as net profit is understated
(d) Gross profit is not affected but net profit is understated

Depreciation – the straight-line method

7.29 A trader depreciates his vehicles at 20% per annum using the straight-line method with proportionate depreciation in the year of acquisition. In addition to the fleet acquired in previous years for £180,000, he acquired a vehicle on 1 May 2011 for £60,000. Calculate depreciation for the year ended 31 December 2010.

a	£12,000	
b	£36,000	
c	£44,000	
d	£48,000	

7.30 A manufacturer owns three machines – the first acquired on 1.1.2006 for £110,000, the second on 1.7.2008 for £90,000 and the third on 1.10.2010 for £130,000. He expects to use each machine for ten years and realise the scrap for £10,000. Using the straight-line method what is his depreciation for the year ended 31.12.2010?

a	£12,000	
b	£21,000	
c	£30,000	
d	£33,000	

7.31 Speedlink owns three trucks acquired as stated below on the left. They expect to use each truck for five years and sell the scrap at 10% of the cost. Their policy is to write off the depreciable cost equally over the five years of each truck's economic life. Calculate the depreciation to be written off in the year ended 31 December 2010.

Date	Cost
1.7.2005	£48,000
1.1.2007	£36,000
1.4.2010	£60,000

a	£18,900	
b	£19,380	
c	£21,600	
d	£22,320	

7.32 A firm owns a fleet of vehicles acquired at a total cost of £264,800. Accumulated depreciation up to the beginning of the current year is £112,400. Vehicles are depreciated at 20% per annum using the straight-line method. The written-down value of the vehicles by the end of the current year would be:

a	£52,960	
b	£99,440	
c	£152,400	
d	£211,840	

7.33 A builder owns three cranes, particulars of which are stated on the right. As at 31 December Year 5 these are reported on the Statement of financial position at £99,000. The cranes are depreciated at 20% per annum, using the straight-line method and calculating depreciation for the months of use. Crane B was sold on 30 June year 6. The depreciation for year 6 would be:

Crane	Acquired on	Cost
A	1.4. Year 1	£60,000
B	1.7. Year 3	£40,000
C	1.10. Year 5	£80,000

(a) £19,800
(b) £23,000
(c) £32,000
(d) £36,000

7.34 An extract of the year-end Trial Balance is shown on the right. A new machine had been acquired for £180,000 on 1 September 2010. Machinery is depreciated at 10% of cost with proportionate depreciation in the year of acquisition. The financial statements for the year ended 30 June 2011 will report:

Trial Balance as at 30 June 2011		
	£'000	£'000
Machinery at cost	860	–
Accumulated depreciation to 30.6.2010	–	216

	Depreciation	Written-down value	
a	£83,000	£561,000	
b	£86,000	£561,000	
c	£86,000	£558,000	
d	£64,400	£579,600	

Depreciation – the reducing balance method

7.35 A firm owns a fleet of vehicles acquired at a total cost of £480,000. Accumulated depreciation up to the beginning of the current year is £212,400. Vehicles are depreciated at 25% per annum using the reducing balance method. The written-down value of the vehicles by the end of the current year would be:

a	£66,900	
b	£147,600	
c	£200,700	
d	£267,600	

7.36 A trader depreciates his vehicles at 40% per annum using the reducing balance method, with proportionate depreciation in the year of acquisition. In addition to vehicles acquired on 1 July 2010 for £180,000, he acquired a vehicle on 1 May 2011 for £60,000. His depreciation for year ended 31 December 2011 will be:

a	£59,200	
b	£73,600	
c	£81,600	
d	£83,200	

7.37 Gateway owns three trucks acquired as stated below on the left. They depreciate their trucks at 25% per year, using the reducing balance method and time apportioning in the year of acquisition. What will be the depreciation to be written off in the Statement of income for the year ended 31 December 2011?

Date	Cost
1.7.2008	£48,000
1.1.2009	£36,000
1.4.2011	£60,000

a	£22,219	
b	£25,126	
c	£25,969	
d	£36,000	

7.38 A builder owns three cranes, particulars of which are stated on the right. The cranes are depreciated at 25% per annum using the reducing balance method, with time apportioning in the year of acquisition and disposal. Crane B was sold on 30 June year 6. The depreciation for year 6 would be:

Crane	Acquired on	Cost
A	1.4. Year 4	£80,000
B	1.7. Year 5	£40,000
C	1.9. Year 6	£60,000

(a) £21,563
(b) £23,750
(c) £25,000
(d) £31,563

7.39 An extract of the year-end Trial Balance is shown on the right. A new machine had been acquired for £180,000 on 1 September 2010. Machinery is depreciated at 25% on the reducing balance method with proportionate depreciation in the year of acquisition. The financial statements for the year ended 30 June 2011 will report:

Trial Balance as at 30 June 2011		
	£'000	£'000
Machinery at cost	920	–
Accumulated depreciation to 30.6.2010	–	424

	Depreciation	Written-down value	
a	£112,750	£383,250	
b	£116,500	£379,500	
c	£157,750	£338,250	
d	£161,500	£514,500	

Depreciation – The sum of the years' digits method

7.40 A machine acquired for £180,000 on 1 January 2008 is expected to have an economic life of five years and a residual value of £30,000. The machine is depreciated using the sum of the years' digits method. The depreciation for the year ended 31 December 2011 would be:

a	£10,000	
b	£20,000	
c	£24,000	
d	£30,000	

7.41 A machine was acquired for £160,000 on 1 July 2007 and another for £200,000 on 1 January 2010. The economic life of each machine is estimated at four years and the residual value 10% of cost. Machinery is depreciated using the sum of the years' digits method. The depreciation for the year to 31 December 2011 would be:

a	£54,000	
b	£62,000	
c	£61,200	
d	£68,400	

Bad and doubtful debts

7.42 When preparing its financial statements, if a business deliberately underestimates the allowance required to cover doubtful debts, it would be:

(a) overstating its performance and understating its liability

(b) overstating its performance as well as its liability

(c) overstating its performance and understating its assets

(d) overstating its performance as well as its assets

7.43 A trade debt of £12,400 is to be written off as bad and the Allowance for doubtful debts increased from £38,200 to £41,900. The amount to be written off against the profit for the year as bad and doubtful debts would be:

a	£8,700	
b	£12,400	
c	£16,100	
d	£54,300	

7.44 Trade debt as at 30 June 2011 amounted to £418,400. Allowance for doubtful debts brought forward as at 1 July 2010 was £18,800. The proprietor wishes a debt of £3,400 to be written off and the Allowance adjusted to cover 5% of debts receivable as at 30 June 2011. Calculate the expenditure for the year.

a	£1,450	
b	£3,400	
c	£5,350	
d	£20,920	

7.45 Trade debts receivable as at 1 April 2010 were £382,400. During the year ended 31 March 2011, sales and sales returns amounted to £859,600 and £18,400 respectively; while £659,800 was received from credit customers and £8,200 was written off as bad. An allowance for doubtful debts is maintained at 4% of debts outstanding. Calculate the expenditure written off in the year to 31 March 2011.

a	£8,200	
b	£6,928	
c	£15,128	
d	£22,224	

7.46 Trade debts receivable as at 1 January 2011 were £474,500. During the year ended 31 December 2011, sales and sales returns amounted to £728,400 and £11,500 respectively; while £752,200 was received from credit customers and £9,800 was written off as bad. An allowance for doubtful debts is maintained at 3% of debts outstanding. Calculate the expense written off in the year to 31 December 2011.

a	£8,447	
b	£9,800	
c	£11,153	
d	£12,882	

7.47 As at 31 December 2011 trade debtors were £1,238,740 and the Allowance for doubtful debts was £39,420. £29,460 of trade debts has been written off already in the year. The age analysis of debtors and percentage allowance usually carried are stated on the right.

Period outstanding	Amount	Allowance
Over 90 days	£12,800	100%
Over 60 days	£84,200	10%
Over 30 days	£279,400	5%
Within credit term	£862,340	0%

The bad and doubtful debts expensed in the year to 31 December 2011 would be:

(a) £4,230
(b) £25,230
(c) £33,690
(d) £35,190

7.48 The year-end Trial Balance includes those stated on the right. Another debt of £12,400 should be written off and the Allowance adjusted to 4% of debts outstanding. Ascertain the amount to be written off as bad debts in the year.

	Dr	Cr
Trade debtors	£284,075	–
Allowance for doubtful debts	–	£16,240
Bad debts	£11,600	–
Bad debt recoveries	–	£5,800

(a) £1,227
(b) £12,827
(c) £18,627
(d) £23,573

General

7.49 Which of the following would be the transaction which decreases both the assets and the liabilities?

(a) A vehicle was acquired paying £32,000
(b) A loan of £25,000 was settled
(c) Goods were purchased for sale from Orlando Ltd for £12,800
(d) Received a cheque for £5,850 from a credit customer

7.50 A Statement of financial position would report prepayments as:

(a) Current liabilities
(b) Current assets
(c) Non-current assets
(d) Deduction from the capital

7.51 On its Statement of financial position a business would report as a current liability the amounts:

(a) It intends to repay within one year of the end of accounting period
(b) It intends to pay immediately after the accounting period
(c) It intends to pay as early as possible but not later than a month after the accounting period
(d) It hopes to repay one day

7.52 When preparing the Statement of financial position as at 31 December 2011 adjustments need to be made for the following:

(a) Stationery remaining unused by the year-end is £5,400
(b) Rent income account includes £6,000 relating to the period after the year-end
(c) A loan given an employee is reported at £4,500 after wrongly crediting to that account an amount of £200 received as interest on the loan
(d) As at the year-end salary accrued and insurance prepaid amount to £22,500 and £4,800 respectively

The effect of making these adjustments would be to include in the Statement of financial position an additional:

	Current asset	Current liability	
a	£14,900	£22,500	
b	£9,500	£33,900	
c	£28,500	£14,900	
d	£10,400	£28,500	

Answers to multiple choice questions

7.1: d 7.2: d 7.3: b 7.4: b 7.5: c 7.6: c 7.7: b 7.8: c 7.9: d 7.10: c 7.11: a 7.12: c 7.13: c 7.14: c 7.15: c 7.16: d 7.17: c 7.18: b 7.19: a 7.20: c 7.21: a 7.22: c 7.23: c 7.24: d 7.25: b 7.26: d 7.27: b 7.28: a 7.29: c 7.30: b 7.31: a 7.32: b 7.33: b 7.34: a 7.35: c 7.36: b 7.37: a 7.38: a 7.39: b 7.40: b 7.41: c 7.42: d 7.43: c 7.44: c 7.45: d 7.46: d 7.47: b 7.48: b 7.49: b 7.50: b 7.51: a 7.52: d

Progressive questions

PQ 7.1 The impact of every transaction on account balances

The following are lists of account balances extracted from the books of a trader at nine different points on the same day. You are to assume that the shift from one point to the next was caused by a single transaction.

	Point 1	Point 2	Point 3	Point 4	Point 5	Point 6	Point 7	Point 8	Point 9
	£	£	£	£	£	£	£	£	£
Non-current asset	40,000	40,000	40,000	40,000	40,000	40,000	40,000	40,000	40,000
Less: Depreciation	(8,000)	(8,000)	(8,000)	(8,000)	(8,000)	(8,000)	(8,000)	(8,500)	(8,500)
	32,000	32,000	32,000	32,000	32,000	32,000	32,000	31,500	31,500
Inventory	18,000	21,000	16,000	16,000	16,000	16,000	16,000	16,000	16,000
Trade receivables	15,000	15,000	23,000	18,200	18,200	18,200	18,200	18,200	18,200
Cash and bank	4,500	4,500	4,500	9,300	7,300	7,100	7,100	7,100	7,000
	69,500	72,500	75,500	75,500	73,500	73,300	73,300	72,800	72,700
	£	£	£	£	£	£	£	£	£
Capital	50,000	50,000	50,000	50,000	50,000	50,000	50,000	50,000	50,000
Add: Net profit	14,000	14,000	17,000	17,000	17,000	16,800	16,500	16,000	16,000
Less: Drawings	(4,000)	(4,000)	(4,000)	(4,000)	(4,000)	(4,000)	(4,000)	(4,000)	(4,100)
	60,000	60,000	63,000	63,000	63,000	62,800	62,500	62,000	61,900
Trade payables	6,500	9,500	9,500	9,500	7,500	7,500	7,500	7,500	7,500
Accrued expense	3,000	3,000	3,000	3,000	3,000	3,000	3,300	3,300	3,300
	69,500	72,500	75,500	75,500	73,500	73,300	73,300	72,800	72,700

Required: Identify each transaction and the amount involved.

PQ 7.2 Period-end adjustments

The year-end Trial Balance of Bill Renton, extracted as at 31 December 2010, includes the items shown with related information below.

Item	Amount	Further information relating to each item
1. Purchases	£214,500	Goods costing £14,500 remain unsold at the year-end
2. Stationery	£3,600	Stationery costing £600 remains unused at the year-end
3. Rent	£15,000	Annual rent for 2010 is agreed at £12,000
4. Salaries	£22,800	Staff salaries of £2,200 remained unpaid at the year-end
5. Vehicle	£18,000	Depreciation of vehicles is estimated at 20% of cost

Required: Show how each of them will appear on the Statement of income for the year ended 31 December 2010 and the Statement of financial position as at that date.

PQ 7.3 Payments in advance and in arrears

Mod Shoes prepares its financial statements annually up to 31 December. It moved into its current premises on 1 November 2009 agreeing a rental of £24,000 per year.

Required: Set out the Rent account of the business for the year ended 31 December 2010, on each of the following alternative bases:
(a) rent is paid quarterly (i.e. every three months) in advance, beginning 1 November 2009;
(b) rent is paid quarterly in arrears, the first payment being made on 31 January 2010.

PQ 7.4 Relations between payments and expense in a new business

Information tabulated below relates to a business which commenced this year.

	During the current year:		As at the year-end:	
Account	Payments	Expense	Prepayment	Accrual
(a) Vehicle maintenance	£135	£160	–	
(b) Insurance	£500		–	£125
(c) Salaries		£2,600	–	£55
(d) Rates		£260	£95	–
(e) Telephone	£290		–	£80

Required: Fill in the blanks in the grid with appropriate figures.

PQ 7.5 Relations between payments and expense in a continuing business

Information stated below is in respect of a business which commenced several years ago.

	Statement of financial position – 31.12.2009		During the year ended 31.12.2010		Statement of financial position as at 31.12.20X7	
	Asset	Liability	Payment	Expense	Asset	Liability
(a) Rent	£400	–	£1,600	£1,600		–
(b) Fuel	–	–	£855		£155	–
(c) Office equipment	£8,000	–	–			–
(d) Motor vehicles	£5,500	–	£2,500			–
(e) Salaries	£300	–	£6,200		–	£400
(f) Insurance	–	£300		£1,200	–	£200
(g) Telephone	£160	–		£420	£100	–

Office equipment and motor vehicles are depreciated at 20% and 25% per annum respectively, using the straight-line method. New vehicles were paid for on 1.1.2010.

Required: Fill in the blanks with appropriate figures.

PQ 7.6 Accounting for expenses on an accruals basis

In his Statement of financial position as at 1 June 2009, Albert, a retailer, reported rent accrued at £400, while insurance prepaid and rates prepaid were reported at £360 and £350, respectively. During the year ended 31 May 2010 the following payments were made:

Date	Item	Amount	Period covered
11.7.2009	Rent	£600	Three months to 30 June 2009
24.9.2009	Insurance	£1,200	One year to 30 September 2010
3.10.2009	Rates	£700	Six months to 28 February 2010
14.11.2009	Rent	£800	Four months to 31 October 2009
16.3.2010	Rent	£800	Four months to 29 February 2010
8.4.2010	Rates	£800	Six months to 31 August 2010

Required: Post these payments to appropriate accounts in the ledger, make the year-end adjustments and identify how each item will be reported in the Statement of income for the year ended 31 May 2010 and the Statement of financial position as at that date.

PQ 7.7 Accounting for renting a photocopy machine (ICSA)

Whatmore College rents a photocopy machine from City Equipment Ltd agreeing to:

(i) pay an agreed rental annually in advance on 1 January and in addition pay three pence per copy taken;

(ii) meet the copy charges by paying £5,000 per quarter in arrears on 31 March, 30 June, 30 September and 31 December.

As at 1 May 2009 annual rental paid in advance amounted to £8,000 while copy charges owed was £1,245. As from 1 January 2010 the annual rental has been increased to £15,000. During the year ended 30 April 2010, the number of photocopies taken was 710,400. Assuming that the college maintains a single account for City Equipment, recording both rentals paid in advance and amount payables for copies taken, set out the City Equipment account for the year ended 30 April 2010.

PQ 7.8 Accounting for income on an accruals basis: 1

The accruals basis, in relation to income, means that income is recognised in each accounting period, not in accordance with the amount received in the period, but in accordance with the amount earned in the accounting period.

	Statement of financial position – 31.12.2009		During the year ended 31.12.2010		Statement of financial position – 31.12.2010	
	Asset	Liability	Receipts	Income	Asset	Liability
(a) Commission earnings	£50	–	£565		£35	–
(b) Interest receivable	£100	–	£900	£1,000		
(c) Rent receivable	–	£150	£1,300		£100	–
(d) Commission earnings	£120	–	£1,600		–	£250
(e) Interest receivable	£100	–	£1,300	£1,500		–
(f) Rent receivable	£500	–		£6,000	–	£500

Required: Fill in the blanks of the grid with appropriate figures.

PQ 7.9 Accounting for income on an accruals basis: 2

Free Range Stores make up accounts to 31 December each year. Premises used by them have an apartment which is rented out to university students at £2,000 per quarter. Particulars of rent received from students have been tabulated below.

Cash received during year 2009		Cash received during the year 2010	
Amount	In respect of the period	Amount	In respect of the period
£2,000	1.1.2009 to 31.3.2009	£2,000	1.10.2009 to 31.12.2009
£2,000	1.4.2009 to 30.6.2009	£2,000	1.1.2010 to 31.3.2010
£2,000	1.7.2009 to 30.9.2009	£2,000	1.4.2010 to 30.6.2010
		£2,000	1.7.2010 to 30.9.2010
		£2,000	1.10.2010 to 31.12.2010
		£2,000	1.1.2011 to 31.3.2011

Required: Calculate for each of the two years, 2009 and 2010, the amounts that should be reported as rental income in the Statement of income and as asset or liability in the Statement of financial position.

PQ 7.10 Bad debt recoveries

As at 1 April 2010 Ronan's trade receivables amounted to £186,500 and his transactions with his customers during the year ended 31 March 2011 are stated on the right. Ronan maintains a 4% allowance for doubtful debts. The amount stated as cash received from customers includes £4,300 received from Maggie Fish whose debt had been written off as bad in the previous accounting period.

Credit sales	£528,400
Bad debts written off	£8,400
Returns inwards	£19,200
Cash received from customers	£471,600

Required:
(a) Explain how the amount received from Maggie Fish should be accounted for.
(b) Set out the Allowance for doubtful debts account showing the amount to be written off as bad debt.

PQ 7.11 Allowance for doubtful debts account over several accounting periods

Rupert Bear's trade debts amounted to £345,500 on 1.1.2010. Further particulars are stated below. He always maintains an Allowance for doubtful debt at 5% of the debts outstanding at the year-end.

	2010	2011	2012	2013
Trade debts as at 31 December	£412,500	£368,400	£548,500	£512,800
Bad debts written off in the year	£18,400	£11,800	£17,650	£14,400

Required: Prepare the Allowance for doubtful debts account showing the amount he would expense as bad debts in each of the four years.

PQ 7.12 Annual adjustment of allowance for doubtful debts

Alex Smith operates a retail business, permitting his customers one month's credit, and maintaining an allowance for doubtful debts calculated as stated in the last column of the table shown below. An allowance for doubtful debts was reported on 1 January 2009 at £2,400. Receivables reported as outstanding for more than 61 days, as at 31 December 2009, include £4,000 which was written off in 2010, and similarly, a corresponding amount reported as at 31 December 2010 includes £1,500 written off in 2011.

Age of receivables	As at 31.12.2009	As at 31.12.2010	As at 31.12.2011	Percentage allowance
One month	£210,000	£312,500	£418,500	0
30 to 45 days	£45,000	£75,000	£64,500	3
46 to 60 days	£28,000	£30,000	£22,000	5
61+ days	£15,000	£20,000	£10,000	10

Required:
Make the necessary entries in the Allowance for doubtful debts account maintained by Alex for each of the three years to December 2011.

PQ 7.13 Receivables and allowances over successive years (ACCA adapted)

You are given the balances on 1 January 2010 as stated on the left and further information of transactions in 2010 as stated on the right:

Trade receivables	£10,000
Allowance for doubtful debts	£400

Sales for the year on credit terms	£100,000
Sales returns during the year	£1,000
Receipts from customers in the year	£90,000
Bad debts written off	£500
Discounts allowed to customers	£400

At the end of year 2010 the allowance for doubtful debts is required to be 5% of trade receivables, after making a specific allowance for a debt of £200 from a customer who went bankrupt. Transactions in 2011 are stated on the right.

Sales in the year (90% on credit)	£100,000
Sales returns (90% relating to credit customers)	£2,000
Receipts from credit customers	£95,000
Offset against amount due to a supplier[a]	£3,000
Bad debt written off in the year	£1,500
Discounts allowed to customers[b]	£500

Footnotes:
(a) An amount due from a customer set off from what is owed to the same party reported as a supplier.
(b) A reduction of amount receivable from a customer as an incentive to obtain early payment.

At the end of 2010 the allowance for doubtful debts is still required to be 5% of trade receivables.

Required: Set out the Trade receivables account and the Allowance for doubtful debts account for the years ended 31 December 2010 and 2011.

PQ 7.14 Trial Balances extracted on same date at different stages of accounting

Mike Russell commenced business on 1 January 2010 with a capital in cash of £100,000. On the same date he acquired some furniture for £10,000 and a vehicle for £20,000. Sales during the year on credit terms amount to £492,000 and he received £458,000 from his credit customers. His payments during the year to 31 December 2010 are summarised as follows:

To trade payables	£436,000	Salaries and wages	£48,000
Postage and telephone	£1,000	Lighting and heating	£2,000
Sales commission	£4,000	Rent	£15,000
Staff welfare	£3,000	Advertising	£9,000

Trade payables as at 31 December 2010 amount to £29,000.

Required:

(a) Account for the above transactions, extracting a Trial Balance as at 31.12.2010.

(b) Account for the closing inventory of £78,000, find the cost of goods sold and extract a second Trial Balance immediately thereafter.

(c) Account for the following year-end adjustments, extracting another Trial Balance after making the adjustments: Mike expects to use his furniture and vehicle for five years and wishes to depreciate both using the straight-line method. He reports that as at 31 December 2010 he owes £4,000 as salaries and £1,000 for heating; while the rent for the shop premises has been agreed at £1,000 per month.

(d) Prepare a Statement of income for the year ended 31.12.2010 and a Statement of financial position as at that date.

PQ 7.15 A basic question from Trial Balance to Statement of financial position sheet

Chrys Lunt, a trader in business for several years, has extracted the year-end Trial Balance from his books of account as shown on the right. He informs you as follows:

(i) Goods costing £72,400 remain unsold at the year-end.

(ii) Salaries amounting to £13,160 and rent of £6,000 remain unpaid on 31 December 2010.

(iii) A trade debt of £4,400 should be written off and an allowance for doubtful debts set up at 5% of debts remaining.

(iv) Depreciation should be written off motor vehicles and furniture at 20% and 5% per annum respectively, using the straight-line method.

Required: Prepare the Statement of income for the year ended 31 December 2010 and set out the Statement of financial position as at that date.

Trial Balance as at 31 December 2010

	£	£
Motor vehicle at cost	150,000	–
Furniture at cost	48,000	–
Accumulated depreciation:		
Motor vehicles	–	80,000
Furniture	–	16,800
Inventory – 31 Dec 2009	52,500	–
Purchases	326,850	–
Sales	–	532,750
Returns inwards	7,250	–
Trade receivables	64,800	–
Trade payables	–	34,250
Salaries	48,540	–
Rent	18,000	–
Other expenses	22,680	–
Capital account	–	80,000
Cash and bank	5,180	–
	743,800	743,800

PQ 7.16 Another Trial Balance to Statement of financial position question

The year-end Trial Balance of a retail trader is shown on the right. You are informed as follows:

(i) Cost of goods in hand on 30 .6. 2010 was £72,000.

(ii) Non-current assets are to be depreciated using the straight-line method, time apportioning for the months of use. Vehicles acquired on 1 October 2009 are expected to have a 20% scrap value after five years of use. Furniture, acquired on 1 July 2009, is expected to be used for ten years with negligible scrap value.

(iii) A debt of £5,000 is to be written off and an allowance for doubtful debt set up at 5% of remaining receivables.

(iv) Rent has been agreed at £3,000 per month. A third of the premises is used as the owner's residence.

(v) £12,000 salary remains unpaid as at year-end.

(vi) Loan obtained from Lucy Brown on 1 August 2009 carries interest at 12% per annum and is repayable by 31 July 2014.

Required: Prepare the Statement of income for the year ended 30 June 2010 and the Statement of financial position as at that date.

Trial Balance as at 30.6.2010		
	£'000	£'000
Motor vehicles	50	–
Furniture	40	–
Purchases	348	–
Sales	–	590
Salaries	78	–
Rent	40	–
Interest paid to Brown	3	–
Receivables/payables	45	27
Inventory – 1 July 2009	42	–
Stationery	12	–
Carriage inwards	14	–
Postage	7	–
Capital account	–	90
Business rates	12	–
Telephone	9	–
Loan from Brown	–	60
Cash book	67	–
	767	767

PQ 7.17 Preparing a business forecast

On 1 January 2010, Sally Sobers submits a business plan to her bank seeking financial assistance. Her plan is to buy ceramic vases, print decorative designs on them and sell them to the retail trade.

- She requires a printing machine, which would cost £10,000, and may be used for five years.
- She intends to buy 10,000 vases in the first year, and step up the purchases each year by 5,000 vases more than the previous year's quantity, during the next three years.
- The current purchase price per vase is £30, but the price is expected to increase by £5 per vase in each of the next three years.
- She expects to sell not less than 8,000 vases in the first year, 14,000 in the second and 18,000 in the third. Her selling price per vase will be £40 in the first year, £45 in the second and £50 in the third.
- She estimated that the overhead would remain at £4 per vase in each of the three years. This does not include depreciation of the machine, which is to be calculated using the straight-line method.
- The cost of inventory on hand at the end of each year is to be calculated on the FIFO cost-flow assumption.

Required: Prepare for Sally a forecast of her business performance in the three years commencing on 1 January 2010 assuming that all her expectations were met and ignoring interest on any finance expected from the bank.

Test questions

Test 7.1 Accounting on the basis of accrual concept

On completion of first year of business Imelda Folly has prepared her Statement of income for the year ended 31 December 2010 and her Statement of financial position as at that date as shown below:

Statement of income for year ended 31 December 2010	
	£
Sales	328,400
Purchases	(178,500)
Gross profit	149,900
Staff salary	(75,500)
Rent	(22,000)
Advertising	(5,400)
Telephone and postage	(1,500)
Stationery	(800)
Sundry expenses	(11,200)
Insurance	(9,000)
Gas and electricity	(3,000)
Net profit for the year	21,500

Statement of financial position as at 31 December 2010		
	£	£
Non-current assets at cost		
Furniture	30,000	
Equipment	60,000	90,000
Current assets:		
Cash in hand	300	
Balance at bank	6,200	6,500
		96,500
	£	£
Capital	50,000	
Profit for the year	21,500	71,500
Loan from Mr Guy Folly		25,000
		96,500

At her request you reviewed the financial statements and have identified the following:

(a) £105,000 due from customers for sales made in the year has not been accounted for on the premise that these amounts were not received until 2011.

(b) Goods costing £45,000 remained unsold at year-end but have not been accounted for.

(c) Expenses remaining unpaid at year-end, but not accounted for, were salary £25,800, advertising £4,500 and one month's rent agreed at £2,000 per month. The loan owed to Guy, Imelda's husband, however, is interest free and repayable only when able.

(d) Insurance, paid on 1 April 2010, was for one year from that date.

(e) Included within sundry expenses are £2,800 paid as membership fees for Imelda's Ladies Club and £1,400 paid as school fees for her son.

(f) Other than an equipment acquired on 1 July 2010 for £15,000, all furniture and equipments were acquired at commencement of business and are to be depreciated at 10% and 20% per annum, using the straight-line method.

Required: Re-draft the financial statements of Imelda's business in compliance with the accruals concept.

Test 7.2 Measuring and accounting for depreciation

Listed below are particulars of non-current assets held on 1 January 2010 by a business owned by Rebecca Brown; another machine was acquired for £60,000 on 1 April 2010.

Asset	Date acquired	Cost	Rate and method of depreciation
Land	1.1.2004	£75,000	No depreciation
Building	1.1.2004	£300,000	2% per annum on straight-line method
Machinery	1.7.2008	£120,000	10% per annum on reducing balance method
Equipment	1.1.2009	£30,000	Sum of the years' digits method; four-year life

Required: Identify the amount expensed as depreciation on each class of asset in the year ended 31 December 2010 and the amounts at which each class of non-current asset will be reported on the Statement of financial position as at 31 December 2010.

Test 7.3 Bad debts and allowance for doubtful debts

As at 31.12.2008	£384,600
As at 31.12.2009	£402,000
As at 31.12.2010	£396,200

The trade receivables in a business owned by Peter Cuthbert were as stated on the left and bad debts written off in each year as stated on the right. Peter consistently maintains an allowance for doubtful debts at 3% of debts outstanding.

2009	£4,820
2010	£3,240

Required: Identify the amount written off as bad debt in 2009 and 2010 and state the amount at which trade receivables will be reported in the Statement of financial position on the last day of each of these two years.

Test 7.4 Preparation of financial statements of a new business

Bill Hardy extracted the year-end Trial Balance at the end of his first year as shown on the right. You are informed:

(i) As at 30 June 2010:
Inventory costing £120,000 remains unsold
Stationery costing £3,000 remains unused
Salary £6,000 and electricity £1,000 remain unpaid.

(ii) Rent for office premises is agreed at £1,500 per month.

(iii) Interest is payable on City Bank loan at 10% per annum.

(iv) Motor vehicles and furniture are to be depreciated at 20% and 10% per annum respectively, using the reducing balance method.

(v) A trade debt of £12,000 should be written off as bad and an allowance set up for doubtful debts at 5% of debts outstanding.

(vi) Sundry expenses reported on the Trial Balance include £15,000 paid as school fee for Bill Hardy's daughter.

Trial Balance as at 30 June 2010

	£'000	£'000
Motor vehicles	420	–
Depreciation – vehicles	–	80
Stationery	12	–
Sales	–	950
Advertising	46	–
Bank a/c	36	–
Staff loans	15	–
Salaries	65	–
Purchases	725	–
Rent	24	–
Sundry expenses	32	–
Trade receivables	172	–
Trade payables	–	119
Furniture	150	–
Depreciation – furniture	–	30
Heat and light	19	–
Cash account	3	–
City Bank loan	–	150
Staff welfare	10	–
Capital account	–	400
	1,729	1,729

Required: Prepare the Statement of income for the first year ending 30 June 2010 and the Statement of financial position as at that date.

Note: The amounts in the Trial Balance are listed under £'000 which means that each amount has been rounded off to the nearest thousand pounds.

Test 7.5 Preparation of financial statements of a continuing business

The year-end Trial Balance of a business owned by Frances Inglish is shown on the right. You have been provided with following information:

Trial Balance as at 30 June 2010		
	£'000	£'000
Motor vehicles	420	–
Accumulated depreciation – vehicles	–	80
Furniture	380	–
Accumulated depreciation – furniture	–	110
Advertising	46	–
Bank account	36	–
Sales	–	958
Allowance for doubtful debt	–	18
Purchases	765	–
Stationery	38	–
Rent	24	–
Inventory on 30 June 2009	114	–
Receivable/payables	405	384
Drawings	20	–
Staff salary	94	
Transport expenses	78	–
Motor vehicle maintenance	14	–
Cash account	6	–
London Bank loan @ 8%	–	200
Staff welfare	10	–
Capital account	–	700
	2,450	2,450

(a) On the basis of an inventory count conducted on 7 July 2010, the cost of inventory in hand was ascertained to be £138,000. During the seven days after 30 June purchases amounted to £7,000 and sales (at cost plus 25%) to £20,000.

(b) Goods costing £4,000 removed by Frances for personal use, and others costing £5,000 given away as prizes in a sales promotion exercise, have not been accounted for.

(c) A new vehicle was acquired on 1 October 2009 for £60,000. Motor vehicles and furniture need to be depreciated in the current year at 20% and 10% per annum respectively, using the straight-line method for vehicles and the reducing balance method for furniture.

(d) £14,000 included in transport expenses is for carriage inwards.

(e) The loan from London Bank was raised in 2008 and is repayable in 2013.

(f) Frances wishes to write off a trade debt of £5,000 and maintain the allowance at 4% of trade receivable.

Required: Prepare the Statement of income for the year ended 30 June 2010 and the Statement of financial position as at that date.

Test 7.6 Focus on reconciliation of inventory

Tony Lamb deals in alarm clocks of a standard make and model. He buys the clocks for £40 each and sells them for £60. The year-end Trial Balance appears as shown on the right. You are informed as follows:

(a) 500 alarm clocks distributed free for advertising purposes have not been accounted for.

(b) Motor vehicles are depreciated at 20% p.a. on the straight-line method and furniture at 10% p.a. using the reducing balance method.

(c) The loan obtained from Tina Small on 1.11.2009 at interest calculated at 10% p.a. is repayable by October 2014.

(d) Rent for office premises is agreed at £24,000 p.a.

(e) Salary £6,000 and audit fees £3,000 remain unpaid at the year-end.

(f) A debt of £4,000 is to be written off and the allowance needs to be adjusted to cover 5% of remaining trade receivables.

(g) An inventory count conducted on 7 October identified that there are 1,830 alarm clocks in the warehouse. Between 1 and 7 October purchases and sales amounted to £2,000 and £1,200 respectively. Any alarm clocks identified as missing should be regarded as those taken by Tony as a gift for members of his family.

Trial Balance as at 30 September 2010		
	£'000	£'000
Motor vehicles	180	–
Furniture	90	–
Accumulated for depreciation:		
Motor vehicles	–	60
Furniture	–	30
Inventory – 30 September 2009	120	–
Purchases	640	–
Sales	–	990
Salaries	72	–
Stationery	12	–
Advertising	39	–
Postage	8	–
Sales commission	5	–
Loan to manager	10	–
Trade receivables	204	–
Trade payables	–	134
Loan from Tina Small	–	150
Light and heat	12	–
Rent	30	–
Allowance for doubtful debts	–	5
Carriages outward	9	–
Cash and bank balance	18	–
Capital – Tony Lamb	–	80
	1,449	1,449

Required: Show your calculation of the alarm clocks removed by Tony and prepare the Statement of financial performance for the year ended 30 September 2010 and the Statement of financial position as at that date.

Note: p.a. stands for per annum.

Chapter 8

Disposal, revaluation and impairment of non-current assets

By the end of this chapter

You should learn:	You should be able to:
■ About the disposal and revaluation of non-current assets	■ Account for disposal of non-current assets
■ About the merits and demerits of reporting non-current assets at current value	■ Prepare a statement of movement on non-current assets in an accounting period
■ About the impairment of non-current assets	■ Account for an asset that is scrapped or traded in for another
	■ Report the asset at current market value rather than at historical cost
	■ Identify the amount of revaluation gain that is realised in each accounting period
	■ Identify and account for impairment loss

8.1 What are non-current assets?

Non-current assets are not specifically defined. Instead they are defined as being assets other than current assets. Current assets, however, are identified as:[1]

(a) Cash in hand and at bank.

(b) Other assets which are either:

- held primarily for the purpose of being traded, or
- are expected to be converted to cash (e.g. inventory, receivables), or
- are expected to be used up (e.g. prepayments, unused stationery)

within the accounting period immediately following the date of the Statement of financial position.

All other assets not referred to in (a) and (b) above are non-current assets. Some among them such as land, buildings, machinery, furniture, office equipment and motor vehicles are identified as *tangible* non-current assets because these have a physical existence, i.e. they can be seen and touched. Other non-current assets such as goodwill and brand name are identified as *intangible* non-current assets because they have no physical existence but nevertheless generate future economic benefit to the business. In this chapter we will focus on accounting for tangible non-current assets.

8.2 Why does a gain or loss arise on the disposal of an asset?

A non-current asset is reported on each Statement of financial position at its written-down value (i.e. its cost less accumulated depreciation until that date). The depreciation written off in each accounting period is based on estimates of (a) the asset's expected economic life and (b) its scrap value on completion of that life. Estimates, by their very nature, may not be accurate. If either or both of the estimates regarding the asset are wrong, the disposal of the asset will result in a gain or loss. The disposal may occur at (a) the end of its estimated economic life or (b) before the end of its estimated economic life.

8.2.1 Disposal at end of its economic life

The sales proceeds are compared with the scrap value. If these are more than the scrap value, then there will be a profit on disposal which is credited to the Statement of income; if these are less then a loss on disposal will be charged as an expense.

To illustrate, let us assume that a haulier's business acquired a vehicle for £40,000 and, estimating the economic life as four years and scrap value as £4,000, wrote off in each of the four accounting periods depreciation of £9,000, i.e. ((£40,000 – £4,000) × 1/4). The written-down value of the vehicle on the last day of the fourth year would be £4,000, i.e. £40,000 – (4 × £9,000). In the unlikely event that the vehicle is sold for £4,000 on the last day of the fourth year there would be no gain or loss on disposal of the asset. On the other hand if, as would be more likely, the vehicle is sold for a different amount or is sold earlier than the last day of the fourth year, a loss or gain on disposal would arise. For example, if sold for £3,000, a loss on disposal of £1,000 would arise.

8.2.2 Disposal before the end of its economic life

In this case the sales proceeds are compared with the written-down value at the date of disposal to determine the amount of any gain or loss. For example, if the asset is sold for £3,000 after completing three years of use, the loss on disposal would be £10,000 i.e. £40,000 – (£9,000 × 3 years) = written-down value of £13,000 – £3,000.

8.3 Accounting for the disposal of a non-current asset

Accounting for the disposal of non-current assets may involve five steps:

Step 1: Depreciate the asset involved for the year of disposal, until the date of disposal. This step will be dispensed with in real life if the policy of the business is to depreciate assets for a full year in the year of acquisition so that no depreciation is charged in the year of disposal.

Step 2: Transfer to a Disposal account the cost of the asset from the asset account as well as the corresponding accumulated depreciation on that asset *up to the date of disposal*. This step is necessary because the amounts relating to the asset are recorded in two separate accounts and the relevant amounts from each of them need to be transferred into a Disposal account to identify the written-down value of that asset at that point of disposal.

Step 3: Record the disposal proceeds debiting the Cash account and crediting the Disposal account.

Step 4: Account for any expenses of disposal, e.g. auctioneer's commission, crediting the Cash account and debiting the Disposal account.

Step 5: Calculate any gain or loss on disposal and transfer it to the Statement of income.

Let us illustrate by reconsidering the case of the haulier. The haulier acquired a vehicle on 1 January 2008, for £40,000, depreciated it using the straight-line method, estimating a useful life of four years and scrap value of £4,000. He disposed of the vehicle on 1 May 2011 for £11,000 paying a commission of £2,000 to the auctioneer. Let us assume that the haulier's accounting periods end on 31 December. The disposal will be accounted for as follows:

Step 1: Depreciate vehicle for four months in 2011: 1/4 of (£40,000 – £4,000) × 4/12 months = £3,000.

Step 2: Transfer to the Disposal account (i) from the asset account the cost of the vehicle and (ii) from the Accumulated depreciation account the whole of the depreciation relating to this asset (i.e.: 1/4 of £40,000 – £4,000) for three years + £3,000 for the four months until 31 May 2011, the date of disposal.

Step 3: Account for the disposal price, posting £11,000 from the Cash Book to the credit of the Disposal account.

Step 4: Account for any related expenses, posting £2,000 from the Cash Book to the debit of the Disposal account.

Step 5: Identify the loss on disposal of £1,000 and transfer it to the Statement of income.

The ledger accounts will then appear as follows:

Motor vehicle account

	£		£
Balance b/f	40,000	Disposal a/c	40,000
	40,000		40,000

Accumulated depreciation of vehicles account

	£		£
Disposal a/c	30,000	Balance b/f	27,000
		Depreciation a/c	3,000
	30,000		30,000

Disposal of motor vehicle account

	£		£
Motor vehicle a/c	40,000	Accumulated depreciation a/c	30,000
Cash – commission	2,000	Cash account – proceeds of sale	11,000
		Statement of income – loss transferred	1,000
	42,000		42,000

Activity 8.1 Disposal of a single non-current asset with no scrap value

Linda, manufacturer of surgical gloves, acquired a machine for £120,000 on 1 January 2006 and depreciates it at 10% per annum, using the straight-line method with time apportionment, and assuming that scrap value would be negligible. She disposed of the machine on 31 March 2011 for £78,000 and incurred £1,000 as expense. Linda prepares her Statement of financial position annually on 31 December.

Required: Account for the disposal to identify the gain or loss on disposal.

Activity 8.2 Disposal of asset with estimated scrap value

Prentice, with a Statement of financial position date of 31 December, acquired a machine for £140,000 on 1 March 2005 and depreciated it using the straight-line method, estimating a scrap value of £20,000 on completion of ten-year use. The machine was sold for £39,000 on 30 June 2011. Expenses of disposal amounted to £2,000.

Required: Set out the Disposal of machine account.

8.4 Disposal of one from a class of assets

When the asset disposed of is one of a group of similar assets, e.g. one of several vehicles, then two points have to be remembered:

1. The transfer to the Disposal account should be the cost and the accumulated depreciation relating only to the particular asset sold.
2. The cost of the asset sold should be removed from the opening balance in the asset account to identify the cost of the assets remaining in use. These assets may have to be depreciated for the whole accounting period, unless any of them had been acquired within the current year.

Activity 8.3 Disposal of one from a class of assets

Henry, engaged in transportation services, owns a fleet of vehicles acquired for £240,000 and written down to £148,000 by 31 December 2010. He depreciates the vehicles at 20% per annum using the straight-line method, assuming that scrap value will be negligible. On 1 April 2011 he acquired another vehicle for £60,000 and on 1 July 2011 sold for £25,000 a vehicle which cost him £80,000 on 1 April 2008.

Required: Set out how these transactions will feature in the financial statements for the year ended 31 December 2011.

8.5 Preparation of a statement of movement of non-current assets

IAS 16[2] requires that every Statement of financial position should be accompanied by a statement tracing the movements during the accounting period in each class of non-current asset and the corresponding accumulated depreciation account. All that needs to be done is to prepare in a statement format all the information in the ledger accounts reporting the asset and the corresponding accumulated depreciation, setting out in separate columns the particulars of each class of non-current asset. For example, the ledger accounts recording the information on motor vehicles in the books of Henry (Activity 8.3) and how the same information is stated in a Statement of movement are shown below:

Motor vehicles account

	£		£
Balance b/d	240,000	Disposal a/c	80,000
Cash a/c	60,000	Balance c/d	220,000
	300,000		300,000
Balance b/d	220,000		

Statement of movement . . .	£
Balance b/f	240,000
Acquisition in the year	60,000
Disposal	(80,000)
Balance c/f	220,000

Accumulated depreciation on vehicles a/c

	£		£
Disposal a/c	52,000	Balance b/d	92,000
Balance c/d	89,000	Depreciation	8,000
		Depreciation	41,000
	141,000		141,000
		Balance b/d	89,000

Accumulated depreciation:	£
Balance b/f	92,000
Depreciation in the year	49,000
Disposal	(52,000)
Balance c/f	89,000
Written-down value	131,000

The same information is required for each class of asset. Accordingly, additional columns would be needed to record the movements for each class, as follows:

Statement of movement of tangible non-current assets:				£	£
	Machinery	Furniture	Equipment	Vehicles	Total
Balance b/f				240,000	
Acquisition in the year				60,000	
Disposal				(80,000)	
Balance c/f				220,000	
Accumulated depreciation:					
Balance b/f				92,000	
Depreciation in the year				49,000	
Disposal				(52,000)	
Balance c/f				89,000	
Written-down value				131,000	

8.6 Two problems in disposal accounting encountered in examinations

In examinations, students frequently encounter two problems when accounting for disposal of assets. These are (a) identifying the opening balance in the asset account and (b) when a disposal has not been fully accounted for by calculating any gain or loss on disposal.

8.6.1 Identifying the opening balance in the asset account

The asset account balance at the commencement of the period needs to be identified because this is needed both for preparing the movement of non-current assets and for calculating the depreciation for the current period. However, the balance that appears on the Trial Balance is the balance that exists on the day the Trial Balance is extracted, i.e. the last day of the accounting period.

To identify the opening balance we need to work back from the Trial Balance figure by adding the cost of any asset that has been sold and deducting the cost of any asset acquired during the accounting period. For example, let us assume that the closing balance in the Motor vehicles account is £120,000 and the cost of vehicles acquired and disposed of in the year were £40,000 and £35,000 respectively; the opening balance (see the ledger account on the right) would be identified as £115,000.

Motor vehicles account

	£		£
Balance b/f	?	Disposal a/c	35,000
Cash a/c	40,000	Balance c/d	120,000
	155,000		155,000
Balance b/d	120,000		

8.6.2 When a disposal has not been fully accounted for

If the Trial Balance includes a *gain or loss* on the disposal of the asset, it could be assumed that the disposal has been correctly and fully accounted for. However, if the Trial Balance reports the *proceeds* on disposal as a credit balance in a disposal account, this is a signal that the transfers of the cost of the asset and the accumulated depreciation to a disposal account have not taken place. The accounting for the disposal transaction needs to be completed by crediting the asset account at cost and debiting the disposal account; debiting the Accumulated depreciation account and crediting the disposal account; and transferring any gain or loss to the Statement of income.

If the cost of the asset disposed of has not been deducted from the asset, the closing asset balance will be overstated. In the above example if the cost of the vehicle sold had not been removed from the asset account, the asset would be included on the Trial Balance at £155,000 (as the closing balance in the Motor vehicle a/c). It is necessary then to remove £35,000 from £155,000 (see on the right) leaving £120,000 in the Motor vehicles account.

Motor vehicles account

	£		£
Balance b/f	115,000		
Cash a/c	40,000	Balance c/d	155,000
	155,000		155,000
Balance b/d	155,000	Disposal a/c	35,000
		Balance c/d	120,000
	155,000		155,000

Activity 8.4 Accounting for asset disposal: confronting two problems

The year-end Trial Balance of Dido Ltd includes the ledger balances stated below. Dido had acquired a machine for £60,000 on 1 March 2010 and on 1 May 2010 sold for £14,000 a vehicle acquired on 1 April 2007 for £30,000. Machinery and vehicles are depreciated at 10% and 20% per annum respectively using the straight-line method.

Trial Balance as at 31 December 2010	£'000	£'000
Machinery at cost	750	–
Motor vehicles at cost	180	–
Accumulated depreciation to 31 December 2009:	–	
Machinery	–	240
Motor vehicles		112
Disposal of motor vehicle (proceeds)		14

Required: Prepare a statement of movement of non-current assets for the year ended 31 December 2010.

Notes:
1. Depreciation has been written off only until 31 December 2009.
2. The Machinery account balance, as at 31 December 2010, would include £60,000, the cost of machinery acquired ten months earlier.
3. The Motor vehicle account balance, on the other hand, will still include the cost of the vehicle sold eight months earlier because Dido Ltd is yet to account for the disposal by removing the cost of that vehicle to a Disposal account.

8.7 Disposal of an asset depreciated on the reducing balance method

If the reducing balance method of measuring depreciation is the one in use, the calculation of the depreciation charge on the assets remaining in use, after a disposal, involves three steps as follows:

Step 1: Identify the cost of the remaining assets by removing *from the opening balance brought forward* in the asset account the cost of the one disposed of.

Step 2: Remove from the opening balance in the Accumulated depreciation account, the amount (i.e. up to the commencement of the year) relating to the asset sold.

Step 3: Calculate the depreciation at the stated percentage of the difference between the answers to steps 1 and 2.

Activity 8.5 An asset disposal with reducing balance method of depreciation

Joey Ltd depreciates machinery at 40% per annum using the reducing balance method. As at 31 December 2009 machinery acquired for £480,000 was reported on their Statement of financial position at £264,000. On 1 July 2010 they sold for £18,000 a machine acquired for £40,000 on 1 April 2008 and acquired a replacement for £60,000 on 1 September 2010.

Required: Set out the ledger accounts recording these transactions in the year ended 31 December 2010.

8.8 Disposal by scrapping or trading-in

As an alternative to disposal by sale, non-current assets may be scrapped at the end of their useful life or may be traded in for another. The accounting entries are just as for disposal by sale. Where disposal takes the form of a trade-in, the value of the asset obtained in exchange should be its own fair value unless the value of the asset surrendered is more evident.

Activity 8.6 Disposal by scrapping or trading in an asset

Machinery acquired for £720,000 is reported at £484,000 on Leyton plc's Statement of financial position as at 31 December 2010. On 1 April 2011 a machine acquired for £120,000 on 1 July 2008 was traded in for another, with a list price of £160,000, the difference in value of £98,000 being paid in cash. On 30 June 2011 Leyton plc scrapped a machine acquired for £180,000 on 1 July 2007. The cost of scrapping amounted to £1,000. Machinery is depreciated at 10% per annum, using the straight-line method and time apportioning for the months in use.

Required: Set out how these transactions will feature in the financial statements for the year ended 31 December 2011.

8.9 Reporting non-current assets at current valuation

As an alternative to reporting at historical cost, IAS 16[3] permits property, plant and equipment to be reported on the revaluation model at their *fair value* (meaning the closest approximation to the value at which they could change hands in a market transaction). In the UK, since 1981, company law has introduced, in addition to the historical cost rule, an *alternative accounting rule*,[4] permitting the reporting of non-current assets at their current value. Should a business opt to report a particular class of asset (say property) at fair value (i.e. current market value) it is essential that all its property (the same class of asset) should be reported at valuation; but there is no compulsion that it should report all its non-current assets at valuation.

8.10 Merits of reporting non-current assets at valuation

1. The current up-to-date values of assets, rather than their depreciated historical cost, may be more relevant to users of financial statements for making economic decisions.
2. The current values may place the business in a better light by reporting a bigger asset base. This is particularly true of assets such as property which increase significantly in value over time. Financial statements reporting such assets at historical cost would understate the value of the total assets of the business.
3. When non-current assets are written up to their higher current values, the correspondingly increased depreciation charge will better reflect the financial performance by matching earnings with the actual cost of the assets consumed in the process.

8.11 Demerits of reporting non-current assets at valuation

1. Whereas the historical costs, based on arm's length market transactions, are objective and verifiable, current values are subjective, representing someone's opinion and quite likely to be volatile.
2. Value can have more than one meaning – such as value in use and realisable value.
3. If an asset is reported at valuation there are requirements that all assets of the same class should be valued and that the valuation should always be updated. Reporting on fair value basis could therefore be expensive.
4. An asset is acquired at a cost which appears justifiable in comparison with the economic benefits expected from the asset. Reporting an asset at a higher market value may not make sense because the improving value may not necessarily imply a corresponding increase in expected economic benefits.
5. When assets are revalued, the depreciation has to be based on the revised value and this may reduce the profit reported by the business.

8.12 Requirements relating to reporting assets at valuation

IAS 16[3] makes the following requirements relating to accounting on a valuation basis.

8.12.1 Revaluation should be of all assets of the same class

All non-current assets of the same class (e.g. land and building are one class, plant and machinery another) should be revalued simultaneously. This is to avoid (i) selective revaluation (cherry-picking), and (ii) reporting assets in financial statements as a mixture of costs and values. However, it is permitted, e.g. where a company has land and buildings located in many countries, to revalue on a rolling basis provided the process is completed within a short period of time and provided revaluation is kept up to date.

8.12.2 The basis of identifying the fair value

- For land and building the fair value is the market value determined on the basis of the current use by appraisal, normally by professional valuers.
- For other non-current assets the fair value is the market value determined by appraisal. The use of official indices for this purpose is permitted, e.g. if the machine was acquired for £525,000 when the related price index was 105 and the index has moved up to 120 by the time of valuation, the current value of the machine would be £600,000 (£525,000 × 120/105). However, if an asset is of such specialised nature that evidence of market value cannot be found, it may be valued at its *depreciated replacement cost*. For example, assume that a machine acquired for £400,000 and depreciated using the straight-line method at 10% per annum is reported on completion of four years of use at £240,000 (£400,000 – 4 × £40,000). If the replacement cost of the machine on this date is found to be £600,000, the depreciated replacement cost is calculated as £600,000 – (4 × £60,000) = £360,000.

8.12.3 Fair valuation should be on the existing use basis

IAS 16 requires that the valuation should be on existing use basis. An alternative use basis of valuation (e.g. land used as a car park may be worth much more if it is to be developed into a shopping centre) may be used only if the change in use is probable, i.e. management is committed to the change in use and necessary planning permission has been obtained.

8.12.4 Frequency of valuation

Unless significant movements in value are known to occur, the valuation could be done every three to five years. Revaluations should be made with sufficient regularity such that the value at which the asset is reported (carrying amount) does not differ materially from its fair value on the date of reporting.

8.13 Accounting for revaluation gain/loss

1. If the asset revalued is one that is not depreciated (say land), the gain or loss on valuation is the difference between the cost and the fair value. For example, if land which cost £400,000 is valued at £600,000 the gain on valuation is £200,000. If, on the other hand, the asset is one that has been depreciated, the gain or loss on valuation is the difference between the fair value and the cost less depreciation up to the date of valuation.
2. Any gain on revaluation should be credited to a *revaluation reserve*, which should appear on the Statement of financial position as part of equity (owner's interest). As we shall see in the next chapter, in a limited company, profits retained by the company (without being distributed to its owners – shareholders) are known as *reserves*. Any reserves available for distribution to shareholders (as dividends) are referred to as *revenue reserves*. Others, not available for distribution, are usually referred to as *capital reserve*. Revaluation surplus is a capital reserve. However, the balance in the revaluation reserve becomes distributable, and should therefore be transferred to revenue reserves, when it becomes realised. The balance in the revaluation reserve becomes realised in the following two circumstances:
   - when the asset to which the gain relates is disposed of, or
   - annually, to the extent depreciation based on valuation exceeds depreciation based on historical cost.
3. Any loss on subsequent revaluation is regarded as an expense and reported on the Statement of income. However, the loss may be offset against any related revaluation surplus held in the reserve, until the surplus on the same asset is exhausted.
4. While a business has an obligation to keep under review its estimate of an asset's scrap value, useful life as well as the depreciation method, these estimates should not be affected by a revaluation exercise alone.

Illustration:

(a) **Identifying revaluation surplus of an asset subject to depreciation:** the revaluation gain is the amount by which the fair value exceeds the carrying value of the asset at the point of revaluation. If a machine acquired for £600,000 is depreciated on the straight-line method, over a ten-year expected life, annual depreciation based on the historical cost would be £60,000. If the machine is revalued after four years at £900,000, this amount would be compared with the written-down value at that date – this is £360,000 (£600,000 less £60,000 × 4 years) which results in a gain on revaluation of 540,000 (£900,000 – £360,000).

(b) **Depreciation of an asset after revaluation:** the fair value of the asset should be depreciated:

(i) using the same method (straight-line) and
(ii) on the basis of the original estimate of useful life (ten years).

Accordingly the depreciation, based on the fair value, spread over the remaining six years of use would be £150,000 (i.e. £900,000/6 years).

(c) **The amount of revaluation gain that is regarded as realised:** We have seen in our illustration that £150,000 would need to written off in each year as depreciation based on the fair value of the machine; whereas based on historical cost the annual depreciation would have been £60,000 (i.e. 10% of £600,000). As a result the annual profit regarded as realised (i.e. available for distribution) is lowered by £90,000 (£150,000 – £60,000). To compensate this, the company law as well as IAS16 confirm that annually Revaluation reserve should be regarded as realised to the extent of additional depreciation arising because of revaluation. This is accounted for by transferring £90,000 annually from the Revaluation reserve to Retained earnings. When this is repeated in each of the six years over which the machine is expected to be used, the whole of the revaluation gain becomes distributable. Note that if the Revaluation gain is reported as £360,000 and the remaining life of the machine, after revaluation, as six, the amount to be so transferred annually could be identified as £90,000 (£360,000/6 years = £90,000). The intention is that the whole of the Revaluation gain should one day become distributable either when the related asset is sold or over the life of that asset.

Activity 8.7 Revaluation of non-current assets as at the end of an accounting period

Equipment used for product design, acquired at a cost of £480,000 and depreciated at 10% per annum, using the straight-line method, was reported in the books of Hickory plc at £264,000 as at 31 December 2010. The directors wish to report the asset at its current market value ascertained on this date as £550,000.

Required: How will the items be reported in the financial statements for the year ended 31 December 2010?

Activity 8.8 Revaluation of a non-current asset at commencement of a period

In the books of Dickory plc machinery acquired at a cost of £800,000 and depreciated at 10% per annum, using the straight-line method, is reported on the Statement of financial position at 31 December 2010 at its written-down value of £320,000. On 1 January 2011 the machinery has been professionally valued at £500,000.

Required: How will these transactions be reported in the financial statements of the company for the year ended 31 December 2011?

8.14 Impairment of a non-current asset

8.14.1 What is impairment of a non-current asset?

We have seen that inventories are written down to the lower of cost and net realisable value. However, this has not been the case with non-current assets. These have been usually reported at their cost less accumulated depreciation until that date. This is referred to as the written-down value or, if preferred, carrying value. If a machine acquired at a cost of £600,000 is written down to £360,000 by 31 December 2010, it will be reported at that amount on the Statement of financial position of that date, even if the net realisable value of the asset is lower. This is because financial statements are prepared on the assumption that the business will remain in operational existence for the foreseeable future (this is known as the 'going concern concept') and, therefore, it is unlikely that the asset will be sold at the lower realisable value. However, there is now an additional test which is based on identifying an asset's recoverable value.

What is recoverable value?

Recoverable amount is the amount that is likely to be recovered either by continuing to use that asset or alternatively by selling it. This is in keeping with the principle that an asset should not be reported at an amount higher than what is likely to be recovered from it. This is why IAS 36 *Impairment of Assets*[5] requires that a non-current asset should not be reported at an amount higher than its *recoverable amount*. Recoverable amount is the asset's *value in use* or its *net realisable value* (*NRV*), whichever is higher.

Recoverable amount

is the higher of

Value in use and **Net realisable value**

The value in use is the present discounted value of future cash flows expected from the asset during its remaining period of use and upon its final disposal. The value in use, on any date, is found by estimating the cash flow that asset is expected to generate during its remaining economic life as well as its scrap value when ultimately sold and discounting both amounts, up to that date, using the market rate of interest applicable to that business. The net realisable value is the amount at which the asset can be disposed of less expenses of disposal. Admittedly, if the NRV of an asset is readily ascertainable, and if that value happens to be higher than the asset's carrying value, there would be no need to either work out the value in use (which is a laborious task) or write down the asset to the recoverable amount.

8.14.2 What if it is not possible to estimate the cash flow from an individual machine?

For purposes of impairment testing it is necessary to estimate the cash flows expected from an asset. It is not always possible to estimate, for example, the cash flow that an individual machine could generate, because several machines together may be involved in one line of activity. In such situations all the machines involved in that activity are regarded together as a *cash-generating unit* and that unit needs to be impairment tested. A cash-generating unit is defined as the smallest identifiable group of assets in relation to which cash flows can be identified and measured.

8.14.3 When is an impairment test required?

In the case of goodwill arising from a business combination (see Chapter 13) and other intangible assets with indefinite useful life (i.e. not amortised) an impairment test should be conducted on the last day of each accounting period. In the case of other assets an impairment test is needed only if and when there is an impairment indicator.

8.14.4 What are impairment indicators?

The impairment indicators may be concerned with the asset (known as internal indicators) or concerned with general market conditions (external indicators). Some of these impairment indicators are listed below.

Internal impairment indicators:

- Asset's performance is affected (say because of involvement in an accident)
- The value of the asset or its output is reduced
- Asset has become obsolete or business restructuring has affected its use
- Asset has been identified as held for disposal.

External impairment indicators:

- Adverse change in the economy, the market or in the technology
- Arrival of a competitor
- Change in interest rate or the expected market rate of return.

8.14.5 Measurement of the impairment loss

For illustration let us focus on the machine acquired for £600,000, and depreciated annually at 10% of cost, and reported at the carrying value of £360,000 on 31.12.2010, upon completion of four years' use. So long as the machine continues in use, and the income it generates in the remaining six years of use is expected to be more than sufficient to match the depreciation in each of these years, there would be no impairment.

On the other hand, let us assume that early in 2011 the machine is involved in an industrial accident and as a result it generates an income of only £100,000 in 2011, and is expected to generate £60,000 and £40,000 in 2012 and 2013 respectively. We need to identify the value in use by discounting the expected earnings. Discounting is done using the interest rate at which the business is able to borrow (assumed at 10% per annum) and that the machine could be sold either immediately or by end of 2013 for £20,000. The value in use is identified as follows:

Earning in 2011 (not discounted)		£100,000
Present value as at 1 January 2011 (the date of impairment test) of:		
Expected earning in 2012	£60,000 × 100/110	£54,545
Expected earning in 2013	£40,000 × 100/110 × 100/110	£33,058
Scrap value at end of 2013	£20,000 × 100/110 × 100/110	£16,529
Value in use, i.e. the present value of what that asset is expected to generate		£204,132

The recoverable value of that machine as at 1 January 2011 would be its value in use of £204,132 because that is more than the net realisable value of £20,000. Accordingly the impairment loss to be written off is £155,868 (£360,000 carrying value less £204,132 recoverable amount).

8.14.6 Accounting for an impairment loss

The amount of impairment loss identified in an accounting period should be accounted for by debiting an Impairment loss account (expense) and crediting an Allowance for impairment account which, like the Accumulated depreciation account, is reported as a deduction from the related asset on the Statement of financial position.

8.14.7 Depreciation of an asset after impairment

In our illustration we found that an impairment loss of £155,868 should be written off the impaired machine as at 1 January 2011, so that the machine is reported on that date at £204,132 (i.e. cost £600,000 less accumulated depreciation up to that date of £240,000 less allowance for impairment £155,868). This machine is expected to remain in use only for three years from 1 January 2011 and should be depreciated in each of these three years by £61,377 (£204,132 less £20,000 scrap value/3 years). On the Statement of financial position as at 31 December 2011 the machine will be reported as shown on the right.

Machine at cost	**£600,000**
Accumulated depreciation (240,000 + 61,377)	(£301,377)
Allowance for impairment	(£155,868)
	£142,755

8.14.8 Reversal of impairment

If, after writing off an impairment loss, in a future year there is a change in the circumstances which caused the impairment, so that the amount written off as impairment loss is assessed to be excessive, the excess in the Allowance for impairment account may be reversed and treated as an income in the year in which the change takes place. However, reversal of impairment is prohibited where the impairment is of goodwill.

Activity 8.9 Impairment of a non-current asset

On 1 January 2005 Hickory plc had acquired machinery costing £800,000 to produce the Dowell model of computer laptops. The machinery was depreciated at 5% per annum using the straight-line method. During the year ended 31 December 2011 the income from sale of this model was only £200,000. A market survey has identified that the sales will only be as stated on the right. The scrap value of this machinery is negligible. The cost of capital for the company is 8% per annum.

Year	Sales
2012	£150,000
2013	£100,000
2014	£60,000

Required: Show how these transactions will be reported on financial statements of this company for the year ended 31 December 2011.

Summary

- Any gain or loss on the disposal of a non-current asset is found by comparing the proceeds from disposal with its carrying value, i.e. cost less accumulated depreciation up to the date of disposal.
- The Statement of financial position should be accompanied by a statement tracing the movements during the accounting period in each class of non-current asset and the corresponding Accumulated depreciation account.
- When a non-current asset is acquired by trading in another, the asset acquired is recorded at its own fair value.
- If a business wishes to account for any non-current asset at a revalued amount, the requirements of IAS 16[2] should be strictly complied with.
- When faced with an impairment indicator, an impairment test of the asset or of the relevant cash-generating unit should be conducted and any resulting impairment loss accounted for.

References

1. IAS 1 *Presentation of Financial Statements*, revised in 1997, effective 1.1.2005, London, International Accounting Standards Board, paragraph 57.
2. IAS 16 *Property, Plant and Equipment*, revised 2003, effective 1.1.2005, London, International Accounting Standards Board, paragraph 73.
3. IAS 16 *Property, Plant and Equipment*, revised 2003, effective 1.1.2005, London, International Accounting Standards Board, paragraphs 31 to 42.
4. Companies Act (2006) London, The Stationery Office.
5. IAS 36 *Impairment of Assets*, revised 2004, effective 1.4.2004, London International Accounting Standards Board.

Suggested answers to activities

8.1 Disposal of a single non-current asset with no scrap value

Disposal of machine account

	£		£
Machine a/c[a]	120,000	Accumulation depreciation[b]	63,000
Cash – expenses	1,000	Cash – proceeds	78,000
Gain – statement	20,000		
	141,000		141,000

(a) Cost of machine sold
(b) Accumulation depreciation:

10% of 120,000 for 5 years	60
10% of 120,000 for 3 months	3
	63

8.2 Disposal of an asset with estimated scrap value

Disposal of machine account

	£		£
Machine a/c	140,000	Accumulated depreciation	76,000
Cash – expenses	2,000	Cash – proceeds	39,000
		Loss on disposal	27,000
	142,000		142,000

Depreciable cost: 140 – 20	£120,000
Depreciation: 120/10 years	£12,000

Accumulated depreciation to 30.6.2011:

2005: 10 months @ 12,000	£10,000
Next five years: 5 @ 12,000	£60,000
2011: 6 months @ 12,000	£6,000
	£76,000

8.3 Disposal of one of several non-current assets

Motor vehicles account

		£'000			£'000
1.1	Balance b/f	240	1.7	Disposal a/c	80
1.4	Cash Book	60	31.2	Balance c/d	220
		300			300
1.1	Balance b/d	220			

Income statement for year 31 December 2011	£'000
Depreciation[e]	(49)
Disposal loss	(3)

Statement of financial position as at 31 December 2011	£'000
Motor vehicle	£220,000
Accumulated depreciation	(£89,000)
	£131,000

Accumulated depreciation on vehicles a/c

	£		£
Disposal a/c[c]	52,000	1.1 Balance b/f[a]	92,000
		1.7 Depreciation[b]	8,000
Balance c/d	89,000	31.12 Depreciation	41,000
	141,000		141,000
		Balance b/d	89,000

Disposal of motor vehicle account

	£		£
Motor vehicle	80,000	Accumulated depreciation	52,000
		Cash – proceeds	25,000
		Loss on disposal	3,000
	80,000		80,000

(a) Accumulated depreciation b/f 240 – 148 = £92,000

(b) 2011 depreciation on machine sold:

20% of £80,000 for six months	8

(c) Accumulated depreciation on machine sold:

2008: 20% of £80 for nine months	12
Next two years: £16 × 2 years	32
2011: as in (b) above	8
Total depreciation to 30 June 2011	52

(d) Depreciation on other machines

20% of £240,000 – £80,000	32
20% of £60,000 for nine months	9
	41

(e) Depreciation = £8,000 + £41,000
= £49,000

8.4 Preparing asset movement statement on the basis of period-end information

Machinery account

	£		£
Balance b/f[a]	690,000		
Cash Book	60,000	Balance c/d	750,000
	750,000		750,000
Balance b/d	750,000		

Accumulated depreciation on machinery account

	£		£
		Balance b/f[b]	240,000
Balance c/d	314,000	Depreciation[c]	74,000
	314,000		314,000
		Balance b/d	314,000

Motor vehicles account

	£		£
Balance b/f[d]	180,000	Balance c/d	180,000
	180,000		180,000
Balance b/d[d]	180,000	Disposal a/c	30,000
		Balance c/d	150,000
	180,000		180,000
Balance b/d	150,000		

Accumulated depreciation on vehicles account

	£		£
Disposal a/c[e]	18,500	Balance b/f[b]	112,000
		Depreciation[f]	2,000
Balance c/d	125,500	Depreciation[g]	30,000
	144,000		144,000
		Balance b/d	125,500

Disposal of motor vehicle account

	£		£
Motor vehicle	30,000	Balance b/f	14,000
Gain on disposal	2,500	Accumulated depreciation[e]	18,500
	32,500		32,500

Movement of non-current assets

	Machinery	Motor vehicle	Total
	£	£	£
Balance b/f	690,000	180,000	870,000
Acquisition	60,000	–	60,000
Disposal	–	(30,000)	(30,000)
Balance c/f	750,000	150,000	900,000

Accumulated depreciation

	£	£	£
Balance b/f	240,000	112,000	352,000
Depreciation	74,000	32,000	106,000
Disposal	–	(18,500)	(18,500)
Balance c/f	314,000	125,500	439,500
Written-down value	436,000	24,500	460,500

(a) Machine: balance on 1.1.2010; 750,000 – 60,000 acquired = 690,000.

(b) Balances in accumulated depreciation accounts are both opening balances.

(c) Depreciation on machinery in 2010:

10% of 690,000 =	69,000
10% of 60,000 for ten months.	5,000
	74,000

(d) Since the cost of the vehicle sold has not been removed from the asset a/c, the opening balance in that account is the same as the closing balance reported on the Trial Balance.

(e) Accumulated depreciation on vehicle sold:

	£
2007: 20% of 30,000 for 9 months	4,500
2008 and 2009: 20% of 30,000 × 2	12,000
2010: 20% of 30,000 for 4 months	2,000
	18,500

(f) Depreciation in 2010 on vehicle sold = £2,000

(g) Depreciation on other vehicles: 20% of (180,000 – 30,000) = £30,000

8.5 An asset disposal with reducing balance method of depreciation

Machinery account

	£		£
Balance b/f	480,000	Disposal a/c	40,000
Cash Book	60,000	Balance c/d	500,000
	540,000		540,000
Balance b/d	500,000		

Depreciation on machine account

	£		£
Accumulated depreciation	3,360	Statement of income	110,240
Accumulated depreciation	106,880		
	110,240		110,240

Accumulated depreciation on machine

	£		£
Disposal[b]	26,560	Balance[a]	216,000
		Depreciation	3,360
Balance c/d	299,680	Depreciation[c]	106,880
	326,240		326,240
		Balance b/d	299,680

Disposal of machine account

	£		£
Machine a/c	40,000	Accumulated depreciation	26,560
Gain	4,560	Cash Book	18,000
	44,560		44,560

(a) Accumulated depreciation on 1.1.2010:
480,000 – 264,000 = £216,000

(b) Depreciation on machine sold:

		£
Cost of the machine	40,000	
2008: 40% of 40,000 for 9 months	(12,000)	12,000
wdv on 31.12.2008	28,000	
2009: 40% of 28,000 for full year	(11,200)	11,200
wdv on 31.12.2009	16,800	23,200
2010: 40% of 16,800 for 6 months	(3,360)	3,360
		26,560

(c) Depreciation on remaining machinery:

		£
Cost of all machinery – 1.1.2010	480,000	
Cost of the machine sold	(40,000)	440,000
Accumulated depreciation on all – 1.1.2010	216,000	
Accumulated depreciation on machine sold	(23,200)	(192,800)
wdv on remaining machine on 1.1.2010		247,200
Depreciation: @ 40% on 247,200		98,880
Depreciation on new: 40% of 60,000 for 4 months		8,000
Total depreciation on machinery remaining		106,880

8.6 Disposal by scrapping or trading in an asset

Income statement to 31 December 2011

	£'000
Depreciation – machinery	(66)
Scrapping machinery	(109)
Loss on trade-in	(25)

Statement of financial position – 31 December 2011

	£'000
Machinery at cost	580
Accumulated depreciation	(197)
	383

Machinery account

	£'000		£'000
Balance b/f	720	Disposal	120
Trade-in a/c	160	Scrapping	180
		Balance c/d	580
	880		880
Balance b/d	580		

Accumulated depreciation – machinery

	£'000		£'000
Disposal[a]	33	Balance[b]	236
Scrap[c]	72	Depreciation[d]	3
		Depreciation[e]	9
Balance	197	Depreciation[f]	54
	302		302
		Balance	197

Machine trade-in account

	£'000		£'000
Machinery	120	Accumulated depreciation	33
Bank	98	Machinery	160
		Loss	25
	218		218

Machine scrapping account

	£'000		£'000
Machine	180	Accumulated depreciation	72
Bank	1	Loss	109
	181		181

(a) 10% of 120 for two years and 9 months = £33
(b) 720 – 484 = £236
(c) 10% of 180 for four years = £72
(d) 10% of 120 for 3 months = £3
(e) 10% of 180 for 6 months = £9
(f) 10% of (720 – 120 – 180) + 10% of 160 for 9 months = £54

8.7 Revaluation of non-current assets as at the end of an accounting period

The Statement of financial position as at 31 December 2010:

As Non-current asset:

Equipment at valuation £550,000

As Equity and reserves:

Revaluation reserve £236,000

Equipment account

	£		£
Balance b/f	480	Accumulated depreciation	216
Revaluation reserve	236	Balance c/d	550
	766		766
Balance b/d	550		

8.8 Revaluation of a non-current asset at commencement of a period

Statement of income year ended 31 December 2011	
	£'000
Depreciation	125

Statement of financial position as at 31 December 2011	
	£'000
Non-current asset:	
Machinery	500
Accumulated depreciation	(125)
	375
Equity and reserves:	
Revaluation reserve	135
Retained earnings[f]	45

Machinery account

	£		£
Balance b/f	800	Accumulated depreciation[a]	480
Revaluation reserve	180	Balance c/d	500
	980		980
Balance b/d	500		

Accumulated depreciation on machine account

	£		£
Machinery a/c	480	Balance b/f	480
	480		480
		Depreciation[e]	125

Revaluation reserve

	£		£
Retained earning[f]	45	Machine a/c	180
Balance c/d	135		
	180		180
		Balance b/d	135

(a) Accumulated depreciation b/f: £800,000 – £320,000 = £480,000
(b) Depreciation based on cost: 10% of £800,000 = £80,000
(c) Machine has been used until 1 January 2011: £480,000/£80,000 = 6 years
(d) Remaining life after revaluation: 10 years originally estimated less 6 years already used = 4 years
(e) Depreciation in 2011 based on new value: £500,000/4 years = £125,000
(f) Realised portion of revaluation reserve: £125,000 (depreciation on valuation basis) – £80,000 (depreciation on cost basis)
The same £45,000 can be arrived at alternatively as £180,000/4 years

8.9 Impairment of a non-current asset

Statement of income year ended 31 December 2011	
	£
Depreciation – machinery	(118,063)[c]
Impairment loss	(87,747)[b]

Statement of financial position as at 31 December 2011	
	£
Machine at cost	800,000
Accumulated depreciation (240,000 + 118,063)	(358,063)
Allowance for impairment	(87,747)
	354,190

(a) Recoverable amount:

		£
Sale in 2011		200,000
PV of sale in 2012	150,000 × 100/108	138,889
PV of sale in 2013	100,000 × 100/108 × 100/108	85,734
PV of sale in 2014	60,000 × 100/108 × 100/108 × 100/108	47,630
		472,253

(b) Impairment loss:

	£
Cost of machine	800,000
Accumulated depreciation to 2010	(240,000)
Carrying value	560,000
Recoverable amount[a]	(472,253)
Impairment loss	87,747

(c) Depreciation: recoverable amount £472,253/four years remaining to 2014 = £118,063

Multiple choice questions

Disposal of assets when the straight-line method of depreciation is in use

8.1 Gain or loss on disposal of an asset is the difference between the sale price of an asset and

(a) the cost of that asset

(b) the cost of the asset less depreciation up to the beginning of the year in which disposal took place

(c) the cost or valuation less depreciation up to the beginning of the year in which disposal took place

(d) the cost or valuation less accumulated depreciation up to the date of disposal

8.2 The only vehicle owned by a company is reported at its cost of £60,000 in the Motor vehicle account, while the depreciation on the vehicle written off in each of the three years of use is reported in an Accumulated depreciation account at £36,000. Which of the following statements is incorrect regarding when the whole £36,000 needs to be transferred away from the Accumulated depreciation account?

(a) When the asset is disposed of

(b) Annually when the financial statements are prepared

(c) When the asset is revalued

(d) When the asset is traded in for another

8.3 A machine acquired for £360,000 on 1 April 2006 and depreciated at 10% of cost per annum was sold for £112,000 on 30 September 2011. Depreciation is time apportioned. Expenses of disposal amounted to £3,000. Identify the gain or loss on disposal of the machine.

a	£161,000 loss	
b	£53,000 loss	
c	£161,000 gain	
d	£53,000 gain	

8.4 A vehicle acquired for £60,000 on 1 September 2005 and depreciated at 20% of cost per annum (time apportioned) was sold for £4,000 on 31 March 2011. Expenses of disposal was £200. What is the gain or loss on disposal?

a	£3,800 gain	
b	£5,800 gain	
c	£3,800 loss	
d	£4,000 gain	

8.5 Machinery acquired for £720,000 was reported at £494,000 on the Statement of financial position as at 30 June 2010. A machine was acquired for £60,000 on 1 December 2010 and another acquired for £120,000 on 1 June 2005 was sold for £52,000 on 30 April 2011. Depreciation is calculated at 10% of cost per annum with time apportionment. Calculate the depreciation in the year ended 30 June 2011 and the gain or loss on disposal of machinery.

	Depreciation	Gain/Loss	
a	£74,500	£4,000 gain	
b	£73,500	£3,000 gain	
c	£85,500	£3,000 loss	
d	£75,000	£8,000 loss	

8.6 As at 31 March 2010 a manufacturer reported at £284,000 machinery which originally cost £480,000. £90,000 had been paid for a new machine on 1 July 2010 and on 1 October a machine which cost £80,000 on 1 January 2007 was sold for £36,000. Annual depreciation is at 10% of cost using the straight-line method. What is the carrying value of machinery as at 31 March 2011 and the gain or loss on the disposal of machinery?

	Carrying value	Gain/Loss	
a	£273,250	£14,000 loss	
b	£490,000	£14,000 gain	
c	£265,250	£18,000 loss	
d	£265,250	£18,000 gain	

8.7 Furniture costing £280,000 was reported at £195,400 on the Statement of financial position as at 31 December 2010. Furniture acquired on 4 May 2011 cost £72,000; while those acquired on 2 July 2006 for £24,000 were discarded on 31 July 2011 and others, acquired for £60,000 on 3 June 2008, were sold for £15,000 on 4 November 2011. Furniture is depreciated at 5% of cost per annum with time apportionment to the nearest number of months of use. Calculate the depreciation expense in the year 2011 and the gain or loss on the discard and the disposal.

	Depreciation	On discard	On sale
a	£15,400	£17,900 loss	£34,750 loss
b	£15,300	£18,000 loss	£36,000 loss
c	£19,500	£19,100 loss	£35,000 loss
d	£19,600	£19,200 loss	£36,000 loss

8.8 A machine acquired for £360,000 on 19 April 2006 and depreciated annually at 10% of cost is sold for £240,000 on 18 August 2011. Full year's depreciation is charged in the year of acquisition and no depreciation in the year of disposal. What is the gain or loss on disposal in the year ending 31 December 2011?

a	£60,000 loss
b	£60,000 gain
c	£24,000 gain
d	£120,000 loss

8.9 Machinery acquired for £720,000 was reported at £494,000 on the Statement of financial position as at 30 June 2010. A new machine was acquired for £60,000 on 1 December 2010 and another, acquired for £120,000 on 1 June 2005, was sold for £52,000 on 30 April 2011. Depreciation is calculated using the straight-line method and assuming ten years' life, but full year's depreciation is charged in the year of acquisition and no depreciation in the year of disposal. What is the depreciation charge in the year ended 30 June 2011 and the gain or loss on the disposal of the machinery?

	Depreciation	Gain/loss
a	£74,500	£4,000 loss
b	£63,500	£14,000 gain
c	£78,000	£60,000 loss
d	£66,000	£4,000 gain

8.10 Machinery, acquired for £400,000, is reported on the Statement of financial position on 31 December 2011 at £218,500 and this includes one acquired for £60,000 on 1 April 2011. Another machine acquired for £90,000 on 1 January 2005 had been sold for £72,000 on 30 April 2011. Depreciation, calculated using the straight-line method and assuming ten years' useful life, is time apportioned. Identify the balances as at 1 January 2011 in the Machine account and Accumulated depreciation a/c.

	Machinery a/c	Accumulated depreciation a/c
a	£412,000	£197,000
b	£430,000	£197,000
c	£490,000	£188,000
d	£430,000	£184,500

8.11 Machinery, acquired at a cost of £660,000, is reported on the Statement of financial position on 30 June 2011 at a carrying value of £431,500. A machine had been acquired for £60,000 on 1 December 2010; while one acquired for £120,000 on 1 June 2005 was sold for £52,000 on 30 April 2011. Depreciation, calculated using the straight-line method and assuming ten years' useful life is time apportioned. Identify the balances as at 1 July 2010 in the Machinery account and Accumulated depreciation a/c.

	Machinery a/c	Accumulated depreciation a/c
a	£720,000	£214,000
b	£652,000	£226,000
c	£720,000	£226,000
d	£720,000	£236,000

8.12 The Trial Balance as at 31 December 2011 reports the Machinery account balance as £360,000 and the balance in Accumulated depreciation (up to 31 December 2010) as £184,200. The balance in the Machine account includes a machine acquired for £72,000 on 1 May 2011. A machine acquired for £60,000 on

1 April 2006 had been sold for £24,000 on 30 September 2011. None of the entries necessary to account for the machine disposal have been made other than crediting the Sales account with the amount received from disposal. Machinery is depreciated using the straight-line method and assuming a useful life of ten years. What is the carrying value (i.e. cost less accumulated depreciation to date) of machinery as at 1 January 2011 and as at 31 December 2011?

	As at 1.1.2011	As at 31.12.2011	
a	£103,800	£116,700	
b	£163,800	£110,700	
c	£103,800	£170,700	
d	£163,800	£115,200	

8.13 The Trial Balance as at 31 December 2011 reports the Machinery account balance as £340,000 and the balance in Accumulated depreciation (up to 31 December 2010) as £144,800. The balance in the Machine account includes a machine acquired for £96,000 on 1 April 2011. A machine acquired for £40,000 on 1 May 2004 had been sold for £18,000 on 30 October 2011. None of the entries necessary to account for the machine disposal have been made. Machinery is depreciated using the straight-line method and assuming a useful life of ten years and residual value estimated at 10% of cost. What is the carrying value of machinery as at 1 January 2011 and as at 31 December 2011?

	As at 1.1.2011	As at 31.12.2011	
a	£99,200	£163,720	
b	£99,200	£151,360	
c	£81,200	£151,400	
d	£81,200	£144,100	

8.14 The Trial Balance as at 31 March 2011 reports the Machinery account balance as £424,000 and the balance in Accumulated depreciation (up to 31 March 2010) as £214,800. The balance in the Machine account includes a machine acquired for £105,000 on 1 August 2010, £15,000 for installing the machine as well as £24,000 paid for a three-year guarantee. The machine is depreciated using the straight-line method and assuming a useful life of ten years. What is the carrying value (i.e. cost less accumulated depreciation to date) of machinery as at 1 April 2010 and as at 31 March 2011?

	As at 1.4.2010	As at 31.3.2011	
a	£89,200	£146,800	
b	£65,200	£173,200	
c	£65,200	£149,200	
d	£89,200	£149,200	

8.15 The Trial Balance as at 30 June 2011 reports the Machinery account balance as £340,000 and the balance in Accumulated depreciation (up to 30 June 2011) as £144,800. The balance in the Machinery account includes a machine acquired for £80,000 on 1 October 2010. A machine acquired for £60,000 on 1 July 2006 had been traded in for another with a list price of £90,000 on 1 March 2011, the difference being paid in cash. The trading-in of machinery has been accounted for correctly. Machinery is depreciated using the straight-line method and assuming a useful life of ten years. What is the carrying value of machinery as at 1 July 2010 and as at 30 June 2011?

	As at 1.7.2010	As at 30.6.2011	
a	£183,200	£177,720	
b	£93,200	£195,200	
c	£192,200	£195,200	
d	£123,200	£177,720	

8.16 A service station in Manchester, acquired for £420,000 and written down to £312,000, was traded in for another in Birmingham with the market value of £600,000. A cash payment of £150,000 was made as part of the trade-in. At what value should the Birmingham service station be reported in accounts?

a	£450,000	
b	£312,000	
c	£600,000	
d	£462,000	

8.17 Aslam Ismail, living in south London, exchanged his service station, acquired for £480,000 and written down to £284,000, for another (nearer his residence) with a market value of £275,000. At what value should Aslam report the service station nearer his residence?

a	£79,000	
b	£480,000	
c	£275,000	
d	£284,000	

Disposal of assets when the reducing balance method of depreciation is in use

8.18 A machine acquired for £400,000 on 1 July 2008 and depreciated at 25% p.a. using the reducing instalment method was sold for £112,000 on 30 April 2011. Depreciation is time apportioned. Expenses of disposal amounted to £1,500. What is the gain or loss on disposal of the machine to be reported in the Statement of income?

a	£67,625 loss	
b	£66,125 loss	
c	£56,750 gain	
d	£58,250 loss	

8.19 Machinery acquired for £800,000 was reported at £494,000 on the Statement of financial position as at 30 June 2010. A machine was acquired for £120,000 on 1 April 2011 and another, acquired for £40,000 on 1 July 2008, was sold for £22,000 on 31 March 2011. The depreciation is written off at 40% per annum using the reducing balance method with time apportionment. Calculate the depreciation written off in the year ended 30 June 2011 and the gain or loss on disposal of machinery.

	Depreciation	Gain/loss	
a	£197,920	£11,920 gain	
b	£213,920	£13,360 gain	
c	£208,160	£11,920 gain	
d	£212,160	£13,360 gain	

8.20 As at 31 December 2010 a manufacturer reported at £424,000 machinery which had originally cost £840,000. A machine was acquired for £80,000 on 1 April 2011 and on 1 July 2011 a machine acquired for £120,000 on 1 April 2008 was sold for £20,000. Machinery is depreciated at 40% per annum on the reducing balance method with time apportionment. What is the carrying value (cost less accumulated depreciation) as at 31 December 2011 and the gain or loss on the disposal of machinery?

	Carrying value	Gain/loss	
a	£286,208	£4,192 gain	
b	£287,936	£1,856 gain	
c	£334,208	£4,448 gain	
d	£292,256	£4,192 loss	

8.21 The Trial Balance as at 31 December 2011 reports the Machinery account balance as £360,000 and the balance in Accumulated depreciation (up to 31 December 2010) as £184,200. The balance in the Machine account includes a machine acquired for £72,000 on 1 May 2011. A machine acquired for £60,000 on 1 April 2008 had been sold for £24,000 on 30 September 2011. None of the entries necessary to account for the machine disposal have been made other than crediting the Sales account with the amount received from disposal. Machinery is depreciated at 40% per annum using the reducing balance method. What is the carrying value (i.e. cost less depreciation to date) of machinery as at 1 January 2011 and as at 31 December 2011?

	As at 1.1.2011	As at 31.12.2011	
a	£163,800	£108,168	
b	£103,800	£106,008	
c	£103,800	£108,168	
d	£163,800	£72,408	

8.22 The Trial Balance as at 31 December 2011 reports the Machinery account balance as £480,000 and the balance in Accumulated depreciation (up to 31 December 2010) as £144,800. The balance in the Machine account includes a machine acquired for £120,000 on 1 April 2011. A machine acquired for £84,000 on 1 May 2009 had been sold for £18,000 on 31 October 2011.
None of the entries necessary to account for the machine disposal have been made. Machinery is depreciated at 40% per annum, using the diminishing balance method. What is the carrying value of the machinery (i.e. cost less accumulated depreciation) as at 1 January 2011 and as at 31 December 2011? No depreciation required in year of disposal.

	As at 1.1.2011	As at 31.12.2011	
a	£197,200	£189,984	
b	£335,200	£278,640	
c	£197,200	£219,504	
d	£215,200	£190,944	

8.23 The Trial Balance as at 30 June 2011 reports the Machinery account balance as £540,000 and the balance in Accumulated depreciation (up to 30 June 2010) as £244,800. The balance in the Machinery account includes a machine acquired for £80,000 on 1 October 2010. A machine acquired for £120,000 on 1 July 2008 had been traded in for another with a list price of £90,000 on 1 March 2011. The trading-in of machinery has been accounted for correctly. Machinery is depreciated at 25% per annum using the reducing balance method. What is the carrying value of machinery (i.e. cost less depreciation) as at 1 July 2010 and as at 30 June 2011? No depreciation required in year of disposal.

	As at 1.7.2010	As at 30.6.2011	
a	£245,200	£303,275	
b	£125,200	£290,150	
c	£245,200	£280,775	
d	£335,200	£175,775	

Disposal of assets when the sum of the years' digits method of depreciation is in use

8.24 Jacobs Ltd paid £480,000 on 1 April 2008 to acquire a reputed brand name and decided to amortise the cost using the sum of the years' digits method estimating five years' useful life. How much would it write off as amortisation of brand name in the year ended 31 December 2011?

a	£128,000	
b	£120,000	
c	£72,000	
d	£64,000	

8.25 Patents reported at £144,000 on the Statement of financial position as at 31 December 2010 were sold for £98,000 on 30 June 2011. These patents were acquired on 1 January 2009 and were being amortised over five years' useful life using the the sum of the years' digits method. Calculate the gain or loss on disposal.

a	£10,000 loss	
b	£31,600 loss	
c	£10,000 gain	
d	£31,600 gain	

Revaluation of non-current assets

8.26 Which of the following is *not* a valid reason for reporting non-current assets at current value rather than cost?

(a) To prevent long-life assets from being reported at out-of-date historical costs

(b) To avoid having to pay higher taxes

(c) To report performance correctly by matching earnings with the proper costs of assets used

(d) To keep owners of the business better informed of their equity in the business

8.27 With regard to reporting property, plant and equipment at their current values, which of the following is *not* a requirement of IAS 16?

(a) If an asset is revalued all assets of the same class should also be revalued

(b) The current value should be found by reference to the value prevailing in the market

(c) It is not allowed to update value by using index numbers relating to that asset's prices

(d) The carrying value of a revalued asset should not materially differ from its current value

8.28 A footwear manufacturer acquired a machine on 1 July 2008 for £180,000 and depreciated it annually at 10% of cost. Being an item of a specialised nature the machine has no market. On 1 July 2011 it learns from the supplier of the machine that replacement of the same machine will cost £210,000. Is revaluation of the machine permitted in the absence of a market and, if so, what will be the gain on revaluation?

a	Cannot revalue	
b	£30,000	
c	£21,000	
d	£336,000	

8.29 A machine acquired for £480,000 on 1 May 2007 and depreciated at 10% per annum using the straight-line method has a market value of £600,000 on 1 May 2011. How much is the revaluation gain to be included in the Revaluation surplus account, if the machine is to be revalued on 1 May 2011?

a	£120,000	
b	£72,000	
c	£360,000	
d	£312,000	

8.30 A machine costing £480,000, depreciated at 10% per annum on cost, was revalued after four years of use at £600,000. How much of the revaluation gain recognised in the accounts may be regarded as realised and transferred to Retained earnings in the fifth year of the machine's use?

a	£52,000	
b	£312,000	
c	£120,000	
d	£72,000	

8.31 Property including buildings was acquired for £840,000. 75% of the cost was assumed to relate to the building which was depreciated using the straight-line method and assuming a useful life of 50 years. On 1 January 2011, on completion of 28 years of useful life, the property was revalued at £1,200,000. 25% of the value may be assumed to relate to land. How much of the revaluation gain is realised in 2011?

a	£622,800	
b	£32,400	
c	£16,364	
d	£28,309	

8.32 A machine costing £720,000 and written down to £432,000 by 1 July 2010 was revalued on that date at £900,000. Twelve years of the machine's useful life remain. What is the revaluation surplus and how much of it may be regarded as realised in the year ended 30 June 2011?

	Revaluation surplus	Realised	
a	£180,000	£180,000	
b	£468,000	£39,000	
c	£180,000	£39,000	
d	£468,000	£15,000	

Impairment of asset

8.33 Bell plc, manufacturers of laptop computers, acquired a machine for £360,000 on 1 January 2008 with an expectation that it could be used for ten years. Depreciation was on the straight-line method. The model for the production of which this machine is used is not Skype capable. In the circumstances, as at 1 January 2011 the sales in 2011 are expected to be £120,000 and in 2012 and 2013 £80,000 and £40,000 respectively. Sale of the model thereafter and the proceeds from disposal of the machine are not expected to be significant. Cost of capital for Bell plc is 8% per annum. What is the impairment loss as at 1 January 2011 and the depreciation written off in the year ended 31 December 2011?

	Impairment loss	Depreciation	
a	£131,632	£76,123	
b	£131,632	£43,877	
c	£23,632	£76,123	
d	£23,632	£114,184	

8.34 A machine acquired for £480,000 on 1 January 2005 and depreciated using the straight-line method assuming 20 years useful life and 10% scrap value was damaged in an accident on 1 January 2011. Although it has been restored to working condition at a cost of £20,000, it is expected to be in operational use for only four more years and the present value as at 1 January 2011 of the cash flow it is expected to generate is £84,000. The machine is expected to have a scrap value of £10,000. What is the impairment loss to be written off on 1 January 2011 and depreciation in the year 2011?

	Impairment loss	Depreciation	
a	£266,400	£21,000	
b	£256,499	£23,500	
c	£286,400	£21,000	
d	£266,400	£23,500	

Answers to multiple choice questions

8.1: d 8.2: b 8.3: b 8.4: a 8.5: b 8.6: a 8.7: a 8.8: b 8.9: d 8.10: b 8.11: c 8.12: a 8.13: b 8.14: c 8.15: b 8.16: d 8.17: c 8.18: a 8.19: c 8.20: d 8.21: b 8.22: d 8.23: c 8.24: c 8.25: a 8.26: b 8.27: c 8.28: c 8.29: d 8.30: a 8.31: d 8.32: b 8.33: c 8.34: a

Progressive questions

PQ 8.1 A basic question involving disposal of a non-current asset

A warehouse was acquired for £180,000 on 1 April 2004. A third of the price was for land which is not depreciated. £30,000 was spent immediately after acquisition to make some structural changes to render the building suitable for the intended use. The cost of the building was depreciated using the straight-line method and assuming a useful life of 50 years. On 30 September 2011 the warehouse was sold for £240,000.

Required: Calculate the gain on disposal of the warehouse.

PQ 8.2 Depreciation using the straight-line method and accounting for disposal

Raymond Industries reported machinery, as at 1 April 2010, at cost at £1,320,000. Particulars of machinery are stated on the right. On 1 July 2010 it sold machine AC504 for £180,000 and replaced it on 1 October 2010 with another PT702 costing £600,000. The policy of the business is to depreciate each machine at 20% per annum using the straight-line method and time apportioning the depreciation expense for the nearest number of months each machine was used in each accounting period.

Acquired on	Machine number	Cost
1.1.2007	AC504	£320,000
1.1.2009	DL201	£480,000
1.10.2009	FN378	£520,000

Required:

(a) Identify the accumulated depreciation relating to each machine as at 1 April 2010.

(b) Show how the transactions stated above would be reported in the Statement of income of the business for the year ended 31 March 2011 and the Statement of financial position as at that date.

PQ 8.3 Depreciation on the reducing balance method and accounting for disposal

Marina operates in the transport industry and owns several vehicles, acquired for a total cost of £540,000 and reported at £296,400 in her Statement of financial position on 31 December 2010.

On 30 June 2011 she sold for £26,200 a vehicle acquired for £60,000 on 1 July 2009.

On 1 September 2011 she acquired another vehicle for £90,000.

On 1 October 2011 she scrapped a vehicle acquired for £40,000 on 1 January 2008.

She depreciates her vehicles at 40% per annum using the reducing balance method.

How will these transactions be reported in her financial statements for the year ended 31 December 2011?

PQ 8.4 How depreciation features on financial statements

The year-end Trial Balance extracted from the books of a business owned by Guy Morris included the ledger balances listed on the right. A third of the property cost relates to land which is not depreciated. A machine was acquired for £400,000 on 1 July 2011; while a vehicle that cost £128,000 on 1 April 2010 was sold on 30 September for £40,000 and the amount credited to the Motor vehicles account. Guy depreciates his assets at the rates shown below:

Class of asset	Method	Annual rate
Building	Straight-line	2%
Machinery	Straight-line	5%
Motor vehicle	Reducing balance	25%

Trial Balance as at 30 September 2011		
	£'000	£'000
Land and building at cost	2,400	–
Machinery	1,600	–
Motor vehicles at cost	720	–
Accumulated depreciation to 30 September 2010:		
Building	–	448
Machinery	–	600
Motor vehicles	–	240

Required:

(a) Show how the information in respect of the three classes of assets will be reported in the Statement of movement of assets of the year ended 30 September 2011 and

(b) identify the gain or loss on disposal of the vehicle in the year.

PQ 8.5 How depreciation, disposal and revaluation feature on financial statements

The year-end Trial Balance of a business owned by Stella Hanson included the ledger balances listed on the right. Stella wishes to report the land and buildings at their current market value on 30 June 2011 and has identified the market value on that date as £4.5 million. A third of the cost/value relates to land, which is not depreciated. Furniture acquired at a cost of £800,000 on 1 January 2008 was sold on 31 March 2011 for £240,000, but other than posting the proceeds to the Disposal account, the sale of furniture is not accounted for. Buildings and furniture are both depreciated, on the straight-line method, at 2% and 10% per annum respectively. Brand name, acquired on 1 July 2010, is to be depreciated on the sum of the years' digits method over an expected economic life of five years.

Trial Balance as at 30 June 2011		
	£'000	£'000
Land and buildings at cost	3,600	–
Furniture at cost	1,600	–
Brand names at cost	720	–
Accumulated depreciation to 30 June 2010:		
Building	–	672
Furniture	–	600
Disposal of furniture	–	240

Required:

(a) Show how these transactions will feature in the Statement of income for the year ended 30 June 2011 and in the Statement of financial position as at that date.

(b) Identify the gain on revaluation of land and buildings.

Test questions

Test 8.1 Preparation of a Statement of movement of non-current assets

Non-current assets were reported on the Statement of financial position as at 31 March 2010 as shown on the right. You are informed as follows:

Statement of financial position as at 31 March 2010			
Non-current assets:	Cost	Accumulated depreciation	£
Land and building	720,000	(96,000)	624,000
Machinery	480,000	(198,000)	282,000
Motor vehicle	330,000	(180,000)	150,000
Brand names	180,000	(108,000)	72,000

(a) As at 1 April 2010 land was valued at £400,000 and buildings at £800,000. Land and buildings are to be reported in accounts at current values. Buildings have been depreciated at 2% per annum assuming that one-third of the cost was for land which is not depreciated.

(b) Machinery has been depreciated at 10% per annum using the straight-line method. Due to changes in consumer preference, the machinery is expected to become obsolete by 31 March 2013. Sale of products from the machinery in the year to 31 March 2011 was £128,000 and the present value as at 1 April 2010 of sales expected in years ending 31 March 2012 and 2013, until obsolescence, is determined as £112,000.

(c) Motor vehicles are depreciated at 25% per annum on the reducing balance method. A vehicle, acquired for £160,000 on 1 April 2008, was sold for £58,000 on 30 November 2010 and replaced next day with another at a cost of £240,000.

(d) Brand names, acquired on 1 April 2008, are being depreciated on the sum of the years' digits method assuming a useful life of five years.

Required: Prepare a statement of movement of non-current assets for the year ended 31 March 2011.

Test 8.2 Basic question with disposal of asset not accounted for at all

A business owned by Philip Saunders sold some of its furniture for £18,000 on 31 December 2010, but had not accounted for the disposal when the year-end Trial Balance was extracted as shown on the right.

You are informed as follows:

(a) Cost of inventory at year-end was £498,000.

(b) Furniture sold on the last day of the period had been acquired for £60,000 on 1 January 2008.

(c) Inventory costing £4,000 removed by Philip for personal use has not been accounted for.

(d) One-fourth of the cost is attributed to land which is not depreciated. Buildings and furniture are depreciated, using the straight-line method, at 2% and 10% per annum respectively.

(e) Interest, at 5% per annum, should be paid on the loan from Mrs Saunders obtained in 2008.

Required: The Statement of income for the year ended 31 December 2010 and the Statement of financial position as at that date.

Trial Balance as at 31 December 2010		
	£'000	£'000
Trade receivables/payables	412	498
Inventory as at 31.12.2009	574	–
Staff salary	295	–
Advertising	172	–
Sales	–	4,942
Purchases	3,358	–
Cash and bank balance	122	–
Capital account	–	1,000
Loan from Mrs Saunders	–	300
Other expenses	214	
Drawings by Mr Saunders	57	
Land and buildings at cost	1,600	–
Furniture at cost	300	–
Accumulated depreciation to 31 December 2009:		–
Building	–	240
Furniture	–	124
	7,104	7,104

Test 8.3 A difficult question involving asset disposal not fully accounted for

The only accounting entries made in respect of £73,000 received on 1 January 2011 as proceeds on disposal of boardroom furniture were posting of that amount to the Disposal account. The furniture disposed of had been acquired for £160,000 on 1 July 2008. The year-end Trial Balance of the business has been extracted from the books as shown below.

Trial Balance as at 31 March 2011		
	£'000	£'000
Land at cost	500	–
Buildings at cost	1,200	–
Furniture at cost	480	–
Motor vehicles at cost	400	–
Brand names at wdv	120	
Accumulated depreciation up to 31.3.2010		
Buildings		168
Furniture	–	106
Motor vehicles	–	180
Vehicle running expenses	27	–
Inventory as at 31.3.2011	544	–
Cash in hand	19	–
Cost of goods sold	4,888	–
Business rates	92	–
Sales	–	6,545
Administrative expenses	528	–
Receivable and payable	372	676
Allowance for doubtful debt	–	16
Bank overdraft	–	54
Advertising expenses	148	–
Capital account	–	1,500
Disposal of furniture	–	73
	9,318	9,318

You are informed as follows:

(a) Goods invoiced to customers for £64,000 have been wrongly accounted for as sale though the customers retain the option to return these goods until a week after the year-end. These goods have been invoiced at cost plus a third.

(b) Brand names acquired on 1 April 2008 are being amortised on the sum of the years' digits method, assuming a useful life of five years.

(c) A new vehicle was acquired for £60,000 on 1 December 2010; while furniture acquired for £40,000 when the business commenced on 1 April 2000 continues to remain in use.

(d) Buildings and furniture are both depreciated on the straight-line method at 2% and 10% per annum respectively; while vehicles are depreciated at 25% per annum on the reducing balance method.

(e) Advertising expenses include £38,000 paid to an advertising agency for a campaign which would commence only from 1 April 2011, while administrative expenses amounting to £42,000 remain unpaid at the year-end.

Required: Prepare the financial statements of this business for the year ended 31 March 2011.

Test 8.4 A more difficult question with asset disposal and revaluation

Jessica Parker is a graduate in management and finance, and is reporting in a current account maintained in the ledger the amounts she may feel free to withdraw at any time from the business. She has extracted the year-end Trial Balance from the books of her business as shown on the right and informs you as follows:

(a) Jessica has been depreciating the buildings on the straight-line method, assuming that a third of the cost relates to land which is not depreciated and assuming the useful life of the buildings to be 50 years. Professional valuers have valued the land and the buildings as at 1 October 2010 as £1 million and £1.6 million respectively. Jessica wishes to incorporate these values into her books but wishes that only amounts legally distributable should be included in her current account.

(b) The only movements in non-current assets were:

  (i) A new vehicle was acquired for £80,000 on 1 January 2011; and

  (ii) a machine acquired for £120,000 on 1 June 2009 was sold on 31 May 2011 for £85,000. The only accounting entries made for recording the disposal were posting the amount received to the Sales account.

Trial Balance as at 30 September 2011		
	£'000	£'000
Land and buildings	2,100	–
Machinery at cost	800	–
Vehicles at cost	600	–
Accumulated depreciation up to 30.9.2010		–
Buildings	–	280
Machinery	–	300
Vehicles	–	240
Inventory as at 30.9.2010	642	–
Cash in hand and at bank	76	–
Purchases	7,584	–
Carriage inwards	158	–
Sales	–	9,333
Return inwards	49	–
Machine maintenance	164	–
Machine selling expenses	2	–
Vehicle running expenses	58	–
Telephone and postage	17	–
Salaries to staff	394	–
Rent	150	–
Receivables and payables	486	693
Allowance for doubtful debts	–	26
Drawings	72	–
Advertising expenses	148	–
Capital account – Jessica	–	2,000
Current account – Jessica	–	628
	13,500	13,500

(c) Rent for several shop premises in main city centres has been agreed at £10,000 per month.

(d) Following expenses remain unpaid at year-end:

Staff salaries £38,000
Advertising £12,000

(e) Machinery is depreciated at 5% per annum using the straight-line method; while vehicles are depreciated at 40% per annum on the reducing balance method.

(f) 60% of owned land and building are used for production activity.

(g) The cost of goods remaining unsold on 30 September 2011 has been identified as £578,000. However, this includes at £42,000 certain goods which, being shop-soiled because they were used for display, may be sold for only £25,000, provided an additional cost of £2,000 is incurred on restoring them to saleable condition. Jessica regards the loss as part of her sales promotion expenses.

(h) £6,000 of trade receivables should be written off and the allowance for doubtful debts adjusted to cover 5% of remaining receivables.

Required: Prepare the Statement of income for the year ended 30 September 2011 and the Statement of financial position as at that date. You must identify carefully any amount Jessica may feel free to withdraw from the business.

PART B

FINANCIAL STATEMENTS OF LIMITED COMPANIES, SOLE TRADERS, GROUPS AND PARTNERSHIPS

Chapter 9

Accounting for limited companies

By the end of this chapter

You should learn:	You should be able to:
■ About the merits and demerits of company formation ■ About shares and debentures ■ About financial statements of companies	■ Account for a share issue, bonus issue and rights issue ■ Account for tax, deferred tax and dividends ■ Prepare financial statements of companies both for internal use and for publication ■ Prepare the Statement of changes in equity (both short form and extended version) ■ Prepare the Statement of comprehensive income

9.1 What is a limited company?

We have, until now, considered the accounting function in a sole trader's business. Let us next focus on a limited liability company – which is the most common type of business entity in the UK, for any business of reasonable size. A business entity acquires limited liability by registering with the Registrar of Companies, a process known as *incorporation*. We begin by setting out the features peculiar to limited companies as follows.

9.1.1 How a company obtains and records its capital

We have seen that in a sole trader's business the capital is provided by the sole trader who, therefore, both owns and manages the business. It is very different for a company in that it may be owned by a minimum of two up to an unlimited maximum number – all identified as *shareholders*. This is possible because the capital of a company is divided into shares issued to shareholders in proportion to the funds they invest and each shareholder is issued with a share certificate as evidence of their legal title to the shares.

Instead of writing up a separate Capital account for each of its numerous shareholders, a company records the total of the capital received in a single *Share capital account.* Particulars of the names of shareholders, their addresses and how many shares each shareholder owns are recorded outside the books of account, in a *Share register* – this information being needed to send out notice of meetings and to pay dividends.

9.1.2 How a company is managed

The management of the company is delegated to a group of specialists, known as directors, who are elected by the shareholders at annual general meetings (AGM). The directors are responsible for managing the company, keeping proper books of accounts and providing shareholders with financial statements so that they can see how the company is performing and what its financial position is at the end of each accounting period. In the UK the financial statements are also filed with the Registrar of Companies and are available for any member of the public to see.

9.1.3 What happens to the profits of a company

In a limited company the profits (or losses) identified in each accounting period are either distributed to shareholders (as dividends) or retained within the company.

- ***Profits distribution to shareholders:*** some (or all) of the company's profit may be distributed to shareholders in the form of *dividends* which are usually expressed as so many pence/cents per share. The directors have the authority to declare and pay one or more *interim dividends* during the accounting period and to recommend a *final dividend,* calculated on the basis of information in the period-end financial statements. The recommended final dividend cannot be declared or paid until approved by the shareholders at the AGM.
- ***Profits retained within the business:*** profits retained by a company for its own use are known as *reserves.* Because these reserves are of the type that may be distributed to shareholders as dividend they are referred to as *revenue reserves.* If any reserve is not permitted to be distributed they are referred to as *capital reserves.*

9.2 How is a limited company formed?

A limited company is formed by registering with the Registrar of Companies – a process known as *incorporation.* As part of this process every company is required to file the following with the Registrar[1]:

An application for registration, which should state:

- the company's proposed name;
- whether the registered office is to be in England and Wales, Scotland or Northern Ireland;
- details of the secretary and director(s);
- details of the share capital;
- whether the liability of each member is to be limited;
- whether the company is to be a private company or a public company.

The application should be accompanied by the following:

1. *A Memorandum of Association* – which is simply a statement by the subscribers (this name refers to those who wish to form a company) that they wish to form a company and that they have each agreed to take at least one share.
2. *Articles of Association* – which contain internal rules setting out the relationship between the company and its members as well as granting certain powers to its directors. If a company does not register its own set of Articles, then there are statutory model articles available.
3. *A statement of capital* which must state:
   - the total number of shares the company intends to issue;
   - the aggregate nominal value of shares (see paragraph 9.7 below);
   - particulars of rights attaching to each class of shares (see paragraph 9.6.3 below);
   - amount paid up on each share and any amount remaining unpaid (see paragraph 9.7 below).

In the UK limited companies are governed by the Companies Act 2006. There are similar requirements in other countries.

There are many advantages and disadvantages to operating as a limited company rather than carrying on business as a sole trader or in partnership.

9.3 Advantages of limited companies

The advantages of operating a business as a limited liability company include the following:

1. **Substantial amounts of capital** can be raised because:
   - there is no limit on the number of persons who may become *shareholders*;
   - the limitation of liability may prompt more people to contribute capital to even a risky venture;
   - individuals may be willing to contribute capital encouraged by the knowledge that they would not be burdened with the management function, which is delegated to a few chosen directors.
2. **Delegation of management:** management may be delegated to those with appropriate skills and expertise, who are known as *directors*.
3. **Limited liability:** each shareholder's liability (obligation to pay for claims against the company) is limited to the amount the shareholder agreed to pay the company for the shares. This is seen by governments as essential for companies wishing to raise capital as potential shareholders are aware of the full extent of their liability if the company should fail. In other forms of business organisation such as sole traders and partnerships, if the business fails the owner's personal assets could be at risk if the business assets are insufficient to meet the business liabilities. However, while protecting the interest of the shareholders by granting them limited liability, company law does place at risk the interests of those (like banks and trade payables) who have a claim on the company because they do not have any recourse to the personal resources of the shareholders or the directors.
4. **Legal entity:** what this means is that, upon incorporation, a company is recognised in law as a person, separate and distinct from the shareholders. Though not endowed with a physical life, in the eyes of the law a company is a separate legal person (referred to as

body corporate) capable of owning property, entering into contracts, suing and being sued in a court of law and undertaking any legal activity (though having to act of course through human agents).

5. **Perpetual succession:** a limited company comes into existence by the legal process of *incorporation*. It will continue to exist until its existence is terminated by another legal process known as *liquidation*. While individual shareholders may change, the company continues to exist. In a partnership, on the other hand, the partnership ceases to exist when one of the partners leaves the partnership.
6. **Transferability of shares:** if a shareholder wishes to transfer a number of shares to another a share transfer form is completed and forwarded to the company secretary who makes the appropriate changes in the share register.

9.4 Disadvantages of limited companies

The disadvantages of operating as a limited company include the following:

1. **Companies are subject to strict legal control**, mainly because of the need to protect (i) the interest of its creditors who are denied recourse to the personal resources of the shareholders and (ii) the interest of the shareholders who have delegated the management to a few. The legal control includes requirements to:
   - maintain proper accounting records and (subject to exemption of small companies) have the financial statements audited;
   - make regular returns (such as the annual return) and file financial statements and a directors' report with the Registrar of Companies, within prescribed time limits;
   - maintain statutory registers such as a Register of Members, Register of Directors and Secretaries and Register of Charges and hold them for public inspection;
   - protect the capital base of the company by, for example, insisting that any distribution to shareholders should only be out of profits determined in accordance with rules prescribed for the purpose.
2. **Publicity**. A significant price a company pays for the many advantages bestowed on it is its inability to protect the confidentiality of information on its performance and position. First, there is the legal requirement that anyone shall be permitted access to the company's statutory registers. Secondly, all information filed with the Registrar of Companies, including the annual financial statements and reports, are available for anyone's inspection.
3. **Delegation of management to a few has its downside**. Despite the efforts by successive company legislation to safeguard the ownership rights of the shareholders and to compel the directors to discharge adequately their stewardship responsibilities, the powers of the directors are substantial and real. For example, they are usually in control of their own levels of remuneration. The government is not inclined to provide statutory control over directors' remuneration and has favoured voluntary regulation.

For example, companies are encouraged to comply with the Combined Code on Corporate Governance[2] which recommends that companies should have non-executive directors (i.e. directors who are not full-time employees of the company) and that the non-executive directors should determine the remuneration of the executive directors. The directors are also in control of the rewards paid as *dividends* to shareholders. The shareholders cannot approve dividends at a level higher than that recommended by the directors. No court of law will compel a company to pay a dividend larger than that proposed by directors. This is because there is an assumption that the directors' proposal has taken into account broader strategy issues such as a potential increase in competition or a planned increase in capital expenditure.

9.5 Types of limited companies

Limited companies are of two types:

- *public companies* which identify themselves using the letters plc at the end of their names;
- *private companies* which use the word Ltd (or Limited) as the last part of their name.

A public limited company (plc) can only start trading if it has a minimum share capital (in the UK[3] this is £50,000 or the euro equivalent) and only public companies may issue securities (shares, debentures) to the public. There is no requirement for a public company to have its securities listed on a recognised stock exchange. If it wishes to have its shares listed and be able to offer shares to the public it has to undergo a prolonged in-depth investigation calculated to protect the reputation of the Stock Exchange and the interests of those who buy and sell in it. Public companies listed on a stock exchange are known as *listed companies*. Listed companies are obliged to comply with certain rules, which are known as *continuing obligations* and which are intended to so regulate the volume and timing of price-sensitive information made available on the company that no-one is given an advantage. Besides, company law makes special requirements from listed companies including the following:

- Publish, along with the annual reports and accounts, a *business review* stating:
  - the main trends and factors likely to affect future developments, performance and position;
  - information on environmental matters, employees and social matters.
- Publish their annual reports and accounts on their website.

Private companies are not allowed to do some things that public companies can, for example:

1. They are prohibited from inviting members of the public to subscribe for their shares.
2. The transfer of shares from one shareholder to another may be restricted. For example, the Articles of Association may require shareholders to offer their shares first to the directors of the company if they wish to sell them. This is known as the right of pre-emption.

On the other hand private companies have some concessions that are not available to public companies, as shown below.

Some concessions given to private companies[4]		Public company
Directors	Can have one director	At least two
Appointment of a company secretary	Optional	Compulsory
Holding of an annual general meeting	Optional	Compulsory
Delivering accounts to Registrar	Within nine months of year-end	Within seven years
Retention of accounting records	For at least three years	For six years

9.6 Shares and loan notes (debentures)

A limited company raises long-term finance by issuing *shares* or *debentures*. All companies issue shares known as Ordinary shares. Other varieties of shares may also be issued, one of which is known as Preference shares.

9.6.1 Ordinary shares

An ordinary share is a portion of a company's capital which entitles the owner to certain rights (such as the rights to attend shareholders' meetings, to elect directors and auditors, to approve financial statements and to declare final dividends) and to share in the profits of the company to the extent approved by the directors.

9.6.2 Preference shares

Preference shares are so called because these shares are given the right to a dividend before a dividend is paid to the ordinary shareholders. Their dividend, unlike that of the ordinary shareholders, is usually at a fixed percentage of the nominal value of their share, e.g. 8% preference shares of £1 each. Preference shares are assumed to be cumulative, irrespective of whether the name expressly confirms this position.[5] This means that the ordinary shareholders cannot be paid a dividend until all arrears (up to and including the current year's preference dividend) are fully discharged. These shares do not usually have a right to vote at meetings, though exceptionally they might have the right if their dividends are in arrears or there is a possibility that the company will cease trading. If it should cease trading, preference shareholders do not automatically have a prior right to the return of their capital unless this was one of the terms of issue.

9.6.3 Rights attaching to shares

Depending on the terms of issue a class of share may have the following rights:

- Right to receive notice of, to attend and to vote at shareholders' meetings.
- Right to receive dividends, but only at amounts recommended by the directors.
- In the event the company is liquidated, the right to participate in any capital distribution.
- If so agreed upon, the right to be redeemed (i.e. the company takes back the share, repays the capital and perhaps an additional compensation which is referred to as 'premium on redemption').

9.6.4 Loan notes or debentures

Loan notes (commonly referred to in the UK as *debentures*) are a written acknowledgement of debt by a company. The acknowledgement is usually made in a document that bears the company's seal and states the rate of interest, the nature and type of any security provided and the terms of repayment. Loan note holders, like shareholders, have the right to receive financial statements and, unlike shareholders, have the right to receive interest on their loan whether the company makes a profit or a loss. Like the preference shareholders, they usually have no voting rights unless their interest is not paid or their capital has not been repaid by the agreed date.

Activity 9.1 Difference between shares and debentures

Rose Petal has identified a company to invest in and seeks your advice on whether she should invest in that company's shares or debentures. How would you advise her?

9.7 Accounting for a share issue

Company law in the UK requires that every share should have a *par value*[6] (also known as nominal value or face value) assigned to the share, for example, shares of 50p or £1 each. In the USA and other countries, shares of no par value are common. Although a committee appointed by the Board of Trade advocated the issue of shares of no par value in the UK,[7] to date no action has been taken to allow this.

9.7.1 Issue of shares at par or at a premium

A company may issue its shares at a price that should be equal to or more than the par value. It cannot issue the share at a price below the par value because company law prohibits issue of shares at a discount. When issuing its shares, a successful company may fix a price that is higher than the share's par value. The extra amount received is known as *share premium*.

For example, if a company issues an ordinary share with a par value of £10 for £12, company law in the UK requires that the par value should be credited to the Share capital account while the excess is credited to a Share premium account (see box on right).

Dr Cash Book	£12	–
Cr Ordinary share capital a/c	–	£10
Cr Share premium a/c	–	£2

How a share premium account may be used

The whole amount received (£12), including the amount recorded in the Share premium account, is part of the capital contributed by the shareholders and is not available for distribution as dividend. However, it is permitted[8] to use the share premium:

1. to pay up new shares for allocation to the shareholders as *bonus shares*; or
2. to write off the expenses of the issue and any commission paid on the issue of the shares in respect of which the premium was received.

Activity 9.2 Accounting for share issue

Orange plc issued 100,000 ordinary shares of 50p each, at 60p each, fully called up and paid up. £3,000 was incurred as expense on the issue.

Required:

(a) Explain how the transactions stated above should be accounted for.

(b) Show how they will be reported on the Statement of financial position at the year-end.

9.7.2 Accounting for issue of shares when shareholders pay in instalments

A company may not always need immediately the full amount of the price at which it issues its shares. For example, a company may issue 10,000 ordinary shares of £1 each at 110p each, but may call for only 80p per share to be paid and the remainder when it is called for. In this situation, at the point of allotting (i.e. issuing) the shares, only the *so far called-up value* of the shares allotted (i.e. 80p less 10p premium on each share) is credited to the Share capital account (see entries on the right).

Dr Called-up capital a/c	£8,000	–
Cr Ordinary share capital a/c	–	£7,000
Cr Share premium a/c	–	£1,000

If we assume that £7,800 is received by the period-end, the amount received is posted from the Cash Book to the credit of the Called-up capital account, which would then report £200 as yet to be received. This amount is shown on the Statement of financial position as an asset – whether current or non-current depending on when that amount is expected to be received.

Activity 9.3 Accounting for issue of shares partly called up

Pink plc issued 100,000 ordinary shares of 50p each, at 60p each, 40p called. By the year-end it had received £32,000 from the issue and had incurred £2,000 as expense on issue.

Required: Set out the ledger accounts recording the share issue and show how their balances will be reported on the Statement of financial position at the year-end.

Clue: The amount called up (40p) on each share includes the premium (10p). Hence, the called-up value of each share at the point of allotment is only 30p.

At any point in time only *the called-up value of the number of shares in issue* as at that point is reported in the Share capital account. Assuming that a company which has issued 10,000 shares of £1 each, 70p called up at the time of issue, makes the remaining call of 30p per share, the call when made is accounted for as shown below. The Share capital account would by then record the fully called up value of £10,000 (i.e. £1 each on 10,000 ordinary shares in issue).

Dr Final call account	£3,000	–
Cr Ordinary share capital a/c	–	£3,000

9.7.3 How is a company affected when shareholders sell their shares?

Once shares have been issued and paid for in full, there is no further entry in the company's financial records if shareholders sell their shares. If a shareholder sells some of his shares, the company has no financial interest in the sale and only needs to have the particulars of the new shareholder to enter in the share register. For example, let us assume that Jane, who was allotted 300 shares, sells them to Jackie at a price far in excess of the issue price. The company will not receive any money on this sale nor will any accounting entry be made in the company's books of account relating to this transfer. The particulars of the number of shares transferred from Jane to Jackie are recorded in the share register (which is not a book of account).

Activity 9.4 Accounting for share transfers between shareholders

Beige plc has in issue 100 million shares of £1 each, 70p called up, and issued at 10p premium. Miriam, who has received an allotment of 5,000 shares from Beige plc, sold her entire holding to Michael at 220p per share.

Required:

(a) Show how the shares in issue will be reported on the Statement of financial position.
(b) Explain how the shares sold by Miriam will be accounted for in the books of Beige plc.
(c) If Beige plc goes into liquidation and its resources prove inadequate to meet its liabilities, how much more will Michael be obliged to pay in respect of the shares he bought from Miriam? Assume that all amounts called had been paid in full by Miriam.

9.8 All-inclusive concept of reporting earnings in each accounting period

There are two schools of thought on which earnings should be recognised (i.e. included) in the Statement of income of the current period. These are as follows:

1. **Current operating profit school**: this advocates that only operating profit, earned in the current year, should be included in the Statement of income.
2. **All-inclusive school:** this is the one adopted by IAS 1. What this means is that all profits/losses recognised in an accounting period should be included within the Statement of income of that period irrespective of whether it is:
   (a) realised;
   (b) arises from operating activities;
   (c) is unusual or normal (in nature or size of its amount);
   (d) expected to recur or not; and
   (e) arises from correction of an estimate made in a prior period.

Accordingly, IAS 1 requires that all items of income or expenses recognised in a period should be included in the Statement of income unless company law or an accounting standard requires otherwise. For example, the profit made on issuing its own shares is credited to a Share premium account and not to the Statement of income and certain items are reported in the Statement of changes in equity which we discuss further in paragraph 9.11 of this chapter.

9.9 Accounting for current tax

Companies are required to pay tax (known as *corporation tax* in the UK) on the profit made in each accounting period. The amount has to be estimated by the company at the date the Statement of financial position is prepared and subsequently agreed with the tax authorities – the final amount is often different from the original estimate.

9.9.1 Accounting for current year's tax

The estimated tax on the year's profit (assumed as £24 for illustration) is accounted for by debiting a Tax (expense) account and crediting a Tax (liability) account.

Taxation (expense) account

	£		
Taxation a/c	24		

Taxation (liability) account

			£
		Taxation a/c	24

When financial statements are prepared at the period-end, the tax expense is included in the Statement of income and the liability is reported in the Statement of financial position as a current liability.

9.9.2 What if the estimated tax liability differs from what tax authorities assess?

At the time of preparing financial statements the tax liability is estimated and the estimate cannot always exactly match the amount the company will be called upon to pay when tax is assessed by tax authorities. If the estimate happens to be lower than the amount assessed, we say that there has been an under-provision. Assuming that the amount set aside last year for tax liability was £120,000 and the amount paid this year to settle the liability is £124,000, the amount of the under-provision will appear, this year, as a debit balance in the Taxation (liability) account (see account on the left). This is transferred by a pair of entries (see on the right) to this year's Taxation (expense) account.

Taxation (liability) account

Bank a/c	£124	Balance b/f	£120
		Balance c/d	£4
	124		124
Balance b/d	4		

Dr Tax (expense) a/c	£4
Cr Tax (liability) a/c	£4

The Statement of income of this year will report as tax expense not only the tax estimated on the current year's profit but also any tax under-provided for the previous year. In the event tax relating to the previous year had been over-provided, a seldom occurrence, there would be a credit balance in the Taxation (liability) which, when transferred to this year's Taxation (expense) account, will reduce this year's tax expense.

9.10 Accounting for deferred tax

Besides current year's tax and under-provision for tax relating to a previous year, the tax expense in an accounting period could include also *deferred tax*, i.e. tax the payment of which is delayed until a future accounting period. We will explain two of the common situations in which the tax relating to income recognised in the current period is accounted for as an expense in that period, but its payment is deferred until a future period.

9.10.1 Income recognised for accounting purposes but not recognised for tax purposes

An example of this is interest income. For accounting, interest is recognised, on the accruals concept, in the period in which it is earned, even if it is not received until the next period. Tax regulations, on the other hand, recognise interest income only when received. For illustration, let us assume that a company reports in its Statement of income for the current period (2010) an operating profit of £400,000 and an interest income of £100,000 although the interest income is not received until the next accounting period. The total income reported by the company would be £500,000. The tax relating to the interest income of £100,000 is delayed, though temporarily, until it is received in 2011. Therefore, interest income is referred to as *taxable temporary difference* and it is a requirement of the Accounting Standard[9] that the tax relating to taxable temporary differences should be accounted for as part of the tax expense in the Statement of income and reported in the Statement of financial position as *Deferred tax*.

Dr Tax (expense) a/c	£20,000
Cr Deferred tax (liability) a/c	£20,000

Let us consider why tax deferred by taxable temporary difference needs to be accounted for. In our illustration, although the profit accounted for in 2010 is £500,000, the taxable profit (i.e. excluding the interest yet to be received) is only £400,000. Assuming that the tax rate for this company is 20%, the current year's tax (in the UK this is payable nine months after the year-end) will be £80,000 (20% of £400,000). The tax relating to the interest income at £20,000 (i.e. 20% of £100,000) would become payable along with tax for 2011 and needs to be accounted for as shown by the accounting entries above. When that is done the total tax expense reported in 2010 (see the Statement of income on the left) would be £100,000 and that matches the amount of income reported for the year at £500,000. The rate of tax for the company (20%) explains the relationship between the tax expense and the profit accounted for in 2010. The deferred tax, not payable until 2012, will be reported as a non-current liability in the Statement of financial position as at 31 December 2010.

Statement of income year ended 31.12.2010		
		£'000
Operating profit		400
Interest income		100
Profit before tax		500
Current tax	80	
Deferred tax	20	(100)
Profit after taxation		400

9.10.2 Tax deferred by capital allowance

As we have learnt already, companies can choose one of several methods for depreciating non-current assets and, depending on the method chosen, their reported profit will differ. To overcome this problem the Tax Department disallows the depreciation expense written off in the Statement of income and replaces it with what they refer to as *Tax capital allowance*. In the UK, on industrial machinery the Tax Department calculates a Tax capital allowance at 25% on the reducing balance method, without taking into account whether the asset was used for the whole or part of an accounting period.

To illustrate let us assume that a company acquires a machine for £600,000 on 1 October 2010 (just three months prior to the period-end) and after depreciating the machine by £15,000 (i.e at 10% per annum on cost, for three months of use) reports an operating profit of £800,000. HMRC disallows the depreciation and replaces it with a tax capital allowance of £150,000 (calculated at 25% of £600,000, ignoring the fact that the machine has been in use for only three months). As a result the taxable profit (see box on the left) is £135,000 less than the accounting profit. However, the tax benefit for the company is temporary because, over the economic life of the asset, the total depreciation as well as the tax capital allowance will be the same amount of £600,000. But in the year 2010 the current tax (assuming a tax rate of 20%) would be £133,000 (20% of the taxable profit of £665,000). If we account for the tax relating to the taxable temporary difference of £27,000 (i.e. 20% of £135,000), the total tax expense included in the Statement of income for 2010 at £160,000 (see working on the left) will be 20% of the profit accounted for in that year (£800,000).

Accounting profit		£800,000
Depreciation disallowed	£15,000	
Tax capital allowance	(£150,000)	
Taxable temporary difference		(£135,000)
Taxable profit		£665,000

Current tax	£133,000
Deferred tax	£27,000
Total tax expense	£160,000

We identified the taxable temporary difference, relating to tax deferred by capital allowance, as £135,000. IAS 12 suggests that the taxable temporary difference should be identified as the amount by which the carrying value of an asset exceeds its *tax base*. Carrying value of an asset is of course the written-down value at the period-end and that, in the illustration we used, is £585,000 (£600,000 less depreciation of £15,000 to that date). The tax base is the corresponding amount to which the asset would have been written down in the books of the tax authorities. The taxable temporary difference (see working below) is £135,000.

(a) Accounting carrying value	£600,000 less £15,000	£585,000
(b) Tax base	£600,000 less £150,000	(£450,000)
Taxable temporary difference (a) – (b)		£135,000

Activity 9.5 Accounting for taxation and deferred tax

Tax on the profit earned in 2010 was provided for at £74,000, and was settled on 1 September 2011 by a payment of £79,000. Current tax on the profits earned in 2011 has been estimated at £84,000. The Deferred tax account reported a balance of £28,000 as at 31 December 2010. As at 31 December 2011 the written-down value of non-current assets was £596,000, whereas the tax base was £456,000. The company pays tax at 25%.

Required: Identify the tax expense of the year 2011.

Activity 9.6 Why tax expense is different from tax liability

At an AGM of shareholders a shareholder wishes to know why the tax expense for the year is reported at £394,000; whereas the tax liability reported among the current liabilities is £378,000.

Required: Explain the possible reason(s) to the shareholder.

9.11 Financial statements of companies for internal use

The financial statements of companies prepared for the *internal use* of the company's board of directors are no different from those we met with in Chapter 4 except that:

(a) On the Statement of income the operating expenses would be listed, not randomly, but grouped under meaningful functional headings.

(b) There will be an additional statement known as a Statement of changes in equity.

9.11.1 Functional grouping of expenses

Functional groupings of operating expenses are usually made within three headings. The first heading, with which we are already familiar, is the cost of sales and it includes all expenses incurred on placing the goods sold in the condition in which and the location from which they are sold. Other headings are distribution costs or administrative expenses.

Distribution costs are expenses related to the selling efforts and delivering to customers of the goods sold and typically include:

- warehousing expenses such as warehouse rent, wages and other remuneration of warehousing staff, depreciation, repairs and maintenance of equipment used in this activity;
- sale promotion costs such as advertising, sale promotion expenses, commission and other remuneration to sales staff, and arguably bad debts (i.e. assuming they arose from bad selling);
- delivery to customer costs such as carriage outwards, depreciation, repair and maintenance of vehicles and remuneration of staff engaged on this activity.

Administrative expenses typically include:

- expenses of administering the company such as staff salaries (including any relating to the directors of the company) and other forms of remuneration, stationery, telephone, postage (unless incurred for delivery), depreciation of equipment used for this activity, bank charges;
- cost of premises such as rent, rates, depreciation of buildings (unless used for production/selling activity), lighting and heating;
- cost of checking on the administration, such as audit fees;
- cost of administrative failure, such as from loss of goods, bad debts (if they arise from inadequacy of credit management), fines and penalties, development cost written off.

9.11.2 The Statement of changes in equity

The word *equity* is used to indicate an element of risk. Normally, ordinary shares are referred to as equity shares because they bear the maximum risk being only entitled to the residual portion of a company's profit, after all claims from creditors, loan creditors and preference shareholders have been met.

Once the profit after tax has been calculated in the Statement of income, the directors have to decide how much to distribute to the shareholders and how much to retain. The profit that is retained from year to year is known as *accumulated profit* or *retained earnings* and forms part of the company's *reserves*. A reserve is any profit retained within the company.

IAS 1 *Presentation of financial statements*[10] requires that the movements in the amount of retained earnings in each accounting period should be traced in a *Statement of changes in equity*, as shown on the right. Note that the statement starts with the accumulated balance of retained earnings brought forward from prior years, adds the profit after tax from the Statement of income of the current period and deducts the dividends paid in the period to ordinary shareholders (only), ending with the amount of retained earnings carried forward to the next period. That amount (£482) is reported on the Statement of financial position as part of the Equity and reserves.

Statement of changes in equity	£
Retained earnings b/f	428
Profit for the year after tax	84
Dividend paid/declared	(30)
Retained earnings c/f	482

9.12 Accounting for dividends

9.12.1 Interim dividends paid

These are posted from the Cash Book to a Dividend account, which is shown as a deduction, not in the Statement of income, but in the *Statement of changes in equity*.

9.12.2 Dividends *declared*

These are accounted for by debiting a Dividend (expense) account and crediting a Dividend (liability) account, as shown below:

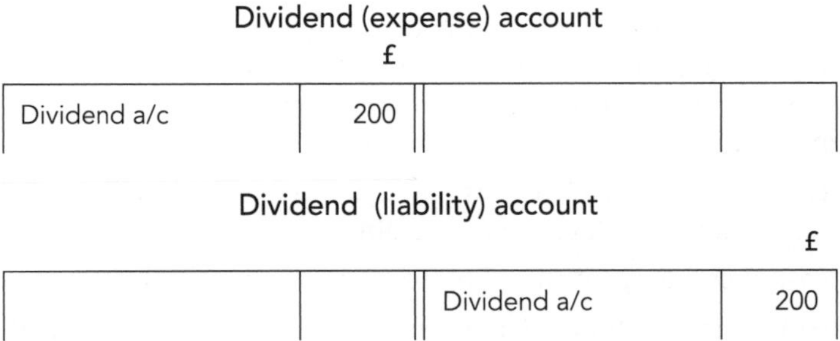

The expense is deducted from the Statement of changes in equity and the liability reported, as a current liability, on the Statement of financial position.

9.12.3 Final dividend *proposed*

Need only be disclosed as a note. It cannot be accounted for because, until it is declared, it would not qualify to be regarded as a liability. As we will see (in Chapter 23), to be regarded as a liability it must be an obligation arising from a past event. The obligating event, in the case of final dividend, is a resolution of the shareholders, which may be expected at their next meeting. Remember, however, that the directors have the power to declare (not just propose) any number of interim dividends.

9.12.4 Preference dividends

Need to be accounted for, irrespective of whether the directors have proposed their payment, if any ordinary dividend has been paid or declared, because preference shares have a priority right. The preference dividend is accounted for by debiting an expense account and crediting a liability account, as shown below.

Preference dividend (expense) account

	£		
Preference dividend a/c	1,000		

Preference dividend (liability) account

			£
		Preference dividend a/c	1,000

The expense (unlike in the case of ordinary dividend) is always included in the Statement of income. The point of inclusion depends on whether the preference shares qualify to be regarded as part of the company's equity capital or, if they are of the redeemable variety,[11] need to be reported on the Statement of financial position as a non-current liability.

(a) **If preference shares are redeemable** the shares will be reported on the Statement of financial position as a non-current liability and the preference dividend, being equivalent to interest paid, is shown on the Statement of income *before* deducting taxation.

(b) **If the preference shares are *not* redeemable**, the shares will be reported, on the Statement of financial position, within Equity and Reserves and the dividend, on the Statement of income, *after* identifying the amount of profit after tax.

Activity 9.7 Accounting for dividends

When preparing the financial statements for 2011 a limited company seeks your advice on how to deal with the items listed below. State your answer by placing a tick in the appropriate grid.

	Statement of income before tax expense	Statement of income after tax expense	Statement of changes in equity	As a footnote
(a) Final dividend paid for 2010				
(b) Interim dividend paid for 2011				
(c) Dividend on redeemable preference shares				
(d) Dividend on preference shares				
(e) Final dividend proposed				
(f) Interim dividend declared				

9.13 When adjustments have to be made to the retained earnings

IAS 8 *Accounting policies, changes in accounting estimates and errors*[12] permits two items, identified below, to be shown as adjustments from the amount of retained earnings brought forward from prior periods. This means that they are included in the statement of changes in equity (rather than in the current period's Statement of income).

9.13.1 Correction of prior period errors

Prior period errors are material omissions or misstatements in previous financial statements. These errors are corrected retrospectively by adjusting the balance brought forward from those years. For example, a material loss arising from a fraud in the previous period, which had not been detected and accounted for when the financial statements of that period were prepared, will be reported in the current period's Statement of changes in equity as a deduction from retained earnings brought forward.

9.13.2 Retrospective effect of adjustments arising from a change of accounting policy

A further item that should be reported in the Statement of changes in equity. *Accounting policy* changes can arise if there is a new policy with regard to (a) recognition, (b) measurement or (c) reporting of an element. Let us try to illustrate with examples as follows:

(a) A change in recognition, e.g. where development cost, regarded as an expense until now, is to be capitalised from this year (provided it meets with the capitalisation criteria stated in Chapter 22).

(b) A change in measurement, e.g. where a company which had not depreciated its buildings until now decides that buildings ought to be depreciated, so that the measure (amount) at which the buildings are reported in the Statement of financial position will be different.

(c) A change in the way items are presented (reported) in the financial statements, e.g. salary paid to staff on production activity, previously shown as part of cost of sales, is now to be included in administrative expenses.

Illustration

Let us assume that a building acquired at a cost of £500,000, six years prior to commencement of the current one, has not been depreciated and that it is now decided to depreciate it using the straight-line method over an estimated life of 50 years. Thus the cost of the building, reported until now as an asset, is to be in part expensed. This is a change of policy and has to be given retrospective effect (i.e. from the date the asset was available for use).

Depreciation would amount to £10,000 (£500,000/50 years) per year. The backlog depreciation (i.e. the portion relating to previous six years) of £60,000 is deducted in the Statement of changes in equity from the retained earnings brought forward; whereas the current year's expense (£10,000) is included, under the appropriate functional heading, in the Statement of income.

Activity 9.8 Accounting for prior period adjustment

Lydall plc seeks your advice on how it should treat the following items, when preparing its financial statements for the year ended 31 December 2011:

(a) £50,000 was paid as an out-of-court settlement to a customer on 7 May 2011, as compensation for injuries suffered in company premises on 24.1.2011.

(b) On 17 January 2012, before 2011 financial statements were approved, following amounts misappropriated by staff are identified:

Misappropriation until 31 December 2010	£148,500
Misappropriation in the year to 31 December 2011	£92,500

The amounts cannot be recovered either from members of staff, who have all been dismissed, or from insurance.

(c) Buildings, not depreciated until now, are to be depreciated. The amount of the depreciation has been calculated as follows:

Backlog until 31 December 2010	£214,800
Current year depreciation in the year to 31 December 2011	£16,200

(d) Corporation tax, in respect of the year ended 31 December 2010, provided for at £79,800, was settled on 1 October 2011 at £76,500.

Note: On Events after the reporting period (formerly post balance sheet events) see Chapter 23.

9.13.3 Changes of estimation are not changes of policy

We have learnt that measurements, for purposes of accounting, are often made on the basis of estimates. The amount estimated could become different because of a change:

- either in the estimation technique; or
- in the assumptions made when making the estimate.

(a) *A change of estimation technique*. For example, let us assume that an entity that has previously depreciated vehicles using the reducing balance method at 40% per year, now proposes to depreciate vehicles using the straight-line method because it believes that the change better reflects the pattern of consumption of economic benefits. This is not a change of accounting policy – it's a change in estimation technique. All that needs to be done is to apply the change prospectively from this year. If the vehicles have been already written down, on the previous technique, to say £300,000 by the beginning of the current year and the remaining useful life of the vehicles is three years, £100,000 (£300,000/3) is written off in each of the remaining three years.

(b) *A change in the assumptions made when making estimates*. Let us assume that a company has chosen the straight-line method for depreciating equipment and has estimated the economic life and scrap value. If equipment had been acquired for £400,000 with an estimated useful life of ten years and nil scrap value, the annual depreciation charge would be £40,000. If, after using the equipment for four years, when the written-down value of the asset is reported at £240,000 (i.e. £400,000 – £40,000 × 4 years), the remaining useful life is re-estimated at only three more years, the annual depreciation from the fifth year would need to be accounted for at £80,000 (i.e. £240,000/3 remaining years).

The impact of any change in estimates, whether arising from the technique used or the assumptions made for making the estimation, is accounted for prospectively, i.e. from the day the change took place.

9.14 Illustration of financial statements prepared for internal use

Let us now prepare the financial statements of Azure plc, for internal use of the directors, bearing in mind that expenses will have to be functionally classified and a Statement of changes in equity is also required.

The year-end Trial Balance of Azure plc is shown below. You are informed as follows:

Trial Balance as at 31 December 2011		
	£'000	£'000
Non-current assets at cost	840	–
Accumulated depreciation – 31.12.2010	–	190
Directors' fees	18	–
2010 final dividend paid	45	–
Inventory – 31 December 2010	294	–
Sales	–	4,154
Rent	30	–
Salaries	312	–
Receivables and payables	505	380
2011 interim dividend paid	36	–
Retained profit b/f	–	214
Taxation account	4	
Advertising	70	–
Allowance for doubtful debts	–	17
Carriage outwards	19	–
Other admin expenses	192	–
6% Preference shares of £1	–	200
8% Debentures – issued 2007	–	50
Interest paid on debenture	2	–
Ordinary shares of 50p each	–	400
Share premium a/c	–	40
Purchases	3,244	–
Cash and bank balance	34	–
	5,645	5,645

(i) The cost of inventory at 31 December 2011 was £328,000.
(ii) Rent has been agreed at £2,000 per month.
(iii) Salaries (£18,000) and audit fees (estimated at £10,000) remain unpaid by year-end.
(iv) A trade receivable of £5,000 should be written off and the allowance for doubtful debts adjusted to cover 5% of the remainder.
(v) Non-current assets are to be depreciated at 20% per annum using the reducing balance method.
(vi) The amount reported as taxation on the Trial Balance is the amount by which tax paid in respect of the previous year exceeded the amount provided for. The tax on current year's profit is estimated at £29,000.
(vii) Directors have proposed a final dividend of 3p per share.

Required: Prepare for the internal use of directors
(a) The Statement of income for the year ended 31 December 2011.
(b) The Statement of changes in equity for the same period.
(c) The Statement of financial position as at 31 December 2011.

The financial statements, for internal use, will be prepared as follows:

The Statement of income for year ended 31 December 2011

	£'000	£'000
Sales		4,154
Inventory – 1.1.2011	294	
Purchases	3,244	
Inventory – 31.12.2011	(328)	(3,210)
Gross profit		944
Distribution costs:		
Advertising	70	
Bad debts[a]	13	
Carriage outward	19	(102)
Administrative expenses:		
Directors' fees	18	
Salaries[b]	330	
Rent[c]	24	
Audit fees	10	
Depreciation[d]	130	
Other expenses	192	(704)
Finance cost[e]		(4)
Profit before tax		134
Taxation[g]		(33)
Profit after tax		101
Preference dividend[f]		(12)
Retained profit		89

The Statement of financial position as at 31 December 2011

	£'000	£'000	£'000
Non-current assets	840	(320)	520
Current assets:			
Inventory		328	
Trade receivables	500		
Allowance for doubtful debts	(25)	475	
Prepaid rent		6	
Cash and bank		34	843
			1,363

	£'000	£'000
Equity and reserves:		
Ordinary shares of 50p	400	
6% Preference shares of £1[f]	200	
Share premium a/c	40	
Retained earnings	222	862
Non-current liabilities:		
8% Debentures		50
Current liabilities:		
Trade payables	380	
Accrued salary	18	
Audit fees payable	10	
Preference dividend	12	
Interest accrued[e]	2	
Taxation	29	451
		1,363

The Statement of changes in equity

	£'000
Retained profit b/f	214
Profit after tax for 2011	89
2010 Final dividend paid[h]	(45)
2011 Interim dividend[h]	(36)
Retained profit c/f	222

Notes: Final dividend proposed on ordinary shares for 2011 is £24,000.[i]

Workings are as follows:

(a) Bad debts £5,000 + (£25,000 – £17,000) = £13,000
(b) Salaries: £312,000 + £18,000 accrued = £330,000
(c) Rent: £30,000 – £6,000 prepaid = £24,000
(d) Depreciation: 20% of (£840,000 – £190,000) = £130,000
(e) Finance cost: 8% of £50,000 = £4,000 of which £2,000 has been paid, leaving £2,000 unpaid.
(f) Preference dividend calculated at 6% of £200,000 needs to be accounted for, because preference shares have priority over the ordinary shares. Preference shares, not being redeemable, are regarded as equity (as per IAS 32). Therefore the preference shares are reported on the Statement of financial position as part of equity and the dividend is shown as a deduction from profit after tax expense has been deducted.
(g) Taxation: under-provision £4,000 for 2010 + current tax £29,000 = £33,000.
(h) Final dividend (on ordinary shares) for 2010 paid in 2011 as well as the interim dividend paid in 2011 are both shown as deductions in the movement of equity.
(i) Final dividend for 2011, yet to be declared, is only disclosed as a Note, calculated as: 400,000 shares of 50p each = 800,000 shares @ 3p = £24,000.

9.15 Financial statements of companies for publication

The financial statements for publication means those that are prepared (i) to be sent out to every shareholder and debenture holder and (ii) to be filed with the Registrar of Companies so that anyone interested could, for a fee, have access to them. When financial statements are prepared for publication care needs to be exercised with regard to their format and the disclosures that are required to be made.

9.15.1 The format of presentation of the Statement of income

The financial statements should be presented in one of the acceptable formats. For the Statement of income IAS 1[10] allows companies a choice between two formats. Format 1 analyses expenses by their function, e.g. cost of sales, distribution costs and administrative expenses. Format 2 analyses expenses according to their nature, e.g. inventories, staff costs, depreciation. Depending on the format chosen the Statements of income would appear as follows:

Format 1

Statement of income for the year . . .	
	£
Revenue	2,400
Cost of sales	(1,580)
Gross profit	820
Other operating income	30
Distribution costs	(142)
Admin expenses	(498)
Profit from operations	210
Finance costs	(12)
Profit before tax	198
Income tax expense	(39)
Profit after tax	159

Format 2

Statement of income for the year . . .	
	£
Revenue	2,400
Other operating income	30
Changes in inventories	(11)
Raw materials used	(1,454)
Staff costs	(560)
Depreciation	(195)
Profit from operations	210
Finance costs	(12)
Profit before tax	198
Income tax expense	(39)
Profit after tax	159

Note: After identifying the profit from operations the presentation in both formats is identical.

9.15.2 The format of presentation of the Statement of financial position

The Statement of financial position, as we already know, is presented as two separate statements – the first reporting the assets and the second the equity and liabilities. A distinction should be drawn between non-current and current, for both the assets and the liabilities. On the format illustrated in IAS 1, current liabilities are stated on the Equity and liability part of the Statement of financial position. The alternative of showing the current liabilities as a deduction from current assets, as is common in the UK, is also permitted.

9.15.3 Disclosure of minimum required information

Companies have to strike a balance between publishing too much information (disclosing sensitive particulars to rivals) and failing to disclose what is required under the company law and various Accounting Standards. In the UK (as well as in many other countries) a company failing to make the necessary disclosures in its financial statements or failing, in any way, to comply with the requirements of Accounting Standards may find itself taken to court by a body set up for this purpose known as *Financial Reporting Review Panel* (FRRP). Examples of items required to be disclosed by the Companies Act and those required to be disclosed *separately* by IAS 1 are listed below:

Disclosures required under UK company law	Separate disclosures required under IAS 1
1. Turnover (sales) with segmental breakdown	1. Write down of inventory to realisable value
2. Depreciation	2. Impairment loss
3. Directors' emoluments (specified details)[a]	3. Disposal of assets
4. Audit fees and expenses	4. Disposal of investments
5. Number of employees with break-down[b]	5. Discontinued operations
6. Employee remuneration[c]	6. Litigation settlements
7. Exceptional items	7. Reversal of provisions

(a) The Secretary of state is empowered to make regulations from time to time specifying details of directors' emoluments to be disclosed. Such disclosures include particulars of share options, long-term incentives and compensation for loss of office.[13]

(b) The average number employed in the financial year needs to be disclosed, with their major categories. Categorisation is left to the nature of business involved.[14]

(c) Employees' remuneration should include, in addition to salaries and wages, social security and pension benefits.[15]

In general, IAS 1 requires that if any income or expense is material, its nature and amount should be disclosed separately. Note also that whereas disclosures required by company law may be in notes, the disclosures required by International Standards may be required to be shown on the face of the published financial statements. For example, when a business discontinues an operation (i.e. abandons or disposes of one of its major lines of business) the income and expenses relating to it need to be specifically identified on the face of the Statement of income, distinguishing between:

(a) profit or loss, after tax, arising from the activities of the discontinued operations, and

(b) any gains/loss arising from disposal or impairment review of the assets/liabilities relating to that operation.

Such information is important because stakeholders need to be aware that a corresponding profit or loss will not arise in the future.

IAS 1[10] also prohibits presentation of any item of income or expense as an *extraordinary item*.

9.16 Illustration of financial statements prepared for publication

Let us illustrate how financial statements prepared for publication need to appear, bearing in mind that information disclosed should neither be excessive nor fall short of the requirements in company law and Accounting Standards. We will use format 1 of the two formats illustrated in IAS1.

Magnolia plc buys processed leather to make vanity bags for sale. Their year-end Trial Balance has been extracted as shown on the right. You are informed as follows:

Trial Balance as at 31 March 2011		
	£'000	£'000
Land and buildings	1,800	–
Machinery	840	–
Office equipment	320	–
Accumulated depreciation – 31.3.2010		
Building	–	360
Machinery	–	416
Office equipment	–	70
Brand name	240	–
Inventory – 31.3.2010	349	–
Other administration expenses	29	–
8% Loan notes	–	200
Investments	180	–
Carriage inwards	34	–
Retained earnings	–	748
Salaries	298	–
Machine maintenance	31	–
Postage and stationery	18	–
6% Preference shares	–	400
Ordinary shares – 20p	–	1,000
Share premium a/c	–	30
Interest on loan notes	8	–
Disposal of machinery	–	29
Rent and rates	282	–
Purchases and sales	2,148	3,768
Interim dividend paid	50	–
Receivables/payables	400	341
Allowance for doubtful debts	–	8
Return inwards	29	–
Cash and bank	37	–
Director's remuneration	122	
Dividend received	–	20
Advertising	149	–
Carriage outwards	26	–
	7,390	7,390

(a) The cost of year-end inventory was £504,000.

(b) On 1 April 2006 £400,000 was paid to acquire an established brand name which was amortised using the straight-line method, anticipating a commercial life of ten years. A market survey carried out on 1 April 2010, however, reveals that the discounted present value of income from the brand, on that date, was £100,000 and that the brand's commercial value may be exploited for only two years from that date.

(c) Expenses need adjustment as follows:

	Accruals	Pre-payments
Other administrative expense	£11,000	–
Rent and rates	–	£12,000
Wages and salaries	£42,000	–

(d) A machine acquired for £60,000 and written down to £44,000 by 1 April 2010 was sold on that date for £29,000.

(e) Buildings are depreciated at 2% per annum using the straight-line method and assuming that a third of the cost relates to land which is not depreciated; machinery and equipment are depreciated at 30% and 20% per annum respectively, using the reducing balance method.

(f) Allowance for doubtful debts is to be maintained at 3% of amount receivable from trade customers.

(f) Audit fee payable is estimated at £25,000.

(g) 6% Preference shares are redeemable at par on 31 March 2014.

(h) Income tax on the year's profit is estimated at £58,000. The under-provision of tax relating to the previous year, amounting to £3,000, is included in other administration expenses.

(i) Expenses should be apportioned as:

	Cost of sales	Admin. expenses	Distribution cost
Salaries	40%	50%	10%
Depreciation of building	50%	25%	25%
Depreciation of equipment	–	100%	–
Rent and rates	40%	30%	30%

Required: Prepare for publication a Statement of income for the year ended 31 March 2011, using format 1 as illustrated in IAS 1 and the Statement of financial position as at that date.

The financial statements prepared for publication will appear as follows:

Statement of income for the year ended 31 March 2011

	£'000
Sales revenue[a]	3,739
Cost of sales[bi]	(2,478)
Gross profit	1,261
Distribution costs[bii]	(300)
Administrative expenses[biii]	(509)
Profit from operation	452
Disposal of machine[c]	(15)
Impairment of brand[d]	(140)
Dividend received	20
Finance cost[e]	(16)
Preference dividend[f]	(24)
Profit before taxation	277
Taxation[g]	(61)
Profit after taxation	216

Statement of changes in equity

	£'000
Balance b/f	748
Profit for the year	216
Interim dividend	(50)
Balance c/f	914

Operating expenses written off include the following

	£'000
Salaries and wages	340
Directors' emoluments	122
Audit fees	25
Depreciation	188

Statement of financial position as at 31 March 2011

	£'000	£'000	£'000
Non-current assets:			
Land and buildings	1,800	(384)	1,416
Machinery	780	(514)	266
Equipment	320	(120)	200
Brand name			50[e]
Investments			180
Current assets:			
Inventory		504	
Trade receivables[i]		388	
Pre-payments		12	
Cash and bank balance		37	941
			3,053

	£'000	£'000
Equity and reserves:		
Ordinary shares of £1	1,000	
Share premium a/c	30	
Retained earnings	914	1,944
Non-current liabilities:		
6% Preference shares[f]	400	
8% Loan notes	200	600
Current liabilities:		
Trade payables	341	
Accrued expenses[h]	86	
Taxation[g]	58	
Preference dividend[e]	24	509
		3,053

(a) Sales revenue: £3,768 – £29 return inwards = £3,739.
(b) Operating expenses have been grouped according their function so that the total may be published as a single amount.

		Cost of sales	Distribution cost	Admin. expenses
Opening inventory		349	–	–
Purchases		2,148	–	–
Salaries and wages	298 + 42 = £340 allocated as 40%/10%/50%	136	34	170
Rent and rates	282 – 12 = £270 prepaid allocated as 40%/30%/30%	108	81	81
Carriage inwards		34	–	–
Machine maintenance		31	–	–
Depreciation of machine	30% of (840 – 60) – (416 – 16)	114	–	–
Depreciation of building	2% of 2/3 of 1,200,000 allocated as 50%/25%/25%	12	6	6
Brand name	Recoverable amount £100/2 years expected life	50	–	–
Closing inventory		(504)	–	–
Other admin. expenses	29 + 11 accrued – 3 under-provision for tax	–	–	37
Depreciation of equipment	20% of 320 – 70	–	–	50
Directors remuneration		–	–	122
Audit fees		–	–	25
Postage		–	–	18
Advertising		–	149	–
Carriage outwards		–	26	–
Bad debts	3% of £400,000 – £8,000 allowance available	–	4	–
		2,478[bi]	300[bii]	509[biii]

(c) Gain on disposal of machine: £29,000 less wdv on date of sale £44,000 = loss of £15,000.
(d) Impairment of brand: carrying value £400 – £160 = £240 less recoverable amount £100,000 = £140,000.
Amortisation of brand: recoverable amount £100,000/2 years = £50,000.
(e) Finance cost is interest at 8% on loan notes of £200,000 = £16,000.
(f) Preference shares are of the redeemable variety. Hence the shares themselves are included within non-current liability; while the dividend payable on them (6% of £400,000) is shown as an expense, and stated before taxation expense.
(g) Taxation expense consists of current tax of £58,000 plus £3,000 under-provision for previous year.
(h) Accrued expenses are £11,000 other admin. expenses + £42,000 salaries + £8,000 interest + £25,000 audit fee = £86,000.

Note the following points of difference between financial statements for publication and the ones for internal use:

1. Sensitive information such as Return inwards and Allowance for doubtful debts are not publicised, but netted off from the appropriate items.
2. Rather than tabulating one by one every item of operating expense only the totals of functional groups are disclosed. However, those operating expenses that are specifically required to be disclosed are listed as footnotes, or in some instances separately identified within the financial statements.

Activity 9.9 Financial statements for publication (format 2)

Set out the Statement of income of Magnolia plc shown in paragraph 9.16 above on format 2 as illustrated in IAS 1.

9.17 The Statement of comprehensive income

The Statement of income is referred to as a Statement of comprehensive income, if it is so prepared as to draw attention to the total gains and losses recognised in an accounting period, including within it any gains or losses (e.g. revaluation gain) which cannot be included in the Statement of income. For example, let us assume that a company identifies its profits for the year before tax as £360,000 and its tax expense for the year is £65,000. Let us assume further that in the same period a revaluation gain of £100,000 has been accounted for. The Statement of income would be as usual, identifying the profit after tax of £295,000 which amount is then included in the Statement of changes in equity as an addition to Retained earnings brought forward. If, on the other hand, a Statement of comprehensive income is to be prepared (see on the left), the revaluation gain recognised in the year, and reported directly in the Statement of financial position, is shown also as an appendage to the Statement of income, adding it to the profit after tax under the heading 'other comprehensive income' so that the total comprehensive income recognised in that year of £395,000 is drawn to the attention of the shareholders. However, the amount included in the Statement of changes in equity will still be £295,000.

Statement of comprehensive income	
	£'000
Profit before tax	360
Taxation	(65)
Profit after tax	295
Other comprehensive income	
Revaluation gain	100
Total comprehensive income	395

Activity 9.10 Preparation of a Statement of comprehensive income

Sylvio plc has extracted its year-end Trial Balance as shown below on the right, after after making most of the year-end adjustments. You are informed as follows:

(a) Buildings, not depreciated until now, need to be depreciated as follows: For 8 years until 31 December 2010: £144,000. For year ended 31 December 2011: £18,000. As at 31 December 2011 the market value of land and buildings has been identified as £1.5 million. Directors wish to report this asset at market value.

(b) The motor vehicles are depreciated at 25% p.a. on the reducing balance method. Office equipment, used for administration, is depreciated at 10% per annum on cost. However, on 1 January 2011 the directors decided that to keep up with changes in technology equipment needed to be replaced by 31 December 2013.

(c) Corporation tax on the year's profit is estimated at £55,000.

(d) Directors have declared a dividend of 4p per share.

Required:

(a) Prepare the Statement of comprehensive income for the year ended 31 December 2011

(b) with the Statement of changes in equity and

(c) the Statement of financial position as at that date.

Trial Balance as at 31 December 2011		
	£'000	£'000
Receivables/payables	348	412
Distribution cost	194	–
Admin. expenses	278	–
Sales	–	4,024
Cost of goods sold	3,165	–
Land and building	1,200	–
Motor vehicles	440	–
Office equipment	540	–
Accumulated depreciation		
to 31 December 2010:		
Office equipment		324
Motor vehicles		240
Inventory – 31.12.2011	395	–
Cash and bank	22	–
Share capital – £1 each	–	1,200
Share premium	–	50
Retained earnings	–	332
	6,582	6,582

9.18 Issue of bonus shares

9.18.1 What is a bonus issue?

Bonus shares (known also as scrip issue and capitalisation issue) are shares issued free (i.e. without any charge) by a company to its ordinary shareholders. A company may take such a step if and when it wishes to:

- prepare the market for a new share issue for cash;
- reward existing shareholders without having to deplete its cash resources by paying a dividend;
- bring the issued capital of the company (i.e. the portion of the capital held as shares by the shareholders) more in line with the amount of its Equity and reserves;
- bring down the market price of its shares (because when a larger number of shares are available the share price may tend to come down) to make the shares more affordable and thereby make more people become shareholders.

9.18.2 Accounting for a bonus issue

If a company with an issued share capital of 10,000 shares of £1 each decides to make a bonus issue of one for every five, the issue of 2,000 bonus shares (i.e. 10,000 × 1/5) is accounted for as shown below:

Dr Bonus issue a/c	£2,000	
Cr Share capital a/c		£2,000

To account for the bonus issue.

Dr Share premium a/c	£2,000	
Cr Bonus issue a/c		£2,000

To write off the cost of the bonus issue.

The cost of bonus shares is preferably charged against the balance in the Share premium account as this account may be applied only for limited purposes (see 9.7.1) and the opportunity to use the account should be taken when it arises. On the other hand a company may write off the cost of its bonus issue against the balance in its Retained earnings, if its intention is to reduce the amount available for distribution to its shareholders.

Activity 9.11 Accounting for a bonus issue of shares

As at the end of the year the Equity and reserves of a public limited company is made up of amounts stated on the right. The directors have resolved to make a scrip issue of one for every five shares, taking care, however, to protect the amounts available for distribution to shareholders.

Ordinary shares of £1	£500,000
Share premium a/c	£90,000
Revaluation reserve	£54,000
Retained earnings	£168,000

Required:

(a) Taking note of the directors' wish, explain how you would write off the cost of the scrip issue.

(b) Set out the Equity and reserves section of the company's Statement of financial position as at the year-end, after the scrip issue has been made.

9.19 Rights issue of shares

9.19.1 What is a rights issue of shares?

This is where a company may permit its shareholders the right to acquire from it (i.e. not from the market) additional shares at a privileged price – i.e. a price lower than the one at which it is currently sold on the share market (but not lower than its par value). Such rights, when granted, need to be restricted. Otherwise shareholders might abuse such rights, buying as many shares as possible at the privileged price and disposing of them at the market price.

9.19.2 Accounting for a rights issue

Assume that a company with an issued capital of 100,000 ordinary shares of £1 each allows its shareholders the right to buy one for every five shares held (observe the restriction of the right by limiting it to one for five) at a price of 120p each whereas the market rate is 150p each (observe the privileged price). If all the shareholders exercise the right (as they probably would) the amount received (20,000 shares @ 120p each = £24,000) will be posted from the Cash Book to the credit of the Share capital account (20,000 @ the par value of £1 each = £20,000) and the excess to the Share premium account (20,000 @ 20p each = £4,000).

Activity 9.12 Accounting for a bonus issue and rights issue

As at 1 January 2011, commencement of an accounting period, Olive plc had a balance of £300,000 in its Share capital account and £45,000 in its share premium account. The shares in issue were ordinary shares of £1 each. The following share issues were made during the year:

On 1 March 2011: a bonus issue of one for every 15 shares
On 1 May 2011: a rights issue of one for every four shares at 120p each
On 1 June 2011: a cash issue of 200,000 ordinary shares of £1 each at 180p each

Required: Show how these transactions will be reported on the Statement of financial position as at 31 December 2011.

9.20 Statement of changes in equity: an extended version

A company may opt[10] to publish an extended version of the Statement of changes in equity, tracing all the changes resulting from transactions with shareholders during the accounting period, i.e. changes in share capital, share premium, as well as every class of reserves. To illustrate let us assume the reserves position of a company is as stated in the boxes shown below:

Equity and reserves as at 1 January 2011
£400,000 ordinary shares of £1 each £124,000 in the Share premium account £312,000 in revaluation reserve £554,000 in retained earnings

Changes in reserves during year 2011:
1. Profit after tax £139,000; dividend paid £32,000 2. Correction of prior period error £96,000 (loss) 3. Revaluation surplus arising in the year £145,000

You are further informed that during the year ended 31 December 2011:

(a) A bonus issue of one for four shares was made and cost written off from Share premium.

(b) A cash issue of 100,000 shares of £1 each was made at 150p each and expenses of issue, amounting to £2,000 – were written off against Share premium.

(c) £22,000, being the extra depreciation arising because of revaluation, was transferred to distributable profit.

A Statement of changes in equity, if prepared so as to trace all transactions with equity holders during the year, will appear as follows:

Statement of changes in equity for year ended 31 December 2011	Share capital	Share premium	Revaluation reserve	Retained earnings	Total
Balance b/f	£400,000	£124,000	£312,000	£554,000	£1,390,000
Bonus issue of shares[a]	£100,000	(£100,000)	–	–	–
Share issue for cash[b]	£100,000	£50,000	–	–	£150,000
Expenses of issuing shares[c]	–	(£2,000)	–	–	(£2,000)
Revaluation of land and building	–	–	£145,000	–	£145,000
Transfer[d]	–	–	(£22,000)	£22,000	–
Prior period adjustment[e]	–	–	–	(£96,000)	(£96,000)
Profit for 2011 after tax	–	–	–	£139,000	£139,000
Dividend paid	–	–	–	(£32,000)	(£32,000)
Balance c/f	£600,000	£72,000	£435,000	£587,000	£1,694,000

(a) 400,000/4 = 100,000 shares of £1 each issued as bonus and the cost written off from Share premium.
(b) 100,000 shares issued at 150p = £150,000; the par value credited to Share capital, remainder to premium.
(c) Expenses of issuing share can be and hence should be written off from Share premium.
(d) Revaluation reserve, when realised, is transferred to Retained earnings.
(e) Correction of a prior period error can be adjusted from opening balance of Retained earnings.

Activity 9.13 Statement of changes in equity

On the right is the capital and reserves section of Crimson plc's Statement of financial position as at 31 December 2011, after recording the following transactions all of which took place in the current year.

As at 31 December 2011	£
Ordinary shares – £1	360,000
Share premium a/c	29,000
Revaluation reserve	84,000
Retained earnings	128,000

1 Jan: A bonus issue of one for three was made.

1 April: Revaluation gain of £46,000 was recognised in respect of land and buildings.

1 Sept: 200,000 ordinary shares of £1 each were issued at 125p each. Expenses amounting to £1,000 were written off against Share premium.

1 Nov: An interim dividend of £20,000 was paid.

31 Dec: Profit before tax for the year was identified as £39,000 and tax estimated at £11,000. £12,000 of revaluation reserve realised in the year ended 31 December 2011.

Required: The Statement of changes in equity tracing all transactions with shareholders in 2011.

Note: This question is quite a challenging one because what is provided is the position at the year-end and we have to trace the steps backwards from there to find the position at the commencement.

Summary

- Most businesses of any significant size in the UK are limited liability companies.
- Operating as a limited company brings many advantages as well as some disadvantages.
- Limited companies can be of two types – public (plc) and private (Ltd) – the latter suffer from some restrictions but enjoy some concessions. Some of the public companies may be listed.
- Limited companies raise finance by issuing shares and loan notes (debentures).
- At any point of time the Share capital account reports the so far called-up value (until that point) of the number of shares in issue.
- If amount received on issue of shares is more than the par value, the excess must be stated as Share premium, which may be used only for a bonus issue or to write off expenses on issuing the same shares.
- Financial statements must be prepared both for internal use and for publication.
- Financial statements prepared for publication should be in the prescribed format.
- Additional disclosures are required of items such as directors' remuneration.
- Tax expense in an accounting period could include, in addition to current tax, adjustment for any under-provision or over-provision in previous year as well as deferred tax.
- Correction of prior period errors and impact of changes in accounting policy on performance in prior periods are shown in the Statement of changes in equity as adjustments from retained earnings brought forward.
- Ordinary dividends paid or declared are reported in the Statement of changes in equity, whereas final dividend proposed is only reported as a note.
- Dividends to preference shares are always included in the Statement of income, ordinarily after tax, but before tax in the event the preference shares are redeemable.
- The Statement of comprehensive income is a Statement of income with additional information included for drawing attention to the total comprehensive income recognised in the accounting period.
- A Statement of changes in equity needs to be published. It may be prepared either in the short format (tracing changes in the Retained earnings only) or in an extended format (tracing changes that have taken place during the year in the Share capital account as well in every one of the reserves).

References

1. Companies Act 2006, section 7 & 8, effective from 1 October 2009, London, The Stationery Office.
2. *The Combined Code on Corporate Governance*, 2006, London, Financial Reporting Council.
3. Companies Act 2006, section 762, London, The Stationery Office.
4. Companies Act 2006, section 59, 271 & 336, London, The Stationery Office.
5. *Henry v Great Northern Railway Company* (1857), 1 De G and J 606.
6. Companies Act 2006, section 542, London, The Stationery Office.
7. The Gedge Committee Report, 1954, Gedge Committee, Cmd 9112, London, HMSO, http://www.bopcris.ac.uk/bopall/ref9192.html.
8. Companies Act 2006, section 610, London, The Stationery Office.
9. IAS 12 *Income Taxes*, issued in 1979, amended in December 2003, London, International Accounting Standards Board.

10. IAS 1 *Presentation of Financial Statements*, revised 2003, effective 1.1.2005, London, International Accounting Standards Board.
11. IAS 32 *Financial Instruments: Disclosure and Presentation*, revised 2003, effective 1.1.2005, London, International Accounting Standards Board.
12. IAS 8 *Accounting Policies, Changes in Accounting Estimates and Errors*, revised 2003, effective 1.1.2005, London, International Accounting Standards Board.
13. Companies Act 2006 s.412, London, The Stationery Office.
14. Companies Act 2006 s.411, London, The Stationery Office.
15. Companies Act 2006 s.411, London, The Stationery Office.

Suggested answers to activities

9.1 Difference between shares and debentures

1. **Status.** The shareholder is a member with rights (such as invitation to participate in shareholders' meetings, elect directors, appoint auditors, receive financial statements), whereas the debenture-holder is only a creditor of the company.
2. **Rewards.** Shareholders are entitled to a dividend only if the company makes distributable profit, as defined by company law, and the amount is paid or proposed by directors and, in the case of final dividend, approved by the shareholders; whereas debenture-holders are entitled to receive interest for each year, irrespective of whether the company makes a profit.
3. **Security**. Debenture-holders may, depending on the terms agreed when they were issued, have a fixed or floating mortgage on the company's assets, so that, in case of need, they may have recourse to these assets to recover their capital plus interest up to that date, whereas the shareholders have no such protection.
4. **In a liquidation of company**. Debenture-holders will rank with creditors (and may even have the added advantage of claiming their dues from any asset on which they are secured), whereas the shareholders may or may not get any return of what they are owed, depending on whether the amount realised from the company's assets is sufficient to pay for the expenses of liquidation (including the liquidator's remuneration) and to repay the claims of outsiders.

9.2 Accounting for share issue

(a) Prime entry for the share issue

(i) £60,000 received on share issue is posted from the Cash Book to the credit of the Share capital account (£50,000) and the Share premium account (£10,000).

(ii) £3,000 expenses on share issue is posted from the Cash Book to the debit of the Share premium account.

(b)

Statement of financial position (extract)	
	£
Capital and reserves:	
Ordinary shares of 50p each	50,000
Share premium a/c	7,000

9.3 Accounting for issue of shares partly called up

Ordinary share capital account

			£
		Called-up capital	30,000

Share premium account

			£
		Called-up capital	10,000

Called-up capital account

	£		£
Share capital	30,000	Cash Book	32,000
Share premium	10,000	Balance c/d	8,000
	40,000		40,000
Balance b/d	8,000		

(b) Statement of financial position (extract)

Current assets:		
Called-up capital not received		£8,000
Capital and reserves:		
Ordinary shares of 50p each 40p called up	£30,000	
Share premium account	£8,000	

9.4 Accounting for share transfers between shareholders

(a) Statement of financial position (extract):

	£'000
Ordinary shares of £1	60,000
Share premium a/c	10,000

(b) No entries in books of account of Beige plc. Share register alone needs to be amended.

(c) Michael needs to pay up to (5,000 shares × 40p remaining call not yet made =) £2,000.

9.5 Accounting for taxation and deferred tax

Taxation (expense) account

Under-provision for previous year	£5,000[a]	Statement of income	£96,000
Current year tax	£84,000		
Deferred tax	£7,000[b]		
	£96,000		£96,000

(a) Under-provision for previous year: £79,000 (paid) – £74,000 (provided) = £5,000

(b) Deferred tax adjustment:

Accounting wdv	£596,000		
Tax base	£456,000		
Taxable temporary difference	£140,000	@ 25% =	£35,000
Deferred tax already accounted for			(£28,000)
Additional deferred tax to be accounted for in 2011			£7,000

9.6 Why tax expense is different from tax liability

The tax liability included within current liability is only the estimated corporation tax on the profits reported in the current period's Statement of income. This amount needs to be agreed with the tax inspectors and settled on the next day after completing nine months from the date of the Statement of financial position. The tax expense reported is not only the tax estimated on current period's profit but will also be:

- increased (or decreased) by under-provision (or exceptionally over-provision) for previous period; and
- increased or decreased by any adjustment needed to the deferred tax account balance.

9.7 Accounting for dividend

Variety of dividends paid declared and proposed	Statement of income before tax expense	Statement of income after tax expense	Statement of movement of equity	As a footnote
(a) Final dividend paid for 2010			x	
(b) Interim dividend paid for 2011			x	
(c) Dividend on redeemable preference shares	x			
(d) Dividend on preference shares		x		
(e) Final dividend proposed				x
(f) Interim dividend declared			x	

9.8 Accounting for prior period adjustment

(a) The obligating event (customer suffering injury within company premises) occurred on 24 January 2011 and, therefore, unless the company's liability is in dispute, it must estimate the liability and account for it on that date and adjust the estimate to £50,000 when it is settled on 7 May. As a result, the compensation to the customer is included as an expense in the Statement of income for the year 2011.

(b) The period after 31 December 2011 and the date on which 2011 financial statements are approved is commonly known as the 'post balance sheet period' and events occurring in that period as 'events after reporting date' (see Chapter 23). The loss from staff misappropriation which occurred in 2011 (£92,500) is included in that year's Statement of income as a loss. The material loss of £148,500 which occurred in 2010, not detected until 2011 financial statements are approved, is reported in the Statement of changes in equity for 2011, as a deduction from the balance of Retained earnings brought forward.

(c) Decision to depreciate buildings which have not been depreciated is a change of policy. IAS 8 requires any change of policy to be given effect retrospectively, i.e. from the time the building was first available for the company's use. Accordingly £214,800, which is backlog depreciation until the beginning of the current accounting period, is accounted for and shown in the Statement of changes in equity for 2011 as a deduction from Retained earnings brought forward. The current year depreciation of £16,200 is included as an expense in the Statement of income for 2011 under an appropriate functional heading.

(d) The correction of an estimate for tax made in the previous year is not a change of policy nor is it a correction of prior period error because firstly the amount is not material and secondly would be expected to arise from year to year because estimates, by their nature, would need correction. Hence the over-provision of £3,300 (i.e. £79,800 – £76,500) is reduced from the tax expense accounted for in 2011.

9.9 Statement of income on IAS format 2

Statement of income on Format 2 for year ended 31 March 2011	
	£'000
Sales revenue	3,739
Change in inventory[a]	155
Raw material consumed[b]	(2,148)
Staff costs[c]	(462)
Depreciation and amortisation[d]	(238)
Other administration expenses[e]	(569)
Audit fees	(25)
Operating profit[f]	452
Loss on disposal of machine	(15)
Impairment of brand	(140)
Dividend received	20
Finance costs	(16)
Preference dividend	(24)
Profit before tax	277
Taxation	(61)
Profit after tax	216

(f) After identifying the operating profit for the year as £452,000, the remaining items are the same in both formats 1 and 2.

Workings:

(a)

	£'000	£'000
Opening inventory	349	
Less: Closing inventory	504	155

Because closing inventory is more than the opening one the difference is added.

(b) It is assumed that all raw materials bought were used up in the accounting period.

(c) Staff costs:

Salaries and wages	340	
Directors' emoluments	122	462

(d) Depreciation/amortisation:

Depreciation of building	24	
Depreciation of machine	114	
Depreciation of equipment	50	
Amortisation of brand	50	238

(e) Other admin. expenses:

Rent and rates	270	
Carriage inwards	34	
Machine maintenance	31	
Postage	18	
Bad debts	4	
Other expenses	37	
Carriage outwards	26	
Advertising	149	569

9.10 Preparation of a Statement of comprehensive income

Statement of comprehensive income year ended 31.12.2011	
	£'000
Sales revenue	4,024
Cost of sale	(3,165)
Gross profit	859
Distribution cost[a]	(244)
Admin. expenses[b]	(404)
Profit before tax	211
Taxation	(55)
Profit after tax[c]	156
Other comprehensive income	
Revaluation gain	462
Prior period adjustment	(144)
Total comprehensive income	474

Statement of financial postion as at 31 December 2011			£'000
Non-current assets:			
Land and buildings at valuation[d]			1,500
Equipment	(432)	(432)[e]	108
Motor vehicles	(290)	(290)[g]	150
Current assets:			
Inventory		395	
Receivables		348	
Cash and bank		22	765
			2,523

Statement of changes in equity:	£'000
Balance b/f	332
Prior period adjustment	(144)
Profit after tax	156
Dividend declared	(48)
Balance c/f	296

		£'000
Equity and reserves:		
Ordinary shares	1,200	
Share premium a/c	50	
Revaluation reserve	462	
Retained earnings	296	2,008
Current liabilities:		
Trade payables	412	
Taxation	55	
Divident declared	48	515
		2,523

Workings:

(a)

	£'000
Distribution cost	
As reported	194
Depreciation on vehicle	50
	244

(b)

	£'000
Admin. expenses	
As reported	278
Depreciation on building	18
Depreciation on equipment	108
	404

(c) Profit after tax is transferred to Statement of changes in equity, irrespective of whether what is being prepared is the Statement of income or the Statement of comprehensive income

(d) **Land and buildings account**

	£		£
Balance b/f	1,200	Accumulated depreciation a/c	162
Revaluation reserve	462	Balance c/d	1,500
	1,662		1,662
Balance b/d	1,500		

Accumulated depreciation on buildings

	£		£
Land and building	162	Balance b/f	144
		Depreciation	18
	162		162

(e) **Equipment account**

	£		£
Balance b/f	540		

Accumulated depreciation on equipment a/c

	£		£
		Balance b/f	324
		Depreciation[f]	108
			432

(f) Depreciation on equipment: £540 – 324/2 yrs =£108

(g) **Motor vehicles account**

	£		£
Balance b/f	440		

Accumulated depreciation on vehicles a/c

	£		£
		Balance b/f	240
		Depreciation[h]	50
			290

(h) Depreciation on vehicle: 25% of 440 – 240 = £50

9.11 Accounting for a bonus issue of shares

(a) The cost of bonus shares (500,000/5 × £1 = £100,000)

- would not be written off against retained earnings because the directors wish to protect the distributable profit;
- would, to the maximum possible extent, be written off from the Share premium account because in no circumstance would it become distributable; and
- thereafter, if necessary, be written off against Revaluation reserve. This is because the Revaluation reserve would become distributable either when the related asset is sold or annually to the extent of additional depreciation arising because of revaluation (see Chapter 8).

(b) Statement of financial position

	£'000
Equity and reserves:	
Ordinary shares of £1 each	600
Revaluation reserve	44
Retained earnings	168

Bonus issue is accounted for as follows:

	£'000
Dr. Share premium a/c	90
Dr. Revaluation reserve	10
Cr. Share capital a/c	100

9.12 Accounting for a bonus issue and rights issue

(a) Bonus issue: 300,000/15 = 20,000 of £1 each.

(b) Rights: 320,000 shares × $^1/_4$ = 80,000 shares
80,000 shares @ 1.20p = £96,000.

(c) Cash issue: 200,000 @ 1.80 = £360,000, £200,000 of it credited to Share capital, remainder to Share premium.

Statement of financial position as at 31 December 2011	
	£
Equity and reserves:	
Ordinary shares of 1 each	600,000
Share premium account	201,000

9.13 Statement of changes in equity

Statement of changes in equity for year ended 31 December 2011	Share capital	Share premium	Revaluation reserve	Retained earnings	Total
Balance b/f[a]	£120,000	£20,000	£50,000	£108,000	£298,000
Bonus issue of shares[b]	£40,000	(£40,000)	–	–	–
Share issue for cash[c]	£200,000	£50,000	–	–	£250,000
Expenses of issuing shares[d]	–	(£1,000)	–	–	(£1,000)
Revaluation of land and building	–	–	£46,000	–	£46,000
Transfer[e]	–	–	(£12,000)	£12,000	–
Profit for 2011 after tax[f]	–	–	–	£28,000	£28,000
Dividend paid	–	–	–	(£20,000)	(£20,000)
Balance c/f	£360,000	£29,000	£84,000	£128,000	£601,000

(a) The technique to be used is to start with the bottom line and then to work upwards to the top.
(b) This is the most difficult step. Before making the new issue of £200,000 on 1 September there were £160,000 shares (i.e. £360,000 – £200,000). That number of shares was reached after giving a bonus of 1 for every 3, i.e. every four shares held after getting the bonus had three before and got one free. Hence the bonus would have been £160,000 × $^1/_4$ = £40,000.
(c) 200,000 shares @ 125p = £250,000; £200,000 to Share capital and the remainder to Share premium.
(d) Expenses of issue can be and should be written off from Share premium.
(e) Realised portion of revaluation gain is transferred to Retained earnings.
(f) Profit after tax is £39,000 less £11,000.

Multiple choice questions

Limited company as a form of business organisation

9.1 Which of the following will *not* be the most compelling reason for investing in a limited company rather than in a partnership?

(a) Limitation of liability

(b) Absence of confidentiality of information on its performance and position

(c) Divorce of management from ownership

(d) Perpetual succession

9.2 Which one or more of the following would you consider to be among the disadvantages of forming a limited company?

(a) Legal control and stringent requirements that have to be complied with

(b) The need to entrust control and decisions to a few

(c) Restrictions on return of capital if in excess of company's requirements

(d) The ease with which the share of ownership could be disposed of

w	a, b & c	
x	b, c & d	
y	a, c & d	
z	c & d	

9.3 Which of the following statements contained in the Articles of Association of Caves would identify it as a private limited company rather than a public limited company?

(a) The liability of each member is limited

(b) The company shall have not less than two directors, each holding office for five years

(c) To qualify for election as a director a member shall own not less than 1,000 shares

(d) A member shall not transfer the shares to another without offering it first to the directors

9.4 As at 31 March 2011 M plc has in issue 100 million ordinary shares of £1 each, 80p called up. On that day Terry paid 120p per share to buy 4,000 ordinary shares from Lester. In the event M plc becomes insolvent and is unable to meet its debts in full, what is the maximum Terry may be required to pay from his personal resources?

a	£ Nothing	
b	£800	
c	£4,000	
d	£2,000	

Shares and debentures

9.5 Which of the following statements is incorrect?

(a) In a company liquidation preference shares are entitled to priority return of capital

(b) Normally preference shares have no votes at meetings of shareholders

(c) Preference shares are always cumulative, even if the name does not confirm the position

(d) Preference shares have priority right to receive dividend

9.6 Which of the following statements is correct?

(a) Ordinary shares could be paid dividend even when a company has negative retained earnings

(b) Debentures will not receive interest in a year when the company makes an operating loss

(c) Preference shares will get dividend only when ordinary shares too receive them

(d) Preference shares and debentures have priority right for a reward over ordinary shares

Share issue

9.7 The share capital of the company consisted of one million shares of £1 each. Those were issued for £1.50, for each of which £1 has been paid. The Statement financial position would refer to this as:

(a) The share capital of the company taken up by subscribers
(b) The issued capital of the company
(c) The paid-up capital of the company
(d) The called-up share capital of the company

9.8 £120,000 recorded in the Cash Book upon issuing 100,000 ordinary shares of £1 each should be credited to which account or accounts?

(a) To a Suspense account
(b) To the Share capital account
(c) £100,000 to the Share capital account and £20,000 to the Share premium account
(d) To the Share premium account

9.9 £360,000, being the proceeds of issuing 600,000 Ordinary shares of 50p each, has been posted from the Cash Book to the credit of the Share capital account. How should this error be corrected?

(a) Dr Cash account £360,000, Cr Share capital account £300,000 and Cr Share premium £60,000
(b) Dr Suspense account £360,000, Cr Share capital a/c £300,000 and Cr Share premium £60,000
(c) Dr Share capital account £300,000, Cr Share premium account £360,000
(d) Dr Share capital account £60,000, Cr Share premium £60,000

9.10 X plc offered for issue ten million ordinary shares of £1 each at 120p per share. Applications were received, however, for only eight million shares and the directors proceeded to allot the shares applied for. Expenses of the issue amounted to £3,000. X plc availed itself of section 610 of the Companies Act, 2006. What will be the balance in the Share premium account, after these transactions are accounted for?

a	£2,000,000	
b	£1,600,000	
c	£1,597,000	
d	£1,997,000	

9.11 Y plc issued 800,000 ordinary shares of 20p each at 25p each. At the point of issue all shares were fully called up. However, by the year-end £15,000 due on the share issue was yet to be received. What will be the amount reported as balance in the company's Share capital account?

a	£200,000	
b	£160,000	
c	£145,000	
d	£185,000	

9.12 £15,000 still to be received, by the year-end, out of the total amount receivable from a share issue should be reported on that company's financial statements as:

(a) An income in the Statement of income
(b) An asset on the Statement of financial position
(c) A loss on the Statement of income
(d) A liability on the Statement of financial position

9.13 The balance appearing on the Ordinary share capital account, at any point of time, is:

(a) The called-up capital of the company ☐
(b) The issued capital of the company ☐
(c) The paid-up capital of the company ☐
(d) The so far called-up value of the number of its shares already in issue ☐

9.14 Z plc allotted one million shares of 50p each, as 35p called up per share, requiring an immediate payment of 45p per share. Accounting entries to record the allotment are:

(a) Dr Share allotment £450,000; Cr Share capital £350,000 and Cr Share premium £100,000 ☐
(b) Dr Share capital £350,000; Dr Share premium £100,000 and Cr Cash £450,000 ☐
(c) Dr Share allotment £350,000; Cr Share capital £250,000 and Cr Share premium £100,000 ☐
(d) Dr Share allotment £500,000; Cr Share capital £400,000 and Cr Share premium £100,000 ☐

9.15 For which one or more of the following reasons could a balance in the share premium be applied?

(a) To issue bonus shares
(b) For distribution to shareholders as dividend
(c) To write down the value of assets, particularly when they are impaired
(d) To write off expenses of and commission on issuing the same shares

w	a & b	
x	b & c	
y	a & d	
z	c & d	

9.16 For which one or more of the following reasons does company law attempt to protect the balance in the Share premium account by specifying the reasons for which alone it may be applied?

(a) It is part of the capital actually contributed by the shareholders
(b) It should be protected from erosion as part of the creditors' buffer
(c) It is not realised in cash
(d) It is immoral to allow a company to make profit by trading in its own shares

w	a & b	
x	b & c	
y	a & c	
z	c & d	

9.17 During the year a company used the balance it had in its Share premium account for all of the following purposes. Which one is correct?

(a) Write off expenses of company formation
(b) Write off the cost of issuing bonus shares
(c) Write off goodwill acquired when another business was bought as a going concern
(d) Write off expenses of issuing shares

w	a & b	
x	b & c	
y	a & d	
z	c & d	

9.18 The directors of a company are considering the use of a large balance in the Share premium account for the purposes listed below. Which among these planned actions is/are not legally permitted?

(a) Write off accumulated losses of prior years
(b) Write down the value of non-current assets to their recoverable amounts
(c) Distribute as dividends
(d) Cancel the calls yet to be made on the shareholders in respect of shares issued

w	a, b & c	
x	b, c & d	
y	a, c & d	
z	All four	

9.19 A company was able to acquire land with a market value of £6 million, by issuing four million ordinary shares of £1 each. When accounting for the acquisition of land and the issue of shares, how much should be credited to the Share premium account?

a	£6,000,000	
b	£2,000,000	
c	£4,000,000	
d	£10,000,000	

9.20 Q plc allotted ten million of its ordinary shares of £1 each, quoted in the market at 180p each, to acquire P Ltd as an ongoing business. The tangible assets of P Ltd had a market value on this date of £15 million. How much has Q plc paid to acquire P Ltd's goodwill?

a	£10,000,000	
b	£15,000,000	
c	£18,000,000	
d	£3,000,000	

Bonus issue/rights issue

9.21 Which of the following actions, when taken by a company, will not change the balance it has on its Share capital account?

(a) Make a fresh issue of shares for cash

(b) Make a rights issue of shares

(c) Receive from the shareholders the calls which were in arrears

(d) Make a call on the partly called-up shares already in issue

9.22 To raise additional finance a company offered its existing shareholders two ordinary shares of 50p each, for every five held by them, at a discounted price of 80p each. This is known as:

(a) Bonus issue of shares

(b) Share option

(c) Rights issue of shares

(d) Scrip issue of shares

9.23 At commencement of a year X plc had in issue 500,000 ordinary shares of £1 each fully called up, and a balance of £90,000 in the Share premium account. During the year they made a bonus issue of three for every twenty shares, using the balance in the Share premium account, and, thereafter, a rights issue of one for every five shares at 180p each. What will be the balances, by the year-end, in the company's Share capital account and Share premium account?

	Share capital	Share premium	
a	£630,000	£149,000	
b	£714,000	£15,000	
c	£690,000	£107,000	
d	£500,000	£90,000	

9.24 Which of the following will be the effect when a company makes a bonus issue of two for every five ordinary shares?

(a) The liquidity of the company will improve

(b) The company will have more capital employed (meaning total assets)

(c) Capital and reserves of the company will increase

(d) The amount of some items within Equity and reserves will change

9.25 Which one or more of the following will be the effect when a company makes a rights issue of one for every three ordinary shares?

(a) The company will have more investments
(b) The company's liquidity will improve
(c) The company's capital and reserves will increase
(d) The company's share premium balance may remain unchanged or increase

w	a, b & c	
x	b, c & d	
y	a, c & d	
z	All four	

9.26

Ordinary shares of 50p	£800,000
Share premium account	£120,000
Retained earnings	£195,500

The Capital and reserves of a company appear as shown on the left. On this day the directors of the company resolve to make a bonus issue of one for every five ordinary shares, using to maximum profits not available for distribution. Which of the following entries is correct?

(a) Dr Share premium £160,000, Cr Share capital £160,000
(b) Dr Share premium £120,000, Cr Share capital £120,000
(c) Dr Retained earnings £160,000, Cr Share capital £160,000
(d) Dr Share premium £120,000, Dr Retained earnings £40,000, Cr Share capital £160,000

9.27

Ordinary shares of 50p	£800,000
Share premium account	£120,000
Retained earnings	£195,500

The Capital and reserves of a company appear as shown on the left. On this day the directors of the company resolve to make a bonus issue of one for every five ordinary shares, for the purpose of enlarging the capital base of the company. Which of the following entries is correct?

(a) Dr Share premium £160,000, Cr Share capital £160,000
(b) Dr Share premium £120,000, Cr Share capital £120,000
(c) Dr Retained earnings £160,000, Cr Share capital £160,000
(d) Dr Share premium £120,000, Dr Retained earnings £40,000, Cr Share capital £160,000

9.28 N plc, with an issued capital of £500,000, in ordinary shares of 20p each, made a rights issue of one for every ten. All rights were taken up. £75,000 received on the issue has been posted from the Cash Book, £50,000 to the credit of Share capital account and the remainder to the credit of a Suspense account. Which of the following entries are needed to correct the error?

(a) Dr Suspense account £25,000, Cr Share premium account £25,000
(b) Dr Bank account £75,000, Cr Share capital account £50,000, Cr Suspense account £25,000
(c) Dr Share premium account £25,000, Cr Suspense account £25,000
(d) Dr Suspense account £25,000, Dr Share capital account £50,000, Cr Bank account £75,000

Financial statements of companies

9.29 The year-end Trial Balance of Quin plc reports £400,000 8% Loan notes (issued 2004) and £16,000 as interest paid. In this regard identify the amounts to be reported as expense in the Statement of income for the year ended 31.12.2011 and as current liability on the Statement of financial position.

	Interest expense	Current liability	
a	£16,000	£32,000	
b	£32,000	£32,000	
c	£32,000	£16,000	
d	£48,000	£16,000	

9.30 Epsilon plc had in issue £400,000 6% Debentures as at 31 March 2010 and on 31 December 2010 redeemed £300,000 of these debentures at 10% premium. Interest on debentures was paid annually in arrears on 31 December. No new debentures were issued. Calculate the interest expense in the year to 31 March 2011.

a	£6,000	
b	£32,500	
c	£19,500	
d	£24,000	

9.31 Clinton plc depreciates machinery at 30% per annum, on the reducing balance method, time apportioning for the nearest months of usage. As at 31.12.2010 machinery costing £720,000 was reported on the balance sheet at £485,600. A machine acquired for £120,000 on 1 July 2009 was sold on 30 September 2011 for £54,000. With regard to machinery, identify the items that would appear on their Statement of income for the year ended 31 December 2011.

	Depreciation	Disposal gain/loss	
a	£140,325	£1,335 loss	
b	£176,325	£17,400 loss	
c	£125,745	£1,335 loss	
d	£140,325	£17,400 loss	

9.32 The commercial exploitation of a product commenced on 1 January 2009. The development cost relating to that product, amortised over five years from that date using the sum of the years' digits method, was reported as £360,000 as at 31 December 2010. What is the amortisation in the year ended 31 December 2011?

a	£120,000	
b	£180,000	
c	£72,000	
d	£96,000	

9.33 Rocky plc, engaged in retailing consumer durables, received £30,000 as dividend from the investments it holds in other companies. This should be reported in current year's financial statements as:

(a) Addition to Retained earnings brought forward in the Statement of changes in equity

(b) As an income after identifying profit from operations, in the Statement of income

(c) As a deduction from administration expenses in the Statement of income

(d) As addition to Equity and reserves total in the Statement of financial position

9.34 A debit balance appearing on the Trial Balance as taxation has been identified as the under-provision for tax relating to the previous year's profit. This amount should be included in the current year's financial statements of a company as:

(a) Part of administrative expenses in the Statement of income

(b) Part of the tax expense reported in the current year's Statement of income

(c) A deduction from the subtotal of Equity and reserves on the Statement of financial position

(d) A deduction from Retained earnings brought forward, in the Statement of changes in equity

9.35 The year-end Trial Balance of Aroma plc reports a debit balance of £4,800 described as taxation. This amount represents an under-provision for previous year's taxation. Taxation on current year's profit is estimated at £72,800. Identify taxation expense to be reported in the current year's Statement of income and, as current liability, in the corresponding Statement of financial position.

	Tax expense	Tax liability	
a	£72,800	£68,000	
b	£68,000	£72,800	
c	£72,800	£77,600	
d	£77,600	£72,800	

9.36 The year-end Trial Balance of Flavour plc reports a credit balance of £1,500 described as taxation. This represents an over-provision for previous year's taxation. Tax on the current year's profit is estimated as £58,200. Identify the taxation expense to be included in current year's Statement of income and, as current liability, in the corresponding Statement of financial position.

	Tax expense	Tax liability	
a	£58,200	£59,700	
b	£59,700	£58,200	
c	£56,700	£58,200	
d	£58,200	£58,200	

9.37 The Trial Balance as at 31 December 2011 reports a debit balance of £3,000 identified as taxation and a credit balance of £27,500 as deferred taxation. The debit balance in the taxation account is the amount by which tax paid in respect of 2010 exceeded the amount provided when that year's financial statements were prepared. Tax on profits in 2011 is estimated at £84,500, while the taxable temporary difference as at 31 December is £98,500. The company pays tax at 20%. Identify the tax expense to be stated in the Statement of income for the year 2011 and the tax liability to be reported in the Statement of financial position as at 31 December 2011.

	Taxation			
	Expense	Current liability	Deferred tax	
a	£73,700	£84,500	£19,700	
b	£79,700	£84,500	£19,700	
c	£84,500	£89,300	£27,500	
d	£95,300	£84,500	£35,300	

9.38 Tax in respect of 2010, accounted for at £148,500, was settled on 1 October 2011 paying £154,400. Tax on the profits in 2011 is estimated at £179,000. As at 31 December 2011 the tax base is £75,800 lower than the written-down value of the corresponding assets. A balance of £18,400 is available in the Deferred tax account. Tax rate applicable is 25%. Identify the tax expense to be included in the Statement of income for 2011 and the tax liability to be reported in the Statement of financial position as at 31 December 2011.

	Taxation			
	Expense	Current liability	Deferred tax	
a	£185,450	£179,000	£18,950	
b	£172,550	£179,000	£17,850	
c	£179,000	£148,500	£18,400	
d	£203,850	£327,500	£37,350	

9.39 Current year's depreciation charge relating to Equipment used for designing products should be included as an expense in the current year's Statement of income, within which of the headings listed below?

(a) Within Administrative expenses

(b) Within Distribution cost

(c) Within Cost of sales

(d) Within Other operating expenses

9.40 A company had to pay £15 million in respect of customers' claims for injuries suffered from goods manufactured and sold in the previous year. When preparing the financial statements for the previous year the company was not aware of it, nor did they provide for these damages. How should the company report the amount paid?

(a) In the current year's Statement of income, describing it as an extraordinary item

(b) In the Statement of changes in equity as a deduction from balance brought forward

(c) In the current year's Statement of income, included as part of Administration expenses

(d) On the Statement of financial position as a deduction from the total of Equity and reserves

9.41 The cost of dividend payable on redeemable preference shares should be included:

(a) As a deduction in the Statement of changes in equity

(b) In the Statement of income as a deduction prior to identifying profit from operations

(c) In the Statement of income before identifying the profit before tax

(d) In the Statement of income after identifying profit after tax

9.42 Which of the following would you not include within the heading Equity and reserves in a company's Statement of financial position?

(a) Revaluation reserve
(b) Share premium account
(c) Redeemable preference shares
(d) Dividend declared

w	a & d	
x	b & d	
y	a & c	
z	c & d	

9.43 To enable stakeholders to make informed decisions, which of the following needs to be reported separately, preferably on the face of the published Statement of income, assuming the amounts are material?

(a) Amount written off as impairment loss of a non-current asset
(b) Profit relating to an activity which has been discontinued in the year
(c) Loss on disposal of machinery
(d) Reversal (no longer needed) of a provision for a customer's claim for damages

w	b and c	
x	a, b & d	
y	a, c & d	
z	All four	

9.44 Which one or more of the following would you report as a liability on a Statement of financial position?

(a) Redeemable preference shares
(b) Retained earnings
(c) Dividend declared
(d) Loan notes

w	a, b and c	
x	b, c & d	
y	a, c & d	
z	All four	

9.45 Which one or more of the following items will be included in the Statement of changes in equity for the year ended 30 September 2011?

(a) Preference dividend paid
(b) Ordinary dividend declared
(c) Backlog depreciation arising because of a change of policy
(d) Gain on revaluation of a non-current asset

w	a and b	
x	b and c	
y	a, c & d	
z	b, c and d	

9.46 The Share capital account of the company reports a balance of £500,000 reporting ordinary shares of 20p each. Directors have declared an interim dividend of 5p per share. What is the amount of the dividend to be accounted for?

a	£125,000	
b	£25,000	
c	£50,000	
d	£75,000	

9.47 The following are particulars of dividends proposed, declared and paid to ordinary shareholders:

January 2011: paid £30,000 as second interim for 2010, declared in December 2010
April 2011: paid £90,000 final for 2010, proposed in December 2010, declared in March 2011
August 2011: paid £45,000 first interim for 2011
December 2011: declared £20,000 as second interim dividend for the year ending 31 December 2011
December 2011: proposed £120,000 final dividend for 2011
January 2012: paid £20,000 as second interim for 2011.

Identify the amount you would include as dividend in the Statement of change in equity for the year ended 31 December 2011 and as liability in the Statement of financial position.

	Equity statement	Balance sheet	
a	£305,000	£140,000	
b	£155,000	£50,000	
c	£185,000	£50,000	
d	£155,000	£20,000	

9.48 When preparing the financial statements for the year a company has included the following in the Statement of changes in equity. Identify the incorrect one.

(a) Ordinary dividend paid

(b) Preference dividend paid

(c) Correction of prior period error

(d) Backlog adjustment arising from a change of policy

9.49 The Development cost account appearing on the year-end Trial Balance includes research expenses of £312,500. £280,000 of this amount had been incurred in prior years. Which of the following is the correct accounting entry for correcting this error?

(a) Dr Research expenses a/c £312,000, Cr Development cost a/c £312,000

(b) Dr Statement of income £32,500, Dr Changes in equity £280,000, Cr Development cost a/c £312,500

(c) Dr Statement of income £312,500, Cr Development cost a/c £312,500

(d) Dr Statement of changes in equity £312,500, Cr Development cost a/c £312,500

9.50 Which one or more of the following is a company obliged to disclose when preparing financial statements for publication?

(a) Depreciation written off

(b) Particulars as well as the impact of any change in accounting policy

(c) Issued capital of the company

(d) Final dividend proposed

w	a, b & c	
x	a, c & d	
y	b, c & d	
z	All four	

Answers to multiple choice questions

9.1: b 9.2: w 9.3: d 9.4: b 9.5: a 9.6: d 9.7: d 9.8: c 9.9: d 9.10: c 9.11: b 9.12: b 9.13: d 9.14: a 9.15: y 9.16: w 9.17: y 9.18: z 9.19: b 9.20: d 9.21: c 9.22: c 9.23: c 9.24: d 9.25: x 9.26: d 9.27: c 9.28: a 9.29: c 9.30: c 9.31: a 9.32: b 9.33: b 9.34: b 9.35: d 9.36: c 9.37: b 9.38: a 9.39: c 9.40: b 9.41: c 9.42: z 9.43: z 9.44: y 9.45: x 9.46: a 9.47: d 9.48: b 9.49: b 9.50: z

Progressive questions

PQ 9.1 Allotment of shares

Genus plc invited application for ten million ordinary shares of £1 each, stipulating that it should receive 20p per share with the application, 70p more per share should be paid at the point the shares are allotted. A final call of 20p per share will be made on a future date. Applications were received for twelve million shares. Those for two million were rejected and the amounts received from them refunded in full. Others were allotted shares on 14 March 2010. By the year-end, 31 December 2010, £39,550 due on the allotment was still to be received.

Required: Set out the Application and allotment account, the Share capital account and the Share premium account recording these transactions and show how they will be reported on the Statement of financial position as at 31 December 2010.

PQ 9.2 Financial statements for internal use – a trading company

Titbits Ltd extracted its year-end Trial Balance as shown on the right and informs you that:

(a) Cost of goods remaining unsold at year-end cost £512,450. Goods costing £18,400 distributed free for sales promotion have not been accounted for.
(b) Besides debenture interest, salaries £11,540 and audit fees £6,000 remain unpaid.
(c) Buildings are depreciated at 2% per annum, using the straight-line method and assuming that one-third of the cost relates to land which is not depreciated. Vehicles are depreciated at 30% per annum on the reducing balance method.
(d) Rent is agreed at £2,000 per month.
(e) 30% of salaries and wages and 20% of telephone, postage, electricity relates to selling and distribution activity.
(f) Income tax on the year's profit is estimated at £112,000.

Required:
Prepare for internal use the Statement of Income for the year ended 30 June 2011 and the Statement of financial position as at that date.

Trial Balance as at 30 June 2011		
	£	£
Ordinary shares of 50p each	–	300,000
Share premium account	–	30,000
Land and buildings at cost	840,000	–
Motor vehicles at cost	180,000	–
Accumulated depreciation to 30.6.2010		
Buildings	–	135,450
Motor vehicles	–	81,000
Sales	–	4,428,200
Inventory – 30 June 2010	428,620	–
Rent	30,000	–
Salaries and wages	124,560	–
8% Debentures	–	400,000
Receivables and payables	562,400	494,640
Advertising	24,400	–
Interim dividend	12,000	–
Telephone, postage, electricity	18,440	–
Cash and bank balance	12,550	–
Retained earnings b/f	–	348,780
Debenture interest paid	16,000	–
Purchases	3,936,500	–
Sales commission	32,600	–
	6,218,070	6,218,070

PQ 9.3 Financial statements for internal use – a manufacturing company

Benham Ltd has in issue six million shares of 50p each, issued at 60p each. Apart from the balances in the Share capital and Share premium accounts, the remaining account balances extracted as at 31 March 2011 have been listed on the right. You are further informed:

(a) Cost of inventory as at 31.3.2011 was £398,000.
(b) Premises have been rented for £5,000 per month and a third of it used for production activity.
(c) A vehicle was acquired for £60,000 on 1 January 2011.
(d) Machinery is depreciated at 5% per annum using the straight-line method; and vehicles at 20% per annum on the reducing balance method.
(e) A debt of £12,000 is to be written off and the allowance for doubtful debts adjusted to cover 5% of remaining receivables.
(f) Reported in the list as taxation is the under-provision for tax relating to previous year. Current year's tax is estimated at £29,000. Ignore deferred tax.
(g) A dividend of 2p per share declared at the year-end has not been accounted for.

	£'000
Machinery at cost	2,800
Motor vehicles at cost	920
Accumulated depreciation – 31 March 2010	
Machinery	420
Motor vehicles	380
Purchases	2,385
Trade receivables	972
Allowance for doubtful debts	32
Rent	48
Staff salary	346
Trade payables	398
Advertising	74
Interest paid	4
Cash and bank balance	11
Bank overdraft	41
Inventory – 31 March 2010	212
Taxation account (debit)	9
Sales	3,282
Retained earnings b/f (credit)	176
Returns inwards	44
Administrative expenses	194
Carriage inwards	21
Investments	340
Dividend income	51

Required:
Prepare for internal use the Statement of income for the year ended 31 March 2011 along with the Statement of changes in equity as well as the Statement of financial position as at 31 March 2011.

PQ 9.4 Financial statements for internal use (CIMA amended)

ABC Ltd extracted its year-end Trial Balance as shown below. You are further informed:

Trial Balance as at 31.3.2011		
	£	£
Freehold land at cost	60,000	–
Buildings at cost	50,000	–
Plant and equipment at cost	120,000	–
Motor vehicles at cost	32,000	–
Accumulated depreciation:		
Buildings	–	20,000
Plant and equipment	–	74,000
Motor vehicles	–	16,800
Inventory – 1 April 2010	74,000	–
Receivables/payables	122,500	99,800
Cash at bank	3,500	–
Sales (all on credit)	–	249,760
Purchases (all on credit)	134,630	–
Returns inwards/outwards	12,900	4,875
Discount allowed/received	3,200	1,850
Admin. expenses	22,150	–
Selling/distribution expenses	6,900	–
Ordinary shares of £1 each	–	100,000
Retained earnings	–	69,695
Suspense account	–	5,000
	641,780	641,780

(a) A vehicle acquired for £14,000 and written down to £6,000 by 31.3.2010 was sold on that day for £5,000. The disposal has not been accounted for other than posting the proceeds to a Suspense account.

(b) Administrative expenses include £4,000, the amount by which tax paid on previous year's profit exceeded the amount provided for.

(c) Cost of year-end inventory was £124,875.

(d) As at the year-end adjustments need to be made as follows:

	Accruals	Prepayments
Admin. expenses	£4,500	£12,000
Distribution costs	£5,300	£8,000

(e) Depreciation should be provided for as:

Buildings at 4% p.a. on cost

Plant and equipment at 20% p.a. on cost

Vehicles at 25% p.a. – reducing balance method.

(f) Tax on the profit earned in the year ended 31 March 2011 is estimated at £15,000.

Required: Prepare for internal use the Statement of income for the year ended 31 March 2011, together with the Statement of changes in equity and the Statement of financial position as at 31.3.2011.

PQ 9.5 Financial statements for publication (from ACCA, CAT 6 amended)

Trial Balance as at 31.5.2011		
	£'000	£'000
Revenue	–	3,500
Discounts received	–	80
Discounts allowed	70	–
Bank balance	147	–
Buildings at cost	1,040	–
Plant at cost	1,200	–
Accumulated depreciation – 1.6.2010		
Buildings	–	160
Plant	–	400
Land at cost	345	–
Purchases	2,170	–
Returns inwards	15	–
Returns outwards	–	17
Heating and lighting	270	–
Admin. expense	60	–
Trade payables	–	1,030
Trade receivables	700	–
Carriage inwards	105	–
Wages and salaries	250	–
10% Loan notes	–	580
General reserve	–	35
Allowance for doubtful debts	–	30
Directors' remuneration	60	–
Retained earnings	–	115
Ordinary shares £1	–	800
Inventory – 1.6.2010	515	–
Share premium a/c	–	200
	6,947	6,947

The Trial Balance of Adnett Ltd is shown on the left.

Additional information:

(a) Cost of closing inventory is £560,000.

(b) There are wages and salaries to be paid of £42,000.

(c) Loan notes interest has not been paid in the year.

(d) Allowance for doubtful debts is to be increased to £40,000.

(e) Plant is to be depreciated at 25% p.a. using the reducing balance method.

(f) Buildings are depreciated at 5% p.a. on cost, allocated as 25% to cost of sales, 50% to distribution cost and 25% to administrative expenses.

(g) On 1 August 2010 Adnett acquired and absorbed another business as a going concern. Adnett paid £85,000 for goodwill and £35,000 for inventory. Acquisition was paid for by the issue of 100,000 ordinary shares of £1 each. The transaction has not yet been recorded in the books of Adnett. As at 31 May 2011 the fair value of goodwill was £68,000.

(h) During May 2011 a bonus issue of one for five was made to ordinary shareholders. This has not been entered in the books. The Share premium account is to be used for this purpose.

(i) Directors have declared a dividend of 3p per share on ordinary shares and have decided to transfer £35,000 from the profits of the company to general reserves.

(j) Tax on profits for the year ended 31 May 2011 is estimated at £70,000.

(k) Expenses are to be apportioned as:

	Cost of sales	Distribution cost	Administration expenses
Discount allowed/received	–	–	100%
Heating and lighting	40%	20%	40%
Wages and salaries	50%	25%	25%
Goodwill impairment	–	–	100%

Required:

(a) Prepare, for external use, the Statement of income for the year ended 31 May 2011 and the Statement of financial position as at that date.

(b) Briefly explain the accounting treatment for purchased goodwill.

PQ 9.6 Financial statements for publication (ACCA amended)

Trial Balance as at 31 December 2011		
	£'000	£'000
Administrative expenses	850	
Interest on loan notes	25	
Distribution expenses	346	
Directors emoluments	150	
Purchases	4,329	
Sales	–	8,900
Rates and insurance	350	–
Dividend paid	46	–
Ordinary shares – £1	–	400
10% Preference shares – £1	–	600
Revaluation reserve	–	650
Retained earnings	–	550
5% Loan notes	–	1,000
Goodwill	300	–
Land and buildings	4,800	–
Accumulated depreciation – building	–	1,750
Plant and machinery	1,500	–
Accumulated depreciation – plant	–	600
Inventory	2,124	–
Trade receivables/payables	1,500	1,750
Bank balance	200	–
Allowance for doubtful debts	–	100
Share premium account	–	180
Deferred taxation	–	40
	16,520	16,520

The year-end Trial Balance of Cheapstake plc, prepared by your predecessor, is shown on the left. You are informed:

(i) The credit control department advises that:
- ~ a debt of £25,000 should be written off;
- ~ allowance should be increased by 50%;
- ~ a debt of £15,000, previously written off, should be accrued.

(ii) Goodwill acquired when the business started is impaired by £120,000.

(iii) Inventory on 31.12.2011 is £1,950,000.

(iv) The buildings are depreciated at 10% per annum and plant and machinery at 20% per annum on cost. The land and buildings are subject to revaluation every three years. The review on 31.12.2011 reduces the value of land and buildings by £300,000. The balance in the Revaluation reserve is gains on revaluation of land and buildings. Assume that a third of the value relates to land.

(v) Allocate as follows

	Distribution %	Administration %
Rates and insurance	50	50
Building depreciation	40	60
Machine depreciation	75	25

(vi) Tax, at 20%, is estimated on current year's profit, at £105,000. The tax base as at 31 December 2011 is £140,000 lower than the written-down value of the corresponding assets.

(vii) There is an outstanding claim of £200,000 from a customer relating to supply of faulty goods. This is not covered by insurance. The outcome is uncertain and the amount of the damage is not quantifiable.

(viii) The amount reported as dividend paid includes one-half of the current year's preference dividend.

Required:

(a) Prepare for publication the Statement of income for the year ended 31 December 2011, together with the Statement of changes in equity and the Statement of financial position as at that date.

(b) Write a note explaining your treatment of information stated in (vii) above.

PQ 9.7 Financial statements for publication – advanced

Trial Balance as at 31 December 2011		
	£'000	£'000
Land and buildings	2,400	–
Plant and equipment	960	–
Motor vehicles	240	–
Accumulated depreciation – 31.12.2010		
Plant and equipment	–	360
Motor vehicles	–	96
Receivables/payables	528	492
Salaries and wages	138	–
Dividend received	–	15
Directors' emoluments	49	–
Rent and rates	27	–
Sales revenue	–	3,284
Trade investments	96	–
Accumulated profit b/f	–	704
Telephone and postage	45	–
Deferred tax	–	21
Purchases	1,594	–
Return inwards	24	–
Allowance for doubtful debts	–	11
Taxation	9	–
Admin. expenses	124	–
Advertising	54	–
6% Redeemable preference shares £1	–	200
Inventory – 31.12.2010	312	–
Ordinary shares – £1 each	–	1,200
Share premium account	–	240
Cash and bank balance	23	–
	6,623	6,623

Year-end Trial Balance has been extracted from the books of Phoenix plc as stated on the left.

You are informed as follows:

(a) Cost of unsold goods, identified as £386,000, includes goods costing £40,000 used for display. These can be sold for only £27,000 provided £3,000 is incurred on restoring their condition.

(b) Land and buildings, though acquired in January 2001, were not depreciated. Directors wish to depreciate buildings assuming that 75% of the cost relates to buildings which are expected to remain in use for 50 years.

(c) £8,000 of receivables is to be written off and the allowance adjusted to cover 5% of receivables.

(d) Expenses in the year need to be adjusted as follows:

	Prepaid	Accrued
Rent and rates	£3,000	–
Salaries and wages	–	£22,000
Directors' emoluments	–	£11,000
Audit fees	–	£10,000

(e) Expenses are to be functionally allocated as follows:

	Cost of sales %	Distribution Cost %	Admin. expense %
Salaries and wages	50	10	40
Rent and rates	–	–	100
Building depreciation	75	25	–
Bad debts	–	100	–

(f) Plant and equipment are to be depreciated at 10% using the reducing balance method, while motor vehicles, including one acquired for £60,000 on 1 July 2011, are depreciated at 20% using the straight-line method.

(g) The amount stated as taxation is the under-provision for the previous year. Current tax, at 20%, is estimated at £179,000; while the taxable temporary difference at the year-end is £120,000.

(h) A bonus issue of one for every four shares was made on 4 January 2011, the cost being written off from the Share premium, followed by a cash issue of 200,000 ordinary shares at 120p each.

(i) A dividend of 5p per share, declared by directors on 31 December, is yet to be accounted for.

Required: Prepare for publication:

(a) A Statement of comprehensive income for the year ended 31 December 2011.

(b) A Statement of changes in equity, for the same period, tracing all movements in equity, and

(c) a Statement of financial position as at 31 December 2011.

Test questions

Test 9.1 Accounting for share issue

On application	250p
On allotment	350p
On first Call	300p
On final Call	200p

Bravo plc invited application for 10,000 ordinary shares of £10 each, payable as stated in the box on the right. By 31 January 2010 applications were received for 16,000 shares. Applications for 4,000 shares, from non-residents, were rejected and application money refunded. On 1 February allotment was made pro rata to other applicants, excess received on application being retained against amounts due on allotment. The first call was made on 1 April 2010. By 30 June 2010:

(a) All amounts receivable on allotment had been received except for the amount due on 1,000 shares that had been allotted.

(b) All amounts receivable on the first call had been received except for the amount due on 500 shares.

(c) The amount due on the final call had been received in advance from those to whom 1,200 shares had been allotted.

Required:

(a) Identify the amount reported in the Share capital account and explain what that amount represents.

(b) Explain the concept of share premium and what a company may apply it for.

(c) Set out the Application and allotment account, First call account, the Share capital account, the Share premium account and the Calls received in advance account, up to 30 June 2010.

(d) Show how the amounts received and receivable will be reported on the company's Statement of financial position as at 30 June 2010.

Test 9.2 Financial statements for internal use

The year-end Trial Balance of Global Ltd is set out on the right. Further information:

(a) Cost of closing inventory was £644,000.

(b) The Trial Balance failed to balance because a folio in the Purchases Day Book had been added as £226,000 instead of £248,000. The difference has been placed in a Suspense account.

(c) Furniture and vehicles are to be depreciated for the year at 5% and 20% per annum, using the straight-line method for furniture and reducing balance method for vehicles.

(d) Directors wish to write off a trade debt of £8,000 and to adjust the allowance to cover 5% of the remaining receivables.

(e) Rent is payable at £10,000 per month.

(f) £44,000 salaries and £3,000 advertising remain unpaid as at the year-end.

(g) Tax on current year's profit is estimated at £138,000.

(h) A dividend of 3p per share, declared by the directors, is yet to be accounted for.

Required: Prepare, for internal use, the Statement of income for the year ended 31 December 2011 and the Statement of financial position as at that date.

Trial Balance as at 31 December 2011

	£'000	£'000
Furniture (cost and depreciation)	640	130
Motor vehicles (cost and depreciation)	280	90
Inventory – 31.12.2010	542	–
Ordinary shares of £1 each	–	400
Share premium a/c	–	80
Purchases a/c	3,248	–
Return outwards	–	35
Rent a/c	140	–
Bank overdraft	–	34
Salaries and wages	314	–
Advertising	56	–
9% Debentures (issued 2009)	–	200
Stationery	21	–
Receivables/payables	648	494
Cash and bank balance	30	–
Interim dividend paid	20	–
Bad debts	11	–
Allowance for doubtful debts	–	39
Interest paid on debentures	9	–
Sales	–	4,241
Suspense a/c	22	–
Accumulated profit b/f	–	282
Sales commission	44	–
	6,025	6,025

Test 9.3 Statement of financial position for publication (ACCA amended)

Share capital – 50p each	£1,000,000
Share premium a/c	£400,000
Suspense a/c	£800,000
Accumulated profit	£7,170,000
Development cost	£570,000
Property, plant, equipment	£5,000,000
Accumulated depreciation – 31.12.2010	£1,000,000
Inventory – 31.12.2011	£3,900,000
Trade receivables	£3,400,000
Overdraft at bank	£100,000
Trade payables	£1,900,000
Allowance for doubtful debts	£100,000
6% Loan notes	£400,000

The balances listed on left are as at 31 December 2011 from the books of Abrador Ltd.

You are informed as follows:

(i) On 31 December 2011 the company issued for cash one million ordinary shares at a premium of 30p each. The proceeds have been posted from the Cash Book to a suspense account.

(ii) Profit for the year, identified without adjusting for information stated as iii, iv and v, is included within accumulated profit.

(iii) Depreciation should be provided on property, plant and equipment at 25% on the reducing balance method.

(iv) A debt of £400,000 should be written off and the allowance adjusted to 3% of receivables.

(v) Income tax on the current year's profit should be accounted for at £125,000.

Required: Prepare for publication the company's Statement of financial position as at 31.12.2011.

Test 9.4 Transfer to reserve, bonus issue and acquisition of a business

Trial Balance as at 30 September 2011		
	£'000	£'000
Land and buildings	2,400	–
Machinery	720	–
Equipment	450	–
Accumulated depreciation to 30.9.2010:		
Buildings	–	648
Machinery	–	360
Equipment	–	270
Directors' fees	78	–
Cash and bank	59	–
Retained earnings	–	291
Purchases	2,117	–
Administration expenses	192	–
Sales	–	3,433
Receivables/payables	496	284
Carriage inwards	74	–
General reserve	–	45
Salaries	296	–
Advertising	54	–
Deferred tax	–	29
Returns inwards	25	–
Allowance for doubtful debt	–	19
Interim dividend paid	45	–
Over-provision for tax	–	4
Rent received	–	30
Delivery expenses	44	–
Dividend received	–	15
Investments	112	–
Inventory – 30.9.2010	316	–
Ordinary shares of £1	–	1,500
6% Preference shares	–	400
Share premium a/c	–	150
	7,478	7,478

The year-end Trial Balance was extracted from the books of Sparrow Ltd as shown on the left.

You are informed as follows:

(a) Included within sales are goods invoiced at £16,000 in respect of which the customers have the option to return until a week after the year-end. These goods were invoiced at cost plus a third.

(b) Cost of inventory held as at 30 September 2011 was £385,000.

(c) A portion of the shop premises has been let out, at £3,000 per month, since 2007.

(d) Buildings are depreciated at 2% of cost per annum assuming that a quarter of the cost related to land which is not depreciated. Directors wish to report land and buildings at their current value which was identified, as at 1 October 2010, as £1 million for land and £1.6 million for the buildings.

(e) New machinery was acquired for £80,000 on 1 April 2011. Machinery is depreciated at 10% per annum using the reducing balance method.

(f) Equipment acquired on 1 October 2008 is depreciated using the sum of the years' digits method over five years.

(g) Tax on current year's profit is estimated at £79,000. Deferred tax needs to be accounted for at 20% of taxable temporary difference which, as at 30 September 2011, is identified at an amount of £180,000.

Required: Prepare for publication the Statement of income for the year ended 30 September 2011 and the Statement of financial position as at that date.

Test 9.5 Financial statements for publication (advanced)

Trial Balance as at 30.4.2012		
	£'000	£'000
Land at cost	1,200	–
Buildings at cost	600	–
Plant and equipment at cost	960	–
Brand names	450	–
Accumulated depreciation – 30.4.2011:		
Building	–	240
Plant and equipment	–	280
Interim dividend paid	60	
Receivables and payables	325	296
Taxation	–	8
Sales revenue	–	5,267
Distribution cost	294	–
Administrative expenses	526	–
Accumulated profit b/f	–	495
Cost of sale	3,283	–
Deferred tax	–	21
Inventory as at 30.4.2012	326	–
Ordinary shares of 50p each	–	1,200
Share premium account	–	240
Cash and bank balance	23	–
	8,047	8,047

Sinclair plc's year-end Trial Balance is stated on the left. The following information is provided:

(i) Directors have resolved to report land and buildings at current values and have ascertained the market values on 1 May 2011 of land and buildings as £3,000,000 and £900,000 respectively. From the date of revaluation buildings have an expected useful life of 30 years.

(ii) Plant and equipment are depreciated at 10% per annum on the reducing balance method; while brand names, acquired on 1 May 2008, are depreciated over a five-year period using the sum of the years' digits method. All depreciation is to be included within cost of sales.

(iii) Amount reported as taxation is the amount by which the amount set aside for the purpose exceeded the amount at which previous year's tax was settled. Current year's tax, at 20%, is estimated at £94,000; while the tax base is lower than the written-down value of corresponding assets by £180,000.

(iv) A cash issue of 100,000 ordinary shares was made at 75p each in May 2011 and on 30 April 2012 directors have declared a second interim dividend of 5p per share.

Required: For publication,

(a) The Statement of comprehensive income for the year ending 30 April 2012.

(b) The Statement of changes in equity tracing all movements with shareholders, and

(c) the Statement of financial position as at 30 April 2012.

Chapter 10

Incomplete records

By the end of this chapter

You should learn:	You should be able to:
■ To deal with incomplete records and single-entry situations	■ Either estimate the profit or loss in the accounting period
■ About the four rules that help in such situations	■ Or prepare financial statements in an incomplete records situation

10.1 What is an incomplete records situation?

Accountants use the expression *incomplete records* to refer to a situation where the accounting records, which had been maintained on the proper double-entry basis, have been partly destroyed (e.g. by fire, flood or deliberate action) so that it is no longer possible to extract a Trial Balance. An alternative situation where a Trial Balance cannot be extracted because accounting records were not maintained on the double-entry system is referred to as *single-entry*.

In either case, the approach to preparing the financial statements depends on the extent of the information that is available.

10.1.1 Where information is insufficient to prepare a Statement of income

There may be insufficient information to prepare a Statement of income which shows the income and expenses for the accounting period. In such a case we need to estimate the profit or loss by comparing the owner's equity at the commencement of the period with that at the end.

This is where we make use of the accounting equation Assets – Liabilities = Equity (see Chapter 4). If the owner's equity at commencement was £400,000 and it has become £600,000 by the end, the inference is that the business has made a profit of £200,000 (£600,000 – £400,000). The inference will be correct provided, during the period, the owner has not removed any business assets for personal use or introduced additional capital. If we assume further that the owner's drawings in the period were £36,000 and additional capital introduced was £50,000, the revised estimate of profit will be:

Equity at end	–	Equity at commencement	+	Drawings	–	Capital introduced	=	Profit
£600,000	–	£400,000	+	£36,000	–	£50,000	=	£186,000

Activity 10.1 Where information is insufficient to prepare financial statements

The tax authorities seek your assistance to estimate the profit made in the year ended 31 December 2011 by a retail shop belonging to Chris Jones. They inform you as follows:

(i) Chris has no income other than from his shop.

(ii) Considering the style and standard of living Chris's living expenses should be at least £1,500 per month.

(iii) The assets and liabilities of his shop are ascertained as stated on the right.

(iv) In June 2011 Chris introduced additional capital of £20,000 left to him by his late uncle.

As at 31 December		
	2010	2011
	£	£
Non-current assets at wdv	180,000	215,000
Inventory at cost	284,200	326,600
Trade receivables	16,500	21,400
Cash and bank balance	11,400	26,800
Trade payables	(165,800)	(158,500)

10.1.2 Where information is sufficient to prepare the financial statements

If we have more information so that, rather than estimate the profit, we are able to prepare both a Statement of income and a Statement of financial position, then we approach the situation as follows:

Step 1: Prepare a *statement of affairs* as at the commencement of the accounting period, identifying the capital at that date. A statement of affairs is similar to a Statement of financial position in that it lists the assets and liabilities with the difference representing the owner's capital. In accounting, the term Statement of financial position is used only where accounting records have been maintained on a double-entry basis and it lists the ledger account balances.

Step 2: Post the information to appropriate ledger accounts. Upon completing this step the records will be on a double-entry accounting basis.

Step 3: Account, by a pair of matching entries (i.e. on the double-entry basis), for every transaction and event during the accounting period that you have been able to identify.

Step 4: This step is necessary only if, after making use of all information, there remains a need to make estimates to prepare the financial statements. Make guesses as best as you can to prepare the Statement of income as well as the Statement of financial position.

10.2 Four rules to remember

When dealing with an incomplete records situation it helps to remember four rules:

1. The five classes of accounts fall within four boxes – (see diagram). Accounts reporting assets and expenses always have debit balances. Those reporting income, capital and liability have credit balances.

Debits	Credits
Asset	Liability/capital
Expense	Income

2. Unless it has been stated otherwise always assume that:
   - purchases and sales of goods (intended for sale) are on credit terms;
   - acquisition/disposal of assets is on cash terms.
3. Take good care to identify whether the information provided is:
   - a payment or expense (e.g. amount of rent paid or the rent payable for the period);
   - a receipt or income (e.g. the amount of income collected or the whole income earned).
4. When less than full information has been provided adopt the crossword puzzle mentality:
   - Identify how many letters (amounts) are needed to complete the word (account).
   - Make a guess only after all clues (information) provided have been fully used.

10.3 Illustration of how the four rules work

Let us illustrate the application of the four rules, assuming that Tim's Retail does not maintain its accounting records on the double-entry basis and that the assets and liabilities of the shop were ascertained on 30 June 2010 as stated on the right.

As at 30 June 2010	
	£'000
Non-current assets	400
Inventory at cost	120
Trade receivables	210
Cash	20
Trade payables	(190)

Step one is taken by presenting the information in the form of a Statement of affairs (see on the right) for the purpose of identifying Tim's capital on 30 June 2010 (commencement of the accounting period) as £560.

Step two is to open the (six) accounts needed to report the balances remembering the first rule, that the accounts reporting assets will each have a debit balance while the Trade payable account and the Capital account will each be reporting a credit balance.

Statement of affairs as at 30 June 2010	
	£'000
Non-current assets	400
Inventory	120
Trade receivables	210
Cash	20
Trade payables	(190)
Capital as at 30.6.2010	560

Step three is to account for every transaction on a double-entry basis. Let us assume that the information listed on the next page is all that has been identified. When accounting for the four transactions we have to bear in mind the second rule that, unless otherwise told, the non-current assets were acquired for cash (credit Cash account and debit the Asset account); whereas the purchases are made on credit terms (debit Purchases account and credit Trade payables account). When accounting for the third and the fourth transactions we have to remember the third rule. Rent reported is the expense (not payment) because £60,000 is the whole of the rental expense for the year. Hence £60,000 is accounted for by debiting the Rent (expense) account and crediting the Rent (liability) account. Transaction four, on the other hand, reports the amount paid (not whole of the expense) as salary. Hence the payment of £80 should be accounted for by crediting the Cash account and debiting Salary (expense) account. After recording each of the four transactions on the double-entry basis, the year-end balances are carried down in the respective ledger account, remembering that closing inventory is accounted for by a credit in the Statement of income and a debit in an asset account, which will appear on the Statement of financial position.

During the year ended 30 June 2011	
	£
1. Non-current assets bought	100
2. Purchases on credit	300
3. Rent payable for the year	60
4. Payment as salary	80
As at 30 June 2011:	
Non-current assets	450
Inventory at cost	190
Trade receivables	285
Cash in hand	30
Trade payables	210
Rent accrued	15
Salary accrued	40

Step four is to fill in the blanks in each account, making guesses as best as possible. For example, in the case of the Non-current asset account the missing item and the related amount can be identified as depreciation of £50. This can be done with equal ease also in the case of the Trade payables account as a cash payment of £280.

Non-current asset account

	£'000		£'000
Balance b/f	*400*	?	?
Cash a/c	100	Balance c/d	450
	500		500
Balance b/d	450		

Trade payables account

	£'000		£'000
?	?	*Balance b/f*	*190*
Balance c/d	210	Purchases	300
	490		490
		Balance b/d	210

The missing item and related amount can be found with equal ease in case of the Rent (liability) account (as cash paid of £45) and in the case of the Salary (expense) account as the total expense in that regard of £120 to be transferred to the Statement of income.

Rent (liability) account

	£'000		£'000
?	?	Rent (expense)	60
Balance c/d	15		
	60		60
		Balance b/d	15

Salary (expense) account

	£'000		£'000
Cash a/c	80	Statement of income	120
Salary accrued	40		
	120		120

In the case of the Trade receivables account, by contrast, guessing the missing items (as sales on the debit side and cash on the credit) would be easy, but guessing the amounts impossible because there are two amounts missing. If we find one then the other can be identified.

Trade receivables account

	£'000		£'000
Balance b/f	*210*	?	?
?	?	Balance c/d	285
Balance b/d	285		

One of these can be found (as £515 received from customers) by completing the Cash account. When this information is included in the Trade receivables account we can identify the other missing amount as credit sales for the year of £590.

Cash account

	£'000		£'000
Balance b/f	20	Non-current asset	100
?	?	Salary	80
		Payables	280
		Rent	45
		Balance c/d	30
	535		535
Balance b/d	30		

Trade receivables account

	£'000		£'000
Balance b/f	210	Cash a/c	515
?	?	Balance c/d	285
	800		800
Balance	285		

We now have all of the information that we require to prepare the financial statements for the year ended 30 June 2011 as follows:

Statement of income for the year ended 30 June 2011

	£'000	£'000
Sales		590
Inventory – opening	120	
Purchases	300	
Inventory – closing	(190)	(230)
Gross profit		360
Rent	60	
Depreciation	50	
Salary	120	230
Net profit		130

Statement of financial position as at 30 June 2011

	£'000	£'000
Non-current assets		450
Current assets:		
Inventory	190	
Trade receivables	285	
Cash in hand	30	505
		955

	£'000	£'000
Capital	560	
Profit	130	690
Current liabilities:		
Trade payables	210	
Salary accrued	40	
Rent accrued	15	265
		955

Activity 10.2 Preparing financial statements from incomplete records

Simon lists his assets and liabilities as shown on the right and provides the following information:

(i) Drawings by Simon £40,000

(ii) Payments to suppliers £1,731,600

(iii) Receipts from customers £2,160,000

(iv) Paid as salary £180,000

(v) Paid for other expenses £154,800

Required: Prepare the financial statements for 2011.

As at 31 December		
	2010	2011
	£	£
Non-current assets	96,400	112,800
Accumulated depreciation	(24,600)	(32,400)
	71,800	80,400
Inventory	234,500	252,800
Trade receivables	43,200	46,800
Bank balance	2,160	?
Trade payables	97,200	109,800

Activity 10.3 The need to distinguish between payments and expenses

On 11 January 2012 Betty assumed duties as accountant in Tongdean, a retail shop. The shop's owner provided her with the following information:

(i) The shop's assets and liabilities are listed on the right.

As at 31 December		
	2010	2011
	£	£
Non-current assets at wdv	240,000	284,000
Inventory at cost	112,400	138,200
Trade receivables	136,800	164,600
Cash and bank balance	12,600	15,400
Trade payables	62,500	77,800

(ii) During the year ended 31 December 2011:

Purchases were £486,200
Rent is agreed at £3,000 per month
£72,000 was paid as salary
£16,400 was paid as other expenses
Proprietor's drawings were £200 per week
Depreciation written off was £32,000
Non-current assets, written down to £60,000, were sold for £48,000.

(iii) As at 31 December 2011 salary (£8,000) and other expenses (£3,000) remain unpaid, while one month's rent had been prepaid.

Required: Prepare the financial statements for the year ended 31 December 2011.

Summary

- Incomplete records refer either to a situation where accounting records are partly lost or one where accounting records have not been maintained on the double-entry system.
- Where information is not sufficient to prepare financial statements, estimates of profit and loss are made.
- When dealing with an incomplete records situation compliance with certain procedural rules may help.

Suggested answers to activities

10.1 Where information is insufficient to prepare financial statements

As at 31 December		
	2010	2011
	£	£
Non-current assets	180,000	215,000
Inventory	284,200	326,600
Trade receivables	16,500	21,400
Cash and bank	11,400	26,800
Trade payables	(165,800)	(158,500)
Capital	326,300	431,300

Capital as at 31 December 2011	£431,300
Capital as at 31 December 2010	(£326,300)
Increase in capital in the year	£105,000
Add: Drawings @ £1,500 for 12 months	£18,000
Less: New capital introduced	(£20,000)
Estimated profit in the year	£103,000

10.2 Preparing financial statements from incomplete records

Statement of income – year ended 31 December 2011

	£	£
Sales		2,163,600
Inventory	234,500	
Purchases	1,744,200	
Inventory	(252,800)	(1,725,900)
Gross profit		437,700
Salaries	180,000	
Expenses	154,800	
Depreciation	7,800[b]	(342,600)
Net profit		95,100

Statement of financial position as at 31 December 2011

	£	£
Non-current assets		112,800
Accumulated depreciation		(32,400)
		80,400
Current assets:		
Inventories	252,800	
Receivables	46,800	
Cash and bank	39,360	338,960
		419,360

	£	£
Capital	254,460	
Net profit	95,100	
Drawings	(40,000)	309,560
Current liabilities:		
Payables		109,800
		419,360

Workings:

Statement of affairs as at 31.12.2010

	£
Non-current asset	96,400
Accumulated depreciation	(24,600)
	71,800
Inventory	234,500
Receivables	43,200
Cash/bank	2,160
Payables	(97,200)
Capital[a]	254,460

Cash account

	£		£
Balance b/f	2,160	Drawings	40,000
Receivables	2,160,000	Payables	1,731,600
		Salaries	180,000
		Expenses	154,800
		Non-current asset	16,400
		Balance[a]	39,360
	2,162,160		2,162,160
Balance b/d	39,360		

Trade receivables account

	£		£
Balance b/f	43,200	Cash Book	2,160,000
Sales[a]	2,163,600	Balance c/d	46,800
	2,206,800		2,206,800
Balance b/d	46,800		

Trade payables account

	£		£
Cash Book	1,731,600	Balance b/f	97,200
Balance c/d	109,800	Purchases[a]	1,744,200
	1,841,400		1,841,400
		Balance b/d	109,800

Non-current asset account

	£		£
Balance b/f	96,400		
Cash Book[a]	16,400	Balance c/d	112,800
	112,800		112,800
Balance b/d	112,800		

Notes:
(a) balancing figures
(b) Accumulated depreciation:
£32,400 – £24,600 = £7,800

10.3 The need to distinguish between payments and expenses

Statement of income for the year ended 31.12.2011

	£	£
Sales		727,300
Inventory	112,400	
Purchases	486,200	
Inventory	(138,200)	(460,400)
Gross profit		266,900
Salaries[b]	80,000	
Rent[c]	36,000	
Asset disposal[e]	12,000	
Expenses[d]	19,400	
Depreciation	32,000	(179,400)
Net profit		87,500

Statement of financial position as at 31.12.2011

	£	£
Non-current assets		284,000
Current assets:		
Inventory	138,200	
Receivables	164,600	
Prepaid rent	3,000	
Cash and bank	15,400	321,200
		605,200

	£	£
Capital	439,300	
Net profit	87,500	
Drawings	(10,400)	516,400
Current liabilities:		
Payables	77,800	
Salary accrued	8,000	
Expense accrued	3,000	88,800
		605,200

Workings:

Statement of affairs as at 31.12.2010

	£
Non-current asset	240,000
Inventory	112,400
Receivables	136,800
Cash/bank	12,600
Payables	(62,500)
Capital[a]	439,300

Cash account

	£		£
Balance b/f	12,600	Rent	39,000
Disposal	48,000	Salary	72,000
Receivable[a]	699,500	Expenses	16,400
		Drawings	10,400
		Non-current asset	136,000
		Payables	470,900
		Balance c/d	15,400
	760,100		760,100
Balance b/d	15,400		

Trade receivables account

	£		£
Balance b/f	136,800	Cash Book	699,500
Sales[a]	727,300	Balance c/d	164,600
	864,100		864,100
Balance b/d	164,600		

Trade payables account

	£		£
Cash Book[a]	470,900	Balance b/f	62,500
Balance c/d	77,800	Purchases	486,200
	548,700		548,700
		Balance b/d	77,800

Non-current asset account

	£		£
Balance b/f	240,000	Disposal	60,000
Cash Book	136,000	Depreciation	32,000
		Balance c/d	284,000
	376,000		376,000
Balance b/d	284,000		

Notes:
(a) Balancing figures
(b) Salaries: 72 + 8 = £80
(c) Rent: 39 paid – 3 prepaid = £36 expense
(d) Expense: 16.4 + 3 = £19.4
(e) Loss on asset disposal: 60,000 – 48,000 = £12,000

Multiple choice questions

Note: Questions 10.6, 10.7, 10.12 and 10.14 involve a knowledge of bank reconciliation which is dealt with in Chapter 15.

Estimation of profit or loss

10.1 The owner's capital in a business was £340,000 on 30 June 2011 and £215,000 a year earlier. In each of the following independent scenarios, given the stated amount of proprietor's drawings and capital introduced within the year, estimate the profit (P) or loss (L).

(a) Drawings during the year were £3,000 per month.

(b) During the year, no drawings; capital introduced was £9,000.

(c) Drawings were £40,000 and capital introduced £20,000.

(d) Drawings were £24,000 and capital introduced £150,000.

(x)		(y)		(z)	
£125,000 P		£161,000 P		£89,000 P	
£116,000 P		£125,000 P		£134,000 P	
£185,000 P		£165,000 P		£145,000 P	
£1,000 L		£251,000 P		£149,000 P	

10.2 Rupert owns a retail shop but does not maintain any accounting records. The Tax Inspector prepared a Statement of affairs for him on 30 June 2011 establishing his capital on that date as £426,500. Making a similar exercise one year later, his capital in the business was established at £596,800. Further inquiries reveal that:

(a) he has no other source of income;

(b) he must be spending not less than £2,000 per month on living;

(c) he educates his son at Harvard spending on average £1,000 per month;

(d) he paid £40,000 in the year for a personal car, selling the old one for £8,000.

What is your estimate of his business profit in the year?

a	£246,300	
b	£170,300	
c	£238,300	
d	£226,300	

Focus on identifying the sales revenue

10.3 Trade receivables as at 30 September 2011 were £24,800 and a year later £42,400. Identify the sales revenue during the year ended 30 September 2012, taking into account the following additional information provided in each of the following independent scenarios:

(a) The amount received from credit customers was £59,500.

(b) Amount received £52,800, debts written off £400 and sales returns £500.

(c) Sales received £49,400, cheques dishonoured £200, discount allowed £100.

(d) £55,680 was received from customers availing of 4% cash discount.

(x)		(y)		(z)	
£41,900		£59,500		£77,100	
£71,300		£70,400		£70,800	
£66,900		£67,300		£66,700	
£75,507		£75,600		£73,280	

10.4 Cash and bank balance of a shop on 31 December 2011 and a year prior to that were £11,200 and £14,500 respectively. During the year ended 31 December 2011 £4,800 was paid out in cash and £39,500 by cheque. Trade receivables were £41,500 on 31 December 2011 and £39,900 a year prior to that date. Taking into consideration the additional information provided in each of the following independent scenarios, identify the sales revenue in 2011.

(a) £3,000 was received from disposal of a non-current asset.

(b) £1,200 due from a customer was offset by contra.

(c) Drawings, not included in the cash payments, were £300 per month.

(d) A debt of £400 was written off and the Allowance for doubtful debts increased by £300.

(x)		(y)		(z)	
£39,600		£46,200		£45,600	
£50,400		£41,400		£43,800	
£46,200		£42,900		£52,800	
£43,300		£43,000		£42,700	

10.5 Jerry, owner of a retail shop, does not maintain proper accounting records. He seeks your assistance to calculate his sales revenue in the year. He habitually banks his daily takings intact, leaving a float of £100 to meet incidental expenses and after taking £20 per day for household expenses. Incidental expenses paid in cash, recorded in his diary, amounted to £26,640. He makes other payments always by cheque and the total cheque payments in the year amounted to £595,400. His bank balance at the beginning of the year was £29,400 and at the end £41,800. His trade receivables were £18,400 at commencement of the year and £22,900 at the end. What was his sales revenue in the year?

a	£646,240	
b	£646,340	
c	£638,860	
d	£638,960	

10.6 Morning Bakers have prepared a summary of their bank statement for the year ending 30 June 2012 as shown on the left. Deposits not cleared were £15,500 on 1.7.2011 and £9,500 a year later; while cheques not presented for payment amounted to £27,400 on 1.7.2011 and £3,000 a year later. All payments are always made by cheque and sales are always strictly on a cash basis. Identify the sales in the year.

Balance on 1.1	£72,450
Lodgements	£184,240
Cheques drawn	(£112,900)
Balance – 31.12	£143,790

a	£190,240	
b	£178,240	
c	£209,240	
d	£181,240	

10.7 In an attempt to identify the sales revenue in 2012 of Pauline's Confectionery, you have prepared a summary of her bank statements as shown on the left. Bank lodgements not cleared were £3,900 on 1.1 and £7,200 on 31.12. A cheque for £500 in payment of December rent is yet to be presented for payment. Pauline makes all her payments by cheque, apart from small incidental payments (amounting to £4,280 in the year) paid out of an imprest she retains of £300. Her trade receivables were £19,400 as at 1 January and £22,700 as at 31 December. Identify her sales revenue in 2012.

Balance on 1.1	£24,580
Lodgements	£492,650
Cheques drawn	(£428,900)
Balance – 31.12	£88,330

a	£495,950	
b	£499,250	
c	£503,530	
d	£7,580	

10.8 Trade payables of Brixton Corner were £248,450 on 30 September 2012 and £195,900 a year prior to that date. Payment to suppliers in the year to 30 September 2012 was £794,700. The cost of inventory on 1 October 2011 was £98,400 and that a year later was £112,250. Identify the sales revenue in the year, in each of the following independent scenarios:

(a) Sales prices were so fixed to yield a gross profit ratio of 10%.

(b) Sale were always made at cost plus 20%.

(c) Sales were made at cost plus a third.

(d) Sales were usually made at cost plus 20%; but sales invoiced at £194,400 during summer were subject to a special discount of 10%.

(x)		(y)		(z)	
£926,000		£916,740		£931,975	
£1,000,080		£1,016,700		£1,059,063	
£1,129,667		£1,041,750		£1,111,200	
£784,080		£978,480		£1,000,080	

Focus on identifying purchases

10.9

As at 30 June	2011	2012
Trade receivable	£49,800	£59,700
Inventory	£39,200	£42,400

Particulars relating to a Newsagent are stated on the left. The cash takings during the year ended 30 June 2012 were £594,800. The sales are made at cost plus 10%. A trade debt of £300 was written off. Identify the amount of purchases in the year ended 30 June 2012.

a	£607,900	
b	£553,200	
c	£608,200	
d	£605,000	

10.10 Payments to suppliers during the year to 30 September 2012 were £486,780, taking advantage of 5% cash discount offered by suppliers. Taking note of the information in the box on the left, identify the amount of purchases in the year.

As at 30 September	2011	2012
Trade payables	£54,500	£65,900

a	£498,180	
b	£546,858	
c	£523,800	
d	£503,304	

10.11 Cash takings from customers during the year were £524,800; while the trade receivables at commencement of the year and at year-end were £84,700 and £94,500 respectively. The cost of inventory in hand was £39,800 at commencement and £42,400 at year-end. Identify the purchases during the year, in each of the following independent scenarios:

(a) Sales were at cost plus 50%.

(b) Gross profit ratio is 25% and carriage inwards amounted to £24,000.

(c) Sales were at cost plus 20% and bad debts written off £3,000.

(d) Gross profit ratio is 50% but goods costing £5,000 are lost in a fire.

(x)		(y)		(z)	
£359,000		£269,900		£537,200	
£513,200		£446,350		£427,550	
£540,200		£450,600		£432,680	
£542,200		£364,000		£274,900	

10.12 A summary of a retailer's bank statements identified that, during the year, cheques for £948,500 were drawn in the name of suppliers. However, cheques drawn in the name of suppliers not presented to the bank were £42,400 at commencement and £59,200 at the end of the year. Trade payables were £214,600 at commencement and £159,400 at the end of the year. Cash discounts received amounted to £9,400. Identify the amount of purchases during the year.

a	£876,500	
b	£885,900	
c	£902,700	
d	£919,500	

Focus on expenses

10.13 Payments for insurance during the year, of £21,900, include an amount of £5,400 paid for a year ending four months after the date of the Statement of financial position. At commencement of the year insurance prepaid was £900. What is the insurance expense in the year?

a	£17,400	
b	£510	
c	£21,000	
d	£19,200	

10.14 According to the bank statement summary for the year, cheques for £14,800 have been drawn in the name of the landlord. However, a landlord's cheque for £1,200 had not been presented for payment at the commencement of the year and another for £2,800 at the year-end. Rent accrued at the beginning of the year was £3,600 and at the end £2,800. What is the year's rent expense?

a	£12,400	
b	£15,600	
c	£17,200	
d	£14,000	

10.15 Browns have rented a photocopying machine from Whites. The contract is that, besides the annual rental, further payments will be calculated at 3p per copy taken. As at 1 April 2011 rental of £3,000 had been paid in advance; while £2,298 was owed in respect of copies taken. During the year ended 31 March 2012, Browns have paid £11,980 to Whites. The invoice shown on the left was received from Whites in March 2012, and remains unpaid as at 31 March, and Browns have made 12,500 copies in the two months to 31 March 2012. Identify the expense Browns should report in the year to 31 March 2012.

Rental for the year to 30 September 2012	£7,200
48,800 copies made until 31 January 2012	£1,464

a	£18,121	
b	£21,721	
c	£17,746	
d	£17,371	

Focus on non-trading income

10.16 In addition to its trading activities a business earns substantial amounts as rent, particulars of which are stated on the left. Rent received during 2012 was £54,800. Identify the rental income it should report on its Statement of income for the year 2012.

As at 31 December	2011	2012
Rent received in advance	£9,800	£5,400
Rent in arrears	£21,500	£32,600

a	£27,600	
b	£93,700	
c	£15,900	
d	£70,300	

10.17 On 1 August 2011 a business invested £400,000 in a fixed deposit account earning interest at 6% per annum. Identify the amount of interest income to be reported in the Statement of income of the business for the year ended 31 March 2012.

a	£18,000	
b	£16,000	
c	£24,000	
d	£12,000	

10.18

Block	Date received	Amount	Period relating to
A	9.4.2007	£2,700	Three months to 30.4.2007
B	11.5.2007	£4,800	Six months to 30.6.2007
C	21.8.2007	£12,000	One year to 31.7.2007
A	7.10.2007	£5,400	Six months to 31.10.2007
C	12.12.2007	£12,000	One year to 31.7.2008

Shown on the left is a summary of rent received by a business from subletting three blocks out of its office premises.

Identify the amount that should be included as rental income in the year ended 31 March 2008 and as an asset or liability on the Statement of financial position as at that date.

	Income	Liability	Asset
a	£36,900	–	£11,700
b	£32,400	£4,000	£11,700
c	£36,400	–	£11,700
d	£32,400	£4,000	£15,700

Focus on non-current assets

10.19 The non-current assets of a business were reported at a written-down value of £548,000 at the year-end and at £472,400 a year prior to it. Depreciation in the year was £51,600. Assets costing £60,000, written down to £21,200, had been sold in the year for £18,000. Identify cost of assets acquired in the year.

a	£144,800	
b	£186,800	
c	£148,400	
d	£2,400	

10.20 Non-current assets have been reported in the Statements of financial position of a business as shown on the left. An asset that cost £40,000, written down to £28,000, was sold in the year for £20,000. What is the cost of non-current assets acquired during the year?

As at 31 March	2011	2012
Non-current assets at cost	£524,000	£578,000
Accumulated depreciation	£98,600	£112,200

a	£40,000	
b	£94,000	
c	£74,000	
d	£82,000	

10.21 Statements of financial position reported non-current assets as shown below. A new asset had been acquired for £120,000 and depreciation of £38,000 written off. An asset was disposed of for £10,000. Identify the gain (G) or loss (L) on the disposal.

As at 31 December	2011	2012
Non-current assets at cost	£498,000	£594,000
Accumulated depreciation	£74,200	£98,600

a	£14,000 L	
b	£14,000 G	
c	£400 L	
d	£400 G	

10.22 During the year land was revalued and the surplus reported as Revaluation surplus; and an asset costing £80,000, written down to £38,000, was sold for £40,000. Identify the cost of any non-current assets acquired during the year ending 30 September 2012.

As at 30 September	2011	2012
Non-current assets at cost	£595,000	£924,000
Accumulated depreciation	£84,400	£97,200
Revaluation surplus	–	£120,000

a	£289,000	
b	£409,000	
c	£329,000	
d	£249,000	

Focus on missing inventory/cash

10.23 Shown below is an extract of the year-end Trial Balance as at 30 June 2012. Sales are always made at cost plus 25%. The cost of inventory as at 30.6.2012 is found to be £54,000. What is the cost of inventory missing?

Inventory as at 30.6.2011	£78,000	–
Sales	–	£490,000
Purchases	£398,000	–

a	£30,000	
b	£84,000	
c	£108,500	
d	£54,500	

10.24 Richard, a newsagent, reported as at 30 June 2011 Trade receivable as £79,400 and the balance at bank as £59,400. Daily takings are banked intact and all payments made by cheque. The total of all cheque counterfoils issued in the year to 30 June 2012 amounts to £394,200. Extracts from the year-end Trial Balance as at 30 June 2012 is shown on the left. Sales are always effected at cost plus 20%. Cost of inventory on 30 June 2012 was £62,500. You have been requested to identify the amount of any cash misappropriated in the year ended 30 June 2012.

Inventory as at 30.6.2011	£48,200
Purchases	£349,400
Bank balance	£11,800
Trade receivable	£81,200

a	£447,920	
b	£65,520	
c	£134,920	
d	£53,720	

Answers to multiple choice questions

10.1a: y 10.1b: x 10.1c: z 10.1d: x 10.2: c 10.3a: z 10.3b: x 10.3c: x 10.3d: y 10.4a: x 10.4b: z 10.4c: x 10.4d: y 10.5: a 10.6: b 10.7: c 10.8a: x 10.8b: x 10.8c: z 10.8d: y 10.9: b 10.10: c 10.11a: x 10.11b: z 10.11c: y 10.11d: y 10.12: d 10.13: c 10.14: b 10.15: a 10.16: d 10.17: b 10.18: b 10.19: c 10.20: b 10.21: c 10.22: a 10.23: a 10.24: d

Progressive questions

PQ 10.1 Three scenarios when financial statements can or cannot be prepared

Assets and liabilities of a retail shop owned by Joe Ross are identified as stated on the right.

As at 31 December		
	2010	2011
	£	£
Non-current assets at wdv	240,000	284,000
Inventory at cost	112,400	138,200
Trade receivables	136,800	164,600
Cash and bank balance	12,600	15,400
Trade payables	62,500	77,800

Scenario (a): Assuming that no more information is available with regard to the business, estimate the profit from this business in 2011.

Scenario (b): Make a revised estimate of the profit John Ross earned from this shop if, in addition to the above information, you have been able to ascertain as follows:

(i) Joe Ross has no income other than from this shop.

(ii) Considering his style of living Joe Ross must be spending not less than £200 per week as household expenses.

Scenario (c): In addition to the information provided in scenarios (a) and (b), you have ascertained as follows:

(i) Purchases in the year ended 31 December 2011 were £486,200.

(ii) Non-current assets were acquired in the year for £60,000.

(iii) Joe's personal diary records that he has drawn £200 per week to meet his household expenses and has paid for business expenses as stated in the box on the right.

	£
Rent	24,000
Salaries	48,800
Other expenses	16,400

Required: Prepare the financial statements for 2011.

PQ 10.2 A basic question on incomplete records

The assets and liabilities of a shop owned by Simon are stated on the right. Transactions in 2011 were as follows:

(i) Drawings by the proprietor £40,000

(ii) Payments to suppliers £1,731,600

(iii) Receipts from customers £2,160,000

(iv) Paid as salary £180,000

(v) Paid for other expenses £154,800

As at 31 December		
	2010	2011
	£	£
Non-current assets	96,400	112,800
Accumulated depreciation	(24,600)	(32,400)
	71,800	80,400
Inventory	235,500	252,800
Trade receivables	43,200	46,800
Bank balance	2,160	?
Trade payables	97,200	109,800

Required: Prepare:

(a) a summarised Cash Book and

(b) financial statements for 2011.

PQ 10.3 Incomplete records with goods taken by the sole trader

Dick Barton, a sole trader, banks all his takings intact and makes his payments by cheque. A summary of his bank statements for the year ended 30 April 2011 is shown on the right.

	£		£
Bank summary:		Trade payables	49,600
Balance at 1.5.2010	1,200	Expenses	12,620
Trade receivables	63,120	Rent	4,000
Cash sales	20,000	Drawings	15,000
		Fixtures	750

A list of his shop's assets and liabilities is shown on the right.

As at 30 April	2010	2011
	£	£
Trade receivables	3,800	5,860
Trade payables	3,320	4,250
Expenses owed	620	930
Inventory at cost	4,350	6,200
Fixtures (net)	1,200	1,500
Rent prepaid	300	500

Required: Prepare:

(a) a Statement of income for the year ended 30 April 2011, and

(b) a Statement of financial position as at that date.

PQ 10.4 Incomplete records involving bank reconciliation

Statement of financial position as at 31 December 2010	
	£
Tangible assets	180,000
Accumulated depreciation	(72,000)
	108,000
Inventory	112,000
Receivables	21,400
Bank balance	12,800
Cash in hand	300
Payables	(32,500)
Capital	222,000

Assets/liabilities as 31.12.2011	
Inventory	£142,800
Receivables	£48,400
Bank balance	£18,500
Cash in hand	£400
Payables	£49,800

Since submitting her last Statement of financial position (as shown on the left) to the Tax Department, Stella Norris has lost the services of her accountant. From particulars in her own diary and by summarising her bank statements she was able to identify the payments made in 2011 as follows:

	Cash	Bank
Paid to suppliers	£12,800	£144,400
Paid as office rent	–	£10,000
Paid as salary to staff	–	£22,000
Paid for office cleaning	£720	£1,500
Paid as other expenses	£940	£2,850
Paid for a vehicle 1.7.2011	–	£18,000

She admits that she takes £200 per week from the till for personal expenses. Her policy is to depreciate tangible non-current assets, including the new vehicle, at 20% p.a. on cost. Listed on the left are her current assets and liabilities.

Required: Prepare:

(a) a summarised two-column Cash Book recording the transactions in 2011, and

(b) the financial statements for the year 2011.

PQ 10.5 Cost of goods taken by the owner (ACCA 1.1 amended)

Bob is a sole trader who does not maintain complete accounting records. He has listed his assets and liabilities as shown on the right, and has prepared, as shown below, a summary of bank and cash transactions. He has taken away goods from inventory for personal use but has not kept any record of their costs. Bob always fixes his selling price by adding 50% to the buying price of goods. There is no wastage.

Asset/liability 30 September	2010	2011
	£	£
Inventory	38,000	46,000
Receivables	119,200	125,000
Prepaid	2,400	2,600
Payables	68,100	77,100
Accruals	3,900	4,600

Bank summary

	£		£
Balance	20,500	Purchases	408,100
Deposits	12,900	Expenses	89,400
Customers	519,400	Drawings	30,000
		Balance c/d	25,300
	552,800		552,800

Cash summary

	£		£
Balance b/f	300	Banked	12,900
Sales	79,000	Purchases	14,200
		Expenses	4,100
		Drawings	47,900
		Balance c/d	200
	79,300		79,300

Required:

(a) Prepare Bob's Statement of income for the year ended 30 September 2011.

(b) Calculate the cost of goods taken by Bob.

PQ 10.6 Adopt the crossword puzzle mentality

Rick Alderman owns a shop. Because of a recent bereavement he has neglected to maintain full accounting records. To prepare the financial statements for the year ended 31 December 2011 he has gathered the following information:

(i) Total operating expenses for the year, other than depreciation, were reported as £214,500 in the year ended 31 December 2010. Corresponding amount for the current year is expected to be 20% more.

(ii) Assets and liabilities of the shop were as stated on the right.

(iii) Apart from new furniture acquired on 1 October 2011, other furniture was all acquired when the business started in January 2009. Furniture is depreciated at 10% per annum using the straight-line method.

(iv) Rick has no other source of income and he draws from the business £400 per week.

(v) Sales are always effected at cost plus 50%.

As at 31 December	2010	2011
	£	£
Furniture at cost	240,000	300,000
Inventory at cost	426,400	316,500
Trade receivables	48,200	64,400
Prepaid rent	6,000	–
Cash and bank	38,600	55,200
Trade payables	185,200	212,600
Accrued expense	12,600	17,800

Required: Prepare the financial statements for Rick's shop for the year ended 31 December 2011.

Test questions

Test 10.1 An easy question (ACCA 1.1 amended)

Aim is a sole trader who does not keep a full set of accounting records. An analysis of his bank transactions is shown below on the left. Aim's other assets and liabilities were as stated below on the right:

	Receipts	Payments
	£	£
Overdraft 1 July 2010	–	32,400
Cash banked	418,200	–
Disposal of motor van	4,500	–
Payment for purchases	–	316,300
New van (on 1.1.2011)	–	22,000
Rent and expenses	–	49,200
Drawings	–	80,400
Overdraft – 30 June 2011	77,600	–
	500,300	500,300

	As at 30 June	
	2010	2011
	£	£
Shop fittings (cost £45,000)	?	35,000
Motor van (cost £18,000)	–	4,000
New motor van	22,000	–
Trade receivables	48,600	44,700
Trade payables	24,200	19,600
Inventories	63,200	58,900
Rent and expenses accrued	13,000	12,500

Notes:

(i) Prior to banking cash takings from customers Aim made payments listed on the right.

Wages	£74,000
Purchases	£13,700
Expenses	£7,400

(ii) Aim depreciates motor van and shop fittings, on a straight-line basis (assuming no residual value) at 20% and 10% per year respectively, depreciating for the full year in the year of purchase and not depreciating in the year of disposal.

Required: Prepare Aim's Statement of income for the year ended 30 June 2011.

Test 10.2 Involves acquisition and disposal of assets

A shop owned by Jeanne Salt informs you that:

(a) Assets and liabilities of the shop are as shown on the right.

(b) Furniture acquired for £16,200 and written down to £5,400 was scrapped during the year.

(c) A vehicle acquired for £54,000 was sold during the year for £30,000 making a gain of £8,000.

(d) Sales in the year amounting to £846,200 yielded a gross profit ratio of 25%.

(e) Expenses incurred in the year include the following:
£68,200 administrative and selling expenses
£2,100 bad debts
£4,200 depreciation on furniture.

(f) No record has been maintained of amounts drawn by Jeanne from time to time.

	As at 31 March	
	2010	2011
	£	£
Furniture at cost	36,400	54,200
Depreciation	(18,200)	?
Motor vehicles	124,000	132,400
Depreciation	(86,800)	(68,400)
Inventory	154,500	216,800
Trade receivables	216,400	254,200
Cash and bank	16,200	9,600
Trade payables	208,300	245,900
Accrued expense	16,400	32,500

Required: Prepare:

(a) the Statement of affairs as at 1 April 2010, and

(b) the financial statements for the year ended 31 March 2011.

Test 10.3 Where a two-column Cash Book is needed

Bruce Drake requests your assistance to prepare the financial statements of his business for the year ended 30 June 2011 and has provided you with the following information:

(i) The shop's assets and liabilities include those listed on the right.

(ii) Motor vehicles acquired for £28,000 and written down to £12,000 were sold in 2011 for £9,000.

(iii) Bruce always banks his takings intact, every day at close of business, leaving a float of £500.

(iv) Rent is agreed at £2,000 per month. Bruce and his family occupy a third of the premises.

(v) A fire in May 2011 destroyed a substantial amount of inventory. An insurance claim was agreed at £30,000.

(vi) Payments made in the year, recorded by Bruce in a diary, are summarised as shown on the right.

(vii) The sales are always effected at cost plus a third.

As at 30 June		
	2010	2011
	£	£
Motor vehicles at wdv	82,000	106,000
Office equipment at wdv	24,500	28,400
Inventory at cost	142,400	96,500
Trade receivables	98,500	118,400
Prepaid insurance	1,200	?
Balance at bank	21,300	19,700
Trade payables	68,600	114,200
Salaries accrued	18,200	15,600

	In cash	By cheque
	£	£
For purchases	12,400	662,800
Rent	–	30,000
Salaries and wages	3,600	108,500
Motor vehicles	–	60,000
Office equipment	–	16,000
Living expenses – family	3,400	14,200
Other expenses	7,800	44,600
Insurance – year to 30.9.2011	–	6,000

Required:

(a) Record these transactions in a two-column Cash Book.

(b) Prepare the financial statements for the year ended 30 June 2011.

Chapter 11

Statements of cash flows

By the end of this chapter

You should learn:

- About the need to focus on cash availability
- Why information in a Statement of cash flows is more reliable than that in other financial statements

You should be able to:

- Prepare a Statement of cash flows and
- Interpret the information in the Statement

11.1 Why a business should focus on its cash resources

The performance of a business entity is usually gauged in terms of its profit-generating ability. Experience teaches, however, that its survival could depend on its cash-generating ability.

To exploit opportunities and to meet its bills as they fall due, the business has to generate the necessary cash – ensuring that the amounts and timing match the needs. On the face of it, it would appear that a company making profit would necessarily have correspondingly more cash. Such an expectation would be met if the additional profit does not get tied up in additional inventory, receivables and non-current assets. An entity making profit but unable to find cash when necessary could face problems such as the following:

1. Failure to settle accounts on time could lead to suppliers stopping supplies and other suppliers refusing or limiting credit. Continuing failure could ultimately lead to liquidation.
2. Lost opportunities for making profit because of inability to find the cash outlay, e.g. for buying new assets or investing in a lucrative new line of business.
3. Enforced borrowing on unfavourable terms to pay its trade or other payables.
4. Inability to placate staff (paying salary on time and granting increases) and shareholders (not paying dividend).

Research[1] shows that more than half of Britain's small businesses collapse because of cash flow problems.

As the availability of cash is so important for its survival, it is usual for a business to prepare and keep updating cash projections (i.e. forecasts). A company that usually settles its debts, say at weekly intervals, may prepare its projections of expected cash inflows and outflows on a weekly basis. This gives forewarning of the extent of any cash shortfall and when it is likely to occur, allowing the company to take timely remedial action, e.g. by delaying payment of some debts or arranging for an overdraft. Such cash forecasts, however, are available only for the internal use of the company's management.

Those external to the business are given a Statement of cash flows, which is no more than a summary of the cash flow in the year that was completed. The expectation is that information on the cash flows in the past year would provide a basis for assessing the company's liquidity, solvency and financial adaptability. This is the reason for the insistence that annual reports published by companies should include its Statement of cash flows.[2]

11.2 Preparation of a Statement of cash flows

A Statement of cash flows is a statement, presented in the format prescribed in IAS 7 *Statements of cash flows*, summarising cash inflows (i.e. receipts) and outflows (i.e. payments) during the year to which the other financial statements relate. The information on the cash inflows and outflows is derived from the information appearing in the Statement of income for that accounting period and in the opening and closing Statements of financial position.

The approach to preparing a Statement of cash flows is, in many ways, similar to the approach we followed when preparing financial statements from incomplete records in Chapter 10. For example, if trade receivables (appearing in the opening Statement of financial position) was £3,000 and credit sales for the year (reported in the Statement of income) is £9,000, the total amount receivable by the year-end would be £12,000 provided no cash had been received from customers. If, however, the closing Statement of financial position reports trade receivables as £4,000, then the cash inflow (received) during the year should be the difference of £8,000.

In view of the similarity of approach for identifying cash flows we should remember the four rules that we applied in Chapter 10:

1. The five classes of accounts fall into four groups – assets and expenses have debit balances while liabilities, capital and income have credit balances.
2. Unless it has been stated to the contrary it should be assumed that:
   - purchases and sales of goods (held for sale) are on credit terms;
   - acquisition/disposal of assets is on cash terms.
3. Care should be taken to identify whether the information provided is:
   - a payment or expense, i.e. the amount paid (cash outflow) or the whole amount payable for the period (expense);
   - a receipt or income, i.e. the amount received (cash inflow) or the whole amount receivable for the period (income).
4. When less than full information has been provided the crossword puzzle mentality should be adopted:
   - Identify how many letters (amounts) are needed to complete the word (account).
   - Make a guess only after all clues (information) provided have been fully used up.

For example, if the information provided is that £11,000 has been paid as rent (note that what is referred to is payment rather than expense) and that £1,000 more is payable for the year, the expense for the year could be identified as £12,000. On the other hand, if the information provided is that rent per month has been agreed at £1,000, making an expense of £12,000 for the year, and that £1,000 of it remains unpaid at the year-end, the cash outflow could be identified as £11,000.

Activity 11.1 Identification of cash inflows and outflows

Income/expense for the year ended 31.12.2011		As at 1.1.2011		As at 31.12.2011	
	£'000		£'000		£'000
Sales	1,680	Trade receivables	245	Trade receivables	368
Purchases	1,246	Trade payables	264	Trade payables	296
Rent	60	Prepaid rent	15	Accrued rent	10
Salaries	246	Accrued salary	32	Accrued salary	46

Required: Calculate the cash inflow/outflow during the year ended 31.12.2011.

11.3 Format of a Statement of cash flows

The information on cash flows during an accounting period, if presented in an account format (see on the right), would be nothing more than a summarised Cash account. Observe that the cash balance of £34 at commencement of the year has increased to £164 by the end, i.e. a net cash inflow of £130 during the accounting period.

Cash account

	£		£
Balance b/f	34	Purchases[a]	514
Sales[a]	852	Rent[a]	11
Disposal of asset[b]	14	Furniture[b]	140
Share capital[c]	50	Salary[a]	58
		Tax[a]	29
		Loan repaid[c]	25
		Interest[a]	9
		Balance c/d	164
	950		950
Balance b/d	164		

The cash inflows are the three amounts received and cash outflows seven amounts paid out during the period.

The Statement of cash flows merely reports the same information in a statement format identifying the net cash inflow during the accounting period as £130, but facilitating better understanding by reporting the cash flows within three headings. You will notice that in the Cash account we have marked six items with a superscript [a]. These are all revenue items, i.e. income items and expense items. These are the items that are included either in the Statement of income or Statement of changes in equity. The remaining four items in the Cash account have been marked either with [b] or [c]. These are items of a capital nature, i.e. those that would affect the information reported on the Statement of financial position – two (marked [b]) on the asset side and other two (marked [c]) on the side reporting Equity and liabilities. The equity and liability side of the Statement of financial position reports how a business has been *financed* and the asset side reports how that amount has been *invested*.

Accordingly IAS7 requires that a Statement of cash flows should:

1. Report the cash flows in each accounting period, within three headings as:
   (a) *Cash flows from operating activities*
   (b) *Cash flows from investing activities*
   (c) *Cash flows from financing activities.*
2. Identify the net increase during the accounting period in the cash and cash equivalent held by the business, along with a reconciliation of the amount held at the commencement of the period with that at the end.

Study the Statement of cash flows (on the right) prepared in the format required by IAS 7.

Statement of cash flows for the year ended xxx		
	£	£
Cash flows from operating activities:		
Sales	852	
Purchases	(514)	
Rent	(11)	
Salary	(58)	
Interest	(9)	
Tax	(29)	231
Cash flows from investing activities:		
Furniture	(140)	
Disposal of asset	14	(126)
Cash flows from financing activities:		
Share capital	50	
Loan repayment	(25)	25
Net increase in cash and cash equivalents		130
Cash at commencement of the period		34
Cash at end of the period		164

Activity 11.2 Cash flow using the direct method

Saddle plc has supplied you with copies of its Statements of financial position and the Statement of income as shown below:

Statements of financial position as at 31 December	2010	2011
	£'000	£'000
Non-current assets:	540	720
Accumulated depreciation	(145)	(190)
	395	530
Investments	115	140
Current assets:		
Inventories	315	418
Trade receivables	412	438
Cash and bank	48	51
	1,285	1,577

Statement of income for the year ended 31.12.2011	£'000
Sales revenue	2,460
Cost of sales	(1,780)
Gross profit	680
Operating expenses	(424)
Operating profit	256
Interest	(24)
Profit before tax	232
Taxation	(48)
Profit after tax	184

→

	£'000	£'000
Capital and reserves:		
Ordinary shares – £1	600	800
Share premium	40	55
Accumulated profit	217	311
	857	1,166
Non-current liabilities:		
12% Loan note	250	200
Current liabilities:		
Trade payables	139	166
Taxation	39	45
	1,285	1,577

Statement of changes in equity

	£'000
Accumulated profit b/f	217
Profit after tax	184
Dividend paid	(90)
Accumulated profit c/f	311

Required: Prepare the Statement of cash flows for the year ended 31 December 2011.

11.4 Why operating profit does not equal cash inflow

If a trader's sales are all on a cash basis, the amount of sales in a year should be equal to the amount of cash inflow in that year. Again, if the trader buys only to replace his sales (i.e. carries no inventory) and buys strictly on a cash basis, we would expect his cash position in the year to have improved by the amount of his gross profit in the year. Finally, if all expenses are paid for immediately (i.e. no accruals or prepayments and no expenses such as depreciation are incurred that do not involve a corresponding cash outflow) we would expect the cash position to have improved by the amount of operating profit.

When answering Activity 11.2 you would have identified the cash inflow from sales as £2,434[a] (see the account on the right). Then you would have identified the purchases in the year as £1,883[b] (see working below on the left) and proceeded to identify cash outflow on purchases as £1,856[c] (see below).

Trade receivables account

	£		£
Balance b/f	412	Cash inflow[a]	2,434
Sales	2,460	Balance c/d	438
	2,872		2,872
	438		

Inventory on 1.1.2011	£315
Purchases	£1,883[b]
	£2,198
Inventory on 31.12.2011	£(418)
Cost of sales	£1,780

Trade payable account

Cash paid	£1,856[c]	Balance b/f	£139
Balance c/d	£166	Purchases	£1,883
	£2,022		£2,022
		Balance b/d	£166

Similarly, you would have identified depreciation written off in the period as £45 (£190 – £145) and, assuming that operating expenses in the year (£424) includes depreciation, the cash outflow in the year on operating expenses would be £379 (£424 – £45). On the basis of this information the cash outflow on operating activities would be £199,000 (see box on the right); whereas the operating profit is identified in the Statement of income as £256,000. The reasons for the difference need to be inquired into. The reasons are as follows:

	£'000
Inflow from sales	2,434
Outflow on purchases	(1,856)
Outflow on expenses	(379)
Net cash inflow	199

The first reason is depreciation. Depreciation decreases operating profit but would not decrease cash in the current year; although in the year when the related asset was acquired there would have been a cash outflow which, in that year, would have been reported as an investing activity. Therefore, to identify the Cash inflow from operating activity, we need to add to operating profit any items (like depreciation and amortisation of an intangible asset) which do not involve a cash outflow in the current year. Hence the cash inflow from operating activity of Saddle plc in 2011 is £301,000 (operating profit of £256,000 + depreciation of £45,000).

The second reason is changes in net current assets. The cash inflow from operating activity of Saddle plc would have been £301,000 if there had been no change in its inventory, receivable and payable positions. Had inventory reported say at £100 at the beginning of the year increased to £140 by the end, £40 of the cash generated by operating activity in that year would have been tied up in that asset. Similarly, if payables at the beginning of the year were £90 and had increased to £95 by the end, the cash flow would have improved by £5.

We are now in a position to identify why the operating profit of Saddle plc for 2011 is £256,000, whereas its cash flow from operating activity is only £199,000. First, the operating profit (£256,000) is increased by depreciation to identify the cash flow from operating activity as £301,000. Then we proceed to identify whether increase (or decrease) in inventory or trade receivables has tied up (or released) cash and whether decrease (or increase) in trade payables has taken (or released) cash. The results are:

Inventory: £315,000 – £418,000 = £103,000 tied up

Receivables: £412,000 – £438,000 = £26,000 tied up

Payables: £139,000 – £166,000 = £27,000 released.

The results of this inquiry (see box on the right) are set out in a Statement of reconciliation of operating profit the publication of which is obligatory, because this statement would add credibility to the information published in a Statement of cash flows.

Reconciliation of operating profit with cash flow

	£'000
Operating profit	256
Depreciation	45
Cash flow from operations	301
Inventory increase	(103)
Receivables increase	(26)
Payables increase	27
Cash flow	199

11.5 Statement of cash flows using the indirect method

The Statement of cash flows illustrated in Section 11.3 identifies individually:

1. the cash inflow from sales;
2. the cash outflow on purchases;
3. the cash outflow on each operating expense such as rent, salary and so on.

Such a presentation is known as the *direct method*. Most companies are reluctant to disclose cash-flow information in such detail. Instead they opt to present their Statement of cash flows on the *indirect method*, illustrated on the right, which is permitted as an alternative by IAS7.

Observe the following points:

1. Both methods of presenting the Cash flow statement identify the cash flow from operating activities as £199,000. Whereas on the direct method the inflow from sales and outflows on purchases and other operating expenses are individually identified, on the indirect method such information is not disclosed. Instead the reconciliation of operating profit is brought into the Statement of cash flows to identify the cash flow from operating activity.
2. Apart from the manner of reporting the cash flow from operating activity there is no difference between the two methods of presenting the Statement of cash flows.
3. We have included all revenue items within the heading 'Cash flow from operating activities'. IAS7, however, permits the following alternative presentations:
   - Interest paid may be included within the heading 'Cash flow from financing activity'.
   - Interest received and dividend received may be included within the heading 'Cash flow from investing activities'.

Statement of cash flows for the year ended 31.12.2011		
	£'000	£'000
Cash flow from operating activities:		
Operating profit	256	
Depreciation	45	
Cash flow from operations	301	
Working capital changes:		
Inventory increase	(103)	
Receivables increase	(26)	
Payables increase	27	
Cash generated from operations:		199
Interest		(24)
Dividend paid		(90)
Tax paid		(42)
		43
Cash flow from investing activities:		
Non-current asset	(180)	
Investments	(25)	(205)
Cash flow from financing activities:		
Share capital	200	
Share premium account	15	
Loan note repaid	(50)	165
Net increase in cash in the year:		3
Cash as at 31.12.2010		48
Cash as at 31.12.2011		51

Activity 11.3 Statement of cash flows using the indirect method

The Statements of financial position of Paddles plc are shown on the right. You are informed as follows:

(i) There was no disposal of non-current assets in the year.
(ii) A dividend of £30,000 was paid in October 2011.
(iii) Debenture interest of £36,000 was paid in the year.
(iv) Tax on current year's profit has been accounted for at £82,000.

Required:

(a) Prepare a Statement of cash flows for 2011.
(b) Make three comments on the information provided by the Statement of cash flows.

Note: The question does not include a Statement of income. In the absence of information on sales, purchases and expenses it is impossible to prepare the Statement of cash flows on the direct method. To prepare the Statement on the indirect method, we need the figure of operating profit and to get that figure we need to prepare a Statement of income based on the information provided.

Statements of financial position as at 31 December

	2010		2011	
	£'000	£'000	£'000	£'000
Non-current assets:	720		820	
Accumulated depreciation	(242)	478	(258)	562
Investments		180		240
Current assets:				
Inventory	590		407	
Trade receivables	332		392	
Cash and bank	11	933	4	803
		1,591		1,605
	£'000	£'000	£'000	£'000
Equity and reserves:				
Ordinary shares of £1	350		500	
Share premium a/c	75		115	
Accumulated profit	137	562	254	869
Non-current liabilities:				
12% Debentures		400		150
Current liabilities:				
Trade payables	478		418	
Accrued expenses	64		72	
Taxation	87	629	96	586
		1,591		1,605

11.6 Cash flow from asset disposal

Upon disposal of any non-current asset the cash flow improves by the amount of the proceeds received. The impact of gain or loss on the cash flow is automatically taken into account when the sale proceeds are recognised as the cash inflow.

For example, let us assume that a vehicle acquired for £20,000 and depreciated by £8,000 (i.e. reported at £12,000) is sold for £15,000. Cash flow improves by the proceeds of £15,000 and this amount includes the gain of £3,000. When we report the proceeds (£15,000) as a cash inflow we should not also report the gain (£3,000) as a cash inflow, because if we do we would be double-counting £3,000.

Having reported the sale proceeds (£15,000) as a cash inflow, when preparing a Statement of cash flows on the indirect method, we should take care to identify whether the reported operating profit does or does not include the gain on disposal. For example, let us assume that the operating profit is stated as £100,000 and the gain on disposal is stated thereafter, separately. It is clear then that the stated operating profit does not include the disposal gain. The operating profit (£100,000) could then be the starting point when preparing the Reconciliation of operating profit. On the other hand, if the operating profit stated as £100,000 includes the disposal gain (£3,000), to avoid double-counting we need to exclude the disposal gain and report £97,000 as the starting point in the reconciliation.

Parallel adjustment may become necessary with regard to expenses such as

- loss on disposal
- impairment of non-current assets.

These are examples of expenses, which, like depreciation, do not involve any cash outflow. But unlike depreciation, these expenses may be shown in the Statement of income after reporting the operating profit. In that event the reported operating profit would be the starting point of the reconciliation. However, in the event any of these expenses has been counted within the company's operating expenses, so that its operating profit is reported after deducting it, then that expense needs to be added to the stated operating profit, just as happens with depreciation.

Activity 11.4 Focus on asset disposal

During the year ended 30 June 2012 Middle plc sold for £78,000 a machine acquired for £200,000 and written down to £52,000. You are provided with an extract of the company's Statement of income as shown on the right. The non-current assets have been depreciated in the year by £28,000 and working capital changes in the year were as stated on the left. The tax liability was reported as £39,000 on 30 June 2011 and as £52,000 on 30 June 2012.

Operating profit	£284,000
Interest paid	(£24,000)
Profit before tax	£260,000
Taxation	(£50,000)
Profit after tax	£210,000
Dividend paid	(£40,000)

Inventory increased by	£18,000
Receivables decreased by	£30,000
Payables increased by	£21,000
Accrued expenses increased by	£4,000

Required: Identify the cash flow from operating activities in the year ended 30.6.2012.

Clue: operating profit stated in the extract includes the gain on machine disposal.

11.7 Cash and cash equivalents

The requirement of IAS 7 is that the Statement of cash flows should trace the movements within the year not only of cash but also of what are known as *cash equivalents*. IAS 7 defines cash equivalents as short-term highly liquid investments (such as bank deposits) that are readily convertible to known amounts of cash and which are subject to insignificant changes in value. We have to remember that when identifying the amount of cash and cash equivalent on any date:

1. We should include any bank balance as well as amounts held in a deposit account provided, *at the date of making the deposit*, there was only a short maturity date of three months or less.
2. We should not include any investments in equity shares because these are not readily convertible to a known amount of cash (their price could change from day to day) and it cannot be said that they are subject to only an insignificant risk of change in value.
3. We should also include (as an offset) any bank overdraft (but not bank loan).

Activity 11.5 Identifying the amount of cash and cash equivalent

In each of the following independent cases identify the total cash inflow or outflow during the year.

As at 30 June	Scenario A		Scenario B		Scenario C	
	2010	2011	2010	2011	2010	2011
Cash in hand	£640	£850	£1,400	£800	£400	£250
Bank current account	£11,200	£24,800	£11,200	–	–	–
Bank overdraft	–	–	–	£4,500	£8,900	£5,400
Bank loan	£30,000	£24,000	£30,000	£24,000	£30,000	£24,000
Bank deposit (three months)	–	–	£2,800	–	£2,000	£3,000
Bank deposit (four months)	–	–	£3,000	£2,000	–	£5,000
Equity investments	£12,000	£15,800	£9,200	£11,400	£15,500	£19,200

Activity 11.6 Statement of cash flows involving asset disposal

Statements of financial position as at 31 December

	2010		2011	
	£'000	£'000	£'000	£'000
Non-current assets:	760		920	
Accumulated depreciation	(288)	472	(318)	602
Investments		186		214
Current assets:				
Inventory	596		397	
Trade receivables	332		392	
Cash and bank balance	5	933	0	789
		1,591		1,605
	£'000	£'000	£'000	£'000
Equity and reserves:				
Ordinary shares of £1	350		500	
Share premium a/c	75		125	
Accumulated profit	137	562	294	919
Non-current liabilities:				
12% Loan notes		400		100
Current liabilities:				
Trade payables	478		396	
Accrued expenses	64		72	
Taxation	87		96	
Bank overdraft	0	629	22	586
		1,591		1,605

The financial statements of Diddle plc are set out on the left. You are informed as follows:

(i) A vehicle costing £72,000 was sold in the year for £54,000.

(ii) Part of the loan notes were redeemed on 1.1.2011 at 25% premium.

(iii) Depreciation amounting to £64,000 was included in the cost of sales.

(iv) Extracts from the Statement of income appear as follows:

	£'000
Operating profit	344
Impairment of investment	(20)
Premium on loan notes	(75)
Dividend received	17
Interest on loan notes	(36)
Profit before tax	230
Taxation	(48)
Profit after tax	182

(v) £25,000 was paid as dividend in 2011.

Required: Prepare the Statement of cash flows for the year ended 31 December 2011.

11.8 Interpretation of a Statement of cash flows

Statement of cash flows year ended 31 December 2011		
	£'000	£'000
Cash flow from operating activities:		
Operating profit	344	
Gain on disposal	(16)	
Depreciation	64	
Cash flow from operations	392	
Working capital movement:		
Inventory decrease	199	
Receivables increase	(60)	
Payables decrease	(82)	
Accrual increase	8	
	457	
Tax paid	(39)	
Dividend received	17	
Dividend paid	(25)	
Interest paid	(36)	374
Cash flow from investing activities:		
Disposal of asset	54	
Non-current assets	(232)	
Investments	(48)	(226)
Cash flow from financing activities:		
Share issue (150 + 50)	200	
Loan redemption	(375)	(175)
Net cash outflow in the year		(27)
Cash and cash equivalent on 31.12.2010		5
Cash and cash equivalent on 31.12.2011		(22)

Set out on the left is a Statement of cash flows of Diddle plc, for the year 2011, you would have prepared when answering Activity 11.6. Bear in mind that this cash flow relates to 2011 and as at the end of that year Diddle's current liabilities amounted to £586,000. Based on the information provided by the Statement of cash flows let us review the liquidity position of Diddle plc.

1. **On the face of it**, it would appear that Diddle's liquidity is poor for the following reasons:
   (a) There has been a cash outflow of £27,000.
   (b) Its cash and cash equivalents have changed from a positive £5,000 to a negative £22,000.
   (c) It had to release £199,000 by running down its holding of inventory and, perhaps, this may have been necessary to overcome liquidity problems.
   (d) Its inability to pay in full the tax liability for 2010 (£87,000) may have been due to liquidity constraints.
2. **Cash flow from operations**, at £392,000, is poor for the following reasons:
   (a) It is not generating sufficient cash in the year from its operating activities to pay off in full its current liabilities (£586,000). Its cash flow ratio, calculated as shown below, is 66.9%.

   £392,000/£586,000 × 100 = 66.9%

   (b) Net of its standing commitments (£87,000 for tax + £36,000 as interest + £25,000 as dividend to maintain it at current levels = £148,000), its 'free cash' generated by operating activity would be only £244,000 (£392,000 – £148,000) and that amounts to only 41.6% (£244,000/£586,000 × 100) of the year-end current liabilities.
3. **Management of working capital**: the cash inflow during the year has been increased from £392,000 to £457,000 by the management of working capital items.

(a) Release of £199,000 from inventory, unless it arose from cash flow constraints, may be attributed to good purchasing management, buying goods that sell readily.
(b) An additional £60,000 has been tied up in receivables. This may be the result of a deliberate strategy to boost sales by extending the credit period allowed to customers.
(c) The need to reduce the levels of payables by £82,000 could well be a symptom of the company's cash flow problems, which probably prompted the suppliers to enforce the credit terms permitted by them.

4. **Investing activities**: most cash outflows (£226,000) have been on investing activities. This is good because it improves the asset base of the company and enhances its future revenue-earning capacity. On the other hand, it could be that the company is building up its asset base to levels more than commensurate with its earning capacity – a situation which accountants diagnose as '*over-capitalisation*'.
5. **Financing activities**: the company is endeavouring to replace loan capital with share capital, thus improving its gearing and, therefore, its position in the share market. Besides, most of its improvement in asset base has been financed by the issue of equity. This is the right strategy.
6. **Conclusion**: overall, though the company's liquidity at the end of the year is worse than that at the beginning, the company appears to be fully aware of the direction in which it is moving, and is taking deliberate steps to achieve its aim. Hence the cash flow problems could well be temporary and part of its management strategy.

11.9 Usefulness of the Statement of cash flows

It is claimed that for making decisions the information provided by a Statement of cash flows is more useful than that provided by a Statement of income. The reasons given to support this claim are as follows:

1. Though profit making is crucial because it provides the motivation for continuing to carry on with a business, cash is the lifeblood of a business because its scarcity:
   (i) affects performance because opportunities for making profit may be missed and because finances may have to be raised at penal rate;
   (ii) affects the ability to meet bills as they fall due and thereby miss discounts, alienating suppliers and other payables; and
   (iii) may even jeopardise its survival.
2. Cash flow is easy to understand and is significant when investment decisions are made.
3. Information in a Statement of cash flows is objective, whereas the performance as reported in a Statement of income depends for its accuracy on:
   (i) choice of accounting policies such as decisions whether or not to depreciate and whether to report assets at cost or at valuation;
   (ii) estimates made on matters such as the useful economic life and scrap value of assets and recoverability of trade receivables;
   (iii) accounting procedures adopted such as choice of depreciation method and the cost-flow assumptions when valuing closing inventory; and
   (iv) expectations such as whether the company will remain in operational existence, and whether the income from its cash-generating units will be at such levels that no impairment loss needs to be accounted for.
4. Information in a Statement of cash flows is less susceptible to manipulation. It is not affected by schemes such as off-balance sheet financing and creative accounting.

Summary

- In running a business it is essential to focus on the availability of cash.
- The Statement of cash flows traces the movements of cash and cash equivalents during the year.
- Cash equivalents cannot include investments in shares nor exclude bank loans; but includes bank deposits (with up to three months' maturity at point of investment) and excludes overdraft.
- A Statement cash flows may be prepared on the direct method or indirect method.
- When preparing the Statement of cash flows on the indirect method care should be taken to ensure that operating profit, used in preparing the Reconciliation, does not include any gain on asset disposal nor exclude loss on disposal as well as impairment of assets.
- A Statement of cash flows should be prepared in IAS 7 format with three headings and identify the net inflow or outflow in the year.
- Focusing on cash is at least as important as focusing on performance, if not more so.

References

1. http://www.insolvencyhelpline.co.uk/ltd-companies/htm
2. IAS 7, (1992), effective 1.1.1994, London, International Accounting Standards Board, retitled in 2007 as Statement of cash flows.

Suggested answers to activities

11.1 Identification of cash inflows and outflows

Trade receivables account (asset)

	£		£
Balance b/f	245	Cash[a]	1,557
Sales	1,680	Balance c/d	368
	1,925		1,925
Balance b/d	368		

Trade payables account (liability)

	£		£
Cash[a]	1,214	Balance b/f	264
Balance c/d	296	Purchases	1,246
	1,510		1,510
		Balance b/d	296

Rent account (expense)

	£		£
Balance b/f	15		
Cash[a]	35	Statement of	
Balance c/d	10	income	60
	60		60

Salaries account (expense)

	£		£
Cash[a]	232	Balance b/f	32
		Statement of	
Balance c/d	46	income	246
	278		278
		Balance b/d	46

Note: (a) Balancing figure, in each account.

11.2 Cash flow using the direct method

Statement of cash flows for the year ended 31.12.2011

	£'000	£'000
Operating activity:		
Sales		2,434
Purchases		(1,856)
Expenses		(379)
Cash flow from operation		199
Interest		(24)
Dividend paid		(90)
Tax paid		(42)
		43
Investing activity:		
Non-current asset	(180)	
Investments	(25)	(205)
Financing activity:		
Share capital	200	
Share premium	15	
Loan note	(50)	165
Cash inflow in the year		3
Cash – 31.12.2010		48
Cash – 31.12.2011		51

Workings:

Non-current asset account

	£'000		£'000
Balance b/f	540		
Cash[a]	180	Balance c/d	720
	720		720
Balance b/d	720		

Accumulated depreciation account

	£'000		£'000
		Balance	145
Balance c/d	190	Depreciation[a]	45
	190		190
		Balance b/d	190

Investments account

	£'000		£'000
Balance b/f	115		
Cash[a]	25	Balance c/d	140
	140		140
Balance b/d	140		

Expenses account

	£'000		£'000
Depn[b]	45	Statement of	
Cash[a]	379	income	424
	424		424

Trade receivables account

	£'000		£'000
Balance	412	Cash[a]	2,434
Sales	2,460	Balance c/d	438
	2,872		2,872
Balance	438		

Trade payables account

	£'000		£'000
Cash[a]	1,856	Balance b/f	139
Balance c/d	166	Purchases[b]	1,883
	2,022		2,022
		Balance b/d	166

Cost of sales

	£'000		
Inventory	315		
Purchases[a]	1,883		
Inventory	(418)		
	1,780		

Share capital account

	£'000		£'000
		Balance b/f	600
Balance c/d	800	Cash[a]	200
	800		800
		Balance b/d	800

Share premium account

	£'000		£'000
		Balance b/f	40
Balance c/d	55	Cash[a]	15
	55		55
		Balance b/d	55

Tax (expense) account

	£'000		£'000
Tax (L)	48	Statement of income	48
	48		48

Tax (liability) account

	£'000		£'000
Cash[a]	42	Balance b/f	39
Balance c/d	45	Tax (exp.)	48
	87		87
		Balance b/d	45

Notes:

(a) Balancing figures in each account.

(b) A figure derived from another account.

11.3 Statement of cash flows using the indirect method

Cash flow statement year ended 31.12.2011	£'000	£'000
Operating activities:		
Operating profit[b]		265
Depreciation[c]		16
Cash from op. activity		281
Changes in working capital:		
Inventory decrease[k]		183
Receivables increase[l]		(60)
Payables decrease[m]		(60)
Accruals decrease[n]		8
		352
Interest paid[i]	(36)	
Tax paid[d]	(73)	
Dividend paid[j]	(30)	(139)
Investing activities:		213
Non-current assets[e]	(100)	
Investments[f]	(60)	(160)
Financing activities:		
Share capital[g]	150	
Share premium[h]	40	
Debenture redemption	(250)	(60)
Net cash outflow		(7)
Cash on 31.12.2010		11
Cash on 31.12.2011		4

Comments on the cash flow

1. Cash flow from operating activity (£352,000) is adequate to service loan capital (£36,000) as well as share capital (£30,000) and to pay tax.
2. Significant cash outflow on investing activity (£160,000) improves the asset base as well as future earning capacity.
3. Replacement of loan capital with equity improves the company's gearing.

Notes:

(a) The balancing figure in each account

(b) Statement of income

	£'000
Operating profit[a]	265
Interest paid[i]	(36)
Profit before tax	229
Taxation	(82)
Profit after tax	147

Change in equity	£'000
Balance b/f	137
Profit after tax	147
Dividend paid[j]	(30)
Balance c/f	254

(c) Accumulated depreciation account

	£'000		£'000
		Balance b/f	242
Balance c/d	258	Depreciation[c]	16
	258		258
		Balance b/d	258

(d) Taxation (liability) account

	£'000		£'000
Cash[a]	73	Balance b/f	87
Balance c/d	96	Tax (expense)	82
	169		169
		Balance b/d	96

(e) Non-current asset account

	£'000		£'000
Balance b/f	720		
Cash[a]	100	Balance c/d	820
	820		820
Balance b/d	820		

(f) Investments account

	£'000		£'000
Balance b/f	180		
Cash[a]	60	Balance c/d	240
	240		240
Balance b/d	240		

(g) Share capital account

	£'000		£'000
		Balance b/f	350
Balance c/d	500	Cash[a]	150
	500		500
		Balance b/d	500

(h) Share premium account

	£'000		£'000
		Balance b/f	75
Balance c/d	115	Cash[a]	40
	115		115
		Balance b/d	115

(i) 12% Debentures account

	£'000		£'000
Cash[a]	250	Balance b/f	400
Balance c/d	150		
	400		400
		Balance b/d	150

(j) Dividend paid: (30)
(k) Inventory: 590 – 407 = (£183)
(l) Trade receivables: 332 – 392 = £60
(m) Trade payables: 478 – 418 = £60
(n) Accruals: 64 – 72 = £8

11.4 Focus on asset disposal

Operating activities:	
	£'000
Operating profit	284
Gain on disposal[a]	(26)
Depreciation[b]	28
Inventory increase[c]	(18)
Receivables decrease[d]	30
Payables increase[e]	21
Accruals increase[e]	4
	323
Interest paid	(24)
Tax paid[f]	(37)
Dividend paid	(40)
Cash generated	222

Notes:

(a) The disposal proceeds, reported as cash inflow, is inclusive of the gain of £26,000. Unless the gain is excluded from operating profit, it will be double-counted.

(b) Depreciation, though an expense, does not involve cash outflow.

(c) Increase of inventory ties up cash.

(d) Decrease in receivables releases cash.

(e) Increases in payables as well as accruals release cash.

(f) Tax: balance b/f + tax expense – closing balance = £37,000.

11.5 Identifying the amount of cash and cash equivalent

	Scenario A	
Opening	640 + 11,200	£11,840
Closing	850 + 24,800	£25,650
	Cash inflow	£13,810

Scenario B	
1,400 + 11,200 + 2,800	£15,400
800 – 4,500	(£3,700)
Cash outflow	£19,100

Scenario C	
400 – 8,900 + 2,000	(£6,500)
250 – 5,400 + 3,000	(£2,150)
Cash inflow	£4,350

11.6 Statement of cash flows using the indirect method

Cash flow statement
year ended 31 December 2011

	£'000	£'000
Cash flow from operating activities:		
Operating profit	344	
Gain on disposal	(16)	
Depreciation	64	
Cash flow from operation	392	
Working capital moves:		
Inventory decrease	199	
Receivables increase	(60)	
Payables decrease	(82)	
Accrual increase	8	
	457	
Tax paid	(39)	
Dividend received	17	
Dividend paid	(25)	
Interest paid	(36)	374
Cash flow from investing activities:		
Disposal of asset	54	
Non-current asset	(232)	
Investments	(48)	(226)
Cash flow from financing activities:		
Share issue (150 + 50)	200	
Loan redemption	(375)	(175)
Net cash outflow in the year		(27)
Cash and cash equivalent on 31.12.2010		5
Cash and cash equivalent on 31.12.2011		(22)

Workings:

Non-current assets

	£'000		£'000
Balance b/f	760	Disposal	72
Cash	232	Balance c/d	920
	992		992
Balance b/d	920		

Accumulated depreciation account

	£'000		£'000
Disposal	34	Balance	288
Balance c/d	318	Depreciation	64
	352		352
		Balance	318

Disposal account

	£'000		£'000
Non-current asset	72	Acc. depn	34
Gain	16	Cash	54
	88		88

Investments account

	£'000		£'000
Balance b/f	186	Impairment	20
Cash	48	Balance c/d	214
	234		234
Balance c/d	214		

Taxation (liability) account

	£'000		£'000
Cash	39	Balance b/f	87
Balance c/d	96	Tax expense	48
	135		135

Multiple choice questions

The concept

11.1 Which of the following statement(s) are correct with regard to preparation of Statements of cash flows?

(a) A Statement of cash flows is less objective than a Statement of income
(b) A Statement of cash flows is a forecast of what a company expects in the next year
(c) If receipts in a year exceed payments the difference is identified as net cash inflow
(d) IAS 7 requires the Statements of cash flows to be prepared under three headings

w	a & b	
x	b & c	
y	a & d	
z	c & d	

Identification of cash inflow from sales

11.2 A company's Statement of financial position reports its receivables as shown on the right. In each of the following independent scenarios, identify the cash inflow from sales in the year ended 30 June 2012:

As at 1 July 2011	£498,500
As at 30 June 2012	£525,400

(a) Its sales were £720,800

x	£720,000	
y	£693,900	
z	£746,900	

(b) Its sales were £988,400 and returns inwards £18,200

x	£693,100	
y	£979,700	
z	£943,300	

(c) Its sales were £920,400, returns inwards £5,500, discount allowed £7,800, and discount reversed £900

x	£881,000	
y	£879,300	
z	£890,300	

(d) Its opening inventory was £328,400, purchases £752,800, closing inventory £412,200 and it effects its sales at prices calculated to yield a gross profit ratio of 25%

x	£809,350	
y	£865,100	
z	£642,100	

Identification of cash outflow on purchases

11.3 Particulars of a company's inventory are stated on the right. Identify the company's cash outflow relating to purchases, in each of the following independent scenarios:

As at 1 January 2011	£218,400
As at 31 December 2011	£244,600

(a) Its purchases were £540,200, and its trade payables £118,400 on 31 December 2010 and £286,400 a year later

x	£372,200	
y	£398,400	
z	£708,200	

(b) Its purchases in the year and returns outwards were £712,800 and £35,600 respectively, while trade payables were £392,600 on 1 January 2011 and £388,500 on 31 December 2011

x	£673,100	
y	£681,300	
z	£707,500	

(c) Its sales in the year ended 31 December 2011, made at prices calculated to yield a gross profit ratio of 20%, were £720,000; whilst its trade payables were £294,200 on 31 December 2010 and £282,800 on 31 December 2011

x	£885,100	
y	£879,300	
z	£613,600	

(d) Its sales in the year ended 31 December 2011, made at prices calculated to yield a profit margin of a fourth of cost, were £988,400; while its trade payables were £294,800 on 31 December 2011 and £312,400 a year earlier

x	£799,320	
y	£834,520	
z	£785,100	

(e) During the year to 31 December 2011 its sales made at cost plus a fifth were £850,200; its carriage inwards £12,400 and its trade payables £324,800 on 31 December 2010 and £298,500 on 31 December 2011

x	£720,260	
y	£734,400	
z	£761,000	

Identification of cash outflows on operating expenses

11.4 Rent on business premises has been agreed at £3,000 per month. £9,000 rent had been prepaid at commencement of the year; whilst two months' rent was in arrears by the year-end. Identify the cash outflow on rent.

a	£36,000	
b	£21,000	
c	£39,000	
d	£51,000	

11.5 As at commencement of the year £112,500 was owed to the advertising agent. His bill for the current year was for £827,200; but this includes £30,000 for future television advertising which needs to be paid next year. However, £49,800 is owed to the agent as at the year-end for services already performed in the current year. Identify the cash outflow in the current year.

a	£734,500	
b	£889,900	
c	£859,900	
d	£764,500	

11.6 Operating expenses for the year amounted to £826,400. Accrued operating expenses were £42,400 at commencement of the year and £58,900 at the year-end. Depreciation of non-current assets in the year was £112,400. Identify the cash outflow on operating expenses in the year.

a	£922,300	
b	£730,500	
c	£809,900	
d	£697,500	

11.7 Operating expenses for the year amounting to £752,400 includes depreciation of £98,400, amortisation of development cost of £35,000 and directors' emoluments of £80,000. Prepaid operating expenses were £32,400 at commencement of the year whilst £72,500 remains accrued by the year-end. Identify the cash outflow.

a	£514,100	
b	£434,100	
c	£647,500	
d	£581,500	

Identification of cash outflows on non-operating expenses

11.8 A company had £400,000 8% Loan notes in issue on 1 January 2011 and repaid £150,000 of it by 30 September. Interest in arrears was £8,000 on 1 January 2011 and £5,000 on 31 December 2011. Identify the cash outflow in respect of interest during the year ended 31 December 2011.

a	£32,000	
b	£24,000	
c	£26,000	
d	£20,000	

11.9 On 1 April 2011, a company had in issue £300,000 6% Loan notes and redeemed a third of it on 30 June 2011 paying a premium of 10%. It pays interest on Loan notes half yearly in arrears on 30 June and 31 December. Identify the cash outflow in respect of interest during the year ended 31 March 2012.

a	£13,500	
b	£15,000	
c	£18,000	
d	£16,500	

Identification of cash inflow from operating income

11.10 A business owns seven flats rented out to staff at £500 per month. All flats were tenanted during the year. As at 1 January 21 months' rent was in arrears and as at 31 December 14 months' rent was in arrears. Identify the cash inflow during the year ended 31 December.

a	£45,500	
b	£42,000	
c	£24,500	
d	£38,500	

11.11 Interest income of a company was £39,400 during the year ended 31 March 2012. Interest receivable was £9,400 as at 31 March 2011 and £10,500 as at 31 March 2012. Identify the cash inflow from interest during the year.

a	£39,400	
b	£38,300	
c	£40,500	
d	£28,900	

Identification of cash flows from acquisition and disposal of non-current assets

11.12 As at 1 April 2011 a business owned non-current assets costing £420,000 written down by that date to £284,400. Depreciation in the year was £54,000. Year-end Statement of financial position reports non-current assets at a written-down value of £582,400. Identify the cash outflow on acquiring non-current assets in the year.

a	£216,400	
b	£162,400	
c	£352,000	
d	£298,000	

11.13 Non-current assets of a company were reported on its Statements of financial position as shown on the right. Identify the cash outflow on acquisition and inflow from disposal in each of the following independent scenarios:

As at 30 June	2011	2012
Cost	£640,000	£580,000
Accumulated depreciation	£(112,800)	£(164,200)

(a) A machine acquired for £120,000 and depreciated by £32,400 was sold in the year for £68,000

	Outflow on acquisition	Inflow upon disposal	
x	£60,200	£68,000	
y	None	£19,600	
z	£59,800	£48,400	

(b) A machine acquired for £150,000 was sold at a loss of £38,400. Depreciation written off in the year was £72,500

x	£150,000	£111,600	
y	£90,200	£90,500	
z	£59,800	£167,300	

(c) Computer equipment acquired for £90,000 was sold at a gain of £12,800. Depreciation written off in the year was £82,400 and expenses of disposal were £3,000

x	£30,200	£71,800	
y	£59,800	£46,200	
z	£30,200	£74,800	

(d) Computer equipment acquired for £30,000 and written down to £18,000 was traded in for another, the difference of £15,000 being paid in cash. A vehicle which cost £88,000 was sold at a loss of £12,400. Depreciation written off in the year was £129,800

x	£25,200	£2,800	
y	£40,200	£9,200	
z	£40,200	£12,800	

Identification of cash flows from issue of shares

11.14 The Statements of financial position reported the balances in Share capital and Share premium accounts as shown on the right. Identify the net cash inflow from the share issue, during the year ended 31 March 2012, in each of the following independent scenarios:

As at 31 March	2011	2012
Share capital	£400,000	£700,000
Share premium	£136,000	£174,000

(a) A bonus issue of one for every four was made, prior to a cash issue of shares

w	£338,000	
x	£238,000	
y	£200,000	
z	£138,000	

(b) A bonus issue of one for every five was made prior to a cash issue of shares and expenses on cash issue amounting to £3,000 were written off from the Share premium account

w	£341,000	
x	£338,000	
y	£220,000	
z	£421,000	

(c) A cash issue was made on 1 May 2011, writing off the commission on the issue amounting to £4,000 and expenses of issue amounting to £2,000, followed by a bonus issue on 1 January 2012: one bonus share for every four issued shares

w	£344,000	
x	£342,000	
y	£338,000	
z	£332,000	

(d) A bonus issue of one for five was made on 1 August 2011, followed on 1 November by a rights issue of one for every twelve at 150p per share and a cash issue on 1 January 2012. Par value of ordinary shares was £1 each. Expenses on issuing shares, written off against Share premium, were £3,000

w	£220,000	
x	£278,000	
y	£335,000	
z	£338,000	

Cash inflow/outflow on Loan notes

11.15 6% Loan notes in issue were reported as £300,000 on 31 March 2011 and as £500,000 a year later. On 1 January 2012 one hundred thousand 6% Loan notes were converted to ordinary shares at the rate of two ordinary shares of £1 each for every £50 Loan note. Identify the cash inflow from issue of Loan notes.

a	£200,000	
b	£300,000	
c	£100,000	
d	£400,000	

11.16 9% Loan notes in issue were reported as £400,000 on 31 March 2011 and as £100,000 a year later. On 31 December 2011 a part of the Loan notes in issue was redeemed at 20% premium. What was the cash outflow on redemption of Loan notes during the year ended 31 March 2012?

a	£387,000	
b	£300,000	
c	£240,000	
d	£360,000	

Preparation of Statement of cash flows on the direct method

11.17 Which of the following items will appear on a Statement of cash flows prepared on the direct method?

(a) Depreciation
(b) Bad debts
(c) Receipts from customers
(d) Payments to suppliers
(e) Dividend received
(f) Dividend paid
(g) Revaluation gain
(h) Proceeds of share issue
(i) Bonus issue of shares
(j) Current year tax yet to be paid

w	a, c, d, e, g, h	
x	b, c, e, f, h, i	
y	c, d, e, f, i, j	
z	c, d, e, f, h	

11.18 When the Statement of cash flows is presented on the direct method which of the following items will be listed under the heading 'Cash flow from operating activities'?

(a) Operating expenses
(b) Depreciation
(c) Cash paid for purchases
(d) Interest paid
(e) Dividend received
(f) Dividend proposed
(g) Tax paid
(h) Proceeds on disposal of non-current asset
(i) Interest received
(j) Gain on disposal of non-current assets

w	a, c, d, e, g, h, i	
x	a, b, c, f, h, j	
y	a, c, d, f, g, h	
z	a, b, c, g, h, i	

11.19 Bearing in mind that IAS 7 permits an alternative classification of a few items when presenting Statements of cash flows, which of the following cash flow items may be reported under the heading 'Cash flow from investing activities'?

(a) Acquisition of non-current assets
(b) Gain on disposal of non-current assets
(c) Interest paid
(d) Proceeds of disposal of non-current assets
(e) Interest received
(f) Dividend received
(g) Dividend paid
(h) Tax paid

w	a, c, e, f, g	
x	a, d, e, f	
y	a, c, e, f, g	
z	b, c, e, f, h	

11.20 Bearing in mind that IAS 7 permits an alternative classification of a few items when presenting Statements of cash flows, which of the following cash flow items may be reported under the heading 'Cash flows from financing activities'?

(a) Amount paid to redeem long-term loans
(b) Dividend received
(c) Gain on revaluation of non-current assets
(d) Proceeds of issuing own shares
(e) Interest paid
(f) Bonus issue of shares
(g) Rights issue of shares
(h) Dividend paid

w	a, d, f, g, h	
x	a, b, c, f, g, h	
y	a, c, d, f, g	
z	a, d, e, g	

11.21 Which of the following items will never appear in a Statement of cash flows?

(a) Gain on disposal of non-current assets
(b) Tax on current year's profit
(c) Proceeds on disposal of non-current asset
(d) Gain on revaluation of non-current assets
(e) Dividend proposed
(f) Bonus issue of shares
(g) Rights issue of shares
(h) Dividend paid

w	a, b, d, e, f	
x	a, b, c, f, g, h	
y	a, c, d, f, g	
z	a, c, d, e, f, g	

Preparation of Statement of cash flows on the indirect method

11.22 Which of the following statements is correct in relation to preparation of a statement of cash flows?

(a) The amount reported as cash generated by operating activity will differ depending on whether the Statement of cash flows is prepared on the direct or indirect method
(b) On the indirect method of preparing Statement of cash flows depreciation is added because depreciation generates cash
(c) Revaluation gain will appear as a cash inflow
(d) Gain on disposal of an asset is shown as a source of cash inflow

w	None	
x	a only	
y	b & c	
z	c & d	

11.23 Which of the following items will appear on a Statement of cash flows prepared on the indirect method?

(a) Depreciation
(b) Bad debts
(c) Receipts from customers
(d) Dividend proposed
(e) Dividend received
(f) Dividend paid
(g) Revaluation gain
(h) Proceeds of share issue
(i) Bonus issue of shares
(j) Current year tax yet to be paid

w	a, c, d, e, h	
x	a, e, f, h	
y	c, d, e, f, j	
z	c, d, e, f, h	

11.24 Cash generated from operating activities has been wrongly identified as £950 as shown below on the left. Which of the following corrections need to be made to identify the cash flow?

Operating profit	£948
Depreciation	(£32)
Inventory increase	42
Receivables decrease	21
Payables increase	(29)
Cash inflow	£950

(a) Depreciation should have been added
(b) Inventory increased should have been deducted
(c) Receivables decrease should have been deducted
(d) Payables increase should have been added

Correct answers are		
w	a and b	
x	a, c and d	
y	b, c and d	
z	a, b and d	

11.25 Which of the following statements are correct with regard to calculation of cash generated by operating activities, when using the indirect method?

(a) Increase in the amount of interest remaining unpaid should be added
(b) Depreciation and amortisation of intangibles should be added
(c) Loss of asset disposal should not be deducted from operating profit
(d) Increase in inventory should be deducted

w	a and b	
x	b and c	
y	b, c and d	
z	a, c and d	

11.26 Operating profit, after deducting loss on asset disposal of £34,000 and depreciation amounting to £58,000, has been reported as £842,500. Changes in working capital items in the year were as shown on the left. Calculate the cash generated by operating activity for inclusion in a Statement of cash flows prepared on the indirect method.

Inventory increased by	£21,000
Receivables decreased by	£54,500
Payables decreased by	£12,500
Accruals increased by	£8,200

a	£929,700	
b	£896,200	
c	£842,500	
d	£963,700	

11.27 A machine acquired for £360,000 and depreciated by £210,000 was sold in the year for £180,000. Operating profit for the year, reported as £980,000, includes the gain on disposal of the machine. Ignoring depreciation and changes in working capital items, the amounts to be included in a Statement of cash flows prepared on the indirect method would be:

	Cash flow from		
	Disposal	Operating profit	
a	£120,000	£950,000	
b	£90,000	£980,000	
c	£180,000	£980,000	
d	£180,000	£950,000	

Answers to multiple choice questions

11.1: z 11.2a: y 11.2b: z 11.2c: x 11.2d: y 11.3a: x 11.3b: y 11.3c: z 11.3d: y 11.3e: y 11.4: b 11.5: c 11.6: d 11.7: a 11.8: a 11.9: b 11.10: a 11.11: b 11.12: c 11.13a: x 11.13b: y 11.13c: z 11.13d: y 11.14a: w 11.14b: x 11.14c: y 11.14d: z 11.15: b 11.16: d 11.17: z 11.18: w 11.19: x 11.20: z 11.21: w 11.22: w 11.23: x 11.24: z 11.25: y 11.26: d 11.27: d

Progressive questions

PQ 11.1 Statements of cash flows on both direct and indirect methods

Statements of financial position of Pilchard Ltd are given below:

Statement of financial position as at 31 March	2011		2012	
	£'000	£'000	£'000	£'000
Non-current assets		780		940
Accumulated depreciation		(240)		(320)
		540		620
Current assets:				
Inventory	324		396	
Trade receivables	438		412	
Cash and bank	12	774	3	811
		1,314		1,431
	£'000	£'000	£'000	£'000
Ordinary shares of £1		600		750
Share premium a/c		100		120
Retained earnings		74		90
		774		960
Non-current liabilities:				
6% Loan notes		200		150
Current liabilities:				
Trade payables	298		265	
Taxation	42		45	
Bank overdraft	–	340	11	321
		1,314		1,431

You are informed as follows:

(i) Shown on the right is an extract of the Statement of income for the year ended 31.3.2012.

	£'000
Operating profit	103
Interest	(12)
	91
Taxation	(45)
Profit after tax	46

(ii) There was no acquisition or disposal of non-current assets during the year.

(iii) Loan notes were redeemed at par on 31 March 2012.

Required:

(a) Prepare a Statement of cash flows for the year ended 31 March 2012 using the indirect method.

(b) Prepare a Statement of cash flows on the direct method, taking account of the following additional information:

(i) Sales in the year were £840,000

(ii) Purchases in the year were £620,000.

Clue: The cash balance at beginning of the year was £12,000 whereas the corresponding amount at the end (£3,000 – £11,000 overdraft) was £8,000 negative. Cash outflow = £20,000.

PQ 11.2 A basic question – either method (CIMA amended)

Statement of income year ended 30 September 2011	£'000
Sales revenue	8,000
Cost of sales	(4,500)
Gross profit	3,500
Other expenses	(1,000)
Interest	(14)
Profit before taxation	2,486
Taxation	(800)
Dividends	(700)
Retained profit	986
Retained earnings b/f	4,400
Retained earnings c/f	5,386

Statement of financial position as at 30 September	2011		2010	
	£'000	£'000	£'000	£'000
Non-current assets (wdv)		8,100		6,800
Current assets:				
Inventories	800		600	
Receivables	670		620	
Bank	80		300	
Current liabilities:				
Trade payables	(420)		(340)	
Dividend declared	(400)		(360)	
Taxation	(635)	95	(595)	225
		8,195		7,025
Long-term loans		(1,200)		(1,400)
		6,995		5,625
		£'000		£'000
Share capital		1,100		1,000
Share premium		509		225
Retained earnings		5,386		4,400
		6,995		5,625

During the year the company acquired non-current assets for £1,900,000 and sold for £80,000 ones written down to £310,000.

Required: Prepare a Statement of cash flows for year ended 30.9.2011.

PQ 11.3 A basic question – on the indirect method (CAT 6 – June 2005 amended)

Statements of financial position as at 31 May	2011	2010
	£'000	£'000
Non-current assets	4,600	2,700
Inventory	580	500
Trade receivables	360	230
Bank	0	170
	5,540	3,600
	£'000	£'000
Equity and reserves:		
Ordinary shares	3,500	2,370
Share premium	300	150
Retained earnings	1,052	470
	4,852	2,990
Non-current liabilities:		
10% Loan note	0	100
Current liabilities:		
Trade payables	450	365
Taxation	180	145
Bank overdraft	58	0
	5,540	3,600

Statements of financial position of Snowdrop Ltd are stated on the left. Additional information:

(i) Statement of income for year to 31.5.2011 includes information stated on the right.

	£'000
Operating profit	1,052
Premium on loan note	(10)
Interest expense	(10)
	1,032
Taxation	(180)
Profit after tax	852

(ii) £270,000 was paid as dividend in the year.

(iii) £700,000 was written off as depreciation in the year.

(iv) During the year non-current assets with a written-down value of £200,000 were sold for £180,000.

(v) Loan notes were redeemed at a premium of 10%.

Required:

(a) Prepare a Statement of cash flows for the year ended 31 May 2011.

(b) Comment on the change in the company's liquidity, based on the information in the Statement of cash flows.

(c) Briefly state some of the ways in which companies could manipulate their year-end cash position.

PQ 11.4 On indirect method involving revaluation (ACCA 1.1 amended)

The following information is available for Sioux, a limited liability company:

Statements of financial position as at 31 December

	2011		2010	
	£'000	£'000	£'000	£'000
Non-current assets:				
Cost or valuation		11,000		8,000
Accumulated depreciation		(5,600)		(4,800)
Net book value		5,400		3,200
Current assets:				
Inventories	3,400		3,800	
Receivables	3,800		2,900	
Cash at bank	400	7,600	100	6,800
		13,000		10,000
	£'000	£'000	£'000	£'000
Equity and liabilities:				
Ordinary share capital	1,000		1,000	
Revaluation reserve	1,500		1,000	
Retained earnings	3,100	5,600	2,200	4,200
Non-current liabilities:				
10% Loan notes		3,000		2,000
Current liabilities:				
Trade payables	3,700		3,200	
Income tax	700	4,400	600	3,800
		13,000		10,000

Summarised Statement of income for the year ended 31 December 2010

	£'000
Profit from operations	2,650
Finance cost (loan note interest)	(300)
	2,350
Income tax expenses	(700)
Net profit for the period	1,650

Notes:

(i) During the year non-current assets which cost £800,000, with a net book value of £350,000, were sold for £500,000.

(ii) The revaluation surplus arose from the revaluation of land that is not being depreciated.

(iii) Additional loan notes were issued on 1 January 2011. Interest is paid half-yearly on 30 June and 31 December.

(iv) £750,000 was paid as dividend.

Required: Prepare a Statement of cash flows for the year ended 31 December 2011.

PQ 11.5 Interpretation of information in the Statement of cash flows

Dynamic plc reports a bank overdraft of £13,000 as at 31 December 2011 whereas a year prior to that date it reported a favourable balance at the bank of £10,000.

Directors of the company are unable to make sense of the information conveyed by the Statement of cash flows prepared for the year as shown on the right. They have requested you to:

(a) Advise them on whether depreciation stated on the Statement of cash flows is itself a source of cash inflow.

(b) Explain how a loss made on disposal of a non-current asset could appear as a source of cash.

(c) Comment on whether the liquidity of the company has become worse in the year 2011. Bear in mind that the current liability of the company has been stated at £312,000 on the Statement of financial position as at 31 December 2011.

Statement of cash flows
Year ended 31 December 2011

	£'000	£'000
Cash flow from operating activity:		
Operating profit	540	
Depreciation	62	
Loss on asset disposal	30	
	632	
Inventory increase	(12)	
Receivables increase	(18)	
Payables increase	10	
Interest paid	(40)	
Tax paid	(35)	
Dividend paid	(20)	517
Cash flow from investing activity:		
Property, plant and equipment	(340)	
Asset disposal proceeds	40	
Investments	(50)	(350)
Cash flow from financing activity:		
12% Loan notes redeemed	(400)	
6% Loan notes	100	
Share issue	110	(190)
Cash outflow in the year		(23)
Cash and cash equivalent on 31.12.2010		10
Cash and cash equivalent on 31.12.2011		(13)

PQ 11.6 Cash flow involving revaluation, deferred tax as well as a bonus issue

Statements of financial position as at 30 June	2012		2011	
	£'000	£'000	£'000	£'000
Land and buildings	2,250		1,800	
Accumulated depreciation	(50)	2,200	(480)	1,320
Equipment at cost	960		800	
Accumulated depreciation	(290)	670	(260)	540
Brand names		288		320
Current assets:				
Inventory	492		378	
Trade receivables	374		312	
Cash and bank	36	902	4	694
		4,060		2,874
	£'000	£'000	£'000	£'000
Equity and reserves:				
Ordinary shares of £1	1,600		1,000	
Share premium	48		240	
Revaluation reserve	904		–	
Retained earnings	703	3,255	478	1,718
Non-current liabilities:				
6% Loan notes	100		400	
Deferred tax	41	141	29	429
Current liabilities:				
Trade payables	482		561	
Taxation	102		89	
Dividend declared	80		50	
Bank overdraft	–	664	27	727
		4,060		2,874

(a) Land and buildings were revalued on 1 July 2011 and £26,000 of the revaluation gain was treated as realised in the year. No new land and buildings were acquired in the year.

(b) Equipment acquired for £70,000 was sold in the year for £12,000.

(c) Extracts from the Statement of income for the year are shown on the right.

	£'000
Operating profit	473
Impairment of equipment	(32)
Premium on redemption of loan	(60)
Interest expense	(18)
Profit before taxation	363
Taxation	(84)
Profit after taxation	279

(d) Included within cost of sales in the year were the following:

£40,000 depreciation of equipment
£32,000 amortisation of brand names and depreciation of buildings.

(e) On 1 July 2010 a bonus issue of one for five was made. The cost of the bonus issue, together with £2,000 expenses of a cash issue which took place in April 2011, has been offset from the balance in the Share premium.

(f) £80,000 dividend was declared in 2011.

Required: Prepare the Statement of cash flows for the year ended 30 June 2012.

Test questions

Test 11.1 A basic question

Statements of financial position of Fixem plc are shown on the right. You are informed:

(i) Non-current assets acquired for £120,000 and written down to £60,000 were sold in the year for £90,000.

(ii) Depreciation of £74,000 was written off in the year.

(iii) Payments in the year include the following:

Interest on loan notes: £16,000
Dividends: £20,000

(iv) Tax on the year's profit has been estimated at £48,000.

Required: Prepare a Statement of cash flows for the year ended 31 March 2012 in the format stated in IAS 7.

Clue: To identify operating profit we need to prepare, as far as possible, extracts of a Statement of income.

Statements of financial position as at 31 March	2011		2012	
	£'000	£'000	£'000	£'000
Non-current assets		540		480
Current assets:				
Inventory	320		365	
Trade receivables	286		298	
Cash and bank	34	640	27	690
		1,180		1,170
	£'000	£'000	£'000	£'000
Share capital	500		400	
Share premium	60		40	
Retained earnings	227	787	120	560
Non-current liabilities:				
8% Loan notes		100		300
Current liabilities:				
Trade payables	245		275	
Taxation	48	293	35	310
		1,180		1,170

Statements of financial position as at 31 December	2011	2010
	£'000	£'000
Non-current assets		
Property, plant	1,400	800
Investments	150	120
Current assets:		
Inventory	485	215
Trade receivables	398	328
Cash and bank	34	16
	2,467	1,479
	£'000	£'000
Equity and reserves:		
Share capital	750	500
Share premium	75	50
Retained earnings	793	420
Non-current liabilities:		
8% Loan notes	200	–
Current liabilities:		
Trade payables	496	425
Taxation	78	59
Dividend declared	75	25
	2,467	1,479

Test 11.2 A simple question with extracts from a Statement of income

Bestow Ltd's Statements of financial position are shown on the left. You are informed as follows:

(a) A plant with a written-down value of £354,000 was sold in the year for £280,000. Depreciation written off in the year amounted to £115,000.

(b) Extracts from the company's Statement of income for the year 2011 appear as stated on the right.

	£'000
Operating profit	530
Dividend received	8
Interest paid	(12)
Profit before tax	526
Taxation	(78)
Profit after tax	448

(c) Tax in respect of 2010 was settled at the amount at which it was accounted for.

(d) Apart from paying in March 2011 the dividend declared reported in the Statement of financial position as at 31 December 2010, Bestow Ltd did not pay any other dividend in 2011.

Required:

(a) Prepare a Statement of cash flows for 2011, and

(b) on the basis of the information in the Statement of cash flows make three comments on any change in the company's liquidity position during the year 2011.

Test 11.3 More difficult question on the indirect method

Statements of financial position		
As at 31 December	2011	2010
	£'000	£'000
Non-current asset		
Property, plant and equipment	1,500	1,200
Accumulated depreciation	(420)	(360)
	1,080	840
Brand name	84	96
Investments	112	74
Current assets:		
Inventory	316	348
Trade receivables	424	416
Cash and bank	29	4
	2,045	1,778
	£'000	£'000
Equity and reserves:		
Share capital	800	650
Share premium	80	50
Retained earnings	468	337
Non-current liability:		
8% Loan notes	100	200
Current liabilities:		
Trade payables	408	425
Taxation	114	62
Bank overdraft	–	24
Dividend declared	75	30
	2,045	1,778

The Statements of financial position of Serendib Ltd are shown on the left. You are given the following information:

(a) A plant acquired for £450,000 was sold in the year, making a gain of £14,000.

(b) During the year property, plant and equipment were depreciated by £129,000 and brand names amortised by £12,000.

(c) Extracts from the Statement of income for the year 2011 are shown on the right.

	£'000
Operating profit	369
Impairment of plant	(11)
Dividend received	5
Premium on loan note	(10)
Interest paid	(12)
Profit before tax	341
Taxation	(120)
Profit after tax	221

(d) Tax on profits earned in 2010 was settled by a payment of £68,000.

(e) Some of the loan notes were redeemed in the year at a premium of 10%.

(f) Expenses on issuing shares in the year, amounting to £2,000, were offset from the Share premium balance.

(g) The dividend declared on 31 December 2010 was paid in February 2011, followed by an interim dividend of £15,000 paid in August 2011.

Required:

Prepare a Statement of cash flows for the year ended 31 December 2011 in the format stated in IAS 7.

Test 11.4 An advanced question on the indirect method

Financial statements of Jupiter plc have been prepared as follows:

Statements of financial position as at 30 June

	2012			2011		
	£'000	£'000	£'000	£'000	£'000	£'000
Non-current assets:						
Land and buildings	1,360	(240)	1,120	1,240	(180)	1,060
Plant and equipment	840	(320)	520	720	(280)	440
Development cost			180			160
Investments			140			100
Current assets:						
Inventory		555			624	
Trade receivables		482			396	
Cash and bank balance		3	1,040		14	1,034
			3,000			2,794

	2012 £'000	2012 £'000	2011 £'000	2011 £'000
Equity and reserves				
Ordinary shares of £1 each	1,000		900	
Share premium account	200		90	
Accumulated profit	1,028	2,228	874	1,864
Non-current liabilities:				
6% Loan notes	–		400	
Deferred tax	47	47	34	434
Current liabilities:				
Trade payables	544		368	
Taxation	122		98	
Dividend declared	20		30	
Bank overdraft	39	725	–	496
		3,000		2,794

The following information should be taken into account:

(a) Shown on the right is information extracted from the company's Statement of income for the year ended 30 June 2012.

	£'000
Operating profit	336
Dividend received	12
Premium on loan notes	(40)
Interest paid	(48)
Profit before taxation	260
Taxation	(86)
Profit after tax	174

(b) Operating expenses written off in the year include the following:

	£'000
Depreciation of buildings	60
Depreciation of plant and equipment	46
Amortisation of development cost	34

(c) A plant which cost £80,000 was sold in the year, incurring a loss of £52,000.

(d) Some of the loan notes were redeemed in the year at a premium of 10%.

Required: Prepare a Statement of cash flows for the year ended 30 June 2012.

Test 11.5 Another advanced question involving revaluation and bonus issue

You have been provided with the Statements of financial position of Solvent plc as follows:

Statements of financial position as at 30 June	2012		2011	
	£'000	£'000	£'000	£'000
Non-current assets				
Property, plant and equipment		3,330		2,210
Investments		240		190
Current assets:				
Inventory	569		468	
Trade receivables	474		392	
Cash and bank	9	1,052	48	908
		4,622		3,308
		£'000		£'000
Equity and reserves:				
Ordinary shares of £1 each	2,000		1,500	
Share premium account	200		150	
Revaluation reserve	806		296	
Retained earnings	793	3,799	345	2,291
Non-current liabilities:				
8% Loan notes	100		300	
Deferred tax	72	172	54	354
Current liabilities:				
Trade payables	394		525	
Taxation	112		108	
Dividend declared	40		30	
Bank overdraft	105	651	–	663
		4,622		3,308

You are informed as follows:

(a) Property, plant and equipment is made up as follows:

	As at 30 June 2011			As at 30 June 2012		
Land and buildings at cost/valuation	£1,800	(£348)	£1,452	£2,000	(£32)	£1,968
Plant and equipment	£1,200	(£442)	£758	£1,800	(£438)	£1,362
	£3,000	(£790)	£2,210	£3,800	(£470)	£3,330

(b) Land and buildings were again revalued as at 1 July 2011 and £38,000 of the revaluation reserve, being the extra depreciation arising because of the revaluation exercise, was transferred to Retained earnings. No further acquisition or disposal of land and buildings took place during the year.

(c) A plant which had been acquired for £180,000 several years earlier and depreciated by £54,000 until the date of disposal was sold resulting in a loss of £39,000.

(d) Extracts from the Statement of income for the year ended 30 June 2012 are are shown on the right.

	£'000
Operating profit for the year	598
Dividend received	30
Interest expense	(28)
Premium on redeeming loan notes	(20)
Profit before taxation	580
Taxation	(130)
Profit after taxation	450

(e) Some of the Loan notes were redeemed during the year at a premium of 10%.

(f) A bonus issue of one for five was made and the cost written off from Share premium.

Required: Prepare a Statement of cash flows for the year ended 30 June 2012.

Chapter 12

Accounting ratios and interpretation of financial statements

By the end of this chapter

You should learn:

- About accounting ratios as a tool of analysis
- Methods of calculating and interpreting the ratios
- About the limitations of accounting ratios

You should be able to:

- Calculate accounting ratios
- Interpret the information in financial statements of a company

12.1 The need to interpret financial statements

Financial statements, together with non-financial ones (such as the chairman's review, directors' report and operational and financial review), communicate information to those who have an interest in the company so that they can make decisions on the basis of the information. As the financial statements are prepared on the basis of information in accounting records, those who use the information need to be confident that these are authentic, accurate and complete. Assuming that they are, many users need help to understand the information and accountants provide that help when they prepare reports interpreting the information. For the interpretation accountants rely heavily on what are known as 'accounting ratios'.

12.2 What is an accounting ratio?

An *accounting ratio* merely compares an amount in a financial statement with another related amount for the purpose of tracing the relationship between them in the hope of drawing meaningful conclusions from the relationship. The relationship could be expressed in one of the following forms:

(a) *Pure ratio form*, e.g. A and B share profits in the ratio 2:1 respectively.

(b) *Fraction form*, e.g. this year's profit is one half of last year's profit.

(c) *Percentage form*, e.g. this year's profit is 50% of last year's.

(d) *Times cover*, e.g. current assets cover current liabilities three times.

It would be futile to trace the relationship between two amounts unless there is a valid reason to expect a meaningful relationship between them, and the form chosen to report the relationship is the one regarded as most appropriate to communicate the relationship. For example, if the sales in an accounting period were £100 and the gross profit £25, the relationship between them is usually expressed in percentage form as (£25/£100 × 100 =) 25%. This is known as the gross profit ratio.

A ratio on its own would not be significant unless whether it is good, bad or normal can be established by comparing it with something we refer to as a comparator. Accountants agree that to be useful the comparison could be with:

1. **Ratios in previous periods**: This is known as *inter-temporal comparison* and aims to establish trends and assess whether the trend is in the correct direction (is it becoming better?).
2. **Forecast ratios** to check whether the relationship is according to what the management expected when they prepared forecasts and budgets.
3. **Ratios in similar businesses**: This is known as *inter-firm comparison.*

A change in the relationship needs careful interpretation. It is tempting to rush to wrong conclusions, e.g. that performance in a period is worse because the gross profit percentage has fallen despite improvement in sales. The lower gross profit ratio need not necessarily raise an alarm because it may have been deliberately intended as a way to expand the customer base or to eliminate a rival.

Activity 12.1 Interpreting a change in ratio

A company's sales have decreased and yet its year-end trade receivables have increased. Suggest possible reasons for the change in relationship between sales and receivables.

12.3 The need to focus the interpretation

One of the first things an accountant does before interpreting financial information is to identify the party requiring the interpretation and what the interests and priorities of that party are. That party could be the management of the business, the owners or those to whom it owes money such as the banks and suppliers. Establishment of this is important because the interests and priorities of each would be different. For example, perhaps:

- the priority of the owners could well be the profitability of the business;
- the priority of management could be continuation of employment and improvement of emoluments;
- the priority of a bank could be liquidity, i.e. the ability to service the overdraft and repay loans.

Notwithstanding the individual priorities, all may have a common interest in the following three areas:

1. ***Profitability***: profit levels are important for owners because dividend levels and share prices depend on them. It is also important to those with a claim on the company because falling profits and incurrence of losses would not only erode its liquidity but also threaten its continuity.
2. ***Liquidity***: the entity's ability to meet its bills and exploit opportunities depends on whether it can find ready cash when needed.

3. ***Stewardship***: i.e. the management performance, bearing in mind their fiduciary relationship with the shareholders who have entrusted them with the management.

Let us illustrate the calculation of accounting ratios by reference to the financial statements of an imaginary company, Oldy plc.

Statement of income year ended 31 December 2011	
	£'000
Sales revenue	34,800
Cost of sales	(22,400)
Gross profit	12,400
Operating expenses	(7,850)
Operating profit	4,550
Impairment loss	(200)
Dividend received	30
Interest paid	(40)
Profit before tax	4,340
Taxation	(890)
Profit after tax	3,450
Preference dividend	(60)
Retained profit	3,390

Change in equity	
	£'000
Balance b/f	18,302
Retained earnings	3,390
Dividend paid	(2,000)
Balance c/f	19,692

Statements of financial position as at 31 December				
	2010		2011	
	£'000	£'000	£'000	£'000
Non-current assets:				
Property, plant and equipment	35,800		37,400	
Accumulated depreciation	(8,240)	27,560	(9,280)	28,120
Development cost		320		510
Investments		390		825
Current assets:				
Inventory	1,840		2,848	
Trade receivables	2,680		3,262	
Cash and bank	110	4,630	140	6,250
		32,900		35,705
	£'000	£'000	£'000	£'000
Capital and reserves:				
Ordinary shares of 50p each	10,000		12,000	
6% Preference shares of £1	1,000		1,000	
Retained earnings	18,302	29,302	19,692	32,692
Non-current liability:				
8% Loan notes	500		500	
Deferred tax	42	542	54	554
Current liabilities:				
Trade payable	2,180		1,607	
Accrued expenses	128		94	
Taxation	748	3,056	758	2,459
		32,900		35,705

Other information:

(a) Oldy's shares are listed on 31 December 2011 at 180p.

(b) Oldy issued 4,000,000 ordinary shares of 50p each on 1 April 2011.

12.4 Ratios to measure profitability

The main focus of shareholders would probably be on dividend levels and capital growth in terms of the market price of their shares. With alternative investment opportunities they need to consider whether to keep the shares or to sell them and invest in another. Crucial to such decisions is the level of the company's earnings in comparison with the amount of capital employed in the company. The ratios that are used for this are the return on capital employed (ROCE), relating profit before interest and tax to the average capital employed, and return on equity (ROE). We will consider each of these.

12.4.1 Return on capital employed: also known as the primary ratio

The focus of this ratio is on the levels of profit attained by the company given the long-term capital used – irrespective of whether the capital has been provided by the owners (equity) or by those who have a prior claim to a return, e.g. loan notes and preference shares. The capital employed is the long-term capital financing the company's assets, i.e. excluding current liabilities.

The long-term capital can be identified in one of two ways:

1. either by deducting current liabilities from the total assets;
2. or adding together equity, reserves and non-current liabilities.

In the case of Oldy plc, for example, the capital employed could be calculated as £32,900 less £3,056 amounting to £29,844, or find the same amount by adding together £29,302 plus £542.

Calculating average capital employed

Additional capital raised during an accounting period has an impact on profit levels which depends on how long before the year-end the additional capital was introduced. If capital is introduced late in the year, the ROCE could appear lower than the return actually achieved on the assets used during the year. We need, therefore, to identify the average capital employed in the year.

The profit figure to use

We have defined capital employed as including preference shares and loan notes. The profit used in the ROCE should, therefore, be before deducting any returns in the form of preference dividends and interest. It is also profit before deduction of tax, so that ROCE identifies the performance without being affected by the tax regime in which a company operates.

The formula

ROCE is calculated as follows:

$$\frac{\text{Profit before interest and tax (PBIT)}}{\text{Average capital employed}} \times 100 \qquad \frac{£4{,}380^{a} \times 100}{£31{,}545^{b}} = 13.9\%$$

(a) £4,340 + £40 = £4,380.
(b) (£29,302 + 542) + (32,692 + 554)/2 = £31,545.

How is the ROCE used?

ROCE is referred to as the primary ratio because it is the most useful ratio to assess the profitability of a business. It facilitates comparison of alternative investment opportunities, e.g. a low ROCE might even suggest that investing in a bank fixed deposit is a better alternative. Management use this ratio when making financing and investment decisions, e.g. when deciding whether to borrow additional funds it would not make sense to borrow paying interest at 8% per annum if the company's ROCE is only 7%. Management also focus on ROCE when evaluating acquisitions and the disposal of lines of activity. For example an activity may be profitable, but the overall ROCE of the company may be improved by disposing of it. Low ROCE may reflect *over-capitalisation*, i.e. returns are not commensurate with the amount of capital invested. The question is how the ROCE can be improved.

How can ROCE be improved?

An answer may be found by considering the make up of the ROCE. Later in this chapter we will learn of net profit margin and define it as net profit before interest/sales × 100. We will also learn of the asset turnover ratio and define it as sales/capital employed × 100. We have just learnt that ROCE is net profit before interest/capital employed × 100.

Consider the relationship among the three ratios as follows:

Net profit ratio **Asset turnover ratio** **ROCE**

$$\frac{\text{Net profit before interest}}{\text{Sales}} \times 100 \times \frac{\text{Sales}}{\text{Capital employed}} \times 100 = \frac{\text{Net profit before interest}}{\text{Capital employed}} \times 100$$

Sales	£34,800
Net profit before interest	£4,380
Capital employed	£31,545

We can see that ROCE is the product of the net profit ratio and asset turnover ratio. Let us study the relationship in the case of Oldy plc (see information on the right). The net profit ratio (£4,380/£34,800 × 100) is 12.6% and the asset turnover ratio (£34,800/£31,545) is 1.1 times. The ROCE is, therefore 12.6% × 1.1 times = 13.9%.

This means that the ROCE of a company can be improved by:

(a) improving the net profit ratio, e.g. by improving GP ratio, reducing costs or increasing non-operating income; and

(b) improving the asset turnover, e.g. either by expanding sales or reducing the asset base.

Possible over-trading

A high ROCE may suggest *over-trading*, i.e. the company is trying to achieve business levels far in excess of what its asset base could support. If the high level of business is likely to continue then the company should endeavour to improve its asset base, e.g. by issuing more shares.

ROCE may be affected by many factors

When interpreting ROCE bear in mind that the ROCE of a company could be affected by many factors, such as:

(a) **Revaluation**: when prices are continuing to rise, a company which opts to revalue their non-current assets is likely to show a lower ROCE because its capital employed is likely to be reported at a higher amount.

(b) **Lease rather than buy**: a company may lease its non-current assets so that it does not have to tie down its resources in buying the assets – the effect on ROCE would be an increased percentage return.

(c) **Continuing with outdated assets**, without replacing them. When assets continue in use their carrying value diminishes (because of depreciation), whereas upon their replacement the asset base would increase and correspondingly ROCE reduce.

(d) **Impact of inflation**: a company that acquired most of its assets when the inflation was low would report a better ROCE than one that acquired similar assets when the prices were higher.

12.4.2 Return on equity (ROE) (also known as return of owners' capital – ROOC)

The focus of this ratio is on the level of profits attained on the capital provided by the owners – i.e. the equity capital. The calculation of ROE differs from that of ROCE because:

(a) The profit figure is the profit before tax but after deducting any portion of profit payable to those with a prior claim (as interest and preference dividend) so as to identify the pre-tax profit available to equity holders.

(b) Comparison is with the equity part of the capital employed, i.e. without including prior charge capital such as those provided by preference shares, loan notes and set aside for deferred tax.

The calculation of ROE is shown in the equation:

$$\frac{\text{Profit before tax (after preference dividend)}}{\text{Average equity capital and reserves}} \times 100 \qquad \frac{£4{,}280^{a} \times 100}{£29{,}997^{b}} = 14.3\%$$

(a) £4,340 – 60 = £4,280; (b) (£10,000 + £18,302) + (£12,000 + £19,692)/2 = £29,997.

Observe that this ratio focuses on the levels of profit achieved on the basis of the capital provided by the equity holders. Accordingly amounts provided by and dividends and interest paid to preference shares and loan notes are excluded. We need to remember that the factors (such as revaluation, leasing and inflation) which affect ROCE would equally affect ROE.

In the case of Oldy plc, ROE (14.3%) is better than ROCE (13.9%) because the company earns 13.9% on its capital employed but was able to find a part of the capital at a lower cost, i.e. preference shares at 6% and loan notes at 8%.

The ROE ratio is useful for assessing the justification for using preference share capital (costing 6% but payable from profit after tax) and loan capital (costing 8% interest which is deductible when calculating tax). ROE is useful also for those providing the equity capital when they consider whether the earning levels are commensurate with the risks involved and how it compares with possible earnings from alternative investments.

12.4.3 Gross profit ratio

The simplistic way of assessing the profitability of a business is to identify the percentage of gross profit it makes on each £ of its sales. This is known as the gross profit ratio and is calculated as shown:

$$\text{Gross profit/Sales} \times 100 \qquad £12{,}400/£34{,}800 \times 100 = 35.6\%$$

The gross profit ratio is not a measure of a company's profit-making ability, it merely reflects the company's trading policy – whether it prefers to sell more at reduced prices or to aim at a higher GP ratio by selling at increased prices. Higher GP ratio would not necessarily reflect greater profit-making ability because a company with low GP ratio and a large sales revenue (such as a supermarket) could well be far more profitable than another dealing say in designer clothing with higher gross profit ratio.

Whether a business can achieve higher levels of gross profit ratio would depend on factors such as:

- Whether it is able to sell at its own price or at prices prevailing in the market.
- Whether there is any restriction on competition with it.
- Whether it is able to obtain its inventory from cheaper sources.
- Whether it is able to cut down on its expenses that are counted within the cost of sale.

However, GP ratio is a useful tool, used by auditors and tax authorities to establish the acceptability of accounting information, e.g. each type of business has a typical gross profit ratio which is seen as the norm and enquiries would be made if a company's percentage was significantly different from the norm.

A change in the gross profit ratio could occur for a variety of reasons.

1. **Commercial reasons:**
   - changes in sale prices prevailing in the market;
   - change in the cost of goods that could not be passed on to consumers;
   - change in the sales mix, e.g. the lines with higher GP ratio are selling less than others.
2. **Management failings:**
   - inadequate controls leading to pilferage by staff and shoplifting by customers;
   - failing to ensure that goods accounted for as opening inventory and purchases are also accounted for either as sales or closing inventory;
   - inaccuracies in inventory-taking;
   - inaccuracies in pricing the items remaining unsold.
3. **Manipulations:**
   - deliberately overstating or understating of closing inventory;
   - changing the cost-flow assumption when pricing unsold inventory;
   - inflating or reducing the sales by changing the basis on which sales are recognised.

12.4.4 Operating profit margin

This ratio establishes how operating profit relates to sales, the operating profit being determined by deducting operating expenses from gross profit. Non-operating income such as dividend received and expenses such as interest paid are not taken into account because these cannot be expected to have a meaningful relationship with sales. The ratio is calculated as follows:

$$\frac{\text{Operating profit}}{\text{Sales}} \times 100 \qquad \frac{£4{,}550}{£34{,}800} \times 100 = 13.1\%$$

Operating profit margin would not signal that one company is superior in profitability to another. Whether the operating profit margin level is satisfactory may only be assessed in comparison with norms such as those achieved by others in the same industry. For example the normal operating profit margin in a manufacturing industry is between 8 and 10%; and in a high-volume low-margin activity like food retailing it is around 3%. A higher ratio than the industry norm will attract competition and cannot be maintained unless there are barriers to entry in forms such as the need for significant initial capital, protection from patents and other special features.

A higher operating profit margin may result from a higher gross profit ratio or, if achieved in identical circumstances, may reflect good management and economy, e.g. good cost control. The areas of control could then be identified by working out additional ratios expressing each operating expense as a percentage of sales and comparing the ratio with those of previous years or of other companies.

Operating profit margin is useful when forecasting future profit trends by applying the ratio to forecasted future sales.

12.4.5 Net profit ratio

The net profit ratio is calculated by tracing a relationship between sales and the net profit before deducting interest and tax as follows:

$$\frac{\text{Net profit before interest and tax}}{\text{Sales}} \times 100 \qquad \frac{£4{,}380^{a}}{£34{,}800} \times 100 = 12.6\%$$

(a) £4,340 + £40 = £4,380.

Other than for identifying reasons for a change in ROCE (see 12.4.1), the net profit ratio may not serve any useful purpose. This is because for calculating this ratio we include non-operating income and expenses (such as dividend received and abnormal items such as impairment loss) which are unlikely to have any meaningful relationship with sales.

Activity 12.2 Possible reasons for a fall in gross profit ratio

Tarrant Electronic report their gross profit for the year, along with comparative figures, arrived at as shown on the right.

Required:

(a) Identify the gross profit ratios.

(b) Explain possible reasons for the change in relationship between sales (which increased) and the gross profit (which decreased).

Year ended 30 June	2012		2011	
	£'000	£'000	£'000	£'000
Sales		884		876
Inventory	128		116	
Purchases	726		652	
Inventory	(164)	(690)	(128)	(640)
Gross profit		194		236

Activity 12.3 Assessment of comparative profitability

Salmon Ltd and Tuna Ltd are both retailers of ready-made garments. Salmon aims at the more expensive end of the market, Tuna at the cheaper end. The financial statements of both companies are shown below:

Statement of income year ended 31.12.2011

	Salmon	Tuna
	£'000	£'000
Sales revenue	2,840	18,460
Cost of sales	(1,988)	(16,712)
Gross profit	852	1,748
Distribution cost	(184)	(216)
Administrative expenses	(429)	(426)
Operating profit	239	1,106
Interest	(40)	–
Profit before tax	199	1,106
Taxation	(39)	(220)
Profit after tax	160	886

Statement of financial position as at 31 December 2011

	Salmon	Tuna
	£'000	£'000
Non-current assets	3,200	1,840
Accumulated depreciation	(648)	(484)
	2,552	1,356
Inventory	548	414
Trade receivables	346	28
Cash and bank	34	12
	3,480	1,810
	£'000	£'000
Ordinary shares of £1	2,000	900
Retained earnings	669	354
8% Loan notes	500	–
Trade payables	266	328
Taxation	45	228
	3,480	1,810

Required: Comment on the comparative profitability of both companies, on the basis of calculating four relevant accounting ratios.

12.5 Ratios to assess liquidity

Liquidity is the entity's ability to muster liquid resources, e.g. cash, as and when needed, to (a) exploit opportunities and (b) meet bills as they fall due. It was once believed that a business suffers liquidity problems because it has insufficient working capital (i.e. current assets less current liabilities) and therefore to assess its liquidity we need to check how many times its current assets cover its current liabilities. Hence the traditional methods used to assess liquidity are as follows:

(a) Check how many times the current assets cover current liabilities, and

(b) check how long (in days) it would take to convert each current asset into cash.

12.5.1 Current ratio or working capital ratio

It has been customary to think (not quite correctly) that the liquidity of a company will be satisfactory if the current assets held at each period-end are at least double its current liabilities so that, in an emergency, it will be possible to settle the current liabilities in full if only 50% of its current assets are realised in cash. The current ratio is calculated as follows:

$$\frac{\text{Current assets}}{\text{Current liability}} \quad \frac{£6{,}250}{£2{,}459} = 2.5 \text{ times}^{a}$$

(a) It is always expressed as a times cover. As a rule of thumb a ratio of two or more has been customarily regarded as satisfactory.

The traditional expectation that to be satisfactory current assets should be double the size of the current liability may not be appropriate in all circumstances. Whether a ratio of two or more is satisfactory depends on:

- Type of business: supermarkets are known to operate with negative working capital whereas one engaged in a long-term contract requires a much larger current ratio.
- Type of product – inventory needs to be kept low if it is a fashion item with a risk of rapid obsolescence.
- Type of customers – whether customers are likely to take the full credit period on offer or to respond to an offer of cash discount for early settlement.
- Relations with banks and availability of a fall-back position.

Care is required when interpreting the current ratio

A low ratio does not necessarily indicate a problem: it may be low because the industry norm is low. For example, supermarkets make their purchases on one month's credit. If we assume that a month's purchase amounts to say £300 million, their current liability at the year-end will be in excess of that amount, whereas the current assets will be much smaller because the sales are strictly on a cash basis and inventory is held at minimum levels because emphasis is on rapid turnover. The resources the supermarket uses to settle the current liability in the month following the year-end would not be the ones reported in the form of current assets on its Statement of financial position. The resources needed are generated by purchases made in the days following the year-end and the sale of those items within a few days. The current assets may be deliberately kept low because of investments in non-current assets to expand the asset base.

What is significant, in the case of Oldy plc, is that the current ratio has improved from 1.5 to 2.5 times within a year. This reflects better management of working capital.

12.5.2 Liquidity ratio or acid test ratio or (as it is sometimes known) the quick ratio

It has been customary also to think that for the liquidity of a business to be regarded as satisfactory, its current assets without including the inventory should be at least equal to the current liabilities. Inventory is left out of the equation on the premise that (a) it is the least liquid of the current assets (arguably) and (b) in a going concern scenario inventory needs to remain on the shelf and available for sale. The ability to meet current liabilities must, therefore, be gauged without relying on liquidating the inventory. Hence the liquidity ratio is calculated as follows:

$$\frac{\text{Current asset} - \text{Inventory}}{\text{Current liability}} \qquad \frac{£6{,}250 - £2{,}848}{£2{,}459} = 1.4 \text{ times}^{a}$$

(a) It is always expressed as times cover. As a rule of thumb a ratio of one or more is regarded as satisfactory.

12.5.4 Inventory days

Inventory days calculates how many days' purchases are tied up in the year-end inventory and this is calculated as follows:

$$\frac{\text{Inventory (year-end)}}{\text{Purchases}} \times 365 \text{ days} \qquad \frac{£2{,}848 \times 365 \text{ days}}{£23{,}408^{a}} = 44.41 \text{ days}$$

(a) Purchases in the year has been calculated as £22,400 + £2,848 – £1,840 = £23,408.

By dividing the purchases in the year by 365 days in a year we establish the purchases per day by Oldy plc as £64.13 and then by dividing the year-end inventory by the purchases per day (£2,848/£64.13) we establish that 44.41 days' purchases are tied down in inventory. It indicates that on average it takes 44.41 days for inventory to be converted into cash. Whether the ratio is satisfactory depends on the product and its trading cycle. The number of inventory days for white goods such as refrigerators and washing machines may be expected to be more than those for products with short shelf lives.

12.5.3 Trade receivable days or receivable collection period

This ratio identifies how many days' sales are tied down in the year-end receivables and is calculated as follows:

$$\frac{\text{Receivables (at year-end)}}{\text{Credit sales in the year}} \times 365 \qquad \frac{£3{,}262}{£34{,}800^{a}} \times 365 = 34.21 \text{ days}$$

(a) We assume that all sales are made on credit terms.

If all sales were made on credit terms, the daily sales are £95.34 (£34,800/365 days) and 34.21 (£3,262/£95.34) days' sales are tied up in receivables. Whether the ratio is satisfactory depends on the credit days permitted to customers. If Oldy is a retailer, selling, as is usual, on one-month credit, the ratio of 34.21 days would be satisfactory.

12.5.4 Trade payable days

This ratio identifies how many days it takes on average to settle trade payables and is calculated as:

$$\frac{\text{Payables (at year-end)}}{\text{Credit purchases in the year}^{a}} \times 365 \text{ days} \qquad \frac{£1{,}607}{£23{,}408^{b}} \times 365 = 25.06 \text{ days}$$

(a) We assume that all purchases were made on credit terms; (b) Purchases in the year has been calculated as £22,400 + £2,848 – £1,840 = £23,408.

Purchases per day are £64.13 (£23,408/365 days) and 25 days' purchases (£1,607/£64.13) remain unpaid at the year-end. Whether the ratio is satisfactory depends on the credit terms agreed with the suppliers. If supplies are purchased on one month's credit the ratio of 25 days means that Oldy plc is not exceeding the credit period. However, by paying earlier than 30 days Oldy is not taking advantage of credit made available by the suppliers.

12.5.5 The working capital cycle

The working capital cycle would identify how much of the capital employed in a business is needed for financing its working capital requirements. We have calculated that in the case of Oldy plc the inventory days are 44.41 and of that the suppliers finance 25.06 days. This leaves a balance of 19.35 days of purchases @ £64.13 per day, which needs to be financed within the company. In addition, trade receivable days of 34.21 @ £95.34 per day need to be financed. Hence Oldy needs to find (see box on the right) £4,503 from its capital employed to finance its working capital cycle.

Inventory: 19.35 days @ £64.13 per day	£1,241
Receivables 34.21 days @ £95.34 per day	£3,262
Total working capital finance	£4,503

12.5.6 The cash flow ratio

The cash flow ratio (which we met with in Chapter 11) is the most useful of the liquidity ratios because it establishes a relationship between the cash generation that may be expected from a company's operating activities with the cash flow requirements to settle the year-end current liability. The calculation is as follows:

$$\frac{\text{Operating profit + depreciation}^{a}}{\text{Current liability (year-end)}} \qquad \frac{£4{,}550 + £1{,}040^{b}}{£2{,}459} = 2.3 \text{ times}$$

(a) Depreciation and similar expenses not involving cash outflow in the current year are added back;
(b) Depreciation has been calculated on the basis of accumulated depreciation figures as £9,280 – £8,240 = £1,040.

Thus the cash generation from Oldy's operating activities in the year has been £5,590 (£4,550 operating profit plus depreciation £1,040 which did not involve a cash outflow in the year) and this is able to cover 2.3 times the amount of its current liability reported at the year-end.

Activity 12.4 Evaluation of liquidity

Refer back to Activity 12.3 for information on Salmon and Tuna. You are further informed as follows:

(a) Their Statement of financial position as at 31 December 2010 includes items shown on the left.

(b) In the year ended 31 December 2010 revenue items were as reported below.

As at 31.12.2010		
	Salmon	Tuna
	£'000	£'000
Inventory	472	328
Trade receivables	298	32
Cash and bank	52	39
Trade payables	217	294
Taxation	38	198

	Salmon	Tuna
	£'000	£'000
Sales	2,140	17,200
Purchases	1,680	14,900
Depreciation	122	78
Operating profit	218	994

Required: Comment on the liquidity of both companies, making inter-temporal as well as inter-firm comparisons based on not less than six sets of accounting ratios calculated for each company.

12.6 Ratios to assess operating performance

The performing efficiency of a business is gauged by calculating how hard it uses its available resources. If a business with a capital base of £100,000 is able to achieve a sales level of ten times that amount (i.e. capital is turned around ten times) it is considered to be more efficient than another achieving comparatively lower levels of asset turnover. Similarly, by calculating turnover ratio for the amount of inventory carried the satisfactoriness of purchasing management can be evaluated. The efficiency of credit management can be evaluated by calculating the receivables turnover ratio and the payables turnover ratio. Let us review these ratios:

12.6.1 Asset turnover ratio

The asset turnover is calculated as follows:

$$\frac{\text{Sales for the year}}{\text{Average capital employed in the year}} \qquad \frac{£34{,}800}{£31{,}545^{a}} = 1.1 \text{ times}^{b}$$

(a) Capital employed as at a particular day may be found by either adding together the non-current assets and the current assets less current liabilities or as done below by deducting current liabilities from the total assets: (32,900 – 3,056) + (35,705 – 2,459) × ½ = £31,545; (b) Asset turnover ratio is always expressed as a times cover.

There is no norm to be regarded as the ideal, but assessment of what is achieved could be done only on the basis of inter-firm or inter-temporal comparisons. If the asset turnover appears by comparison to be excessively high it would indicate 'over-trading' (i.e. trying to do too much business with too little capital). One example of it could be when a company attempts to maintain revenue levels without keeping the asset base modernised and up to date – a situation in which you will find a rapid decline in the carrying value of non-current assets and corresponding increase in asset turnover.

To investigate changes in the asset turnover ratio we could work out separately the *non-current asset turnover ratio* and the *current asset turnover ratio*. A company could prove more profitable than another by improving its asset turnover, even if the operating profit margin remains identical for both.

Non-financial ratios

Many business entities go even further to demonstrate the superiority of their operating performance when they calculate physical ratios such as:

- sales per square metre of selling space;
- sales per sales staff.

12.6.2 Inventory turnover ratio

The ratio identifies the number of times the inventory has been turned around (i.e. sold and replaced). Increase in this ratio indicates improvement in the buying function, i.e. focus on buying only those that can be quickly sold. It is calculated as follows:

$$\frac{\text{Cost of sales}}{\text{Average inventory}} \qquad \frac{£22{,}400}{(1{,}840 + 2{,}848) \times {}^{1}/_{2}} = 11 \text{ times}$$

The more frequent the turn around the greater is the profit, not only because there is profit margin at each cycle, but also because of decrease in capital tied up in inventory, storage costs and insurance as well as loss from obsolescence.

Care when interpreting

The inventory turnover would differ in accordance with whether the entity is a wholesaler, retailer, exporter, importer, trader or manufacturer having regard, for example, to how long the manufacturing process takes. The ratio has by necessity to be high in businesses such as bakery, dairy and any that deal with perishables or products with a limited sell-by date. Besides, the inventory turnover ratio is usually exaggerated because entities tend to fix their accounting period to end when their inventory holdings are at the lowest. We need also to bear in mind that the inventory turnover ratio is susceptible to manipulations by such means as deliberately running down inventory holdings, postponing reordering, conducting heavily discounted sales by year-end and undertaking an aggressive write-down of inventory.

12.6.3 Trade receivables turnover

Although a business sells goods on credit in an effort to promote its sales, it remains conscious that amounts tied up in trade receivables are unproductive. That is why it sets a credit period and endeavours to enforce it. One measure of the success of its enforcement of the credit period is the trade receivable turnover, calculated as follows:

$$\frac{\text{Credit sales}}{\text{Average receivables}} \qquad \frac{£34{,}800}{(2{,}680 + 3{,}262) \times {}^{1}/_{2}} = 11.7 \text{ times}$$

Whether the ratio is satisfactory can only be judged in accordance with the nature of business, the type of product, the kind of customers, the credit terms on offer by competitors, the length of credit offered by the business, whether the business offers discounts for prompt payment and so on. A high ratio is generally better because it means that less of the amounts generated by credit sales remain tied up in trade receivables – however, care is needed that the pressure to increase the rate of turnover does not adversely affect the level of sales. On the other hand, a low receivables turnover ratio can be an indication of poor credit management.

The importance of sound credit management

Unless proper credit management is enforced the survival of the business can be in jeopardy. It was reported[1] that 4,818 companies failed during the first quarter of 2006 and of the 34 industries surveyed by Experian, 22 recorded an increase in business failures in the first quarter of 2006.

12.6.4 Trade payables turnover

To maximise the benefits from financial resources available to it a business should aim at the lowest possible trade payable turnover, without alienating its suppliers. The payables turnover ratio is calculated as follows:

$$\frac{\text{Credit purchases}}{\text{Average payables}} \quad \frac{£22{,}400 + £2{,}848 - £1{,}840 = £23{,}408^{a}}{(£2{,}180 + £1{,}607)/2 = £1{,}894} = 12.4 \text{ times}$$

(a) Cost of sales + closing inventory minus opening inventory would provide the figure of purchases.

Activity 12.5 An assessment of operational efficiency

Statement of income year ended 30 June 2011	
	£'000
Sales revenue	16,425
Cost of sales	(9,855)
Gross profit	6,570
Expenses	(3,942)
Operating profit	2,628

Mackeral plc's capital employed as at 30 June 2011 is £7.5 million. A summary of their Statement of income appears on the left. Directors are proposing to raise £1.5 million additional capital by a share issue and expect that their performance next year will be as shown on the right.

Assuming that their expectations materialise:

Statement of income year ended 30 June 2012	
	£'000
Sales revenue	21,600
Cost of sales	(12,960)
Gross profit	8,640
Expenses	(5,076)
Operating profit	3,564

Required:

(a) Calculate for each of two years the return on capital employed, identifying how much of the improvement arises from asset turnover and how much from the improvement in operating profit margin, and

(b) explain how exactly the directors are planning to improve the company profitability.

12.7 Level of risk to equity shareholders

Companies finance their activity by issuing shares or loan notes. A company which obtains loan-finance is said to be *geared* and *'highly geared'* if the loan capital is more than 50% of the total capital employed in the company. The level of gearing is measured by one of the following two ratios.

12.7.1 Gearing (or leverage) ratio

This ratio focuses on the proportion of capital employed provided by those other than equity holders, i.e. preference shares and loan notes. It is calculated as follows:

$$\frac{\text{Prior charge capital}}{\text{Total capital employed}} \times 100 \qquad \frac{£1{,}000^{a} + £500^{b}}{£32{,}692 + 554} \times 100 = 4.5\%$$

Any capital provider with a right to receive a return prior to equity holders is regarded as 'prior charge' capital. Hence preference shares[a] and loan notes[b] are in that category. Oldy plc is geared, but to be regarded as highly geared the ratio should exceed 50%.

Companies may raise capital by issuing loan notes or preference shares, so long as investment opportunities arise which give them prospects of improving their ROCE. However, in the process they could become highly geared. High gearing is not necessarily detrimental so long as the company has prospects of improving profit. However, in the event there is a fall in profit levels there will be a more than proportionate impact on the amount of profit available to equity holders.

12.7.2 Debt equity ratio

The debt equity ratio is merely an alternative formula for measuring the level of gearing and is calculated as follows:

$$\frac{\text{Prior charge capital}}{\text{Equity capital (including reserves)}} \times 100 \qquad \frac{£1{,}000 + £500}{£12{,}000 + £19{,}692} \times 100 = 4.7\%$$

When gearing is measured this way, to be regarded as highly geared, the ratio needs to be more than 100%.

Activity 12.6 How high gearing affects equity shareholders

	£'000
Ordinary shares	4,000
6% Preference shares	3,000
Reserves	500
	7,500
8% Loan notes	5,000
	12,500

Extracts from Sardine plc's Statement of income for the year ended 30 September 2011 are shown on the right and particulars of capital employed, as at 30 September 2011, are shown on the left. Assume that tax is calculated at 20% of profit.

Statement of income year ended 30.9.2011	£'000
Operating profit	945
Interest on loan	(400)
Profit before tax	545
Income tax	(80)
Profit after tax	465
Preference dividend	(180)
Retained profit	285

Required:

(a) Calculate the extent of the company's capital gearing.

(b) Identify how high gearing affects equity shareholders by working out the percentage fall in the retained profits (available for ordinary shares) if there is a 20% fall in operating profit.

12.8 Share market ratios

If a company is one listed on a stock exchange (i.e. share market), when making decisions such as whether to hold the shares, buy more, or dispose of existing holdings, investors consider the following accounting ratios:

12.8.1 Earnings per share (EPS)

Every company listed on any stock exchange is required to publish a figure of EPS in the hope that it would assist the investor to make an estimate of what each equity share in the company may be able to earn. EPS is calculated as follows:

$$\frac{\text{Profit after tax} - \text{Preference dividend}}{\text{Weighted average number of ordinary shares}} \times 100 \qquad \frac{£3{,}450 - £60}{23{,}000^{a}} \times 100 = 14.7\text{p}$$

(a) Since four million shares had been issued on 1 April 2011, the weighted average number of shares in issue in the year would be (20,000,000 shares × 3/12 months) + (24,000,000 shares × 9/12 months) = 23,000,000 shares.

EPS is always expressed in pence and is calculated to one decimal place. The aim is to identify how much of the current year's earnings is potentially available, after deducting tax as well as amounts payable to those with a prior claim, to each of the ordinary shares in issue and ranking for dividend in that year. It is possible that a company may issue ordinary shares towards the end of its accounting period with a warning that these shares would not rank for any dividend payment in that period. Those who hold shares or wish to buy shares in a company listed on a stock exchange view EPS as the indicator of the earning ability of the equity shares in a company.

Activity 12.7 Earnings per share

	£'000
Ordinary shares of 50p each	900
6% Preference shares	100
Share Premium account	120
Retained earnings	90
	1,210

The equity and reserves portion of Sardine plc's Balance sheet as at 31 December 2011 is shown on the left and an extract from the Statement of income ending on that date is shown on the right. 300,000 Ordinary shares of 50p each were issued on 1 May 2011. No dividends were paid in the year.

	£'000
Operating profit	158
Interest	(30)
Profit before tax	128
Taxation	(25)
Profit after tax	103

Required: Calculate the basic earnings per share for the year ended 31 December 2011.

Clue: If after issuing 300,000 shares there are 1,800,000 (900,000/0.50p) ordinary shares in issue, then in the four months to 1 May 2011 the ordinary shares in issue would have been 1,500,000.

12.8.2 Price earnings ratio

The price earnings (PE) ratio calculates how many years earnings are represented by the share price. By comparing the market price of each share with that share's earning power

(EPS) an attempt is made to gauge the confidence the market has in that company. A high PE ratio reflects a high level of market confidence that there will be a growth in the share price. Usually the PE ratio of a high-quality blue chip may be 15 or more, whereas the PE ratio of companies without market appeal may be 8 or even less. The market appeal of a company may depend on many factors, some of which are listed in the box on the right.

Factors that usually affect the price earnings ratio:

- Overall mood of share market
- Prospects within the industry
- The company's own history
- Market's view of the company's prospects
- Volume of shares being traded at any time

The PE ratio is calculated as follows:

$$\frac{\text{Market price per share}}{\text{Earnings per share}} \qquad \frac{180\text{p}}{14.7\text{p}} = 12.2 \text{ times}$$

It appears that there is a high market confidence in the growth of Oldy plc's share prices.

12.8.3 Dividend cover

Dividend cover measures whether the company will be able to continue paying dividends at the current levels. It is calculated as follows:

$$\frac{\text{Earnings per share}}{\text{Dividend per share}} \qquad \frac{14.7\text{p}}{8.3^{a}} = 1.8 \text{ times}$$

(a) £2,000/24,000 shares = 8.3p per share.

This is an important ratio that needs to be taken account of – particularly if the company's earnings are volatile. A dividend cover of 1.8 indicates that earnings are almost twice the amount paid out as dividend. In percentage terms the dividend is only 56.5% (8.3/14.7 × 100) of the earnings. This means that unless the earnings fall by more than 43.5% the company will be able to maintain dividends at current levels.

12.8.4 Dividend yield

This ratio identifies what percentage return the dividend represents when considered in the light of the amount tied up in the share. The amount tied up in each share is the amount at which it can be sold, i.e. the market price of the share. The calculation is as follows:

$$\frac{\text{Dividend per share}}{\text{Price per share}} \times 100 \qquad \frac{8.3\text{p}}{180\text{p}} \times 100 = 4.6\%$$

The dividend yield on the shares in Oldy plc may not compare well with possible returns from alternative investments, if, for example, the return on a bank fixed deposit is that amount or higher.

12.8.5 Earnings yield

Since the dividend a company pays would depend on the directors' dividend policy, a more meaningful comparison of the return from investing in the shares could be by identifying an earnings yield by expressing the earnings per share (rather than the dividend) as a percentage of the market price of each share. Earnings yield is calculated as follows:

$$\frac{\text{Earnings per share}}{\text{Price per share}} \times 100 \qquad \frac{14.7\text{p}}{180\text{p}} \times 100 = 8.2\%$$

The earnings yield on the shares in Oldy plc may perhaps be more comparable with alternative earning possibilities.

12.8.6 Interest cover

This ratio is useful for providers of loan capital (rather than equity capital). It measures the possible impact of a fall in profit levels on the interest payments and is calculated as follows:

$$\frac{\text{Profit before interest and tax}}{\text{Interest expense}} \qquad \frac{£4{,}340 + £40}{£40} = 110 \text{ times}$$

The holders of loan notes in Oldy plc can rest assured that their interest payments are well covered (110 times) by its earnings.

Activity 12.8 Investor's dilemma

Gloria seeks your advice on whether she should invest in ordinary shares of Minnow plc or Mullet plc. Shares of both companies have a par value of £1 and she has provided you with the information stated on the right.

	Minnow	Mullet
Earnings per share	18p	24p
Market price per share	252p	192p
Dividend paid per share	5p	15p

12.9 Limitations of accounting ratios

12.9.1 Ratios indicate symptoms

Accounting ratios are to the accountant what physical symptoms are to the doctor. A reading from a thermometer or a blood pressure gauge would in itself have no significance unless the medical practitioner is able to interpret the reading. The relationship traced by an accounting ratio is only a symptom. The symptoms need to be interpreted and for that other corroboration may be required such as:

1. **Other ratios**, e.g. if asset turnover is rising quickly calculate the non-current asset turnover ratio as well as the current asset turnover ratio to check whether there is a fall in either. Then explore further. If the current asset turnover is also rising, continue to check inventory turnover, receivable turnover and so on.
2. **Identify any bias**: every effort must be made to identify possible bias. For example, an owner of a business proposing to sell it may be tempted to inflate the profit. Whereas, if a management buy-out is being considered, the temptation would be to deflate profit level to buy the business at a lower price.
3. **Seek corroboration** from alternative sources such as from credit agencies, bank references, comments in trade press and so on.

The usefulness of an accounting ratio depends on the skill of the analyst using it, interpreting it and identifying reasons as well as corrective action.

12.9.2 Ratios can be calculated and expressed in different ways

Other than for earnings per share,[2] there is no Accounting Standard prescribing a formula or assisting with the interpretation of any accounting ratio. As a result the ratio arrived at could differ, depending on how it has been worked out.

Calculating a ratio in a different way

For example, we calculated the ROCE by dividing profit before interest and tax (referred to as PBIT) by average capital employed and worked out the average by adding together the capital employed at the end of an accounting period and that at the beginning and dividing the total by two, i.e. we found the simple average. It would be more appropriate had we used the weighted average. For example, Oldy plc raised an additional £2,000,000 by issuing shares on 1 April 2011, so that the issued share capital was £10 million for the first three months and £12 million for the remaining nine months, so that the weighted average issued capital would be (£10,000,000 × 3/12 + £12,000,000 × 9/12 =) £11,500,000. Assuming that retained earnings accrued consistently throughout the year its simple average would be (£18,302 + £19,692/2 =) £18,997. Adopting this approach, the average capital employed would have been calculated as (£11,500 + 18,997 =) £30,497 rather than £31,545.

Expressing a ratio in a different way

The way a ratio is communicated may also be questioned. For example, we calculated the dividend cover using the formula (earnings per share/dividend per share) and reported the ratio in times cover form as 1.8 times. But when interpreting it we reversed the formula as dividend per share/earnings per share expressing the relationship in percentage terms, to identify that dividend amounted to 56.5% of the earnings, so that unless earnings fell by 43.5% (reciprocal) the current levels of dividend can be maintained.

12.9.3 Accounting ratios need comparators

A ratio, in isolation, would be of little use, unless the ratio has a norm with which it can be compared or a standard against which it can be judged. The relationship traced by a ratio would be meaningful only in comparison with:

- what the relationships were in the past;
- what relationships were aimed at when the business established its budget;
- what relationship competitors and others achieve in the same industry.

Such a comparison may not always be meaningful because the comparator may not always be the ideal attainable. Comparative information may be obtained from membership of a trade association where members submit their financial data and receive an inter-firm comparison report, which compares each member's performance with the other members whilst maintaining each firm's anonymity. A typical inter-firm comparison report calculates the company's own ratios and a quartile analysis of the ratios of all members, so that the company can assess its own position in comparison with the average for the industry, i.e. whether the company is within the best quartile or the worst.

12.9.4 Ratios are no more than red flags

The ratios are simply red flags that should raise questions. Accounting ratios are incapable of providing answers to the numerous questions raised by the users of accounting reports.

All that they can do is to provide a basis for comparison and to indicate trends. For example, we learnt that the ROCE of Oldy plc for the year is 13.9%. This does not tell us what the yield could have been in the circumstances of the business or how best such a yield could be improved.

12.9.5 Knowledge of a business's commercial thinking is essential

A relationship traced by a ratio would be meaningless unless it is interpreted in the light of the circumstances of the business involved. For example, a business may deliberately build up high inventory levels, resulting in poorer inventory turnover ratio as well as deterioration of the liquidity ratio. But this may be a deliberate move either to launch a significant sales push or in anticipation of a price rise. An interpretation of accounting ratios, without full awareness of the attendant circumstances, may well lead to erroneous conclusions and hence, decisions. Besides, the symptoms revealed by the same set of ratios are capable of several, sometimes conflicting, interpretations. For example, significantly high inventory turnover ratio and receivable turnover ratios may well be interpreted as signs respectively of super buying efficiency and effective credit control. What these ratios may mask is that the entity is losing business because of inadequate inventory levels to meet customer needs and that customers are being alienated by an overly severe credit policy.

12.9.6 Trends are vital

More important than a relationship currently existing is the trend in relationships, over the years. The trend throws into relief the significance of any change taking place. Taking note of such changes is crucial where the ratios are used as the basis for predicting the future.

12.9.7 Inter-firm comparison is meaningless unless the companies are comparable

The companies with which the comparison is made should:

- be in the same lines of activity;
- carry on the same type of business – manufacturer, wholesaler or retailer;
- use identical accounting policies – on all matters such as asset valuation, depreciation, cost-flow assumption, deferral of development cost;
- be engaged in similar business practices on matters like buying/leasing assets, dealing in consignment goods, debt factoring;
- be financed similarly with identical gearing levels.

12.9.8 Inflation distorts ratios

The size of the capital employed in a company will depend on the price levels prevailing when most of its non-current assets were acquired. For example, given the steadily rising price levels, a company which acquired its assets in the recent past may well appear to be better endowed (though reporting a lower ROCE) than another which commenced long years ago, merely because the latter acquired its assets when the value of money was higher.

12.9.9 Year-end figures are not always representative

Most companies choose their year-end date when their inventory levels are the lowest. As a result inventory turnover levels reported tend to be exaggerated.

12.9.10 Ratios can be deliberately manipulated

Manipulation may take the form of window dressing, e.g. delaying purchases until after the year-end. The manipulation could also take forms such as off-balance sheet financing or a finance lease engineered to appear as an operating lease.

12.10 Interpreting financial information by other means

There are, of course, alternative ways of placing the information in a financial statement in proper perspective. These include:

1. **Graphical representations** such as *pie charts* and *bar charts* drawn to portray the comparative sizes of each item, say in a Statement of income, as slices of a pie or as bars, each proportional in size to the amount or percentage it represents.
2. **Component percentages** can be used to equate the focal point of attention in a financial statement to 100 and then express all other significant amounts as percentages of that figure.

Statement of income for year ended 31.12.2011	
	£'000
Sales revenue	950
Cost of sales	(665)
Gross profit	285
Administrative expenses	(152)
Distribution cost	(56)
Interest	(12)
Profit for the year	65

For example, if information in the Statement of income on the left is presented as component percentages, the sales revenue is equated to 100 and the remaining items of expenses presented as what percentage each of them represents, as shown on the right. For reporting as percentage, the individual expenses could be classified by function (as we have) or by type of expense (as salary, advertising).

Statement of income year ended 31.12.2011	
	£'000
Sales revenue	100%
Cost of sales	(70)%
Gross profit	30%
Administrative expenses	(16)%
Distribution cost	(6)%
Interest	(1)%
Profit for the year	7%

Expression as a percentage is useful for the purpose of cost control – first by establishing how it relates to sales and secondly for inquiring whether it is increasing more than in proportion to increase in sales. Once the need for control is identified action may be taken using methods such as follows:

- establishment expense – moving the head office from the city centre to a less expensive location;
- administrative expense – by downsizing or making middle managers redundant;
- selling expense – by pruning advertising or sales commission;
- distribution costs – by using own delivery fleet rather than carriers;
- finance costs – by seeking cheaper source of finance or renegotiating loan terms.

Summary

- Accounting ratios are the main tools of analysis used for interpreting information in the financial statements.
- Accounting ratios trace, in one of four different forms, the relationship between two amounts reported in financial statements with a view to drawing conclusions from that relationship and from movements in that relationship.
- Accounting ratios are only useful as signals identifying symptoms which need proper diagnosis, interpretation and appropriate action.

References

1. http://www.prnewswire.co.uk/cgi/news?release?id=169387.
2. IAS 33 *Earnings Per Share*, IASB issued 1997, London, International Accounting Standards Board.

Suggested answers to activities

12.1 Interpreting a change in ratio

The adverse change in relationship between sales and trade receivable could have arisen because of any one or more of the following reasons:

(a) Commercial reasons:
- the credit terms allowed by competitors in the industry may have changed;
- because of keener competition in the market, extended credit may be the only way to survive;
- because of a change in customer base – the new customers may be ones who could negotiate better credit terms;
- extension of credit period may be a strategy to survive in a declining market;
- company may have taken debt indemnity insurance and hence be willing to extend credit period.

(b) Financial reasons: with improvement in liquidity position there could have been a decision to offer improved credit terms to customers.

(c) Administrative reason such as break-down in credit control.

12.2 Possible reasons for a fall in gross profit ratio

(a) Gross profit ratio 2012: £194,000/£884,000 × 100 = 21.9%
2011: £236,000/£876,000 × 100 = 26.9%

(b) Possible reasons for fall in gross profit ratio:
- Commercial reasons:
  - market price for the product has fallen;
  - costs (purchase price, processing costs, carriage inwards, freight duty) and so on have increased and they could not be passed on to the customer by increasing sale price;
  - an adverse variation in sales mix, i.e. more is sold of less profitable items.
- Accounting errors:
  - not establishing the correct cut-off to ensure that all goods accounted for as opening inventory and purchases are included within closing inventory unless they have been sold;
  - error in inventory-taking such as failing to include some items in the count or overlooking items in bonded warehouse or with customers on sale or return basis;
  - error in ascribing cost to the items listed on the inventory sheet.

- Failure of internal controls:
  - pilferage of goods by staff;
  - shoplifting by customers;
  - failure to account for goods removed by owner.
- Manipulation of accounts calculated to deliberately understate the entity's performance.

12.3 Assessment of comparative profitability

	Salmon		Tuna	
(a) Gross profit ratio	£852,000/£2,840,000 × 100 =	30%	£1,748,000/£18,460,000 × 100 =	9.5%
(b) Operating profit ratio	£239,000/£2,840,000 × 100 =	8.4%	£1,106,000/£18,460,000 × 100 =	6%
(c) ROCE	£239,000/£3,169,000[a] × 100	7.6%	£1,106,000/£1,254,000[b] × 100 =	88.2%
	(a) £2,000,000 + £669,000 + £500,000 = £3,169,000		(b) £900,000 + £354,000 = £1,254,000	
(d) Return on equity	£199,000/£2,669,000 × 100 =	7.5%	£1,106,000/£1,254,000 × 100 =	88.2%

Comments:

1. Catering to customers at the upper end of the market, Salmon Ltd is able to fix its sale prices high, earning a gross profit ratio of 30%; whereas Tuna Ltd's gross profit ratio is only 9.5% because its trading policy is higher turnover with lower margins.
2. Higher gross profit ratio is reflected in a higher operating profit ratio as well for Salmon – 8.4% compared to 6%. However, as we shall see when considering operating efficiency, Salmon incurs a higher proportion of its earnings on administration and distribution expenses.
3. The ROCE identifies Tuna (88.2%) as far more profitable than Salmon which earns only 7.6%; calling into question whether it is justified in borrowing loan notes at 8%. Though considering the type of customers it caters to it has to maintain a better selling environment, with consequent capital cost, there arises a suspicion whether it is over-capitalised. On the other hand Tuna could be over-trading.
4. Salmon's ROE is lower than ROCE because it services loan notes at a rate (8%) higher than what it earns (7.6%). In the absence of any prior charge capital Tuna's ROE is the same as its ROCE.

12.4 Evaluation of liquidity

	Salmon . . .				Tuna . . .			
	2010 £'000		2011 £'000		2010 £'000		2011 £'000	
Current ratio	822/255	3.2 times	928/311	3 times	399/492	0.8 times	454/556	0.8 times
Liquidity ratio	310/255	1.2 times	380/311	1.2 times	71/492	0.14 times	40/556	0.07 times
Inventory days	472/1,680 × 365	102 days	548/2,064 × 365	97 days	328/14,900 × 365	8 days	414/16,798 × 365	8.9 days
Receivable days	298/2,140 × 365	50.8 days	346/2,840 × 365	44.5 days	32/17,200 × 365	0.7 days	28/18,460 × 365	0.5 days
Payable days	217/1,680 × 365	47 days	266/2,064 × 365	47 days	294/14,900 × 365	7 days	328/16,798 × 365	7 days
Cash flow ratio	218 + 122/255	1.3 times	239 + 142/311	1.2 times	994 + 78/492	2.2 times	1,106 + 96/556	2.2 times

Comments:

1. Though dealing in the same product (garments) the companies cannot be compared because:
   (a) They are operating in two diverse markets – Salmon is at the upper end where convenience and facilities matter more than the price; whereas Tuna operates at the opposite extreme, pruning down profit margins and focusing on sales volume.
   (b) Their trading practices are obviously different – Salmon buying probably on one month's credit and selling also on similar terms; whereas Tuna is selling mostly on cash terms and buying predominantly on cash terms.
2. Considering the trading practices, the normal rule of thumb is probably applicable to Salmon; and it is faring well under that rule. Current ratio at three is well above the ratio of two regarded as comfortable and is being maintained at that level over the two years. Similarly, the liquidity ratio at 1.2, maintained at the same level over the two years, compares well with one regarded as ideal. If we assume, as is normal in retail trade, that its customers have been allowed 30 days' credit, the control over receivable (credit management) is not satisfactory; but the trend is improving because the receivable days have fallen from over 50 days to 44.5 days.

   Payable days remain at 47. This may not be a satisfactory position unless six weeks' credit period has been agreed with suppliers. Inventory is being held for more than three months. Though the inventory days too are improving the position is still not satisfactory if we bear in mind that (a) demand for ready-made garments could be volatile, changing as it would with fashion trends, and (b) there is a cost attaching to holding high inventory in the form of storage costs, insurance and risks of obsolescence. However, those to whom Salmon owes money need not be too concerned with its liquidity position because it continues to generate sufficient cash every year (as seen from the cash flow ratio) to settle what it owes (1.2 times).
3. It is evident that the trading practices of Tuna are such (doing business mainly on cash terms and focusing on quick turnover rather than high margins) that the normal rule of thumb would not apply to it. Hence there need not be any concern that its current ratio is so much below two and the liquidity ratio so much below one. Its cash-generating ability continues to cover its current liability by more than twice. It takes only eight to nine days to convert its inventory into cash. Its receivable days and payable days, though not quite meaningful in the context of its trading practices, show that cash is collected from its sales within less than a day and payables do not remain unpaid for more than seven days, over the two-year period.

12.5 An assessment of operational efficiency

	Year to June 2012 £'000		Year to June 2012 £'000	
ROCE	2,628/7,500 × 100	35%	3,564/9,000 × 100	39.6%
Net profit ratio	2,628/16,425 × 100	16%	3,564/21,600 × 100	16.5%
Total asset turnover	16,425/7,500	2.19 times	21,600/9,000	2.4 times

Proof: ROCE is the product of net profit ratio × total asset turnover

16% × 2.19 times = 35%	16.5% × 2.4 times = 39.6%

How directors plan to achieve improved profitability:

1. By pruning down operating expenses (as seen in the workings below) while gross profit remains constant at 40% of sales, the operating expenses are reduced from 24 to 23.5% of sales.
2. By making the company's assets work harder: improving total asset turnover from 2.19 times to 2.4 times.

Workings	2011	2012
GP ratio	6,570/16,425 × 100 = 40%	8,640/21,600 × 100 = 40%
Operating expenses to sales	3,942/16,425 × 100 = 24%	5,076/21,600 × 100 = 23.5%

12.6 How high gearing affects equity

(a) Capital gearing expresses 'prior charge capital' (i.e. preference shares and loan notes) as a percentage of total capital employed: (5,000 + 3,000)/12,500 × 100 = 64% (highly geared).

(b) 20% fall in operating profit will reduce the retained profit (available to ordinary share holders (see working) to £104,800. That is a fall of (285 – 104.8) £180,200. Expressed as a percentage it is a (180,200/285,000 × 100) 63.2% fall. Thus the amount available for ordinary shareholders would suffer by a more than proportionate impact whenever there is a decrease in profit, in a highly geared company.

	£'000
Operating profit	756
Interest on loan	(400)
Profit before tax	356
Taxation @ 20%	(71.2)
Profit after tax	284.8
Preference dividend	(180)
Retained profit	104.8

12.7 Earnings per share

Weighted average number of shares in issue in 2011		
		£'000
1.1 to 1.5	1,500,000 × 4/12 months	500
1.5 to 31.12	1,800,000 × 8/12 months	1,200
		1,700

	£'000
Profit after tax	103
Preference dividend	(6)
Available for ordinary shares	97

EPS: £97,000/1,700,000 shares × 100 = 5.7p

12.8 Investor's dilemma

Ratios:

	Minnow £'000		Mullet £'000	
Price earnings ratio	252/18	14	192/24	8
Dividend yield	5/252 × 100	2%	15/192 × 100	7.8%
Earnings yield	18/252 × 100	7.1%	24/192 × 100	12.5%
Dividend cover	18/5	3.6 times	24/15	1.6 times

Comments:

1. Although dividend yield is low (2% compared to Mullet's 7.8%) and earnings yield (at 7.1%) is not substantially more than the market rate on bank fixed deposits, if Gloria is aiming at long-term investment she should invest in Minnow plc for the following reasons:
   - PE ratio at 14 is almost as high as what could be expected on blue-chip companies.
   - High PE ratio reflects the market confidence in that company and such confidence is usually translated into more demand for shares in that company and, therefore, further increase in its share price, opening the door for making capital gains whenever these shares are disposed of.
   - Minnow's policy is obviously to plough back profits into further expansion of its activities rather than paying out as dividend.
   - Given the high dividend cover (3.6 times), even in the unlikely event of a fall in profits Minnow will be able to maintain its current levels of dividend payment.
2. On the other hand, if Gloria is to retire from work and seeks an investment capable of providing an income, she is advised to invest in Mullet plc because the dividend yield from it is almost 8% per annum and the earnings yield a very attractive 12.5% per annum. She must remember, however, that a fall in Mullet's profits will impair its capacity to maintain dividends at current levels.

Multiple choice questions

The concept

12.1 Which of the following statements are correct?

(a) Accounting ratios should always be expressed as a percentage

(b) An accounting ratio compares two amounts appearing on the Statement of financial position

(c) An accounting ratio traces the relations between two amounts in financial statements

(d) An accounting ratio may be expressed in one of four alternative forms

w	a & b	
x	a & c	
y	b & c	
z	c & d	

Gross profit ratio

12.2 Sales in the year ending 31 March 2012 were £43,200. Identify the gross profit ratio, as a percentage, in each of the following independent situations:

(a) Gross profit for the year was £5,400

x	20%	
y	12.5%	
z	25%	

(b) Goods are sold at a consistent price fixed at cost plus a third

x	25%	
y	20%	
z	10%	

(c) Opening inventory, purchases, carriage inwards and closing inventory were £4,400, £21,400, £1,200 and £5,400 respectively

x	40%	
y	33%	
z	50%	

12.3 Which of the following conclusions could be drawn if the gross profit ratio falls from 25 to 18%?

(a) There has been a deliberate change in trading policy

(b) There has been a mistake in counting or valuing closing inventory

(c) There has been an increase in costs which could not be passed on to the customers

(d) There has been shoplifting by customers or pilferage by staff not accounted for

w	a & b	
x	a, b & c	
y	b, c & d	
z	All four	

12.4 Which one or more of the following will reduce a company's gross profit ratio?

(a) Increasing profit margins added to cost

(b) Omission from closing inventory of items with customers on sale or return basis

(c) Inability to pass on increasing cost of purchase to customers

(d) During rising prices, identify the cost of closing inventory on LIFO instead of FIFO

w	a & b	
x	a, b & c	
y	b, c & d	
z	c & d	

12.5 Which one of the following will reduce a company's gross profit ratio, when sales are increasing?

(a) Decision to increase the quantity of inventory held

(b) Increase in advertising costs and expenses of delivering to customers

(c) Decision to extend the credit period allowed to customers

(d) Adverse change in the sales mix, i.e. lower sales of more profitable lines

12.6 Which one of the following could cause a significant increase in a company's gross profit ratio?

(a) Loss of goods by customer shoplifting or pilferage by staff

(b) Inclusion in closing inventory of goods for which invoices are yet to be received

(c) Increase in the sales volume

(d) Failure to account for goods removed for own use by the proprietors

Return on capital employed ratio (ROCE) and return on equity ratio (ROE)

12.7 Which of the following ratios is known as the primary ratio?

(a) Earnings per share

(b) Return on capital employed ratio

(c) Price earnings ratio

(d) Liquidity ratio

12.8 As at 31 March 2011 a listed company had no loan notes in issue and its capital employed was £3.9 million. Shown on the right are summaries of the liability side of its Statement of financial position as at 31.3.2012 and Statement of income for the year ended on that date. Which of the following is the correct calculation of its ROCE ratio and the ROE ratio?

	£'000
Ordinary shares	2,500
Share premium	150
Reserves	1,450
	4,100
9% Loan notes	400
Current liability	1,500
	6,000

	£'000
Operating profit	746
Interest on loan	(36)
Profit before tax	710
Taxation	(150)
Profit after tax	560
Dividend paid	(120)
Retained profit	440

	Return on capital employed ratio		Return on equity ratio		
a	£710,000/£4,000,000 × 100 =	17.75%	£440,000/£4,000,000 × 100 =	11%	
b	£746,000/£4,200,000 × 100 =	17.76%	£710,000/£4,000,000 × 100 =	17.75%	
c	£746,000/£4,000,000 × 100 =	18.65%	£710,000/£4,100,000 × 100 =	17.32%	
d	£746,000/£4,200,000 × 100 =	17.74%	£710,000/£4,100,000 × 100 =	17.32%	

Working capital ratio and liquidity ratio

12.9 In which line of business would you expect the working capital ratio to be higher?

(a) Supermarket

(b) Dealer in white goods such as refrigerators, washing machines and cookers

(c) Construction industry

(d) Retail trader

12.10 A company's Statement of financial position reports its current assets and current liabilities as shown on the right. Which of the following is the correct calculation of the company's working capital ratio and liquidity ratio?

Current assets:	£'000
Inventory	548
Trade receivables	486
Prepayments	12
Cash and bank	32

Current liability:	£'000
Trade payable	392
Accrued expense	48
Taxation	118
Dividend declared	60

	Working capital ratio		Liquidity ratio	
a	(548 + 486 + 12 + 32)/(392 + 48 + 118 + 60)	1.7	(486 + 12 + 32)/(392 + 48 + 118 + 60)	0.9
b	(486 + 12 + 32)/(392 + 48 + 118 + 60) × 100	86%	(548 + 486 + 12 + 32)/(392 + 118 + 60)	1.9
c	(548 + 486 + 12 + 32)/(392 + 48 + 118)	1.9	(486 + 12 + 32)/(392 + 48 + 118 + 60)	0.9
d	(486 + 12 + 32)/(392 + 48 + 118 + 60)	0.9	(548 + 12 + 32)/(392 + 48 + 118 + 60)	1.0

Inventory days

12.11 Prichard's sales in the year ended 31 December 2011 were £390,000. The sales produced a gross profit ratio of 30%.

(a) If the cost of inventory on 31 December 2010 was £78,000 and that of 31 December 2011 was £96,000, what would be his inventory days?

x	128 days	
y	109 days	
z	120 days	

(b) If Prichard reports his inventory days as 90, and the cost of closing inventory as £54,000, what would have been the cost of his opening inventory?

x	£108,000	
y	£135,000	
z	£54,000	

(c) What will be Prichard's sales in 2011, if he consistently so fixes his sale prices to produce a gross profit ratio of 20% and reports his opening inventory as £54,000, purchases as £292,000 and inventory days as 60?

x	£298,000	
y	£357,600	
z	£372,500	

12.12 (a) What consequence will you expect if the inventory days are reduced from 78 to 64?

(i) Profitability of the business will improve

(ii) Liquidity of the business will improve

(iii) Operational efficiency of the business will improve

x	i only	
y	i & ii	
z	i, ii & iii	

(b) In which one or more of the following circumstances will it not be sensible to reduce inventory days?

(i) When the business is already suffering cash shortage

(ii) When the business is unable to meet the demand for its products

(iii) When suppliers are already pressing for payment of overdue bills

x	i & ii	
y	ii only	
z	iii only	

Trade receivable days

12.13 Afford Mills is in business as a wholesale dealer in textiles. Sales in the year ended 30 June 2010 were £365,000 and Afford allows its customers 45 days' credit, with sales taking place consistently throughout the year.

(a) If, following 25% increase in sales in the year ended 30 June 2011, there is an increase in the amount of trade receivables, the increase in receivables will need to be funded by:

(i) obtaining more credit from suppliers

(ii) retaining more profit within the business

(iii) introducing additional capital

x	i and ii	
y	i, ii, and iii	
z	ii, and iii	

(b) It is not sensible for Afford Mills to reduce the credit period allowed to its customers to less than 45 days when:

(i) competitors allow 45 days

(ii) business is short of cash

(iii) Afford is attempting to increase its sales

x	ii and iii	
y	i and ii	
z	i and iii	

(c) It is not sensible for Afford Mills to extend the credit period allowed to customers to more than 45 days when:

(i) the business has cash flow problems

(ii) the business is unable to meet the customers' demand for more goods

(iii) the customers are not buying as much as they did earlier

x	i and iii	
y	ii and iii	
z	i and ii	

12.14 Marlin's wholesale reported its sales in the year ended 30 June 2012 as £511,000.

(a) If her trade receivables on 30 June 2012 were £63,000, calculate her receivable days.

x	60 days	
y	45 days	
z	30 days	

(b) If her receivable days are calculated to be 63 days, ascertain her trade receivables as at 30 June 2012.

x	£126,400	
y	£321,930	
z	£88,200	

(c) If in the year ended 30 June 2013 the sales are expected to increase by 20%, while receivable days remain 63, ascertain the trade receivables as at 30 June 2013.

x	£105,840	
y	£88,200	
z	£3,552,667	

(d) If her sales in the year ended 30 June 2013 are expected to be 10% lower than those in the previous year and if one-sixth of these sales remain outstanding by that year-end, ascertain the receivable days.

x	54 days	
y	61 days	
z	45 days	

Trade payable days

12.15 A business would attempt to negotiate extended credit period from its suppliers if:

(a) It experiences cash flow problems

(b) It wishes to negotiate better trade discounts

(c) It wishes to extend credit period allowed to its customers

(d) It wishes to earn more cash discounts

x	a & c	
y	b, c & d	
z	b & d	

12.16 A business should endeavour to reduce its payable days if:

(a) It breaches credit period allowed by suppliers
(b) It wishes to improve its sales
(c) It wishes to reduce bad debts
(d) It has cash surplus to its needs

w	a & b	
x	b & c	
y	a & d	
z	c & d	

12.17 A fall in trade payable days may signal:

(a) A reduction in profitability
(b) An improvement in liquidity
(c) Worsening operational efficiency

12.18 In respect of the year ended 31 December 2011 Hussain reports his purchases as £624,000 and his trade payables by the year-end as £114,000. His payable days would be:

a	94 days	
b	67 days	
c	48 days	

12.19 In respect of the year ended 31 March 2011 Akbar reports his purchases as £578,160 and his trade payable days as 54 days. Ascertain his trade payable as at 31 March 2011.

a	£92,400	
b	£85,536	
c	£72,840	

12.20 Which of the following may be expected to improve a company's liquidity?

(a) Increase of the inventory days
(b) Reduction of trade payable days
(c) Reduction of trade receivable days
(d) Repayment of loan notes

Cash flow ratio

12.21 Your advice is sought by a bank which is considering a request for substantial overdraft facility from Fairways, a supermarket with sales outlets spread throughout the UK. The operating profit of Fairways for the year ended 30 June 2010 was £4,428,500, after writing off £84,500 as depreciation. Shown on the right are items reported on Fairways' Statement of financial position as at 30 June 2010. Which of the accounting ratios stated on the right will you draw the bank's attention to when considering the overdraft requested?

	£'000
Inventory	324
Trade receivables	16
Cash and bank	12
Current liabilities	842

a	Net current liability	£352,000–£852,000	£490,000	
b	Current ratio	£352,000/£842,000	0.41	
c	Liquidity ratio	£28,000/£842,000	0.03	
d	Cash flow ratio	£4,428,500 + £84,500/£842,000	5.4 times	

Operating efficiency

12.22 In which line of business would you expect the inventory turnover ratio to be higher?

(a) Supermarket
(b) Dealer in white goods such as refrigerators, washing machines and cookers
(c) Construction industry
(d) Greengrocer

12.23 A company reports its net profit ratio as 5.4% and its total asset turnover as 7 times. Which of those stated on the right is the correct calculation of the company's ROCE?

a	5.4/7 = 0.7%	
b	5.4 × 7 = 37.8%	
c	5.4 + 7 = 12.4	

12.24 A company's sales in the year ended 31 March 2011 were £948,200 and its operating profit £182,750. Its assets and liabilities at the year-end were as stated on the right. Which of the following is the correct calculation of the asset turnover and current asset turnover?

	£'000
Non-current assets	417,500
Current assets	298,400
Current liability	154,200

	Total asset turnover		Current asset turnover		
a	£561,700/£948,200 × 100	59.2%	£144,200/£948,200 × 100	15.2%	
b	£948,200/£561,700	1.7 times	£948,200/£144,200	6.6 times	
c	£715,900/£948,200 × 100	75.5%	£298,400/£928,200 × 100	32.1%	
d	£948,200/£715,900	1.3 times	£928,200/£298,400	3.1 times	

12.25 During the year ended 30 June 2012 a company's sales were £498,400. As at 30 June 2011 the cost of its inventory was £98,200 and its trade payables £124,600. Identify its inventory turnover ratio in each of the following independent scenarios:

(a) Its purchases in the year ending 30 June 2012 were £392,400 and the cost of year-end inventory £112,400.

w	3.7 times	
x	26.8%	
y	3.5 times	
z	28.0%	

(b) As at 30 June 2012 its cost of inventory was £74,200 and trade payables £114,800; while it paid £294,800 to its suppliers during the year ended 30 June 2012.

w	3.1 times	
x	32.4%	
y	3.3 times	
z	27.9%	

(c) As at 30 June 2012 the cost of its inventory was £148,200 and throughout the year it sold its goods at consistent prices calculated at cost plus 25%.

w	3.2 times	
x	3.0 times	
y	27.50%	
z	3.6 times	

12.26 Which of the following changes in accounting ratios would please a company management concerned with cash flow problems in their company?

(a) Increase in gross profit ratio ☐

(b) Increase in inventory turnover ☐

(c) Decrease in payables turnover without obtaining extended credit period from suppliers ☐

(d) Decrease in trade receivables turnover ☐

Capital gearing

12.27 Which of the following steps will result in lowering the capital gearing of a company?

(a) Pay dividends to its shareholders

(b) Make a bonus issue of shares to ordinary shareholders

(c) Make a rights issue of ordinary shares

(d) Issue loan notes with a long redemption date

12.28 Which of the following statements is/are correct?

(a) It is always bad to invest in a highly geared company

(b) Redemption of long-term loans will reduce a company's gearing

(c) Paying dividends to its shareholders will increase its capital gearing

(d) If loan notes form less than 5% of a company's capital employed it is not geared

w	b only	
x	a & b	
y	b & c	
z	b & d	

12.29 A listed company's capital employed as at 31 December 2012 was £8,000,000. This amount includes the items shown on the right. Which capital gearing calculation shown below would you accept as correct?

	£'000
8% Loan notes	500
6% Preference shares	2,000

(a) £500,000/£8,000,000 × 100 = 6.25%

(b) £500,000 + £2,000,000/£8,000,000 × 100 = 31.25%

(c) £2,000,000/£8,000,000 × 100 = 25%

(d) £8,000,000 – £500,000 – £2,000,000/£8,000,000 × 100 = 68.75%

Share market ratios

12.30

Operating profit	£5,000,000
Interest paid	(£80,000)
Profit before tax	£4,920,000
Taxation	(£994,000)
Profit after tax	£3,926,000

Extracts from a listed company's Statement of income for the year ended 30 June 2012 are shown on the left, while its Statement of financial position reports:

As Share capital, ordinary shares of 50p each	£5,000,000
As Non-current liability: 8% Loan notes	£1,000,000

Calculate the earnings per share for 2012 in each of the following independent scenarios:

(a) During the year ended 30 June 2012 the company did not pay any dividend or issue any shares.

w	98.4p	
x	39.3p	
y	39p	
z	50p	

(b) The company has also in issue £500,000 6% Preference shares; but during the year ended 30 June 2012 no shares have been issued nor dividend paid.

w	39.3p	
x	39p	
y	97.8p	
z	77.9p	

(c) The company has also in issue £500,000 6% Preference shares which, as at 30 June 2011, were in arrears for three years' dividend. During the year ended 30 June 2012 no shares were issued nor any dividend paid.

w	39.3p	
x	39p	
y	97.8p	
z	77.9p	

(d) The company made an issue of 2 million ordinary shares of 50p each on 1 April 2012 at 70p each and paid a dividend of 3p per share on 29 June 2012.

w	60.4p	
x	46.2p	
y	39.3p	
z	39p	

12.31 Four companies in the same line of business and with identical trading practices and accounting policies report their earnings per share as shown on the left. Which of these companies would you say is the most profitable one?

	Equity shares in issue	EPS
W plc	4 million ordinary shares of £1 each	21p
X plc	20 million ordinary shares of 50p each	12p
Y plc	200 million ordinary shares of 20p each	5p
Z plc	500 million ordinary shares of 10p each	3p

a	W plc	
b	X plc	
c	Y plc	
d	Z plc	

12.32

Earnings per share	24p
Market price per share	192p
Dividend per share	8p

Information relating to Bamby plc is stated on the left. Identify the share market ratios using information stated on the right.

	PE ratio	Dividend yield	Earnings yield	
a	8	4.2%	12.5%	
b	12.4%	33.3%	8	
c	8	24	33.3%	

Answers to multiple choice questions

12.1: z 12.2a: y 12.2b: x 12.2c: z 12.3: z 12.4: y 12.5: d 12.6: b 12.7: b 12.8: b 12.9: c 12.10: a 12.11a: z 12.11b: x 12.11c: z 12.12a: z 12.12b: y 12.13a: y 12.13b: z 12.13c: z 12.14a: y 12.14b: z 12.14c: x 12.14d: y 12.15: x 12.16: y 12.17: b 12.18: b 12.19: b 12.20: c 12.21: d 12.22: d 12.23: b 12.24: d 12.25a: w 12.25b: y 12.25c: z 12.26: b 12.27: c 12.28: y 12.29: b 12.30a: x 12.30b:x 12.30c: x 12.30d: x 12.31: d 12.32: a

Progressive questions

PQ 12.1 A basic interpretation of financial statements

Small Fry's business submits to you the following financial statements:

Statement for income for the year ended 31.12.2012

	£	£
Sales		625,000
Inventory on 31.12.2011	54,500	
Purchases	415,000	
Depreciation – machinery	18,000	
Inventory on 31.12.2012	(62,500)	
Cost of sale		(425,000)
Gross profit		200,000
Administrative expenses		(118,000)
Distribution cost		(48,000)
Interest on loan		(9,000)
Profit for the year		25,000

Statement of financial position as at 31.12.2012

Non-current assets:	Cost	Accumulated depreciation	£
Machinery	180,000	(45,000)	135,000
Motor vehicles	27,000	(12,000)	15,000
			150,000
Current assets:			
Inventory		62,500	
Trade receivables		31,250	
Cash and bank		6,250	100,000
			250,000
		£	£
Capital		100,000	
Profit for the year		25,000	125,000
Loan notes			75,000
Trade payables			50,000
			250,000

Required: Assess:
(a) the profitability;
(b) the liquidity; and
(c) the operational efficiency of this business.

Calculate not less than two ratios on which you will base your assessment.

PQ 12.2 Return on capital employed

Stated below are particulars with regard to six different companies 'a' to 'f'. Each of these companies has borrowed £2,500 at 8% interest per annum. Fill the shaded grids with appropriate figures.

	Sales	Net profit after interest	Interest on loan notes	Capital employed	Net profit ratio	Asset turnover	Return on capital employed
(a)	£10,000	£800	£200	£5,000	?	?	?
(b)	£15,000	?	£200	£8,000	12%	?	?
(c)	£10,000	?	£200	?	5%	?	20%
(d)	?	£800	£200	?	?	4	20%
(e)	?	?	£200	£10,000	10%	4	?
(f)	£20,000	?	£200	?	?	4	10%

PQ 12.3 Profitability – inter-firm comparison (CAT 6 amended)

Aber and Cromby are two retail businesses in the leisurewear market. Your manager has asked you to review the performance of both businesses from the financial statements which are provided below:

Statements of income year to 31 October 2011

	Aber	Cromby
	£'000	£'000
Revenue	5,500	7,200
Cost of sales	(4,400)	(5,040)
Gross profit	1,100	2,160
Expenses	(610)	(1,685)
Profit from operations	490	475
Finance cost	(15)	(15)
Profit before tax	475	460
Tax	(200)	(180)
Net profit	275	280

Statements of financial position as at 31 October 2011

	Aber		Cromby	
	£'000	£'000	£'000	£'000
Non-current assets		3,750		7,200
Inventory	125		360	
Receivables	500		190	
Bank	30	655	0	550
		4,405		7,750
	£'000	£'000	£'000	£'000
Equity and reserves:				
Ordinary shares of $1		3,000		7,000
Reserves		1,080		410
		4,080		7,410
Non-current liabilities:				
Loan notes		75		110
Current liability:				
Trade payables	200		205	
Tax	50		20	
Overdraft	0	250	5	230
		4,405		7,750

Required:

(a) Calculate the following ratios for each:
   (i) Gross profit percentage
   (ii) Return on capital employed
   (iii) Earnings per share.

(b) Comment on the performance of each as indicated by each of the ratios.

(c) Explain the limitations of using ratios as the basis for analysing performance.

PQ 12.4 Liquidity and performance on inter-temporal comparison (ACCA 1 amended)

Extracts from the financial statements of Apillon for the year ended 31 March 2011 and 2012 are given on the right.

Note a: sales revenue includes a cash sale of £300,000 in 2011 and £100,000 in 2012.

Statement of income year ended 31 March

	2011		2012	
	£'000	£'000	£'000	£'000
Sales revenue (note a)		3,100		3,800
Opening inventory	360		540	
Purchases	2,080		2,580	
Closing inventory	(540)	(1,900)	(720)	(2,400)
Gross profit		1,200		1,400
Expenses		(900)		(1,100)
Net profit		300		300

Required:

(a) Calculate the following for each year:
   (i) Current ratio
   (ii) Quick ratio (acid test)
   (iii) Inventory turnover ratio
   (iv) Trade receivable days
   (v) Trade payable days.

(b) Make four brief comments on the changes in the position of the company as revealed by changes in these ratios and/or in the amounts stated in the financial statements.

Statements of financial position	2011		2012	
	£'000	£'000	£'000	£'000
Current assets:				
Inventory	540		720	
Trade receivables	450	990	700	1,420
Current liabilities:				
Trade payables	410		690	
Bank overdraft	20	430	170	860

PQ 12.5 Stock market ratios (CAT 6 amended)

Nicola is thinking of investing in a limited company called Tresven. She seeks your help to calculate and interpret some ratios so as to assist her with the decision. Summarised financial statements of Tresven are shown on the right. Additional information:

(i) Dividend paid in the year is $10 million.

(ii) Market price of Tresven share 150c.

(iii) Tresven's major competitor is Hilday the ratios for which have been calculated as shown on the right.

Statement of income year ended 31.10.2012	$'000
Sales revenue	23,420
Cost of sales	(8,245)
Gross profit	15,175
Expenses	(2,460)
Operating profit	12,715
Finance costs	(50)
Profit before tax	12,665
Income tax	(1,515)
Net profit	11,150

Statement of financial position as at 31.10.2012	$'000	$'000
Non-current assets		31,000
Current assets:		
Inventory	1,450	
Trade receivables	2,500	
Cash	50	4,000
		35,000
	£'000	£'000
Capital and reserves:		
Ordinary shares $.50		25,000
Reserves		7,520
		32,520
Current liabilities:		
Trade payables	860	
Tax	620	1,480
Loan notes		1,000
		35,000

Dividend per share	10 cents
Dividend cover	5 times
Earnings per share	20 cents
Price earnings ratio	13.4
Earnings yield	15%
Interest cover	100 times

Required:

(a) Calculate for Tresven the ratios which have been calculated for Hilday.

(b) Comment on Tresven's ratios.

PQ 12.6 Interpretation from an investor's focus

William had commenced in business with capital provided by his mother. The financial statements for the period from 1 April 2009 have been submitted to you as shown below.

Statement of income year ended 31 March	2010	2011
	£	£
Sales	70,000	98,000
Cost of sales	(42,000)	(63,000)
Gross profit	28,000	35,000
Overheads:		
Variable[a]	(14,000)	(24,500)
Fixed[b]	(8,400)	(11,200)
Net profit (loss)	5,600	(700)

Statements of financial position as at 31 March	2009	2010	2011
	£	£	£
Non-current assets	49,000	49,000	56,000
Current assets:			
Inventory	3,500	7,500	4,000
Trade receivables	–	9,700	16,800
Bank balance	9,100	2,400	–
Current liabilities:			
Trade payables	(2,100)	(3,500)	(9,600)
Bank overdraft	–	–	(2,800)
Capital employed	59,500	65,100	64,400

(a) Expenses that change with sales; (b) Expenses that do not change with sales.

In an effort to persuade his mother to lend him a further amount, William points out that:

1. The sales in the year ended March 2011 were 40% more than that in the previous year and he estimates that his sales in the year to March 2012 would probably be around £150,000.
2. The net loss in the second year results from the increase in fixed costs because of renting more commodious premises big enough to allow for the anticipated expansion in sales.
3. A cash injection is urgently needed to maintain the business at the intended scale. Currently the business is unable to comply with the suppliers' term of one month's credit and the inventory levels are inadequate to meet customer demand.
4. The bank overdraft has not been negotiated.

The mother's concern, however, is that William is capable of earning around £7,000 per year if he finds employment and she herself could earn 8% per year on her savings.

Required: Your advice is sought by William's mother.

PQ 12.7 Preparing financial statements from accounting ratios

The following information is available for the period ended 31 May 2011:

1. Working capital as at 31 May 2011 was £11,500.
2. Drawings during the year were £3,000.
3. Depreciation of non-current assets during the year @ 10% on cost was £1,500. No new non-current assets were acquired during the period.
4. Assume that inventory and trade payables remained constant throughout the year.
5. General expenses (without depreciation) was 25% of sales.
6. The following ratios applied:

   Acid test ratio was 1.25 times; Current ratio was 1.5 times; Total asset turnover was 2 times; Inventory turnover: 5 times; Trade receivables turnover: 8 times.

Required: Prepare the Statement of income for the year ended 31 May 2011 and a Statement of financial position as at that date.

Test questions

Test 12.1 A comprehensive question on ratio analysis

The financial statements for the current year (2011) and the preceding one are summarised below:

Statements of financial position as at 30 September

2010		2011
£		£
	Non-current assets:	
70,000	Premises	150,000
65,000	Plant and equipment	162,000
135,000		312,000
	Current assets:	
51,200	Inventory	85,300
29,700	Trade receivables	55,700
15,600	Cash and bank	3,500
96,500		144,500
231,500		456,500
£		£
100,000	Share capital £1 each	120,000
25,000	Share premium account	30,000
36,000	Retained earnings	50,600
161,000		200,600
	Non-current liability	
–	7% Loan notes	100,000
	Current liabilities:	
52,300	Trade payables	131,100
18,200	Taxation	24,800
231,500		456,500

Statement of income for year to 30 September

2010		2011
£		£
386,400	Sales	764,200
29,600	Inventory on 1.10.	51,200
310,720	Purchases	682,400
(31,200)	Inventory on 30.9.	(85,300)
(309,120)	Cost of sales	(648,300)
77,280	Gross profit	115,900
(43,400)	Admin. expenses	(37,650)
(14,680)	Distribution cost	(24,650)
–	Interest	(7,000)
19,200	Profit before tax	46,600
(4,600)	Taxation	(20,000)
14,600		26,600

You are required to comment on:

(a) the profitability

(b) the liquidity

(c) the operational performance and

(d) the capital structure of Burstow Ltd, supporting your answer with pertinent accounting ratios.

Test 12.2 Working capital cycle (ACCA 1.1)

(a) Explain the meaning of the term 'working capital cycle' for a trading company.

(b) Calculate the working capital cycle in days from the information provided on the right.

(c) State one advantage to a business of keeping its working capital cycle as short as possible.

	£'000	£'000
Sales (all on credit)		1,000
Less:		
Opening inventory	100	
Purchases	800	
Closing inventory	(200)	(700)
Gross profit		300
Receivables at year end		250
Payables at year end		150

Test 12.3 A comprehensive inter-firm comparison

Miss New Rich has decided to take advantage of the slump in the share market and has identified two listed companies, Rose plc and Daisy plc, for making her investment. She has obtained the financial statements of both companies, extracts from which are shown on on the right.

Further information provided:

	Rose	Daisy
Depreciation in year 2011	£132,000	£194,000
Inventory on 31.12.2010	£296,000	£602,000
Price per share – 31.12.2011	215p	190p

You are required to assess the following aspects of each company, calculating the ratios identified:

(a) Profitability on the basis of:
  (i) ROCE
  (ii) ROE

(b) Liquidity on the basis of:
  (i) Liquidity ratio
  (ii) Cash flow ratio

(c) Operating efficiency on the basis of:
  (i) Asset turnover
  (ii) Inventory turnover

(d) Investment prospects on the basis of:
  (i) Earnings per shares
  (ii) Price earnings ratio.

Statements of income year ended 31 December 2011

	Rose plc	Daisy plc
	£'000	£'000
Sales revenue	3,250	8,690
Cost of sales	(1,960)	(6,780)
Gross profit	1,290	1,910
Distribution cost	(214)	(432)
Administrative expense	(496)	(698)
Operating profit	580	780
Interest paid	–	(72)
Profit before taxation	580	708
Income tax	(120)	(140)
Profit after taxation	460	568

Statements of financial position as at 31 December 2011

	Rose plc	Daisy plc
	£'000	£'000
Non-current assets:		
Property, plant and equipment	1,740	2,520
Current assets:		
Inventory	248	648
Trade receivables	312	592
Cash and bank balance	40	–
	2,340	3,760
	£'000	£'000
Equity and reserves:		
Ordinary shares of £1 each	1,000	1,500
Share premium account	100	150
Retained earnings	780	796
Non-current liability:		
12% Loan notes	–	600
Current liabilities:		
Trade payables	286	344
Taxation	114	168
Bank overdraft	–	52
Dividend declared	60	150
	2,340	3,760

Test 12.4 Interpretation of information in financial statements (advanced)

Extracts from Chambers plc's financial statements are shown:

Statement of financial position as at 31 December

	2011		2010	
	£'000	£'000	£'000	£'000
Non-current assets:				
Property, plant and equipment		960		840
Current assets:				
Inventory	516		492	
Trade receivables	478		346	
Cash and bank balance	32	1,026	3	841
		1,986		1,681

	£'000	£'000	£'000	£'000
Equity and reserves:				
Ordinary shares – £1	900		600	
Share premium account	100		30	
Retained earnings	460	1,460	321	951
Non-current liabilities:				
8% Loan notes	100		300	
Deferred tax	38	138	27	327
Current liabilities:				
Trade payables	297		342	
Taxation	46		31	
Dividend declared	45	388	30	403
		1,986		1,681

Statement of income year ended 31 December

	2011	2010
	£'000	£'000
Operating profit	229	224
Asset disposal	20	–
Interest expense	(24)	(48)
Profit before tax	225	176
Taxation	(41)	(35)
Profit after tax	181	141

Statement of cash flows

	£'000	£'000
Cash flow from operating activities		
Operating profit	229	
Depreciation	98	
Inventory	(24)	
Receivables	(132)	
Payables	(45)	
Interest paid	(24)	
Tax paid	(15)	
Dividend paid	(30)	57
Cash flow from investing activities		
Non-current asset	(298)	
Asset disposal	100	(198)
Cash flow from financing activities		
Share issue	370	
Loan redemption	(200)	170
Cash inflow in the year		29
Cash and cash equivalent 31.12.2010		3
Cash and cash equivalent 31.12.2011		32

Required: On the basis of the information provided, assess any change in the profitability as well as liquidity position of Chambers during the year ended 31 December 2011, calculating not less than four accounting ratios to support your assessment of each aspect.

Chapter 13

Consolidation of financial statements

By the end of this chapter

You should learn:

- The identity of a parent, subsidiary and associate
- The need to prepare consolidated financial statements
- The method of preparing consolidated financial statements

You should be able to:

- Prepare a Consolidated Statement of financial position and a Consolidated Statement of income

13.1 The need to prepare consolidated financial statements

It is now a common practice for a company to invest some of its resources in one or more other companies, usually by buying shares in these organisations. If company Alpha buys all the shares or most of the shares in company Beta, and hence has all or most of the votes at the shareholders' meetings of Beta, Alpha will be able to elect the directors of and control the operations of Beta. To be in a position to control Beta, Alpha should have more than 50% votes in Beta. If it has, Alpha is known as the *parent* and Beta as a *subsidiary*. The parent and all its subsidiaries are together known as a '*group*' of companies. In such a situation the Statement of income and the Statement of financial position prepared for each company will not reflect the totality of activities carried out by and the resources at the disposal of the whole group. To assess the profitability, liquidity and operating efficiency, the parent and all its subsidiaries constituting the group need to be considered together. This is why it has become common practice, and also there is a legal requirement,[1] to prepare group accounts in the form of *Consolidated Statement of financial position* and *Consolidated Statement of income*.

Activity 13.1 Identification of a parent and subsidiary

Alpha has 100% of the ordinary shares in Beta, 60% of the shares in Delta and 30% of the shares in Gamma. Each share has one vote at the shareholders' meetings. Would you identify Beta, Delta and Gamma as subsidiaries of Alpha?

13.2 Consolidation of Statements of financial position

Consolidation of Statements of financial position is merely the aggregation of two (or more) Statements of financial position, subject to certain *consolidation adjustments*. We will first learn to aggregate the Statements of financial position of two companies before we consider the consolidation adjustments in turn.

Alpha's Statement of financial position	
	£
Non-current assets	500
Investments in Beta	300
Current assets	100
	900
	£
Ordinary shares	600
Retained earnings	200
	800
Current liabilities	100
	900

Beta's Statement of financial position	
	£
Non-current assets	250
Current assets	150
	400
	£
Ordinary shares	300
Retained earnings	60
	360
Current liabilities	40
	400

To start with we will assume that Alpha invested £300 to incorporate (as distinct from buying from some one else) Beta, and one year later each has prepared its own Statement of financial position as shown on the left. Observe that Alpha reports its investment of £300 in Beta as an asset; whereas Beta reports that amount as its capital. Though legally Alpha is a separate entity and so is Beta, since Beta is owned and controlled by Alpha, in commercial substance Alpha and Beta would act together because they constitute a single group with a legal obligation to report their financial position at the end of each accounting period in a Consolidated Statement of financial position (see on the right) by adding together, line by line, the items reported in each company's separate Statement of financial position.

However, the Consolidated Statement of financial position we have prepared has a major flaw in that there is a double-counting of the amount invested by Alpha (£300) – showing that amount both as an asset (investment) and as a liability (Beta's share capital).

The aim is to report the assets available to the group and the liabilities of the group.

Consolidated Statement of financial position as at xxxxx		
		£
Non-current assets	500 + 250	750
Investments in Beta		300
Current assets	100 + 150	250
		1,300
		£
Share capital – Alpha		600
Share capital – Beta		300
Retained earnings	200 + 60	260
		1,160
Current liabilities	100 + 40	140
		1,300

Consolidated Statement of financial position as at xxxxx		
		£
Non-current assets	500 + 250	750
Current assets	100 + 150	250
		1,000
Share capital – Alpha		600
Consolidated retained earnings	200 + 60	260
		860
	100 + 40	140
Current liabilities		1,000

Therefore, an amount owed by one member of the group to another within the group cannot be reported both as an asset and as a liability. We need therefore to cancel that amount from both sides, so that the Consolidated Statement of financial position is prepared as shown on the left.

Observe that

(a) We have offset Alpha's investment against Beta's share capital, and

(b) We have identified the retained earnings of the parent and the subsidiary together as the *Consolidated retained earnings*.

The *cancellation of inter-company debt* (what one company within the group owes another) is the first basic consolidation adjustment.

Activity 13.2 Consolidation of a subsidiary incorporated by the parent

On 1 January 2011 Alpha invested £500 to incorporate Beta. A year later each company had prepared its own Statement of financial position as shown on the right.

Required: Prepare the Consolidated Statement of financial position of the Alpha group as at 31 December 2011.

Statements of dinancial position as at 31 December 2011		
	Alpha	Beta
	£	£
Non-current assets	840	530
Investments in Beta	500	–
Current assets	280	140
	1,620	670
	£	£
Ordinary shares	1,000	500
Retained earnings	310	80
	1,310	580
Current liabilities	310	90
	1,620	670

13.3 Where the subsidiary is acquired rather than incorporated

In the case considered so far Alpha incorporated Beta. On the other hand, if Alpha acquires Beta from some one else – say Henry – after Henry has incorporated it, Alpha may have to pay Henry more than what Henry invested in Beta. That excess paid to Henry is known as *goodwill*. For example, let us assume that Henry incorporated Beta investing £300 and that immediately after incorporation Alpha paid £360 to Henry to acquire from him all his shares in Beta. The excess paid (£60) is for goodwill. Goodwill is required to be recognised as an asset on the Consolidated Statement of financial position and continue to be so reported year after year unless it is impaired (i.e. its value is lost).

Let us assume also that when Henry invested £300 in Beta he accounted for it in Beta's books by posting £200 to the credit of the Capital account and the remainder (£100) to the credit of the Share premium account. Goodwill paid for by Alpha is identified by cancelling its investment to acquire Beta (£360) with the Share capital and Share premium in Beta (see on the right)

Calculation of goodwill in Beta		
	£	£
Investment by Alpha		360
Beta's share capital	200	
Share premium	100	(300)
Goowill		60

Activity 13.3 Acquisition of a fully owned subsidiary immediately upon incorporation

Maureen incorporated Beta on 1 January 2011 investing £450. She recorded £400 in the Share capital account and £50 in a Share premium account. On the same day, immediately after incorporation, Alpha paid Maureen £480 to acquire all her shares in Beta. A year later both companies drafted their own Statements of financial position as shown on the right.

Required: The Consolidated Statement of financial position of the Alpha group as at 31 December 2011. Assume that goodwill is not impaired by the end of the first year after acquisition.

Statements of financial position as at 31 December 2011		
	Alpha	Beta
	£	£
Non-current assets	920	440
Investments in Beta	480	
Current assets	240	180
	1,640	620
	£	£
Ordinary shares	900	400
Share premium	90	50
Retained earnings	210	90
	1,200	540
Current liabilities	440	80
	1,640	620

In the event Alpha is able to strike a bargain, it may be able to acquire the subsidiary for less than what it is worth. For example, if Alpha pays only £300 to acquire the whole of a subsidiary with capital and reserves adding up to £400, instead of having to pay a premium (goodwill) on acquisition, Alpha would have made a gain on acquisition of £100 (£400 – £300). This gain is known as *negative goodwill* and it is recognised immediately as a gain in the Consolidated retained earnings.

13.4 The acquisition of a subsidiary later than upon incorporation

Next, let us assume that Felix incorporated Beta, investing £500 and recording £100 of that amount in a Share premium account (rather than Share capital) and that by the end of the first year Beta makes a profit of £120. If Alpha wishes to buy from Felix all of his shares in Beta, the minimum Felix will expect to receive is £620 (£500 invested + £120 profit). If Alpha is required to pay £750 for acquiring all of Felix's shares, Alpha will be paying £130 (see working on the right) as goodwill. The portion of a subsidiary's profit earned by it prior to the date of its acquisition is referred to as pre-acquisition profit and that, being a part of what the parent pays for, needs to be offset from the investment for identifying goodwill. Such offsetting is known as *'freezing of subsidiary's pre-acquisition profits'* and this is the second basic consolidation adjustment. The consequence of this adjustment is that what is reported as the consolidated retained earnings will include (a) the whole of the parent's earnings and (b) only the post-acquisition portion of the subsidiary's earnings.

Calculation of goodwill		
	£	£
Alpha's investment in Beta		750
Beta's share capital	400	
Share premium	100	
Pre-acquisition profit	120	(620)
Goowill paid		130

Activity 13.4 A wholly owned subsidiary acquired later than incorporation

Ibrahim incorporated Beta on 1 April 2010, investing £360. A year later, on 1 April 2011, Alpha paid £500 to Ibrahim to acquire all his shares in Beta. By that date Beta's retained earnings were £90.

Impairment of goodwill, estimated at £15, should be written off.

Required: Prepare the Consolidated Statement of financial position of the Alpha group as at 31 December 2012.

Statements of financial position as at 31 March 2012	Alpha	Beta
	£	£
Non-current assets	900	440
Investments in Beta	500	–
Current assets	340	280
	1,740	720
	£	£
Share capital	800	300
Share premium	80	60
Retained earnings	490	210
	1,370	570
Current liabilities	370	150
	1,740	720

13.5 Fair valuation of the subsidiary's assets

Beta's Statement of financial position as at 31 December 2011	
	£
Share capital	400
Share premium	50
Retained earnings	270
	720

The expression 'fair value' means market value, i.e. the price at which an asset may be sold. Let us consider a situation where Sarina owns Beta. She invested £450 when she incorporated it, crediting £50 of that amount to a Share premium account. By the end of the seventh year, on 31 December 2011, the share capital and reserves of Beta were reported as stated on the left. Note that Beta's profit until that date was £270. If Alpha acquired this business on this date, paying £1,000 for all of Sarina's shares, it would appear that Alpha paid £280 for goodwill because that is the difference between the price paid for control and Beta's net assets on that date. The situation, however, will be different if we learn that Beta's Statement of financial position as at 31 December 2011 reports at £100 land acquired many years earlier at that cost, and the current fair value (market value) of that land is £300. There is no reason why Sarina should sell the land to Alpha at any price other than its current fair value. Therefore, to identify the correct amount paid as goodwill, Beta should first make the accounting entries necessary to report the land at its market value by debiting the Land account with £200 (the gain on fair valuation) and crediting a Fair valuation account. Both accounts involved will then appear as follows:

Land account

	£		
Balance b/f	100		
Fair valuation a/c	200		

Fair valuation account

			£
		Land a/c	200

The land has a fair value of £300 on the date Beta was acquired. Hence the gain on fair valuation is a pre-acquisition gain which, like the subsidiary's pre-acquisition profit of £270, needs to be frozen by being offset from Alpha's investment, for identifying the goodwill paid for by Alpha. Goodwill is identified as £80 (see the working on the right).

Calculation of goodwill		
	£	£
Alpha's investment in Beta		1,000
Beta's:		
Share capital	400	
Share premium	50	
Fair valuation of land	200	
Pre-acquisition profit	270	(920)
Goowill paid		80

Therefore, there is a need to fair value the identifiable non-monetary assets of the subsidiary on the date of the acquisition. There are two reasons for this as follows:

(a) to identify the cost of that asset to the group – the land costs Alpha £300;

(b) to correctly identify the amount Alpha pays for Beta's goodwill.

Fair valuation of subsidiary's identifiable non-monetary assets on the date of acquisition is the third basic consolidation adjustment.

A subsidiary's assets such as receivables, bank balance and cash in hand cannot have a fair value different from the value at which each of them is reported in the books of account. These assets are known as *monetary assets*. Monetary assets are defined as assets for which the value receivable is legally fixed. For example, if £5,000 is receivable from Thomas, a customer, he cannot be required to pay more on the excuse that the value of money has gone down because of inflation. What needs to be fair valued are the subsidiary's identifiable *non-monetary assets*. The word *identifiable* is used to point out that the subsidiary may well own an asset (like a brand name) which is not recorded in its books and will yet have to be fair valued for identifying the amount paid for goodwill.

Activity 13.5 Fair valuation of subsidiary's assets on the date of acquisition

Alpha paid £1,000 to acquire the whole of Beta's equity on 1 April 2008 when:

(a) investments held by Beta were quoted in the share market at £210; and

(b) Beta's retained earnings were £180.

In 2010 a goodwill impairment of £20 was written off.

Required: Prepare the Consolidated Statement of financial position of the Alpha group as at 31 March 2012.

Statements of financial position as at 31 March 2012

	Alpha	Beta
	£	£
Non-current assets	1,000	780
Investments in Beta	1,000	120
Current assets	480	320
	2,480	1,220
	£	£
Share capital	1,200	600
Share premium	180	60
Retained earnings	590	390
	1,970	1,050
Current liabilities	510	170
	2,480	1,220

13.6 Cancellation of inter-company debts

We have seen in 13.2 above that there is a need to cancel inter-company debts to prevent double-counting the same amount both as an asset and as a liability on the Consolidated Statement of financial position. We identified the cancellation of inter-company debt as the first basic consolidation adjustment when we came across the first example of such cancellation. That was when we cancelled the parent's investment with the subsidiary's Share capital and all reserves as at the date of acquisition. Similarly, there is a need to cancel whatever the parent and the subsidiary may owe each other. Another example would be when the parent reports its own subsidiary as a trade receivable. Let us assume, for illustration, that the parent and the subsidiary have reported their trade receivables and payables as at 31 December 2011 as stated below and that the receivables reported by the parent includes an amount of £40 due from the subsidiary.

Parent:	
	£
Trade receivables	150
Trade payables	95

Subsidiary:	
	£
Trade receivables	120
Trade payables	80

In this situation, if we report on the Consolidated Statement of financial position trade receivables as £270 (£150 + £120) and trade payables as £175 (£95 + £80), we would again be double-counting the inter-company debt, i.e. £40 due to the parent by the subsidiary, reporting that amount both as an asset and as a liability. We have, therefore, to cancel the inter-company debt of £40 from both trade receivables and trade payables, when we report in the Consolidated Statement of financial position the trade receivables of the group as £230 (£150 – £40 + £120) and the trade payables of the group as £135 (£95 + £80 – £40).

Activity 13.6 Cancellation of inter-company debts

Statements of financial position, as at 31 December 2011, of Alpha and its fully owned subsidiary, Beta, include items stated below. Trade receivables reported by Alpha includes £70 receivable from Beta. Identify the amounts of receivables and payables to be stated in the Consolidated Statement of financial position as at 31 December 2011.

Alpha's	
	£
Trade receivables	540
Trade payables	428

Beta's	
	£
Trade receivables	348
Trade payables	296

On the matter of cancelling inter-company debt, it will be useful to remember three points:

1. The inter-company debts should not be cancelled until both companies agree on the same amount. Disagreement would usually arise because, as at the year-end, cash or goods may remain in transit from one company in the group to another.
2. If the disagreement arises because of an item in transit (cash or goods), irrespective of the direction in which the item is moving (from the parent to subsidiary or in reverse direction), habitually make the adjustment in the parent's books.
3. If the disagreement arises because there is an error in one party's books of account, make the correction in that party's books.

Activity 13.7 Cancellation of inter-company debts involving items in transit

Statements of financial position as at 31 March 2012 of Alpha and its fully owned subsidiary Beta include items stated on the right. Alpha's trade receivables include £80 due from Beta; whereas the corresponding amount reported as payable by Beta is only £50. The difference is because goods invoiced by Alpha to Beta at £20 and a remittance of £10 from Beta to Alpha are in transit on that date. Identify the amounts at which the items stated above would to be stated in the Consolidated Statement of financial position as at 31 March 2012.

Alpha's	
	£
Inventory	300
Trade receivables	400
Cash and bank	12
Trade payables	250

Beta's	
	£
Inventory	200
Trade receivables	300
Cash and bank	10
Trade payables	150

Remember also that there may be other examples of inter-company debts that deserve similar cancellation. Some examples are as follows:

- interest receivable/payable;
- rent receivable/payable;
- dividend receivable/payable (provided it has already been declared).

For example, a dividend declared by the subsidiary will be reported as a liability by the subsidiary. If the subsidiary is one fully owned by the parent, when the parent accounts for the dividend it expects to receive from the subsidiary it would record the dividend as its income and as an asset. The dividend receivable (asset) reported by the parent and dividend declared (liability) reported by the subsidiary would be another situation of inter-company debt which needs to be cancelled so that the same item is not reported both as an asset and as a liability in the Consolidated Statement of financial position.

13.7 Elimination of unrealised profit

In the event the parent sells goods to the subsidiary, and the sale is effected at the price the goods cost the parent, then any portion of these goods remaining unsold with the subsidiary at the year-end will be reported by the subsidiary at its cost, which is also the cost to the group. On the other hand, if the parent's cost is £400 and the parent invoices the goods to the subsidiary at £600 (i.e. making a profit of £200) we then need to check whether any portion of the goods remains with the subsidiary by the year-end. This is because £200 profit recognised by the parent would not be earned (accountants call it *realised*) until the goods are sold to someone outside the group. If the subsidiary is able to sell all the goods for £750 by the year-end, from the group's perspective, the parent's profit of £200 as well as the subsidiary's profit of £150 would be realised by then.

On the other hand, if a quarter of these goods remain unsold with the subsidiary by the year-end, these goods will be reported as inventory on the subsidiary's Statement of financial position at (£600 × $^1/_4$) £150. That amount is what the goods cost the subsidiary, but is not what these goods cost the group. The group cost of the inventory remaining with the subsidiary is £100. When the subsidiary reports these goods at its own cost of £150, that amount includes a profit made by the parent against the subsidiary. Hence, as at the year-end a quarter of the profit the parent made against the subsidiary would remain unrealised and, therefore, needs to be eliminated by removing the unrealised amount of £50 from the parent's earnings and from the subsidiary's inventory. This is known as *elimination of unrealised profit*, and this is the fourth basic consolidation adjustment.

Activity 13.8 Elimination of unrealised profit

When Alpha acquired the whole of Beta's equity on 1 January 2011, Beta's retained earnings were £100. The Statements of financial position of both companies, a year later, include the items reported on the right. Inventory reported by Beta includes £40 goods invoiced to it by Alpha. Alpha had purchased these goods for £30.

Statements of financial position as at 31.12.2011		
	Alpha	Beta
	£	£
Inventory	540	420
Retained earnings	398	240

Required: How will the inventory and the consolidated retained earnings be reported on the Consolidated Statement of financial position of the Alpha group as at 31 December 2011?

There are three reasons why unrealised profit needs to be eliminated:

1. The Consolidated Statement of financial position is prepared from the point of view of the group – i.e. treating the parent and the subsidiary together as a single entity. An entity cannot make a profit from itself.
2. If unrealised profit is not eliminated it becomes possible to improve the earnings of a group by merely shifting goods from one to another within the group.
3. It is a requirement of company law and Accounting Standards that inventory should be reported at cost. Hence, when the Consolidated Statement of financial position is prepared from the group's point of view it should report the inventory at the cost to the group.

In relation to eliminating unrealised profit it will be useful to remember three points:

1. There would be a portion of profit unrealised not only because some goods sold at a profit by one member of the group remain with another as at the year-end, but also because goods in similar circumstances may remain in transit. For example, if the year-end inventory with the subsidiary had been invoiced to it by the parent at £80 and further goods invoiced to the subsidiary at £40 remain in transit, and assuming the cost of these goods to the parent were £60 and £30 respectively, the total of unrealised profit that needs to be eliminated from the parent's retained earnings would be £30 (£20 + £10).
2. The unrealised profit should be eliminated from the retained earnings of the party who made that profit. In our illustrations we have consistently assumed that it is the parent who made the unrealised profit and, accordingly, eliminated it from the parent's retained earnings. Alternatively, if the unrealised profit had been made by the subsidiary, the elimination has to be from the subsidiary's retained earnings.
3. When calculating the unrealised profit to be eliminated care should be taken to clarify whether the profit involved has been expressed as a gross profit ratio or as a profit margin (see Chapter 6 for the difference). For example, let us assume that goods invoiced by the parent at £120 remains with the subsidiary by the year-end. If the invoicing had been done at cost plus 25%, the unrealised profit would be £24 (£120 × 25/125). On the other hand, if the invoicing had been at a price calculated to produce a gross profit ratio of 25%, the unrealised profit would be £30 (25% of £120).

Activity 13.9 Fully owned subsidiary with four consolidation adjustments

Alpha acquired all of Beta's equity for £780,000 on 1 July 2009 when:

(i) Beta's retained earnings were £125,000.

(ii) Beta's investments had a market value of £200,000.

You are further informed as follows:

(a) Beta's inventory includes at £90,000 goods invoiced to it by Alpha. These goods have cost Alpha £60,000.

(b) Receivables reported by Alpha includes an amount of £80,000 due from Beta. Beta's payables, on the other hand, includes only £65,000 as due to Alpha. The difference arises because of cash in transit.

Required: Prepare the Consolidated Statement of financial position of the Alpha group as at 30 June 2012.

Statements of financial position as at 30 June 2012		
	Alpha	Beta
	£'000	£'000
Non-current asset	740	580
Investments	820	140
Current assets:		
Inventory	398	245
Trade receivables	412	315
Cash and bank	38	20
	2,408	1,300
	£'000	£'000
Ordinary shares of £1	1,200	500
Share premium	90	50
Retained earnings	570	265
Current liabilities:		
Trade payables	398	375
Taxation	90	60
Dividend declared	60	50
	2,408	1,300

13.8 Where the subsidiary is one partly owned

13.8.1 What is a partly owned subsidiary?

We have defined a subsidiary as a company within the control of the parent. To be within control, the parent need not always own 100% of the subsidiary's shares. If Alpha holds more than 50% shares in Beta and if each share has a vote the majority of directors in Beta will be those appointed by Alpha and Alpha is, therefore, able to control Beta's resources and activities, and so Beta is a subsidiary of Alpha.

13.8.2 The consolidation of a partly owned subsidiary

Although the subsidiary is one that is partly owned, the consolidation is done, as we have studied, by adding together, line by line, all the assets and liabilities of the parent with those of the subsidiary, making every one of the basic consolidation adjustments we have met with, which are listed below:

1. cancel all inter-company debts;
2. freeze all pre-acquisition profits of the subsidiary;

3. fair value all identifiable non-monetary assets of the subsidiary, on the date of acquisition; and
4. eliminate all unrealised profit.

However, when consolidating a partly owned subsidiary the following additional steps become necessary:

1. A Consolidated Statement of financial position reports in full all of the assets and liabilities of the group, irrespective of whether they are held by the parent or the subsidiary. It is, therefore, required that the goodwill reported on it should not be just the portion of it acquired by the parent. In a fully owned subsidiary we have been identifying the goodwill paid for by the parent by comparing the price paid by the parent to acquire control with the net assets of the subsidiary at that date. In a partly owned subsidiary there would be others holding the remaining shares in the subsidiary, and they are referred to as *Non-controlling interest* (NCI). For identifying the goodwill relating to the NCI we need to place a value on the portion of the subsidiary's net assets belonging to the NCI. The common way of doing this is to value the number of shares held by the NCI at the market price of the shares on the date of subsidiary's acquisition. For example, if the subsidiary's share capital is 100 shares of £1 each and 80% of it had been acquired by the parent, the 20 shares belonging to the NCI are valued at the market price on the date of acquisition (assumed to be £3 each) at £60. Alternatively, if the parent had paid £260 to acquire an 80% holding, the value of the remaining 20% is identified proportionately as £65 (260 × 20/80). The second method of placing a proportionate value on the portion of subsidiary belonging to the NCI is questionable because the parent could well have paid a higher price for acquiring control, taking into consideration the synergy effects of acquisition (i.e. advantages that could be gained by conducting the operations of both companies together).
2. The amount so identified as the value of the NC1 on the date of acquisition is accounted for by a pair of entries as follows:
   (a) as addition to the parent's investment, so that the total of both may be matched with the subsidiary's net assets (i.e. Share capital, Share premium, fair valuation gain and pre-acquisition profit) on the date of acquisition to identify the *whole* goodwill; and
   (b) as the value of the NCI's interest in the subsidiary on the date of the acquisition.
3. The subsidiary's post-acquisition retained earnings (after any adjustment such as for additional depreciation arising from fair valuation of subsidiary's assets) is shared between the Consolidated retained earnings and the NCI, in accordance with their respective percentage shareholding.
4. Any impairment of goodwill, if and when identified, is written off against consolidated retained earnings and the NCI according to their respective shareholding.
5. In a situation where the subsidiary is one fully owned by the parent, any dividend declared and reported as a liability by the subsidiary would be cancelled as a consolidation adjustment with the dividend receivable (asset) reported by the parent. This would not be true when the subsidiary is a partly owned one. For example, if the subsidiary reports a dividend declared of £100 and the parent owns only 80% of the subsidiary, the parent would report only £80 as dividend receivable from the subsidiary. Upon cancellation of the inter-company debt, in this situation, £20 of the dividend declared by the subsidiary will not be cancelled, because that is the amount payable to those holding non-controlling interest in the subsidiary. Therefore, that amount should be reported separately, as a current liability, in the Consolidated Statement of financial position.

6. The Consolidated Statement of financial position, on any date, reports the amount owed to the NCI on that date (i.e. value of the NCI on the date of acquisition, plus its share of adjusted post-acquisition profits of the subsidiary less its share of any goodwill impairment) either as a non-current liability or within equity and reserves. IFRS 3[2] permits both alternatives.

13.8.3 Illustration of consolidation with a partly owned subsidiary

Statements of financial position as at 31.12.2011		
	Alpha	Beta
	£'000	£'000
Non-current assets:		
Property, plant	900	400
Investments	675	35
Current assets:		
Inventory	242	228
Trade receivables	198	185
Cash and bank	35	22
	2,050	870
	£'000	£'000
Equity and reserves:		
Ordinary shares of £1	1,000	400
Share premium account	150	40
Retained earnings	504	170
Current liabilities:		
Trade payables	212	196
Taxation	84	24
Dividend declared	100	40
	2,050	870

Alpha plc paid £640,000 to acquire 80% of equity in Beta plc on 1 January 2010 when:

- Beta's land and buildings had a fair value that exceeded the book value by £120,000;
- Beta's retained earnings were £90,000; and
- Beta's shares were quoted at 185 pence per share.

Draft Statements of financial position of both on 31 December 2011 are shown on the left.

You are informed as follows:

(a) If Beta had reported its land and buildings at the fair value it would have had to write off an additional depreciation of £10,000 per year.

(b) Trade receivables reported by Alpha includes £50,000 due from Beta; whereas the corresponding amount reported by Beta was only £32,000. The difference has arisen because of goods in transit.

(c) As at the year-end Beta's inventory includes those purchased from Alpha at £42,000. Alpha invoices Beta at cost plus a third.

Required: Prepare the Consolidated Statement of financial position of the Alpha group as at 31 December 2011.

Let us proceed with preparing the Consolidated Statement of financial position of Alpha group by taking the following steps:

Step a We fair value Beta's land and buildings, increasing it by £120,000, so that the Consolidated Statement would report the asset at what it cost Alpha. The gain is a pre-acquisition one that needs to be frozen. Once fair valued, depreciation needs to be written off from the revised cost of the buildings at £10,000 per year for the two post-acquisition years. This would reduce Beta's property, plant and its *post*-acquisition profit by £20,000.

Step b To identify the full amount of goodwill in Beta (not just the amount acquired by Alpha) we need to place a value on the NCI's share in Beta's net assets on the date of acquisition and we could do that using the market price of Beta's shares on the date of acquisition, i.e. 185p. 20% of 400,000 shares @ 185 pence = £148,000.

Step c By comparing the price paid for the acquisition of 80% interest by Alpha as well as the value of the NCI on the same date (£148,000) with the net assets of Beta on that date (see box below) we identify the goodwill in Beta on that date as £138,000.

Alpha's investment		£640
NCI in Beta		£148
Net assets in Beta:		
Share capital	400	
Share premium	40	
Fair valuation	120	
Pre-acquisition profit	90	(£650)
Goodwill in Beta		£138

Step d Alpha's receivables include £50,000 due from Beta whereas the corresponding amount admitted by Beta is £32,000. The difference (£18,000) is identified as arising because of goods in transit and it must be moving from Alpha to Beta because Beta is the customer to whom goods are sold. After removing the goods in transit from Alpha's receivables (to report it as part of inventory) both parties would agree that they owe each other £32,000 which is cancelled.

Step e The unrealised profit, in this instance, is made by Alpha and is calculated as:

£42,000 (held by Beta) + £18,000 (in transit) = £60,000

The unrealised profit is £60 × $^1/_4$ = £15,000

The unrealised profit of £15,000 is removed from inventory as well as Alpha's retained earnings.

Step f Beta's post-acquisition profit of £80,000 (£170,000 less £90,000 pre-acquisition portion), net of the additional depreciation (£20,000), is shared between consolidated retained earnings and the NCI in their respective ratios as 80% and 20%. Therefore, the amount owed to the NCI as at 31 December 2011 is reported as £160,000 (see working below) within Equity and reserves.

	£'000
Non-controlling interest	
As valued at acquisition	148
Post-acquisition profit b[1]	12
	160

b[1]: 20% of (£80,000 post-acquisition profit – £20,000 depreciation).

Step g Alpha is entitled to £32,000 (80% of £40,000) dividend declared by Beta. The dividend receivable has not been accounted for by Alpha because if it had been Alpha would have reported as a current asset a dividend receivable of £32,000. Hence, the dividend receivable needs to be accounted for in Alpha's books, as an income (which is included within Alpha's retained earnings) and as a current asset. Then the dividend receivable (£32,000) reported as an asset by Alpha is cancelled against dividend declared reported as a liability by Beta, leaving £8,000 (dividend owed to the NCI) which is reported separately, as a current liability, in the Consolidated Statement of financial position.

Step h Consolidated retained earnings are stated as £569,000 (see working below).

		£'000
Consolidated retained earnings		
As reported by Alpha		504
Unrealised profit[e]		(15)
Dividend receivable from Beta[g]		32
Beta's profit as reported	170	
Pre-acquisition profit – frozen[c]	(90)	
Post-acquisition profit	80	
Additional depreciation[a]	(20)	
Adjusted post-acquisition profit	60	48
		569

Step i Investments held by Alpha are included in the Consolidated Statement of financial position net of its investment in Beta.

Step j Only the parent's Share capital and Share premium are reported in the consolidated statement. This is because the whole of the subsidiary's Share capital and Share premium were cancelled when determining the goodwill in step c.

The Consolidated Statement of financial position of the Alpha group would appear as shown below:

Consolidated Statement of financial position as at 31 December 2011

		£'000	£'000
Non-current assets:			
Property, plant	900 + (400 + 120[a] – 20[a])	1,400	
Goodwill[c]		138	
Investments	(675 – 640[i]) + 35	70	1,608
Current assets:			
Inventory	242 + 228 + 18[d] – 15[e]	473	
Trade receivables	(198 – 18[d] – 32[d]) + 185	333	
Cash and bank balance	35 + 22	57	863
			2,471

		£'000	£'000
Equity and reserves:			
Ordinary shares of £1[j]		1,000	
Share premium account[j]		150	
Consolidated retained earnings[h]		569	1,719
Non-controlling interest[f]			160
Current liabilities:			
Trade payables	212 + (196 – 32[d])	376	
Taxation	84 + 24	108	
Dividend payable to non-controlling interest[g]		8	
Dividend declared		100	592
			2,471

Activity 13.10 Consolidation of a partly owned subsidiary

Alpha paid £520 to acquire 360 shares in Beta on 1 April 2009 when:

(i) Beta's retained earnings were £80 and

(ii) Beta's property had a market value which exceeded the book value by £100.

(iii) Beta's share were quoted at 140 pence each.

You are informed as follows:

(a) Alpha's trade receivables includes £85 due from Beta; Beta agrees with the amount subject to £15 cash remaining in transit.

(b) Beta's inventory includes goods invoiced to it by Alpha at £80. Alpha invoices Beta at cost plus a third.

(c) Based on fair value Beta should have written off an additional depreciation of £5 per year in each of the three post-acquisition years.

(d) As at 31 March 2012 goodwill in Beta was valued at £6.

Required: Prepare the Consolidated Statement of financial position of the Alpha group as at 31.3.2012.

Statements of financial position as at 31 March 2012

	Alpha	Beta
	£	£
Non-current assets:		
Property, plant and equipment	900	500
Investments	780	40
Current assets:		
Inventory	380	210
Trade receivables	420	285
Cash and bank	30	15
	2,510	1,050
	£	£
Share capital – £1 each	1,500	600
Share premium	120	60
Retained earnings	542	180
Current liabilities:		
Trade payables	215	148
Taxation	58	32
Dividend declared	75	30
	2,510	1,050

13.9 Consolidation of Statements of income

13.9.1 The consolidation schedule and consolidation adjustments

The task of preparing the Consolidated Statement of income involves the preparation of a *consolidation schedule* including within it the information from the individual Statements of income of both the parent and the subsidiary, making the following consolidation adjustments:

1. *Cancel all inter-company transactions* such as:
   - sales with cost of sales;
   - interest income with interest expense;
   - rent income with rent expense;
   - dividend received with dividend paid.

   This is necessary so that the group can report the income it earned and the expenses it incurred during the accounting period, excluding transactions that took place within the group.

2. *Eliminate any unrealised profit* from the column of the company making that profit so that the realised gross profit of the group may be identified. This is because when reporting from the group's perspective any profit one member of the group makes from another is not realised until the goods are sold to someone outside the group.
3. *Account for any additional depreciation* that may arise because of the fair valuation exercise. For example, if a machine that cost the subsidiary £400 is depreciated by it at 10% of cost, the depreciation written off by the subsidiary (based on its historical cost) would have been £40. If at acquisition the machine was fair valued upwards, an additional depreciation would need to be accounted for and included as an addition to the cost of sale reported by the subsidiary.
4. *Any impairment of goodwill* that occurred in the current year is deducted from the subsidiary's column (so that the NCI too would share the loss), after identifying the operating profit.
5. *Remove the post-tax profit of the subsidiary for the year, to the extent it relates to Non-controlling interest*, so that the group's post-tax profit may be identified. If the parent holds say 80% of equity in a subsidiary, the whole of the income earned and expenses incurred by the subsidiary is consolidated so as to report the total performance of the assets within the group's control. After reaching the amount of subsidiary's 'profit after tax' the portion of it attributable to Non-controlling interest is removed, so as to identify the group share.
6. *If the acquisition of the subsidiary happened part way through the current year*, the subsidiary's income and expenses included within the consolidation schedule should only be those of the subsidiary relating to the post-acquisition period of the current year. This is because the Consolidated Statement of income should report the income and expenses of the group and, therefore, it cannot include any income or expenses of the subsidiary before it joined the group.

   For example, let us assume that in the year 2012 the parent and the subsidiary have reported their sales as £800 and £400 respectively and that the acquisition was on 31 March 2012; the sales of the group, to be reported on the Consolidated Statement of income, for the year ended 31 December 2012 would be £1,100 (£800 + (£400 × 9/12 months).

13.10 The Consolidated Statement of changes in equity

The Consolidated Statement of changes in equity reports only the changes to the extent they relate to the parent company's shareholders. Accordingly in the group's Statement of changes in equity:

(a) Only the (i) *group share* of (ii) the *adjusted* (iii) *post-acquisition* retained earnings of the subsidiary, earned prior to the current year is reported, in the subsidiary's column, as the balance brought forward from prior years. To illustrate let us assume as follows:

   (i) Alpha acquired 80% of Beta on 1.1.2010 when Beta reported retained earnings of £120.

   (ii) As at 1 January 2012 Beta reports, in its Statement of changes in equity, retained earnings brought forward of £380.

   (iii) On the basis of fair valuation done at the point of acquisition an additional depreciation of £5 should be written off in each of the post-acquisition years (2010 and 2011).

On the Consolidated Statement of changes in equity, the subsidiary's column would state £200 as the retained earnings brought forward (see the calculations in the box on the right).

Beta's retained earnings brought forward	£380
Less: Pre-acquisition portion that is frozen	(£120)
Post-acquisition portion of retained earnings b/f	£260
Less: additional depreciation (£5 × 2 years)	(£10)
Adjusted post-acquisition retained earnings b/f	£250
The group portion: 80% of £250	£200

(b) If any goodwill impairment had been written off prior to the current year (assume £20) the group portion only (i.e. 80% of £20) is shown in the adjustment column of the Consolidated Statement of changes in equity, as a deduction from the Retained earnings brought forward.

(c) Only the parent's dividend paid or declared in the year is included in the Consolidated Statement of changes in equity.

13.11 Preparation of the Consolidated Statement of income illustrated

Alpha and its 80% owned subsidiary Beta have drafted their Statements of income for the year ended 31 December 2011 as shown below on the left. You are informed as follows:

Statements of income year ended 31 December 2011

	Alpha	Beta
	£	£
Sales revenue	800	500
Cost of sales	(500)	(300)
Gross profit	300	200
Expenses	(180)	(120)
Operating profit	120	80
Dividend received	16	–
Interest expense	(40)	(10)
Profit before tax	96	70
Taxation	(24)	(15)
Profit after tax	72	55

Statement of changes in equity

	£	£
Balance b/f	324	175
Profit after tax	72	55
Dividend paid	(40)	(20)
Balance c/f	356	210

(a) Alpha acquired Beta on 1 January 2008. On the date of acquisition Beta's retained earnings were £60 and goodwill in Beta was identified as £80.

(b) During the year ended 31.12.2011 Alpha invoiced goods to Beta at £75.

(c) On the basis of the goods remaining with Beta and in transit unrealised profit has been identified as £4.

(d) On the basis of fair valuations done on the day of acquisition Beta should have written off additional depreciation amounting to £5 per year.

(e) In view of stiff competition facing Beta an impairment loss of £10 was written off goodwill in the year ended 31 December 2010. A further impairment of £20 needs to be written off in the current year.

Required: Prepare a Consolidated Statement of income, along with a Statement of changes in equity, for the Alpha group, for the year ended 31 December 2011.

For preparing a Consolidated Statement of income it would be convenient to draft a consolidation schedule, making the following adjustments:

(a) Cancel the inter-company sale (£75) both from the sales and the cost of sales.

(b) Similarly cancel the dividend income earned by Alpha from Beta – 80% of £20 paid by Beta. This cancellation cannot be shown on the consolidation schedule, as we have done for inter-company sale, because a Statement of changes in equity is not prepared for the subsidiary.

(c) Unrealised profit, made by Alpha, is eliminated from Alpha's column in the consolidation schedule, before identifying the realised portion of its gross profit.

(d) The additional depreciation arising because of the fair valuation exercise, in the current year, will increase Beta's cost of sale to £305 (£300 + £5) and that related to three post-acquisition years will reduce Beta's post-acquisition profit (see g below).

(e) Impairment of goodwill in the current year (£20) is included in Beta's column of the consolidation schedule (so that the NCI too would share the loss); while that written off in the previous year is shown, only to the extent of the group's share (80% of £10 = £8), as a deduction from the Retained earnings brought forward in the Statement of changes in equity.

(f) 20% of the subsidiary's profit after tax £6 (20% of £30) relates to Non-controlling interest and is removed to identify the group portion of the subsidiary's profit in the current year.

(g) The Consolidated Statement of changes in equity reports, within Retained earnings brought forward, only the group portion of the adjusted post-acquisition profit (see working on the right) of the subsidiary: 80% of £100 = £80.

Beta's profit b/f	£175
Pre-acquisition portion forzen	(£60)
Post-acquisition portion of subsidiary	£115
Adjustment for depreciation £5 × 3 yrs	(£15)
Adjusted post-acquisition profit of subsidiary	£100

(h) The Consolidated Statement of changes in equity reports any dividend paid or declared in the current year by the parent (only).

The Consolidated Statement of income (along with the workings in the form of a consolidation schedule) is shown below:

Consolidation schedule year ended 31 December 2011				
	Alpha	Beta	Adjusted	Consolidated
	£	£	£	£
Sales revenue	800	500	(75)[a]	1,225
Cost of sales	(500)	(305)[d]	75[a]	(730)
Unrealised profit	(4)[c]	–	–	(4)
Gross profit	296	195	–	491
Expenses	(180)	(120)	–	(300)
Operating profit	116	75	–	191
Impairment of goodwill	–	(20)[e]	–	(20)
Interest expense	(40)	(10)	–	(50)
Profit before taxation	76	45	–	121
Taxation	(24)	(15)	–	(39)
Profit after taxation	52	30	–	82
Non-controlling interest	–	(6)[f]	–	(6)
Group profit for the year	52	24	–	76

Consolidated statement of changes in equity

	£	£	£	£
Retained earnings b/f	324	80[g]	(8)[e]	396
Group profit for the year	52	24	–	76
Dividend paid	(40)[h]	–	–	(40)
Retained earnings c/f	336	104	(8)	432

Activity 13.11 Consolidated Statement of income

Alpha had acquired 70% of the equity in Beta on 1 April 2009 when Beta's retained earnings were £400. Both companies have drafted their Statement of income as shown on the right.

You are informed as follows:

(a) During the current year Beta has sold goods for £500 to Alpha. Beta sells to Alpha at cost plus 25%.

(b) As at 31.12.2012 inventory held by Alpha includes goods invoiced to it by Beta at £800. In addition goods invoiced at £200 are in transit.

(c) 75% of interest expense of Beta was paid to Alpha.

Required: Prepare a consolidation schedule to identify the amounts that should be included in the Consolidated Statement of income.

Statements of income year ended 31.12.2012	Alpha	Beta
	£	£
Sales revenue	7,400	3,800
Cost of sales	(4,500)	(2,100)
Gross profit	2,900	1,700
Expenses	(1,800)	(900)
Operating profit	1,100	800
Dividend from Beta	210	–
Interest income	30	–
Interest paid	–	(40)
Profit before tax	1,340	760
Taxation	(480)	(140)
Profit after tax	860	620

Changes in equity:	Alpha	Beta
	£	£
Balance b/f	2,140	1,100
Profit after tax	860	620
Dividend paid	(400)	(300)
Balance c/f	2,600	1,420

13.12 An associate company

If a company (investor) does not have sufficient votes (50% +) to control the company it has invested in (investee) but is still in a position to significantly influence the operating and financial decisions of the investee, the investee company is known as an *associate*. There is a presumption that if the investor holds 20% or more votes in an investee, the investee is an associate. Investments in an associate company should be accounted for on the *equity method*, i.e. at cost plus the group share of the associate's post-acquisition profits.[3]

Let us assume that Alpha paid £300 to acquire 25% of equity in Delta when Delta's retained earnings were £100 and that by 31 December 2012 (when the Consolidated Statement of financial position is to be prepared for the group), Delta's retained earnings have increased to £160 – i.e. a post-acquisition earning by Delta is £60. On the Consolidated Statement of financial position as at 31 December 2012, Alpha will report its investments in Delta, on the equity method, at (£300 + 25% of £60) £315. This is achieved by the following pair of accounting entries recording £15:

(a) Debit Investment in associate account (reporting an asset of £315).

(b) Credit an 'Income from associates' which is included in the investor's Statement of income.

Summary

- A parent is an entity able to control another and the one controlled is a subsidiary; both together constitute a group.
- Groups are legally obliged to prepare a Consolidated Statement of financial position and Consolidated Statement of income.
- Consolidation is merely an aggregation of items appearing in their separate financial statements, subject to a number of consolidation adjustments.
- If the parent acquires control of a subsidiary paying a premium price, the premium paid is known as goodwill which is reported as an asset year after year unless it is impaired. On the other hand if the parent makes a gain on the acquisition, the gain is known as negative goodwill and is immediately included within Consolidated retained earnings and the NCI in accordance with their respective shareholding in the subsidiary.
- With regard to consolidation of the Statements of financial position there are four basic adjustments as follows:
  - Cancel inter-company debts, mainly to avoid double-counting.
  - Eliminate unrealised profit, i.e. profit made by one member of the group from another.
  - Freeze subsidiary's pre-acquisition profit because it is part of the package paid for by the parent, and needs to be taken into account when identifying the premium paid, i.e. goodwill.
  - Fair value the subsidiary's identifiable non-monetary assets to identify what that asset is costing the parent and to identify the amount paid as goodwill.
- Further adjustments to remember when the subsidiary is one that is partly owned:
  - To establish the subsidiary's goodwill on the date of acquisition, the Non-controlling interest in the subsidiary on the date of acquisition needs to be valued.
  - The subsidiary's post-acquisition earnings and any loss from impairment of goodwill are shared by the parent and the NCI according to their percentage share of ownership.
- With regard to consolidation of Statements of income the basic adjustments are as follows:
  - Inter-company transactions (those between members of the group) should be cancelled.
  - Unrealised profit should be eliminated from whichever group member made it, so as to identify the realised gross profit.
  - Subsidiary's expenses may need to be adjusted by, for instance, additional depreciation arising from the fair valuation exercise.
  - The portion of current year's profit of the subsidiary relating to the NCI is eliminated only after identifying profit after taxation.
  - The Consolidated Statement of changes in equity reports only the retained earnings relating to the group members.
- If company Alpha makes sufficient investment in company Gamma so as to exercise significant influence over Gamma's operating and financing decisions, Gamma is regarded as an associate and the investment is accounted for on the equity method. Holding 20% or more votes creates a presumption that the investee is an associate.

References

1. Companies Act (2006), section 399, London, The Stationery Office.
2. IFRS 3 (2008) *Business Combinations*, London, International Accounting Standards Board.
3. IAS 28 (2008) *Investments in Associates*, London, International Accounting Standards Board.

Suggested answers to activities

13.1 Identification of parent and subsidiary

Beta and Delta are subsidiaries of Alpha; Gamma is not.

13.2 Consolidation of a subsidiary incorporated by the parent

Consolidated Statement of financial position as at 31 December 2011		
		£
Non-current assets	840 + 530	1,370
Current assets	280 + 140	420
		1,790
Ordinary shares (parent)		1,000
Consolidated reserves	310 + 80	390
Current liabilities	310 + 90	400
		1,790

Note: Alpha's investment of £300 in Beta has been offset against Beta's Share capital.

13.3 Acquisition of a fully owned subsidiary immediately upon acquisition

Consolidated Statement of financial position as at 31 December 2011		
		£
Non-current assets	920 + 440	1,360
Goodwill		30
Current assets	240 + 180	420
		1,810

		£
Share capital (parent only)		900
Share premium (parent only)		90
Consolidated reserves	210 + 90	300
Current liabilities	440 + 80	520
		1,810

Identification of goodwill in Beta		£
Alpha's investment in Beta		480
Beta's share capital	400	
Beta's Share premium	50	(450)
Goodwill		30

13.4 A wholly owned subsidiary acquired later than incorporation

Consolidated Statement of financial position as at 31 March 2012

		£
Non-current assets	900 + 440	1,340
Goodwill	50 – 15 impairment	35
Current assets	340 + 280	620
		1,995

		£
Share capital (parent only)		800
Share premium (parent only)		80
Consolidated reserves	490 + 120 – 15 impairment	595
		1,475
Current liabilities	370 + 150	520
		1,995

Calculation of goodwill:		£
Alpha's investment in Beta		500
Beta's share capital	300	
Share premium	60	
Pre-acquisition profit	90	(450)
Goodwill		50

13.5 Fair valuation of subsidiary's assets on the date of acquisition

Consolidated Statement of financial position as at 31 March 2012

		£
Non-current assets	1,000 + 780	1,780
Goodwill	70 – 20 impairment	50
Investments	120 + 90 fair valuation	210
Current assets	480 + 320	800
		2,840

		£
Share capital (parent only)		1,200
Share premium (parent only)		180
Consolidated reserves	590 + (390 – 180) – 20 impairment	780
		2,160
Current liabilities	510 + 170	680
		2,840

Calculation of goodwill:	£	£
Alpha's investment in Beta		1,000
Beta's Share capital	600	
Share premium	60	
Pre-acquisition profit	180	
Fair valuation gain	90	(930)
Goodwill		70

13.6 Cancellation of inter-company debt

Trade receivables: (540 – 70[a]) + 348	£818
Trade payables: 428 + (296 – 70[a]) =	£654

(a) Inter-company debt cancelled from both parties.

13.7 Cancellation involving items in transit

Inventory	300 + 200 + 20[a]	£520
Receivables	(400 – 20[a] – 10[a] – 50[b]) + 300	£620
Cash/bank	12 + 10 + 10[a]	£32
Payables	250 + (150 – 50[b])	£350

(a) Items in transit; (b) amount agreed on by both parties.

13.8 Elimination of unrealised profit

Consolidated statement of financial position 31.12.2011		
Inventory	540 + 420 – 10[a]	£950
Consolidated reserves:	(398 – 10[a]) + (240 – 100[b])	£528

(a) Unrealised profit made by Alpha; (b) pre-acquisition profit frozen by offset from investment for identifying the goodwill.

13.9 Fully owned subsidiary with four consolidation adjustments

Consolidated Statement of financial position as at 30 June 2012			
			£'000
Non-current assets	740 + 580		1,320
Goodwill[a]			45
Investments	(820 – 780) + (140 + 60[b])		240
Current assets:			
Inventory	398 + (245 – 30[c])	613	
Trade receivables	(412 – 15[d] – 65[e]) + 315	647	
Cash and bank	38 + 20 + 15[d]	73	1,333
			2,938

			£
Equity and reserves:			
Ordinary shares of £1 each		1,200	
Share premium account		90	
Consolidated retained earnings[f]		730	2,020
Current liabilities:			
Trade payables	398 + (375 – 65[e])	708	
Taxation	90 + 60	150	
Dividend declared		60	918
			2,938

(a) Calculation of goodwill.

		£'000
Alpha's investment		780
Beta's:		
Share capital	500	
Share premium	50	
Fair valuation[b]	60	
Pre-acquisition profit	125	(735)
Goodwill		45

(b) Fair valuation gain on investments.
(c) Unrealised profit of Alpha in Beta's inventory (£90,000 – £60,000) = £30,000.
(d) Cash in transit from Beta to Alpha.
(e) Inter-company debt agreed by both.
(f) Consolidated retained earnings:

Alpha's		570
Unrealised profit[c]		(30)[c]
Dividend receivable from Beta		50
Beta's retained earnings	265	
Pre-acquisition – frozen	(125)	140
		730

(g) Dividend receivable from Beta, accounted for as an asset by Alpha, is fully cancelled from dividend declared reported as a current liability by Beta.

13.10 Consolidation of a partly owned subsidiary

Consolidated Statement of financial position as at 31 March 2012			£
Non-current assets:			
Property, plant	900 + (500 + 100 fair value – 15 depreciation)		1,485
Goodwill[c]	16 – 10 impairment		6
Investments	(780 – 520) + 40		300
Current assets:			
Inventory	380 + 210 – 20 unrealised	570	
Trade receivables	(470 – 15 transit – 70) + 285	620	
Cash and bank	30 + 15 + 15 transit	60	1,250
			3,041

			£
Equity and reserves:			
Ordinary shares of £1 each		1,500	
Share premium account		120	
Consolidated retained earnings[e]		585	2,205
Non-controlling interest[d]			366
Current liabilities:			
Trade payables	215 + (148 – 70 inter-company)	293	
Taxation	58 + 32	90	
Dividend payable to non-controlling interest		12	
Dividend declared		75	470
			3,041

(a) Alpha's percentage holding:
360/600 × 100 = 60%.

(b) Value of NCI at acquisition:
40% of £600 @ 140p = £336.

(c) Goodwill:

Alpha's investment		520
NCI's value		336
Share capital	600	
Share premium	60	
Fair valuation	100	
Pre-acquisitionprofit	80	(840)
		16

(d) Non-controlling interest:

Value at acquisition	336
Post-acquisition retained:	
40% of £85	34
40% of impairment	(4)
	366

(e)

Consolidated retained	542
Unrealised profit	(20)
Dividend from Beta	18
Beta's profit: 60% of £85	51
Goodwill impairment	(6)
	585

13.11 Consolidated Statement of income

Consolidation schedule

	Alpha	Beta	Adjustment	Consolidation
	£	£	£	£
Sales revenue	7,400	3,800	(500)[a]	10,700
Cost of sales	(4,500)	(2,100)	500[a]	(6,100)
Unrealised profit	–	(200)[b]	–	(200)
Gross profit	2,900	1,500	–	4,400
Expenses	(1,800)	(900)	–	(2,700)
Operating profit	1,100	600	–	1,700
Interest income	30	–	(30)[a]	–
Interest expense	–	(40)	30[a]	(10)
Profit before tax	1,130	560	–	1,690
Taxation	(480)	(140)	–	(620)
Profit after tax	650	420	–	1,070
Non-controlling interest	–	(126)[c]	–	(126)
Group profit	650	294	–	944
Changes in equity	£	£	£	£
Retained earnings b/f	2,140	490[d]	–	2,630
Group profit for the year	650	294	–	944
Dividend[e]	(400)	–	–	(400)
Retained earnings c/f	2,390	784	–	3,174

(a) Inter-company sales cancelled and inter-company interest cancelled.
(b) Unrealised profit eliminated: 25/125 × 800 + 200 = £200.
(c) Non-controlling interest = 30% of £420 = £126.
(d) Group share of Beta's post-acquisition retained earnings brought forward: 70% of £1,100 – 400 = £490.
(e) Only the parent company's dividend paid or declared.

Multiple choice questions

Concepts – the group

13.1 Which of the following companies would qualify to be regarded as subsidiaries of Alpha?

(a) Beta in which Alpha has 15% votes and a place on the board of directors
(b) Delta in which Alpha has 52% votes but no place on the board of directors
(c) Gamma in which Alpha has 25% shares and two places on the board of directors
(d) Theta in which Alpha holds 100% votes and all places on the board of directors

w	a & c	
x	b & c	
y	b & d	
z	a & b	

13.2 Which of the following would qualify a company to be regarded as a parent of another?

(a) A parent: both it and its subsidiary must be in the same line of business
(b) A parent should own majority shares in the subsidiary
(c) A parent should control the majority of the votes at subsidiary's shareholders' meetings
(d) A parent and the subsidiary should both have the same persons as their directors

Concepts – Consolidated Statement of financial position

13.3 Which of the following statement(s) is/are correct with regard to preparation of consolidated financial statements?

(a) To be a subsidiary a parent should hold 100% of its equity shares
(b) Consolidation is merely the addition together of two Statements of financial position
(c) In consolidation a subsidiary and an associate are treated identically
(d) Consolidated Statement of financial position excludes assets not owned by the group

w	a & b	
x	b & c	
y	a & d	
z	None	

13.4 Which of the following statement(s) apply when consolidating Statements of financial position?

(a) All inter-company balances should be cancelled
(b) The group share of the whole of subsidiary's profit is included within group profit
(c) Inter-company profit should be eliminated unless it is realised by sale to an outsider
(d) Subsidiary's asset values need to be updated at the end of each accounting period

w	a & c	
x	b & c	
y	a & d	
z	a & b	

13.5 With regard to preparing Consolidated Statements of financial position which of the following statements is/are correct?

(a) The Consolidated Statement of financial position reports only parent's goodwill
(b) Any unrealised profit made by a subsidiary should be eliminated from its profit
(c) An amount owed to each other within the group needs to be cancelled
(d) Only the group portion of any unrealised profit need be eliminated

w	a	
x	c	
y	b & c	
z	a & b	

13.6 When preparing a Consolidated Statement of financial position the identifiable non-monetary assets of the subsidiary need to be fair valued for which of the following reasons?

(a) To inform the acquired company what its assets are worth in the market
(b) To comply with the practice followed over the years
(c) To report each of the subsidiary's assets at what it cost the group to acquire
(d) To identify the amount paid for goodwill as the residual not attributed to other assets

w	a, b & c	
x	b, c & d	
y	a, c & d	
z	c & d	

13.7 When preparing a Consolidated Statement of financial position the identifiable non-monetary assets of the subsidiary need to be fair valued. Which of the following assets of the subsidiary need to be fair valued?

(a) Land and buildings appearing in the books of the subsidiary
(b) Trade receivables reported on the subsidiary's Statement of financial position
(c) Brand name the cost relating to which the subsidiary has already fully written off
(d) Inventory reported on the subsidiary's Statement of financial position

w	a, b & c	
x	b, c & d	
y	a, c & d	
z	c & d	

13.8 Which of the following statements are incorrect with regard to preparation of a Consolidated Statement of financial position?

(a) Gain on fair valuation of a subsidiary's asset is a pre-acquisition profit
(b) Non-controlling interest does not deserve any portion of fair valuation gain
(c) If an asset is not reported in the subsidiary's ledger it need not be fair valued
(d) Gain on fair valuation of subsidiary's asset inflates the cost of goodwill

w	a, b & c	
x	b, c & d	
y	a, c & d	
z	c & d	

13.9 When preparing a Consolidated Statement of financial position any profit made by one member of the group against another should be eliminated unless it has been realised by disposal to someone outside the group. Which of the following is/are the reason(s) for this?

(a) Because an entity cannot make a profit against its own self
(b) Because it is fashionable to do so
(c) Because subsidiary's assets needs to be reported at the amount each cost the group
(d) Because the unsold goods may have to be returned to the party purchased from

w	a, b & c	
x	b, c & d	
y	a & c	
z	c & d	

13.10 A parent owns two-thirds of the subsidiary's equity. As at a year-end the subsidiary's inventory includes goods sent to it by the parent invoiced at £360,000. Parent has purchased these goods for £300,000. Which of the following are the correct entries for eliminating unrealised profit?

(a) Debit the subsidiary's retained earnings and credit the subsidiary's inventory with £45,000
(b) Debit the parent's retained earnings and credit the subsidiary's inventory with £60,000
(c) Debit the subsidiary's retained earnings and credit the subsidiary's inventory with £60,000
(d) Debit the parent's retained earnings and credit subsidiary's inventory with £45,000

13.11 What is the amount of the unrealised profit to be eliminated if the parent's year-end inventory includes at £540,000 goods invoiced to it by its 60% owned subsidiary at cost plus 25%?

a	£64,800	
b	£81,000	
c	£108,000	
d	£135,000	

13.12 Subsidiary's inventory at the year-end included £180,000 purchased from its parent. Further goods invoiced by the parent at £45,000 were in transit. The parent invoices the subsidiary at cost plus 20%. The amount of unrealised profit that needs to be eliminated from the parent's retained earnings would be:

a	£36,000	
b	£30,000	
c	£38,333	
d	£37,500	

13.13 When preparing a Consolidated Statement of financial position, the pre-acquisition portion of subsidiary's retained earnings needs to be frozen by offsetting it from the cost of investments. Which of the following is/are the reason(s) for this?

(a) That portion of profit has been paid for by the parent as part of its investment
(b) It is not ethical for the parent to claim profits made before a company became a subsidiary
(c) To establish the true cost to the parent of acquiring the subsidiary's goodwill
(d) Otherwise group profits are inflated by acquiring subsidiaries with high retained earnings

w	b & d	
x	b & c	
y	a & c	
z	c & d	

13.14 Any amount owed by one member of a group to another needs to be cancelled when preparing the Consolidated Statement of financial posiition. As at the year-end the parent's receivable includes £90 due from the subsidiary; whereas the subsidiary reports that it owes only £60 to the parent. The difference has arisen because of cash in transit. Which is the correct way of dealing with the situation when preparing the Consolidated Statement of financial position?

(a) Cancel £90 from parent's receivable, 60 from subsidiary's payable and include £30 with cash
(b) Cancel £60 from both receivable and payable
(c) Cancel £90 from both receivable and payable
(d) Cancel £90 from receivable and £60 from payable

13.15 As at the year-end the parent's Statement of financial position reports rent receivable as an asset at £600 and this includes £150 due from the subsidiary. Subsidiary reports rent payable as £150. Which of the following will be included in the Consolidated Statement of financial position?

(a) Rent receivable as an asset at £600 and rent payable as a current liability at £150

(b) Rent receivable as an asset at £450 and rent payable as a current liability at £150

(c) Rent receivable as an asset at £450 and report nothing within Current liabilities as rent payable

(d) Rent receivable as an asset at £600 and report nothing as current liability

13.16 The parent paid £480 to acquire 75% of 300 ordinary shares issued by the subsidiary on 1 January 2012 when shares in the subsidiary were quoted at 180p per share and the equity and reserves of the subsidiary were reported as £350 and fair valuation of its assets identified a gain of £50. What is the goodwill of the subsidiary on this date?

a	£180	
b	£130	
c	£215	
d	£240	

13.17 Which of the following statements is/are correct with regard to accounting for goodwill?

(a) Goodwill needs to be written off as soon as it is identified

(b) Goodwill is reported continuously as an asset unless it is impaired

(c) Goodwill should be amortised over an estimated useful life

(d) Goodwill should be amortised over an estimated useful life not exceeding 20 years

w	b & c	
x	c & d	
y	a	
z	b	

13.18 If the capital and reserves, including fair valuation gain of a subsidiary, is £5,400 and the parent acquires the whole of it for £4,000, the difference of £1,400 would be known as:

(a) Goodwill

(b) Gain on acquisition

(c) Badwill

(d) Negative goodwill

13.19 How is a negative goodwill reported on the Consolidated Statement of financial position?

(a) As a negative asset – i.e. shown on the asset side but as a deduction

(b) As a reserve, which may preferably be titled a capital reserve

(c) Included fully in the Consolidated retained earnings

(d) A tenth of it is included in Consolidated reserves and the remainder reported as a reserve

Concepts – Consolidated Statement of income

13.20 With regard to preparing a Consolidated Income statement which of the following statements are correct?

(a) Only the group portion of subsidiary's sales, cost of sales and expenses are included

(b) Non-controlling interest is identified immediately after consolidating operating profit

(c) Consolidated movement of equity includes only the parent company's dividend

(d) Only the group portion of the subsidiary's post-acquisition profit is brought forward in the Consolidated changes in equity

w	a, b & c	
x	c & d	
y	a, c & d	
z	b & d	

13.21 When preparing a Consolidated Statement of income, inter-company transactions are cancelled. Which one or more of the following would you say is the reason for this step?

(a) That is how it is expected to be done
(b) Otherwise group earnings can be inflated by one within the group earning from another
(c) Otherwise the same amount is double-counted both as an income and expense
(d) Failure to do so would be bad for the group image

w	b & d	
x	b & c	
y	a & c	
z	c & d	

13.22 Though a subsidiary is only partly owned, the whole of the subsidiary's sales, cost of sales and expenses are aggregated with those of the parent to report the group's income and expenses. Which one or more of the following is/are the justification for this?

(a) That is how it is expected to be done
(b) That is a legal requirement
(c) Otherwise the group would appear to be doing poorly with adverse effect on share price
(d) To report the income generated by and expenses incurred by the group as a whole

w	b & d	
x	b	
y	a & c	
z	d	

13.23 For identifying the group profit for the current year at which of the following points is the profit relating to non-controlling interest removed?

(a) After identifying the gross profit
(b) After identifying the operating profit
(c) After identifying the net profit before tax
(d) After identifying the profit for the year after tax

Consolidated statement of financial position – finding the goodwill

13.24 Alpha paid £300,000 on 1.1.2010 to acquire 80% of Beta. On that date Beta had in issue one hundred thousand ordinary shares of £1 each issued at 120p each, but quoted on this date at 145p. Identify the goodwill in Beta in each of the following alternative situations.

(a) On 1.1.2010 Beta's retained earnings were £30,000 and the fair value of its identifiable assets the same as their book value

w	£170,000	
x	£200,000	
y	£199,000	
z	£212,500	

(b) On 1.1.2010 Beta's retained earnings were £60,000 and the fair value of their identifiable assets £80,000 more than their book value

w	£89,000	
x	£60,000	
y	£75,000	
z	£169,000	

(c) On 1.1.2010 Beta's earnings were £50,000 and while their non-current assets had a fair value £80,000 more than the book value, the investments held by Beta had a fair value £30,000 less than the book value

w	£59,000	
x	£30,000	
y	£37,500	
z	£129,000	

(d) On 1.1.2010 Beta had an accumulated loss of £40,000, though its non-current assets had a fair value which exceeded the book value by £120,000

w	£120,000	
x	£149,000	
y	£96,000	
z	£69,000	

Consolidated Statement of financial position – finding the non-controlling interest

13.25 Alpha paid £750,000 to acquire 60% of equity in Beta on 1 January 2010. Beta's Statement of financial position as at 31 December 2012 reports its Share capital as £500,000, Share premium as £50,000, and Retained earnings as £320,000. Identify the non-controlling interest to be included in the Consolidated Statement of financial position as at 31 December 2012 in each of the following independent situations: Beta's shares have a par value of £1 each.

(a) On 1 January 2010 Beta's retained earnings were £200,000 and the fair value of Beta's identifiable non-monetary assets were equal to the book value. The value of non-controlling interest on the date of acquisition is to be identified on the basis of the price paid by Alpha to acquire control

w	£548,000	
x	£848,000	
y	£348,000	
z	£750,000	

(b) On 1 January 2010 Beta's retained earnings were £160,000, the fair value of its non-current assets exceeded their book value by £100,000 and Beta's shares were quoted at 225p each

w	£450,000	
x	£528,000	
y	£978,000	
z	£514,000	

(c) On 1 January 2010 Beta's retained earnings were £180,000, the fair value of its non-current assets was £90,000 more than the book value and Beta's shares were quoted at 240p each. As at 31 December 2012 £10,000 of profits reported by Beta is unrealised because they related to sales made to Alpha

w	£864,000	
x	£536,000	
y	£532,000	
z	£480,000	

(d) On 1 January 2010 Beta reported an accumulated loss of £120,000, though the fair value of its non-current assets exceeded their book value on that date by £50,000 and Beta's shares were quoted at 255p each

w	£590,000	
x	£686,000	
y	£368,000	
z	£878,000	

Consolidated Statement of financial position – finding the Consolidated Retained earnings

13.26 As at 31 December 2012 the retained earnings reported in their own Statement of income by Alpha was £394,500 and by Beta £240,000. Identify the Consolidated Retained earnings as at 31 December 2012 on each of the following independent scenarios.

(a) Alpha acquired 75% of Beta's equity on 1 January 2008 when Beta's retained earnings were £80,000

w	£514,500	
x	£574,500	
y	£454,500	
z	£634,500	

(b) Alpha acquired 90% of Beta's equity on 1 January 2010 when Beta's retained earnings were £120,000; and during the year ended 31 December 2012, an unrealised profit of £20,000 had to be eliminated from Alpha's retained earnings. Ignore fair valuation adjustments

w	£614,500	
x	£502,500	
y	£583,500	
z	£482,500	

(c) Alpha acquired 80% of Beta's equity on 1 January 2010 when Beta's retained earnings were £180,000. During the year ended 31 December 2012 an unrealised profit of £20,000 had to be eliminated from Beta's retained earnings

w	£426,500	
x	£422,500	
y	£570,500	
z	£634,500	

(d) Alpha acquired 60% of Beta's equity on 1 January 2010 when Beta's retained earnings were £140,000. During the year ended 31 December 2012 an unrealised profit of £20,000 had to be eliminated from Beta's retained earnings and £10,000 written off as impairment of goodwill

w	£418,500	
x	£436,500	
y	£408,500	
z	£516,500	

(e) Alpha acquired 80% of Beta's equity on 1 January 2011 when Beta reported a retained loss of £90,000. Fair valuation recognised at acquisition was £120,000 and, as a result, an additional depreciation needs to be written off at £5,000 per annum

w	£650,500	
x	£578,500	
y	£658,500	
z	£654,500	

(f) Alpha acquired 80% of Beta's equity on 1 January 2011 when Beta's retained earnings were £90,000. Fair valuation gain was £100,000 and as a result the additional depreciation that needs to be written off is £15,000. Negative goodwill on acquisition of Beta was £58,000

w	£502,500	
x	£560,500	
y	£548,500	
z	£536,900	

Consolidation – finding goodwill, non-controlling interest and retained earnings

13.27

Statement of financial position as at 31.12.2012

	Alpha	Beta
	£	£
Assets	400	300
Investment in Beta	400	–
	800	300
	£	£
Shares of £1 each	600	200
Retained earnings	200	100
	800	300

Draft Statements of financial position are stated on the left. Alpha acquired 160 shares in Beta for £400 on 1 January 2008 when Beta's retained earnings were £40, the fair valuation of its non-current assets £80 more than the book value and Beta's shares were quoted at 225p each. Based on fair value Beta should have written off additional depreciation of £4 per year.

Required:

(a) Identify Beta's goodwill as at 1 January 2008.

x	£210,000
y	£180,000
z	£170,000

(b) At what amount will non-controlling interest be reported on the Consolidated Statement of financial position as at 31 December 2012?

x	£72,000	
y	£108,000	
z	£98,000	

(c) What is the amount of consolidated retained earnings reported in the Consolidated Statement of financial position as at 31 December 2012?

x	£300,000	
y	£264,000	
z	£232,000	

Consolidated Statement of income – identifying the group profit

13.28 Trading particulars of Alpha and its 75% controlled subsidiary Beta are shown on the right. During the year Alpha sold goods to Beta for £90,000 and a third of these goods remain unsold with Beta by the year-end. Alpha invoices goods to Beta at cost plus 20%. Identify the realised gross profit of the group.

	Alpha	Beta
Sales	£720,000	£325,000
Cost of sales	(£480,000)	(£190,200)

a	£230,600	
b	£274,800	
c	£369,800	
d	£241,100	

13.29 Trading particulars of Alpha and its 60% controlled subsidiary Beta are shown on the right. During the year Alpha sold goods to Beta for £84,000 at cost plus a third. As at the year-end £16,000 of the goods sent by Alpha remained unsold with Beta while goods invoiced at £8,000 remained in transit. Identify the realised gross profit of the group.

	Alpha	Beta
Sales	£690,000	£495,000
Cost of sales	(£420,000)	(£284,600)

a	£374,400	
b	£390,400	
c	£474,400	
d	£359,400	

13.30 Individual Statements of income of Alpha and its 80% owned subsidiary Beta report the information shown on the right. A fourth of the interest paid by Beta was received by Alpha. During the current year Beta has invoiced goods for £210,000 to Alpha at cost plus a fifth. £60,000 of these goods remained unsold with Alpha by the year-end. Identify the consolidated group profit for the year.

	Alpha	Beta
Gross profit	690,000	£397,000
Expenses	(£420,000)	(£265,000)
Interest received	£5,000	–
Interest paid	–	(£20,000)
Taxation	(£58,000)	(£25,000)

a	£292,000	
b	£281,000	
c	£277,600	
d	£297,000	

13.31 Individual Statements of income of Alpha and its 80% owned subsidiary Beta report the information shown on the right. A third of the interest paid by Beta was received by Alpha. During the current year Alpha has invoiced goods for £180,000 to Beta at cost plus a fourth. £40,000 of these goods remained unsold with Beta by the year-end. During the year goodwill in Beta was impaired by £30,000. Identify the consolidated group profit for the year.

	Alpha	Beta
Gross profit	740,000	£496,000
Expenses	(£440,000)	(£276,600)
Interest received	£7,000	–
Interest paid	–	(£21,000)
Taxation	(£54,000)	(£40,000)

a	£403,000	
b	£346,320	
c	£401,000	
d	£375,000	

Consolidated Statement of income – the movement of equity

13.32 The individual Statements of financial position of the parent and the subsidiary, as at 31 December 2012, report their retained earnings as £540,000 and £297,000 respectively. The profit after tax in the year ended 31 December 2012 was £124,000 for the parent and £96,000 for the subsidiary. Parent acquired two-thirds of the equity in the subsidiary on 1 January 2010 when the subsidiary's retained earnings were £120,000. Assume that no dividends were declared or paid by either company in the year 2012. In the Consolidated Statement of changes in equity for the year ended 31 December 2012:

(a) What would be the balance b/f from previous years for the parent?

x	£540,000	
y	£664,000	
z	£416,000	

(b) What would be the balance b/f from previous years for the subsidiary?

x	£134,000	
y	£118,000	
z	£54,000	

(c) What would be the current year's profit for the subsidiary?

x	£96,000	
y	£64,000	
z	£32,000	

13.33 The end portion of the individual Statements of income of Alpha and its subsidiary Beta are shown on the right. Alpha acquired 75% of Beta three years earlier. Identify the amounts that should be reported on the Consolidated Statement of changes in equity as

	Alpha	Beta
Profit after taxation	£580	£240
Dividend declared	(£200)	(£80)
Retained profit	£380	£160

(a) the consolidated profit for the current year and

(b) dividend declared

	Profit for the year	Dividend	
a	£760,000	£200,000	
b	£580,000	£280,000	
c	£560,000	£200,000	
d	£820,000	£260,000	

Answers to multiple choice questions

13.1: y 13.2: c 13.3: z 13.4: w 13.5: y 13.6: z 13.7: y 13.8: x 13.9: y 13.10: b 13.11: c 13.12: d 13.13: y 13.14: a 13.15: c 13.16: c 13.17: z 13.18: d 13.19: c 13.20: x 13.21: x 13.22: z 13.23: d 13.24a: y 13.24b: w 13.24c: z 13.24d: x 13.25a: w 13.25b: z 13.25c: y 13.25d: x 13.26a: w 13.26b: z 13.26c: w 13.26d: x 13.26e: w 13.26f: y 13.27a: z 13.27b: z 13.27c: z 13.28: c 13.29: c 13.30: c 13.31: b 13.32a: z 13.32b: z 13.32c: y 13.33: a

Progressive questions

PQ 13.1 Fully owned subsidiary incorporated by the parent

Alpha plc incorporated Beta plc on 1 January 2012, investing £150 and recording, in the books of Beta, £100 as share capital and the remainder as share premium. The Statements of financial position of both companies have been prepared as shown on the right.

Required: The Consolidated Statement of financial position of the Alpha group as at 31 December 2012.

Statements of financial position as at 31 December 2012		
	Alpha	Beta
	£	£
Non-current assets	400	120
Investments	150	–
Current assets	150	60
	700	180
	£	£
Share capital	400	100
Share premium account	80	50
Reserves	220	30
	700	180

PQ 13.2 Fully owned subsidiary acquired immediately upon incorporation

Alpha plc paid £180 to acquire the whole of the equity in Beta plc on 1 January 2012, immediately upon Beta's incorporation. The Statements of financial position of both companies, a year after acquisition, are shown on the right. You are informed that trade receivables reported by Alpha includes £72 due from Beta.

Required: The Consolidated Statement of financial position of the Alpha group as at 31 December 2012.

Statements of financial position as at 31 December 2012	Alpha	Beta
	£	£
Non-current assets	840	90
Investments	240	20
Current assets:		
Inventory	280	80
Trade receivables	310	112
Cash and bank	20	18
	1,690	320
	£	£
Ordinary shares of £1 each	800	100
Share premium account	160	50
Retained earnings	515	55
Trade payables	215	115
	1,690	320

PQ 13.3 Consolidation involving items in transit and unrealised profit

Alpha paid £405,000 to acquire 300,000 shares of £1 each in Beta plc, immediately after Beta's incorporation. The Statements of financial position of both companies have been prepared as shown on the right.

You are informed that as at 31 December 2012:

(a) Trade receivables reported by Alpha includes £112,000 due from Beta.

(b) Goods invoiced by Alpha at £48,000 and a remittance of £24,000 by Beta are in transit.

(c) Inventory in the hands of Beta includes those invoiced to it by Alpha at £72,000.

(d) Alpha invoices Beta at prices calculated to produce a gross profit ratio of 25%.

(e) There has been no impairment of goodwill.

Required: Prepare the Consolidated Statement of financial position of the Alpha group as at 31 December 2012.

Statements of financial position as at 31 December 2012	Alpha	Beta
	£'000	£'000
Non-current assets:		
Property, plant and equipment at cost	960	420
Accumulated depreciation	(240)	(160)
	720	260
Investments	430	30
Current assets:		
Inventory	484	188
Trade receivables	319	296
Cash and bank	17	16
	1,970	790
	£'000	£'000
Equity and reserves:		
Ordinary shares of £1 each	800	300
Share premium account	80	60
Retained earnings	521	89
Current liabilities:		
Trade payables	494	312
Taxation	75	29
	1,970	790

PQ 13.4 Consolidation involving pre-acquisition profit and fair valuation

Alpha plc paid £820,000 to acquire all of the equity shares in Beta plc on 1 January 2010 when:

(i) Beta had retained earnings amounting to £80,000.

(ii) Investments held by Beta had a market value of £120,000.

The Statements of financial position of both companies as at 31 December 2012 have been prepared as shown on the right.

You are informed as follows:

(a) As at 31 December 2012 Alpha's trade receivables include £114,000 receivable from Beta. However, goods invoiced at £42,000 and £30,000 cash are in transit.

(b) Inventory held by Beta on 31.12.2012 includes goods invoiced to it by Alpha at £118,000. Alpha invoices Beta at cost plus a third.

(c) £10,000 needs to be written off as impairment of goodwill.

Required: The Consolidated Statement of financial position of the Alpha group as at 31 December 2012.

Statements of financial position as at 31 December 2012

	Alpha	Beta
	£'000	£'000
Non-current assets:		
Property, plant and equipment at cost	740	520
Accumulated depreciation	(210)	(180)
	530	340
Investments	920	80
Current assets:		
Inventories	428	312
Trade receivables	516	475
Cash and bank	24	13
	2,418	1,220
	£'000	£'000
Equity and reserves:		
Ordinary shares of £1 each	1,200	600
Share premium account	60	60
Retained earnings	492	220
Current liabilities:		
Trade payables	398	259
Taxation	148	21
Dividend declared	120	60
	2,418	1,220

PQ 13.5 Partly owned subsidiary

Alpha plc acquired 800,000 ordinary shares of 50p each in Beta plc for £760,000 on 1 April 2010 when:

(i) Beta had an accumulated profit of £90,000.

(ii) The market value of Beta's land was £460,000.

(iii) Beta's shares were quoted at 92 pence each.

The Statements of financial position of both companies appear as shown on the right.

You are informed as follows:

(a) Receivables reported by Alpha include £42,000 due from Beta. The corresponding amount reported by Beta is £18,000. Goods invoiced by Alpha at £16,000 are in transit. The remainder of the difference arose from cash in transit.

(b) £32,000 of goods reported by Beta have been invoiced to it by Alpha.

(c) Alpha invoices Beta at cost plus a third.

Required: The Consolidated Statement of financial position of the Alpha group as at 31 March 2012.

Note: The par value of each share is 50p.

Statements of financial position as at 31 March 2012

	Alpha	Beta
	£'000	£'000
Non-current assets:		
Land at cost	400	100
Other tangible assets	720	450
Investments	780	60
Current assets:		
Inventory	544	240
Trade receivables	386	198
Cash and bank	42	15
	2,872	1,063
	£'000	£'000
Ordinary shares of 50p each	1,600	600
Share premium account	160	30
Accumulated profit	691	210
Current liabilities:		
Trade payables	349	194
Taxation	72	29
	2,872	1,063

PQ 13.6 Consolidation of Statement of financial position (CAT 6)

Draft statements of financial position of Spyder and its subsidiary Phly are shown on the right. The following information is available:

(1) Spyder purchased 480 million shares in Phly some years ago when Phly had a credit balance of £95 million in reserves, and shares in Phly were quoted at 130p.

(2) At the time of acquisition Phly's land and buildings were valued at £70 million more than their book value.

(3) Phly's inventory as at 31.10.2012 includes goods sold to it by Spyder at a price giving Spyder £12 million profit.

(4) As at 31.10.2012 Phly owes Spyder £25 million for goods purchased.

Required:
(a) Calculate the goodwill on acquisition.
(b) Prepare the Consolidated Statement of financial position as at 31 October 2012.
(c) Explain the accounting treatment of intra-group trading and inter-company balances when preparing consolidated financial statements.

Statements of financial position as at 31.10.2012

	Spyder	Phly
	£'000	£'000
Non-current assets:		
Land and buildings	315	278
Plant	285	220
Investments in Phly shares	660	–
Current assets:		
Inventory	357	252
Trade receivables	525	126
Bank	158	30
	2,300	906
	£'000	£'000
Equity and reserves:		
Ordinary shares of £1 each	1,500	600
Reserves	580	215
	2,080	815
Current liabilities:		
Trade payables	220	91
	2,300	906

PQ 13.7 Consolidation of Statements of income

Alpha plc paid £760,000 to acquire two-thirds of Beta plc's equity on 1 April 2010 when Beta plc had an accumulated profit of £90,000.

You are informed as follows:

(a) During the year ended 31 March 2012, Alpha plc invoiced goods to Beta plc at £360,000.

(b) As at 31 March 2012 Beta plc's inventory included £32,000 of goods invoiced to it by Alpha plc; while £16,000 more of these goods were in transit.

(c) Alpha invoices Beta at cost plus a third.

Required: The Consolidated Statement of income for the Alpha group for the year ended 31 March 2012.

Statements of income year ended 31.3.2012

	Alpha	Beta
	£'000	£'000
Sales revenue	1,760	1,180
Cost of sales	(942)	(756)
Gross profit	818	424
Expenses	(482)	(275)
Operating profit	336	149
Dividend from Beta	16	–
Profit before taxation	352	149
Taxation	(72)	(29)
Profit after tax	280	120
Movement of equity:	£'000	£'000
Balance b/f	501	114
Profit after tax	280	120
Dividend paid	(90)	(24)
Balance c/d	691	210

PQ 13.8 Consolidation of Statements of income (CAT 6)

The summarised Statements of income of two companies, Liverton and Everpool, for the year ended 31 May 2012 are shown on the right. Liverton acquired 3,000,000 ordinary shares in Everpool for £3,500,000 on 1 June 2010. At that time the retained earnings of Everpool were £200,000 and its shares quoted at 110p each. Further information:

(i) Everpool's total share capital consists of 4,000,000 ordinary shares of £1 each.
(ii) At 31 May 2011 Liverton had valued the goodwill arising from the acquisition of Everpool at £300,000. An impairment review of this goodwill at 31 May 2012 valued it at £230,000.
(iii) During the year ended 31 May 2012 Liverton sold goods costing £110,000 to Everpool for £200,000. At 31 May 2012, 60% of these goods remained in Everpool's inventory.

Statements of income year ended 31 May 2012	Liverton	Everpool
	£'000	£'000
Sales revenue	6,400	2,600
Cost of sales	(3,700)	(1,450)
Gross profit	2,700	1,150
Distribution cost	(1,100)	(490)
Administrative expenses	(700)	(320)
Profit from operations	900	340
Dividend from Everpool	150	–
Profit before tax	1,050	340
Tax	(400)	(90)
Net profit for the period	650	250

Required:
(a) Calculate the goodwill arising on the acquisition of Everpool.
(b) Prepare the Consolidated Statement of income of Liverton for the year ended 31 May 2012.
(c) Explain the criteria that should be met for a company to be accounted for as an associate company.

PQ 13.9 Consolidation of Statements of financial position and Statement of income (CAT 6)

Following are the financial statements relating to Black, a limited liability company, and its subsidiary Bury.

Statement of income year ended 31.Oct.2010	Black	Bury
	£'000	£'000
Sales revenue	245,000	95,000
Cost of sales	(140,000)	(52,000)
Gross profit	105,000	43,000
Distribution cost	(12,000)	(10,000)
Administrative expense	(55,000)	(13,000)
Profit from operations	38,000	20,000
Dividend from Bury	7,000	–
Profit before tax	45,000	20,000
Tax	(13,250)	(5,000)
Net profit for the year	31,750	15,000

Statements of financial position as at 31 October 2010	Black	Bury
	£'000	£'000
Non-current assets:		
Property, plant and equipment	110,000	40,000
Investments – 21 million shares in Bury	28,000	–
Current assets:		
Inventory	9,360	3,890
Trade receivables and dividend receivable	14,640	6,280
Bank	3,500	2,570
	165,500	52,740
	£'000	£'000
Equity and reserves:		
Ordinary shares of £1 each	100,000	30,000
General reserves	9,200	1,000
Accumulated profit	27,300	9,280
	136,500	40,280
Current liabilities:		
Trade payables	9,000	2,460
Dividend declared	20,000	10,000
	165,500	52,740

The following information is also available:

(a) Black purchased its ordinary shares in Bury on 1 November 2006 when Bury's balance in General reserves was £0.5 million and the balance in Accumulated profit was £1.5 million.

(b) At 1 November 2009 the goodwill arising from acquisition of Bury was valued at £6,000,000. Black's impairment review of this goodwill at 31 October 2010 valued it at £5,000,000.

(c) During the year ended 31 October 2010 Black sold goods which originally cost £12 million to Bury. Black invoiced Bury at cost plus 40%. Bury still has 30% of these goods in inventory as at 31 October 2010.

(d) Bury owed Black £1.5 million at 31 October 2010 for some goods Black supplied during the year.

(e) Value the non-controlling interest in Bury on the date of acquisition in proportion to the amount paid for control by Black.

Required:
(a) Calculate the goodwill arising on acquisition of Bury.
(b) Prepare the Consolidated Statement of income for the year ended 31 October 2010.
(c) Prepare the Consolidated Statement of financial position as at 31 October 2010.

PQ 13.10 Consolidated statements of income and financial position – advanced

Though shares in Minor plc were quoted on this day at 145p each, Major plc paid £680,000 to acquire 400,000 ordinary shares of £1 each in Minor plc on 1 April 2010 when:

(i) Minor's retained loss amounted to £60,000; and

(ii) the fair value of property, plant and equipment held by Minor was £600,000, though that of its investments was £25,000.

On the day of acquisition Major acquired at par £100,000 8% Loan notes issued by Minor.

The Statements of income for the year ended 31 March 2012 have been prepared by both companies, as shown on the right, and the Statements of financial position as set out on the right and below.

Further information is available as follows:

Statements of income year ended 31.3.2012		
	Major	Minor
	£'000	£'000
Sales revenue	2,654	1,280
Cost of sales	(1,894)	(942)
Gross profit	760	338
Operating expenses	(413)	(186)
Operating profit	347	152
Interest income	8	–
Interest expense	–	(12)
Profit before taxation	355	140
Taxation	(115)	(20)
Profit after taxation	240	120

Statement of changes in equity:	£'000	£'000
Balance b/f	383	(45)
Profit after taxation	240	120
Dividend declared	(60)	(25)
Balance c/f	563	50

(a) Based on fair value Minor needs to write off additional depreciation amounting to £5,000 p.a.

(b) Interest payable on the loan notes has been accrued by both companies, but remains unpaid.

(c) During the year ended 31 March 2012 Minor plc invoiced goods to Major plc at £180,000. Minor invoices Major at prices calculated produce a gross profit of 25%. The amount invoiced in the year includes those invoiced at £20,000 not received by Major until 4 April 2012.

(d) Inventory held by Major, as at the year-end, includes goods invoiced by Minor at £40,000.

(e) Trade payables reported by Major includes £65,000 owed to Minor. Corresponding amount reported by Minor is £90,000. The difference, unless explained otherwise, may be attributed to cash in transit.

(f) Major plc has not accounted for the dividend declared by Minor plc.

(g) Fair value of goodwill in Minor, as at 31 March 2012, is estimated at £200,000.

Statements of financial position as at 31 March 2012

	Major plc		Minor plc	
	£'000	£'000	£'000	£'000
Non-current assets:				
Property, plant and equipment		760		450
Investments		810		30
Current assets:				
Inventory	372		228	
Trade and interest receivables	395		154	
Cash and bank	38	805	28	410
		2,375		890
	£'000	£'000	£'000	£'000
Equity and reserves:				
Ordinary shares of £1 each	1,200		500	
Retained earnings	563	1,763	50	550
Non-current liabilities:				
8% Loan notes		–		150
Current liabilities:				
Trade payables	390		132	
Accrued expenses	35		14	
Taxation	127		19	
Dividend declared	60	612	25	190
		2,375		890

Required: Prepare the Consolidated Statement of income for the Major group for the year ended 31 March 2012 and the Consolidated Statement of financial position as at that date.

Test questions

Test 13.1 Consolidation of Statements of financial position – basic

Alpha paid £300 to acquire 240 shares in Beta on 1 April 2010 when:

(a) Beta's reserves stood at £40.

(b) Fair value of Beta's land, which is not depreciated, was £100 more than the book value.

(c) Beta's shares were quoted at 120p.

You are informed that as at 31 March 2012:

(i) Receivables reported by Alpha includes £30 due from Beta and Beta agrees with it.

(ii) Goodwill in Beta was valued at £62.

Required: Prepare the Consolidated Statement of financial position as at 31 March 2012.

Statements of financial position as at 31 March 2012

	Alpha	Beta
	£	£
Non-current assets	800	320
Investment in Beta	450	–
Current assets	320	180
	1,570	500
	£	£
Ordinary shares of £1 each	900	300
Reserves	455	125
Current liabilities	215	75
	1,570	500

Test 13.2 Consolidation of Statements of financial position – stage 2

Alpha paid £450 to acquire 300 ordinary shares in Beta on 1 July 2010 when:

(i) Beta's Retained earnings were £40;

(ii) Fair value of Beta's property plant was £120 more than the book value; and

(iii) Beta's shares were quoted at 130p each.

You are informed as follows:

(a) As at 30 June 2012 Receivables reported by Alpha included £80 due from Beta; whereas the corresponding amount reported by Beta was £62. Goods in transit on this date were £15. The remainder of the difference arose from cash in transit.

(b) Based on fair valuation Beta should have depreciated its property and plant by £4 more per annum.

(c) As at 30 June 2012 Beta's inventory included goods invoiced to it by Alpha at £75. Alpha invoices Beta at prices calculated to produce a gross profit ratio of 20%.

Required: Prepare the Consolidated Statement of financial position as at 30 June 2012.

Statements of financial position as at 30 June 2012

	Alpha		Beta	
	£	£	£	£
Non-current assets:				
Property, plant		980		510
Investments		495		30
Current assets:				
Inventory	320		180	
Trade receivables	428		260	
Cash and bank	32	780	20	460
		2,255		1,000
	£	£	£	£
Equity and reserves:				
Ordinary shares of £1		1,200		400
Retained earning		585		280
Current liabilities:				
Trade payables	318		235	
Taxation	92		45	
Dividend declared	60	470	40	320
		2,255		1,000

Test 13.3 Consolidation of Statements of financial position – stage 3

When Alpha paid £1,200 to acquire 640 ordinary shares in Beta on 1 January 2010:

(i) There was a gain of £300 and £40 on the fair valuation of Beta's property, plant and equipment and brand names respectively.

(ii) Beta's retained earnings were £120; and

(iii) Beta's shares were quoted at 160p each.

You are informed as follows:

(a) Trade receivables reported by Alpha includes £145 due from Beta. The amount reported by Beta is different because of the following:

- goods in transit at £32
- cash in transit of £15.

(b) Inventory held by Beta on 31 December 2012 includes goods invoiced by Alpha at £96. Alpha invoices Beta at cost plus a third.

(c) Based on fair valuation Beta should have written off an additional depreciation of £15 per annum on property, plant and equipment and additional amortisation of £5 per annum on brand names.

(d) A dividend of 5p per share, declared by the directors of Beta on 31 December 2012, has not been accounted for by either company.

(e) There was no impairment of goodwill.

Required: Prepare the Consolidated Statement of financial position.

Statements of financial position as at 31.12.2012

	Alpha		Beta	
	£	£	£	£
Non-current assets:				
Property, plant and equipment		2,440		1,200
Brand names		180		80
Investments		1,380		35
Current assets:				
Inventory	592		492	
Trade receivables	645		384	
Cash and bank	22	1,259	29	905
		5,259		2,220
	£	£	£	£
Equity and reserves:				
Ordinary shares of £1		3,000		800
Retained earning		1,189		580
Non-current liabilities:				
8% Loan notes	150		200	
Deferred tax	34	184	12	212
Current liabilities:				
Trade payables	614		589	
Taxation	122		39	
Dividend declared	150	886	–	628
		5,259		2,220

Test 13.4 Consolidation of Statements of financial position – advanced

Alpha plc paid £1,480 to acquire 2,400 shares in Beta plc. On the date of acquisition Beta plc had an accumulated loss of £180, though its property, plant and equipment had a fair value which exceeded the book value by £200. However, the development costs reported at £40 on that date failed to meet Alpha group's capitalisation criteria. On the date of acquisition by Alpha, Beta's shares were quoted at 140p each. You are further informed as follows:

Statements of financial position as at 31.12.2012

	Alpha		Beta	
	£	£	£	£
Non-current assets:				
Property, plant and equipment		1,540		1,600
Development cost		480		160
Investments		1,980		54
Current assets:				
Inventory	592		572	
Trade and other receivables	645		496	
Cash and bank	22	1,259	8	1,076
		5,259		2,890
	£	£	£	£
Equity and reserves:				
Ordinary shares of 50p each		3,000		1,500
Retained earnings		1,189		620
Non-current liability:				
8% Loan notes	150		100	
Deferred tax	34	184	27	127
Current liabilities:				
Trade payables	614		494	
Taxation	122		74	
Dividend declared	150	886	75	643
		5,259		2,890

(a) Trade payables reported by Alpha includes £196 owed to Beta; whereas Beta's books report that an amount of £206 is due from Alpha. Inquiries reveal that Beta has not been informed of £10 charged by Alpha on Beta as management services fees for the year.

(b) Inventory reported by Alpha includes goods invoiced to it at £125 by Beta. Beta invoices Alpha at cost plus 25%.

(c) Though Beta continues to capitalise its development cost the amounts capitalised still fail to meet the group's capitalisation criteria.

(d) Included within Alpha's receivables is £250 it paid when acquiring at par 8% Loan notes issued by Beta. The current year's interest on the loan notes has already been accounted for by both companies. An amount of £170 (including £20 interest for the current year) remains in transit.

(e) Based on fair valuation Beta should have depreciated its property, plant and equipment by £8 in each of the five post-acquisition years until 31 December 2012.

(f) Dividend receivable from Beta has been accounted for in Alpha's books.

Required: Prepare the Consolidated Statement of financial position as at 31 December 2012.

Test 13.5 Consolidation of statements of income – basic

Alpha acquired 75% of Beta on 1 January 2010 when Beta's retained earnings were £140 and the fair value of the subsidiary's identifiable non-monetary assets was almost the same as the book value. Both companies have prepared their Statement of income as shown on the right.

You are informed as follows:

(a) During the year Alpha sold goods to Beta, for £240, invoicing the goods at cost plus 20%.

(b) 25% of the goods sold by Alpha to Beta remained in the hands of Beta at the year-end.

Required: Prepare the Consolidated Statement of income for the year ended 31 December 2012.

Statements of income year ended 31 December 2012		
	Alpha	Beta
	£	£
Sales revenue	1,480	740
Cost of sales	(1,060)	(480)
Gross profit	420	260
Distribution cost	(142)	(82)
Administrative expenses	(113)	(68)
Operating profit	165	110
Interest	(20)	(12)
Profit before taxation	145	98
Taxation	(30)	(18)
Profit after taxation	115	80

Test 13.6 Consolidation of statements of income – stage 2

Alpha paid £3,600 to acquire 2,400 ordinary shares in Beta on 1 January 2010 when:

(i) Beta's Share capital consisted of 3,000 ordinary shares of £1 each, quoted at 160p each;

(ii) Beta's reserves stood at £840; and

(iii) the fair value of Beta's identifiable non-monetary assets exceeded the book value by £560.

The Statements of income prepared by both companies are shown on the right. You are informed as follows:

(a) During the year Beta sold goods to Alpha for £480, invoicing them at cost plus 20%. Goods invoiced at £96 remain with Alpha at the year-end, while those invoiced at £24 remain in transit.

(b) 75% of interest expense incurred by Beta was paid to Alpha.

(c) Depreciation, if calculated on the basis of fair values, should have been £20 more per year.

(d) As at 31 December 2012 goodwill in Beta was valued at £100.

Statements of income year ended 31 December 2012		
	Alpha	Beta
	£	£
Sales revenue	8,200	1,280
Cost of sales	(5,450)	(920)
Gross profit	2,750	360
Distribution cost	(694)	(58)
Administrative expenses	(826)	(122)
Operating profit	1,230	180
Dividend from Beta	40	
Interest income	30	
Interest expense	–	(40)
Profit before taxation	1,300	140
Taxation	(240)	(30)
Profit after taxation	1,060	110

Required: Prepare the Consolidated Statement of income for the year ended 31 December 2012.

Test 13.7 Consolidation of statements of income – advanced

Alpha paid £4,800 to acquire 3,000 ordinary shares of £1 each in Beta on 1 January 2010 when:

(i) Beta's share capital consisted of 4,000 ordinary shares of £1 each;

(ii) Beta's reserves stood at £720; and

(iii) the fair value of Beta's identifiable non-monetary assets exceeded the book value by £780.

The Statements of income prepared by both companies are as shown on the right.

You are further informed as follows:

(a) During the year Alpha sold goods to Beta, invoicing them at £320. As at the year-end 25% of these goods remain with Beta. Alpha invoices Beta at cost plus a third.

(b) Based on fair value Beta should have written off £20 more per year as depreciation.

(c) Two-thirds of Beta's interest payments were to Alpha.

(d) The goodwill in Beta was valued at £1,000 on 31 December 2011 and at £840 as at 31 December 2012.

Required: Prepare the Consolidated Statement of income and the Statement of changes in equity for the year ended 31 December 2012.

Statements of income year ended 31 December 2012

	Alpha	Beta
	£	£
Sales revenue	8,200	1,280
Cost of sales	(5,450)	(920)
Gross profit	2,750	360
Distribution cost Beta	(694)	(58)
Administrative expenses	(826)	(122)
Operating profit	1,230	180
Dividend received	60	
Interest income	20	
Interest expense	–	(30)
Profit before taxation	1,310	150
Taxation	(240)	(30)
Profit after taxation	1,070	120

Statement of changes in equity	£	£
Balance brought forward	3,930	1,480
Profit after taxation	1,070	120
Dividend paid	(300)	(80)
Balance carried forward	4,700	1,520

Chapter 14

Accounting for partnerships

By the end of this chapter

You should learn:	You should be able to:
■ About partnerships and how they function	■ Prepare financial statements of a partnership
■ The rules governing partnership if there is no agreement	■ Account for admissions and retirement of partners
■ About appropriating profits among partners	■ Account for dissolution of a partnership
■ The adjustment of partners' interests upon admission/retirement	■ Convert a partnership to a limited company

14.1 What is a partnership?

A business entity, as it grows in size and variety of activities, may require more resources than what a single proprietor can provide in terms of time, finance and skills. It is for such reasons that a sole trader seeks one or more persons to form a partnership.

In the UK the formation of a partnership requires no formality such as registration or entering into an agreement. The legal definition, provided by the Partnership Act, 1890, is that partnership is 'a relationship which subsists between persons carrying on a business in common with a view to profit'.

This means, irrespective of whether it has been registered or an agreement signed, in the eyes of the law a partnership exists if it has the three features stated in the box on the right.

1. Co-ownership of assets
2. Conduct of a business
3. Intention to share profits/losses

14.2 Legal framework of partnerships

Partnership is a long established form of business organisation that has been governed by the Partnership Act 1890. The main provisions of that Act are as follows.

14.2.1 The number of partners

There can be from 2 to a maximum of 20 partners, unless permission is obtained from the Registrar of companies to exceed that limit. Such permission is given only to members of certain professions such as accountants, solicitors and stock exchange brokers.

14.2.2 Partners' obligations and entitlements

Partners are free to mutually agree among themselves on what their obligations and entitlements are. However, in the absence of agreement on any matter the provisions of section 24 (partially listed below) would apply.

- Profits and losses are shared equally among partners
- No salary to be paid to any partner
- No interest to be allowed on partners' capital balances
- No interest to be charged on any partner's drawings
- Interest to be allowed on partners' loans at 5% per year
- Every partner shall introduce capital
- Every partner is entitled to partake in management
- Admission of a new partner requires unanimous consent

If an outgoing partner is not paid in full his entitlements, section 42 of the Act requires interest to be paid on that partner's entitlements either at 5% p.a. or at such rate as a court would determine as attributable to the use of the assets of the partner concerned.

14.2.3 Partners' liabilities

Each partner assumes unlimited liability for all debts of the business. This means that if the partnership assets prove insufficient to meet the partnership debts in full, each partner is legally regarded as jointly and severally liable to make good the shortfall. This means that the private possessions of each partner are at risk. To appreciate how great the risk involved is, we should bear in mind that each partner has the right to make management decisions and enter into agreements and contracts that commit the partnership. This could result in risky commitments that the other partners might not have wanted.

14.3 A partnership agreement

Although a partnership may exist without any written agreement, in view of these liabilities and in order to avoid future disagreements, it is a good idea to have a formal partnership agreement. Such an agreement among partners, usually referred to as a *Partnership deed*, would typically include agreement on areas such as those stated in the box overleaf.

How the profit are shared needs to be agreed among partners. They could, if they so wish, agree to share the profits and losses equally or they may agree to adjust each partner's share taking into account:

(a) each partner's capital contribution, by allowing interest at an agreed rate on their capital balances;

(b) each partner's effort contribution by providing for payment of salaries; and

(c) whether any partner should be penalised if drawings were made before the year-end by charging interest, at an agreed rate, on the amounts drawn.

1. Capital and profits
   - Agreed ratio of each partner's capital
   - Profit-sharing arrangements
   - Limitations on partners' drawings, if any
2. Authority
   - Authority to obtain loans and enter contracts
   - Authority to change the nature of business
   - Authority to admit a new partner
   - Any additional responsibility and reward
3. Accounts
   - Requirements on accounts and audits
   - That audited accounts are binding on all

To be valid the agreement need not necessarily be a written one. Under partnership law, an oral agreement or one which may be inferred from past behaviour (referred to as 'in the course of dealing') also creates inferred terms.

14.4 Limited liability partnerships

Traditionally those providing legal and audit services do so as partnerships. In the recent past, however, there has been a proliferation of legal actions for professional negligence and the compensation claims have been so large that they could not be met from the assets of the partnership and by the insurance cover, placing at risk the personal assets of the partners. The professions sought a form of business organisation in which they could continue as partners and at the same time limit their liability. As a result of their intense lobbying the Limited Liability Partnerships Act 2000 (LLP) has created an additional form of business entity with limited liability. Let us summarise the main features of an LPP as follows:

1. Those who form an LPP are identified as 'members' and, if preferred, two or three of the members may be identified as 'designated members' who would then be responsible for complying with the legal requirements. If no-one is so designated, then every member is regarded as a designated member. The management and decision making is the responsibility of every member.
2. The LLP should be registered with the Registrar of Companies, and upon registration an LPP, like a limited company, is recognised as a legal entity.
3. The advantage of operating as an LLP rather than as a partnership is that each member's liability is limited to the amount he agreed to contribute as capital. This means any claims on an LLP should be met out of the assets of the LLP. The personal assets of its members are protected, as happens for shareholders of a limited company.
4. Since those with a claim on an LLP cannot have recourse to the personal assets of the members, the law requires that, like a company, an LLP should maintain proper books of accounts, have them audited, deliver financial statements (within nine months of each year-end) to the Registrar of Companies, and file annual returns. However, the concessions allowed to small companies are extended also to LLPs.

14.5 Partners' Capital accounts and Current accounts

Partners usually draw out monies for their personal use during the year in anticipation of profits being agreed at the end of the year. This means that there is a potential risk that individual partners might draw out monies that exceed their share of the potential profit. The effect of this would be twofold. First, excessive drawings may reduce working capital to an unsatisfactory level and secondly, a partner may draw out monies that had been contributed as capital. As a precaution against this partners usually agree that capital contributions should be recorded in a Capital account and that such amount should not normally be regarded as available for their withdrawal until the partnership is dissolved.

A separate account, called a *Current account*, is opened to record amounts that partners are entitled to draw during an accounting period. The share of the profits when identified at the year-end is credited to the current account and amounts drawn out debited to it.

Activity 14.1 Sharing profits among partners

Jack and Jill are in business as partners without any formal agreement. Their Trial Balance as at the year-end appears as shown on the right. During the year Jack's drawings amounted to £35,000 and Jill's to £16,000.

Required:

(a) Show the partners' Capital accounts and the Current accounts in columnar format (i.e. with a column for every partner in each account).

(b) Prepare the Statement of financial position of the partnership as at 30 June 2012.

Trial Balance as at 30 June 2012

	£'000	£'000
Non-current assets	840	–
Depreciation – 30.6.2012	–	380
Inventory – 30.6.2012	648	–
Receivables and payables	584	596
Profit for the year	–	260
Partners' drawings	51	–
Capital account:		
Jack	–	600
Jill	–	300
Cash and bank	13	–
	2,136	2,136

14.6 Charges on profit and appropriation of profit

Profit, in a partnership, is the amount available to be shared among the partners, for whatever they have done in their roles of partners. We already know that as partners each of them has to contribute capital and take part in management. If they receive any interest on capital or salary, these are rewards for merely doing what they should do as partners.

It is possible that partners may choose to play one (or more) additional role. For example, a partner may give a loan to the partnership and receive as a reward interest on that loan. This reward is not as a partner but for playing an additional role as a moneylender. Similarly, a partner may provide the business premises and receive a rent for playing the additional role as a landlord. Amounts paid to partners for playing any additional role are regarded as proper deductions (in accounting we refer to them as *charges*) when identifying partnership profit. Any interest on capital or salary paid to partners is not regarded as charges because these are part of what they receive for merely doing what they should in their role as partners. These are known as *appropriations*.

Let us illustrate by assuming that:

- Tom and Dick are partners, contributing as capital £200,000 and £100,000 respectively, and have agreed to share profits equally after allowing interest on capital at 5% per annum, and paying a salary to Dick of £2,000 a month.
- Tom has provided a loan of £100,000 to the partnership at interest agreed at 7% per annum.
- Dick, as the owner of premises used for the business, is to receive rent at £4,000 per month.
- The gross profit for the year is £400,000 and expenses without including any payment to partners is £120,000.

Both Tom and Dick have received rewards known as interest on loan and rent for playing additional roles as moneylender and landlord respectively. These payments, though to partners, are for playing roles that are not expected of partners. These are, therefore, treated as charges against profit, which have to be deducted before identifying the amount of profit available to be shared among the partners. Taking into account these charges, the partnership profit is identified as £225,000 (see the box on the right). That is the amount available to be *appropriated* (that being the word accountants use for sharing of profit) between Tom and Dick as rewards for whatever function each performed in the role of partners. When appropriating the profit of £225,000, in our illustration, they have agreed to allow interest on capital so as to be fair to Tom whose capital contribution is more than that of Dick and have agreed to pay a salary to Dick, probably because Dick gives more time to partnership business. They have agreed to share the remainder of the profit equally. See the appropriation of the partnership profit between the two partners as set out on the left. If there has been no such agreement, section 24 of the Act would apply and the partnership profit appropriated between them equally.

Gross profit	£400,000
Expenses	(£120,000)
Interest (to Tom)	(£7,000)
Rent (to Dick)	(£48,000)
Partnership profit	£225,000

Partnership profit		£225,000
Interest on capital:		
Tom	£10,000	
Dick	£5,000	(£15,000)
Salary to Dick		(£24,000)
Profit share:		
Tom	£93,000	
Dick	£93,000	(£186,000)

Activity 14.2 Distinguishing a charge from an appropriation

Tom, Dick and Harry are partners sharing profits in the ratio 2:1:1, respectively, after allowing Tom a salary of £3,000 per month and interest on capital account balances at 6% per annum. The year-end Trial Balance is stated on the right. You are informed as follows:

(a) The cost of inventory at the year-end was £412,000.

(b) Dick as owner of the premises is to receive rent of £4,000 per month.

(c) £30,000 drawn by Tom as salary is included within the balance in the Salaries account.

(d) Non-current assets are to be depreciated at 20% per annum, using the reducing balance method.

Required: Set out:

(a) partners' Current accounts in columnar form;

(b) the Statement of income for the year ended 31 March 2012 and the Statement of financial position as at that date.

Clue: One way of sorting out the amount drawn by Tom as salary is to transfer that amount from the Salaries account to Tom's Current account, proceed to identify partnership profit and, at the time of appropriation, give Tom the credit for the full salary due to him.

Trial Balance as at 31 March 2012

	£'000	£'000
Non-current assets	640	–
Depreciation – 31.3.2011	–	300
Inventory – 31.3.2011	365	–
Rent paid to Dick	40	–
Salaries	214	–
Interest paid to Tom	9	–
Receivables and payables	544	428
Purchases	2,172	–
Postage and telephone	32	–
Sales	–	3,096
Advertising	165	–
Current accounts:		
Tom	–	126
Dick	–	34
Harry	12	–
12% Loan from Tom	–	100
Cash and bank balance	92	–
Other admin expenses	349	–
Capital account:		
Tom	–	300
Dick	–	150
Harry	–	100
	4,634	4,634

14.7 Interest on partners' drawings

It is normal for partners to make drawings during the year to meet their personal living expenses. If each partner draws the same amount, then none is being disadvantaged. If one draws more than another then it is only fair that this should be taken into account when sharing profits at the end of the year. One way of doing this is to credit the Appropriation account with interest and debit the partner's Current account.

14.7.1 Calculation of interest when drawings are at irregular intervals

For illustration, let us assume that the accounting period ends on 31 December, that partners agree to charge interest on drawings at 6% per year and that a partner draws £5,000 on 1 March. Interest of £250 (£5,000 × 6/100 × 10/12) is charged on the partner by debiting his Current account and crediting the Appropriation account. Individual calculations such as these have to be made in respect of each amount drawn if the drawings are at irregular intervals.

14.7.2 Calculation of interest when partners draw the same amount and at regular intervals

If a partner draws the same amount at regular intervals, interest may be calculated on the total amount drawn for the *average* period. For example, if partner X draws £3,000 per month consistently on the first day of each month, the total amount drawn in the year would be £36,000. Assuming that the year ends on 31 December, the average period for which these drawings would have been outstanding is calculated as follows:

The first amount, drawn on 1 January, would have been outstanding for 12 months, the second for 11 months and so on until the last, drawn on 1 December, would have been outstanding for 1 month. Hence 12 + 11 + 10 + 9 + 8 + 7 + 6 + 5 + 4 + 3 + 2 + 1 = 78 divided by 12 separate drawings = 6.5 months.

Interest is therefore charged on £36,000 at whatever rate has been agreed for the average period of 6.5 months.

Similarly, if a regular amount is drawn on the last day of each month the average period works out at 5.5 months, while if the drawing is half way through each month the average period works out to six months.

Activity 14.3 Calculation of interest on partners' drawings

Sun, Moon and Star are partners who make up their accounts to 31 December each year. Their agreement provides that interest is chargeable on their drawings at 6% per annum.

- **Scenario 1:** Sun draws £5,000 on 31.3.2012, Moon draws £8,000 on 1.7.2012 and Star draws £20,000 on 1.8.2012 and £6,000 more on 1.10.2012.
- **Scenario 2:** Sun, Moon and Star each draw £2,000 per month regularly, Sun drawing on the first day of each month, Moon drawing on the last day and Star in the middle of each month.
- **Scenario 3:** Sun drew £4,000 per month on the first day of each month, up to and including 1 September 2012. Moon drew £5,000 per month, on the last day of each month, but commencing on 31.3.2012. Star drew regularly throughout the year in the middle of each month, but the amount drawn was £2,000 per month until 15.6.2012 and £3,000 per month thereafter.

Required: Determine the amount of interest to be charged in respect of each partner's drawings in each of the above alternative scenarios.

14.8 Accounting for interest on partners' drawings

The interest charged on partners' drawings is not an additional income for the partnership. It is merely a device used to ensure that when profits are shared the extent of their drawings is taken into account. To illustrate let us assume that Peter and Paul are partners, sharing profits equally, that the year's profit has been identified as £300,000, but when sharing it interest needs to be charged on Peter at £800 and on Paul at £200.

Statement of income (Appropriation section)		
	£	£
Partnership profit		300,000
Interest on drawing:		
Peter		800
Paul		200
Profit share:		
Peter	150,500	
Paul	150,500	(301,000)

The appropriations will be as shown above on the right. We need to appreciate that the partnership profit is £300,000 (and not £301,000) and that is the amount shared by the partners, Peter receiving £149,700 (£150,500 – £800) and Paul receiving £150,300 (£150,500 – £200).

14.9 Admission of a new partner – profit-share adjustments

14.9.1 Profit-sharing ratios after new admission

When a partner is admitted to a share of profit, the new profit-sharing ratio among all partners should be mutually agreed. In examination questions when an agreed share of profit is assigned to a new partner, it is usual to assume that the remainder is shared among the continuing partners in the ratio in which they shared profits until then. For example, let us assume that Peter and Paul, who shared profits in the ratio 2:1, respectively, admit John to a fourth share of the profit. In the absence of any more information it is assumed that the quarter share of profit is given to John by Peter and Paul in the ratio 2:1, respectively; the new profit sharing ratio is calculated as shown on the right.

Peter	2/3rd less (2/3rd of 1/4th given to John)	6/12th
Paul	1/3rd less (1/3rd of 1/4th given to John)	3/12th
John	(2/3rd of 1/4th from Peter) plus (1/3rd of 1/4th from Paul)	3/12th

Simplified, Peter, Paul and John will from now share profits in the ratio 2:1:1, respectively, i.e. the relationship between Peter and Paul remains 2:1.

14.9.2 Where the admission is during an accounting period

If there is a change either in the number of partners or the ratio of their profit sharing during the course of an accounting period, it becomes necessary to determine the profit or loss up to the date of the change separately from that of the period after the change. It is necessary then to prepare the Statement of income with two columns, the first identifying the profits to be shared by former partners (or, if it is only a change in the ratios, in the former profit-sharing ratio) and the second the profit to be shared in the changed ratios. To accurately identify the gross profit made in each period may be difficult because it would then be necessary to conduct an inventory-taking on the date of the change. A practical alternative is to apportion the year's gross profit between the two periods. If the sales are even through the year, then the apportionment could be on a time basis. If, however, sales are not even, e.g. sales are seasonal, then the gross profit should be apportioned on the basis of sales in each of the two periods. Since selling and distribution costs are related to sales, these too are apportioned to the two periods on the ratio of sales in each period, whereas administration expenses are apportioned on a time basis (i.e the number of months in each period).

To illustrate let us assume that Peter and Paul, equal partners, admit John as an equal partner on 1 July 2012 and that during the year ended 31 December 2012 the performance of the partnership was as stated in the box on the left. If we assume that sales as well as all expenses accrued evenly throughout the year, the profit in the first half of the year would be £125 (£250/2) to be shared equally between Peter and Paul and that in the second half £125 to be shared equally among Peter, Paul and John. On the other hand, if John was so clever that sales in the second half of the year were double those in the first half, then we have to apportion the gross profit as well as distribution costs to the two halves on the sales ratio of 1:2 respectively, whereas administrative expenses are apportioned on a time basis

Year 2012	
	£
Sales	1,800
Cost of sale	(1,200)
Gross profit	600
Distribution cost	(150)
Admin. expenses	(200)
Profit	250

(i.e. six months in each period). (See working on the right.) On this basis the profit in the first half of the year is £50 and that in the second half £200.

		Up to June	After June
Gross profit	Sales ratio 1:2	£200	£400
Distribution costs	Sales ratio 1:2	(£50)	(£100)
Admin. expenses	Time basis 1:1	(£100)	(£100)
Profit for the year		£50	£200

14.9.3 Where the new partner is given a minimum income guarantee

As an inducement to accepting the partnership, either the firm or one of the continuing partners may guarantee the incoming partner's income from the partnership at a specified amount per year. This could be of particular interest when a manager taken into partnership needs to maintain a base level of income. For illustration, let us assume that John had previously been a manager with the partnership and was admitted to a fourth share of profit on 1 September (four months prior to year-end) on a guarantee that his share of partnership profit would not be less than £18,000 per year; and further assume that during the year ended 31 December his share of the partnership profit was £1,000 as interest on capital and £3,000 as share of profit. This means that John's share of partnership profit is £4,000 which is less than the £6,000 guaranteed – (four months at £18,000 per year). The shortfall of £2,000 is, therefore, credited to John's Current account and debited to the Current account of the partner (or partners) who gave the guarantee.

Activity 14.4 Admission of a new partner during an accounting period

Penny and Sally have been sharing profits and losses in the ratio 3:2 respectively, after allowing Penny a salary of £2,000 per month and interest on partners' fixed capitals at 6% per annum. They admitted Molly to a sixth share of profits from 1 October 2012 on the following terms:

(i) Salary to Penny and interest on capital are to continue.

(ii) Molly's share of income from the partnership is guaranteed by Penny at £120,000 p.a.

Further information:

(i) Inventory on 31.12.2012 was £586,000.

(ii) Sales in each month after Molly's admission were 50% better than they had been in each month prior to her admission.

(iii) Motor vehicles and furniture need to be depreciated at 20% and 10% respectively, using the reducing balance method.

Trial Balance as at 31 December 2012

	£	£
Motor vehicles	320	–
Accumulated depreciation	–	170
Furniture	280	–
Accumulated depreciation	–	120
Inventory – 31.12.2011	524	–
Salaries	288	–
Rent	48	–
Advertising	72	–
Sales	–	3,159
Drawings:		
Penny	50	–
Sally	28	–
Receivables and payables	752	514
Other admin. expenses	96	–
Capital:		
Penny	–	500
Sally	–	300
Molly	–	200
Cash and bank	241	–
Purchases	2,264	–
	4,963	4,963

Required: Prepare the Statement of income for the year ended 31 December 2012 and the Statement of financial position as at that date.

Clue: If profit for each month before 1 October was £100, the sales in each month after that date would have been £150. Hence the sales in each period would be (£100 × 9) : (£150 × 3) = i.e. 2:1 ratio.

14.10 Admission/retirement of a partner – fair value adjustments

14.10.1 What is fair valuation?

The fair value of an asset is the value at which the asset can be sold or acquired in the market. Fair valuation then is adjusting the value of an asset from the value at which it is accounted for (known as carrying value) to the current market value.

14.10.2 Why do non-current assets need to be fair valued?

The historical cost or the depreciated cost at which non-current assets are reported in partnership books would not fairly reflect their market value as at the date of admission of a new partner or retirement of an existing one. This is equally true of an asset, like goodwill, which may not be recorded in the books at all. A partly recorded (or, as in the case of goodwill, an unrecorded) asset represents a gain that has not been recorded in the books on the premise they are not yet realised and unless adjusted for any partner whose share of profit is reduced by the change in the profit-sharing arrangement would suffer a loss.

14.10.3 Illustration of a fair value adjustment

To learn how such unrecorded gains are adjusted for, whenever there is a change in profit-sharing arrangements, let us assume that:

- Peter and Paul have been sharing profits in the ratio 2:1 respectively and, after admission of John, would be sharing profits in the ratio 2:1:1 respectively; and
- on the date of John's admission land, recorded at £100, has a market value of £400.

Leaving the unrealised gain (of £300) to remain unrecorded would be prejudicial to Paul's interest. This can be seen by considering Paul's share if the land were sold prior to John's admission and comparing it with his share if the land is sold after John's admission. If the land is sold prior to John's admission, Paul's share would have been (1/3rd of £300) £100 whereas after the admission his share would only be (1/4th of £300) £75. If Paul is not to suffer this reduction in his share of profit, prior to John's admission either the land should be sold or (as is usually done) the land should be revalued, accounting for the revaluation as shown below on the right. Note that the revaluation gain is credited to existing partners' Capital accounts (rather than Current accounts) because the gain (being unrealised) would not be available for the partners' withdrawal and the existing partners are sharing the revaluation gain in the old ratio.

Dr Land account	£300	–
Cr Peter's Capital a/c	–	£200
Cr Paul's Capital a/c	–	£100

Activity 14.5 When and why assets of a partnership need to be fair valued

(a) Identify three circumstances in which assets of a partnership need to be fair valued.

(b) Explain why the partnership assets need to be fair valued in the stated circumstances.

Activity 14.6 Accounting for fair valuation adjustment

Hickory and Dickory are in partnership with a capital of £500,000 and £400,000 and sharing profits in the ratio 2:1, respectively. On 1.1.2012 they admit Dock, with a capital of £300,000, to a fourth share of the partnership profits. A property, recorded in the books at £280,000, has a market value on 1.1.2012 of £400,000. Explain what you would suggest to protect the interests of the existing partners, given they wish to keep property reported at £280,000.

14.11 What is goodwill and how it is adjusted for?

Goodwill is the amount of the difference between the value at which a whole business can be sold, as a going concern, and the amount at which its net assets are recorded in the books. Let us assume that Peter and Paul's interest in a partnership (whether recorded in Capital accounts or Current accounts) is £600, being the net assets of the partnership. If the business could be sold as a going concern for £900 on that date, the goodwill of the business is £300. When goodwill is not recorded there is a potential gain that has not been recorded in the books and so has not been shared by the partners. With the prospect of profit-sharing arrangements changing, say when John is admitted to partnership (let us continue with the assumptions made when we considered John's admission), there is a need to protect the interests of any of the continuing partners whose percentage share of profit is reduced by the change. We could act as we did in the case of the land, when we protected Paul's interest by increasing the carrying value of the land from cost to current value. Similarly, when the value of the whole business, as a going concern, is more than the amount at which its net assets are recorded, we could identify the difference as goodwill, and protect the interests of the continuing partners by accounting as shown in the box on the right. When we do that the continuing partners would share the gain the way they would have shared it had the business been sold without admitting John to partnership.

Dr Goodwill a/c	£300	–
Cr Peter's Capital a/c	–	£200
Cr Paul's Capital a/c	–	£100

However, goodwill, unlike land, is an intangible asset, the existence of which cannot be verified nor can it be realised unless the whole business is sold as a going concern. For these reasons not everyone likes goodwill to remain recorded in the books of account and reported in the Statement of financial position. The partners might, therefore, decide after John's admission to write the goodwill out of the books.

The writing off is done in such a way that all partners (including the new one) get back credit if goodwill is ever recorded again in the books. The accounting entries to write off goodwill are as shown on the left. The effect of these entries, the first set recording the goodwill and the second set

Dr Peter's Capital a/c	£150	–
Dr Paul's Capital a/c	£75	–
Dr John's Capital a/c	£75	–
Cr Goodwill a/c	–	£300

eliminating it from the books, is that the balance in the Capital account of the new partner (John) will be £75 less than the amount he contributes as his capital. For example, if he brings in £200 as his capital, after the goodwill adjustment (credit Peter and Paul in their old ratio of 2:1 and debit Peter, Paul and John in their new profit-sharing ratio of 2:1:1), the balance in John's Capital account would be only £125. That is because he would have paid £75 for his share (1/4th) of the unrecorded goodwill (£300). Assuming that the capital balances held by Peter and Paul, prior to John's admission, were £500 and £300 respectively, the partners' Capital accounts, after goodwill adjustment and John's admission, will appear as follows:

Capital account

	Peter	Paul	John		Peter	Paul	John
Goodwill – in new ratio	£150	£75	£75	Balance	£500	£300	–
				Goodwill – in old ratio	£200	£100	–
Balance c/d	£550	£325	£125	Bank account	–	–	£200
	£700	£400	£200		£700	£400	£200
				Balance b/d	£550	£325	£125

Observe that because of goodwill adjustment the amount lost by John (£75) is gained by Peter (£50) and Paul (£25). Effectively John compensates Peter and Paul for their respective share of goodwill remaining unrecorded in the books of the partnership.

Activity 14.7 Accounting for unrecorded goodwill

Knight and Tower, sharing profits as 3:2, respectively, admit Rook to a sixth share of profit. Goodwill of the business on this date is valued at £180,000.

Required: Set out the accounting entries needed to adjust for goodwill in each of the following alternative scenarios:
(a) Goodwill is to be stated in the books at £180,000.
(b) Goodwill is not to appear in the books of account.
(c) Goodwill, stated in the books already at £45,000, is to be retained at that amount.

14.12 Death or retirement of a partner

When a partner dies or retires from the partnership he or she (or the estate) is entitled to an appropriate share of: (i) the profit or loss up to that date and (ii) any unrecorded gain (or loss) as at that date. Unless the partner's entitlement can be fully discharged on that date, the outgoing partner is also entitled to interest at an agreed rate. If there is no agreement on the rate, section 42 of the Partnership Act provides for an interest rate of 5% per annum.

14.13 Revaluation account

Whenever there is a change in profit-sharing arrangements (be it on an admission or retirement) all assets and liabilities need to be restated at their market value on the date of the change. We have considered the accounting treatment when a single asset is revalued. Where there are a number of changes in value involved, it may be more convenient to credit the gains and debit the losses to a Revaluation account, so that the net gain (or loss as the case may be) is credited (or debited) to the partners' Capital accounts as a single figure, in the ratio in which they shared profits before the change.

If the partners do not intend to incorporate the new values into the books of account, instead of writing up a Revaluation account on a double-entry basis, a Memorandum Revaluation account may be written up (outside the books of account) to ascertain the net gain or loss on revaluation which is then accounted for as adjustments to the partners' Capital accounts.

To illustrate let us again consider the case of Peter and Paul sharing profits in the ratio 2:1 respectively and, upon admission of John to partnership, sharing profits in the ratio 2:1:1. Let us assume also that several assets, including goodwill, fair valued on the date of admission, identifies a net fair valuation gain (i.e. gain on some assets reduced by losses on others) of £300. If the assets involved are to be adjusted to their fair values, debits in the accounts recording those assets will be matched by credits in the Capital accounts of Peter and Paul in their old ratio of 2:1 respectively. If the gain is then to be removed from the ledger accounts in which they were recorded, then the credits in those ledger accounts will have to be matched by debits in the Capital accounts of all three partners (Peter, Paul and John) in their new profit-sharing ratio.

The net effect of these two sets of accounting entries on the Capital accounts of the partners is shown on the right.

Fair valuation gain of £300	Peter	Paul	John
Credited in old ratio (2:1)	Cr £200	Cr £100	–
Debited in new ratio (2:1:1)	Dr (£150)	Dr (£75)	Dr (£75)
Net effect on Capital accounts	Cr £50	Cr £25	Dr (£75)

On the other hand, if the partnership wishes to do the fair valuation adjustment without making entries in the various accounts recording the assets, they could (a) identify the net fair valuation gain of £300 by writing up a Memorandum Revaluation account (which would not appear on the ledger) and, having so identified the net gain, (b) account only for the net impact of the fair valuation adjustment on the partners' Capital accounts by passing the entries stated on the right.

Cr Peter's Capital a/c	£50
Cr Paul's Capital a/c	£25
Dr John's Capital a/c	£75

14.14 Dissolution of a partnership by piecemeal disposal

When partners wish to terminate the partnership, ideally they would seek to dispose of their business as a going concern because in that way they would get a price for their goodwill. Should this prove impossible, it would become necessary to sell each asset as best as possible, discharge the liabilities, settle the expenses of the dissolution and share whatever remains among the partners.

Let us illustrate such a piecemeal disposal assuming that Rose and Ivy, sharing profits in the ratio 2:1, respectively, decide to terminate their partnership with effect from 31 December 2012 when their position was reported on the Statement of financial position as shown on the right. The dissolution progressed as follows:

- The non-current assets were sold for £295.
- £35 of trade receivable proved irrecoverable.
- Inventory was sold for 20% more than the cost.
- Trade payables were settled subject to 10% discount.
- The dissolution expenses were met at £5.
- The partners' claims were met and the books closed.

Statement of financial position as at 31 December 2012

	£	£
Non-current assets	600	
Accum. depreciation	(240)	360
Inventory	415	
Trade receivables	385	
Cash and bank	25	825
		1,185

	£	£
Capital:		
Rose	500	
Ivy	300	800
Current a/c:		
Rose	£15 Cr	
Ivy	£10 Dr	5
Rose Loan account		100
Trade payables		280
		1,185

The accounting for the dissolution will be done as follows:

1. Every asset (other than cash and bank) is transferred to a Realisation account. This is because the aim is to realise these assets by selling them.
2. The amount raised on disposal of each asset is recorded in the Cash Book and posted to the credit of the Realisation a/c.
3. The amount paid (£5) as dissolution expenses is posted from the Cash Book to the debit of the Realisation account.
4. The amount paid to settle payables (£280 less £28) is posted from the Cash Book to the liability account and the gain on settlement (£28) transferred to the Realisation account.
5. The balances in partners' Current accounts are transferred to their Capital accounts (because faced with closure of business distinguishing what they can withdraw from what they cannot makes no sense).
6. The difference in the Realisation account represents a loss or gain on dissolution and this is appropriated among the partners in their profit-sharing ratio.
7. Any partner's loan is settled, prior to distributing remaining cash according to how they deserve.

The accounts will appear as follows:

Realisation account

	£		£	£
Non-current assets	600	Cash a/c:		
Accumulated depreciation	(240)	Non-current assets	295	
	360	Inventory	498	
Inventory	415	Receivables	350	1,143
Trade receivables	385			
Cash – expenses	5	Payables		28
	1,165			
Gain – Rose	4			
Ivy	2			
	1,171			1,171

Trade payables account

	£		£
Cash a/c	252	Balance b/f	280
Realisation	28		

Cash Book

	£		£
Balance b/f	25	Expenses	5
Realisation	1,143	Trade payables	252
		Rose loan	100
		Capital – Rose	519
		Ivy	292
	1,168		1,168

Partners' Capital accounts

	£	£		£	£
	Rose	Ivy		Rose	Ivy
Current a/c – transferred	–	10	Balance b/f	500	300
Cash Book – balancing	519	292	Current a/c – transferred	15	–
			Realisation a/c – gain	4	2

If a partner wishes to take over any of the assets of the partnership it is customary to recover from that partner the amount that asset cost the partnership. If the asset is a non-current one, which has been depreciated, the amount recovered from the partner is usually the depreciated cost, unless the partnership insists on valuing the asset and seeks to recover that value.

When, in a dissolution of a partnership, the assets are disposed of piecemeal, the amounts realised by disposal of each asset as the realisation process progresses should be disbursed in the sequence stated below on the right. If anyone with a claim on the partnership has a charge (mortgage) on an asset, the proceeds on the realisation of that asset should be paid to the party with the charge. As is shown in the box on the right, the claims of outsiders have precedence over those of the partners. After meeting all claims of outsiders and settling any amount received as loan from any partner (along with interest at the agreed rate right up to the date it is settled), the remaining cash is distributed among the partners exactly according to what claim each partner has, after adjusting their claims with the gain or loss on dissolution.

1. Expenses of dissolution
2. Claims of outsiders (e.g. payables, bank)
3. Amount obtained from partners as loan
4. Partners' claims (as Capital and Current)

Activity 14.8 Piecemeal dissolution of a partnership

Ebb and Flow, who shared profits in the ratio 3:2, respectively, decided to terminate their partnership with effect from 31 March 2012 when their Statement of financial position was prepared as shown on the right. The dissolution progressed as follows:

1. Flow took over a vehicle which had had cost £30,000 and was written down by that date to £26,000.
2. Remaining vehicles, furniture and inventory realised £54,000, £92,000 and £718,000 respectively.
3. Trade receivables were collected subject to writing off £74,000 as irrecoverable.
4. Dissolution expenses were £18,000.

Required: Set out a Dissolution account, the Cash Book and the partners' accounts recording the closure of the partnership books.

Statement of financial position as at 31.3.2012

	Cost	Depreciation	£'000
Furniture	420	168	252
Motor vehicle	280	140	140
Inventory		625	
Trade receivables	460		
Allowance for doubtful debt	(24)	436	
Cash and bank		72	1,133
			1,525

	Ebb	Flow	£'000
Capital accounts	400	400	800
Current accounts	(104)	21	(83)
Loan – Flow			150
Trade payables		562	
Bank overdraft		96	658
			1,525

14.15 Disposal of a partnership as a going concern

If a partnership business is disposed of as a going concern, all of its assets including cash and bank balance, as well as its liabilities, would be sold for the agreed price.

Let us assume, this time, that the business owned by Rose and Ivy was sold as a going concern for a consideration received in cash of £950, on 31.12.2012. Remember the partnership net asset on that date was £905 (total assets £1,185 and current liabilities £280). Net assets reported at £905 were sold for £950 giving the partners a gain on disposal of £45, if we assume that there were no expenses of realisation. The Realisation account will confirm this position as shown on the left.

Realisation account

	£		£
Non-current asset	600	Payables	280
Accumulated depreciation	(240)	Cash	950
	360		
Inventory	415		
Receivables	385		
Cash and bank	25		
	1,185		
Gain:			
Rose	30		
Ivy	15		
	1,230		1,230

The following points need to be noted:

(a) The assets that are sold, in a going concern scenario, include cash and bank balance.
(b) The balance (£280) in the Payables account is transferred to the Realisation account so that the net assets £905 (£1,185 – £280) could be compared with the amount (£950) for which they were sold, identifying the gain on disposal as £45.
(c) The gain on disposal (£45) is appropriated among the partners in their profit-sharing ratio.
(d) The amount received on disposal (£950) is paid to partners in accordance with their respective claim stated in their Capital account, after settling Rose's Loan account.

Cash Book

	£		£
Balance b/f	25	Realisation a/c	25
Dissolution a/c	950	Rose Loan	100
		Capital:	
		Rose	545
		Ivy	305

Capital accounts

	£ Rose	£ Ivy		£ Rose	£ Ivy
Current a/c	–	10	Balance b/f	500	300
Cash a/c	545	305	Current a/c	15	–
			Dissolution a/c	30	15
	545	315		545	315

Activity 14.9 Disposal of a partnership as a going concern

Ebb and Flow, who shared profits in the ratio 3:2, respectively, prepared their Statement of financial position on 31.3.2012 as stated in Activity 14.8. Flow agreed to take over the bank overdraft as well as a vehicle, which cost £30,000 and had been written down by this date to £26,000. Subject to this the business, other than Flow's loan, was taken over by Wave Ltd for a consideration payable in cash of £982,000.

Required: Show the closure of partnership books.

In the context of a business disposal, the expression *purchase consideration* could, but does not always, refer to the total price paid for the assets. If the acquirer does not assume responsibility for discharging the liabilities, then (but then alone) the purchase consideration will equal the price fetched by the assets. When a business is disposed of as a going concern it is usual for the acquirer to take over the assets together with liabilities. In that case, the purchase consideration is arrived at by deducting, from the sum of the agreed price for all of the assets, the amount of any liabilities taken over.

Activity 14.10 Determination of the purchase consideration

George owns a car acquired for £24,000, using a loan of £6,000 from Finco Ltd. When he advertised the car for sale, John Smith agreed to buy it for £25,000.

Required:
(a) Account for the disposal of the car in George's books in each of the following scenarios:
Scenario (1): George undertakes to settle the Finco Ltd loan.
Scenario (2): as part of the deal John Smith undertakes to discharge the Finco Ltd loan.
(b) Explain whether the sale price of the vehicle and the purchase consideration are the same amount in both scenarios.

Upon a disposal of a business the purchase consideration may not always be received in cash. Instead the agreement with the acquirer may be that the purchase consideration should be discharged by an allotment of the acquiring company's shares and possibly debentures. When shares are received in discharge of the purchase consideration there would be a need:

1. **To account for the shares as an asset in the books of the partnership.** The shares are accounted for as investments (an asset), valued at the agreed value at which the shares were allotted. For example, if 100,000 ordinary shares of £1 each had been allotted at £1.25 per share (i.e. with a premium of 25p per share), the shares received will be valued at £125,000 and accounted for by crediting the Acquirer's account and debiting an Investment account.
2. **For the partners to agree on the ratio in which each partner is to be allotted these shares.** In the absence of an agreement (and in an examination, in the absence of instructions to the contrary) the shares may be allotted in one of two ways as follows:
   - If it is the wish of the partners that they should continue to receive dividends from the company in the same ratio as the one in which they shared partnership profits, the shares may be allotted in the partnership profit-sharing ratio.
   - If the wish of the partners is that they should own the company in the ratio in which they owned the partnership, the shares may be allotted in the ratio of their respective capital balances.

Activity 14.11 Purchase consideration calculated based on asset values

After preparing their Statement of financial position as shown on the right, Gerenia and Petunia sold their business, as a going concern, to Foliage Ltd, on the basis of the following valuations:

- Land and buildings at £960,000
- Motor vehicles at £90,000
- Receivables subject to an allowance of 10%
- Goodwill at £150,000.

Foliage Ltd undertook to discharge the purchase consideration as follows:

(i) allotment to partners in their profit-sharing ratio of 1,500,000 ordinary shares of £1 each, in Foliage Ltd at 110p each; and

(ii) payment of the balance in cash.

Dissolution expenses amounted to £5,000. Gerenia and Petunia have been sharing profits in the ratio 2:1.

Required: (a) The Realisation account and (b) the partner's Capital accounts showing the closure of the partnership books.

Statement of financial position as at 30 June 2012

		£'000	£'000
Land and buildings		840	
Accumulated depreciation		(196)	644
Motor vehicles		260	
Accumulated depreciation		(156)	104
Inventory		574	
Receivables	480		
Allowance	(24)	456	
Cash and bank		96	1,126
			1,874

	£'000	£'000
Capital accounts:		
Gerenia		800
Petunia		600
Current accounts:		
Gerenia	(74)	
Petunia	(16)	(90)
Trade payables	492	
Accrued expenses	72	564
		1,874

If a value has been attributed to each of the assets and liabilities of the partnership, the purchase consideration could be identified as the sum of all asset values less the amount of liabilities taken over. However, there are occasions when not all of the assets acquired from a partnership have been attributed a value. For example, if no value has been attributed to the partnership goodwill, it would not be possible to identify the purchase consideration using this method. Instead, the amount of the purchase consideration is calculated by attributing a value to whatever is received from the acquirer, in discharge of the purchase consideration, i.e. shares, loan notes and cash.

Activity 14.12 Purchase consideration arrived at by valuing what is received in discharge

Gerenia and Petunia, sharing profits in the ratio 2:1, respectively, have finalised their Statement of financial position on 30 June 2012 as stated in Activity 14.11. Their business is sold to Foliage Ltd, on this date, valuing land and buildings and vehicles at £960,000 and £90,000, respectively. Trade receivables are to be taken over subject to 10% allowance for doubtful debts. The purchase consideration is to be discharged by:

(i) an allotment to the partners in their profit-sharing ratio of 1.5 million ordinary shares of £1 each in Foliage Ltd, at 110p per share; and

(ii) payment of £88,000 in cash.

Dissolution expenses amounted to £5,000.

Required: Close the books of the partnership.

Clue: No value has been attributed to goodwill. Therefore, the purchase consideration should be calculated by adding the values of whatever is received (shares and cash) from Foliage Ltd to discharge the purchase consideration.

14.16 Opening the books of a newly formed acquiring company

A company newly formed to take over the business from a partnership will set about opening its own books of account as follows.

14.16.1 Record the assets acquired

Every class of asset acquired is debited in an appropriate asset account at the value at which it is taken over and credited to a *Purchase of business account*. There may be a difference between how we account for non-current assets and current assets:

(a) Non-current assets: each non-current asset is accounted for at the value at which it is acquired. For example, if a machine acquired by the partnership for £600 and written down to £360 is taken over, the company would record the machine at £360, i.e. on the assumption that it was acquired at its book value. On the contrary if, for the purpose of acquisition, the machine was valued at £450, the company would record the machine at £450.

(b) Current assets: trade receivables are treated differently. For example the partnership may have reported the receivables at £400 and maintained an Allowance for doubtful debts of £18; whereas the company may take over the asset subject to an allowance of

10%, i.e. £40 and not £18. The company will record the trade receivables at £400 (that being the amount due from customers) and record in its own Allowance for doubtful debts account £40 (being the 10% allowance the company wishes to maintain on the receivables), crediting the Purchase of business account with £360 (i.e. £400 – £40).

14.16.2 Record the liabilities taken over

Every liability taken over from the partnership is credited to an appropriately named liability account (e.g. Trade payables, Loan note) and debited to the Purchase of business account. By this point the Purchase of business account has been credited with all of the assets and debited with all of the liabilities, showing as its balance the net amount payable to the partnership, i.e. the Purchase consideration.

14.16.3 Record the discharge of purchase consideration

As we learnt in Chapter 9, it is a requirement of company law that shares issued by a company should be accounted for in the Share capital account at their nominal value (i.e. the value stated on the share certificate). If a £1 share is issued at £1.25, the excess of 25p over the par value (which is known as the premium) is accounted for in a Share premium account.

Activity 14.13 Opening the books of a company

A partnership business carried on by Gerenia and Petunia was acquired by Foliage Ltd with effect from 30 June 2012. Particulars of this acquisition are as stated as part of Activity 14.11.

Required: Set out the Purchase of business account in the books of Foliage Ltd and the Statement of financial position immediately upon acquisition of the partnership business.

14.17 Converting the books of the partnership to those of a company

As an alternative to closing the partnership books and then opening a new set of books for the company, it may be decided to convert the partnership books to those of the company. There is then the choice of (i) keeping the asset and liability values unchanged or (ii) changing the values to the agreed values. We will consider each of these choices.

14.17.1 Keeping the asset and liability values unchanged

If, after the conversion, the company wishes to continue to report its assets and liabilities at the same values at which they were in partnership books, all that needs to be done is as follows:

1. Transfer the balances in each partner's account (Capital as well as Current) to the credit of the Purchase of business account, which would then report the value at which partnership net assets are taken over.
2. Debit the Purchase of business account with the consideration paid for acquiring the business, i.e. the shares, cash and any other item that may be part of the consideration.

3. The amount by which the value of the consideration exceeds the amount due to the partners for the net assets taken over is the amount paid for goodwill.

To illustrate let us assume that Pansy and Begonia, who shared profits in the ratio 3:2, respectively, drafted their Statement of financial position as at 31 March 2012 as shown on the left and decided to convert their business from that date into a company named Flora Ltd. The purchase consideration, agreed at £1,250, is to be settled by an allotment to the partners of 1,000 ordinary shares of £1 each at 120p per share and a payment of £50 in cash. In the absence of any more information we may assume that Flora took over each asset and liability of the partnership at the values at which they were recorded in the books of the partnership.

Statement of financial position as at 31 March 2012

	£	£
Non-current assets		600
Inventory	320	
Receivables	440	
Cash and bank	80	840
		1,440
	£	£
Capital accounts:		
Pansy	600	
Begonia	300	900
Current accounts:		
Pansy	96	
Begonia	(16)	80
Payables		460
		1,440

To convert the partnership books of account to those of Flora Ltd, all that needs to be done is as follows:

1. Transfer the balances in both partners' account to a Purchase of business account.
2. Account for the discharge of purchase consideration by crediting the Share capital account with £1,000, crediting the Share premium account with £200, crediting the Cash Book with £50 and debiting the total (£1,250) in the Purchase of business account. The difference in the Purchase of business account (see below) is the amount paid by Flora Ltd to acquire the goodwill of the partnership. The Statement of financial position of Flora Ltd, immediately after acquisition, will appear as shown on the right.

Flora Ltd – Statement of financial position as at 1 April 2012

		£
Non-current assets		600
Goodwill		270
Current assets:		
Inventory	320	
Receivables	440	
Cash and bank (80 – 50)	30	790
		1,660
		£'000
Equity and reserves:		
Ordinary shares of £1	1,000	
Share premium account	200	1,200
Payables		460
		1,660

Purchase of business account

	£		£
Begonia – Current	16	Pansy – Capital	600
Share capital	1,000	Begonia – Capital	300
Share premium a/c	200	Pansy – Current	96
Cash	50	Goodwill	270
	1,266		1,266

14.17.2 Changing the values of assets/liabilities taken over

If any of the partnership assets are not taken over, e.g. the partners might decide to keep the partnership cars for their personal use, or if any are taken over at a value different from the book value, the amount of the goodwill will be different. For example, if Flora took over the partnership non-current assets at a value of £750 (instead of £600), the difference of £150 is debited to the Non-current asset account and credited to the Purchase of business account to record the fact that the net assets acquired are worth not £980, but £150 more. Accordingly the amount paid for goodwill will be not £270, but £150 less.

Activity 14.14 Conversion of partnership books to those of a company

Refer back to the information stated in Activity 14.11. You are required to convert the books of the partnership into those of Foliage Ltd.

Required: Set out the Statement of financial position of Foliage Ltd immediately after the conversion to a company.

Summary

- A partnership is a relationship based on co-ownership of assets, conduct of a business and intention to share consequent profits and losses.
- A written partnership agreement is known as a Partnership deed and sets out how the partnership is to be conducted with respect to capital and profits, authority and accounts.
- The Limited Liability Partnerships Act provides for limited liability partnerships.
- Any reward to a partner for serving in an additional role (than as a partner) is a charge to be deducted before the partnership profit is identified; whereas any rewards to partners for merely doing what they should in their role as partners is an appropriation of partnership profit.
- Interest charged on partners' drawings is not a partnership income. It is merely an adjustment to determine how partnership profit should be shared among partners.
- Fair valuation of partnership assets, including goodwill, is necessary whenever there is a change in profit-sharing arrangements, to protect the interest of any partner adversely affected by the change.
- When a partnership is dissolved the partnership books must be closed or converted to those of a company.

Suggested answers to activities

14.1 Sharing profits among partners

(a)

Capital accounts

	£ Jack	£ Jill		£ Jack	£ Jill
			Balance b/f	600	300

Current accounts

	£ Jack	£ Jill		£ Jack	£ Jill
Drawings	35	16	Profit	130	130
Balance c/d	95	114			
	130	130		130	130
			Balance b/d	95	114

Statement of income year ended 30 June 2012

	£'000	£'000
Profit		260
Shared:		
Jack	130	
Jill	130	(260)

(b)

Statement of financial position as at 30 June 2012

	£'000	£'000	£'000
Non-current assets	840	(380)	460
Current assets:			
Inventory		648	
Trade receivables		584	
Cash and bank		13	1,245
			1,705

	£'000	£'000
Capital a/cs:		
Jack	600	
Jill	300	900
Current a/cs:		
Jack	95	
Jill	114	209
		1,109
Current liabilities:		
Trade payables		596
		1,705

14.2 Distinguishing a charge from an appropriation

(a)

Current accounts

	Tom £'000	Dick £'000	Harry £'000		Tom £'000	Dick £'000	Harry £'000
Balance b/f	–	–	12	Balance b/f	126	34	–
Salary drawn[a]	30	–	–	Rent a/c	–	8	–
				Interest on loan	3	–	–
				Salary	[a]36	–	–
				Interest on capital	18	9	6
Balance c/d	175	62	5	Profit share	22	11	11
	205	62	17		205	62	17
				Balance b/d	175	62	5

Note:

(a) Alternatively, as done with rent and interest on loan, instead of debiting Tom salary drawn and then crediting him with his salary entitlement, he could have been credited with the difference of £6,000.

(b)

Statement of income for year ended 31 March 2012

	£'000	£'000
Sales		3,096
Inventory – 1.4	365	
Purchases	2,172	
Inventory – 31.3	(412)	(2,125)
Gross profit		971
Admin expenses:		
Salary (214 – 30)	184	
Rent (40 + 8)	48	
Depreciation	68	
Postage/telephone	32	
Other expenses	349	(681)
Distribution costs:		
Advertising		(165)
Interest on loan		(12)
Profit for the year		113
Tom's salary		(36)
Interest on capital:		
Tom	18	
Dick	9	
Harry	6	(33)
Share of profits:		
Tom	22	
Dick	11	
Harry	11	(44)

Statement of financial positin as at 31 March 2012

	£'000	£'000	£'000
Non-current assets	640	(368)	272
Current assets:			
Inventory		412	
Receivables		544	
Cash and bank		92	1,048
			1,320

	£'000	£'000
Capital a/cs:		
Tom	300	
Dick	150	
Harry	100	550
Current a/cs:		
Tom	175	
Dick	62	
Harry	5	242
		792
12% Loan from Tom		100
Current liabilities:		
Trade payables		428
		1,320

14.3 Calculation of interest on partners' drawings

Scenario one	Sun:	£5,000 @ 6% for nine months		= £225
	Moon:	£8,000 @ 6% for six months		= £240
	Star:	£20,000 @ 6% for five months	= £500	
		plus £6,000 @ 6% for three months	= £90	= £590
Scenario two	Sun:	£24,000 @ 6% × 6.5 months		= £780
	Moon:	£24,000 @ 6% × 5.5 months		= £660
	Star:	£24,000 @ 6% × 6 months		= £720
Scenario three	Sun:	£36,000 @ 6% × (12 + 4/2 =) 8 months		= £1,440
	Moon:	£50,000 @ 6% × (9 + 0/2 =) 4.5 months		= £1,125
	Star:	£12,000 @ 6% × (11.5 + 6.5/2 =) 9 months	= £540	
		£18,000 @ 6% × (5.5 + 0.5/2 =) 3 months	= £270	= £810

14.4 Admission of a new partner during an accounting period

Statement of income for the year ended 31 December 2012

	£'000	£'000	£'000
Sales for the year			3,159
Inventory – 31.12.2011		524	
Purchases		2,264	
Inventory – 31.12.2012		(586)	(2,202)
Gross profit for the year			957
	Total for year	**9 months to 30.9.12**	**3 months to 31.12.12**
Gross profit[b] on turnover basis		638	319
Admin expenses:[c]			
Salaries	288		
Rent	48		
Depreciation – furniture	16		
Other expenses on time basis	96		
	448	(336)	(112)
Distribution cost on turnover basis:			
Depreciation – vehicles	30		
Advertising	72		
	102	(68)	(34)
Profit		234	173
Salary – Penny		(18)	(6)
Interest on capital:			
Penny		(22.5)	(7.5)
Sally		(13.5)	(4.5)
Molly		–	(3)
Profit share:			
Penny		(108)	(76)
Sally		(72)	(51)
Molly		–	(25)

Statement of financial position as at 31 December 2012

	£'000	£'000	£'000
Non-current assets:			
Furniture	280	(136)	144
Motor vehicles	320	(200)	120
Current assets:			
Inventory		586	
Receivables		752	
Cash and bank		241	1,579
			1,843
		£'000	**£'000**
Capital a/cs:			
Penny		500	
Sally		300	
Molly		200	1,000
Current a/cs:			
Penny		186	
Sally		113	
Molly		30	329
			1,329
Current liabilities			
Trade payables			514
			1,843

Notes:

(a) New profit-sharing ratio after Molly's admission:

Penny: 3/5th of 5/6th = 3/6th =	1/2
Sally: 2/5th of 5/6th = 2/6th =	1/3
Molly	1/6

(b) Turnover ratio:

Till 30 September = 9 months × 100 = 900 =	2/3
After 1 October = 3 months × 150 = 450 =	1/3

(c) Time basis:

Till 30 September = 9 months	3/4
After 1 October = 3 months	1/4

Partners' Current accounts

	Penny	Sally	Molly		Penny	Sally	Molly
	£'000	£'000	£'000		£'000	£'000	£'000
Drawings	50	28	–	Up to 30 September:			
Molly – guarantee[d]	2	–	–	Salary	18	–	–
				Interest on capital	22.5	13.5	–
				Profit share[a]	108	72	–
				After 1 October:			
				Salary	6	–	–
				Interest on capital	7.5	4.5	3
				Profit share	76	51	25
Balance c/d	186	113	30	Penny – guarantee[d]	–	–	2
	238	141	30		238	141	30
				Balance b/d	186	113	30

(d) Guarantee: The guarantee of £120,000 for the year works out to £30,000 for the 3 months Molly was a partner. As a partner she has received £3,000 as interest and £25,000 as share of profit, leaving a shortfall of £2,000 to be made good by Penny.

14.5 When and why assets of a partnership need to be fair valued

(a) Assets of a partnership need to be fair valued whenever there is an alteration in the profit-sharing arrangements among partners. Such alterations arise:

- (i) on a change of the profit-sharing arrangement among continuing partners;
- (ii) on admission of a new partner;
- (iii) on retirement or death of a continuing partner.

(b) The need for fair valuation arises because if an asset (as is usual with goodwill) is not recorded or is recorded at lower than its fair value on the date of change in profit-sharing arrangements, the unrecorded portion of the asset represents unrecognised profit which partners are entitled to share in the ratio from which they are proposing to change. If such gain is not adjusted for, the interest of those partners whose share of profit is going to be detrimentally affected by the change will be affected.

14.6 Accounting for fair valuation of an asset

To fair value the property, the Property account is debited with the gain on fair valuation of £120,000 crediting the existing partner's Capital accounts, in their current profit-sharing ratio of 2:1, respectively. In view of the partners' wish to continue reporting the property at its historical cost of £280, the gain recorded in the Property account is reversed, crediting the Property account and debiting all partners' Capital accounts in the new profit-sharing ratio of 2:1:1. The effect of these two pairs of entries on the Capital accounts of the partners will be as shown on the left. Hence the entries shown on the left would be sufficient to adjust for the fair valuation.

Accounting entries needed:	£'000	£'000
Dr: Dock's Capital a/c	30	–
Cr: Hickory's Capital a/c	–	20
Cr: Dickory's Capital a/c	–	10

14.7 Adjusting for goodwill

(a) If goodwill is to be recorded at full value:

	£'000	£'000
Dr Goodwill a/c	180	–
Cr Knight Capital a/c	–	108
Cr Tower Capital a/c	–	72

(b) If goodwill is not to appear in the books:

	£'000	£'000
Dr Rook's Capital a/c	30	–
Cr Knight Capital a/c	–	18
Cr Tower Capital a/c	–	12

(c) If goodwill is to remain recorded at existing value:

	£'000	£'000
Dr Rook Capital a/c	22.5	–
Cr Knight Capital a/c	–	13.5
Cr Tower Capital a/c	–	9

14.8 Piecemeal dissolution of a partnership

Dissolution account

	£'000	£'000		£'000	£'000
Furniture	420		Flow – vehicle		26
Depreciation	(168)	252	Cash a/c:		
Motor vehicle	280		Vehicle	54	
Depreciation	(140)	140	Furniture	92	
			Inventory	718	
Inventory		625	Receivables	386	1,250
			Loss:		
Receivables	460		Ebb		117
Provision	(24)	436	Flow		78
Cash – expenses		18			
		1,471			1,471

Partners' Capital accounts

	Ebb £'000	Flow £'000		Ebb £'000	Flow £'000
Current a/c	104	–	Balance b/f	400	400
Vehicle a/c	–	26	Current a/c	–	21
Dissolution	117	78			
Cash a/c	179	317			
	400	421		400	421

Cash account

	£'000		£'000
Balance b/f	72	Expenses	18
Dissolution a/c	1,250	Bank overdraft	96
		Trade payables	562
		Flow – loan a/c	150
		Capital – Ebb	179
		Flow	317
	1,322		1,322

14.9 Disposal of a partnership as a going concern

Realisation account

	£'000	£'000		£'000
Furniture	420		Flow – vehicle	26
Depreciation	(168)	252	Trade payables	562
			Wave Ltd	982
Motor vehicle	280			
Depreciation	(140)	140		
Inventory		625		
Receivables	460			
Provision	(24)	436		
Cash and bank		72		
Gain:				
Ebb		27		
Flow		18		
		1,570		1,570

Cash and bank account

	£'000		£'000
Balance b/f	72	Dissolution a/c	72
Wave Ltd	982	Flow loan a/c	150
		Ebb Capital a/c	323
		Flow Capital a/c	509
	1,054		1,054

Wave Ltd account

	£'000		£'000
Dissolution a/c	982	Cash and bank	982
	982		982

14.10 Determination of the purchase consideration

Scenario (1) **Disposal of vehicle account**

	£		£
Vehicle a/c	24,000	Cash a/c	25,000
Gain – disposal	1,000		
	25,000		25,000

Scenario (2) **Disposal of vehicle account**

	£		£
Vehicle a/c	24,000	Finco Loan	6,000
Gain – disposal	1,000	Cash a/c	19,000
	25,000		25,000

In both scenarios the sale price of the vehicle is the same, agreed at £25,000. Purchase consideration is that portion of sale price given by the buyer (John Smith) to the seller (George). In scenario one, Smith gives the whole of the agreed sale price to George. Therefore the sale price and the purchase consideration are the same. In the second scenario, because Smith takes over the loan, the portion he will give George (i.e. the purchase consideration) is only £19,000 and this is not the same as the vehicle's sale price.

14.11 Purchase consideration based on asset values

(a)

Realisation account

	£'000	£'000		£'000
Furniture	840		Trade payables	492
Depreciation	(196)	644	Accruals	72
Vehicles	260		Foliage Ltd	1,738
Depreciation	(156)	104		
Inventory		574		
Receivables	480			
Allowance	(24)	456		
Cash and bank		96		
Expenses		5		
Gain:				
Gerenia		282		
Petunia		141		
		2,302		2,302

(b)

Partners' Capital accounts

	Gerenia £'000	Petunia £'000		Gerenia £'000	Petunia £'000
Current a/c	74	16	Balance b/f	800	600
Investments	1,100	550	Gain on realisation	282	141
Cash Book	–	175	Cash Book	92	–
	1,174	741		1,174	741

Calculation of the purchase consideration is shown on the right.

Land and buildings	960
Motor vehicle	90
Goodwill	150
Inventory	574
Receivables (480 – 48)	432
Cash and bank	96
Trade payables	(492)
Accrued expenses	(72)
	1,738

14.12 Purchase consideration arrived at by valuing what is received in discharge

The answer is the same as for Activity 14.11 because the information provided is identical, except that this question does not place a value on goodwill. Therefore, the purchase consideration is calculated (see on the right) by valuing items received from Foliage in discharge of the purchase consideration.

Purchase consideration is calculated as:	
	£'000
Value of shares: 1,500,000 @ £1.10	1,650
Cash received	88
	1,738

14.13 Opening the books of a company

To record assets and liabilities		£'000	£'000
Dr	Goodwill account[a]	150	–
Dr	Land and buildings account	960	–
Dr	Motor vehicles account	90	–
Dr	Inventory account	574	–
Dr	Trade receivables account	480	–
Cr	Trade payables account	–	492
Cr	Accrued expenses account	–	72
Cr	Allowance for doubtful debts account	–	48
Cr	Purchase of business account	–	1,642
		2,254	2,254
To record discharge of purchase consideration			
Dr	Purchase of business account	1,650	
Cr	Ordinary Share capital a/c	–	1,500
Cr	Share premium a/c	–	150
		1,650	1,650

Purchase to business account

Journal[b]	1,650	Cash Book	96
Cash Book[c]	88	Journal[b]	1,642
	1,738		1,738

Note:
(a) The balancing amount.
(b) We will learn of the Journal in Chapter 16.
(c) (175 – 92) + 5 expense.

14.14 Conversion of partnership books to those of a company

Purchase of business account

	£'000		£'000
Current:		Capital:	
Gerenia	74	Gerenia	800
Petunia	16	Petunia	600
Motor vehicle	14	Land and buildings	316
Allowance for doubtful debts	24	Goodwill	150
Share capital	1,500		
Share premium	150		
Cash Book	88		
	1,866		1,866

Land and buildings account

	£'000		£'000
Balance b/f	840	Accumulated depreciation	196
Purchase of business	316	Balance c/d	960
	1,156		1,156
Balance b/d	960		

Motor vehicles account

	£'000		£'000
Balance b/f	260	Accumulated depreciation	156
		Purchase of business	14
		Balance c/d	90
	260		260
Balance b/d	90		

Statement of financial position as at 30 June 2012

			£'000
Non-current assets:			
Land and buildings			960
Motor vehicles			90
Goodwill			150
Inventory		574	
Trade receivables	480		
Allowance for doubtful debts	(48)	432	
Cash and bank (96–88)		8	1,014
			2,214

		£'000
Capital and reserves:		
Ordinary shares of £1 each		1,500
Share premium a/c		150
Current liabilities:		
Trade payables	492	
Accrued expenses	72	564
		2,214

Multiple choice questions

The concept of partnership

14.1 Which of the following characteristics should exist to recognise a business as a partnership?

(a) The business needs to be registered with the Registrar of Companies

(b) The business needs to have more than one owner

(c) The owners should have written an agreement to conduct business as partners

(d) There needs to be co-ownership, a business and intention to share profits

14.2 With regard to a partnership agreement which of the following statements are correct?

(a) Agreement may be an oral one

(b) The agreement can be inferred from the manner of their past behaviour

(c) The agreement should be printed, legally attested and registered

(d) The agreement may be a written one

a	a & b	
b	a, b & c	
c	a, b & d	
d	b, c & d	

14.3 With regard to a partnership business which of the following statements are correct?

(a) Every partner has to participate in management

(b) Every partner needs to contribute equal amounts as capital

(c) The number of partners may be from two to any number

(d) Each partner has unlimited joint and several responsibility to meet partnership debts

a	a & b	
b	a & d	
c	b & d	
d	c & d	

14.4 With regard to a partnership agreement which of the following statements are correct?

(a) A partnership agreement is not essential

(b) The agreement can be inferred from the manner of their past behaviour

(c) The agreement should be printed, legally attested and registered

(d) The agreement may be a written one

a	a & b	
b	a, b & c	
c	a, b & d	
d	b, c & d	

14.5 Which of the following matters would you suggest should be dealt within a partnership agreement?

(a) How they propose to share profits

(b) Whether salary and interest on capital needs to be allowed

(c) Whether every partner may admit to partnership anyone of their choice

(d) Whether there should be restrictions on what a partner may draw out for their own use

a	a & c	
b	a, b & c	
c	All four	
d	b, c & d	

14.6 Which one or more of the following statements is/are correct with regard to the application of section 24 of the Partnership Act 1890?

(a) Section 24 applies to all partnerships

(b) Section 24 applies only if the partnership agreement states that it would

(c) Section 24 applies only if there is no partnership agreement

(d) Section 24 applies on any aspect not covered in the partnership agreement

a	c & d	
b	b & c	
c	c only	
d	d only	

14.7 In a situation where section 24 of the Partnership Act applies, which one or more of the following statements are correct?

(a) Profits and losses have to be shared equally

(b) If any partner contributes more capital interest may be allowed at 5%

(c) No interest can be paid on a loan received from a partner

(d) No interest may be charged on amounts drawn by any partners

a	a & c	
b	b & c	
c	a & d	
d	c & d	

14.8 With regard to a business carried on as a partnership which one or more of the following statements are correct?

(a) A partner may agree to join on condition he would risk only his capital amount

(b) As a sleeping partner, a partner may be excused from management responsibility

(c) By agreement a partner may require interest on his loans at 12% per annum

(d) If registered with the Registrar of Companies as a Limited Liability Partnership partners' liability could be restricted to the amount of capital contributed.

a	c & d	
b	b & c	
c	a & d	
d	b & d	

14.9 For which one or more of the following reasons would you advise partners to have their financial statements professionally audited?

(a) So that each partner may feel assured that his/her interests are protected.

(b) It is a legal requirement

(c) To avoid disputes and possible litigation

(d) It enhance the prestige of the business

a	a & d	
b	b & c	
c	a & c	
d	c & d	

14.10 Where a partnership maintains separate Capital accounts and Current accounts for each partner, which one or more of the following should be credited to the Current accounts?

(a) Share of profit from the partnership

(b) Gain on fair valuing an asset or recording partnership goodwill

(c) Unpaid portion or any rent, salary or interest due to a partner

(d) Additional capital introduced by a partner during the year

a	a & d	
b	b & c	
c	a & c	
d	c & d	

14.11 Which one or more of the following are charges (rather than appropriation) of profit among partners?

(a) Salary payable to a partner

(b) Rent payable to a partner

(c) Interest payable to a partner on any loan received by the partnership

(d) Interest allowed on partners' capital account balances

a	c & d	
b	b & c	
c	a & c	
d	a & d	

14.12 In which of the following circumstances would you suggest that a partnership agreement should provide that salary and interest on capital should be allowed to partners?

(a) If there is a difference in the effort contribution made by all partners

(b) If there is a difference in the amount contributed as capital by each partner

(c) If that is fashionable in the trade or business carried on by the partnership

(d) If one or more partners are cleverer than others

a	c & d	
b	b & c	
c	a & b	
d	a & c	

14.13 In which of the following circumstances is there a need for fair valuing partnership assets and recording any partnership goodwill?

(a) When a new partner is admitted

(b) When an existing partner retires or dies

(c) Whenever the partnership prepares its financial statements

(d) When there is a change in the profit-sharing arrangements among existing partners

a	All four	
b	b, c & d	
c	a & c	
d	a, b & d	

14.14 Having recognised goodwill in specific circumstances, for which of the following reasons are partners usually reluctant to continue recording goodwill in their books?

(a) Goodwill is an intangible asset

(b) Goodwill does not bring in future economic benefit

(c) Goodwill cannot be realised unless the whole business is sold as a going concern

(d) Goodwill is a fiction of business imagination

a	All four	
b	b, c & d	
c	a & c	
d	a, b & d	

14.15 Whenever there is a change in the profit-sharing arrangements among partners, which of the following need adjustments?

(a) Goodwill not recorded or partly recorded in the books

(b) Work in progress which is usually not recorded in partnership of professionals

(c) Any asset not recorded at its fair value on that date

(d) Partnership joint life policy where the premiums paid have been written off

a	All four	
b	b, c & d	
c	a, c & d	
d	a, b & d	

14.16 With regard to interest charged on partners' drawings which one or more of the following statements is/are correct?

(a) Interest is charged to ensure partners do not draw their profit share at all

(b) Interest is charged to discourage drawings prior to the year-end

(c) Irrespective of the date of drawing interest is payable for the whole accounting year

(d) Interest is an additional earning for the partnership

a	a & b	
b	c & d	
c	b only	
d	b & d	

14.17 Which of the following is the correct way of accounting for interest charged on a partner's drawings?

(a) Debit an expense account (to be shown in Income statement) and credit Current account

(b) Debit Current account and credit in the appropriation section of the Statement of income

(c) Debit in the appropriation section of the Income statement and credit Current account

(d) Debit Current account and credit an income account (to be added to partnership gross profit)

14.18 With regard to death or retirement of a partner which of the following statement(s) is/are correct?

(a) When a partner leaves his dues should be settled at once

(b) If retiring partner's dues are not immediately settled interest becomes payable at 5%

(c) A deceased partner's dues, if not immediately settled, are recorded as an estate

(d) Interest on a deceased partner's dues is a charge (rather than appropriation) of profit

a	a, b & c	
b	b, c & d	
c	a & b	
d	c & d	

14.19 When a partnership is dissolved piecemeal, and the following claims need to be met out of the cash realised, which is the correct sequence in which these claims have to be met?

(a) Any partner's loan (b) Return capital and current account balances

(c) Expenses of dissolution (d) Outsider's claims (payables and accruals)

x	a, b, d & c	
y	c, d, a & b	
z	b, c, a & d	

Appropriation of partnership profit

14.20 Anton, Berty and Carol are in partnership without an agreement. However, Carol is entitled to rent from the partnership at £2,000 per month, while Berty has provided a loan of £50,000 to the partnership. The partnership profit for the year ended 31 December 2008, without deducting rent payable to Carol and any interest to Berty, is £438,400. Identify the share of partnership profit each partner is entitled to.

	Anton	Berty	Carol	
a	£137,300	£139,800	£161,300	
b	£137,300	£137,300	£137,300	
c	£137,300	£137,300	£161,300	
d	£137,300	£139,800	£137,300	

14.21 Alfred, Ben and Charles are in partnership without an agreement. The partnership profit for the year ended 31 March 2012, after writing off £58,400 as bad debts, has been determined as £398,000. The partners have agreed, however, that Alfred should bear £28,000 of the bad debt. Identify the share of partnership profit each partner is entitled to.

	Alfred	Ben	Charles	
a	£142,000	£142,000	£142,000	
b	£132,667	£132,667	£132,666	
c	£114,000	£142,000	£142,000	
d	£123,334	£123,333	£123,333	

14.22 Akbar, Bashir and Cader are in partnership with an agreement that provides for a salary of £2,000 per month to Akbar, interest of their fixed capital balances at 6% per annum and profit sharing in the ratio 3:2:1 respectively. Capital account balances of Akbar, Bashir and Cader were £500,000, £300,000 and £200,000 respectively. Profit for the year ended 31 March 2012 was £728,400. Identify the partnership profit each partner is entitled to in that year.

	Akbar	Bashir	Cader	
a	£137,300	£139,800	£161,300	
b	£214,800	£214,800	£214,800	
c	£268,800	£232,800	£226,800	
d	£376,200	£232,800	£119,400	

14.23 Eddie, Fredie and Girly, with capital balances of £300,000, £200,000 and £200,000, are in partnership, sharing profits and losses in the ratio 2:2:1 respectively, after allowing Girly a salary of £1,500 per month, and all partners interest at 8% per annum on their capital account balances. Rent is payable to Girly at £3,000 per month. Profit for the year ended 30 June 2012, without deducting rent, has been calculated at £104,000. Identify the partnership profit each partner would be entitled to in respect of the year ended 30 June 2012.

	Eddie	Fredie	Girly	
a	£21,600	£13,600	£32,800	
b	£21,600	£13,600	£68,800	
c	£26,400	£18,400	£35,200	
d	£12,000	£12,000	£6,000	

14.24 Lambert and Mirza were in partnership without any agreement. They admitted Newton to partnership on 1 October 2012. Profit of the partnership for the year ended 31 December 2012 was £714,000. Determine each partner's share of profit in each of the following independent scenarios:

(a) Assuming that profit accrued consistently throughout the year

	Lambert	Mirza	Newton	
x	£238,000	£238,000	£238,000	
y	£357,000	£357,000	–	
z	£327,250	£327,250	£59,500	

(b) If sales in each of the three months after admission of Newton was double that in the previous nine months

x	£309,400	£309,400	£95,200	
y	£238,000	£238,000	£238,000	
z	£327,250	£327,250	£59,500	

(c) If sales in the three months after admission of Newton was double that in the previous nine months and you are informed that when arriving at the profit of £714,000 for the year, distribution cost of £280,400 and administrative expenses of £989,100 have been written off

x	£284,673	£284,672	£144,655	
y	£238,000	£238,000	£238,000	
z	£327,250	£327,250	£59,500	

(d) Profits accrued consistently throughout the year but at admission, Newton's share of partnership profit was guaranteed by the partnership at £240,000 per annum

x	£137,300	£139,800	£161,300	
y	£237,000	£237,000	£240,000	
z	£327,000	£327,000	£60,000	

(e) Profits accrued consistently throughout the year but at admission Newton's share of partnership profit was guaranteed by Lambert at £240,000 per annum

x	£326,750	£327,250	£60,000	
y	£146,750	£327,250	£240,000	
z	£268,800	£232,800	£226,800	

(f) Profits accrued consistently throughout the year but at admission, Mirza was assured by Lambert that if Newton's share of profit exceeds £200,000 per annum, Lambert will bear the whole of the excess

x	£326,750	£327,250	£60,000	
y	£317,750	£336,750	£59,500	
z	£322,500	£332,000	£59,500	

14.25 Mary, Nelly and Olive are in partnership on the basis of an agreement which provides for equal sharing of profits after allowing Mary salary at £3,000 per month, but requires interest to be charged on drawings at 6% per annum. Mary drew her salary regularly at the end of each month. Partnership profit for the year ended 30 June 2012 was £312,700. Identify the share of partnership profit of each partner in each of the following independent scenarios:

(a) Mary drew an additional £10,000 on 1 December 2011 while Nelly drew £20,000 on 1 January and Olive £15,000 on 1 April 2012

	Mary	Nelly	Olive	
x	£128,275	£92,025	£92,400	
y	£92,625	£92,625	£92,625	
z	£127,491	£91,242	£91,617	

(b) Nelly and Olive each drew £2,000 per month, Nelly mid-way through the month and Olive on the last day of each month

x	£127,774	£91,053	£91,113	
y	£104,234	£104,233	£104,233	
z	£128,694	£91,973	£92,033	

14.26 Peter and Quintus were in partnership sharing profits in the ratio 3:2 respectively. They admitted Rufus for a fourth share of profit. What will be the new profit-sharing ratio of all three partners in each of the following independent scenarios:

(a) If the examiner gives no instruction whatever

	Peter	Quintus	Rufus	
x	3	2	1	
y	9	6	5	
z	1	1	1	

(b) If Peter and Quintus agreed to hand over equally the portion of profit Rufus is being admitted to

x	3	2	1	
y	19	11	10	
z	1	1	1	

(c) If partners agree that the whole of the share Rufus is entitled to should be given up by Peter

x	7	8	5	
y	3	2	1	
z	1	1	1	

Valuation of goodwill

14.27 Red and Blue, partners, are finalising accounts annually on 31 December, and report their performance as shown on the right. Crimson was admitted to a fourth share of partnership profits on 1 September 2012. What will be the value of goodwill on that date using each of the following alternative formulae:

2009	Profit	£267,000
2010	Loss	£75,000
2011	Profit	£324,000
2012	Profit	£480,000

(a) Goodwill is to be valued at two year purchase of the average profit of the three years preceding the date of valuation

x	£444,000	
y	£344,000	
z	£666,000	

(b) Goodwill is to be valued at two year purchase of the average profit for the three years ending on the date of valuation

x	£344,000	
y	£404,000	
z	£438,667	

(c) Goodwill is to be valued at two year purchase of the average profit for the three years preceding the date of valuation, giving a weight to the first, second and the most recent of these years of 1:2:3 respectively

x	£363,000	
y	£726,000	
z	£463,000	

(d) Goodwill is to be valued at the capitalised amount at 16% per annum of the average annual profits for three years preceding the date of valuation

x	£5,781,250	
y	£1,387,500	
z	£1,075,000	

(e) Goodwill is to be valued at the capitalised value at 10% of the average super profit for three preceding years. Super profit is defined by the partners as the excess profit after taking into account a fair remuneration for services of both partners at £2,000 per month for each and a reasonable return at 6% per annum on the capital employed of £800,000.

x	£760,000	
y	£76,000	
z	£840,000	

Accounting for fair valuation

14.28 Rose and Ivy, sharing profits in the ratio 2:1 respectively, and finalising annual accounts on 31 December, admit Liby for a fourth share of profit on 1 March 2012. Until Liby's admission the balances in the Capital accounts of Rose and Ivy were £300,000 and £200,000 respectively. Liby introduced £200,000 as capital. Their partnership agreement provides for a salary to Rose of £2,000 per month and interest on capital at 6% per annum. Apart from the adjustment to the profit-sharing ratio other terms of the agreement are to continue after the admission of Liby. Profit for the year ended 31 December 2012 was £480,000 and it may be assumed to have accrued consistently throughout the year. Identify the share of profit each partner would be entitled to in each of the following alternative scenarios:

(a) If goodwill, not appearing in the books, is valued on Liby's admission at £300,000 and is to be recorded in the books

	Rose	Ivy	Liby	
x	£258,833	£123,417	£97,750	
y	£264,333	£123,167	£92,500	
z	£234,833	£123,166	£92,500	

(b) If goodwill, not appearing in the books, is valued on Liby's admission at £300,000, and should be adjusted for, but is not to appear in the books

	Rose	Ivy	Liby	
x	£261,833	£121,917	£96,250	
y	£240,333	£123,167	£92,500	
z	£264,333	£123,167	£92,500	

(c) If goodwill, reported already in the books at £120,000, is valued at £300,000 on the date of Liby's admission and is to be reported in the books at the new value

	Rose	Ivy	Liby	
x	£241,833	£126,417	£87,750	
y	£265,833	£126,417	£87,750	
z	£263,333	£122,667	£94,000	

(d) If goodwill, reported in the books at £120,000, is valued on Liby's admission at £300,000. However, the partners have decided that goodwill should not appear in the books

	Rose	Ivy	Liby	
x	£263,333	£122,667	£94,000	
y	£239,333	£122,667	£94,000	
z	£261,833	£121,917	£96,250	

(e) On the date of Liby's admission, non-current assets reported at £400,000 had a fair value of £760,000 and goodwill not recorded in the books is valued at £300,000. The partners have decided to report non-current assets at their fair value but not to record goodwill in the books

	Rose	Ivy	Liby	
x	£240,333	£123,167	£92,500	
y	£267,333	£124,667	£88,000	
z	£264,333	£123,167	£92,500	

Dissolution of partnership

14.29 The Statement of financial position as at 31 March 2012, of Sarah and Terry, sharing profits equally, reported their position as on the right. Current assets included £30,000 cash. Expenses of dissolution amounted to £4,000. Answer the questions below treating each as an independent scenario:

Tangible non current assets	£180,000
Current assets	£120,000
Current liabilities	£80,000

(a) On a piecemeal dissolution sale of the assets realised £240,000 and liabilities were discharged subject to 10% discount. Identify the gain or loss on dissolution of the partnership

x	Loss £26,000	
y	Loss £56,000	
z	Gain £30,000	

(b) Sarah's capital and current accounts totalled £140,000. She took over from the partnership a vehicle acquired for £30,000 and depreciated by £8,000, while the remaining assets were sold for £280,000 and liabilities discharged subject to 20% discount. How much will Sarah receive on closure of the partnership?

x	£125	
y	£142	
z	£140	

14.30 The Statement of financial position as at 30 June 2012, of Green and Amber, equal partners, appear as on the right. Current assets include £30,000 cash. Colourlights Ltd acquired the partnership on this date as a going concern.

Tangible non-current assets	£180,000
Current assets	£120,000
Current liabilities	£80,000

The total of the Capital and Current account balances of Green and Amber, on this date, were £150,000 and £70,000 respectively.

(a) If goodwill was valued at £50,000, while tangible non-current assets and current assets were valued at £240,000 and £110,000 respectively, what is the purchase consideration receivable by the partners from Colourlights?

x	£400,000	
y	£320,000	
z	£480,000	

(b) If the current liabilities of the partnership included a bank overdraft of £26,000 which is not taken over, goodwill was valued at £60,000, while tangible non-current assets and current assets were valued at £220,000 and £100,000 respectively, what is the purchase consideration receivable by the partners from Colourlights?

x	£326,000	
y	£380,000	
z	£434,000	

(c) If Colourlights agreed to discharge the purchase consideration by an allotment to Green and Amber, in their profit-sharing ratio, of 300,000 ordinary shares of £1 each at 120p each and a payment of £40,000 in cash, how much would Colourlights be paying for the partnership goodwill, assuming that all assets were taken over at book value?

x	£400,000	
y	£180,000	
z	£100,000	

(d) If Colourlights valued the tangible non-current assets of the partnership at £240,000 and agreed to discharge the purchase consideration by an allotment equally to both partners of 800,000 ordinary shares of 50p each, at 60p per share, and an issue to Amber of £50,000 6% Loan notes, how much would have been paid for goodwill?

x	£170,000	
y	£200,000	
z	£250,000	

(e) If Colourlights valued the tangible non-current assets at £300,000 and as purchase consideration agreed to allot equally to both partners one million ordinary shares of 20p each at 25p per share and in addition pay £50,000, how much will Green receive in cash when the dissolution of the partnership is completed?

x	£105,000	
y	£50,000	
z	£65,000	

Conversion of partnership books to a company's

14.31 The Statement of financial position as at 31 March 2012, of Rose and Pink, equal partners, appears as shown on the right. Current assets include £30,000 cash. Colours Ltd acquired the business on this date as a going concern. The total of the Capital and Current account balances of Rose and Pink, on this date, were £200,000 and £150,000 respectively. Partners have resolved to convert their books of account into those of a company.

Tangible non-current assets	£300,000
Current assets	£140,000
Current liabilities	£90,000

(a) If purchase consideration is to be discharged by an allotment of 400,000 ordinary shares of £1 each at 120p per share and a payment of £20,000 in cash, what amounts will be reported in the Statement of financial position of Colours Ltd as goodwill and cash upon the conversion?

	Goodwill	Cash	
x	£150,000	£20,000	
y	£50,000	£10,000	
z	£150,000	£10,000	

(b) If in addition to the information in (a) above you are informed that at conversion the tangible non-current assets are fair valued at £380,000 and an allowance for doubtful debts set up at £5,000, at what value will Colours Ltd report goodwill immediately after the conversion?

	Goodwill	
x	£75,000	
y	£65,000	
z	£225,000	

Answers to multiple choice questions

14.1: d 14.2: c 14.3: b 14.4: c 14.5: c 14.6: d 14.7: c 14.8: a 14.9: c 1410: c 14.11: b 14.12: c 14.13: d 14.14: c 14.15: a 14.16: c 14.17: b 14.18: b 14.19: y 14.20: b 14.21: c 14.22: d 14.23: a 14.24a: z 14.24b: x 14.24c: x 14.24d: z 14.24e: x 14.24f: z 14.25a: x 14.25b: z 14.26a: y 14.26b: y 14.26c: x 14.27a: y 14.27b: z 14.27c: x 14.27d: z 14.27e: x 14.28a: y 14.28b: z 14.28c: z 14.28d: x 14.28e: y 14.29a: x 14.29b: z 14.30a: y 14.30b: x 14.30c: y 14.30d: z 14.30e: y 14.31a: z 14.31b: x

Progressive questions

PQ 14.1 Partnership appropriation with no agreement

Trial Balance as at 31 December 2012		
	£'000	£'000
Furniture at cost	280	–
Accumulated depreciation – furniture	–	112
Motor vehicles at cost	240	–
Accumulated depreciation – vehicles	–	72
Inventory – 1.1.2012	112	–
Salaries	96	–
Trade receivables	215	–
Trade payables	–	165
Rent for shop premises	24	–
Advertising	18	–
Purchases	497	–
Carriage inwards	12	–
Sales	–	748
Returns inwards	32	–
Partners' drawings	54	–
Allowance for doubtful debts		7
Cash in hand and at bank	24	–
Capital accounts:		
A	–	200
B	–	200
C	–	100
	1,604	1,604

A, B and C carried on a business in partnership. They extracted their year-end Trial Balance as shown on the left. You are informed as follows:

(i) Goods costing £20,000 removed by partner A for personal use have not been accounted for.

(ii) Inventory costing £152,000 remains unsold.

(iii) Shop premises belong to partner B and rent is agreed at £3,000 per month.

(iv) Furniture and vehicles are to be depreciated at 10% and 20% per annum respectively, using the straight-line method.

(v) £8,000 salaries remain unpaid.

(vi) £15,000 of trade receivables should be written off and allowance for doubtful debts adjusted to cover 5% of remaining receivables.

(vii) Partners A, B and C drew £2,000, £1,500 and £1,000 respectively each month.

Required:

(a) Partner's Capital accounts in columnar form.

(b) Partner's Current accounts in columnar form.

(c) The Statement of income of the partnership for the year ended 31 December 2012.

(d) The Statement of financial position as at that date.

PQ 14.2 Partnership appropriation when there is an agreement

Trial Balance as at 31 March 2012		
	£	£
Land and buildings	580,000	–
Furniture	210,000	–
Motor vehicles	150,000	–
Accumulated depreciation to 31.3.2011:		
Buildings	–	30,000
Furniture	–	48,000
Motor vehicles	–	72,000
Purchases	1,245,000	–
Allowance for doubtful debts	–	8,000
Current a/c:		
X	13,100	–
Y	–	9,000
Z	–	8,000
Salaries	127,000	–
Rent	10,000	–
Loan from Partner Z	–	50,000
Advertising	18,600	–
Sundry expenses	28,200	–
Sales	–	1,822,250
Admin expenses	127,000	–
Inventory – 1.4.2011	198,000	–
Trade receivables	263,900	–
Trade payables	–	121,400
Bank overdraft	–	2,150
Capital a/c:		
X	–	300,000
Y	–	300,000
Z	–	200,000
	2,970,800	2,970,800

The year-end Trial Balance of a business run by X, Y and Z as partners is shown on the left. The partnership agreement provides that:

- X will receive a salary of £3,000 per month.
- Interest will be allowed on fixed capital at 5% per annum.
- Interest to be charged on drawings at 4% p.a.
- X, Y and Z are to share profits and losses in the ratio 3:2:1 respectively.

Further information:

(i) Premises have been rented from Partner Y at £1,000 per month.

(ii) The cost of goods remaining unsold at the year-end is £248,000. £30,000 of these goods, however, are shop-soiled and can only be sold for £21,000 after reconditioning them at a cost of £5,000.

(iii) Salaries account includes the following:
- £30,000 taken as salary by partner X
- £15,000 drawn by partner Y on 1.7.2011
- £10,000 drawn by partner Z on 1.1.2012.

(iv) The loan of £50,000 was obtained from partner Z when the business commenced in 2006.

(v) Trade receivables of £3,900 should be written off and the Allowance for doubtful debts adjusted to cover 4% of remaining debts.

(vi) Land acquired at a cost of £200,000 is not to be depreciated. Buildings, furniture and vehicles are to be depreciated at 2%, 10% and 20% per annum respectively, on cost.

Required:

(a) The partners' Current accounts in columnar format.

(b) the Statement of income for the year ended 31 March 2012 and the Statement of financial position as at that date.

PQ 14.3 Appropriation with a partner admission (ACCA)

For a number of years you have been employed in a senior position by a firm of certified accountants. The two partners, Checke and Tikk, have now offered to take you into the firm as a junior partner with effect from 1 April 2012. Hitherto Checke and Tikk have contributed £50,000 and £30,000, respectively, as their capital. They receive interest on capital at 5% per annum and share profits in the ratio 3:2, respectively.

After admission to the partnership you will be expected to continue managing the practice for which you will receive exactly half your present annual salary of £14,000 as partnership salary. You will also be expected to contribute £20,000 as capital for which you will receive interest at 5% per annum. The profit-sharing ratio will then be altered to give you one-sixth share of profits and losses, without disturbing the relative shares of the other two partners.

For the year ended 31 March 2012 the total amount appropriated by the two partners was £34,000.

Required: Prepare a statement showing the details of the amounts appropriated to Checke and Tikk during the year ended 31 March 2012 together with details of amounts which would have been appropriated if you had been taken into partnership on 1 April 2011.

PQ 14.4 Sharing profits with a new partner

Sydney carried on a retail trade with a capital of £400,000 as at 1 July 2011, in premises owned by Carton, paying rent agreed at £5,000 per month. As from 1 January 2012 Carton was admitted to 40% of partnership profit, on the basis of the following agreement:

(a) Goodwill of the business, valued at £100,000, should not appear in the books of the business.

(b) Carton should bring in £200,000 as his capital.

(c) Sydney should receive a salary of £2,000 per month.

(d) Rent on premises belonging to Carton should be reduced to £1,000 per month.

(e) Interest should be allowed on capital accounts at 6% per annum.

Profit for the year to 30 June 2012, after charging rent only up to 1 January 2012, and without deducting any amount due to either Sydney or Carton under the partnership agreement, has been ascertained to be £150,000. Assume that profit accrued evenly throughout the year.

Required: Show the appropriation of profit for the year ended 30 June 2012 among the partners.

PQ 14.5 Formation of a new partnership (CAT 6)

Statements of financial Position as at 31 May 2012

	Little	Sutton
	£'000	£'000
Non-current assets:		
Freehold property	110	–
Plant and equipment	25	70
Current assets:		
Inventory	15	12
Trade receivables	10	8
Bank and cash	15	8
	175	98
	£'000	£'000
Capital	160	79
Current liabilities:		
Trade payables	15	19
	175	98

A Little and B Sutton were two sole traders in the same line of business. On 1 June 2012 they decided to merge their businesses to form a partnership called Little Sutton. It was agreed that Little and Sutton will share profits in the ratio 2:1. Their Statements of financial position have been prepared as shown on the left. Additional information:

(i) On 1 June 2012 the freehold property was valued at £120,000 and plant and equipment held until now by Sutton was valued at £55,000.

(ii) Goodwill agreed at £35,000 for Little and £25,000 for Sutton is not to be carried in partnership books.

(iii) All assets and liabilities of the separate businesses were taken over by the partnership.

Required: The Statement of financial position of the partnership as soon as it was formed, and identify the advantages and disadvantages of operating as a partnership.

PQ 14.6 Admission of a new partner in the year and retirement of another

Trial Balance as at 31 December 2010		
	£'000	£'000
Capital accounts:		
Alpha	–	500
Beta	–	300
Gamma	–	400
Drawings:		–
Alpha on 1 September 2010	15	
Beta	30	
Sales		1,500
Inventory – 31.12.2010	214	–
Cost of sales	624	–
Operating expenses	222	–
Land and buildings at wdv	860	–
Furniture at wdv	280	–
Depreciation – furniture	40	–
Depreciation – buildings	14	–
Salaries	36	
Advertising	48	–
Receivables/payables	484	312
Bank	145	–
	3,012	3,012

Alpha and Beta were in partnership sharing profits in the ratio 2:1 respectively, after allowing salary at £3,000 per month to Beta and interest on capital at 6% per annum. No interest is charged on drawings. On 1 May 2010 Gamma was admitted to a fourth share of profit and he brought in as his capital £400,000. On 1 September Alpha retired, but agreed to leave his entitlements behind, as a loan, on which interest was agreed at 10% per annum.

Goodwill, which is not to appear in the books of the partnership, was valued at £240,000 on 1 May 2010 and at £300,000 on 1 September 2010.

You may assume that sales and expenses of the partnership accrued consistently throughout the year.

Required:

(a) Show how you appropriated the partnership profits in the year ended 31 December 2010.

(b) Set out the partnership's Statement of financial position as at 31 December 2010.

Round off to nearest £'000.

PQ 14.7 Piecemeal dissolution of a partnership (ACCA)

Statement of financial position as at 31 December 2012			
Non-current assets:	Cost	Accumulated depreciation	£
Land and buildings	350,000	(50,000)	300,000
Plant and machinery	220,000	(104,100)	115,900
Motor vehicles	98,500	(39,900)	58,600
Current assets:			
Inventory		110,600	
Trade receivables		89,400	
Cash and bank		12,600	212,600
			687,100
			£
Capital – Alpha		233,600	
Beta		188,900	
Gamma		106,200	528,700
Loan from Delta at 10% p.a.			40,000
Trade payables			118,400
			687,100

Alpha, Beta and Gamma were in partnership for many years sharing profits and losses in the ratio 5:3:2, respectively, and making up their accounts to 31 December each year. Alpha died on 31 December 2012 and the partnership was dissolved as from that date. The Statement of financial position as at that date is shown on the left. Dissolution progressed as follows:

(i) Land and buildings were sold for £380,000 and machinery for £88,000. Beta and Gamma took over the cars they were using valued at £9,000 and £14,000 respectively, and the remaining cars were sold for £38,000.

(ii) Inventory was taken over by Gamma at an agreed value of £120,000. £68,400 was collected from trade receivables and the remainder taken over by Gamma at an agreed value of £20,000.

(iii) Payables were all settled for £115,000.

(iv) Delta's loan was settled on 31 March 2013 along with interest until that date.

(v) Expenses of dissolution were met at £2,400.

Required: Set out the (a) Realisation account, (b) Capital accounts and (c) Cash Book recording the closure of the partnership by 31 March 2013.

PQ 14.8 Disposal of a partnership as a going concern

Statement of financial position as at 31 March 2012		
Non-current assets:		£'000
Property, plant	740	
Accumulated depreciation	(280)	460
Investments		80
Current assets:		
Inventory	482	
Trade receivables	320	
Cash and bank	8	810
		1,350
		£'000
Capital – Lock	500	
– Stock	300	
– Barrel	200	1,000
Current – Lock	4 Cr	
Stock	8 Dr	
Barrel	6 Dr	(10)
Trade payable		328
Bank overdraft		32
		1,350

Lock, Stock and Barrel were in partnership sharing profits and losses in the ratio 3:2:1 respectively. Their Statement of financial position as at 31.3.2012 was prepared as shown on the left. They decided to form a company to take over the business on the following basis:

(a) Lock would take over the investments, valuing them for the purpose at £95,000, and also take responsibility for the bank overdraft.

(b) LSB Ltd will take over the business as a going concern for a consideration to be discharged as follows:

- allotment to the partners, in their profit sharing ratio, of 800,000 ordinary shares of £1 each at 1.20p each;
- issue to Lock of £100,000 6% Loan note at par; and
- payment of £20,000 in cash.

The decisions were carried out and expenses of dissolution were met at £3,000.

Required:

(a) Set out the closure of the partnership books.

(b) Assuming that LSB Ltd valued property and plant at £600,000 and took over the receivables subject to an allowance of 5%, set out LSB's:

(i) Purchase of business account

(ii) The opening Statement of financial position.

PQ 14.9 Conversion of a partnership to a limited company

Answer question PQ 14.8 again, but this time on the basis that Lock, Stock and Barrel have decided to convert the partnership books of account into those of LSB Ltd (rather than opening a new set of books for the limited company).

PQ 14.10 Another conversion of a partnership to a limited company

Andrew, Berty and Clive, who carried on a partnership business, sharing profits in the ratio 2:2:1 respectively, have drafted their Statement of financial position as at 30 June 2012 as shown below:

Statement of financial position as at 30 June 2012

	Cost	Accumulated depreciation	£'000
Property	400	–	400
Furniture	320	(140)	180
Motor vehicles	280	(112)	168
Current assets:			
Inventory		396	
Trade receivables	480	465	
Less: Allowance for doubtful debts	(15)	35	
Cash and bank balance			896
			1,644

			£'000
Partners' accounts	Capital	Current	
Andrew	600	100 Cr	700
Berty	500	180 Dr	320
Clive	400	60 Dr	340
Current liabilities:			
Trade payables			284
			1,644

The partnership was converted to a limited company on this date. The company, registered as Abec Ltd, took over all the assets and liabilities of the partnership on the basis of the following agreement:

(a) Property was taken over at its current market value of £550,000.

(b) Trade receivables were taken over subject to adjusting the allowance to cover 5% of receivables.

(c) Purchase consideration was discharged by an allotment to partners, in their profit-sharing ratio, of 1,000,000 ordinary shares of £1 each in Abec Ltd at 150p per share and a payment of £20,000 in cash.

Required: Set out the accounts that need to be written up to convert the partnership books to those of Abec Ltd and the Statement of financial position of Abec Ltd on the day it opened its books of account.

Test questions

Test 14.1 Appropriation of profit – basic level

	Andy	Berty	Camron
Interest on capital	£750	£500	£250
Interest on drawings	(£30)	(£65)	(£25)
Interest on loan	£90	–	–
Rent	–	–	£18,000
Salary	–	£12,000	£6,000
Residual profit	£24,000	£18,000	£12,000
	£24,810	£30,435	£36,225

In respect of the year ended 31 March 2012, partners Andy, Berty and Camron have been told that the partners' entitlements are as stated on the left.

Required:

(a) Identify the amount of the partnership profit in the year ended 31 March 2012.

(b) Camron points out that the appropriation has failed to take into account a guarantee he was given, when he joined the partnership three years earlier, that his share of profit would be at minimum £20,000 per annum. Taking the guarantee into account, identify the amount of current year's profit each partner will be able to draw out.

Test 14.2 Partnership with an agreement – basic

Trial Balance as at 31 December 2012		
	£'000	£'000
Sales revenue	–	1,474
Furniture and fittings	180	–
Motor vehicles at cost	240	–
Accumulated depreciation:		
Furniture and fittings	–	54
Motor vehicles	–	160
Returns inwards	34	–
Returns outwards	–	19
Trade receivables	184	–
Bad debt written off	9	–
Salaries	112	–
Rent	18	–
Carriage inwards	29	–
Inventory at 31.12.2011	284	–
Capital a/c – Sarah	–	300
Capital a/c – Betty	–	100
Purchases	998	–
Advertising	32	–
General expenses	94	–
Discount allowed	8	–
Allowance for d. debts	–	14
Trade payables	–	124
Current a/c – Sarah	–	32
Current a/c – Betty	14	–
Cash and bank	41	–
	2,277	2,277

Sarah and Betty were in partnership sharing profits and losses in the ratio they contributed their capital, after allowing interest at 6% per annum on their fixed Capital account balances and allowing Betty a salary of £2,000 per month. The premises used by the business belong to Sarah who has been promised a rent of £2,000 per month. The Trial Balance extracted at the year-end is set out on the left. You are informed as follows:

(i) Salaries account includes £22,000 drawn by Betty.

(ii) Goods costing £8,000 removed by Sarah for personal use have not been accounted for.

(iii) As at the year-end advertising £9,000 and general expenses £12,000 remain unpaid.

(iv) Trade receivables of £4,000 should be written off and the allowance for doubtful debts adjusted to cover 5% of remaining trade receivables.

(v) Depreciation should be written off on furniture and motor vehicles at 10% and 20% per annum respectively, using the reducing balance method.

(vi) Cost of year-end inventory has been ascertained to be £364,000. This includes at £24,000 the cost of some shop-soiled items which are expected to be sold for £17,000 after reconditioning them at a cost of £2,000.

Required:

The Statement of income for the year ended 31 December 2012 and the Statement of financial position as at that date.

Test 14.3 Admission of a partner and goodwill adjustment – basic

Trial Balance as at 31 December 2012		
	£'000	£'000
Non-current assets	840	–
Accumulated depreciation	–	198
Capital:		
M	–	200
N	–	200
Cash introduced by Q	–	150
Current assets	124	–
Profit for the year		216
	964	964

M and N were in partnership sharing profits in the ratio 2:1 respectively, until Q was admitted to a fourth share of profits on 1 July 2012. Goodwill was valued on that date at £120,000 but is not to appear in the books of the partnership. The Trial Balance of the partnership extracted at the year-end is set out on the left. The partnership agreement provides for interest on capital account balances at 5% per annum.

Required: The Statement of income for the year ended 31 December 2012 and the Statement of financial position as at that date.

Test 14.4 Admission of a new partner – advanced

Blue and Green were in partnership, sharing profits in the ratio 2:1 respectively, after allowing 4% per annum interest on capital and paying Green a salary of £1,000 per month. Red worked as their office manager and was paid a salary of £1,000 per month. Red was admitted to partnership as from 1 January 2012 on the basis of the following agreement:

- Green, Blue and Red are to share profits in the ratio 2:1:1 respectively, after continuing to allow interest on capital at 4% per annum and continuing to pay Green a salary of £1,000 per month.
- Red's loan is to be regarded as his capital and, as a partner, Red will cease to receive any salary.
- Land is to be revalued and recorded at £450,000.
- Goodwill, valued at £240,000, is not to be recorded.

Trial Balance as at 31 March 2012		
	£'000	£'000
Land at cost	300	–
Machinery	1,200	–
Motor vehicles at cost	180	–
Accumulated depreciation to 31.3.2012		
Machinery	–	360
Motor vehicles	–	120
Inventory at 31.3.2012	394	–
Selling expenses	16	
Sales revenue	–	1,440
Trade receivables	266	
Capital – Green	–	800
Capital – Blue	–	400
6% Loan from Red	–	400
Cost of goods sold	972	–
Salaries and postage	117	–
Telephone and postage	28	–
Advertising	32	–
Trade payables	–	198
Drawings by partners	39	–
Current a/c – Green	–	42
Current a/c – Blue	27	–
Other expenses	174	–
Cash and bank	15	–
	3,760	3,760

The year-end Trial Balance of the partnership is shown on the left. You are further informed as follows:

(i) Salary drawn by Green, regularly on the last day of each month, is included in the Salaries account.

(ii) Interest paid on Red's loan, until his admission to partnership, is included within Other expenses; while the salary drawn by him until that date is included in the Salaries account.

(iii) Reported in the Drawings account are the following:

- £2,000 drawn regularly per month by Green.
- £1,000 drawn regularly per month by Blue.
- £1,000 per month drawn by Red after 1.1.2012.

(iv) Assume that income and expenses, unless indicated otherwise, accrued consistently throughout the year.

Required: The Statement of income for the year ended 31 March 2012 and the Statement of financial position as at that date.

Test 14.5 Piecemeal dissolution of a partnership – basic

Statement of financial position as at 31 December 2012	£'000
Non-current assets at cost	890
Accumulated depreciation	(240)
	650
Investments	45
Inventory	328
Receivables	180
Cash and bank balance	36
	1,239
	£'000
Capital a/cs:	
Alpha	500
Beta	300
Current a/cs:	
Alpha	44
Beta (debit balance)	(9)
Trade payables	380
Accrued expenses	24
	1,239

Alpha and Beta, in partnership, and sharing profits in the ratio 3:2 respectively, drafted their Statement of financial position as set out on the left, and decided to dissolve their partnership. The dissolution progressed as follows:

(i) Alpha took over a vehicle which was acquired for £54,000 and had been depreciated by this date to £30,000; while Beta took over the investments at an agreed value of £54,000.

(ii) Inventory realised £218,000 and receivables were collected subject to 20% write-off.

(iii) Trade payables were settled receiving a discount of 10%.

(iv) Non-current assets realised £450,000.

(v) Expenses of dissolution amounted to £11,000.

Required: Record these transactions showing the closure of the partnership books.

Test 14.6 Conversion of partnership into a company – advanced

Rosy, Serah and Terese carried on a business in partnership, sharing profits in the ratio 2:1:1 respectively, and their Statement of financial position on 31 March 2012 was prepared as shown on the right. They decided to convert their business into a limited company from that date, on the following basis:

(a) Rosy would take over at a value of £10,000 the vehicle she had been using and take personal responsibility for the bank overdraft. The vehicle used by Rosy had been acquired by the partnership for £40,000 and depreciated by £8,000 as at the date of conversion.

(b) The limited company, named RST Ltd, will take over the machinery at a value of £200,000 and trade receivables subject to an Allowance for doubtful debts of 5%.

(c) The purchase consideration is to be discharged as follows:

   (i) Allotment to Rosy, Serah and Terese, in their profit-sharing ratio, of 500,000 ordinary shares of £1 each at 120p each.

   (ii) Payment of £14,000 in cash.

Required:

(a) Set out the Realisation account, the Cash account and the partners' Capital accounts, recording the closure of the partnership books, assuming the cash adjustments were made among the partners.

(b) Set out the Statement of financial position of RST Ltd, as soon as it was opened.

Statement of financial position as at 31 March 2012

			£'000
Non-current assets:			
Machinery	300	(120)	180
Motor vehicles	180	(120)	60
Current assets:			
Inventory		324	
Trade receivables	280		
Allowance	(15)	265	
Cash and bank		16	605
			845

		£'000
Capital accounts:		
Rosy	300	
Serah	100	
Terese	100	500
Current account:		
Rosy	74 Cr	
Serah	26 Cr	
Terese	18 Dr	82
Current liabilities:		
Trade payables	229	
Bank overdraft	34	263
		845

PART C

ACCOUNTING FOR CURRENT ASSETS AND LIABILITIES

Chapter 15

Bank account and bank reconciliation

By the end of this chapter

You should learn:

- Typical entries in a bank account
- The need for and method of bank reconciliation
- About cash discount and how it is accounted for
- How petty cash is controlled on an imprest system

You should be able to:

- Write up a two-column and three-column Cash Book
- Prepare bank reconciliation statements
- Operate a petty cash system

15.1 The balance in a bank account

We learned in Chapter 2 that, for the sake of security and convenience, a business would operate a bank account. In that chapter we illustrated accounting for deposits made into the bank and payments made out of the bank by drawing cheques. There are, of course, many other ways in which the balance held in the bank may increase or decrease.

We learned that the balance held with a bank would increase whenever a deposit is made of cash or cheques. The balance could also increase for reasons such as:

- **Credit transfers** where customers choose to settle amounts due by instructing their bank to settle the dues by electronically transferring the amount from their bank account to that of the business. When the business is advised of the receipt by the bank, it debits the Bank account and credits the account of the customer involved.
- **Mandates** issued by a business to its bank to collect any amounts due to it (say dividends from companies in which the business has invested). As with credit transfers the business makes accounting entries in its books upon receiving information from the bank by debiting the bank account and crediting the appropriate income account (say dividend received account).
- **Receiving sale proceeds electronically when the customer uses a debit card** which authorises the issuer of the card to make immediate transfer from the customer's bank to

that of the business. The transfer is accounted for with a debit in the bank account and a credit in the Sales account.

The accounting is different in a situation where the customer uses a **credit card** to settle the sale proceeds. The credit card authorises the issuer of the card (say Barclays) to accept responsibility for settling the sale proceeds. Upon receiving an authorisation from the issuer of the credit card, the transaction is accounted for with a credit in the Sales account and a debit in an account opened in the name of the issuer of the credit card. The amount due from the credit-card issuer is settled when the amount is received from them.

- **Bank loan**, which, on approval by the bank, is accounted for by a debit in the Bank account and credit in a Bank loan account.

We learned also that normally the bank balance of a business decreases on the basis of instructions the business sends to its bank by writing out cheques. The balance at bank could decrease also for other reasons such as:

- **Standing orders** issued by the business to its bank to transfer, at specified intervals, a stated amount from its account to that of a third party. This method of payment is often used when the amount is known and the payment is needed at regular intervals. Examples are rent and trade subscriptions.
- **Direct debit** instructions given by the business to its bank authorising it to pay whatever amount is requested, from time to time, by a third party. This is a convenient method of making payments when (as with electricity, gas and telephone) the amount that needs to be paid varies.
- **Bank charges and loan interest**: the bank recovers its charges (as well as interest on any loans provided by it) from the bank account held with it. On receiving the bank's intimation of this the bank account is credited and the appropriate expense account debited.
- **Payments made using BACS** which is an acronym for Bankers' Automated Clearing Services and used commonly to pay staff salary.
- **Withdrawal of cash from the bank** either by writing out a 'cash cheque' or using a debit card to draw cash from an automatic teller machine (ATM).

15.2 The two-column Cash Book

We have learned that the Cash account and the Bank account may be written up separately, but it is more convenient to use parallel columns on the same folio of the Cash Book to account for both Cash account and Bank account. Such a Cash Book is known as a *two-column Cash Book*. A folio in the two-column Cash Book appears as follows:

Cash Book

Date	V	Particulars	F	Cash	Bank	Date	V	Chq no	Particulars	F	Cash	Bank
2012				£	£	2012					£	£
1.5		Balance b/f		26,450	–	1.5		–	Bank a/c	C	25,000	–
1.5	x	Cash a/c	C	–	25,000	1.5	x	A001	Rent a/c		–	1,200
1.5	x	Sales a/c		2,250	–	1.5	x	–	Wages a/c		24	–

The folio column remains to be filled in with the folio number of the account to which each amount is posted, after the posting is done. Note that when a deposit is made into the bank the debit entry and the credit entry appear on the same Cash Book folio, with the letter C entered in the folio column. The letter C (which is an abbreviation for the word *contra*, meaning 'opposite' in Latin) indicates that the corresponding second entry is on the opposite side of the same folio.

Activity 15.1 Writing up a two-column Cash Book

Baker and Co's had cash in hand of £455 and cash at bank of £7,540 on 1 July 2012 when the following transactions took place:

(i) Paid £1,450 to Salt Ltd, a trade creditor, by cheque no 0475.

(ii) Received a cheque for £1,245 from Paul May, a trade debtor.

(iii) Paid £150 for advertising by cheque no 0476.

(iv) Cash sales £478.

(v) Paid £35 in cash for office cleaning material.

(vi) Sales of £725 were paid for by debit card.

(vii) Paid £1,800 as rent by standing order.

(viii) Bank advised a credit transfer for £840 had been received from June Kelly, a trade debtor, and bank charges of £40 had been taken from the account.

(ix) Deposited £2,000 (cheque £1,245 + cash £755) into the bank account.

(x) Drew £200 from an ATM cash machine.

Required: Record these transactions in a two-column Cash Book.

15.3 Accounting in the books of the bank

Let us assume that Drake Stores opened a bank account on 1 July, making two deposits on the same day and writing out three cheques. When these transactions are recorded, the bank account of Drake Stores will report a debit balance of £3,400 at the end of the day as follows:

Bank account

Date	Particulars	£	Date	Chq no	Particulars	£
1.7	Cash a/c	4,000	1.7	001	Joe Ritter's a/c	1,200
1.7	Cash a/c	1,450	1.7	002	Rent a/c	500
			1.7	003	Advertising a/c	350
			1.7	–	Balance c/d	3,400
		5,450				5,450
2.7	Balance b/d	3,400				

The bank in turn will need to write up its own books of account and, obviously, it will do so from its own point of view. For instance, when it receives the first deposit of

£4,000 from Drake Stores, the bank would record the amount as a receipt (debit) in its Cash Book and post the amount to the credit of an account opened in the name of the customer – Drake Stores. If both deposits made and the three cheques drawn on the bank are all accounted for in the bank's books, the account written up for the customer – Drake Stores – in the bank's books (see on the right) would be a mirror image of the bank account written up in Drake Stores' books. At regular intervals, the bank sends to its customer a copy of that customer's account in its own ledger. This is known as the *bank statement*. On receiving the bank statement Drake Stores gets confirmation of the accuracy of the balance reported in its own bank account.

Drake Stores' account

Date	Particulars	£	Date	Particulars	£
1.7	Chq 001	1,200	1.7	Cash a/c	4,000
1.7	Chq 002	500	1.7	Cash a/c	1,450
1.7	Chq 003	350			
1.7	Balance c/d	3,400			
		5,450			5,450
			2.7	Balance b/d	3,400

Observe that the bank's statement confirms a credit balance because from its own point of view Drake Stores represents a liability. Although the business and the bank are accounting for the same transactions, they are each doing so from their own point of view.

Theoretically the balance reported by the bank should be the same as that reported by its customer. However, this is not so in real life because of reasons such as the following:

1. The bank may not give credit to the business for the deposits the business made until these are cleared or realised. Clearing is a process in which a cheque deposited in a bank is presented to and is settled by the bank to which the cheque is addressed – a process which usually takes around three days.
2. Cheques issued by the business may not be presented by the payee promptly to the bank for payment. There could be time lag, e.g. due to postal delay.

Let us, therefore, next assume a scenario in which:

- the second deposit by Drake Stores of £1,450 was a cheque drawn by a customer of Drake Store and this cheque is not cleared (and, therefore, the deposit not recorded in the bank's books) until three days later;
- the cheque 002 for £500 drawn by Drake Stores in the name of its landlord was not presented to Drake's bank for payment until a week later.

In this scenario the bank would confirm Drake Stores' bank balance as at the end of business on 1 July as £2,450 (see the bank statement on the right). This balance does not agree with the bank balance of £3,400 stated in Drake's Cash Book. Let us be clear that neither party has made a mistake and yet the balances reported by each do not match, merely because each is reporting on the basis of information available up to that point of time.

Drake Stores' account

Date	Particulars	£	Date	Particulars	£
1.7	Chq 001	1,200	1.7	Cash a/c	4,000
1.7	Chq 003	350			
1.7	Balance c/d	2,450			
		4,000			4,000
			2.7	Balance b/d	2,450

15.4 The need for a bank reconciliation statement

Reconciliation is the process of agreeing information from two different sources. If the two sources are independent of each other, the reconciliation of the information provided by each would corroborate the other. In the real world the amount stated in a bank statement, as a customer's bank balance on a particular date, is unlikely to be the same as the bank balance in that customer's Cash Book. The main reasons are as follows.

15.4.1 Items not appearing in the bank statements

(a) Deposits into the customer's bank account awaiting clearance, i.e. not yet accounted for by the bank and not, therefore, appearing in the bank statement and (b) cheques issued by the customer but yet to be presented to the bank for payment and not, therefore, appearing in the bank statement.

15.4.2 Items not appearing in the Cash Book

The Cash Book of the customer may not have been written up with particulars of transactions that have been recorded by the bank but are not known to the customer until a bank statement is received. For example (a) amounts paid in directly to the business's bank account (such as by credit transfers or mandates), (b) amounts paid out by the bank on the instructions of the customer (such as on standing order, by direct debit or BACS) and (c) amounts recovered by the bank from the customer's bank account (bank charges and interest).

15.4.3 Errors in the Cash Book

A cheque payment of £6,000 recorded as £600, for example.

15.4.4 Errors in the bank's accounting

The customer's account has been credited wrongly with a deposit made by another of its customers.

If, for one or more of these reasons, the balance reported in a bank statement disagrees with the bank balance stated in the Cash Book, a *bank reconciliation statement* is prepared.

15.5 Preparing a bank reconciliation statement

The aim of preparing a bank reconciliation statement is to ensure that the Cash Book (and hence the Statement of financial position) reports a bank balance which is not only accurate but is also one that has been confirmed by the bank. The reconciliation is always as at a specific date. The date does not necessarily have to be the last day of the accounting period nor even the last date of a calendar month. Reconciliation could well be the balance as at any date – say 7 May.

The procedure of preparing a bank reconciliation statement is as follows:

1. Trace each item in the bank statements to the bank account in the Cash Book to identify every item appearing in the bank statement but not in the Cash Book.

2. Trace each item in the bank account (of the Cash Book) to the bank statement to identify:
   - bank deposits awaiting clearance; and
   - cheques drawn but not appearing in the bank statement because they are yet to be presented to the bank for payment.

Referring back to Drake Stores, a comparison of the information in Drake Stores' Cash Book with that in the corresponding account written up by the bank identifies that the differences arise from a deposit of £1,450 awaiting clearance and a cheque for £500 that has not been presented to the bank for payment. A bank reconciliation statement is prepared (see on the right) to explain the reason for the two amounts differing.

Bank reconciliation statement as at 1 July 2012	
	£
Balance as per bank statement	2,450
Add: Deposits awaiting clearance	1,450
Less: Cheques drawn not presented	(500)
Balance as reported in the Cash Book	3,400

15.6 Need to amend the Cash Book prior to reconciliation

The bank statement, when received, may contain information which the business may not be aware of until then. For illustrating this aspect, let us assume that the bank statement received by Drake Stores at the end of business on 1 July reports a balance of £938 (see on the right). A comparison of the information in the bank statement with that recorded in Drake Store's Cash Book has identified four differences between them as:

Drake Stores in account with **Midwest Bank plc**			
Particulars	Debit	Credit	Balance
Deposit	–	£4,000	£4,000
Charges	£12	–	£3,988
Chq 003	£350	–	£3,638
s/o Rates	£1,500	–	£2,138
Chq 001	£1,200	–	£938

- The Cash Book fails to record £12 recovered by the bank as bank charges as well as £1,500 paid as business rates by the bank, acting on a standing order issued by Drake Stores.
- The bank statement fails to record (a) the deposit (of a customer's cheque) for £1,450 awaiting clearance and (b) the cheque 02 for £500 (paid as rent) which is yet to be presented.

The first step to achieving a reconciliation is for Drake Stores to amend its Cash Book to include the payment of the bank charges and the rates, which the cashier has overlooked and which need to be accounted for, to identify the amount Drake Stores actually holds in its bank account. Next we should inquire into why the amount reported in the bank statement (£938) differs

Bank account (in Drake Stores' Cash Book)

	£		£
Balance b/f	3,400	Bank charges	12
		Rates a/c	1,500
		Balance c/d	1,888
	3,400		3,400
Balance b/d	1,888		

from the correct amount held in the bank and prepare the bank reconciliation statement (see on the right) so that it could be proven that the information conveyed in the bank statement is consistent with that reported in the Cash Book, after it has been amended.

Bank reconciliation statement as at 1 July 2012	
	£
Balance as per bank statement	938
Add: Deposits awaiting clearance	1,450
Less: Cheque 02 yet to be presented	(500)
Balance as per Cash Book	1,888

Activity 15.2 A bank reconciliation statement

Reward Bros' Cash Book reported a bank balance on 14 September 2012 of £17,240 which did not match the balance reported in the bank statement. Inquiries revealed that:

(i) bank deposits totalling £15,940 were awaiting clearance;
(ii) cheques to the value of £8,450 drawn by Reward Bros were yet to be presented to the bank;
(iii) a bank charge of £25 made by the bank had not yet been recorded in the Cash Book.

Required: Prepare a bank reconciliation statement as at 14 September 2012 using the two-stage approach by first identifying the correct bank account balance which should appear in the Cash Book and then reconciling that adjusted balance with the balance stated in the bank statement.

It is possible that the Cash Book may report a bank overdraft (i.e. a credit balance in the bank account reporting a liability which arises when payments made out of the bank exceed the amount deposited with them); whereas, because of substantial value of cheques yet to be presented to the bank for payment, the bank statement may report a favourable bank balance.

Activity 15.3 A bank reconciliation involving an overdraft

The bank account in the Cash Book reports an overdraft of £7,250 as at 19 July 2012, whereas the bank statement reports a favourable (credit) balance. The difference has arisen because of:

(i) deposits awaiting clearance on that day £11,450;
(ii) cheques yet to be presented for payment £30,340.

Required: Prepare a bank reconciliation statement as at 19 July 2012.

Activity 15.4 Correcting the Cash Book prior to reconciliation

The Bank account in the Cash Book reports a balance of £11,400 as at 10 December 2012 whereas the corresponding amount in the bank statement is an overdraft of £2,450. When preparing the reconciliation, the cashier detects the following:

(i) bank charges of £35 have been entered twice in the Cash Book;
(ii) cheques drawn to the value of £18,850 do not appear in the bank statement;
(iii) business rates of £1,200 paid by standing order is not recorded in the Cash Book.

The remainder of the difference arises from deposits awaiting clearance.

Required: Prepare:
(a) an amended bank account in the Cash Book;
(b) a bank reconciliation statement.

15.7 Cash discount or settlement discount

Having agreed with its customer a credit period of say 30 days, a business may offer a discount as an inducement to receive prompt payment. Such discounts are known as *cash discounts* or *settlement discounts*. A business may opt to allow a cash discount to its credit customers rather than pay interest on a bank loan. Similarly, the business may earn cash discounts by early settlement of suppliers' accounts. A cryptic message appearing on an invoice may state – Terms 5/7 n/30. What this message means is that:

5/7 announces a 5% cash discount if the invoice is settled within seven days;

n/30 confirms the 30 days' credit period approved for the customer.

15.8 The three-column Cash Book

15.8.1 Accounting for discount allowed

A customer who owes £100 and avails himself of a 5% cash discount will send in a cheque for £95 and would expect the whole of his debt to be cleared. To facilitate this, the normal practice is to build in a discount column on the receipt side of the Cash Book so that when recording the amount of the cheque in the Cash Book, the discount entitlement of the customer could be recorded at the same time in the discount column. When posting to the Trade receivables ledger the customer's account is credited with both the cheque amount and the discount allowed amount from the prime entry in the discount column. The total of the discount column is periodically posted to the debit of a Discount allowed account in the Nominal ledger.

To illustrate, let us assume that a 5% cash discount was offered to customers and that two customers, Ted Smith and Jude Burns, sent in the appropriate net amounts in settlement of £10,000 owed by Ted and £20,000 owed by Jude. The amounts received are debited in the Cash Book and credited to the individual customers' accounts. It is part of the cashier's duty, immediately after recording the amounts received, to calculate the appropriate cash discount each customer becomes entitled to and enter that amount in the discount column on the debit side of the Cash Book. The accounts would be as follows:

Cash Book (receipt side)

Date	F	Particulars	F	Discount	Cash	Bank
2012				£	£	£
4.7		Ted Smith's a/c		500	9,500	–
5.7		Jude Burns' a/c		1,000	19,000	–
		Total (expense)		1,500		

Ted Smith's account

		£			£
Sales Day Book	?	10,000	Cash a/c	?	9,500
			Discount allowed a/c	?	500
		10,000			10,000

Jude Burns' account

		£			£
Sales Day Book	?	20,000	Cash a/c	?	19,000
			Discount allowed a/c	?	1,000
		20,000			20,000

Discount allowed account

		£			
Cash Book	?	1,500			

Note that the double-entry to record the discount allowed is to credit each customer's account with the appropriate discount entitlement and debit Discount allowed account with the periodical total of the discount column. This means that the entry made in the Cash Book does not constitute one of the pair of entries accounting for discount allowed. Hence the discount column in the Cash Book serves only as a subsidiary book of accounts.

Activity 15.5 Accounting for discount allowed

Ridleys Novelties is a wholesaler, selling to retailers on one month's credit and allowing them 4% cash discount if their remittance is received within a week of sale. The receipts from customers during March 2012 were as follows:

Date	Customer	Cheque	Received within seven days
4.3	Robinson Ltd	£25,800	£17,280 of the amount
9.3	Tomlinson Bros	£13,440	Whole amount
14.3	Samuel and Son	£43,200	Whole amount
17.3	Patricia and Co.	£19,500	£14,400 of the amount
25.3	Gamage plc	£16,800	Whole amount

Required: Account for the above transactions, showing the prime entry as well as the ledger accounts. Assume that discounts allowed are posted in total at the end of the month.

15.8.2 Accounting for discount received

Discounts earned by a business from paying its suppliers within agreed periods are accounted for similarly. The cashier makes the prime entry in a Discount column built, this time, on the credit side of the Cash Book. The pair of entries to account for discount received are made when each supplier's account is debited individually and the Discount received (income) account is credited in total, usually periodically.

Activity 15.6 Accounting for discount received

Ridleys Novelties purchases its supplies on one month's credit, on terms which allow 6% discount if payment is made within a week of purchase. Payments to suppliers in May 2012 were as stated on the right. All payments, other than the one on 6 May, were made within the discount period.

Date	Customer	Cheque
2.5	Bragabout plc	£68,150
6.5	Tellaround plc	£22,500
16.5	Whocares plc	£32,524
24.5	Sowhat plc	£27,072

Required: Account for these payments showing the prime entry as well as the ledger accounts.

A Cash Book with Discount columns built into its either side is called a *three-column Cash Book* and would appear as shown below:

Cash Book

Date	V	Particulars	F	Disc	Cash	Bank	Date	V	Chq	Particulars	F	Disc	Cash	Bank
2012					£	£	2012						£	£

15.9 Dishonour of a customer's cheque and reversal of discount allowed

A cheque received from a customer and duly deposited in the bank may be returned by the bank usually with an endorsement *refer to drawer*. There could be a number of reasons why the bank has not credited the account, e.g. the customer has forgotten to sign it or has dated it wrongly (say as 5 May 2022 instead of 5 May 2012) or, more seriously from the business point of view, because the customer has insufficient funds to meet the cheque. Whatever the reason may be for the cheque being dishonoured, upon receiving the cheque back from the bank, the business would draw the situation to the attention of the customer and account for the dishonour (i.e. return of the cheque) by crediting the bank account and debiting the account of the customer concerned.

If the customer had already been allowed a cash discount, then it will be cancelled by reversing the ledger entries. For example, assuming that Ted Smith had been allowed a cash discount of £500 on an invoiced amount of £10,000, the accounting entries recording the reversal of discount will be as shown on the right.

Dr Ted Smith' account	£500
Cr Discount Allowed a/c	£500

15.10 The petty cash systems

15.10.1 Importance of proper petty cash systems

Many organisations, ranging from charities to universities to businesses, have a need to pay for some day-to-day items in cash. Although the amounts might not be large in relation to an organisation's overall cash resources, the control of petty cash is taken very seriously, e.g. The National Council for Voluntary Organisations (NCVO) states that petty cash systems demand a level of care that is disproportionate to their actual financial importance. This is because of the element of moral hazard: amounts of hard cash kept on the organisation's premises represent a level of temptation to theft and fraud not shared by most other aspects of the operating systems.

If it is not properly controlled, petty cash payments can involve significant losses, as illustrated by the following information on fraud committed in 2009:

> 2009 saw the highest number of cases of serious fraud by managers and employees (123) since the Fraud Barometer began. There was a major increase in fraud by company managers coming to court, with £335m of cases compared to £129m in 2008. Employees also racked up far higher losses, with cases worth £232m, more than double the £100m figure for 2008.
>
> KPMG's annual fraud barometer

15.10.2 A typical petty cash system

A typical petty cash system would be as follows:

- The cashier pays the person responsible for the petty cash (we will refer to such a person in this chapter as a petty cashier although it could be any named responsible person in an organisation) an agreed amount, say £50. The actual amount will depend on the nature of the business, the number of employees who require petty cash and the length of the period before the cashier reimburses the amount paid out. The agreed amount the petty cashier starts with is known as the *imprest*.
- The petty cashier is authorised only to pay specified types of routine expenses (such as for travelling, buying postage stamps, buying stationery and so on) and up to an agreed limit for each individual payment (say £10). Petty cashiers are usually warned against giving loans to staff.
- Every petty cash payment must be supported by a *petty cash docket*, explaining its nature, bearing the signature of the payee and to which should be attached, where possible, external evidence of the payment, e.g. a used rail ticket.
- At agreed intervals (say every week) the petty cashier should produce to the cashier the vouchers (dockets) to support the payments and the petty cash balance in hand and the two together should make up the amount of the imprest. At this point the cashier reimburses the petty cashier with the amount of petty cash payments so that the petty cashier commences each period with the same amount as imprest. For example, if the imprest is £50 and in a given week the payments (supported by vouchers) is £38, after checking on £12 in hand and vouchers for £38, the cashier pays £38 to the petty cashier and takes custody of the vouchers for £38.
- The petty cashier should write up a Petty Cash Book recording the imprests received from the cashier and the petty cash payments made with payments analysed by main categories. The weekly or monthly totals of these categories, rather than the individual payments, are posted to the appropriate nominal accounts.

15.10.3 Petty Cash Book

The cashier, however, still remains responsible for accounting for all cash receipts and payments, and is required to maintain control of the petty cash payments by setting up a sound petty cash system.

To illustrate, let us assume that on 17 January there was an opening petty cash balance of £14 and a reimbursement of £86 was made on that date to bring the balance back to the imprest of £100. The Petty Cash Book with analysis columns would appear as follows:

Petty Cash Book

Receipts			Payments				Analysis				
2012	Folio	£	2012	V	Particulars	£	Travel	Cleaning	Car expenses	Postage	Stationery
Balance b/f		14.00	17.1	PC51	Bus fare	2.40	2.40	–	–	–	–
17.1	CB1	86.00	18.1	PC52	Rubber stamp	11.00	–	–	–	–	11.00
			18.1	PC53	Postage stamp	4.50	–	–	–	4.50	–
			19.1	PC54	Petrol for car	18.00	18.00	–	–	–	–
			19.1	PC55	Mopping floor	7.50	–	7.50	–	–	–
			19.1	PC56	Taxi to bank	4.50	4.50	–	–	–	–
			20.1	PC57	Servicing car	22.00	–	–	22.00	–	–
			20.1	PC58	Desk stapler	7.60	–	–	–	–	7.60
			21.1	PC59	Janitor's tip	3.00	–	3.00	–	–	–
			21.1	PC60	Car wipers	7.50	–	–	7.50	–	–
						88.00	24.90	10.50	29.50	4.50	18.60
			21.1		Balance c/d	12.00	NL21	NL16	NL32	NL19	NL8
		100.00				100.00					
Balance b/f		12.00									

When, as shown above, the Petty Cash Book is written up with analysis columns, the weekly (or monthly) totals are posted to the nominal accounts, debiting Travelling account with £24.90, Cleaning account with £10.50 and so on.

Activity 15.7 Is the Petty Cash Book a main or subsidiary book of account?

We have seen that the Petty Cash Book is a book of prime entry in which the first entry is made of routine payments by the petty cashier.

Required: Is the Petty Cash Book a subsidiary book of accounts or, like the Cash Book and the ledgers, one of the main books of account which has to be included in a Trial Balance?

Summary

- In a two-column Cash Book, the Cash account and the Bank account are written up in adjoining columns on the same folio.
- Bank statements report the position from the banker's point of view.
- Bank reconciliation is undertaken on any day, to establish the accuracy of the bank balance as shown in the Cash Book by reconciling it to the balance reported on the bank statement.
- In a three-column Cash Book, there is an additional column on each side for making the prime entry for cash discounts, both allowed and received.
- An imprest system is a way of controlling petty cash.
- A Petty Cash Book could operate either as a subsidiary book or as one of the main books of account.

Suggested answers to activities

15.1 Writing up a two-column Cash Book

Cash Book

Date	V	Particulars	F	Cash	Bank	Date	V	Chq	Particulars	F	Cash	Bank
2012				£	£	2012					£	£
1.7		Balance b/f		455	7,540	1.7		J475	Salt Ltd a/c		–	1,450
1.7		Paul May's a/c		1,245	–	1.7		J476	Advertising a/c		–	150
1.7		Sales a/c		478	–	1.7		–	Office cleaning		35	–
1.7		Sales a/c		–	725	1.7		–	Rent a/c		–	1,800
1.7		June Kelly's a/c		–	840	1.7		–	Bank charges		–	40
1.7		Cash a/c	c	–	2,000	1.7		–	Bank a/c	c	2,000	–
1.7		Bank a/c	c	200		1.7		–	Cash a/c	c	–	200
									Balance c/d		343	7,465
				2,378	11,105						2,378	11,105

15.2 A bank reconciliation statement

As at 14 September 2012	
	£
Bank balance as per Cash Book	17,240
Less: Bank charges not recorded	(25)
Corrected balance at bank	17,215
Add: Cheques yet to be presented	8,450
Less: Deposits awaiting clearance	(15,940)
Balance as per bank statement	9,725

15.3 A bank reconciliation involving an overdraft

Bank reconciliation statement as at 19 July 2012	
	£
Overdraft as reported in the Cash Book	(7,250)
Add: Deposits awaiting clearance	(11,450)
	(18,700)
Less: Cheques yet to be presented	30,340
Favourable balance as per bank statement	11,640

15.4 Correction of Cash Book prior to the bank reconciliation

Bank account (in the Cash Book)

	£		£
Balance	11,400	Business rates	1,200
Bank charges	35	Balance c/d	10,235
	11,435		11,435
Balance b/d	10,235		

Bank reconciliation statement as at 10 December 2012	
	£
Balance at bank as per Cash Book	10,235
Add: Cheques yet to be presented	18,850
	29,085
Less: Deposits awaiting clearance	(31,535)
Bank overdraft as per bank statement	(2,450)

15.5 Accounting for discount allowed

Cash Book (receipts side)

Date	V	Particulars	F	Discount	Cash	Bank
2012				£	£	£
4.3		Robinsons Ltd		720	25,800	–
9.3		Tomlinson Bros		560	13,440	–
14.3		Samuel & Sons		1,800	43,200	–
17.3		Patricia and Co		600	19,500	–
25.3		Gamage plc		700	16,800	–
				4,380		

Discount allowed account

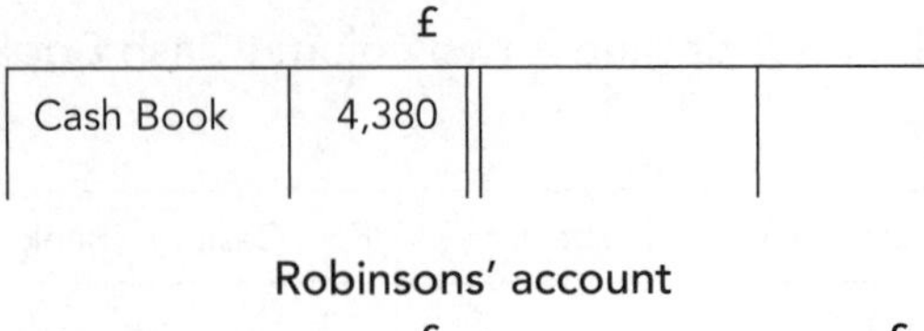

	£		
Cash Book	4,380		

Robinsons' account

	£		£
Balance b/f	?	Cash a/c	25,800
		Cash Book	720

Samuel & Sons account

	£		£
Balance b/f	?	Cash a/c	43,200
		Cash Book	1,800

Tomlinson's account

	£		£
Balance b/f	?	Cash a/c	13,440
		Cash Book	560

Patricia and co account

	£		£
Balance b/f	?	Cash a/c	19,500
		Cash Book	600

Gamage plc account

	£		£
Balance b/f	?	Cash a/c	16,800
		Cash Book	700

15.6 Accounting for discount received

Cash Book (payments side)

Date	V	Chq	Particulars	F	Discount	Cash	Bank
2012					£	£	£
2.5			Bragabout plc		4,350	–	68,150
6.5			Tellaround plc		–	–	22,500
16.5			Whocares plc		2,076	–	32,524
24.5			Sowhat plc		1,728	–	27,072
					8,154		

Bragabout plc's account

	£		
Bank a/c	68,150		
Cash Book	4,350		

Whocares plc's account

	£		
Bank a/c	32,524		
Cash Book	2,076		

Discount received account

			£
		Cash Book	8,154

Sowhat plc's account

	£		
Bank a/c	27,072		
Cash Book	1,728		

15.7 Is the Petty Cash Book a main or subsidiary book of account?

Whether the Petty Cash Book is a main or a subsidiary book of account depends on the accounting arrangements within each particular business.

As a main book of account. In the example used for illustration the Petty Cash Book is regarded as one of the main books of account. The weekly reimbursement (£86) is posted from the Cash Book to the Petty Cash Book. The weekly totals of each classification of expenses are posted from the Petty Cash Book to the respective nominal accounts. Thus the Petty Cash Book is part of the double-entry system. Therefore, when a Trial Balance is prepared the balance in the Petty Cash Book should also be included in it.

As a subsidiary book. An alternative arrangement could be to use the Petty Cash Book as only a prime entry book falling, like the day books, outside the double-entry system. In that case a Petty Cash account is maintained in the ledger. The amounts of the reimbursements are posted from the Cash Book to the Petty Cash account. The Petty Cash Book is then only used as a book of prime entry on the basis of which the weekly total payment of £88 is credited to the Petty Cash account and debited to the various individual nominal accounts as appropriate. Within this alternative arrangement the Petty Cash Book, being outside the double-entry system, would be a subsidiary book of account. Instead of the balance in the Petty Cash Book being included in the Trial Balance, it will be the one in the Petty Cash account.

Multiple choice questions

Two-column Cash Book

15.1 The balance in a Bank account appearing in the Cash Book:

(a) Will always be on the debit side ☐

(b) Will always be on the credit side ☐

(c) Will always be either on the debit side or credit side ☐

(d) If it has a balance it could be on either side ☐

15.2 The credit entries in a Bank account:

(a) Should each be supported by a sequential cheque number ☐

(b) Should each be supported by a cheque number which depends on when the cheque was posted ☐

(c) Will not be supported by a cheque number only when payment is by BACS or standing order ☐

(d) Will not be supported by a cheque number when payment is by BACS or standing order or when cash is drawn out from ATM or when the bank recovers bank charges ☐

15.3 A cheque for £1,000 received from Rebecca Jones, a customer, is accounted for as:

(a) Debit Bank account and credit Rebecca Jones' account ☐

(b) Debit Rebecca Jones' account and credit Cash account ☐

(c) Debit Cash account and credit Rebecca Jones' account ☐

(d) Debit Cash account and credit Sales account ☐

15.4 The bank statement reports a credit transfer of £400 from a customer on 29 July. Accounting entries for this are:

(a) A debit in the Cash account and a credit in the account of the debtor concerned ☐

(b) A debit in the Bank account and a credit in the Cash account ☐

(c) A debit in the account of the debtor concerned and a credit in the Bank account ☐

(d) A debit in the Bank account and a credit in the account of the customer concerned ☐

15.5 The accounting entry required when the bank advises that a bank loan has been approved is:

(a) Debit Bank account credit Cash account
(b) Debit Bank account credit Bank loan account
(c) Debit Cash account credit Bank loan account
(d) Debit Cash account credit Bank account

15.6 The accounting entry to record bank charges deducted from the Bank account of the business is:

(a) Debit Interest account credit Bank account
(b) Debit Bank charges account credit Bank account
(c) Debit Cash account credit Bank charges account
(d) Debit Bank charges account credit Cash account

15.7 A cheque drawn by Dawn Toby, a trade customer, is received back from the bank marked 'r/d':

(a) Debit Bank account and credit Cash account
(b) Debit Dawn Toby's account and credit Bank account
(c) Debit Bank account and credit Dawn Toby's account
(d) Debit Cash account and credit Bank account

15.8 A contra entry in the Cash Book means that:

(a) Debit and credit entries are on the same folio of the Cash Book
(b) Debit and credit entries are on any folio but in the Cash Book
(c) Debit must be in the Cash account and the credit in the Bank account
(d) Debit must be in the Bank account and the credit in the Cash account

Bank reconciliation (note: o/d stands for overdraft)

15.9 Confirm whether the following statements are true or false by placing a tick in grid 'x' if true and grid 'y' if false.

x y

(a) A debit balance in the Bank account in the Cash Book appears as a credit balance in the bank statement
(b) A Bank reconciliation statement is not part of the double-entry system
(c) An overdraft in the bank statement is reported as a current asset
(d) If the bank reconciliation starts with a debit balance from the bank account in the Cash Book, the bank charges appearing in the bank statement would be added
(e) A cash payment as petty cash imprest would appear in the bank statement
(f) If the bank reconciliation statement started with a favourable balance as stated on the bank statement, unpresented cheques would be deducted
(g) Every credit entry in the Bank account of the Cash Book will be on the basis of a cheque
(h) A reconciliation statement is prepared because the Bank account in the Cash Book is always correct and the bank statement is not
(i) The Bank account in the Cash Book cannot report a credit balance unless the bank has already approved overdraft facilities
(j) An instruction to a bank to pay a specified amount at stated intervals is a standing order

15.10 What would be the bank balance as at 11 May 2012 as reported in the bank statement in each of the following circumstances?

(a) As at this date the deposits awaiting clearance are £18,240 and cheques yet to be presented for payment are £21,590; while the bank balance as recorded in the Cash Book was £9,480

x	£6,130	
y	£12,830 o/d	
z	£12,830	

(b) As at this date the Cash Book reports a bank balance of £21,800; while cheques yet to be presented amount to £21,560 and deposits yet to be credited by the bank amount to £36,240

x	£7,120	
y	£21,800	
z	£36,480 o/d	

(c) As at this date the Cash Book reports a bank balance of £11,450, without recording bank charges of £35. Deposits awaiting clearance and cheques yet to be presented amount to £49,240 and £29,780 respectively

x	£30,875	
y	£8,010 o/d	
z	£8,045 o/d	

(d) The Cash Book reports a bank balance of £4,250, without recording a credit transfer from a customer of £7,200 and a standing order payment of £4,500. Deposits awaiting clearance were £22,400 and the value of cheques yet to be presented on this date was £9,480

x	£19,870	
y	£5,970 o/d	
z	£11,370 o/d	

(e) As at this date the Cash Book reports a bank overdraft of £9,850. Cheques yet to be presented and deposits awaiting clearance on this date amount to £15,250 and £21,820 respectively

x	£3,280	
y	£3,280 o/d	
z	£16,420 o/d	

15.11 The balance at bank as at 17 July 2012 is stated on the bank statement as £18,450. Cheques yet to be presented to the bank on this date amount to £19,720. Assuming that the balance in the Bank account written up in the Cash Book differs only because of circumstances stated in each of the following, what is the bank balance to be reported in the Statement of financial position as at 17 July 2012?

(a) The deposits awaiting clearance on that date amount to £32,475

x	£5,695	
y	£18,450	
z	£31,205	

(b) Bank balance stated in the Cash Book is £17,240. A Trade Association subscription of £450 paid by direct debit and a dividend of £3,000 collected on a mandate are yet to be recorded in the Cash Book. Any difference is deposit awaiting clearance

x	£17,240	
y	£19,790	
z	£20,690	

(c) The Cash Book reports a bank balance on that date of £11,420. Deposits awaiting clearance amount to £29,460. Any difference may be attributed to credit transfers from customers and standing order payments not recorded in the Cash Book

x	£1,680	
y	£8,710	
z	£28,190	

(d) The Cash Book reports an overdraft of £7,650, having carried over a bank balance of £21,460 from one folio of the Cash Book to the next as £12,460 and having recorded twice bank charges of £25. Any difference is deposit awaiting clearance

x	£1,375	
y	£1,400	
z	£16,700	

15.12 The bank statement reports an overdraft of £17,455 as at 27 May 2012. As at that date cheques to the value of £14,280 have not been presented for payment and deposits amounting to £39,450 await clearance. If other circumstances are as described in each of the following situations, ascertain the bank balance that would be reported in the Cash Book, prior to correcting what has been stated below:

(a) A cheque for £12,480 written in favour of Guy Soloman, a supplier, has been entered in the Cash Book as £12,840, and an automated credit from Niel Tudor, a customer, for £3,500 is yet to be recorded in the Cash Book

x	£3,855	
y	£4,655	
z	£11,655 o/d	

(b) The Cash Book fails to record the dishonour of a cheque for £22,500 from Moss, a customer, £18 charged as bank commission and £17,500 collected by the bank on a dividend mandate

x	£12,733	
y	£2,707 o/d	
z	£37,607 o/d	

(c) A credit balance of £7,240 at bank has been carried forward from one folio of the Cash Book to the next as a debit balance and £500 drawn from the ATM (cash machine) has not been entered in the Cash Book

x	£7,185	
y	£22,695	
z	£6,265 o/d	

(d) A cheque for £6,500 drawn in favour of Maria Sayes, a trade payable, was lost and replaced by another. Apart from entering both cheques as credits in the Cash Book no other entry has been made

x	£1,215	
y	£14,215	
z	£29,625 o/d	

15.13 The following differences between the Cash Book entries and information in the bank statement have been identified:

(i) An amount incorrectly credited to the company's account by the bank

(ii) Lodgements into bank not reported in the bank statements

(iii) Dishonour of a cheque deposited into the bank

(iv) Bank loan interest recovered by the bank

(v) Cheques drawn by the company yet to be presented to bank.

	In Cash Book	In Bank reconciliation	
a	iii, iv	i, ii, v	
b	i, ii, iii	iv, v	
c	iii, iv	i, ii, v	
d	ii, iv, v	i, iii	

Which set of alternatives correctly analyses treatment of these?

Reconciliation with supplier's statement

15.14 Shoemart's ledger reports that it owes £128,900 to Whites, a supplier; whereas the corresponding figure stated in Whites' monthly statement is £154,700. The difference is found to have arisen from:

(a) A purchase invoice for £73,500 has been posted to Whites' account as £37,500

(b) Whites have overlooked a 4% cash discount entitlement when a cheque for £33,600 was paid to them

(c) The difference arises from returns for which the credit note is yet to be received

The amount of purchases returns is:

a	£8,800	
b	£11,600	
c	£1,544	
d	£60,400	

Discount allowed and received

15.15 Which of the following is the most appropriate description of cash discount?

(a) A reduction in price permitted when items are purchased in bulk

(b) A reduction permitted for inducing someone to pay up ahead of permitted credit period

(c) A reduction in price allowed by one trader to another

(d) A refund of amount overcharged when the customer was invoiced

Reversal of discount allowed

15.16 The prime entry for reversing a discount allowed to a customer would be in:

(a) The credit side of the Cash Book

(b) The debit side of the Cash Book

(c) The Sales Day Book

(d) Neither of the above

15.17 Upon dishonour of a customer's cheque for £4,275 the accounting entries for reversing a 5% discount allowed would be:

(a) Debit the Cash account and credit the customer with £225

(b) Debit the customer's account and credit the Discount allowed account with £225

(c) Debit the Discount allowed account and credit the customer's account with £225

(d) Debit the customer's account and credit the Cash account with £225

Petty cash system

15.18 Which of the following statements is incorrect?

(a) The petty cashier is reimbursed regularly to make up the cash balance to the imprest

(b) Every payment made by the petty cashier should be supported by evidence

(c) In an emergency the petty cashier may give staff loans of small amounts

(d) The Petty Cash Book could be either a subsidiary book or a main book of accounts

15.19 If the Petty Cash Book is treated as merely a subsidiary book of accounts, £78 paid by the cashier to restore the petty cash balance to the level of the imprest should be accounted for as:

(a) Debit Petty Cash Book and credit Cash account

(b) Debit Petty cash account and credit Cash account

(c) Debit Petty cash account and credit Bank account

(d) Debit Cash account and credit Petty cash account

15.20 The Petty cash float, fixed at £100, is reimbursed on the last day of the month. It is decided that from 1 August 2012 the float should be increased to £120. Petty cash expenses paid in July 2012 are summarised as: Stationery £9.50; Office cleaning £21.45; Travelling £14.45; Staff tea £21.55; Postage £19.60; Miscellaneous expenses £9.25. What is the amount of reimbursement the petty cashier would receive on 1 August 2012?

a	£4.20	
b	£24.20	
c	£95.80	
d	£115.80	

General

15.21 The owner of a shop draws a cheque on his personal bank account to pay for shop rent. This should be accounted for as:

(a) Credit Bank account in the Cash Book and debit Drawings account ☐
(b) Debit Bank account and credit Capital account ☐
(c) Credit Bank account in the Cash Book and debit Rent account ☐
(d) Credit Capital account and debit Rent account ☐

Answers to multiple choice questions
15.1: d 15.2: d 15.3: a 15.4: d 15.5: b 15.6: b 15.7: b 15.8: a 15.9a: x 15.9b: x 15.9c: y 15.9d: y 15.9e: y 15.9f: x 15.9g: y 15.9h: y 15.9i: y 15.9j: x 15.10a: z 15.10b: x 15.10c: z 15.10d: y 15.10e: z 15.11a: z 15.11b: y 15.11c: z 15.11d: x 15.12a: x 15.12b: x 15.12c: y 15.12d: x 15.13: a 15.14: b 15.15: b 15.16: d 15.17: b 15.18: c 15.19: b 15.20: d 15.21: d

Progressive questions

Note: Though not true in real life, assume that cheques received from customers are immediately paid into the bank account.

PQ 15.1 A basic question on the three-column Cash Book

On 1 January 2012 a business had a capital of £300 and £350 non-current assets, £50 cash in hand and a bank overdraft of £100. The transactions in the month ended 31 January were as stated on the right.

Cash sales	£500
Credit purchase from P	£400
Wages paid in cash	£100
Amount paid into bank	£370
Credit sales to Q	£300
Paid P £270 by cheque after deducting 10% discount	
Q settled £200 due from him less 5% discount	
Wages paid by cheque	£100
Bank charges notified	£30
Received balance due from Q subject to 4% discount	

Required:
(a) Record these transactions in a three-column Cash Book and post them to appropriate ledger accounts.
(b) Extract a Trial Balance as at 31 January.

PQ 15.2 Two-column Cash Book

As at 16 May Olive Retail had £425 in cash and a bank balance of £15,200. Among others the following transactions took place in May:

Date	Transaction
16.5	Paid £24 in cash for stationery
	Paid £2,400 for purchases by cheque no 54
	Paid £65 for advertising in cash
	Cash sale £345

Date	Transaction
17.5	Received a cheque for £1,250 from Peter, a customer
	Paid £1,500 as rent by cheque no. 55
	Paid £5,800 to Rocco, a supplier, by cheque no. 56
	Cash sale £840
	Received a cheque for £1,600 from Rick, a customer
	Deposited in bank all amounts in hand leaving £400
	Instructed bank to pay £225 as rates monthly on 21st of each month
18.5	A loan of £10,000 is approved by the bank
	Cash sales £980
	Paid £22,500 for a vehicle by cheque no 57
	Received a cheque for £1,500 from Brown, a customer
	Deposited £1,000 in bank
19.5	Cash sales £450
	Received cheque for £2,800 from Tim, a customer
	Paid £450 for advertising by cheque no 58
	Paid £1,650 by cheque no 59 to Black, a supplier
	Paid £45 in cash for motor vehicle fuel
20.5	Drew £500 from ATM to pay weekly wages
	Brown's cheque is received back marked R/D
	Received a cheque for £850 from Pat, a customer
	Bank advises credit transfer of £1,800 from Morris
	Paid £850 as wages in cash
	Bank charges £30 for unauthorised overdraft
	Switch card sales £245
	Paid £240 for advertising by cheque no 60
	Paid £42 in cash for staff tea.

Required: Write up a two-column Cash Book drawn with all the columns.

PQ 15.3 Amending the Cash Book and preparing a bank reconciliation (ACCA)

The Cash Book of a business shows a favourable bank balance of £3,856 at 30 June 2012. After comparing the entries in the Cash Book with the entries on the related bank statement you find that:

(i) Cheques amounting to £218 entered in the Cash Book have not yet been presented for payment to the bank.

(ii) An amount of £50 entered on the Bank account of the Cash Book has not been banked.

(iii) An amount of £95 has been credited by the bank to the account in error.

(iv) The bank has credited and then debited the bank statement with an amount of £48, being A. Jones' cheque which it forwarded on 1 July 2012 marked 'insufficient funds – return to drawer'.

(v) Interest of £10 has been charged by the bank, but not yet entered in the Cash Book.

(vi) A cheque from a customer entered in the Cash Book as £88 had been correctly entered by the bank as £188.

Required:

(a) Show the additional entries to be made in the Cash Book and bring down the corrected balance.

(b) Prepare a bank reconciliation statement.

PQ 15.4 A bank reconciliation with an overdraft

A trader's Cash Book reported a bank overdraft of £5,240 as at 14 September 2012. Inquiries revealed the following:

(i) Deposits amounting to £11,600 are yet to be cleared as at that date.

(ii) The Cash Book does not record trade subscriptions of £30 and business rates of £240 paid by standing order.

(iii) £14 bank charges have been entered twice in the Cash Book.

(iv) Cheques amounting to £18,250 were not presented to the bank until after this date.

(v) A bank overdraft of £2,400 has been carried forward from one folio of the Cash Book to the next as a favourable balance of £2,400.

Required: Prepare a bank reconciliation statement as at 14 September identifying the actual balance at bank.

PQ 15.5 Reconciliation with a missing item

As at 30 September 2012 the Cash Book reports a bank overdraft of £10,240 whereas the bank statement reports a favourable balance of £5,680. Inquiries reveal as follows:

(i) A cheque for £14,750 drawn in favour of Jerry Ross has been entered twice in the Cash Book.

(ii) Deposits awaiting clearance on this date amount to £4,800.

(iii) A credit transfer of £2,400 from Mandy Pitman, a customer, and bank charges of £15 are yet to be recorded in the Cash Book.

(iv) Any difference may be attributed to cheques drawn but yet to be presented to the bank.

Required: Show the corrected Cash Book balance and prepare a bank reconciliation statement as at 30 September.

PQ 15.6 A simple true-to-life question

Given below is the bank column of the Cash Book of Roger Retail and on the right the relevant bank statement:

Cash Book (Bank column only)

Dr		£	Cr		£
1.9	Alfred & Co	3,650	1.9	Balance b/d	5,420
2.9	Cash a/c	3,200	2.9	Electricity	46
4.9	Brandon plc	1,200	2.9	Robert Ltd	92
4.9	Cash a/c	4,225	3.9	Sarah & Co	110
5.9	Carlyle Ltd	3,200	4.9	Advertising	249
6.9	Dudley & Son	900	4.9	Timothy	75
6.9	Edward Ltd	1,400	5.9	Ulster Trade	4,190
			6.9	Balance c/d	7,593
		17,775			17,775

Bank statement	Dr	Cr	Balance
September	£	£	£
1.Balance			5,420 Dr
2. Deposit		3,200	2,220 Dr
5. Deposit		4,225	2,005 Cr
5. Gas – direct debit	145		1,860 Cr
5. Alfred & Co		3,650	5,510 Cr
6. Bank charges	32		5,478 Cr
6. Robert Ltd	92		5,386 Cr
6. Advertising	249		5,137 Cr
6. Timothy	75		5,062 Cr

Required:

(a) Update the Cash Book to obtain the corrected balance.

(b) Prepare a bank reconciliation statement as at 6 September.

Note: Debit balance in the bank statement is an overdraft.

PQ 15.7 Tracing items for a bank reconciliation statement

An extract from the Cash Book of Olive May Retail, along with particulars of its banking and a copy of the bank statement for the period, are shown below:

Bank account in the Cash Book

2012		£	2012	Chq		£
16.5	Balance b/f	15,200	16.5	54	Purchases	2,400
17.5	Cash a/c[a]	3,971	17.5	55	Rent a/c	1,500
18.5	Bank loan	10,000	17.5	56	Rocco a/c	5,800
18.5	Cash a/c[b]	2,500	18.5	57	Vehicle a/c	22,500
20.5	Morris[d]	1,800	19.5	58	Advertising	450
20.5	Sales – switch	245	19.5	59	Black a/c	1,650
20.5	Cash a/c[c]	3,650	20.5	–	Cash – ATM	500
			20.5	–	Brown's a/c	1,500
			20.5	–	Charges	30
			20.5	60	Advertising	240
			20.5	–	Balance c/d	796
		37,366				37,366

Notes:

(a) Bank deposit on 17.5:

Peter's cheque for	£1,250
Rick's cheque for	£1,600
Cash	£1,121
	£3,971

(b) Bank deposit on 18.5:

Brown's cheque	£1,500
Cash	£1,000
	£2,500

(c) Bank deposit on 20.5:

Tim's cheque	£2,800
Pat's cheque	£850
	£3,650

(d) Credit transfer from Morris.

Olive May Retail in account with
CITI BANK plc 501, Pall Mall, London SW1 5PD

2012	Particulars	Debits	Credits	Balance
17.5	Balance b/f	–	–	£15,200
17.5	Loan	–	£10,000	£25,200
17.5	Deposit	–	£1,121	£26,321
18.5	Morris credit transfer	–	£1,800	£28,121
18.5	Deposit	–	£1,000	£29,121
19.5	Chq 54	£2,400	–	£26,721
20.5	Deposit – cheque	–	£1,600	£28,321
20.5	Chq 57	£22,500	–	£5,821
20.5	Automatic Teller	£500	–	£5,321
20.5	Chq 56	£5,800	–	£479 o/d
20.5	Bank charges	£30	–	£509 o/d
20.5	Switch	–	£245	£264 o/d
20.5	Deposit – cheque	–	£1,250	£986

Required:

(a) Trace each item entered in the Bank account of the Cash Book into the bank statement and then trace each item reported in the bank statement into the Cash Book for the purpose of identifying:
- deposits awaiting clearance;
- cheques yet to be presented;
- any item not recorded in the Cash Book.

(b) Prepare a bank reconciliation statement as at 20 May 2012.

PQ 15.8 Bank reconciliation statements as at two dates

Shown below is the Bank account in Bill Sach's Cash Book and next to it (on the right) the bank statement for the period ended 26 January 2012:

Bank account						
Date	Details	Bank	Date	Chq	Details	Bank
2012		£	2012			£
21.1	Balance	1,260	21.1	26	P. Godwin	1,200
22.1	Cash a/c	4,440	21.1	27	Purchases	1,360
22.1	Loan a/c	8,000	23.1	28	Cash a/c	600
23.1	Cash a/c	2,150	23.1	29	Equipment	2,000
26.1	Cash a/c	1,840	23.1	30	Electricity	760
26.1	Balance	2,210	24.1	31	Lucy Gill	1,180
			24.1	32	Rent	1,500
			25.1	33	S. Nathan	750
			25.1	34	Stationery	650
			25.1	35	M. Shaw	2,600
			26.1	36	Salaries	5,460
			26.1	37	R Spring	1,280
			26.1	38	Heating	560
		19,900				19,900
			1.2		Balance	2,210

Bill Sachs in account with Midwest Bank				
2012	Details	Debit	Credit	Balance
21.1	Balance	–	–	£150 o/d
21.1	Deposits	–	£3,250	£3,100
22.1	Loan	–	£8,000	£11,100
23.1	Chq 28	£600	–	£10,500
23.1	Chq 26	£1,200	–	£9,300
23.1	S/O – rates	£400	–	£8,900
24.1	Chq 25	£1,620	–	£7,280
24.1	Dividend	–	£1,500	£8,780
24.1	Chq 29	£2,000	–	£6,780
25.1	Chq 24	£220	–	£6,560
25.1	Deposit	–	£4,440	£11,000
25.1	Charges	£55	–	£10,945
25.1	Chq 31	£1,180	–	£9,765
26.1	Deposit	–	£2,150	£11,915
26.1	Chq 35	£2,600	–	£9,315

Notes: S/O is standing order to pay rates. Dividends were collected by the bank on a mandate.

Required: The bank reconciliation statements as at 21 January 2012 and again as at 26 January 2012.

PQ 15.9 Focus on discounts allowed and received

5% if payment is received at least by the third day; or 3% if payment is received after 3 days but within the calendar month.

Ted Smile, a wholesaler, buys his requirements on a month's credit from three reputed suppliers – Alpha, Beta and Gamma. All of them allow 10% settlement discount if purchases are paid for within three days. Ted in turn has approved a month's credit to his customers – Peter, Paul, James, John and Mark – who have all been offered cash discount on the scale stated in the box above. They have been warned, however, that goods sold cannot be returned after three days from the date of sale. Ted Smile has received the same warning from his suppliers.

On 1st May 2012 Ted owed Alpha, Beta and Gamma £214,600, £346,500 and £126,400, respectively. £38,500 of the amount owed to Beta was in respect of purchases made on 30 April 2012; while the rest of the purchases had been made earlier. A break-down of amounts due from customers as at 1 May 2012 is as follows:

	Peter	Paul	James	John	Mark
Sales on 29/30 April 2012	£25,600	–	£12,500	–	£4,200
Sales prior to 28.4.2012 but within April	£114,200	£69,300	£36,700	£136,800	£12,400
Total receivable	£139,800	£69,300	£49,200	£136,800	£16,600

Transactions within the week commencing on 1 May 2012 include the following:

Date	Transactions
1.5	Sales to Paul £22,200, to John £18,000 and to Mark £6,000 Purchases from Alpha £16,400 and from Gamma £15,600 Return to Beta of goods bought on 30.4.2012 for £6,500 Paid Beta in full by cheque no 287 Received a cheque in full settlement from James
2.5	Sales to Peter £17,500 Mark returns goods sold for £1,200 Returned to Alpha goods purchased for £1,800 Received cheques in full settlement from John and Mark
3.5	Sales to James £13,600 and to Paul £8,200 Purchased from Alpha £16,400 and from Gamma £11,200 Returned to Beta goods bought for £1,500
4.5	Sales to Peter £7,400, Paul £8,600 and John £4,500 Purchased from Alpha for £6,500 and from Gamma for £12,500 Paid £214,600 to Alpha by cheque no 296
5.5	Mark's cheque is returned by the bank endorsed Refer to drawer Sales to Peter £11,200 and to James £26,400 Received a cheque from Peter for £159,261 Settled Gamma in full by cheque no 299

Required: Show how these transactions will be reported in appropriate ledger accounts, identifying whether each account will be in the Sales ledger, Purchases ledger or Nominal ledger.

PQ 15.10 Petty cash system (AAT)

The Petty Cashier of Jockfield received £300 on 1 May 2012 as petty cash float. A summary of payments during the month is stated on the right.

May		£	May		£
2	Postage	18	18	Stationery	9
3	Travelling	12	19	Cleaning	23
4	Cleaning	15	20	Postage	13
7	Petrol for van	22	24	Servicing van	43
8	Travelling	25	26	Petrol	18
9	Stationery	17	27	Cleaning	21
11	Cleaning	18	29	Postage	5
14	Postage	5	30	Petrol	14
15	Travelling	8			

Required:

(a) Rule up a Petty Cash Book with analysis columns for expenses on cleaning, motor expenses, postage, stationery, travelling.

(b) Enter the payments during the month.

(c) Enter the amount received to restore the imprest and carry down the balance.

(d) Explain how double-entry is completed.

Test questions

Test 15.1 Preparation of a bank reconciliation statement

The following items were identified in the course of bank reconciliation as at 31 May 2012:

(i) The bank balance on that day as per the Cash Book was £46,400.

(ii) Bank charges of £36 have been entered twice in the Cash Book.

(iii) A favourable balance at bank of £23,400 has been carried forward from one folio of the Cash Book to the next as £32,400.

(iv) The debit side of the Bank account in the Cash Book has been added as £64,250 instead of £64,150.

(v) £11,400 received from John Curry, a customer, by credit transfer is not accounted for in the Cash Book.

(vi) £3,900 paid as insurance by direct debit is not accounted for in the Cash Book.

(vii) Deposits not cleared by this date were £22,700 and cheques yet to be presented £36,840.

Required: Prepare a bank reconciliation statement as at 31 May 2012.

Test 15.2 Bank reconciliation starting with the bank statement figure

Simon's Corner Shop received its bank statement reporting an overdraft, as at 14 May 2012, of £29,800. Inquiries revealed the following:

(i) A payment by cheque of £72,800 to a supplier has been entered in the Cash Book as £78,200.

(ii) Deposits awaiting clearance on this date amounted to £32,400.

(iii) Bank charges of £14 have been entered twice in the Cash Book.

(iv) The Cash Book did not record the following:

- £400 paid by standing order as subscription to London Chamber of Commerce;
- £54 charged by the bank as interest on the overdraft;
- £12,500 received from a customer by credit transfer.

(v) Cheques amounting to £18,500 are yet to be presented to the bank.

Required:
(a) Prepare a bank reconciliation statement as at 14 May 2012.
(b) Show the Bank account in the Cash Book incorporating the necessary corrections.

Test 15.3 Writing up a columnar Cash Book (Welsh Joint Education Committee)

The following information relates to the receipts and payments of Paul Wallis for the month of April, 2012:

(i) The balances brought forward at 1 April were: Cash £100 Bank £400 (overdrawn)

(ii) Cheques were received during the month:

April 4 – J Parnell £1,450 (after discount allowed of £50)
April 8 – F Abbey £800

(iii) Received in cash: April 12 Cash sales £360

(iv) Cheques issued by Paul:

April 14 – R Cooper £580 (after discount received of £20)
April 16 – M Collins £320

(v) Payments made in cash:

April 18 – Wages £150
April 22 – Stationery £10

(vi) A standing order of £200 was paid to Wrexham Gas on April 24 from Paul's account and he had instructed his bank to honour a direct debit to the Nation Building Society for £250 paid on the 26th of each month.

Required: Paul's updated Cash Book for the month of April, 2012.

Test 15.4 A three-column Cash Book

On 1.1.2012 Hilda Stores had £650 in hand and £12,740 at the bank. The transactions on that day were as follows:

(i) Paid £450 for advertising by cheque no 476.

(ii) Paid £13,800 to Peter Tell, a supplier, by cheque no 477, taking advantage of 8% cash discount on offer.

(iii) Received a cheque for £7,600 from Guy Thomas, a customer, who is entitled to 5% cash discount.

(iv) Cash sales £2,350.

(v) Paid £120 for staff tea.

(vi) Received a cheque for £6,175 from Jerry Wren, a customer, who is entitled to 5% cash discount.

(vii) Paid £5,850 by cheque no 478 to Peter Paul, to settle amount due to them, net of 10% cash discount.

(viii) Mike Saunter, to whom goods had been sold two days earlier for £7,500, returns the goods sold for £300, and settles his remaining balance in full, taking advantage of 5% cash discount on offer for prompt payment.

(ix) Deposited all amounts at bank leaving a cash float of £1,000.

Required: Record these transactions in a three-column Cash Book and post them to the ledger accounts.

Test 15.5 Incomplete records involving bank reconciliation

John Dyson is in business trading wholesale in consumer durables. He purchases from reputable suppliers and sells at a price calculated to yield a profit margin of 25% on cost. His accounts are in a state of disarray and you have been assigned the task of preparing the financial statements for the year ended 30 September 2011. You have been able to obtain from his auditors the Statement of financial position as at 30 September 2010 shown on the right.

Your investigations reveal as follows:

(i) Unpaid invoices as at 30.9.2011 amount to £196,700.

(ii) Trade receivables as at 30.9.2011 were confirmed by circularising them at £168,500.

(iii) Non-current assets are depreciated at 20% per annum using reducing balance method.

(iv) Cost of inventory as at 30 September 2011 was £284,600.

(v) John always banks the whole of his takings, maintaining a float of only £300, and has summarised the payments made from this float as follows:

£12,400 paid to suppliers;
£9,600 paid for other expenses; and
£11,800 drawings by John.

Statement of financial position as at 30.9.2010

	Cost	Accumulated depreciation	WDV
Furniture	60,000	(24,000)	36,000
Equipment	45,000	(10,400)	34,600
Inventory		242,600	
Trade receivables		312,400	
Cash in hand		51,600	
Bank balance		300	606,900
			677,500
		£	£
Capital		312,500	
Profit for the year		98,600	
Drawings		–11,800	399,300
Current liabilities:			
Trade payables		245,400	
Accrued expenses		32,800	278,200
			677,500

(vi) Bank statements for the year ended 30.9.2011 have been summarised as set out on the right. Deposits not cleared were £17,500 on 30.9.2010 and £24,400 a year later. A cheque for £46,800 drawn in favour of a supplier on 27 September 2011 was not presented to the bank for payment until a week later.

	£		£
Balance – 1.10.2010	27,200	Purchases	724,500
Bank lodgement	962,300	Rent	36,000
		Salaries and wages	88,400
		Furniture – 1.1.2011	80,000
		John's life insurance	15,000
		Other expenses	27,400
		Balance – 30.9.2011	18,200
	989,500		989,500

Required: The Statement of income for the year ended 30 September 2011 and the Statement of financial position as at that date.

Chapter 16

The Journal and correction of errors

By the end of this chapter

You should learn:

- About the Journal as an important book of prime entry
- The style of presenting journal entries
- About the Suspense account and correction of errors

You should be able to:

- Journalise transactions which have no other prime entry
- Correct accounting errors
- Place and eliminate a balance in a Suspense account

16.1 The need for a Journal

We saw in Chapter 3 that postings to ledger accounts are only made after a transaction has first been entered in a book of prime entry. We saw in Chapter 2 that the prime entries for all cash transactions are made in the Cash Book and in Chapter 5 that the prime entries for all credit transactions are made in appropriately named Day Books. Historically, the prime entries for all non-cash transactions were made in a book which is known as Journal. The word 'journal', in French, means a daily record or diary. However, as the number of transactions grew, specialised Journals were needed to make the prime entry for repetitive transactions such as purchases, sales, and their returns. Though we identified them as 'Day Books' it is not uncommon to refer to them as Sales Journal, Purchases Journal and so on.

Today the Journal (or sometimes identified as General Journal to distinguish it from the specialised ones) is used for first recording a transaction which cannot be recorded in any other book of prime entry.

Activity 16.1 The books of account

(a) What are the books of prime entry you are familiar with so far and what is entered in each?

(b) What are the main books of account and why are they referred to as that?

(c) What are the subsidiary books of account and why are they so regarded?

16.2 Transactions usually journalised

The act of recording a transaction in a Journal is referred to as *journalising*. The transactions that are journalised are those for which there is no specialised book of prime entry. Depending on the nature of business, further specialised Journals could be used for recording any repetitive transaction. The transactions typically recorded in the (general) Journal include the following:

1. opening entries made either when starting a business or when opening a new set of books;
2. acquisition or disposal of non-current assets on credit terms;
3. correction of errors and transfers between ledger accounts;
4. year-end adjustments such as accounting for closing inventory (Chapter 6) and adjustments for accruals, prepayments, depreciation and bad debts (Chapter 7);
5. reversal of settlement discount (Chapter 15);
6. closing entries – i.e. either closing the nominal accounts when the balances are transferred to the Statement of income or closing all the accounts when the business is closed down.

16.3 The style of presenting a journal entry

Every journal entry takes the form of an instruction identifying the accounts to be debited and the ones to be credited and ends with a *'narration'* which explains briefly the reason for making the entry and which customarily commences with the word 'being'.

The following is an example of a journal entry to record the acquisition on credit terms of a motor vehicle for £18,000 from Belgravia Garages.

Date	Voucher	Particulars		F	Debit	Credit
2012					£	£
11.2	D721	Motor vehicles account	Dr		18,000	–
		To Belgravia Garages account			–	18,000
		Being acquisition of a vehicle on three-month credit term				

We need to remember the following:

1. As is true of all prime entries, every entry in the journal should be supported by and cross-referenced to a voucher evidencing the transaction.
2. It is customary (though not always observed today) to:
   (a) First name the account to be debited and then, on a second line, the account to be credited.
   (b) The name of the account to be debited ends with 'Dr' and the name of the account to be credited begins with 'To' so that the journal entry reads as Motor vehicles account debtor to Belgravia Garages account.
3. When the instruction in a journal entry is carried out, debiting one account and crediting the other, the folio number on which each of these accounts are is stated in the journal.

If the accounting for a single transaction involves more than a pair of ledger accounts, rather than making several journal entries, a *composite journal entry*, as shown below, may serve the purpose. Observe the use of the word 'sundries' on the first line of the journal entry. This is because if there is more than one account that has to be debited, it is conventional to start the journal entry with the word 'Sundries' and to identify the accounts that should be debited by naming them after naming the account to be credited. If the debits as well as the credits are to be made in more than one account, the first two lines of the journal entry conventionally read 'Sundries Dr To Sundries'.

Sundries Dr	£	£
To General Stores account	–	30,000
Furniture account	10,000	
Motor vehicles account	15,000	
Computer account	5,000	
Being acquisition of assets		

The journal is useful because:

(a) it shows the pair of entries (the debit and the credit) accounting for each transaction;
(b) it records the folio in which each of the two entries is made;
(c) it explains briefly the reason for making the entry.

16.4 Journal entries for opening new books of account

If capital is introduced in the form of cash, the prime entry is in the Cash Book and the second entry in the Capital account. If capital introduced also includes non-cash items then a journal entry becomes necessary for recording such items.

For example, if Patrice Kemel commences business on 1 January 2012 introducing as his capital £18,000 in cash and furniture £10,000, we know how the cash will be accounted for. To account for the furniture a journal entry (as shown on the left) would be needed. If a variety of assets are introduced, one way of accounting would be to write up more journal entries. An alternative way is to write up a composite journal entry, as described above. For example, if Kemel introduced also a car valued at £20,000 as part of his capital, the composite journal entry would be written up as shown on the right and, after the entries in the journal have been posted, Kemel's Capital account would appear as shown below, reporting the total capital as £48,000.

Furniture account Dr	£10,000	–
To Capital account	–	£10,000
Being capital introduced by Kemel		

Sundries Dr	–	–
To Capital account	–	£30,000
Furniture account	£10,000	–
Motor vehicles account	£20,000	–
Being assets introduced by Kemel at commencement of business as part of capital		

Capital account

			£
		Cash account	18,000
		Journal	30,000
			48,000

Activity 16.2 The capital introduced consists of assets and a liability

Dave Porter commenced business introducing his car valued at £30,000, furniture valued at £12,000, £25,000 in cash as well as a bank loan of £10,000. Set out the prime entry for the capital introduced at commencement of business.

16.5 Journal entry for acquisition of a non-current asset on credit terms

Non-current assets acquired on credit terms also need to be journalised, to provide the prime entry for the debit in the appropriate asset account and a credit in an account opened in the name of the supplier. The invoice from the supplier should not be recorded in the Purchases Day Book because, in the event that happened, the credit in the supplier's account would be correct but the debit (as part of the total) in the Purchases account would be incorrect.

Activity 16.3 Acquisition of an asset on credit terms

(a) Why is it an error to record the acquisition of a non-current asset on credit terms in the Purchases Day Book?

(b) Acquired from Electroplastics Ltd, on credit terms, a photocopying machine for £80,000 and software such as toners and ribbons for £2,400. Show the prime entry for this transaction.

16.6 Journal entries for transfers between accounts

When we studied year-end adjustments (Chapter 7) we found that prior to preparing the Statement of income we had to make many transfers. For example, any prepaid portion of an expense had to be transferred to an asset account and a debt not expected to be recovered transferred from the asset account to an expense account. Each of these transfers would require a journal entry.

Cost of machine	38,500
Travel expenses	9,200
Cash refund	2,300

Let us consider a more difficult transfer – that of Raymond, the Procurement Manager who left for Japan with an imprest of £50,000 to buy a machine. Upon his return he refunds £2,300 and submits a report as shown on the left. The prime entries both for cash paid to Raymond and amount refunded by him would be in the Cash Book and when posted would show £47,700 as due from Raymond. Transfers necessary to clear that amount would require a journal entry as shown on the right.

	£	£
Sundries Dr		
To Raymond's advance	–	47,700
Machinery account	38,500	–
Travel expenses account	9,200	–
Being transfers		

16.7 Correction of errors

An accounting entry, if wrong, is not allowed to be corrected by rubbing it out or using correcting fluid. Instead, any correction needs to follow the normal double-entry rules with an appropriate debit and credit. The prime entry for such correction is made in the journal.

For example, a common error requiring correction would be when a credit sale is posted to a wrong customer perhaps with a similar name. Let us assume that a sale of £6,500 to Joe Nathan has been posted in error to Jim Nathan. There would probably be a letter of protest from Jim Nathan. The error is corrected by a journal entry shown below. The credit entry when made in Jim's account removes the error; while the debit in Joe's account makes him the debtor for the goods he has received.

Joe Nathan's account Dr	£6,500	–
To Jim Nathan's account	–	£6,500
Being correction of error in posting		

Activity 16.4 Correction of error

An invoice for 24,000 from Carmart Ltd, for an office vehicle, has been entered in the Purchases Day Book. Set out the journal entry for correcting this error.

16.8 Alternative approaches to error correction

If the accounting error is more complicated than one which requires merely a transfer from one account to another, there are two alternative ways of correction. To illustrate let us assume that a credit sale of £18,400 to Rick Jones has been entered as £8,400 in the Sales Journal (first error) and posted to Rob Jones (second error). The simplest way of correcting this error is first to reverse both wrong entries recording the sale (making the first journal entry on the right) and then account for the sale correctly (see the second journal entry). A quicker way is to combine these two journal entries, focusing (see the third journal entry) on correcting the balances in each of the three accounts.

Sales account Dr	£8,400	
To Rob Jones account		£8,400
Being correction of error		

Rick Jones account Dr	£18,400	–
To Sales account	–	£18,400
Being correction of error		

Rick Jones account Dr	£18,400	–
To Rob Jones account	–	£8,400
Sales account	–	£10,000
Being correction of error		

16.9 The need for journal entries to be authorised

A journal entry could well be used to cover misappropriations. For example, having misappropriated the amount received from a customer, the balance in that customer's account could be transferred by a journal entry to either a nominal account (e.g. Staff training) or to the account of another customer whose balance is to be written off as irrecoverable. Therefore, every journal entry *must* be authorised by a responsible manager.

16.10 Suspense account

16.10.1 Why is a Suspense account opened?

Suspense is associated with uncertainty. It might simply be that an amount was received and at the time it was not clear who it should be credited to. In the circumstances the amount is credited to a *Suspense account* until the uncertainty is cleared.

When the totals of the two sides of a Trial Balance are not equal and the reason for the inequality is uncertain, the Trial Balance is made to balance by inserting the amount of the difference in a Suspense account. The intention is to make the totals on either side of the Trial Balance equal when the newly set up Suspense account balance is also listed on it. When, upon detecting the cause (or probably causes) of the difference, the uncertainty is resolved, the amount placed in the Suspense account is transferred to the appropriate ledger account(s) and the Trial Balance would then be in balance.

16.10.2 Accounting entries to set up and to eliminate a Suspense account

A journal entry is required to place the difference in a Suspense account and more journal entries required when the errors are detected and rectified, and as we will see, not every journal entry will consist of a pair of matching debit and credit.

To illustrate, let us assume that £300 received from customer Ted Smith had not been posted to the customer's account. The result will be that the credit side of the Trial Balance will be £300 less than the debit. To correct this imbalance, until its cause is investigated and remedied, £300 is placed on the credit side of a Suspense account, which is then included in the Trial Balance and it would balance. The posting to the credit side of the Suspense account is authorised by the journal entry shown on the right. This journal entry, unlike those met with so far, requires only a single credit entry to be made. This is because if a matching debit entry is also made in another account the Trial Balance will again become imbalanced. When, in due course, the cause of the imbalance (failure to post to the credit of the customer's account) is detected, a second journal entry (see on the right) authorises the transfer of the credit from the Suspense account to the customer Ted Smith's account.

To Suspense account	–	£300
Being trial balance difference placed in suspense		

Suspense account	Dr	£300	–
To Ted Smith's account		–	£300
Being correction of double-entry error			

Activity 16.5 Placing and eliminating a balance in the Suspense account

The copy sales invoice to Jim Wallace for £24,000 has been posted to the customer's account as £42,000. You are required to prepare journal entries to:

(a) place in a Suspense account the resulting difference in the Trial Balance; and
(b) eliminate the Suspense account balance when the error is detected and corrected.

Sales Day Book Date: 7 May 2012			
Voucher	Customer	F	Amount
G712	Sally Davies	L85	£1,468
G713	Joe Brooks	L74	£945
G714	Peter Folly	L39	£3,250
G715	Mike Brown	L93	£1,875
	Sales a/c	L12	£7,838

Similar treatment is required if there is a casting error in one of the Day Books. For example, let us assume that a folio in the Sales Day Book (shown on the left) has been overcast by £300, i.e. added as £7,838 instead of £7,538. This wrong total would have been credited to the Sales account, whereas each of the four customers would have been individually debited with the value of each invoice. As a result the debit side of the Trial Balance will be £300 less than the credit side, and until the cause of the imbalance is identified the journal entry shown on the right wil require £300 to be entered in a Suspense account. When, in due course, the overcastting of the Sales Day Book is detected, another journal entry (shown on the left) will authorise the transfer of the debit balance of £300 from the Suspense account to the Sales account, so that the amount reported as sales is reduced to the correct amount of £7,538.

Suspense a/c *Being difference in Trial Balance placed in suspense*	Dr	£300	–

Sales account To Suspense account *Being correction of overcast in Sales Day Book folio xx*	Dr	£300	– £300

16.11 Preparing financial statements without clearing the Suspense

A Suspense account balance signals the existence of accounting errors and the failure to detect and correct them. Hence, financial reports such as the Statement of income and the Statement of financial position should not be prepared until the balance in a Suspense account is cleared. However, in rare circumstances, there may arise a need to present the financial reports while the Suspense account balance remains uncleared. In such circumstances a Suspense account balance, if a debit, may be reported among assets and, if a credit, included on the Equity and liabilities side of the Statement of financial position. This is not, of course, a satisfactory situation and every step should be taken to clear the balance held in suspense as quickly as possible. The worst case scenario is when the Suspense account balance is written off, i.e. added to an expense if a debit or offset from an expense if a credit. The immateriality of the amount of the Suspense account balance is usually the excuse for this unsatisfactory treatment. The danger of doing this is that while the amount so eliminated may appear insignificant in itself, it could be the net effect of several significant errors.

16.12 Recalculation of profits after correcting errors

Some errors, such as the one where sales were posted to a wrong customer, would not affect the profit or loss reported in the Statement of income nor the overall financial position reported on the Statement of financial position. On the other hand, other errors, such as the failure to post a supplier's invoice to the Trade payables account, will result in the liability being understated. Similarly, the overcasting of the Sales Day Book would have resulted in the sales (i.e. income) being over-stated. Hence, in such cases, when errors are detected and rectified, the reported performance and position will require amendment.

Activity 16.6 Performance/position reported without eliminating Suspense account

For the year ended 31 December 2012 Tim Blunt reported a gross profit of £184,500 and a net profit of £79,800, reporting the Trial Balance difference in a Suspense account. Subsequently, the following accounting errors were detected:

(a) A folio in the Purchases Day Book had been added as £144,800, instead of £114,800.

(b) £4,500 paid to Molly Poe, a supplier, has not been posted to her account.

(c) Three months' rent of £6,000, remaining unpaid, has not been accounted for.

Required:
(a) Set out the journal entries needed to correct the errors.
(b) Show the Suspense Account, and
(c) calculate the revised Gross profit and Net profit for the year ended 31 December 2012.

Summary

- The journal is another subsidiary book of account. It was once the only book of prime entry but is now used for making prime entry for any transaction which cannot be recorded in any other book of prime entry.
- A Suspense account would be unnecessary unless the Trial Balance fails to balance; but should it become necessary a journal entry is needed to set it up and another for eliminating it.

Suggested answers to activities

16.1 The books of account

(a) The prime entry books:	What they record:
Cash Book	All cash transactions
Purchases Day Book	Credit purchases
Sales Day Book	Credit sales
Purchases Returns Day Book	Returns of credit purchases
Sales Returns Day Book	Returns of credit sales
Journal	All other transactions

(b) Main books of account:
Cash Book and the ledgers. These alone record transactions on a double-entry basis and hence these alone are listed in a Trial Balance.

(c) Subsidiary books of account:
The four Day Books and the Journal

16.2 Capital consists of assets

		£	£
Sundries	Dr		
To Sundries			
Motor vehicles account		30,000	–
Furniture account		12,000	–
Capital account		–	32,000
Bank loan account		–	10,000
Being assets and liability introduced as capital			

16.4 Correction of error

Motor vehicles account	Dr	£24,000	–
To Purchases account		–	£24,000
Being correction of error			

The invoice for £24,000 recorded in the Purchases Day Book would have been debited to the Purchases account, and requires transfer to the Motor vehicles account.

16.3 Acquisition of an asset on credit terms

(a) If the invoice for acquiring an asset is recorded in the Purchases Day Book, the individual entry will be posted to the credit of the supplier's account (which is correct); but the corresponding debit will be made in the Purchases account rather than the asset account. This is because the periodical total of the Purchases Day Book is debited to the Purchases account.

(b) Journal entry:

		£	£
Sundries	Dr		
To Electroplastics Ltd a/c		–	82,400
Office Equipment a/c		80,000	–
Stationery a/c		2,400	–
Being acquisition on credit terms of a photocopy machine and its software			

16.5 Placing and elimination of a Suspense account balance

(a) To place the Trial Balance difference in Suspense

To Suspense a/c	–	£18,000
Being a credit shortfall in the Trial Balance placed in a Suspense account		

(b) To eliminate the amount placed in suspense:

Suspense account	Dr	£18,000	–
To Jim Wallace a/c		–	£18,000
Being correction of error			

16.6 Performance/position reported without eliminating Suspense account balance

(a) Journal entries:

1	Suspense a/c	Dr	£30,000	–
	To Purchases a/c		–	£30,000
	Being correction of error			
2	Molly Poe's a/c	Dr	£4,500	–
	To Suspense a/c		–	£4,500
	Being correction of error			
3	Rent a/c	Dr	£6,000	–
	To Rent accrued a/c		–	£6,000
	Being correction of error			

(b) Suspense account

Journal 1	30,000	Balance b/f	25,500
		Journal 2	4,500
	30,000		30,000

(c)

Impact on	Gross Profit	Net Profit
As reported	£184,500	£79,800
Journal entry 1	£30,000	£30,000
Journal entry 2	–	–
Journal entry 3	–	(£6,000)
Revised profits	£214,500	£103,800

Multiple choice questions

Journal entries

16.1 Which of the following statements is incorrect? In the double-entry accounting system maintained manually, a journal entry:

(a) Should be substantiated by the appropriate voucher and authorised at the proper level
(b) Is needed only in the absence of other suitable book of prime entry for the transaction
(c) Should always consist of a single debit entry matched by a corresponding credit entry
(d) Should always end with a narration explaining the need for it

16.2 The journal entry to account for the acquisition on credit of factory machinery from Millet plc should require which of the following:

(a) Debit Machinery account and credit Cash account
(b) Debit Factory account and credit Millet plc account
(c) Debit Machinery account and credit Millet plc account
(d) Debit Millet plc account and credit Machinery account

16.3 Iain Blake commenced business introducing as his capital furniture worth £21,000, a car valued at £30,000 and £48,000 in cash. The journal entry for recording this would require:

(a) Debit in the Cash account and credit in the Capital account
(b) Debit in the three asset accounts, including cash and a credit in the Capital account
(c) Debit in the two asset accounts other than cash and a credit in the Capital account
(d) No journal entries

16.4 The prime entry for the acquisition of a Cash Book, ledgers and a journal for £240 from W. Smith Ltd on credit would be in the:

(a) Purchases Day Book
(b) Journal
(c) Cash Book
(d) None of the above

Correction of errors

16.5 If an amount paid for servicing vehicles has been posted in error to the Motor vehicles account the journal entry necessary to correct this error should require which of the following:

(a) Debit Cash account and credit Motor vehicles account
(b) Debit Vehicle maintenance account and credit Motor vehicles account
(c) Debit Motor vehicles account and credit Vehicle maintenance account
(d) Debit Vehicle maintenance account and credit Cash account

16.6 A repayment of £15,000 has been posted to Jerry Blake's Loan account, whereas £3,000 of this amount was paid as interest on the loan. To correct this error the journal entry would require:

(a) Debit Interest on loan account and credit Jerry Blake's Loan a/c with £3,000
(b) Debit Interest on loan account and credit Jerry Blake's Loan a/c with £15,000
(c) Debit Cash account and credit Jerry Blake's Loan a/c with £3,000
(d) Debit Jerry Blake's Loan a/c and credit Interest on loan account with £3,000

16.7 If a credit sale of £15,400 to Peter Smith had been entered in the Sales Day Book as £14,500, the journal entry for correcting the error should require which of the following:

(a) Debit Peter Smith's account and credit Sales account with £900

(b) Debit Cash account and credit Sales account with £900

(c) Debit Peter Smith's account and credit Sales account with £15,400

(d) Debit Sales account and credit Peter Smith's account with £900

16.8 The invoice relating to the acquisition on credit of office equipment for £24,500 from Globe Ltd was entered in the Purchases Journal. To correct this error which of the following needs to be done:

(a) Journal entry: Debit Office equipment a/c and credit Globe Ltd a/c with £24,500

(b) Journal entry: Debit Globe Ltd a/c and credit Office equipment a/c with £24,500

(c) Journal entry: Debit Office equipment a/c and credit Purchases a/c with £24,500

(d) Journal entry: Debit Office equipment a/c and credit Purchases Day Book

16.9 A sale of £7,800 to Peter Blowes has been posted to Paul Blowes. To correct this the journal entry should require which of the following:

(a) Debit Sales account and credit Paul Blowes account with £7,800

(b) Debit Peter Blowes account and credit Sales account with £7,800

(c) Debit Sales account and credit Paul Blowes account with £15,600

(d) Debit Peter Blowes account and credit Paul Blowes account with £7,800

16.10 Inquiries undertaken after the failure of the Trial Balance to balance revealed that the difference was wholly due to carrying down the Cash account balance of £74,800 as £47,800. No suspense account was set up. To correct this error which of the following courses of action is necessary?

(a) No journal entry: Debit the Cash account with £27,000

(b) Journal entry: Debit Cash account and credit Suspense account with £27,000

(c) Journal entry: Debit Suspense account and credit Cash account with £27,000

(d) Journal entry: Debit Cash account and credit Sales account with £27,000

16.11 A sale to Roy Rogers for £21,400 has been posted to the customer's account as £24,100. The Trial Balance failed to balance but the difference has not been placed in a Suspense account. The journal entry for correcting this error should require which of the following:

(a) Debit Sales account and credit Roy Rogers' account with £2,700

(b) Credit Roy Rogers' account with £2,700 (with no corresponding second entry)

(c) Debit Suspense account and credit Roy Rogers' account with £2,700

(d) Debit Roy Rogers' account and credit Suspense account with £2,700

Suspense account

16.12 Which of the following errors will disturb the balancing of the Trial Balance?

(a) Recording a sales invoice for £5,600 as £6,500 in the Sales Journal

(b) Failing to record a purchase invoice for £54,000 in the Purchases Journal

(c) Recording in the Purchases journal an invoice for acquiring an asset for £60,000

(d) Adding up the Returns inwards journal as £11,400 instead of £12,600

16.13 Identify whether you agree (yes) or disagree (no) with the following definitions:

	y: Yes	z: No
(a) Error of omission – not entered in any book of prime entry		
(b) An entry error – wrong amount entered in the appropriate book of prime entry		
(c) Duplication error – a transaction entered twice in a book of prime entry		
(d) Error of commission – posted to the correct side of the wrong account of same class		
(e) Error of principle – posted to the correct side of the wrong account of another class		
(f) Double-entry error – not posted or posted to the wrong side		
(g) Transposition error – figures in an amount switched around when entering/posting		
(h) Compensating error – an error which does not disturb the Trial Balance		

16.14 Which of the following will disturb the balancing of the Trial Balance?

(a) Entering a wrong amount in a book of prime entry

(b) Posting to an asset account instead of an expenditure account

(c) Entering an acquisition of an asset, on credit terms, in the Purchases Day Book

(d) Error in adding up a book of prime entry

16.15 If the only accounting error is each of those stated below, identify the amount of the Trial Balance difference which will be placed in a Suspense account:

(a) A folio in the Purchases Journal was added as £34,680 instead of £36,480

x	Dr 3,640	
y	Cr 1,800	
z	Dr 1,800	

(b) £4,200 paid to solicitors for conveyancing a property has been written off as legal expenses instead of being added to the cost of the property

x	Dr 4,800	
y	None	
z	Cr 2,400	

(c) £2,400, being the prepaid portion of insurance, was brought forward from the previous year as a credit balance in the nominal account

x	Dr 4,800	
y	None	
z	Cr 2,400	

(d) £218,400 paid to a supplier has been posted to the supplier's account as £214,800

x	Cr 3,600	
y	Dr 3,600	
z	Dr 218,400	

(e) A sale of £13,600 was recorded in the Sales Journal as £3,600 and posted to Guy Bernard, the customer, as £6,300

x	Dr 2,700	
y	Dr 12,700	
z	Cr 2,700	

(f) The recovery of staff loan, on pay-sheet, at £300 per month for nine months in the year has not been accounted for

x	Cr 2,700	
y	Dr 2,700	
z	None	

(g) The year-end Trial Balance records the balance of £116,200 in the Sales returns account as a credit balance

x	Dr 116,200	
y	Dr 232,400	
z	Cr 232,400	

16.16 In each of the following questions the difference in Trial Balance has been placed in a Suspense account. If the only error is subsequently detected to be the one identified below, the correcting journal entry should require:

(a) An invoice for £16,500 from Ken Bros, for goods purchased for sale, was not posted to Ken Bros' account

(w) Debit Purchases account and credit Ken Bros with £16,500 ☐
(x) Debit Purchases account and credit Ken Bros with £33,000 ☐
(y) Debit Ken Bros and credit Suspense account with £16,500 ☐
(z) Debit Suspense account and credit Ken Bros with £16,500 ☐

(b) £12,500 received from customer Sally Peter was posted to the debit of her account

(w) Debit Suspense account and credit Cash account with £12,500 ☐
(x) Debit Suspense account and credit Sally Peter's account with £12,500 ☐
(y) Debit Sally Peter's account and credit Cash account with £12,500 ☐
(z) Debit Suspense account and credit Sally Peter's account with £25,000 ☐

(c) Cash Book balance of £132,600 has been carried forward from one folio to the next as £123,600

(w) Journal entry: Debit Cash account and credit Suspense account with £123,600 ☐
(x) Journal entry: Debit Cash account and credit Suspense account with £9,000 ☐
(y) Journal entry: Debit Suspense account and credit Cash account with £9,000 ☐
(z) No journal entry: Debit Cash account and credit Suspense account with £9,000 ☐

(d) Prepaid rent of £12,000 has been brought down as a credit balance in the Rent account

(w) Debit Rent account with £24,000 ☐
(x) Debit Suspense account and credit Rent account with £24,000 ☐
(y) Debit Rent account and credit Suspense account with £12,000 ☐
(z) Debit Rent account and credit Suspense account with £24,000 ☐

(e) A sale of £4,200 to David Smith was recorded in the Sales Journal as £2,400 and posted to Derrik Smith as £240

(w) Debit Derrik and credit David £4,200 ☐
(x) Debit David £4,200, credit Sales £1,800, credit Derrik £240 and credit Suspense £2,160 ☐
(y) Debit Sales £2,400, debit David £2,160, credit Suspense £2,160 and credit Sales £1,800 ☐
(z) Debit David £2,400, debit Suspense £2,160, credit Sales £2,400 and credit Derrik £240 ☐

(f) A credit note for £640 issued to a customer Alex Bell has been recorded in the Return Inwards Journal as £460 and posted to the debit of Alex Bell's account

(w) Debit Return inwards £180, debit Suspense £460 and credit Alex Bell £640 ☐
(x) Debit Suspense £920, debit Return inwards £180 and credit Alex Bell £1,100 ☐
(y) Debit Return inwards £640, debit Suspense £460 and credit Alex Bell £1,100 ☐
(z) Debit Suspense £920, debit Return inwards £180, credit Alex Bell £1,100 ☐

(g) A cheque for £4,650 drawn in the name of Phil Sawyer, a supplier, has been recorded in the Cash Book as £465, but not posted to Phil's account

(w) Debit Phil Sawyer £4,650 to Suspense account £4,650 ☐

(x) Debit Phil Sawyer £465, credit Suspense £465 (£4,185 will be posted from the Cash Book) ☐

(y) Debit Phil Sawyer £4,650, credit Cash Book £4,185, credit Suspense account £465 ☐

(z) Debit Phil Sawyer £4,650, debit Suspense account £465 and credit Cash Book £5,115 ☐

16.17 The difference in the year-end Trial Balance was placed in a Suspense account. Subsequent inquiries revealed the following errors. Upon correction of all of them the Suspense account was fully eliminated. What was the amount placed in suspense?

(i) Sales account total has been added as £128,500 instead of £138,500

(ii) Return inwards of £3,200 was not posted to the customer

(iii) Carriage inwards amounting to £6,500 was listed as a credit balance

a	£200 Dr	
b	£200 Cr	
c	£6,700 Dr	
d	£6,700 Cr	

16.18 The credit side of the Trial Balance was £11,200 lower than the debit side. The difference was placed in suspense. The correction of which of the following errors will reduce the Suspense account balance:

(a) A cash sale of £3,400 has been posted as £4,300 ☐

(b) A credit sale of £2,150 has not been posted to the customer ☐

(c) Stationery acquired on credit terms for £340 has been recorded in the Purchases Journal ☐

(d) A credit note for £900 from a supplier has not been entered in Returns Outwards Day Book ☐

The impact of error corrections on performance and position

16.19 An invoice for goods for sale, £54,500, was posted to the supplier's account as £5,450. The resulting difference in Trial Balance was placed in a Suspense account and then adjusted with the Sundry expenses account. The impact of correcting this would be:

	Gross profit	Net profit	Net assets	
a	–£54,500	–£54,500	–£54,500	
b	–	–£49,050	–£49,050	
c	–£56,400	–£49,050	+£49,050	
d	–£49,050	–£49,050	+£49,050	

16.20 £12,000 received from a credit customer was posted to the debit of the customer's account. Resultant difference in the Trial Balance was placed in a Suspense account and then that balance adjusted with Sundry expenses. The impact of correction:

	Gross profit	Net profit	Net assets	
a	–	–£24,000	–£24,000	
b	–£12,000	–£12,000	–£12,000	
c	+£12,000	+£12,000	+£12,000	
d	–£24,000	–£24,000	–£24,000	

16.21 When reporting the profit and year-end position for 2012 a business did not take into account:

(i) Cost of goods lost by fire £56,400

(ii) Related insurance claim admitted at £45,000

The impact of correcting these errors would be:

	Gross profit	Net profit	Net assets	
a	+£56,400	+£56,400	+£56,400	
b	–	+£45,000	+£45,000	
c	+£56,400	+£45,000	+£45,000	
d	+£56,400	–£11,400	+£45,000	

16.22 After financial statements for 2011 were prepared it is discovered that credit notes for £4,000 issued by suppliers have not been accounted for. The impact of correcting this error would be:

	Gross profit	Net profit	Net assets	
a	–	–£4,000	–£4,000	
b	+£4,000	–	–£4,000	
c	+£4,000	+£4,000	+£4,000	
d	–£4,000	–£4,000	–£4,000	

16.23 When reporting the performance for 2011 and its position at the end, a business failed to take account of goods costing £45,000 removed by the owner and building depreciation of £18,000. The impact of correcting these errors would be:

	Gross profit	Net profit	Net assets	
a	+£45,000	+£27,000	–£18,000	
b	–£45,000	–£63,000	–£63,000	
c	+£63,000	+£45,000	+£45,000	
d	+£63,000	+£63,000	+£63,000	

General

16.24 The working capital (or net current assets) of a business is:

(a) The capital introduced by the proprietor at commencement of business

(b) Current assets less current liabilities

(c) Capital plus liabilities which are not expected to be paid within twelve months of period-end

(d) Non-current assets plus current assets less current liabilities

16.25 Which of the following statements is correct? If a business acquires a vehicle for £36,000, making a downpayment of £15,000 and undertaking to pay the remainder a year later:

(a) Net assets will increase by £36,000

(b) Net assets will increase by £21,000

(c) Net assets will not change

(d) Net assets will decrease by £21,000

16.26 If, as at the commencement of an accounting period, the account named below has a balance as stated in respect of each, what would that balance represent:

(a) Trade creditors account – a credit balance

(b) Rent account – a debit balance

(c) Stationery account – a debit balance

(d) Accrued expenses account – a credit balance

(e) Insurance account – a debit balance

(f) Trade debtors account – a debit balance

(g) Salaries account – a credit balance

(h) Rent receivable account – a debit balance

(i) Staff loan account – a debit balance

Amount payable	Amount receivable	Unused expense
x	y	z

16.27 Which of the following should be the first action when making a prime entry for a transaction?

(a) Enter the transaction in the appropriate book of prime entry

(b) Decide on the ledger account to be debited and the one to be credited

(c) Post the transactions to the appropriate ledger accounts

(d) Study the voucher to identify the nature of the transaction

16.28 The amount paid by a business as premium on the owner's life insurance is accounted as:

(a) Debit Drawings account and credit Cash account

(b) Debit Insurance account and credit Cash account

(c) Debit Capital account and credit Cash account

(d) Debit Insurance account and credit Accruals account

16.29 Shown on the right is an extract of the year-end Trial Balance. At which of the following points of the accounting process has the Trial Balance been extracted?

	Debit	Credit
Machinery account	£580,000	–
Provision for depreciation	–	£312,600
Depreciation account	£84,200	–

(a) At the beginning of the accounting period

(b) On the last day of the accounting period prior to making any year-end adjustments

(c) On the last day of the accounting period prior to writing off depreciation for the year

(d) On the last day of the accounting period after writing off depreciation for the year

16.30 When the Trial Balance extracted from the books of Kevin Enterprises at the year-end failed to balance, the difference was placed in a Suspense account. Identify the amount that would have been placed in suspense as a result of each of the following errors:

	X	Y	Z
(a) A folio in the Purchases Journal has been undercast by £1,800	Dr 3,640	Cr 1,800	Dr 1,800
(b) £4,200 paid for conveyancing has been written off instead of capitalising	Dr 4,800	None	Cr 2,400
(c) £2,400 prepaid insurance has been brought forward from the previous year as a credit balance	Dr 4,800	None	Cr 2,400
(d) £218,400 paid to a supplier was posted to the supplier as £214,800	Dr 3,600	Cr 3,600	Dr 218,400
(e) A sale of £13,600 was recorded in the Sales Journal as £3,600 and posted to the customer's account as £6,300	Cr 2,700	Dr 2,700	Dr 12,700
(f) The recovery of staff loan at £300 per month for nine months in the year has not been accounted for	None	Cr 2,700	Dr 2,700

Answers to multiple choice questions

16.1: c 16.2: c 16.3: c 16.4: b 16.5: b 16.6: a 16.7: a 16.8: c 16.9: d 16.10: a 16.11: b 16.12: d 16.13a: y 16.13b: y 16.13c: y 16.13d: y 16.13e: y 16.13f: y 16.13g: y 16.13h: y 16.14: d 16.15a: z 16.15b: y 16.15c: x 16.15d: y 16.15e: z 16.15f: z 16.15g: y 16.16a: z 16.16b: z 16.16c: x 16.16d: z 16.16e: x 16.16f: x 16.16g: x 16.17: b 16.18: b 16.19: b 16.20: a 16.21: d 16.22: c 16.23: a 16.24: b 16.25: c 16.26a: x 16.26b: z 16.26c: z 16.26d: x 16.26e: z 16.26f: y 16.26g: x 16.26h: y 16.26i: y 16.27: d 16.28: a 16.29: c 16.30a: z 16.30b: y 16.30c: x 16.30d: x 16.30e: x 16.30f: x

Progressive questions

PQ 16.1 Opening the books of a retail outlet

Sheila West commenced a retail outlet introducing as part of her capital Furniture £36,000, Motor vehicle £24,000, Inventory £48,000 and Cash £4,000. She has arranged with her bank that the business would take over also her personal bank loan of £12,000.

Required: Set out the prime entry for accounting for this transaction.

PQ 16.2 Journal entries to account for transactions

During the year ended 30 June 2012 Jeremy Transporters entered into the following transactions:

(a) Bob Salmon, a customer experiencing cash flow problems, hands in his vehicle valued at £15,000 in part settlement of the amount of £18,000 due from him. Jeremy agrees to waive the remainder of the debt.

(b) £12,000 was paid to repair a vehicle. It was agreed that 50% of the cost of repair should be deducted from the salary of the foreman whose negligence necessitated the repair. Accordingly, from November 2011, for eight months the foreman was paid a salary of £2,400 per month instead of £3,000 per month. The part recovery of the repair bill, and the amount yet to be recovered, need to be accounted for.

(c) A vehicle acquired at a cost of £28,000 and written down to £15,000 was taken over by the owner for personal use.

Required: Set out the journal entry necessary to account for each of the above transactions.

PQ 16.3 Trial Balance difference placed in a Suspense account

The Trial Balance extracted from the books of City Grocers on 31.3.2012 failed to balance. The difference was placed in a Suspense account. Since then the following errors have been detected:

(a) A folio in the Purchases Day Book has been cast as £214,600 instead of £213,400.

(b) £800 paid to Lal Jason, a supplier, had not been posted to his personal account.

(c) A daily total in the Sales Returns Day Book of £1,700 was not posted to the nominal account.

(d) £120 paid for stationery was posted to the Office equipment account.

(e) £4,000 paid as rent was posted as £400.

(f) £360 paid for advertising was posted as £630.

(g) £3,000 received from Mike Shane, a customer, was posted to the debit side of the customer's account.

(h) £4,200, the total of Return Outwards Day Book was debited to the Sales returns account in the Nominal ledger.

(i) A sale of £6,250 to Joe Rogers was recorded as £2,650 and posted to Jill Rogers as £265.

(j) Prepaid rent amounting to £6,000 was brought forward from the previous year as a credit balance in the nominal account.

Required:

(a) Set out the journal entries necessary for correcting each error.

(b) On the basis that the correction of the above errors eliminates the whole balance placed in suspense, show the Suspense account.

PQ 16.4 Clearing the amount placed in suspense (ACCA)

Chi Knitwear Ltd is an old-fashioned firm with a handwritten set of books. A Trial Balance is extracted at the end of each month, and a Statement of income and a Statement of financial position are computed. This month, however, the Trial Balance will not balance, the credits exceeding the debits £1,536. You are required to help and after inspection of the ledgers discover the following errors:

(i) A balance of £87 on a customer's account has been omitted from the schedule of debtors, the total of which was entered as Trade receivable in the Trial Balance.

(ii) A small piece of machinery purchased for £1,200 had been written off to repairs.

(iii) The receipt side of the Cash Book had been undercast by £720.

(iv) The total of one page of the Sales Day Book had been carried forward as £8,154, whereas the correct amount was £8,514.

(v) A credit note for £179 received from a supplier has been posted to the wrong side of his account.

(vi) An electricity bill for the sum of £152, not yet accounted for, is discovered in a filing tray.

(vii) Mr Smith, whose past debts to the company had been the subject of an Allowance for doubtful debts, at last paid £731 to clear his account. His personal account has been credited but his cheque has not yet passed through the Cash Book.

Required:
(a) Write up the Suspense account.
(b) Set out the journal entries correcting the errors.

PQ 16.5 Clearing the suspense to prepare financial statements (University of Oxford)

Patrice has produced the following draft Trial Balance as at 31 March 2012. Subsequent investigation reveals the following points:

	£	£
Sales		47,200
Purchases	11,600	
Opening inventory	1,800	
Sundry expenses	6,200	
Motor vehicle	4,300	
Accumulated depreciation – vehicle		2,600
Receivables and payables	3,600	2,000
Cash at bank and in hand	400	
Capital		7,300
Premises	28,000	
Suspense account	3,200	
	59,100	59,100

(i) An office computer was purchased for £1,500 during the year and was debited to the Purchase account rather than than an Office equipment account. No depreciation is to be charged on the computer in its first year in the business.

(ii) An invoice for goods received from a supplier Katy Ltd for £800 has been mislaid and no entry has been made.

(iii) A payment of £220 for sundry expenses has been entered correctly in the Cash Book but posted as £20.

(iv) The total of the Purchases Returns Journal of £1,000 has not been posted to the General ledger. Correct entries have been made in the individual accounts in the Sales ledger.

(v) £500 received from a customer, correctly entered in the Cash Book, has not been posted.

(vi) The total of the Sales Returns Journal of £3,200 is not posted to the General ledger, though correct entries have been made in the individual accounts in the Sales ledger.

(vii) £1,300 paid to a supplier and correctly entered in the Cash Book has not been posted.

(viii) The cost of inventory as at 31 March 2012 has been ascertained at £2,400.

(ix) Depreciate equipment by £300 and Motor vehicles by £400. Ignore depreciation of premises.

Required:
(a) Journal entries to correct the errors.
(b) Show the Suspense account.
(c) Statement of income for the year ended 31 March 2012.
(d) the Statement of financial position as at that date.

PQ 16.6 Profit identified without correcting errors (CIMA)

After calculating net profit for the year ended 31 March 2012 WL extracted the Trial Balance on the right which failed to balance and the difference was placed in a Suspense account. Further inquiries were then made, and the following errors were identified:

	£	£
Land and building at cost	10,000	–
Building – depreciation at 31.3.2012	–	2,000
Plant at cost	12,000	
Plant – depreciation at 31 March 2012	–	3,000
Inventory	2,500	–
Trade receivables	1,500	–
Bank	8,250	–
Trade payables	–	1,700
Rent prepaid	400	–
Wages accrued	–	300
Capital account	–	19,400
Profit for the year ended 31 March 2012	–	9,750
	34,650	36,150

(i) A Payable account had been debited with £300 sales invoice (which had been correctly recorded in the Sales account).

(ii) The Heat and light account had been credited with £150 paid for gas.

(iii) G. Gordon has been credited with a cheque for £800 received from another customer, G. Goldman.

(iv) The Insurance account contained a credit entry for insurance prepaid of £500, but the balance had not been carried down and hence omitted from the above Trial Balance.

(v) Purchase returns had been overcast by £700.

Required:

(a) Prepare journal entries to correct each of the above errors.
(b) Open the Suspense account at 31 March 2012 and enter the relevant corrections.
(c) Recalculate the net profit for the year to 31 March 2012.
(d) Prepare a Statement of financial position as at 31 March 2012.

PQ 16.7 Financial statements prepared without clearing suspense (AAT)

When Debbie Brown extracted her Trial Balance at March 2012 she found that it did not agree. She opened a Suspense account, prepared her Statement of income and drew up her Statement of financial position as stated on the right. Subsequent checking of her accounting records revealed the following errors which when corrected eliminated the Suspense account:

Statement of financial position as at 31 March 2012

	£	£
Non-current assets:		
Shop fittings	1,500	
Accumulated depreciation	(300)	1,200
Delivery van	3,200	
Accumulated depreciation	(800)	2,400
Current assets:		
Inventory	2,917	
Trade receivables	2,154	
Cash and bank	1,223	6,294
		9,894
	£	£
Capital 1 April 2011	7,500	
Profit for the year	5,497	
Drawings	(5,000)	7,997
Trade payables		1,888
Suspense account		9
		9,894

(i) A cheque for £260 for acquiring a new display stand on 31 March 2012 has been entered correctly in the Cash Book but posted to the Shop fittings account as £200.

(ii) A credit note from XY Ltd for £60 has not been entered in the Return Outwards Day Book but posted to XY's a/c as £66.

(iii) Bank charges £21 appearing in the Cash Book are not posted.

(iv) An invoice for £139 for sales to Thompson correctly entered in the Sales Day Book was posted to Thompson as £193.

(v) A debit balance of £223 in Smith's a/c at 31.3.2012 was carried down as £253 and included in the Trial Balance at that figure.

Required:

(a) Journal entries necessary to correct the errors.
(b) The Suspense account.
(c) Statement of revised profit for the year.
(d) The corrected Statement of financial position as at 31 March 2012.

PQ 16.8 Suspense account cleared after preparing financial statements

Mackie Stores proceeded to finalise its accounts for the year ended 31.12.2012, by placing the difference in the Trial Balance in a Suspense account and reporting the Suspense account balance as a current asset on its Statement of financial position, as shown on the right. Early in 2013 attempts were made to clear the Suspense account, detecting the following errors:

(a) £17,000, being the cost of goods returned to suppliers, was posted to the credit of the supplier's account.
(b) £24,000 paid for advertising has been posted as £42,000.
(c) £58,000 paid to suppliers was not posted.
(d) £48,000 paid for carriage inwards was posted to the Carriage outwards account.
(e) £14,000, being the cost of goods removed for personal use by the proprietor, has not been accounted for.

Mackie Stores has reported a gross profit of £758,000 for the year ended 31 December 2012.

Statement of financial position as at 31 December 2012

	Cost	Dep.	£'000
Non-current assets	640	(280)	360
Current assets:			
Inventory		546	
Trade receivables		396	
Suspense account		74	
Cash and bank		54	1,070
			1,430
		£'000	£'000
Capital		750	
Net profit for the year		198	
Drawings		(50)	898
Current liabilities:			
Trade payables		498	
Accrued expenses		34	532
			1,430

Required:

(a) Set out the journal entries to rectify the errors detected in 2013, bearing in mind that the Statement of income has already been prepared.
(b) Ascertain the corrected gross profit and net profit for the year ended 31 December 2012.
(c) Set out the amended Statement of financial position as at 31 December 2012.

Test questions

Test 16.1 Correction of errors – basic

The following accounting errors were detected in the course of the annual audit:

(a) £16,000, the cost of furniture acquired for office use from Smiths Ltd, has been recorded in the Purchases Day Book.
(b) £1,050 paid for servicing vehicles has been posted to the Motor vehicles account.
(c) £6,400 received from Bob Martin, a credit customer, has been posted in error to the Sales account.
(d) A sale of £9,400 to Joe Budd has been recorded in the Sales journal as £4,900 and posted to Jill Budd.

Required: Set out journal entries necessary for correcting the errors.

Test 16.2 Correction of errors – more difficult

The audit of the books of Collin Drake, dealer in word processors, during the year to 30 April 2012 revealed the following errors and omissions:

(a) A sale invoiced to Sue Robert at £14,200 was recorded in the Sales Journal as £12,400.
(b) A purchase invoice of £16,450 from Tex Bros was omitted from the Purchases Journal.
(c) An invoice of £400, again from Tex Bros, but this time for stationery, was listed in the Purchases Journal.
(d) £11,500 received in respect of a debt written off in the previous year was credited to the Sales account.
(e) £16,000 paid on 1 August 2011 for office equipment was posted to the Stationery account. Such equipment is usually depreciated at 10% per annum on the straight-line method.
(f) Included in the Rent and rates account is £2,000 paid as property tax on Collin's private residence.

Required: Set out the Journal entries necessary for rectifying each of the above errors.

Test 16.3 Impact of error corrections on reported profit

The draft financial statements of Collin Drake have identified the gross profit and net profit for the year ended 30 April 2012 as £976,800 and £172,400 respectively. Thereafter the following errors were detected:

(a) A sale invoiced to Sue Robert at £14,200 was recorded in the Sales Journal as £12,400.
(b) A purchase invoice of £16,450 from Tex Bros was omitted from the Purchases Journal.
(c) An invoice of £400, again from Tex Bros, but this time for stationery, was listed in the Purchases Journal.
(d) £11,500 received in respect of a debt written off in the previous year was credited to the Sales account.
(e) £16,000 paid on 1 August 2011 for office equipment was posted to the Stationery account. Such equipment is usually depreciated at 10% per annum on the straight-line method.
(f) Included in the Rent and rates account is £2,000 paid as property tax on Collin's private residence.

Required: Identify the impact the correction of errors would have on the gross profit and net profit for the year.

Test 16.4 Trial Balance difference placed in a Suspense account

When the Trial Balance extracted from the books of Darwin Stores on 31 March 2012 failed to balance, the difference was placed in a Suspense account. Subsequent inquiries confirm the imbalance to have arisen because of the following errors:

(a) A sale of £9,600 to Sally Brown was not posted to the customer.

(b) A monthly total of the Return Inwards Journal had been posted to the nominal account as £12,400, instead of £21,400.

(c) A credit note issued for £1,200 to Peter Collins, a customer, recorded in the Returns Inwards Journal, has been posted to the debit of the customer's account.

(d) The balance of £4,250 in the Return outwards account was stated in the Trial Balance as a debit balance.

Required:
(a) The journal entries for correcting the errors.
(b) The Suspense account.

Test 16.5 Elimination of the Suspense account to finalise accounts

The Trial Balance stated below was extracted from the books of Joe's Retail on the last day of its accounting period, having placed in a Suspense account the amount by which it failed to balance. Subsequent inquiries revealed as follows:

Trial Balance as at 30.6.2012		
	£'000	£'000
Non-current assets	2,460	–
Accumulated depreciation	–	1,640
Depreciation	369	–
Rent	24	–
Salaries	476	–
Sales	–	2,872
Cash and bank	133	–
Inventory – 30.6.2012	416	–
Sales commission	78	–
Receivable/payable	396	509
Cost of sales	1,708	–
Advertising	84	–
Drawings	115	–
Telephone/postage	28	–
Stationery	17	–
Capital	–	1,250
Suspense account	–	33
	6,304	6,304

(a) A folio of the Sales Journal was undercast by £30,000.

(b) Goods included in Purchases at £24,000 were not included in the Inventory because they remained in transit on the day of the count.

(c) £12,000 paid as sales commission was posted as £21,000.

(d) One month's rent of £3,000, prepaid as at 1 July 2011, has been brought forward in the Rent account as a credit balance.

(e) Salary and rent, amounting to £36,000 and £6,000 respectively, remain unpaid as at 30 June 2012.

(f) Goods costing £16,000 removed by Joe for his own use have not been accounted for.

Required:
(a) Journal entries for correcting the errors and making adjustments.
(b) The Statement of income for the year ended 30 June 2012 and the Statement of financial position as at that date.

Test 16.6 Preparation of financial statements – advanced

Jill Grey operates the Town Shop on premises leased for ten years from 1.1.2009 paying £200,000 for the period. The upper floors of the premises contain two flats. Jill occupies one and has let out the other at £250 per week. She has also invested cash surplus to immediate requirements of the shop in savings certificates. The year-end Trial Balance of the shop appears as shown on the right. You are informed as follows:

(a) Inventory taken on 7 January 2013 reveals the cost of unsold goods in hand as £312,000 and unused stationery as £3,000. During the seven days after 31 December purchases amounted to £11,000, Sales (at cost plus 40%) amounted to £28,000, and stationery has been acquired for £1,000.

(b) A debt of £8,000 is to be written off and the allowance for doubtful debts adjusted to cover 10% of the amount outstanding.

(c) Salary and electricity of £18,000 and £3,000 respectively remain unpaid as at 31 December 2012.

(d) Jill estimates that a tenth of the cost of the lease may be allocated to each flat and depreciates furniture at 10% per annum, using the reducing balance method.

(e) One third of the cost of electricity and gas is to be recovered from Jill.

(f) Interest of £4,000 earned on savings certificates is yet to be accounted for.

Required: The Statement of income for the year ended 31 December 2012 and the Statement of financial position as at that date.

Trial Balance as at 31.12.2012		
	£'000	£'000
Lease of shop premises	120	–
Furniture at cost	200	–
Depreciation to 31.12.2011	–	30
Inventory as at 31.12.2011	248	
Sales	–	1,424
Investments (saving certificates)	45	–
Electricity and gas	21	–
Rent received account	–	15
Postage and telephone	14	–
Purchases	987	–
Receivables and payables	148	267
Salaries	302	–
Advertising	44	–
Stationery	16	–
Allowance for doubtful debts	–	11
6% Loan from Jack Grey	–	300
Carriage inwards	24	–
Capital account	–	200
Cash and bank balance	78	–
	2,247	2,247

Chapter 17

Control accounts

By the end of this chapter

You should learn:	You should be able to:
■ About control accounts and their usefulness	■ Prepare Control accounts ■ Reconcile the balance in a Control account with the sum of the corresponding individual balances

17.1 Introduction to Control accounts

17.1.1 What is a Control account?

A *Control account* is one which records in total the balances reported by a large number of corresponding individual ledger accounts. If we consider trade receivables, for example, there may be numerous accounts of individual customers written up in a Trade receivables ledger, each reporting the amount receivable from every customer. If we write up a Trade receivables control account, using all the information that went into each customer's individual account, we could arrive at a single amount reporting what is receivable from all the customers.

17.1.2 Why is a Control account written up?

The need for writing up a Control account was appreciated when, before the computer age, business entities found the extraction of Trial Balances a time-consuming and laborious process because they had to extract balances from a large number of personal accounts reporting receivables and payables. As a solution to this they decided to maintain just one account to record in total the transactions with all customers and, similarly, another to record in total those with all suppliers. These became known as Control accounts.

17.1.3 Can a Control account replace individual personal accounts?

Merely because we write up a Trade receivables control account identifying the total receivable from all the customers we cannot dispense with writing up a separate account for each customer because we have to keep track of how much is receivable from each, send them monthly statements and pursue the customers until we receive what is due to us.

17.1.4 How is it possible to write up a Control account as well as individual personal accounts?

Either the Control account or the individual customers' accounts will have to be maintained on a memorandum basis, i.e. outside the double-entry system. Let us consider both scenarios in turn:

(a) **Where the Control account is maintained on a memorandum basis.** The accounting for credit sales is carried out as we have seen in Chapter 5, debiting each individual customer's account with the value of every invoice and crediting periodic totals to the credit of the Sales account. Then the particulars of transactions with credit customers, obtained from different sources (see paragraph 17.2), are collated to write up a Trade receivables control account, on a memorandum basis, to identify the amount receivable from all customers.

(b) **Where individual customer's accounts are maintained on a memorandum basis.** In this scenario the pair of entries recording credit sales will take the form of posting the periodic totals from the Sales Day Book to the credit of the Sales account and debit of the Trade receivables control account. In addition, on a memorandum basis, personal accounts maintained for each customer in the Trade receivables ledger (which is then referred to as a 'subsidiary ledger') is debited with the value of every invoice.

There is a third scenario. If a company prefers to write up the Control account as well as the individual customers' accounts on a double-entry basis, that is possible. In the General ledger, the periodic totals of the Sales Day Book are posted to the Sales account and the Receivables control account, so that the control account is within the double-entry system, as in scenario (a) described above. Then, in the Sales ledger too, when the value of each invoice is debited to respective customers, the total of the periodic sales is credited to an Impersonal ledger control account. When maintained this way, the Sales ledger too is able to extract its own Trial Balance whenever necessary. This system is known as '*self-balancing ledgers*' (in Activity 17.5 below, the journal entries have been prepared assuming that City Stores operates with self-balancing ledgers).

17.1.5 Why is the name Control account used?

The name Control account is used because (a) the information used for writing it up is provided by different people (see paragraph 17.2), and (b) when the balance in the Control account matches the sum of the balances in all the customers' accounts in the Trade receivables ledger, the accuracy of the work of those writing up the accounts in the Trade receivables ledger may usually be presumed.

17.1.6 Alternative names for Control accounts

In practice you will find that a Control account is called differently in different businesses and in different computer accounting packages. For example the Trade receivables control account is referred to also as Sales ledger control account, Sold ledger control account or, in the UK, as Debtors control account. Similarly, the Trade payables control account is also referred to as Purchase ledger control account or Bought ledger control account or, in the UK, as Creditors control account.

17.2 The steps for writing up a Control account

We have learnt why a Control account is written up. Let us now study how it is written up, taking for illustration a retail shop owned by Mike Otherton.

Step 1: Obtain from the head of the Trade receivables ledger a list (see on the right) of amounts receivable on a particular date (say 1 May 2012) from all credit customers.

Trade receivables as at 1 May 2012	
	£
Mat Robert	1,000
Ivy Samuel	1,250
Rita Timothy	5,200
	7,450

Step 2: Obtain particulars of credit sales in the month. This information is obtained from the Sales Day Book and assuming that the shop is small and posting is done only at the end of each month, the Sales Day Book for the month of May will appear as on the right.

Sales Day Book May 2012	
	£
Mat Robert	6,000
Ivy Samuel	4,150
Rita Timothy	9,050
	19,200

Step 3: Obtain from the Cashier particulars of amounts received from credit customers in the month of May. If the Cash Book is equipped with analysis columns, the Cashier would easily be able to provide the information stated on the right.

Extract from the Cash Book	
	£
Mat Robert	900
Ivy Samuel	1,250
Rita Timothy	3,000
	5,150

Step 4: Use the information obtained from each of the above three steps to prepare a Trade receivables control account (shown on the right), reporting the total amount due from all credit customers on 31 May 2012 as £21,500.

Trade receivables control account

	£		£
Balance b/f	7,450	Cash	5,150
Sales	19,200	Balance c/d	21,500
	26,650		26,650
Balance b/d	21,500		

17.3 Control account corroborates the accuracy of individual balances

In the meantime those working on the Sales ledger would have continued to post the accounts they would write up for each individual customer (see on the right) with information obtained from the Sales Day Book, Sales Returns Day Book and the Cash Book and, upon balancing the accounts of the customers at the month-end, extract a list of amounts due from each of them as shown below. The accuracy of the amount (£21,500) reported as receivable (the sum of the list of receivable balances) is corroborated by the balance carried down in the Sales ledger control account.

Mat Robert's account

	£		£
Balance b/f	1,000	Cash a/c	900
Sales Day Book	6,000	Balance c/d	6,100
Balance b/d	6,100		

Ivy Samuel's account

	£		£
Balance b/f	1,250	Cash a/c	1,250
Sales Day Book	4,150	Balance c/d	4,150
Balance b/d	4,150		

Rita Timothy's account

	£		£
Balance b/f	5,200	Cash a/c	3,000
Sales Day Book	9,050	Balance c/d	11,250
Balance b/d	11,250		

List of customers as at 31 May 20X7

	£
Mat Robert	6,100
Ivy Samuel	4,150
Rita Timothy	11,250
	21,500

If the sum of the individual customers' balances can be so corroborated by being matched with an independently ascertained total, we may presume the absence of any mistake in the work of the Sales ledger personnel. Otherwise, we would expect the list of balances to be reviewed and any error detected and rectified. However, it is possible that the two amounts would not match because of errors not in writing up the individual customer's accounts but in writing up the Control account. For example, if there is an overcasting in the Sales Day Book (£19,200 added wrongly as £20,200) the Control account balance (based on the wrong total of £20,200) would not match with the sum of individual customers' balances, and the mistake then would be in the Control account, although the Trial Balance would still balance when the Control account debit balance is included in it because the Sales account credit is also incorrect.

17.4 Benefits of writing up Control accounts

There are several benefits from maintaining Control accounts, including:

- It confirms the accuracy of the work of those writing up numerous personal accounts of individual customers and suppliers if the total of the individual ledger balances is the same as the Control account balance.

- It is quicker to prepare a Trial Balance because a single balance in the Receivables control account (as well as Payables control account) is available for inclusion in the Trial Balance rather than to balance off, extract and list out the balances in a large number of personal accounts maintained for each customer and supplier.
- It enables the tracing of errors by localising the error, if possible, to one of the subsidiary ledgers, so that there is no need to check all the accounts when looking for an error. For example, if a Trial Balance balances when it includes the balance in the Trade receivables control account, but does not when the total of individual customer's balances is substituted, the presumption (which may be wrong) is that the error is in the Trade receivables ledger.

17.5 The Trade receivables ledger control account

A Trade receivables control account would include every entry usually made in any customer's account. Study the Trade receivables control account shown below – presented as a pro forma, i.e. as a sample. We are already familiar with how every individual customer's account is posted with sales, amounts received, sales returns, bad debts, discounts allowed, cheques dishonoured as well as reversal of discounts.

Pro forma Trade receivables control account

Balance b/f	xx	Balance b/f[a]	x
Sales (on credit)	xxx	Cash/cheques	xxx
Dishonoured cheques	xx	Discounts allowed	x
Discount (reversed)	xx	Sales returns	x
		Bad debts written off	x
		Set off by contra[b]	x
Balance c/d[a]	x	Balance c/d	xx
Balance b/d	xx	Balance c/d[a]	x

However, on the pro forma, there are two items that have been marked as [a] and [b] which we need to know about.

The first marked [a] arises from the fact that it is possible for one or more customers, with an account in the Trade receivables ledger, to have a credit balance. This could occur for a number of reasons, e.g. we may have received an overpayment or we may, after receiving full payment, have allowed a credit either for defective goods or for goods returned.

The second marked [b] is known as *offset by contra*, which simply means that an amount receivable from a customer needs to be reduced by any amount owed to the same party. A business could possibly purchase from the same party to whom it also sells. If we name that party Imran, Imran could be among Trade receivables, with say £10,000 due from him, and at the same time also among our Trade payables with an amount of say £2,000 that we owe him. In these circumstances it is likely that we would receive only the net amount of £8,000 from Imran in full settlement. When the amount received is posted to the Trade receivables control account, Imran's balance of £2,000 will remain as part of both Trade receivables and Trade payables, unless we cancel both by crediting the Trade receivables control account and debiting the Trade payables control account with £2,000. This is known as Offset by contra.

Activity 17.1 Trade receivables control account balance

Jerry Smith's trade receivables as at 1 January 2012 were £12,500 and his transactions in the two months commencing on that date include those stated on the right.

Required: Ascertain the balance he would carry down in his Trade receivables control account as at 31.1.2012 and 29.2.2012.

During 2012	January	February
Cash sales	£1,500	£2,400
Credit sales	£15,500	£18,600
Returns by credit customers	£200	£540
Settlement discount allowed	£160	£210
Collection from credit customers	£13,650	£16,250
Reversal of discount allowed	£40	–
Bad debts written off	£240	£180
Recovery of debt written off in 2011	–	£80

Activity 17.2 Writing up the Trade receivables control account

Balances in customers' accounts as at 1 March 2012:	
Debit balances	£148,650
Credit balances	£14,200

Information from the Journal in March 2012:	
Bad debts written off	£12,460
Discount reversed	£1,200
Offset by contra	£22,660

Totals for March 2012:	
Sales Day Book	£984,050
Sales Returns Day Book	£62,450
Discount column (in Cash Book receipt side)	£11,600
Receipts from credit customers	£846,240

Credit balance in Sales ledger on 31.3.2012	£24,280

Required: Prepare the Trade receivables control account for the month of March 2012.

17.6 Trade payables control account

To write up a Trade payables control account the information necessary is obtained as follows:

- Opening balances: by extracting a list of balances from each individual supplier's account, at the commencement of the period, from the Trade payables ledger. All balances in suppliers' accounts will normally be credits. Exceptionally, however, one or more of them could have a debit balance.
- Credit purchases: from the periodic totals of the Purchases Day Book.
- Purchases returns: from periodic totals of the Return Outwards Day Book.
- Payments to suppliers: by analysing the payment side of the Cash Book.
- Discounts received: from the periodic totals of the Discount column on the payment side of the Cash Book.
- Set off by contra would be journalised.

A pro forma Trade payables control account is shown on the right.

Pro forma Trade payables control account

Balance b/f	x	Balance b/f	xx
Cash/cheque	xxx	Purchases (credit)	xxx
Purchase returns	x		
Discount received	x		
Set off by contra	x		
Balance c/d	xx	Balance c/d	x
Balance c/d	x	Balance b/d	xx

Activity 17.3 Trade payables control account

Carmen owes his suppliers £224,200 on 1 March 2012. His transactions include those stated on the right.

Required: Ascertain the Purchase ledger control account balances as at 31 March and 30 April 2012.

In 2012	March	April
Purchases for cash	£11,500	£8,600
Purchases on credit	£286,400	£296,800
Payments to credit suppliers	£256,200	£288,500
Returns to credit suppliers	£12,500	£9,600
Cash discount earned	£11,200	£5,400

Activity 17.4 Writing up a Purchases ledger control account

Balances in suppliers' accounts as at 1 July 2012:	
Debit balances	£11,450
Credit balances	£214,840

Totals for July 2012:	
Purchases Day Book	£627,550
Purchases Returns Day Book	£22,340
Discount column (Cash Book receipt side)	£42,800
Payments to suppliers	£586,750

Journal information:	
Offset by contra	£22,660

Debit balance in Payables ledger 31.7.2012	£5,160

Required: Prepare the Trade payables control account for the month ending on 31 July.

Activity 17.5 Offset by contra – assuming self-balancing ledgers

As at 30 June 2012 an amount of £24,500 owed to City Stores is reported in the Trade payables control account and £7,200 due from the same party reported in the Trade receivables control account, though set-off has been agreed with City Stores.

Required: Set out in the form of journal entries how the set-off should be accounted for.

17.7 When a Control balance fails to corroborate individual balances

When the Control account balance fails to match the sum of the list of corresponding individual account balances the error could be in either amount or both. Focusing only on the Trade receivables ledger, let us consider a series of errors with a view to identifying whether the error would affect (indicated as Yes) or not affect (indicated as No) the sum of the list of balances (identified as Sum) or the Control account balance (identified as Control) or both:

Nature of error	Sum	Control
1. A transaction not entered in the appropriate book of prime entry	Yes	Yes
2. A transaction entered at the wrong amount in the book of prime entry	Yes	Yes
3. Error in casting a book of prime entry	No	Yes
4. Posting a wrong amount to the correct side of the customer's account	Yes	No
5. Posting to the wrong side of the customer's account	Yes	No
6. Error in extracting a balance in a customer's account	Yes	No
7. Error in adding up the list of individual customers' balances	Yes	No
8. Listing a credit balance in the customer's account as a debit	Yes	No
9. Error in casting the Control account	No	Yes
10. Not including a transaction in the Control account	No	Yes
11. Including an item on the wrong side of the Control account	No	Yes
12. Not recording an offset by contra	Yes	Yes

If the Control account balance does not match the total of the list of balances, either might be incorrect (see 17.3) and this means both amounts need to be reviewed and after identifying why they failed to match, an attempt should be made to reconcile the two.

For illustration let as assume that as at 31 March 2012 the Sales ledger control account reports a balance of £548,400 whereas the list of individual customers' balances amounts to £544,968. Inquiries revealed the following errors:

(a) A credit note for £600 issued to a customer was entered in the Returns Inwards Day Book as £60.

(b) Cash discount of £34 allowed to a customer has been posted to the debit of that customer's account.

(c) A folio in the Sales Day Book has been added as £17,600 instead of £18,600.

(d) An invoice for £17,200 has been posted to the customer's account as £12,700.

The errors need to be rectified as follows:

(a) The credit note, which reduces the amount receivable from customers, has been entered in the book of prime entry at an amount £540 lower than actual. The wrong amount would have been posted individually in the customer's account and as part of the total in the Sales ledger control account. Therefore the difference of £540 should reduce both the sum of the list and the Control account balance.

(b) Cash discount posted to the wrong side of the customer's account would have increased the list of balances by double the amount £34 × 2 = £68. The error affects only the sum of the list.

(c) Undercasting of the Sales Day Book by £1,000 affects only the Control account which records the totals.

(d) The invoice for £17,200 would have been entered in the Sales Day Book and included in the total recorded in the Trade receivables control account. Posting the smaller amount would have resulted in a lower sum on the list of receivables.

The reconciliation of the sum of the list of customers' balances with the Sales ledger control account balance will be as follows:

Reconciliation of the sum of the individual Trade receivable balances with the balance in the Trade receivables control account as at 31.3.2012	Sum of the list of balances	Control account
Balances as reported	£544,968	£548,400
(a) Error in entering a credit note in the book of prime entry	(£540)	(£540)
(b) Discount allowed posted to the wrong side of customer's account	(£68)	–
(c) Undercasting of the Sales Day Book	–	£1,000
(d) Sales invoice not posted to the customer	£4,500	–
Corrected and reconciled balances	£548,860	£548,860

Activity 17.6 Reconciliation with Control account

Simon's year-end Trial Balance (with other items reported in summary) is shown below. Although the totals on both sides of the Trial Balance are the same, the sum of the list of individual trade receivables and payables, amounting to £203,000 and £147,000 respectively, failed to match the Control account balances. Further inquiries revealed the following:

(i) A folio in the Sales Day Book has been added as £18,600 instead of £14,600.

(ii) £9,000 offset by contra between the Trade receivables ledger and Trade payables ledger is not reflected in the Control account balances.

Trial Balance as at 30.6.2012	£'000	£'000
Purchases/sales	632	984
Trade receivables control	216	–
Trade payables control	–	156
All other item balances	2,944	2,652
	3,792	3,792

Required:

(a) Prepare a reconciliation of the Control account balances with the sum of individual personal accounts balances.

(b) Set out any journal entry needed to correct errors.

(c) Prepare a revised Trial Balance including in it the corrected Control account balances.

17.8 Control accounts for other assets and liabilities

We have learnt the use of a Trade receivables control account to control Receivables and a Trade payables control account to control Payables and produce totals quickly for use in a Trial Balance. The same principle is applied to other assets and liabilities, e.g. Non-current assets and Inventories. For example, a Motor vehicles account reports the total cost of all vehicles in use. Particulars of each vehicle (such as those listed in the box on the right) are recorded in a Motor vehicles register. The sum of the cost of all

A Motor vehicle register may contain particulars of each vehicle. These may include the following:

1. The make and model
2. The registration number
3. The chassis number
4. Engine capacity
5. The cost and improvement
6. Who keeps custody
7. Supplier's particulars
8. Any guarantee/warranty
9. Mileage particulars
10. Service history
11. Major repairs
12. Insurance particulars

motor vehicles reported on the register should equal the balance in the Motor vehicles account.

We have also studied (Chapter 9) that limited companies write up in the ledger a single Share capital account recording the total of the so far called-up value of all shares in issue. Particulars of each shareholder and the value of shares held by each are reported in a Share register.

Summary

- Control accounts are written up, either within the double-entry system or outside it (on a memorandum basis), as a means of verifying the accuracy of the amounts reported as Trade receivables and Trade payables.
- Control accounts are of benefit also for speeding up the preparation of a Trial Balance and for isolating an accounting error to a particular subsidiary ledger.
- Since the information for writing up the Control account comes from different people who are independent of each other, it is a useful control tool.
- Though usually identified with the Trade receivables and Trade payables, the Control accounts are used also to account for other assets, liabilities and share capital.

Suggested answers to activities

17.1 Trade receivables control account balance

Trade receivables
control account – January 2012

	£		£
Balance b/f	12,500	Returns	200
Credit sales	15,500	Discount allowed	160
Discount reversed	40	Cash received	13,650
		Bad debts	240
		Balance c/d	13,790
	28,040		28,040

Trade receivables
control account – February 2012

	£		£
Balance b/f	13,790	Returns	540
Credit sales	18,600	Discount allowed	210
		Cash received	16,250
		Bad debts	180
		Balance c/d	15,210
	32,390		32,390

17.2 Trade receivables control account

Trade receivables control account

	£		£
Balance b/f	148,650	Balance b/f	14,200
Sales	984,050	Sales returns	62,450
Discount allowed – reversal	1,200	Discount allowed	11,600
		Cash Book	846,240
		Bad debts written off	12,460
		Creditors ledger – contra	22,660
Balance c/d	24,280	Balance c/d	188,570
	1,158,180		1,158,180
Balance b/d	188,570	Balance b/d	24,280

17.3 Trade payables control account balance

Trade payables control account – March 2012

	£		£
Cash – paid	256,200	Balance b/f	224,200
Return outwards	12,500	Purchases	286,400
Discount received	11,200		
Balance c/d	230,700		
	510,600		510,600

Trade payables control account – April 2012

	£		£
Cash – paid	288,500	Balance b/f	230,700
Return outwards	9,600	Purchases	296,800
Discount received	5,400		
Balance c/d	224,000		
	527,500		527,500

17.4 Trade payables control a/c

	£		£
Balance b/f	11,450	Balance b/f	214,840
Purchase returns	22,340	Purchases	627,550
Discount received	42,800		
Cash book	586,750		
Debtors ledger contra	22,660		
Balance c/d	161,550	Balance c/d	5,160
	847,550		847,550
Balance b/d	5,160	Balance b/d	161,550

17.5 Offset by contra – assuming self-balancing ledgers

In the General ledger:			
Payables' control a/c	Dr	£7,200	–
To Receivables' control a/c		–	£7,200
Being offset by contra			
In the Payables ledger:			
City stores a/c	Dr	£7,200	–
To Impersonal ledger adjustment a/c		–	£7,200
Being offset by contra			
In the Receivables ledger:			
Impersonal ledger adjustment a/c	Dr	£7,200	–
To City Stores a/c		–	£7,200
Being offset by contra			

17.6 Reconciliation with control account

(a) Reconciliation of the Control account balances with the sum of the individual personal account balances:

	Trade receivables ledger (£'000)	Trade payables ledger (£'000)
Balances in the Control accounts	216	156
Casting error in the Sales Day Book	(4)	–
Failure to record the amount offset by contra	(9)	(9)
Sum of the individual personal account balances	203	147

(b) Journal:

Sales a/c	Dr	£4,000	–
To Trade receivable control a/c		–	£4,000
Being correction of error			
Trade payables control a/c	Dr	£9,000	–
To Trade receivables control a/c		–	£9,000
Being correction of error			

(c) Revised Trial Balance (summarised) as at 30 June 2012:

	£'000	£'000
Purchases/sales	632	980
Trade receivables control a/c	203	–
Trade payables control a/c	–	147
All other items	2,944	2,652
	3,779	3,779

Multiple choice questions

Items in a Control account

17.1 The information for preparing a Control account is obtained from:

(a) The Cash Book
(b) The ledger
(c) The books of prime entry
(d) The General Journal

17.2 Which of the following will not appear in the Trade receivables control account?

(a) Amounts received from credit customer
(b) Cash sales
(c) Credit sales
(d) Bad debts written off

17.3 Which of the following will not appear in the Trade payables control account?

(a) Discount allowed
(b) Credit purchases
(c) Returns outwards
(d) Amounts paid to trade creditors

17.4 The periodical totals of the Returns Inwards Day Book are:

(a) Debited to the Trade receivables control account
(b) Credited to the Trade receivables control account
(c) Debited to the Trade payables control account
(d) Credited to the Trade payables control account

17.5 The periodic totals of the Discount column on the receipt side of the Cash Book are:

(a) Debited to the Trade payables control account
(b) Credited to the Trade payables control account
(c) Credited to the Trade receivables control account
(d) Debited to the Trade receivables control account

17.6 Offset by contra is accounted for by:

(a) A debit in the Trade payables control and a credit in the Trade receivables control accounts
(b) A debit in the Trade receivables control and a credit in the Trade payable control accounts
(c) A combination of entries stated in (a) above as well as in (d) below
(d) A debit and a credit respectively in the account of the particular customer appearing in the Trade receivables and in the Trade payables ledger

£204,950

Preparing a Trade receivables control account

17.7 As at 1.8. 2012 the Trade receivables ledger had £216,400 debit balances and £11,450 credit balances. Credit sales in August were £582,550 and sales returns £31,600. £498,200 has been received from credit customers. Identify the debit balance at the month-end assuming that the only additional information provided was as stated in each of the following alternative scenarios:

(a) Discount allowed was £14,400 and credit balances at the month-end were £19,750

(x) £166,600 ☐

(y) £254,750 ☐

(z) £263,050 ☐

(b) £235,000 of the amount received from trade receivables was net of 6% cash discount, and £14,800 of the amount received from customers was in respect of a debt written off as bad in the previous month. Credit balances in the Trade receivables ledger by the month-end was £9,240

(x) £266,740 ☐

(y) £267,640 ☐

(z) £281,540 ☐

(c) A trade debt of £9,500 was written off as bad in August and a cheque for £14,100 received from a customer has been returned dishonoured by the bank. Upon receipt of this cheque the customer had been allowed 6% cash discount. Discount allowed in the month was £9,400 and credit balances in the Trade receivables ledger by the month-end was £7,200

(x) £261,000 ☐

(y) £261,900 ☐

(z) £270,400 ☐

(d) In August £11,500 was offset by contra, £4,840 was allowed as cash discount and £2,100 was written off as bad. Credit balances in the Trade receivables ledger at the month-end was £14,200

(x) £253,460 ☐

(y) £258,290 ☐

(z) £276,450 ☐

Writing up a Trade payables ledger control account

17.8 During October 2012, purchases, purchases returns and amounts paid to suppliers were £728,450, £11,200 and £682,500 respectively. As at 1 October a list of Trade payables ledger balances included £149,550 credit balances and £7,400 debit balances. Identify the total of credit balances in the Trade payables ledger, at the month-end, assuming that the only additional information provided is as stated in each of the following alternative scenarios:

(a) Payments to trade payables include £280,250 paid taking advantage of 5% cash discount offered by the suppliers and by the month-end the debit balances in the Trade payables ledger amounted to £5,200

(x) £176,900 ☐

(y) £167,350 ☐

(z) £182,100 ☐

(b) During the month of October offset by contra amounted to £15,800; while at the month-end the debit balances in the Trade payables ledger amounted to £8,700

(x) £169,800 ☐

(y) £161,100 ☐

(z) £201,400 ☐

17.9 Place a tick in one of the following grids to identify which of the four alternatives is the correct analysis of the side in which the items listed below will appear in a Trade receivables control account.

(i) Cash sales
(ii) Credit sales
(iii) Discount allowed
(iv) Carriage inwards
(v) Reversal of discount allowed
(vi) Receipts from credit customers
(vii) Allowance for doubtful debts
(viii) Recovery of bad debt previously written off
(ix) Offset by contra
(x) Return inwards
(xi) Return outwards
(xii) Bad debt written off

	On the debit side	On the credit side	On neither side	
a	i, ii, iv	iii, viii, vi, ix, x	v, vii, xi, xii	
b	ii, v	iii, vi, vii, ix, x	i, iv, viii, xi, xii	
c	ii, v	iii, vi, ix, x, xii	i, iv, vii, viii, xi	
d	ii, v, viii	iii, iv, vi, vii, ix, xi	i, x, xii	

Focus on the concept

17.10 Which of the following statements relating to a Control account is correct?

(i) A Control account is always written up on a memorandum basis
(ii) A Control account may be part of the double-entry system or outside it
(iii) If a Control account is maintained the individual customers' accounts need not be
(iv) Customers' accounts may be written up on a double-entry basis or outside it

a	i, ii & iv	
b	ii, iii & iv	
c	ii & iv	
d	iii & iv	

17.11 Which of the following would be normal reason for a credit balance appearing in the Trade receivables ledger?

(i) A customer may occasionally be also a supplier
(ii) A customer could have returned some goods after paying for them
(iii) A customer may have paid without realising his cash discount entitlement
(iv) Offset by contra exceeded the amount receivable from that customer

a	ii & iii	
b	i & ii	
c	iii & iv	
d	ii & iv	

17.12 Which of the following would be valid reasons for writing up Total or Control accounts?

(i) It becomes possible to expedite the preparation of Trial Balances
(ii) It could be part of the company's internal control system
(iii) It is fashionable to write up Control accounts
(iv) It would become possible to localise any error to one of the subsidiary ledgers

a	ii, iii & iv	
b	i, ii & iii	
c	i, ii & iv	
d	i, iii & iv	

17.13 If the Trade receivables control account balance differs from the sum of individual receivable balances:

(a) The Control account balance has to be the correct amount receivable from customers
(b) The sum of the individual balances has to be the correct amount receivable from customers
(c) Neither amount may be the correct amount receivable from customers
(d) Control account balance would be correct if the Trial Balance balances when it is included in it

Reconciliation of sum of individual balances with Control account balance

17.14 The sum of the debit balances extracted from the Trade receivables ledger is different from the debit balance carried down in the Trade receivables control account. Inquiries revealed the following errors. Identify, by placing a tick in the appropriate grid, whether the correction of the error would involve (x) an adjustment to the sum of the list of Receivable balances or (y) an adjustment to the Control account balance or (z) adjustments to both.

	List	Control	Both
	x	y	z
(a) A trade debt has been omitted from the list			
(b) A customer with a credit balance has been listed as a debit balance			
(c) A folio of the Sales Day Book was added as £214,500 instead of £254,500			
(d) A debt regarded as irrecoverable has not been written off			
(e) £1,400 received from a customer has been posted to the debit of his account			
(f) Debt collection fees recovered from a customer are not recorded in Control a/c			
(g) A Returns Inwards Day Book folio was added as £9,450 instead of £9,400			
(h) A sale of £12,400 was posted to the customer as £1,240			
(i) An invoice for £16,000 recorded as £1,600 in the Sales Day Book			
(j) A dishonoured cheque has been posted to the credit of the customer's account			
(k) A credit note received from a supplier has been entered in the Sales Day Book			
(l) A customer's account balance was extracted as £2,480 instead of £3,480			

17.15 If a Trial Balance balances when the Trade receivables control account balance is included in it and does not when the sum of the list of customers' account balances is included, it would be obvious that the error is in:

(a) The individual customers' accounts in the Trade receivables ledger

(b) The Trade receivables control account

(c) Either the Receivables control account or the individual accounts of the Receivables ledger

(d) Neither the Receivables control account nor the individual customers' accounts

17.16 As at 31 March 2012 the Trade receivables control account balance was reported as £296,400 and this did not agree with the sum of the individual customers' balances. The following errors were discovered:

(a) A dishonoured customer's cheque for £4,500 has been posted to the credit of the customer's a/c

(b) Return Inwards Day Book was added as £17,600 instead of £27,600

(c) A copy sales invoice of £42,800 has been recorded as £24,800 in the Day Book

(d) £11,500 offset by contra is entered on the debit side of the Control account

Identify the Trade receivables as at 31 March 2012

a	£263,400	
b	£290,400	
c	£292,900	
d	£281,400	

17.17 The sum of the individual customers' balances as at 30 September 2012 was £492,800. This did not agree with the balance in the Receivable control account. The following errors have been discovered:

(a) Total of the discount column on the receipt side of the Cash Book was overcast by £1,800

(b) A sales invoice for £8,200 was not entered in the Sales Day Book

(c) £5,400 offset by contra is not recorded in both Personal ledger control accounts

(d) A cheque for £3,000 received from a customer has been debited to his account

Identify the trade receivables as at 30 September 2012.

a	£495,000	
b	£493,200	
c	£498,000	
d	£489,600	

17.18 The Receivables control account balance, as at 30 June 2012, was £412,500. This did not agree with the sum of individual customers' balances. The following errors have since been discovered:

(a) A copy debit note for £900 sent with goods returned to a supplier was entered in the Sales Journal.

(b) £40 paid for carriage outwards was debited in error to the customer's account.

(c) A sales invoice for £1,750 has not been posted to the customer's account.

(d) Return Inwards Journal has been undercast by £3,000.

Identify the sum of the individual customers' balances as found before correction.

a	£409,410	
b	£406,890	
c	£407,750	
d	£410,790	

17.19 Which of the following errors will not cause the Trade receivables control account balance to disagree with the sum of the list of individual ledger balances?

(i) A credit note for £900 issued to a customer has not been entered in the Returns Inwards Journal

(ii) A sales invoice for £6,400 has been posted to the customer as £4,600

(iii) The customer's list includes a credit balance of £1,800 as a debit balance

(iv) Discount column on receipt side of Cash Book has been overcast by £1,400

(v) £350 discount allowed to a customer has been posted to his account as £35

a	ii only	
b	ii & iii	
c	i only	
d	iii & iv	

Correction of errors

17.20 The difference in a Trial Balance was placed in a Suspense account and subsequently, upon correction of the following errors, the Suspense account balance was fully cleared:

(a) £380, the weekly total of the Discount column on the payment side of the Cash Book, has been posted to the debit of Discount allowed account

(b) £12,450 offset by contra was incorrectly debited to the Trade receivables control account and credited to the Trade payables control account

(c) A supplier's credit note for £4,800 has not been posted

(d) Bank charges amounting to £24 have not been accounted for

The balance placed in suspense would have been:

a	£4,040 Dr	
b	£4,420 Dr	
c	£5,180 Cr	
d	£5,560 Cr	

Reconciliation of personal ledger balances

17.21 Sheila, a cosmetics retailer, buys her supplies from Eumigs. As at 1 April Sheila owed Eumigs £29,450. She has received two invoices from Eumigs for purchases during April for £54,550 and £48,500. Another invoice from Eumigs of £23,300 and a remittance of £80,640 by Sheila are in transit as at 30 April. When making the remittance Sheila took into account a cash discount of 4%. A monthly statement received from Eumigs shows the amount due from Sheila as £155,800. Identify the amount Sheila owes Eumigs as at 30 April.

a	£23,300	
b	£71,800	
c	£75,160	
d	£155,800	

17.22 Raymond, a dealer in motor spares, received a statement from his supplier Sedan plc requesting the balance to be paid as £179,500, whereas Raymond's own Trade payables ledger shows that £98,440 was owed. Inquiries reveal:

(a) A remittance of £45,000 by Raymond is still to be received by Sedan

(b) Raymond is yet to receive an invoice for £32,500 from Sedan

(c) Raymond is not aware that Sedan has refused a cash discount of £560 because the cheque did not reach him within the stipulated time

How much is the discrepancy remaining to be investigated?

a	£3,000	
b	£3,560	
c	£4,120	
d	£12,500	

General

17.23 Which of the following is an appropriate description of current assets?

(a) Assets which are readily convertible into cash

(b) Assets intended to be used or converted into cash within the next accounting period

(c) Assets which are not fixed to the ground (like buildings)

(d) Assets capable of motion (such as motor vehicles)

17.24 Which of the following would not be listed among current assets?

(a) Trade receivables

(b) Opening inventory

(c) Closing inventory

(d) Prepaid expenses

17.25 Which of the following would not be an appropriate description of working capital?

(a) Current assets minus current liabilities

(b) Capital employed in a business minus the amount tied up in non-current assets

(c) The amount of business resources available to finance the day-to-day operations

(d) The amount of capital introduced by the owner to carry on with the business operations

17.26 Simple Simon's capital at commencement of the year was £234,500 and at the year-end was £258,400. Identify the profit he made in the year, in each of the following alternative scenarios:

(a) He drew £3,000 per month for his household expenses

(x) £12,100

(y) £23,900

(z) £59,900

(b) His drawings were £2,000 per month plus an additional £3,500 over Christmas

(x) £3,600

(y) £27,500

(z) £51,400

(c) His drawings were £2,500 per month; but he introduced £10,000 as additional capital during the year

(x) £40,000

(y) £43,900

(z) £53,900

17.27 Determine the amount of current assets and current liabilities that will result as at 31 December 2012 from all of the following adjustments:

(i) Rent income account includes £3,600 received as rent for four months from 1 December 2012

(ii) The debit balance in the Insurance account includes £9,600 paid for the year ending 31 March 2013

(iii) A supplier's invoice for stationery amounting to £800 is yet to be received

(iv) Telephone bill for £1,240, received on 2 January 2013 and yet to be accounted for, includes £600 rental for the year to 30 June 2013.

	Current asset	Current liability	
a	£300	£4,740	
b	£3,900	£2,700	
c	£2,700	£3,500	
d	£2,400	£4,440	

17.28 On 1 January 2012 Paul borrowed £60,000 from his friend Peter agreeing to repay the amount in five equal instalments commencing from 1 January 2012. Ignore interest. How will the amount owed to Peter be reported in Paul's Statement of financial position as at 31 December 2012?

(a) £60,000 as non-current liability

(b) £60,000 as current liability

(c) £12,000 as current liability and £36,000 as non-current liability

(d) £18,000 as current liability and £48,000 as non-current liability

17.29 Stated below are a list of accounting documents each identified by a letter stated in front. State in the grid on the right the appropriate identifying letter to name the document being described:

(a) Invoice (b) Receipt (c) Statement (d) Credit note (e) Cash sales memo (f) Voucher

(i) Document sent to customers every month to confirm the transactions during the month

(ii) A written acknowledgement of amount received

(iii) One or more written evidence of transactions accounted for

(iv) A note to inform a customer that his account has been credited with any returns

(v) The evidence usually available to support a cash purchase

(vi) A document advising the customer that his account has been debited

Answers to multiple choice

17.1: c 17.2: b 17.3: a 17.4: b 17.5: c 17.6: a 17.7a: z 17.7b: x 17.7c: x 17.7d: x 17.8a: y 17.8b: x 17.9: c 17.10: c 17.11: a 17.12: c 17.13: c 17.14a: x 17.14b: x 17.14c: y 17.14d: z 17.14e: x 17.14f: y 17.14g: y 17.14h: x 17.14i: z 17.14j: x 17.14k: z 17.14l: x 17.15: c 17.16: d 17.17: a 17.18: b 17.19: c 17.20: a 17.21: b 17.22: a 17.23: b 17.24: b 17.25: d 17.26a: z 17.26b: z 17.26c: y 17.27: d 17.28: c 17.29i: c 17.29ii: b 17.29iii: f 17.29iv: d 17.29v: e 17.29vi: a

Progressive questions

PQ 17.1 Trade receivables control and Trade payables control accounts

The following information relates to the personal accounts of a trader during March 2012:

	£		£
Cash purchases	62,400	Return inwards	26,450
Credit purchases	264,600	Return outwards	11,500
Carriage inwards	102,450	Cash sales	102,450
Carriage outward	412,200	Credit sales	412,200
Paid to suppliers	198,500	Bad debts	3,800
Settlement discount allowed to customers			15,950
Settlement discount received from suppliers			9,450
Receipts from customers			368,500
Dishonour of cheques received from customers			6,650
Reversal of discount allowed to customers			350
Debt collection expense charged to customers			150
Debt recovered by contra offset			15,500
Interest charged on a customer who persistently overstepped credit period			225

	Trade receivables balances		Trade payables balances	
As at 1 March 2012	Debit balance	£348,250	Debit balances	£9,400
	Credit balance	£16,200	Credit balances	£225,700
As at 31 March 2012	Credit balance	£17,200	Debit balance	£11,500

Required:

(a) The Trade receivables control account

(b) The Trade payables control account

PQ 17.2 Wrongly prepared Control account and reconciliation (London Examinations)

Barney Ltd has recently appointed a new accountant who has produced a Sales ledger control account for the month of May 2012 as follows:

	£		£
Opening debtors	45,230	Opening credit balances in the Trade receivables ledger	260
Cash and cheques received	189,630	Sales invoices	175,320
Closing credit balances on the Trade receivables ledger	150	Credit notes issued to customers	450
		Bad debts written off	2,300
		Provision for doubtful debts	3,000
		Contra Trade payables ledger	180
		Closing debtors (balancing figure)	53,500
	235,010		235,010

The actual list of Trade receivables ledger balances at 31 May, after deducting credit balances, was £27,480. Three errors were identified as follows:

(a) A credit balance of £120 at 31 May had been added to the list of closing debtors.

(b) The debit balance of Ted Brown (£340) had been listed as Ted Bragg.

(c) The debit balance of Sophie Tree (£490) has been omitted from the list.

Required:

(a) Re-drafted Sales ledger control account

(b) A reconciliation of the sum of the list of Trade receivables ledger balances with the balance in the Control account.

PQ 17.3 Errors affecting the Trade payables control account (ACCA)

The following errors have been discovered:

(a) An invoice for £654 has been entered in the Purchases Day Book as £456.

(b) A prompt payment discount of £100 from a supplier has been completely omitted from the books.

(c) Purchases of £250 had been entered on the wrong side of the supplier's account in the Trade payables ledger.

(d) No entry had been made to record an agreement to contra an amount of £600 owed against an amount of £400 receivable from the same party.

(e) A credit note of £60 from a supplier had been entered in the Control account as if it was an invoice.

Required: The numerical effect on the Trade payable control account balance of each of the above errors.

PQ 17.4 Reconciliation of Payables control account with individual balances

In the books of Morden Textiles, the Trade payables ledger control account reports as at 31.12.2012 a credit balance of £326,200 and a debit balance of £4,500. The list of individual trade payable balances extracted from the Trade payables ledger on the same date shows credit balances totalling £333,600 and debit balances of £2,800. The following errors have been identified since then:

(a) A debit balance of £1,700 in a supplier's account has been listed, in error, as a credit balance.

(b) A credit note received from a supplier for £3,600 is still to be accounted for.

(c) A contra entry of £8,200 with the Trade receivables ledger is posted to the credit side of the Trade payables control account.

(d) A Returns Outwards Day Book folio is added as £43,000 instead of £40,000.

(e) The remainder of the error arose from the failure to post a payment to the supplier's account.

Required: Prepare a reconciliation of Trade payables ledger balances with those in the Control account.

PQ 17.5 Trade receivables control and reconciliation (ACCA)

The Receivables control account of C Ltd is on the right. A list of individual customer balances at the month-end shows debit balances as £54,468.59 and credit balances as £520.80. The following facts have now been discovered:

Trade receivables control account

	£		£
Balance b/d	70,814.16	Balance b/d	1,198.73
Sales	54,738.36	Sales returns	2,344.39
Dishonour of cheque	607.15	Cash Book	68,708.27
Debt collection fees	108.81	Contra	378.82
		Bad debts	474.16
Balance c/d	1,194.26	Balance c/d	54,358.37

(1) No entries have been made in the Sales ledger for the debt collection fees and bad debts written off.

(2) The Sales Day Book has been overcast by £500.

(3) The Sales returns Day Book has been undercast by £10.

(4) A credit balance of £673.46 has been taken as a debit balance when listing the customer balances.

(5) The account of a customer who settled by contra was debited with £378.82.

(6) A debit balance on a customer's account of £347.58 has been stated in the list as £374.85.

(7) The dishonoured cheque had been entered in the Sales ledger as credit £601.75.

Required:

(a) Correct the Trade receivables control account.

(b) Reconcile the corrected Control account balance with the sum of the individual balances.

PQ 17.6 Trade receivables control and reconciliation (CAT amended)

At 30 November 2012 the balance on the Trade receivables control account in Elizabeth's General ledger was £39,982. The total of the list of balances on the customers' personal accounts was £39,614. Elizabeth discovered the following errors:

(i) An invoice for £288, correctly entered in the Sales Day Book has not been posted to the customer's account.

(ii) A payment of £1,300 was accepted in full settlement of a balance of £1,309. No entry was made to record the discount.

(iii) A credit note issued to a credit customer for £120 was incorrectly treated as an invoice.

(iv) An addition error on a personal account meant that the balance was understated by £27.

(v) A customer had lodged a payment of £325 directly to Elizabeth's bank account. The balance in the personal account was adjusted, but no entry was made in the Control account.

(vi) A folio in the Sales Day Book was added as £466 instead of £644.

(vii) A credit balance of £47 on a customer's account was listed as a debit balance.

Required:

(a) The Trade receivables control account, including the necessary correcting entries.

(b) Prepare a reconciliation of control account balance with sum of the list of balances.

(c) State the amount and description of the item to be included in the Statement of financial position.

PQ 17.7 Reconciliation of Control account balance with sum of individual balances

On 31 March 2012, the Trade receivables control account, maintained as part of the double-entry system by Bruce Stationers, showed a debit balance of £346,800 and a credit balance of £16,200. These do not agree with the sum of the balances extracted from the individual accounts in the Trade receivables ledger. Subsequent inquiries reveal as follows:

(a) A sale of £12,400 has been posted to the customer in the Trade receivables ledger as £21,400.

(b) On 19 March 2012 total of the Sales Day Book has been added as £116,400 instead of £114,800.

(c) The dishonour of a cheque for £6,800 has been posted to the credit of the customer's account.

(d) A credit balance of £2,800 in a customer's account has been listed as a debit balance in the list of balances.

(e) The Discount column on the Receipt side of the Cash Book has been added as £21,600 instead of £22,200.

(f) A payment of £160 for delivering goods to a customer's residence has been posted in error to the customer's account (as well as the Control account) instead of the Delivery expense account in the Nominal ledger.

(g) £2,600 written off as bad debt has not been entered in the Control account.

(h) Because of a casting error when balancing a customer's account, £26,700 is reported as receivable from that customer whereas the correct amount should be £29,700.

(i) A debt-collecting expense of £650 incurred in obtaining judgement against a trade receivable remains unpaid. This item is still to be charged to the customer in the Sales ledger and to be included in the Control account.

(j) The recovery of £7,200 in respect of debts written off in the previous year has been posted to the credit of the Control account.

(k) The recovery of a debt of £8,200 by offset contra is yet to be recorded in either of the Control accounts.

(l) A 5% settlement discount, claimed by a customer from whom a cheque for £4,275 was received, though approved is still to be accounted for.

Required: Prepare a reconciliation of the Trade receivables ledger balances with the balances in the Control account, identifying the sum of the individual Trade receivable ledger balances prior to embarking on the reconciliation.

PQ 17.8 Control accounts with a Suspense account (ACCA)

A Trial Balance has an excess of debits over credits of £14,000 and a Suspense account has been opened to make it balance. It is later discovered that:

(a) The discounts allowed balance of £3,000 and the discount received balance of £7,000 have been entered on the wrong side of the Trial Balance.

(b) The Trade payables control account balance of £233,786 has been included in the Trial Balance as £237,386.

(c) An invoice of £500 had been omitted from the Sales Day Book.

(d) The balance on the current account with the senior partner's wife had been omitted from the Trial Balance.

Required:
(a) Set out how you would make the necessary corrections and
(b) show the Suspense account, assuming that the corrections eliminated the balance placed in it.

PQ 17.9 Correction of errors and suspense account (ACCA)

(a) An inexperienced bookkeeper has drawn up a Trial Balance for the year ended 30 June 2012.

Required: Draw up a 'corrected' Trial Balance, debiting or crediting any residual error to a Suspense account.

	Dr	Cr
	£	£
Allowance for doubtful debts	200	
Bank overdraft	1,654	
Capital		4,591
Trade payable		1,637
Trade receivable	2,983	
Discount received	252	
Discount allowed		733
Drawings	1,200	
Office furniture	2,155	
General expenses		829
Purchases	10,923	
Returns inwards		330
Rent and rates	314	
Salaries	2,520	
Sales		16,882
Inventory as at 1 July 2011	2,418	
Accumulated depreciation of furniture	364	
	24,982	25,002

(b) Further investigation of the Suspense account ascertained in (a) above reveals the following errors:

(i) Goods bought from J. Jones amounting to £13 has been posted to his account as £33.

(ii) Furniture which has cost £173 had been debited to the General expenses account.

(iii) An invoice from Suppliers Ltd for £370 had been omitted from the Purchases account, but credited to Suppliers Ltd account.

(iv) Sales on credit to A Hope Ltd for £450 had been posted to the Sales account, but not to the Sales ledger.

(v) The balance on the Capital account had been incorrectly brought forward in the ledger, and should have been £4,291.

(vi) An amount of £86 received from A Blunt, a customer, in settlement of his account had been treated as a cash sale.

(vii) Discount allowed has been under-totalled by £35.

Required: Prepare Journal entries correcting each of the above errors and write up the Suspense account.

Test questions

Test 17.1 Preparation of Control accounts – basic (AAT)

The financial year of The Better trading Company ended on 30 November 2012. You have been asked to prepare a Total receivables account and a Total payables account. (Note: Total account is another name for Control account.) You are able to obtain the following information for the financial year from the books of original entry:

Sales: Cash	£344,890
Credit	£268,187
Purchases: Cash	£14,440
Credit	£496,600
Receipts from credit customers	£250,570
Payments to suppliers on credit	£403,970
Discounts allowed	£5,520
Discounts received	£3,510

Refunds given to cash customer	£5,070
Balance in the Sales ledger set off against the balance in the Purchases ledger	£70
Bad debts written off	£780
Increase in the provision for bad debts	£90
Credit notes issued to credit customers	£4,140
Credit notes received from credit suppliers	£1,480

According to the audited financial statements for the previous year, Receivables and Payables as at 1 December 2011 were £26,555 and £43,450 respectively.

Required: Draw up the relevant Total (Control) accounts.

Test 17.2 Wrongly prepared Sales ledger control account

A new member of accounting staff prepared the Trade receivables control account as shown as on the right. Every amount stated on it, other than the closing debit balance, is correct. However, the amount stated as collection from customers includes an amount of £4,200 received from a debt that was written off as unrecoverable when financial statements were prepared in the previous year's financial statements.

Required: A revised Trade receivables control account.

Sales ledger control account

	£		£
Balance b/f	34,850	Balance b/f	720
Sales (on credit)	49,200	Bank – receipts	29,550
Bad debt	400	Bank – dishonoured	1,425
Discount allowed	260	Discount reversed	75
Offset by contra	2,000	Sales returns	480
Balance c/d	540	Balance c/d	55,000
	87,250		87,250
Balance b/d	55,000	Balance b/d	540

Test 17.3 Reconciliation of Control balance with sum of the individual receivables

As at 31 May 2012 the Sales ledger control account debit balance was £408,900, whereas the sum of the individual trade receivables accounts was £407,360. Investigations revealed the following errors:

(a) The discount column on the receipt side of the Cash Book was added as £2,850 instead of £1,750.

(b) A cheque for £3,500 received from Betty Brown has been posted to the debit of her personal account.

(c) £4,840 receivable from John Brass, regarded as irrecoverable, has not been written off.

(d) £7,950 due from Sam Black, set off by contra, is not recorded in the Control account.

(e) A folio of the Sales Day Book has been added as £28,800 instead of £23,800.

(f) Any difference between the two sets of balances has arisen because of a credit balance in Mary Ratner's account having been listed as a debit balance in the list of customers' balances.

Required: Set out a reconciliation of the two sets of balances.

Test 17.4 Reconciliation of Control balance with the sum of individual balances

Camberwell Ltd's Trade receivables control account balances as at 31 March 2012 were as stated in the box on the right; whereas the sum of the individual account balances in the Sales ledger was £717,840. Inquiries revealed the following:

Debit balances	£748,250
Credit balances	£8,200

(a) The Sales Returns Day Book has been overcast by £800.

(b) £4,900 offset by contra, though recorded in the personal ledgers, was not posted to the Control accounts.

(c) A sales invoice for £19,810, though recorded in the Sales Day Book, has not been posted.

(d) £3,200, being the daily total of the Discount column on the receipt side of the Cash Book, has not been posted to the Control account.

(e) A customer's account balance has been carried down as £15,400 whereas it should have been £18,400.

(f) A debt write-off of £4,500 was not entered in the customer's account or in the Control account.

(g) A credit balance of £8,200 in the Trade receivables ledger has been included in the list as a debit balance.

(h) A customer's balance omitted from the list accounts for the difference.

Required: Set out a reconciliation of the Trade receivables control account balance with the sum of individual Trade receivables ledger balances.

Chapter 18

Accounting for Sales tax (VAT) and payroll

By the end of this chapter

You should learn:

- How to account for Sales tax collected from customers and paid to suppliers of goods and providers of services
- How to calculate net pay and account for pay-sheet recoveries

You should be able to:

- Account for Output VAT and Input VAT
- Account for pay and pay-sheet recoveries

18.1 Introduction to Sales tax

Sales tax, known as Value Added Tax (VAT) in the UK, is an indirect tax, *not* on the trader, but on the final consumer of goods and services. The trader is required by the government to register for the purpose and is then authorised to add VAT to the amount usually charged on customers for goods and services provided to them.

From the amount so collected the trader is entitled to offset any VAT he incurs on his own purchases and expenses and remit the difference to (or receive back the difference from) the appropriate department which, in the UK, is HM Revenue and Customs Department.

For purposes of VAT administration the calendar year is divided into four equal quarters – ending on 31 March, 30 June, 30 September and 31 December – and the trader is required to make the remittance not later than 19 days after the end of each quarter. At the time of writing the standard rate of VAT in the UK is 17.5% and will become 20% in 2011.

18.2 Accounting for Sales tax collected from customers

Sales tax collected from customers is known as *Output VAT*. The amount collected is a liability owed to the government.

(a) **VAT on Cash sales:** if we assume that the normal sale price of an item is £100, the trader has to make the sale, adding VAT calculated at the the standard rate of 17.5% for £117.50 and to account for the cash sale as shown on right.

Debit: Cash account	£117.50
Credit: Sales account	£100.00
Credit: HM Revenue and Customs a/c	£17.50

(b) **VAT on Credit sales:** credit sales are similarly subject to VAT. The sales income is accounted for, as usual, VAT free, whereas the Trade receivables are recorded inclusive of VAT (being the amount to be collected), and the difference (being the amount owed to the government) is reported as a liability (see entries on the right).

Debit: Receivables	£117.50
Credit: Sales account	£100.00
Credit: HM Revenue and Customs a/c	£17.50

18.3 Accounting for Sales tax on purchases and expenses

VAT paid by a trader on purchases and expenses is known as *Input VAT*. Normally a trader (if registered for VAT) is able to recover his Input VAT as an offset from the Output VAT.

Let us assume that the normal price of purchases (i.e. without adding VAT) is £60. The supplier would have invoiced the trader for £70.50 (£60 + 17.5%) and the purchases would be accounted for as shown on the left. If, within any quarter, the Output VAT is more than Input VAT the difference is payable on the 19th day after the end of that quarter. If the position is reversed a cheque for the difference would be received from the VAT office. Assuming the trader's transactions were a single credit sale and a corresponding purchase, the account reporting the VAT liability will appear as shown on the right. If £7 remains unpaid by the year-end, it will be reported as a current liability on the Statement of financial position.

Debit: Purchases	£60.00
Debit: Revenue and Customs	£10.50
Credit: Trade payable	£70.50

HM Revenue and Customs account

	£		£
Purchases Day Book	10.50	Sales Day Book	17.50
Balance c/d	7.00		
	17.50		17.50
		Balance b/d	7.00

Similarly, when the trader pays for any expense (such as telephone, stationery, advertising) the amount paid will include VAT; but the VAT element is debited to the VAT account and the expense accounted for VAT free. Note that because the trader would have accounted for purchases excluding VAT, the cost of any inventory remaining at the year-end should also be reported without the VAT.

Activity 18.1 Accounting for Sales tax

A VAT-registered trader's credit purchases and sales, without including VAT, were £380,000 and £420,000 respectively. VAT rate applicable is 17.5%. £4,800 was paid as VAT. Set out (a) how these transactions will appear on a Trial Balance and (b) the HM Revenue and Customs account.

18.4 Prime entry for sales and purchases liable to Sales tax (VAT)

The prime entry for cash sales and purchase would, as usual, be in the Cash Book, but the amount recorded will be inclusive of the VAT. When posting, say, a cash purchase of £117.50 inclusive of VAT, care should be taken to debit the Purchases account only with £100 and the VAT account with £17.50.

To facilitate the accounting for credit sales, the Sales Day Book is equipped with two additional columns (see on the right). The sale price, inclusive of VAT, is entered in the Total[a] column and amounts in that column posted individually to the debit of respective accounts of each customer.

Sales Day Book	F	Total[a]	Sale[b]	VAT[c]
Marco & Co		£3,525	£3,000	£525
Petro Ltd		£2,350	£2,000	£350
Paulo & Son		£4,700	£4,000	£700
		£10,575	£9,000	£1,575

The sale price, without VAT, is entered in a second column[b] and the total of that column credited to the Sales account. The VAT included in each invoice is recorded in a third column[c] and the total of that column (Output VAT) is posted to the credit of the VAT account.

Activity 18.2 Sales Day Book with VAT analysis column

Richard, a wholesale dealer, reports his sales (inclusive of VAT at 17.5%) as stated below. You are required to record the sales in a Sales Day Book and post them to ledger accounts assuming that the Sales account is in Nominal ledger folio 21, VAT account in the General ledger folio 78. The accounts of the customers Pointer, West, Holmes and Upton are in the Sales ledger folios SL28, SL61, SL39 and SL22 respectively.

2012	Invoice	Customer	£
5.1	SN458	B.K. Pointer	3,102
11.1	SN459	Sheila West	7,520
17.1	SN460	P.S. Holmes	9,400
24.1	SN461	D. Upton	3,525

The Purchases Day Book, if similarly formatted, would facilitate posting of the total of the column recording Purchases excluding VAT to the debit of the Purchases account, and the total of the VAT column recording Input VAT to the debit of the VAT account. The individual suppliers' invoices for purchases (inclusive of VAT) are posted to the credit of the appropriate supplier's account.

18.5 How Sales tax is calculated and features in financial statements

Let us consider some matters we should bear in mind when calculating and accounting for transactions involving VAT.

1. ***Cash discount***: if cash discount is on offer as an inducement for prompt settlement of the invoice the Output VAT is calculated on the amount that would be received if

the customer utilises in full the discount on offer. For example, study the invoice issued by Longman plc (on the right). The terms offered by Longman is that Nancy is entitled to a cash discount of 5% if she settles the amount within seven days. Irrespective of whether she settles within seven days, VAT is calculated at 17.5% of £40,000 less the cash discount on offer of 5% of £40,000, i.e. 17.5% of £38,000.

Longman plc

CUSTOMER: Nancy Doe — Bill and tax point
REFERENCE: 784562 — DATE: 31.7.2012

Item	PRICE	QTY	TOTAL
Longs pc Model G 524	£ 1,000	40	£ 40,000
Current net total			40,000
VAT @ 17.5%			6,650
Brought forward total			0
Total balance now due			46,650

TERMS: 5/7 n/30
REGISTERED IN ENGLAND: NO. 6245895
VAT REG. NO: 326 4791 27

2. ***Non-current assets***: Input VAT on acquisition of non-current assets can usually be recovered, so that all non-current assets are accounted for without including VAT. Exceptionally, however, VAT cannot be reclaimed on motor vehicles (except in specified circumstances such as when the vehicles are for sale or are intended to be used for hire as a taxi or for driving instruction). Accordingly motor vehicles are accounted for at cost including VAT.
3. ***Entertainment expenses***: Input VAT cannot be reclaimed in respect of entertainment expenses (unless it relates to staff). Accordingly entertainment expenses are accounted for with the Input VAT added on.
4. ***Bad debt***: when Trade receivables are written off (bad debts) the Output VAT included therein can be reclaimed (i.e. offset from Output VAT), provided the following conditions are met:
   - The debt written off is more than six months old.
   - The debt has in fact been written off in the books of account and
   - the customer involved has been notified
5. ***Items removed by the owner for own use***: if the owner removes any goods for own use, in keeping with the principle that VAT is a tax on the consumer, the owner needs to be charged VAT. This means that if the Input VAT had been reclaimed when the goods were purchased, VAT becomes payable when goods are removed for personal use, and should be credited to the VAT account.

Activity 18.3 Reporting Sales tax on financial statements

A trader, registered for VAT, commenced business in the year with a capital in cash of £180,000. His purchases and sales, inclusive of VAT at 17.5%, were £446,500 and £493,500. 20% of goods purchased remain in hand at the year-end. He paid £141,000 for furniture and £47,000 as expenses (both inclusive of VAT at 17.5%); besides paying £22,500 as salary and £375,000 to suppliers. During the year he received £412,000 from customers and £20,500 as VAT refund. He wrote off £9,400 as bad debts and 20% of cost of furniture as depreciation. Set out how the transactions will be reported in the year's financial statements.

Note:

- Each amount reported in the question is inclusive of VAT, i.e. amount + 17.5%. Hence the VAT included in purchases (for example) is calculated as £446,500 × 17.5/117.5 = £66,500.
- The trader's purchases are accounted for without VAT. Hence any inventory in hand at the year-end should be reported without the VAT.

Activity 18.4 Accounting for goods removed by proprietor for own use

Set out the journal entry to account for goods costing £235,000 (inclusive of VAT at 17.5%) removed by the proprietor for own use.

18.6 VAT regulations in the UK

18.6.1 Who is eligible for VAT registration?

The VAT Act 1994 requires:

- compulsory registration of those whose taxable supplies in the previous twelve consecutive months exceeded a specified threshold (£70,000 as of October 2010); and
- optional registration of those whose taxable supplies within the subsequent 12 months are expected to exceed the threshold.

Those not registered cannot invoice customers for Output VAT and also cannot claim back their Input VAT. This means that Input VAT a trader pays in respect of purchases, expenses and non-current assets is accounted for as part of the respective expenses and cost of the asset.

18.6.2 Exempted from VAT

Some activities (see examples stated in the box on the right) are exempt from VAT. Those engaged in these activities need not register for VAT. The downside, however, is that they cannot reclaim any Input VAT they suffer.

Exempt from VAT
■ Education and training ■ Medical care ■ Physical education and sports ■ Banking and insurance ■ Lottery and bingo games

18.6.3 VAT at zero rate

The activities listed below on the right are liable to VAT but the VAT is calculated at zero per cent, so that nothing is payable as Output VAT; whereas, being VAT registered, they are able to reclaim any Input VAT. Hence those engaged in these activities are in a privileged position, because they have neither to invoice nor collect VAT from their customers.

Examples of items zero rated for VAT
■ Goods sold abroad ■ Food and drinks (except in catering trade) ■ Water and sewerage services ■ Books, newspapers and periodicals ■ Drugs and medicine on prescription ■ Children's clothing and footwear

18.6.4 The standard and reduced rates of VAT

The standard rate of VAT is currently 17.5% (20% from 2011). There is a reduced rate of 5% on domestic fuel and power and on the installation of energy-saving material.

18.6.5 The obligations arising from VAT registration

All the rules are contained in 'Notices' issued by HM Revenue and Customs. These may be found on their website www.hmce.gov.uk/. If a business is registered for VAT it is obliged to charge VAT, at the appropriate rate, on all sales and services liable to VAT and to issue a VAT receipt.

18.6.6 Issuing a VAT invoice to the customer

Every VAT invoice issued to customers should include the following information:

- VAT registration number of the business issuing the invoice;
- the tax point, i.e. the date when the transaction is presumed to have occurred for VAT purposes;
- the rate of VAT.

18.7 Salaries and wages

Let us now consider the accounting treatment of gross pay, deductions on pay-sheet, pay-sheet recoveries, accountability to HM Revenue and Customs for amounts deducted from pay-sheet as NI and PAYE and the accounting treatment of all these.

18.7.1 Gross and net salaries and wages

Payments made to an employee for work done, when calculated either at hourly rate (£5 per hour) or at piece rate (£10 per unit produced), are usually referred to as '*wages*'. On the other hand, when the pay is agreed at a monthly or annual rate, it is known as '*salary*'. In either case the employee may, in addition to basic pay, be entitled also to overtime, allowances (e.g. London weighting to compensate for the higher cost of living in London), bonus and other incentives. The total entitlement, before making any deductions, is referred to as '*Gross pay*'. From the gross pay one or more of the following deductions are made:

(a) *Pay as you earn* (PAYE) is the amount of income tax deducted from the employee's pay. The intention is to assist the employee to settle (hopefully) the income tax payable in respect of the earnings. The employer is obliged to make this deduction at a rate as instructed by HMRC and remit the amount to them at monthly intervals. To inform the employer of the amount to be deducted, HMRC allots to each employee liable to pay income tax a tax code, and provides the employer with Tax Code Tables showing the percentage to deduct from pay as PAYE.

(b) *National Insurance contribution* (NI) is a legally obligatory contribution the employee makes to become entitled to, in due course, free state benefits such as when disabled, out of work, on maternity leave or upon retirement. The government may change the rate at which the contribution is calculated. In addition to the amounts so deducted from employees' pay, the employer too has to make his own contribution to National Insurance.

(c) *Contributions to a pension scheme* could be another deduction, if the employer has agreed to pay an occupational pension after retirement and requires the employee also to contribute a stated percentage of pay for this benefit. In such a situation, in addition to the amounts deducted from employees' pay, the employer too may be obliged to make his own regular contribution to maintain the funds at levels sufficient to meet the pension payments when they become due.

(d) Other voluntary contributions such as for recovery of a loan obtained from the employer, membership of a social club or for charitable purposes.

In the UK PAYE and National Insurance contributions are obligatory under law and are, therefore, known as statutory deductions. The amount the employee receives, after deductions, is known as *Net pay* or more commonly *'take-home pay'*. The statutory deductions as PAYE and NIC together with the employer's own NI contribution are required to be remitted to HMRC by the 19th of the following month.

Activity 18.5 Net salary payable and amount to be remitted to HMRC

A trader's gross salary to staff for a month is £417,000. PAYE is deductible at 6%, while NI contribution is 5% by staff and 10% by the employer. Calculate (a) the Net salary payable for the month and (b) the amount to be remitted to HMRC as PAYE and as NIC contribution.

18.7.2 Accounting for salaries and wages

The amount of an employer's expense, in respect of employees, consists of:

(a) the gross wages and

(b) the amount the employer is obliged to pay as his own contribution to National Insurance.

Activity 18.6 Writing up the Wages and salaries account

Based on the information provided in Activity 18.5 above, write up the Salaries account in the books of the trader.

To properly account for this expense, a Wages (or salaries) Book is written up with appropriate columns to show the make up of each pay packet – detailing each addition and deduction. To illustrate let us assume that the Wages Book of a business appears as follows:

Wages Book for week ending 6 May 2012

	Basic pay	Overtime	Merit bonus	Gross wages	Deductions				Net Wages
					PAYE	NI	Loan	Total	
	£	£	£	£	£	£	£	£	£
Louise Tolworth	420	60	–	480	(96)	(38)	(15)	(149)	331
A. Salmon	360	20	–	380	(72)	(30)	(25)	(127)	253
Terry Smith	540	40	20	600	(120)	(48)	(40)	(208)	392
Guy Boswell	380	30	–	410	(82)	(33)	(10)	(125)	285
	1,700	150	20	1,870	(370)	(149)	(90)	(609)	1,261

Let us assume also that the business is obliged to pay 10% of gross wages as the employer's contribution to National Insurance. The accounting entries will be as follows:

(a) Net pay (£1,261) when paid is posted from the Cash Book to the Wages account.

(b) The total deductions (£609) is debited to the Wages account so that the expense is fully recorded in the Wages account at £1,870. Corresponding credits are £370 to PAYE account, £149 to the National Insurance account and £90 to the Staff loan account. The amounts so reported as liabilities need to be settled on appropriate dates.

(c) The employer's contribution to National Insurance, calculated at 10% of £1,870, is debited to the Wages account and credited to the National Insurance account.

Hence, the total expense which will, in due course, be reported in the Statement of income is made up of the gross pay (£1,870) plus the employer's NI contribution of £187.

Activity 18.7 Accounting for pay-sheet recoveries

The year-end Trial Balance includes, as shown on the right, the net salary paid and the payments to HMRC. PAYE deductions are 10% of gross pay and National Insurance contribution is at 6% from employees and 9% from employer. Determine the amounts of expense to be stated in the Statement of income and the liability to be reported, if unpaid, on the Statement of financial position.

Salaries (net)	£166,740
Payments to HMRC	
– as PAYE	£17,250
– as National Insurance	£27,500

Note: The net salary paid (after deducting 10% PAYE and 6% NIC) is 84% of gross salary.

Summary

- The trader registered for VAT collects VAT on behalf of the government.
- When registered for VAT, the Output VAT collected by the trader when he sells is not his income but a liability to be paid over to the government, and the Input VAT he pays on his purchases and some expenses are recovered as a set-off. Hence VAT is not normally an expense for the trader.
- The trader is not entitled to recover VAT relating to acquisition of vehicles and on entertainment.
- The trader has to report his trade receivables as well as payables with VAT added on because he is responsible for collecting the VAT on receivables and paying the VAT on payables.
- When a receivable is written off as bad, the VAT element within it is recoverable; and if the trader removes for own use any goods intended for sale, VAT relating to them becomes payable.
- The salaries and wages reported as expense by a business are made up of (a) gross salary + (b) the employer's contribution to National Insurance.

Suggested answers to activities

18.1 Accounting for Sales tax

Trial Balance as at xxxx

	£	£
Purchases	380,000	–
Sales	–	420,000
Trade payables	–	446,500
Trade receivables	493,500	–
HMRC	–	2,200

HMRC account

	£		£
Purchase Day Book	66,500	Sales Day Book	73,500
Bank account	4,800		
Balance c/d	2,200		
	73,500		73,500
		Balance b/d	2,200

18.2 Sales Day Book with VAT analysis column

The Sales Day Book						
20X5	Voucher	Customer	Folio	£	Sales	VAT
5.1	SN458	B.K. Pointer	SL28	3,102	2,640	462
11.1	SN459	J.N. Curry	SL61	7,520	6,400	1,120
17.1	SN460	P.S. Holmes	SL39	9,400	8,000	1,400
24.1	SN461	D. Upton	SL22	3,525	3,000	525
				23,547	20,040	3,507
					NL21	RL78

Sales account NL21

			£
		Sales Day Book	20,040

VAT account RL78

			£
		Sales Day Book	3,507

18.3 Reporting Sales tax on financial statements

Statement of income for the year ended xxx	£	£
Sales		420,000
Purchases	380,000	
Inventory	(76,000)	(304,000)
Gross profit		116,000
Expenses		(40,000)
Salaries		(22,500)
Bad debts		(8,000)
Depreciation		(24,000)
Profit for the year		21,500

Statement of financial position as at xxxx	£	£
Furniture	120,000	
Accumulated depreciation	(24,000)	96,000
Current assets:		
Inventory	76,000	
Receivables	72,100	
VAT receivable	1,900	
Bank balance	27,000	177,000
		273,000
		£
Capital	180,000	
Profit for year	21,500	201,500
Payables		71,500
		273,000

VAT calculations:
On sales: 493,500 × 17.5/117.5 = £73,500
On purchases: 446,500 × 17.5/117.5 = £66,500
On furniture: 141,000 × 17.5/117.5 = £21,000

Workings:

Bank account

	£		£
Capital a/c	180,000	Furniture	141,000
Receivable	412,000	Expenses	47,000
VAT refund	20,500	Salaries	22,500
		Payable	375,000
		Balance	27,000
	612,500		612,500
Balance b/d	27,000		

VAT account

	£		£
Purchases	66,500	Sales	73,500
Furniture	21,000	Bank refund	20,500
Expenses	7,000		
Bad debts	1,400	Balance c/d	1,900
	95,900		95,900
Balance b/d	1,900		

18.4 Accounting for goods removed by proprietor for own use

Drawings a/c	Dr	£235,000	–
To Trading a/c		–	£200,000
VAT account		–	£35,000
Being goods removed by proprietor			

18.5 Net salary payable

(a) Net salary payable 89% of £417,000	£371,130
(b) PAYE to be remitted 6% of £417,000	£25,020
(c) NIC contribution:	
Employees': 5% of £417,000	£20,850
Employer's: 10% of £417,000	£41,700

18.6 Writing up the Wages and salaries account

Wages and salaries account

	£		
Bank a/c – net pay	371,130		
PAYE – deducted from employees	25,020		
NIC – deducted from employees	20,850		
Gross pay	417,000		
NIC – employer's contribution	41,700		
Total expense	458,700		

18.7 Accounting for pay-sheet recoveries

Salaries account

	£		£
Cash Book	166,740	Income statement	216,365
PAYE[a]	19,850		
NI contribution[b]	11,910		
NI contribution[c]	17,865		
	216,365		216,365

PAYE account

	£		£
Cash Book	17,250	Salaries a/c	19,850
Balance c/d	2,600		
	19,850		19,850
		Balance b/d	2,600

National Insurance contribution a/c

	£		£
Cash Book	27,500	Salaries a/c	11,910
Balance c/d	2,275	Salaries a/c	17,865
	29,775		29,775
		Balance b/d	2,275

Calculations:

(a) PAYE = 166,740 × 10/84 = £19,850
(b) NI Contribution – Employees = 166,740/84 × 6 = £11,910
(c) NI Contribution – Employer = 10% of (166,740 + 19,850 + 11,910) = £17,865

Multiple choice questions

Value Added Tax – theory

18.1 The Value Added Tax is an expense to be suffered by:
- (a) The final consumer of the goods on which they are levied
- (b) All traders dealing with goods on which they are levied
- (c) Limited companies dealing with goods on which they are levied
- (d) All traders, registered for VAT, dealing with goods on which they are levied

18.2 Which of the following is not a VAT rate in the UK?
- (a) The standard rate of 17.5%
- (b) The concession rate of 10%
- (c) The reduced rate of 5%
- (d) The zero rate of 0%

18.3 In the UK Value Added Tax is administered by:
- (a) HM Revenue and Customs Department
- (b) The local borough
- (c) The Board of Trade

18.4 Which of the following purposes would a purchase invoice serve?
- (i) To inform of the amount that has to be paid to the supplier in the transaction
- (ii) As evidence to support the entry in the relevant book of prime entry
- (iii) To claim back the related VAT from HMRC
- (iv) To authenticate the purpose for which the supplier should be paid

a	All	
b	i, ii & iii	
c	ii, iii & iv	
d	i, iii & iv	

18.5 A VAT account debit balance reported in the year-end Trial Balance would represent:
- (a) The amount recoverable from the VAT department
- (b) The amount payable to the VAT department
- (c) The amount to be treated as an expense in the Statement of income
- (d) The amount to be treated as an income in the Statement of income

Value Added Tax – prime entry

18.6 Which of the following would be an appropriate book of prime entry for VAT on credit sales?
- (a) The Cash Book
- (b) The Sales Day Book
- (c) The VAT book
- (d) The Journal

18.7 Which of the following is the prime entry book for recording cash sales including 17.5% VAT?
- (a) The Cash Book
- (b) The Sales Day Book
- (c) The VAT book
- (d) The Journal

18.8 The prime entry book for recording a cheque for £14,664 received net of 4% cash discount is:

(a) The Cash Book
(b) The Sales Day Book
(c) The VAT book
(d) The Journal

18.9 The Sales Day Book formatted with a separate column to record VAT reports £485,000 in the column that is posted to the Sales account and VAT rate is 17.5%. How and at what amount will the related VAT be posted?

(a) £84,875 as a debit
(b) £84,875 as a credit
(c) £485,000 as a credit
(d) £569,875 as a credit

18.10 If a VAT-registered trader formats his Sales Day Book to record VAT amounts in a separate column, the total of that column should be periodically posted to:

(a) Debit of VAT account
(b) Credit of VAT account
(c) Debit of Total sales ledger control account
(d) Credit of Total sales ledger control account

18.11 Tom purchased raw materials for £3,760 from Harry and used them to manufacture goods which were sold to Dick for £9,870. Harry and Tom are VAT registered, but Dick is not. Prices stated are inclusive of VAT at 17.5%. The VAT cheque to be sent by each party to the VAT department is:

	Harry	Tom	Dick	
a	£560	£910	£0	
b	£658	£910	£1,070	
c	£560	£1,470	£1,070	
d	£658	£910	£0	

18.12 Agnes paid £4,000 to buy a gas cooker from Linda and sold it for £5,000 plus VAT to Sally who, in turn, sold it for a VAT inclusive price of £7,050 to Catherine, a customer. Agnes and Sally are VAT registered; while Linda is not. VAT rate is 17.5%. How much VAT would Agnes and Sally have to pay?

	Agnes	Sally	
a	£175	£1,050	
b	£875	£175	
c	£875	£1,050	
d	£875	£1,234	

Value Added Tax – accounting

In a VAT-registered trader's books and assuming the VAT rate of 17.5% unless advised otherwise.

18.13 Credit sales invoiced to customer at £282,000 inclusive of VAT should be accounted for as:

(a) Debit Trade receivables £282,000, credit Sales account £282,000
(b) Debit Trade receivables £240,000, credit Sales account £240,000
(c) Debit Trade receivables £282,000, credit Sales account £240,000, credit VAT account £42,000
(d) Debit Trade receivables £240,000, Debit VAT account £42,000, credit Sales account £282,000

18.14 A purchase invoice, inclusive of VAT, for £9,400, should be accounted for as:

(a) Debit Purchases account £9,400, credit Trade payable £9,400 ☐
(b) Debit Purchases account £8,000, debit VAT account £1,400, credit Trade payable £9,400 ☐
(c) Debit Purchases account £8,000, credit Trade payable £8,000 ☐
(d) Debit Purchases account £9,400, credit Trade payable £8,000, credit VAT account £1,400 ☐

18.15 Payment by cheque for expenses, liable to VAT, of £14,100 should be accounted for as:

(a) Debit Expense account £12,000, debit VAT account £2,100 and credit Bank account £14,100 ☐
(b) Debit Expense account £14,100, credit Bank account £14,100 ☐
(c) Debit Expense account £14,100, credit Bank account £12,000 and credit VAT account £2,100 ☐
(d) Debit Expense account £12,000, credit Bank account £12,000 ☐

18.16 Payment by cheque of £5,640 for customer entertainment should be accounted for as:

(a) Debit Customer entertainment account £5,640, credit Bank account £5,640 ☐
(b) Debit Customer entertainment account £4,800, credit Bank account £4,800 ☐
(c) Debit Customer entertainment account £4,800, debit VAT a/c £840, credit Bank account £5,640 ☐
(d) Debit Customer entertainment account £5,640, credit VAT a/c £840, credit Bank account £4,800 ☐

18.17 Payment by cheque for furniture for office use of £14,100 should be accounted for as:

(a) Debit Furniture account £14,100, credit Bank account £14,100 ☐
(b) Debit Furniture account £12,000, credit Bank account £12,000 ☐
(c) Debit Furniture account £14,100, credit Bank account £12,000, credit VAT account £2,100 ☐
(d) Debit Furniture account £12,000, debit VAT account £2,100, credit Bank account £14,100 ☐

18.18 Payment of £35,250 by cheque for an office vehicle should be accounted for as:

(a) Debit Motor vehicles a/c £35,250, credit Bank account £35,250 ☐
(b) Debit Motor vehicles a/c £30,000, credit Bank account £30,000 ☐
(c) Debit Motor vehicles a/c £30,000, debit Vat a/c £5,250, credit Bank account £35,250 ☐
(d) Debit Motor vehicles a/c £35,250, credit Bank account £30,000, credit VAT account £5,250 ☐

18.19 When selling goods with a list price of £20,000 a trade discount of 10% was allowed and a settlement discount of 4% offered if payment is received within a week. The payment was not received; but the goods were returned by the customer in full. The credit note to be issued to the customer should be for:

a	£20,000	
b	£17,280	
c	£18,000	
d	£21,024	

18.20 To write off a trade debt of £11,750, in the books of a VAT-registered trader:

(a) Debit Bad debts account £11,750, credit Trade receivable account £11,750 ☐
(b) Debit Bad debts account £10,000, credit Trade receivable account £10,000 ☐
(c) Debit Bad debts £11,750, credit VAT account £1,750, credit Trade receivable account £11,750 ☐
(d) Debit Bad debts a/c £10,000, debit VAT account £1,750, credit Trade receivable a/c £11,750 ☐

18.21 To account for increasing the Allowance for doubtful debts by £4,935:

(a) Debit Bad debts account £4,935, credit Allowance for doubtful debts account £4,935

(b) Debit Bad debts account £4,200, credit Allowance for doubtful debts account £4,200

(c) Debit Bad debts £4,935, credit VAT account £735, credit Allowance for doubtful debts £4,200

(d) Debit Bad debts £4,200, debit VAT account £735, credit Allowance for doubtful debts £4,935

18.22 If VAT payable at beginning of the month was £22,800, and during the month purchases and sales at VAT-inclusive prices were £92,120 and £128,968 respectively, the balance in the VAT account by the end of the month would be:

a	£28,288 credit	
b	£28,288 debit	
c	£17,312 credit	
d	£17,312 debit	

18.23 The list price of goods sold was £72,000. A trade discount of 10% and 5% cash discount are on offer. The VAT to be included on the invoice would be:

a	£9,800	
b	£10,773	
c	£11,340	
d	£12,600	

18.24 A trader's opening inventory was reported as £38,600. His purchases during the year inclusive of VAT were £569,875. He reports that a fifth of goods purchased during the year remains unsold by the year-end. The cost of sales for the year and the closing inventory reported as an asset will be:

	Cost of sales	Closing inventory	
a	£426,600	£113,975	
b	£426,600	£97,000	
c	£494,500	£113,975	
d	£418,880	£104,720	

18.25 Goods costing £6,815 (inclusive of VAT) removed by a sole trader for personal use should be accounted for as:

(a) Debit Drawings account and credit Purchases account £6,815

(b) Debit Drawings account and credit Purchases account £5,800

(c) Debit Drawings account £6,815, credit Purchases account £5,800, credit VAT account £1,015

(d) Debit Drawings account £6,815, credit Trading account £5,800, credit VAT account £1,015

18.26 A telephone bill for £3,290 (inclusive of VAT) remaining unpaid should be accounted for as:

(a) Debit Telephone expense £2,800, debit VAT account £490, credit Bank account £3,290

(b) Debit Telephone expense £2,800, debit VAT account £490, credit Accrued expenses £3,290

(c) Debit Telephone expense £3,290, credit Accrued expenses account £3,290

(d) Debit Telephone expense £3,290, credit VAT account £490, credit Accrued expense account £2,800

18.27 A trader, registered for VAT but dealing only in zero-rated goods, pays £15,040, by cheque, to acquire office equipment. He should account for it as:

(a) Debit Office equipment a/c £12,800, debit VAT account £2,240, credit Bank account £15,040

(b) Debit Office equipment a/c £12,800, credit Bank account £12,800

(c) Debit Office equipment account £15,040, credit Bank account £15,040

(d) Debit Office equipment account £15,040, credit Bank account £12,800, credit VAT a/c £2,240

18.28 A trader registered for VAT reports his purchases, sales and expenses for the year as £92,120, £116,090 and £16,920 respectively. The amounts reported are all inclusive of VAT at 17.5%. The Statement of Financial position as at the year-end will report VAT as:

a	£1,050 payable	
b	£1,050 receivable	
c	£1,234 payable	
d	£3,570 payable	

18.29 A trader registered for VAT reports his purchases, sales and expenses for the year as £138,180, £174,135 and £25,380. Additionally he paid £35,250 for an office vehicle and £15,040 for office equipment. The amounts stated are all inclusive of VAT at 17.5%. The Statement of financial position as at the year-end will report VAT as:

a	£665 payable	
b	£665 receivable	
c	£4,585 receivable	
d	£5,915 payable	

18.30 A trader registered for VAT but dealing in products zero rated for VAT acquired a vehicle, computers for office use and furniture for £47,000, £7,990 and £15,040 respectively. These prices are all inclusive of VAT at 17.5%. How much VAT refund can he expect to receive in respect of these transactions?

a	£10,430	
b	£3,430	
c	£2,240	
d	£1,190	

18.31 A trader registered for VAT acquired a machine on one month's credit. The list price of the machine is £180,000. The trader is offered 10% trade discount and 6% cash discount if payment is made within a week. Transactions of this type attract VAT at 17.5%. What is the VAT-inclusive price he will be invoiced for?

a	£180,000	
b	£190,350	
c	£188,649	
d	£178,929	

18.32 As at 5 June £74,850 was owed as VAT. During the week commencing on that date purchases were £141,000 (excluding VAT) and sales £423,000 (inclusive of VAT). Assuming that there were no other transactions involving VAT the amount owed as VAT by the end of the week would be:

a	£21,725	
b	£36,525	
c	£113,175	
d	£127,875	

18.33 Goods with a list price of £37,500 were returned to the supplier. When purchased the supplier had allowed 5% trade discount and had offered 4% cash discount for settlement within a week. The amount to be posted from the Returns Outwards Book to the VAT account would be:

a	£6,234 debit	
b	£5,972 debit	
c	£5,985 debit	
d	£5,985 credit	

18.34 As at 1.6.2012 a customer owed £11,400 for goods sold ten days earlier. Sales made on 7 June were invoiced at £60,000 plus £9,975 VAT, with an offer of 5% cash discount if paid for within a week. £22,325 was received on 11 June. The amount receivable from the customer would be:

a	£49,075	
b	£57,875	
c	£58,050	
d	£59,050	

Payroll – theory

18.35 Which of the following are statutory payroll deductions in the UK?

(i) Save as you earn (SAYE)

(ii) Pay as you earn (PAYE)

(iii) Pension contribution

(iv) National Insurance contribution

a	i & ii	
b	i, ii & iii	
c	ii, iii & iv	
d	ii & iv	

18.36 PAYE and NIC deductions from employees, until remitted, are accounted for as:

(a) an income
(b) an expense
(c) a liability
(d) an asset

18.37 PAYE and NIC deductions from employees are normally required to be remitted to HMRC at:

(a) weekly intervals
(b) monthly intervals
(c) quarterly intervals
(d) half yearly intervals

18.38 HMRC allocates a PAYE Code to each employee so that:

(a) the employee's pay may be determined according to family circumstances
(b) the employee's tax deductions may take account of tax allowance and relief entitlement
(c) the employee's National Insurance contribution may be determined accordingly
(d) the employee's cost of living allowance may take into account family circumstances

18.39 The acronym BACS, commonly used for payroll, stands for:

(a) Bank Automated Clearing Services
(b) Bank Automatic Clearing System
(c) Bank Automatic Credit Services
(d) Bank Automated Credit System

18.40 Which of the following is *not* a payroll function?

(a) Check gross pay entitlement of each employee
(b) Verify accuracy of pay-sheet deductions
(c) Prepare and distribute payslips
(d) Notify promotional prospects and when next increment is due

Accounting for pay sheet recoveries

18.41 The year-end Trial Balance as at 31 December reports a staff loan of £10,000 as an asset. Monthly recoveries of £500 made from pay-sheet, from August, should be accounted for as:

(a) Debit Cash Book, credit Staff loan a/c with £2,500
(b) Debit Staff loan, a/c credit Cash Book with £2,500
(c) Debit Salaries account, credit Staff loan account with £2,500
(d) Debit Staff loan account, credit Salaries account with £2,500

18.42 The amount to be written off as expense in the year should be:

(a) The gross salary payable for the year
(b) The net salary paid after making all pay-sheet recoveries
(c) The gross salary payable for the year plus employer's contribution to National Insurance
(d) The net salary paid plus the amount of all pay-sheet recoveries made

18.43 Gross staff salary for the month is £218,400. Pay-sheet deductions to be made are loan recovery (£1,450), PAYE 10%, National Insurance 6%. Employer's contribution for National Insurance is payable at 9%. Ascertain the net salary payable for the month and the amount to be remitted as total National Insurance contribution.

	Net salary	N.I. Contrib.	
a	£183,456	£30,664	
b	£182,006	£30,664	
c	£183,456	£32,760	
d	£182,006	£32,760	

18.44 The only pay-sheet recovery is national insurance contribution at 6%. Employer's contribution is 9%. By the year-end net salary paid is £154,630 and the total amount remitted as the National Insurance contribution is £21,400. Ascertain the amount of salary to be reported as expense and as liability for National Insurance.

	Expense	Liability	
a	£179,305	£3,275	
b	£164,500	£3,275	
c	£163,908	£4,269	
d	£178,660	£2,630	

18.45 Gross staff pay for December is £38,500. All employees contribute to National Insurance and the pension fund at 6% and 9% respectively of gross salary; while the employer's contribution is 9% and 12% respectively of gross salary. Staff loan recovered from the pay-sheet in December is £7,450. Identify the amount of expense to be included in the Statement of income and the amount of the net pay for the month.

	Expense	Net Pay	
a	£33,180	£25,275	
b	£38,500	£32,545	
c	£40,630	£32,545	
d	£46,585	£25,275	

Calculation of gross wages

18.46 Emil's and Basil's wages are calculated at £4.20 and £4.50 per unit produced. Minimum wage per week is £360. Any employee producing more than 80 units per week is paid at £5 per unit for the excess. In week 43 Emil produced 105 units and Basil 64 units. The weekly gross pay for that week would be:

	Emil	Basil	
a	£441	£288	
b	£461	£360	
c	£461	£288	
d	£441	£360	

18.47 Workers at a factory are required to work for 40 hours per week at minimum. Any excess hours are reckoned as overtime and paid at time and a half. Weekend hours are paid at double time. During a week, Peter, on an hourly rate of £7.50, worked 64 hours of which eight were at the weekend. Paul, on an hourly rate of £6, worked 72 hours of which 16 were at the weekend. Calculate the gross wages for each.

	Peter	Paul	
a	£540	£576	
b	£660	£696	
c	£600	£696	
d	£600	£576	

Answers to multiple choice questions

18.1: a 18.2: b 18.3: d 18.4: d 18.5: a 18.6: b 18.7: a 18.8: a 18.9: b 18.10: b 18.11: a 18.12: b 18.13: c
18.14: b 18.15: a 18.16: a 18.17: d 18.18: a 18.19: d 18.20: d 18.21: a 18.22: a 18.23: b 18.24: b 18.25: d
18.26: b 18.27: a 18.28: a 18.29: b 18.30: b 18.31: c 18.32: c 18.33: c 18.34: c* 18.35: d 18.36: c 18.37: b
18.38: b 18.39: a 18.40: d 18.41: c 18.42: c 18.43: d 18.44: a 18.45: d 18.46: b 18.47: d

* Discount allowed: £22,325 × 117.5 × 100 × 5/95 = £1,000.

Progressive questions

PQ 18.1 Accounting for sales and sales returns with VAT – basic (CIMA)

Shown on the right is the Sales and Returns Inwards Day Book of XY, a sole trader, who employs a bookkeeper to maintain her accounting records, but maintains a nominal ledger herself.

DATE	CUSTOMER	GOODS	VAT	TOTAL
2012		£	£	£
Feb-07	ANG Ltd	4,600	805	5,405
Feb-10	John's Stores	2,800	490	3,290
Feb-14	ML Limited	1,000	175	1,175
Feb-17	ML Limited	(600)	(105)	(705)
Feb-25	ANG Ltd	1,200	210	1,410
		9,000	1,575	10,575

Required:

(a) Explain the meaning of the entry on 17 February.

(b) Explain how the realisation concept will have been applied in determining the above entries.

(c) Post the above transactions to the appropriate accounts in the nominal ledger and in the customers' personal accounts.

(d) Why is an Allowance for doubtful debts set up?

PQ 18.2 Accounting for purchases with VAT – basic (CCEA)

Study the following invoices received by J. Kennedy & Co Ltd and answer the questions which follow.

INVOICE

Robert and Co
22, High Street
Bangor

Invoice No 2597

To: J. Kennedy & Co Ltd
48 Runcorn Lane
Dungannon

Order No D 24
Date: 1 April 20X6

ITEM	Quantity	Price	Total
	£	£	£
Jumpers blue Code 346V	6	20	120
VAT at 17.5%			21
			141

INVOICE

K. Summers
The Mill
Ballycastle

Invoice No RT34

To: J. Kennedy & Co Ltd
48 Runcorn Lane
Dungannon

Order No D 25
Date: 4 April 20X6

Item	Quantity	Price	Total
	£	£	£
Jumpers code T582K	10	40	400
VAT at 17.5%			70
			470

(a) Make the necessary entries in J. Kennedy's Purchases Day Book showing clearly the totals of each column.

(b) Make the necessary entries in J. Kennedy's General Ledger.

PQ 18.3 Accounting for transactions with VAT (CIMA)

Pollt Ltd has a year-end of 31 December. At 30 November 2012 the balances stated on the right appear in its ledger. Following transactions took place in December 2012:

VAT owing to Customs and Excise	£3,250
Bank overdraft	£6,250
Trade receivables	£127,000

(i) Sales of £85,000 plus VAT are made on credit.

(ii) A motor car costing £8,000 plus VAT is bought and paid for by cheque.

(iii) Materials are purchased on credit for £27,000 plus VAT.

(iv) Materials costing £3,000 plus VAT are returned to the supplier and a refund given by cheque.

(v) Administration expenses of £2,400 plus VAT are incurred and paid for by cheque.

(vi) A VAT refund of £1,567 for the quarter ended 31 Oct. 2012 is received by cheque from HMRC.

(vii) Customers pay the balance outstanding at 30.11.2012 by cheque, deducting £2,000 cash discount.

(viii) Suppliers are paid £42,000 by cheque.

VAT is 17.5% in all cases.

Required:
(a) Prepare the VAT account for December 2012, showing the closing balance.
(b) Calculate the bank balance at 31 December 2012.

PQ 18.4 Financial statements of a trader not familiar with VAT accounting

John Richard, registered for VAT purposes, extracted his Trial Balance as shown on the right. You are informed as follows:

(a) VAT-inclusive prices of £9,400 and £23,500 paid on 1 January 2012 for furniture and motor vehicles respectively are included in the corresponding asset accounts.

(b) Furniture and motor vehicles are depreciated using the reducing balance method, at 10% and 20% per annum respectively, time apportioning for the months in use.

(c) Inventory as at 30 June 2012 cost £17,390 inclusive of VAT.

(d) £1,410 (inclusive of VAT) receivable from a customer is to be written off as bad.

(e) The VAT rate is 17.5%.

Trial Balance as at 30 June 2012	£	£
Sales inclusive of VAT	–	101,332
Purchases inclusive of VAT	67,680	–
Inventory 30.6.2011 without VAT	8,840	–
Furniture account	20,600	–
Accumulated depreciation on furniture	–	4,740
Motor vehicles	51,000	–
Accumulated depreciation on vehicle	–	7,500
Expenses inclusive of VAT	20,075	–
Entertainment inclusive of VAT	440	–
Receivables and payables	7,140	4,230
Payments of VAT	212	–
Cash and bank	1,815	–
Richard's Capital account	–	60,000
	177,802	177,802

Required: Prepare the Statement of income for the year ended 30 June 2012 and the Statement of financial position as at that date.

PQ 18.5 Payroll accounting (CIMA)

The details stated on the right relate to the payroll of XYZ Ltd for the week ended 27 October 2012. The company pays the employees £5.00 per hour plus an overtime premium of £2.50 per hour in excess of the normal working week. The summary of the employees' time sheet for the same week is stated below on the left. Hours worked, stated below, include 500 overtime hours on capital expenditure and 80 overtime hours on customers' jobs recoverable from them.

Net wages paid	£34,000
PAYE deducted	£16,500
National Insurance:	
Employees'	£2,900
Employer's	£3,300

Hours worked on customers' jobs	8,260
Hours worked on company capital expenditure	1,350
Non-productive hours	940
	10,550

Required:
(a) Show the journal entry for the wages of the company for week ended 27 October 2012, including an appropriate narrative.
(b) Explain the treatment of costs incurred on the company's capital expenditure and the implications for profit measurement.

PQ 18.6 Accounting for pay-sheet recoveries and National Insurance

The Carpet Store extracted its Trial Balance on the last day of its accounting period as stated on the right. You are informed as follows:

(a) A housing loan of £20,000 given to the Store Manager on 1 November 2011 is being recovered from his pay at £400 per month, commencing from November pay. The recoveries have not been accounted for.

(b) Staff salary has been accounted for merely by posting to that account the net salary paid to staff.

(c) Reported as National Insurance is the amount remitted. The National Insurance contribution at 8% of gross pay is deducted on the pay-sheet and the employer's contribution is 10%.

Required: Set out the Statement of income for the year ended 31 March 2012 and the Statement of financial position as at that date.

Trial Balance as at 31 March 2012		
	£'000	£'000
Non-current assets	660	238
Inventory – 31.3.2012	614	–
Staff salaries	320	–
Receivables/payables	512	468
Other admin expenses	486	–
Cost of sales	3,642	–
National Insurance	56	–
Sales	–	4,990
Loan to manager	20	
Distribution costs	263	–
Capital account	–	900
Cash and bank	23	–
	6,596	6,596

PQ 18.7 Involves VAT and payroll (CIMA)

At the beginning of September 2012, GL had the following balances on the accounts of three customers:

A. Barton £400 C. Dodd £1,200 F. Gray £340

During September, the following sales and returns took place for the above customers:

Sales

- on 3 September to A. Barton goods £200 less trade discount of 20%, plus VAT at 17.5%
- on 8 September to C. Dodd goods £800, plus VAT at 17.5%
- on 12 September to C. Dodd goods £360 plus VAT at 17.5%

Sales returns

- on 5 September from A. Barton 25% of the goods sold to him on 3 September
- on 18 September from C. Dodd goods of £120 plus VAT at 17.5%

The balance at the bank was £347 overdrawn on 1 September 2012.

The following bank transactions took place during September 2012:

4 Sept	A. Barton paid the amount outstanding at 1 September, less 5% discount			
8 Sept	C. Dodd paid the amount outstanding at 1 September, less 2.5% cash discount			
10 Sept	Paid J. Swinburn, a supplier, for an invoice of £1,200, less 5% cash discount			
15 Sept	Paid VAT of £832 to Customs and Excise, re the quarter ended 31 August 2012			
17 Sept	Paid P. Taylor, a supplier, £400 less 5% cash discount			
20 Sept	Paid by cheque for a motor car costing £9,550 including £150 vehicle tax and VAT at 17.5%			
22 Sept	C. Dodd paid the invoice of 8 September, less the credit note of 18 September. There was no cash discount allowed on this payment			
25 Sept	Received a cheque from F Gray for 50% of his debt; the remainder is to be written off as bad			
30 Sept	Paid wages to employees, made up as follows:			
	Gross wages	£2,500	Income Tax deducted under PAYE	£300
	Employees' National Insurance	£200	Employer's National insurance	£200
30 Sept	Banks receipts from trade receivables	£10,500		
	Paid cheques to trade payables	£11,200		

GL has a computerised Trade Receivable Ledger system which produced an aged trade receivables printout as at 30 September 2012 as shown on the right.

Current month	£12,000
30 to 60 days	£7,500
60 to 90 days	£3,600
over 90 days	£1,100

The balance on the Allowance for doubtful debts account at 1 September 2012 was £450 credit. No further allowance for doubtful debts has been made since then.

(i) The 'Current month' total includes £60 for discounts allowed to debtors not recorded in the Sales ledger.

(ii) The '30 to 60 day' total includes a balance of £200 to be taken as a contra entry in the Purchase ledger.

(iii) The 'over 90 days' total includes a trade receivable of £240 to be written off as bad debt.

(iv) The company has decided to amend the Allowance for doubtful debts to the amounts stated on the right.

Over 90 days	20%
60 to 90 days	10%
30 to 60 days	5%
current month	nil

Required:

(a) Write up a Cash Book for September 2012, with columns for Bank and Cash discount, and balance off at 30 September 2012. You are not required to complete the double-entry except where asked to do so in part (b) below.

(b) Write up the ledger accounts (in date order) for A. Barton, C. Dodd and F. Gray.

(c) Calculate the change in the Allowance for doubtful debts.

PQ 18.8 Revising the Statement of financial position (ACCA)

Steadfast Stores Ltd has drafted its Statement of financial position as set out below.

Statement of financial position as at 31 March 2012

	£	£		Cost	Accumulated depreciation	£
Capital			Non-current assets:			
Ordinary shares			Freehold property	20,000	3,000	17,000
£1 each fully paid		30,000	Fixtures and fittings	24,000	9,000	15,000
Share premium		5,000				
Retained earnings		9,000		44,000	12,000	32,000
		44,000	Current assets:			
Current liabilities:			Inventory at cost		9,500	
Trade payables	7,100		Trade receivables		7,700	
Dividend	3,000	10,100	Balance at bank		4,900	22,100
		54,100				54,100

Since preparing the draft the following information has become available:

(i) Goods received from B. Brown in February 2012 on a sale or return basis and all unsold as at 31 March 2012 have been regarded as outright purchases at the pro forma invoice cost of £4,000 by the accountant of Steadfast Stores Ltd. Steadfast Stores intends to return these goods.

(ii) The bank balance reported is without making any accounting entry for two cheques, stated below on the right:

	£
L. Barnes – stationery	160
K. Keeper – payment in advance for goods to be delivered in June 2012	240

(iii) The inventory-taking took place on 6 April 2012 instead of on the accounting year-end. During the period from 31 March 2012 to 6 April 2012 transactions stated on the right took place.

Note: Steadfast Stores Ltd obtains a uniform rate of gross profit of 25% on selling price.

	£
Sales were	16,000
Sales returns were	300
Purchases were	4,700
Purchases returns were	180

(iv) The company acquired a quantity of stationery in March 2012 at a special price of £1,000. The acquisition of this stationery, none of which has been used yet, has been charged to fixtures and fittings. Assume that the depreciation charge for the year ended 31 March 2012 has not been affected by this item.

(v) One of the stock sheets prepared on 6 April 2012 was undercast by £300.

(vi) Adjustments have not been made in the accounts for discounts received from suppliers of £340 during the year ended 31 March 2012.

Required: The corrected Statement of financial position as at 31 March 2012 of Steadfast.

PQ 18.9 Correction of errors involving the Suspense account (CIMA)

VB Limited, a chemical company, extracted a Trial Balance from its ledgers on 30 April 2012 and found that the sum of the debit balances did not equal the sum of the credit balances. A Suspense account was opened and used to record the difference. VB Limited does not use Control accounts for its customers and supplier accounts. The company carried out an investigation into the causes of the difference and found the following:

1. Cash sale of £246 has been posted to the debit of Sales returns account.
2. An invoice to a customer for £1,249 had been posted to the customer's account as £1,294.
3. Bank charges of £37 had not been entered in the Cash Book.
4. Value Added Tax £45 had been included in the sum posted to the purchases account from a supplier's invoice.
5. A contra entry of £129 had been debited to the customer account and credited to the supplier account.
6. An invoice for rates for the six-month period ending 30 September 2012 amounting to £13,500 had not been entered in the ledgers and remained unpaid on 30 April 2012.
7. A carriage invoice of £52 had been debited to carriage outwards but it related to the purchase of goods from a supplier of the company.
8. A bad debt of £40 which should have been written off had been forgotten and remained as a balance in the customer account.
9. The purchase on credit of a motor van costing £5,400 before deducting trade-in allowance of £1,200 from an old van had been recorded only by making a debit entry (of £5,400) in the motor van expenses account. The net book value of the old van at the time of the transaction was £1,350.

Required: Show the journal entries necessary to correct each of the above (including narrative), and state the effect of each correction on the profit of the company for the year ended 30 April 2012.

Test questions

Test 18.1 Accounting for purchases and sales with VAT added – AAT (abridged)

Listed on the right are some of the balances, at close of business on 31 May 2012, in the books of MEL. VAT has been calculated to the nearest pound at 17.5%.

Following transactions took place on 1 June 2012:

	Dr	Cr
Customers:	£	£
Autoparts Ltd	24,617	
Salfords Stores Ltd	41,561	
Motormania	27,124	
Other customers	627,341	
Suppliers:		
Carmart Imports Ltd		28,413
Lombard Products Ltd		56,987
Lucas and Co.		33,792
Other suppliers		492,853
Cash Book	4,120	
VAT account		71,089

(a) Sales invoices issued

	Total	VAT	Net
	£	£	£
Autoparts Ltd	5,492	818	4,674
Salfords Stores Ltd	3,396	506	2,890
Motormania	6,156	917	5,239
Other customers	22,696	3,380	19,316
	37,740	5,621	32,119

(b) Purchase invoices received

	Total	VAT	Net
	£	£	£
Carmart Imports Ltd	8,371	1,247	7,124
Lombard Products Ltd	7,727	1,151	6,576
Lucas and Co.	5,820	867	4,953
Other suppliers	12,676	1,888	10,788
	34,594	5,153	29,441

(c) Credit note issued

	Total	VAT	Net
Motormania	£168	£25	£143

(d) Payments made:

	£
Lombard Products Ltd	2,958
Cash purchases	1,363

(cash purchases includes VAT £203)

(e) Cash receipts:

Motormania	£1,550

Required:

(a) Open the account with appropriate balances at commencement of 1 June 2012.

(b) Enter each transaction in appropriate books of prime entry.

(c) Post the transactions.

(d) Prepare a list of balances in the relevant accounts after you have posted the transactions.

Test 18.2 Preparing financial statements with VAT involved

Tom Kelaart, registered for VAT, is familiar with accounting for VAT and has extracted the year-end Trial Balance as shown on the right. He informs you that:

Trial Balance as at 31 December 2012		
	£	£
Sales exclusive of VAT	–	180,200
Purchases exclusive of VAT	128,600	–
Inventory on 31.12.2011	10,800	–
Furniture account	32,500	–
Accumulated depreciation on furniture	–	14,750
Motor vehicles account	21,000	–
Accumulated depreciation on vehicle	–	4,000
Expenses exclusive of VAT	23,630	–
Salaries and wages	54,800	–
Entertainment with VAT	4,400	–
Trade receivables and payables	11,640	8,850
Cash and bank	430	–
Tom' Kelaart's capital	–	80,000
	287,800	287,800

(a) Invoices received after 31 December 2012 confirm that VAT-inclusive prices of £21,150 and £4,935 remain unpaid in respect of furniture (delivered on 1 October 2012) and goods for sale (delivered on 29 December 2012). These are yet to be accounted for.
(b) In addition December salary amounting to £4,500 remains unpaid.
(c) Inventory conducted on 31 December 2012 reveals the cost (inclusive of VAT) of goods in hand to be £17,390. However, goods taken by Tom for his own use have not been accounted for. The cost of these goods, inclusive of VAT, was £4,700.
(d) Furniture is depreciated at 10% per annum using the reducing balance method and vehicles at 20% per annum on cost. Depreciation is time apportioned for the nearest months of use.
(e) Tom wishes to set up an Allowance for doubtful debts at 5% of trade receivables.
(f) The VAT rate is 17.5%.

Required: Prepare the Statement of income for the year ended 31 December 2012 and the Statement of financial position as at that date.

Test 18.3 Including VAT and pay-sheet recovery adjustments

Ryan, registered for VAT, extracted the year-end Trial Balance as shown on the right. He informs you that:

Trial Balance as at 31 March 2012		
	£'000	£'000
Non-current assets	760,000	–
Accumulated depreciation	–	214,000
Inventory 31.3.2011	255,000	
Purchases/Sales	625,800	994,400
Salaries	173,420	–
Loan to Jane Dunn	10,000	–
Telephone/postage	5,800	–
Trade receivables	216,500	–
Trade payables	–	194,800
Allowance for doubtful debts		8,400
VAT account	–	1,540
Electricity	1,820	–
Other expenses	12,850	–
Cash and bank	1,950	–
Capital account	–	650,000
	2,063,140	2,063,140

(a) The following invoices relating to the period are yet to be accounted for:
£29,140 from supplier of goods for sale already delivered
£235 for telephone calls up to 31 March 2013.
(b) Unsold goods in hand at year-end, at cost inclusive of VAT, amounted to £334,875.
(c) The £10,000 Loan given to Jane Dunn, the sales manager, is being recovered from her pay in 20 equal instalments from May 2011.
(d) The salaries account includes only the net salary paid and amounts remitted to HMRC, £15,800 as PAYE and £14,860 as National Insurance. PAYE is deducted at 10% and employees' contribution to National Insurance at 6%. The employer's contribution is 9%.
(e) A trade debt of £23,500 is to be written off and the allowance for doubtful debts adjusted to 4% of trade receivables.
(f) Non-current assets are depreciated at 10% per annum using the reducing balance method.
(g) VAT rate is 17.5%.

Required: The financial statements for the year ended 31 March 2012.

PART D

THE CONCEPTUAL FRAMEWORK

Chapter 19

Conceptual framework of accounting

By the end of this chapter

You should learn:

- Who will benefit from establishing a conceptual framework
- The identity of the stakeholders in a business entity
- The main areas of interest each group has and their information needs
- The assumptions made when preparing financial statements
- The working rules applied when preparing financial statements
- The qualitative characteristics that information in financial statements should possess
- The definition of the main elements in financial statements

19.1 Financial reports

The financial reports are vehicles used by a business to communicate the financial effects of its activities to those outside. These reports, intended to meet the information needs of a wide range of users, include:

- financial statements such as the Statement of income, the Statement of financial position and the Statement of cash flows, along with explanatory notes;
- narrative reports such as the chairman's statement, directors' report and operating and financial review.

Limited companies are legally required to make the reports available to shareholders and to members of the public as documents of public record, filed with the Registrar of Companies. Listed companies are required, in addition, to publish their annual reports and accounts on their website. The format of these reports, as well as their content, is specified in company law. The amount of information to be disclosed has grown over the years because successive legislations have identified the need, often on an ad hoc basis, e.g. requiring disclosures such as of staff salary, number employed, political donations and charitable donations. Each additional disclosure has been designed usually to deal with shortcomings identified by investigations into company failures or to deal with matters of public concern such as the level of directors' remuneration.

It has been recognised by the accounting profession that there is a need for a proactive approach[1] to disclosure requirements. As part of this approach it is now appreciated that the financial reports could be made more meaningful if their contents and format of presentation were determined after considering the following:

- Who are the different parties (known as *stakeholders*) with a legitimate claim for information from a business?
- What are the main areas of interest that each of those parties has?
- Which items of information will be of relevance to those areas of interest?
- What are the qualitative characteristics which these parties will expect of the information provided to them?
- Which vehicles will prove most effective for communicating the identified information?

In this chapter we will learn of the results of this proactive approach taken by the International Accounting Standards Board and stated in their *Framework for Preparation and Presentation of Financial Statements.*[1]

Activity 19.1 Limitations of financial statements

Based on your studies so far, do you feel that the information communicated in the Statement of income and the Statement of financial position is adequate to properly assess the performance and position of a business?

19.2 Who benefits from a conceptual framework?

Let us start by inquiring into who will benefit from the effort to establish a conceptual framework within which the accounting and reporting functions should be carried out. The main beneficiaries will be as follows:

1. **Those responsible for setting and reviewing Accounting Standards**. Before IASC published its *Framework for the Preparation and Presentation of Financial Statements* in 2001, the Standards that were issued tended to be set to solve specific problems. For example, in the UK the publication of SSAP 19 'Investment Property' (since emulated by the IASB when they published IAS 40) was the response of standard-makers to pressure from those who sought a special accounting treatment for properties acquired as an investment. This was seen by many as an ad hoc, reactive and fire-fighting approach to deal with a specific problem. Besides, standard-making usually took the form of identifying various extant practices in use when accounting and reporting, and identifying one or more among them as the best practice. Moreover, in the absence of a conceptual framework on which the Standards could be founded, the pronouncements in different Standards were not always mutually consistent.

   Establishing a framework sets out a generally acceptable accounting theory, based on clearly defined concepts, so that the standard-setters are able to formulate Standards on a consistent basis, avoiding inconsistencies between pronouncements in different Standards.

2. **Those responsible for maintaining financial records and preparing financial reports.** If there is a conceptual framework preparers of financial statements could benefit when having to make decisions such as (a) identifying the accounting treatment that best suited their circumstances, whenever Accounting Standards permitted alternative treatments, and (b) identifying the most appropriate accounting treatment when a transaction to be recorded is not covered by any extant Standard. An additional benefit would be being able to justify their accounting treatment to those for whom the financial statements are intended.
3. **Those for whom the financial statements are intended.** If there is an agreed conceptual framework, the stakeholders could better understand the meaning of the information communicated to them as well as the limitations of the recording and reporting functions, so that they are well placed to make informed decisions.
4. **The auditors will benefit** because an understanding of the underlying concepts will assist them when forming their opinion on whether financial statements give a fair view and when having to justify why they are unable to attest to the truth and fairness of a set of financial statements.

19.3 Identification of the stakeholders

The *stakeholders* are parties who have a legitimate claim for information from profit-oriented entities. They have been identified in the *Framework*[1] as follows:

- **Investors** being those who have provided or intend to provide risk capital.
- **Lenders** (present and prospective) being the providers of loan capital.
- **Suppliers** being providers of goods/services on credit terms.
- **Employees** whose financial security and prospects are entwined with those of the entity.
- **Customers** who expect to be served as well as serviced by the entity.
- **Government** with its various agencies, each with a different focus ranging from revenue collection, compliance with regulations and public welfare.
- **The public** whose welfare is affected by the activities of the entity.

19.4 Main areas of stakeholder interest

The main areas of interest to a range of stakeholders may be identified as follows:

1. **Discharge of stewardship.** In a limited company, although the resources of the entity are usually owned by numerous shareholders, the management of those resources (the stewardship) is entrusted to a few directors. The divorce of ownership from management places the management in a *fiduciary* (position of trust) relationship with the owners and hence with a responsibility to account to the owners for:
   - protection, proper application and efficient use of the resources;
   - achieving returns on the resources at levels that are acceptable to the owners.

2. **Profitability** of the entity's activities: the level of profit expected by the shareholders may depend on the nature of business and extent of commercial risk it involves. For example, in a retail business there might be an expectation of steady growth and customer satisfaction is important; whereas in a pharmaceutical business there might be long periods of low profits, or even losses, whilst new products are being developed. In every business, however, in the long term, profitability is paramount because losses erode the capital base of the entity and may, in time, jeopardise its very existence. Profitability is of course the motivation for operating a business and is, therefore, one of the measures used for assessing stewardship.

3. **Liquidity** provides the means to settle debts and to achieve financial adaptability. It is gauged on the basis of the ability of the business to:

   - meet its bills as and when they fall due;
   - have the resources to avail itself of profit-making opportunities.

   Financial adaptability is the entity's ability to take effective action to alter the amount and timing of its cash flows so that it can respond to unexpected needs or opportunities, e.g. being able to finance a long period of product development. If liquidity is weak then this will:

   - raise alarm bells with suppliers and loan creditors with regard to the creditworthiness of the entity;
   - mean incurring higher costs on any borrowing;
   - mean missing out on profit-making opportunities;
   - mean that shareholders will have to invest more capital to provide the necessary funds.

4. **Solvency** is the ability of the entity, in the event it is wound up, to meet in full all claims on its resources. If the entity is a limited company then lenders need to be careful because the shareholders only have an obligation to contribute the amount they agreed to pay for their shares. If the company runs out of funds the lenders and suppliers to whom the company owes money could be in danger of not being paid.

5. **National goals and public welfare obligations** can impact on an entity in its aim to maintain customer loyalty, social image and a conducive operating environment. For example:

   - national goals include pressures for regional development, non-discriminatory employment policies and ethical standards and absence of bribery and corruption;
   - public welfare may be advanced by measures such as protecting the environment, providing employment, conserving foreign exchange holdings, improving the standard of living.

6. **Employee welfare** encourages staff morale and productivity, and ranges from, for example, benefiting from employee suggestions on one hand to avoiding industrial action at the other extreme. The extent to which an entity secures the welfare of its staff may be gauged not only on the basis of remuneration levels but also taking into account other aspects of interest to employees, such as the following:

   - rate of staff turnover;
   - training and staff development facilities and promotional prospects;
   - work ethics, office atmosphere, grievance redress and staff motivation;
   - debt relief, medical facilities, retirement benefits;
   - participation in the management process.

Activity 19.2 Economic decisions based on information in financial reports

It is claimed that a range of stakeholders depend on financial reports to make crucial economic decisions. Identify two such economic decisions the shareholders have to make.

19.5 The information needs of all stakeholders are not the same

The objective of financial reports is to provide information that is useful to those for whom they are prepared. The same set of financial reports is expected to satisfy the information needs of a variety of stakeholders we have identified above. The problem is that their interests do not always coincide. For example:

- A supplier considering an entity's application for credit would find the annually prepared financial statements and reports inadequate for the purpose and would have to fall back on reports of Credit Protection Agencies.
- A bank, placed in similar circumstances, would find it necessary to insist on additional information such as management reports, budgets and monthly cash flow forecasts.

The information needs of different stakeholders may even be in conflict. For example, to assess the security available to it a bank may prefer the borrower's Statement of financial position to be prepared on a break-up value basis; whereas an investor is more interested in one prepared on a going concern basis.

Activity 19.3 Areas of stakeholder interest

Fill in the words Very, Highly and Potentially in the following grid to state your opinion of the extent of interest each identified group of stakeholders would have in the specified areas:

Stakeholders	Stewardship	Profitability	Liquidity	Solvency	Employee welfare	National goals
1. Investors						
2. Lenders						
3. Suppliers						
4. Employees						

The reports that companies publish annually are expected to provide sufficient information for all stakeholders to make informed economic decisions. However, as we have seen, different groups of stakeholders need to make different decisions, and the information they need for the purpose is not the same. The International Accounting Standards Board (IASB) considers, however, that there is a degree of overlap in the information requirements of the different groups to the extent that all of them are interested, to varying degrees, in an entity's:

- financial performance as seen in the Statement of income;
- financial position as seen in the Statement of financial position;
- ability to generate cash and respond to unexpected needs and opportunities.

In view of this overlap the IASB assumes that, if an entity satisfies the information needs of shareholders, then the information needs of other stakeholders will also be satisfied. Other groups of stakeholders should be aware of this assumption so that, when making their decisions, they would regard the information in financial statements only as a broad frame of reference against which to identify more specific information they should seek and obtain.

19.6 Underlying assumptions when preparing financial statements

When preparing financial statements the following assumptions are made:

1. Separate entity
2. Going concern
3. Money measurement
4. Stable value of money.

19.6.1 Separate entity

When accounting for transactions, it is assumed that the entity in respect of which the accounting records are maintained is separate from (i) its owner or owners and (ii) other entities owned by the same person(s). For example, looked at from the point of view of the business entity, the capital contributed by the owner is a liability and is accounted for as such, whereas from the point of view of the one who contributed it, the capital would be an asset. Similarly, in early chapters when dealing with sole traders, we observed that payment of school fees for the owner's child is accounted for as drawings and not as a business expense. In a strictly legal sense the assumption of separate entity is true only with regard to limited companies which, on incorporation, are recognised as separate entities not only distinct from but also having rights against those who own it. Without such a clear demarcation, which incorporation provides, it is difficult to identify the thin line dividing the resources and activities of the entity from those of its owner, although this is necessary for both accounting and tax purposes.

19.6.2 Going concern

The financial statements are prepared on the assumption that the entity will continue in operational existence for the foreseeable future and that there is no intention or necessity to close down the business or to significantly curtail the scale of its operations. It is on the basis of the assumption that the entity will remain a going concern that:

(a) a non-current asset continues to be reported at depreciated historical cost, even if its realisable value is lower, in the expectation that the asset will continue to remain in use;

(b) a distinction is drawn between current and non-current assets and liabilities because such distinctions have a meaning only when the business continues to trade; and

(c) significant obligations such as compensation payable to staff, in the event of cessation of business, are ignored in the expectation that there is no risk of cessation of business.

Going concern is one of two underlying assumptions held out in IAS on the basis of which financial statements are prepared. That is why those responsible for preparing financial statements are required to satisfy themselves that there are no problems affecting the ability of the entity to continue. For example, they need to consider:

- adequacy of both working and long-term capital;
- operational prospects such as the size of the order book, market share, market trends and intensity of competition;
- availability of resources including raw material, manpower and know-how.

However, as we have seen, financial statements prepared on an assumption of going concern may not be adequate for evaluating aspects such as the security available to a lending bank which may also have to consider prospects of a forced realisation of assets in the event of an emergency.

Activity 19.4 The going concern assumption

Unless expressly stated otherwise, financial statements are assumed to have been prepared on the premise that the entity will remain in the business as a going concern for the foreseeable future, at the current scale.

Required: Explain how assets and liabilities are identified, measured and reported in financial statements on the basis of the assumption that the entity will continue in operation at the current scale of operation for the foreseeable future.

19.6.3 Money measurement

It is assumed that everything that needs to be accounted for can be measured in terms of money. It is possible to account for the resources of a business in physical measures, without necessarily involving money values. The assets of an entity could be expressed, for example, as consisting of *x* acres of land, *y* tons of coal and *z* bales of textiles. The advantage of comparing physical measures is that it would be clear whether there has been a growth or decline over time, e.g. an acre of land remains the same in extent today as it was centuries ago. The disadvantage of measuring in physical terms, however, is that the physical values cannot be aggregated so as to identify the total wealth of an entity in a single figure, for example, receivables, payables and cash cannot be aggregated with physical measures such as acres. Without aggregation, using a common unit of measurement such as the £, it is not possible to compare different entities or the same entity over time.

For these reasons accountants measure assets and liabilities in terms of money. Accountants in each country use their national currency as the yardstick for measuring transactions and events for the purpose of accounting. We in the UK use the pound sterling. Money values, when established by market transactions, are traditionally accepted as objective and reliable for reporting an entity's performance and position. The disadvantage is that any transaction or event which cannot be measured in terms of money is not accounted for in the financial statements. This shortcoming has been increasingly realised by the accounting profession and has led to companies providing more narrative comment in their annual financial reports.

Activity 19.5 Business information which money cannot measure

Accountants measure everything they account for in money terms. Accordingly they assume that what is not measurable in terms of money need not be accounted for. They are aware, however, of significant areas which cannot be measured in terms of money and yet are of interest to those for whom accounting reports are intended.

Required:
(a) Identify some business information which money cannot measure, but which may be important to the successful running of a business.
(b) Explain how such information is communicated to those interested in it.

19.6.4 Stable value of money

Information in financial statements recording money values would be meaningless unless we assume that the value of money remains stable over time. Measuring in terms of money values, however, gives rise to problems such as the following:

1. Whereas physical measures (e.g. acres) remain a stable measure over time, monetary measures do not. A pound sterling today is worth less than 66% of its value 10 years ago and around 20% of its value 30 years ago.
2. Each asset does not always have a constant money value over time. For example, because of limitation in supply, land has increased in money value over time.
3. Measurements made in money are distorted by variations in exchange rate. For example, a machine bought from Japan 20 years ago may be worth much more today because of the appreciation of the exchange value of the Japanese yen.

Yet money remains the yardstick of accounting measurement because it provides the only means of aggregating non-current assets, current assets and current liabilities and making possible comparisons over time and between entities. Accountants have to choose whether to assume that money is stable in value or to adjust all of the figures in the financial statements to take account of the changes in money value. Accountants have opted for the former.

On the basis of this assumption, the financial statements seem to imply that an entity earning £20 million this year has performed better than when it earned £19 million a year earlier and that an entity X with net assets of £100 million is better resourced than an entity Y with £90 million. Neither of these assertions may be valid if, because of inflation, the value of money has diminished. For example:

1. If there is an inflation of 10%, the earning this year of £20 million is worth only (£20 × 100/110) = £18.18 million in terms of last year's money values, so that the performance this year is worse.
2. If the entity Y acquired most of its assets in 1960, when the Retail Price Index was 12.5, and has the same £ amount of assets in 2010 as the entity X which acquired its assets in 2004 when the Retail Price Index was 163, then clearly entity Y is far better resourced than entity X.

A variation in the value of money, therefore, not only distorts comparison over time and with other entities, but also inhibits performance reporting as well as position reporting. For example, performance reporting is bound to be distorted to the extent that earnings measured in terms of current (lower) monetary units are compared with expense at least some of which (like depreciation of assets and opening inventory) is measured in monetary units of a prior period. Position reporting is distorted as well because the assets reported on a historical cost basis will be stated at different money values that prevailed at the time each of them was acquired.

Accountants are fully conscious that measurements are distorted by changing values of their unit of measurement. The distortion is of course greater in times of more pronounced inflation. That is why the accounting profession tends to intensify its efforts at finding a solution to the problem during periods of accelerated inflation, as was the case in the 1970s when they actively searched for ways of accounting for price-level changes. Currently inflation is low and there is little pressure to take it into account.

Activity 19.6 Alternative to historical cost accounting

Accounting on the basis of historical cost is valid only if it is assumed that the value of money remains constant over time. This constraint would be overcome if accounting used current values rather than historical costs.

Required: Explain the reluctance to record accounting information using current values.

19.7 Working rules

There are a number of working rules that are complied with when accounting for transactions to be reported in financial statements. These are:

1. Time interval rule
2. Accruals including matching rule
3. Realisation rule
4. Historical cost rule
5. Valuation rules
6. Non-aggregation rule.

19.7.1 Time interval rule

In the distant past, the accounts for voyages and trade across the seas were based on *the venture concept* and prepared financial statements only when the venture was completed and all of the merchandise as well as the ship had been sold. This meant that there was no need to make estimates such as how long the non-current assets would last and the value of inventory. At the present day, however, stakeholders require information with greater frequency. This is achieved by following the time interval rule which requires accounting information to be provided to stakeholders at regular intervals – in the UK the Companies Act 2006 requires companies to publish their financial reports annually. We will learn in the next chapter that replacement of the venture concept with the time interval rule is responsible for many of the problems accountants face.

19.7.2 Accruals including matching rule

When financial statements are prepared in compliance with the time interval rule there is a need to ensure that in each accounting period the income accounted for in that period is properly matched with the expenses incurred in the earning process. To achieve this matching, the accruals rule requires that:

1. income must be accounted for in the period in which it is earned irrespective of whether the related cash is received in that period or not; and
2. expense is accounted for in the period in which it is incurred irrespective of whether it has been paid for in that period or not.

If this rule is not complied with a business would be in a position to report improved profit by a mere expedience of delaying payments until the next period. Generally accounting in compliance with the accruals rule would not constitute a problem in cases such as expenses remaining unpaid and earnings yet to be received. But problems could arise, for example, with regard to non-current assets where matching the amount earned by using an asset within an accounting period can be done only on the basis of assumptions relating to the asset's life and its scrap value.

A reciprocal of the accruals rule is that a cost incurred in a period should be deferred to the next period if the relationship of that cost to an earning in the next can be established or justifiably assumed. This is the reason why the cost of unsold purchases is reported as an asset at the end of each accounting period and written off in the next when the items are sold.

19.7.3 Realisation rule

The realisation rule requires that income should not be recognised in the Statement of income until it has been realised, i.e. either received in cash or the ultimate realisation in cash is reasonably assured. Realisation requires all uncertainties relating to the earning process to have been substantially resolved. The ideal and prudent approach would be to define income as realised when:

1. The production is completed so that there is no uncertainty as to the readiness of product for sale.
2. The sale has been agreed so that there is no uncertainty as to whether a buyer can be found and on the sales price.
3. The sale proceeds have been received.

If realisation in the form of cash were a necessary condition for accounting for income, then credit sales would not be accounted for as income. In practice the last condition that the sales proceeds should have been received is relaxed and considered to have been satisfied if there is a reasonable assurance of receiving it. Consequently, credit sales are regarded as income and give rise to an asset (referred to as trade receivables) provided there is reasonable certainty that the cash will be received. We saw in Chapter 7 that an Allowance for doubtful debts is created and deducted from the profit if there is no reasonable certainty.

In the UK company law states that only profits realised by the financial year-end should be included in the Statement of income and that distribution to shareholders can only be made out of realised profits.[2] This requirement is part of the effort company law makes to safeguard the interests of those who have a claim on the company by protecting intact the capital base of the company.

Activity 19.7 Realisation rule inhibits performance reporting

Two sisters, Tessa and Vanessa, commenced separate businesses on 1.1.2012 each with capital of £50,000 in cash. On that day each invested their whole capital in 50,000 ordinary shares of £1 each at par. By 31 December 2012 these shares were quoted on the London Stock Exchange at 120p per share. Tessa sold her shares on that date but Vanessa held on to hers expecting the shares to go up even further.

Required:

(a) Set out the Statement of financial position of each sister as at 31 December 2012.

(b) State whether you regard Vanessa's performance in the year as poorer than Tessa's.

A major problem with the realisation rule is the determination of the precise point at which income may be regarded as having been realised. This is the topic we will focus on in the next chapter. Professionals, such as solicitors, who are usually not permitted by rules of professional etiquette to sue their clients for professional fees, have regarded their fee income as earned only when received in cash. A club or association may also adopt the same attitude. It is important to note that the point at which the income may be regarded as realised, though critical to accounting, may not always be clear. The practice in this area has still not been standardised in the UK.

19.7.4 Historical cost rule

The historical cost (actual amount paid) is the time-hallowed method accountants have always used to measure the resources of an entity as well as the expenses. The value is based on the amount actually paid and, being established by an arm's length market transaction, it is objective, verifiable (in that the amount can be checked) and reliable. Since historical cost rule has been applied over the years, profit reported on this basis is generally understood and accepted.

The shortcomings of accounting on the historical cost rule should, however, be admitted.

1. *Resources are not reported at their current worth.* The Statement of financial position, reporting resources at their historical cost, fails to reflect the current value of the resources available to the entity. There is a further problem as the amounts stated on that Statement become meaningless because assets are stated at costs paid at different times when money values, depending on the inflation rate, may have been different. There has been an attempt to get over this by allowing companies to revalue their non-current assets on a regular basis. The Companies Act of 1981 introduced the *alternative accounting rule* permitting assets to be accounted at the market value rather than cost. However, not all companies take advantage of this. Most continue to report non-current assets on the historical cost rule.
2. *Resources may be omitted from the Statement of financial position.* The value of of an asset is not reported on the Statement of financial position unless a payment has been made when acquiring it, e.g. players by football clubs.
3. *Performance is not accurately reported.* This occurs because the Statement of income matches current period's earnings against expenses, some of which might have been incurred at an earlier date when money may have had a different value. The extent of the mismatch depends on the level of inflation and the time gap between the payment

and the use of assets. In addition, it does not recognise the loss suffered through holding monetary assets (such as receivables and bank balance) while prices are rising and causing an erosion in the purchasing power of such assets.

19.7.5 Valuation rules

Some of the valuation rules accountants adopt are as follows:

- Non-current assets are valued at cost less depreciation at the reporting date (Chapter 7).
- Inventory is valued at cost or lower net realisable value (Chapter 6).
- Trade receivables are valued at their expected cash realisable value (Chapter 7).
- A liability is stated at the amount of cash or cash equivalent which is considered to be necessary to fully discharge the obligation existing at the reporting date.

19.7.6 Non-aggregation rule

This rule (referred to in Chapter 6) applies when, with regard to assets such as inventory, cost is compared with realisable value for determining which is lower. The rule requires that the comparison should be done separately for each individual asset or for groups of fungible (meaning interchangeable) assets.

Activity 19.8 IASB's underlying assumptions

We have come across many accounting concepts, of which some are assumptions we make and others are rules we comply with when accounting for transactions. However, IASB's Framework has named two among them as underlying assumptions.

Required:
(a) What are these two underlying assumptions?
(b) Why are they identified as underlying assumptions?

19.8 Capital maintenance

To understand the concept let us focus on a taxi business owned by Dave. Dave invested a capital of £20,000 to buy a vehicle with an estimated economic life of five years. If he measures his annual profit without depreciating the vehicle and draws out the whole of the profit year after year, at the end of the five years he would need to invest £20,000 more to buy another vehicle. What this means is that the amount of his annual drawing included in part a repayment to him of the capital he invested in the business. If, on the other hand, he were to provide for depreciation at 20% of the cost annually, he would have reduced the amount of the annual profit by £4,000 and not taken out this amount as drawings. As a result he would have, by the end of the vehicle's economic life, retained within the business £20,000 (£4,000 × 5) and so maintained the money capital of £20,000 available for reinvestment. This is known as *maintenance of money capital*.

Capital maintenance is protection of the money capital and depreciation of non-current assets helps in this process. But depreciation would not protect the *real capital*, unless the value of money remains unchanged during this period and the price of vehicles remains unchanged, so that £20,000 would be sufficient to replace the vehicle. In such circumstances Dave's business can continue to operate at the same capacity as before and, therefore, he would have maintained his real capital as well. On the contrary, if the price of vehicles increased during the period, £20,000 may only be sufficient to buy a smaller vehicle. This means that while his money capital is maintained, his real capital (i.e. the operating capacity of the business) is not.

19.9 Qualitative characteristics of information in financial statements

The company law prohibits directors of a company from approving financial statements unless 'they are satisfied that the financial statements show a *true and fair view* of the assets, liabilities, financial position and the profit or loss'.[3] The *Framework*[1] suggests that the financial statements would convey a true and fair view if they are prepared in accordance with Accounting Standards and if the information they contain possesses identified qualitative characteristics which make the statements useful. To place them in a proper perspective the qualitative characteristics identified in the *Framework* may be structured[4] as follows:

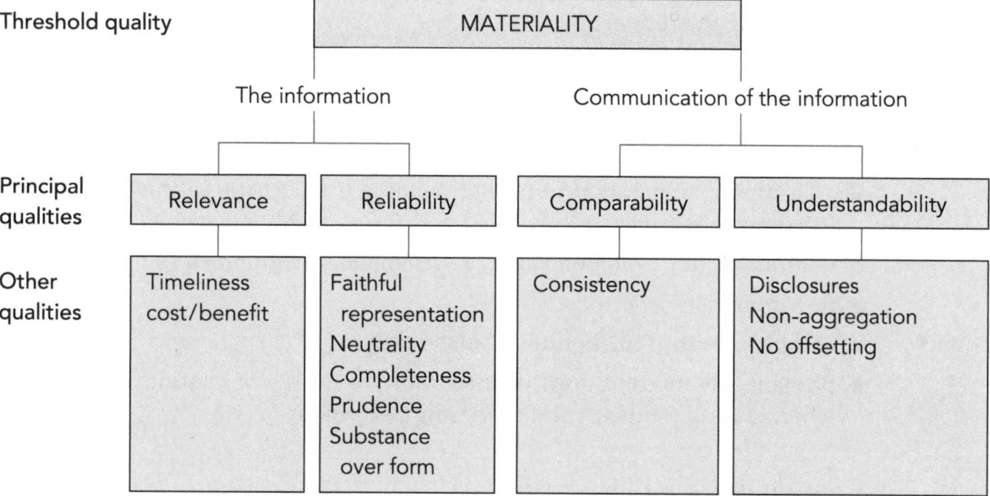

19.9.1 Materiality

In accounting, materiality means the significance of the information to the stakeholders. Information is regarded as material if, by nature or amount, it is significant for those who have to make decisions. For shareholders a significant item of information is one that could influence decisions such as whether to buy, retain or sell shares in a company. There are many situations where accountants have to exercise their discretion with regard to materiality, for example:

1. Deciding whether to capitalise an item as an asset or write it off as an expense, e.g. is it an asset if a company has spent £5,000 on tools? The answer would be influenced by the size of the company, being Yes if preparing the financial statements of a carpenter and No if preparing the financial statements of a multinational company.

2. Deciding whether to report an item separately because of its size, e.g. should bad debts of £10,000 be separately disclosed or included in the selling expenses? Again, it depends on the size of the organisation and other factors such as comparison with:
   - other items in the whole report;
   - size of related items (in this case Trade receivables);
   - comparative figure of the previous year;
   - the amount it was expected to be.
3. Deciding whether to report an item separately because of its nature, e.g. should the fact that the directors have started to sell their shares be disclosed as material? The answer would be influenced by the surrounding circumstances. It might be significant to the shareholders if it is linked with other considerations such as a falling trend in the profits or loss of a major customer or known disagreement amongst the directors.

19.9.2 Relevance

Relevance is the usefulness of that information for making economic decisions. The usefulness could arise because of the significance of the information for:

- confirming or correcting past evaluations and assessments;
- evaluating or assessing the present;
- predicting the future.

19.9.3 Reliability

Reliability requires the information to be:

- a faithful representation of reality, i.e. does it reflect the substance of a transaction and its commercial effect?
- neutral, i.e. free from deliberate or systematic bias intended to influence decisions;
- free from material error;
- complete (within the bounds of materiality);
- prudent, i.e. in conditions of uncertainty a degree of caution should have been used when making estimates and exercising judgement.

19.9.4 Relevance/reliability trade-off

It has been recognised that stakeholders may require information before the annual report is published. There is, therefore, a requirement for companies to produce half-yearly and even quarterly reports. Such reports cannot be checked for completeness as thoroughly as the annual reports and it is accepted when determining the relevance and reliability of information to be included in financial statements that one has to make a trade-off, taking into account the need for timeliness, cost–benefit and completeness.

Activity 19.9 Conflict between qualities of information

Relevance and reliability are accorded equal primary status as principal characteristics of information to be included in financial statements. Discuss the possibility of conflict between the two qualities and how such conflict should be resolved.

19.9.5 Comparability

Comparability means that the information communicated has been identified, measured and presented in such a way that it is comparable over time and, where possible, with those of other similar entities. It is achieved through:

- consistency in the treatment of transactions within each accounting period, from one period to the next and also, ideally, between different entities;
- disclosure of accounting policies to show that there has been consistent treatment or to allow the stakeholders to take any inconsistency into account when making comparisons.

For example, company A may appear to be performing better than company B unless company A discloses that its accounting policy is not to depreciate its buildings. International Financial Reporting Standards contribute to comparability by:

- reducing the options available to different entities when accounting for similar transactions;
- requiring the disclosure of accounting policies and changes in accounting policies.

In order to maintain consistency the IASB requires the consistent adoption of an *accounting policy* unless there is a good reason for a change, in which case the change should be explained and the effect of the change on the information presented identified.

19.9.6 Understandability

Understandability is whether the users of financial statements will be able to recognise the significance of the information. This depends on both the preparer of the financial statements and the users themselves. For example:

1. The statutory authorities and the IASB have required the preparers to format the statements in a way that assists understanding, e.g. that the Statement of income is required to be so formatted as to report sales revenue, cost of goods sold, distribution costs and administrative expenses in that sequence and to explain any unusual items such as an unusually high level of bad debts.
2. The users are assumed to have a reasonable knowledge of the business, economic activities and accounting and to be willing to study the information with reasonable diligence. However, information on complex matters which needs to be included because of its relevance to decision making should not be left out merely because it would be too difficult for certain users to understand.

19.9.7 Neutrality

Also known as objectivity, neutrality means that the preparers of the financial statements have not presented a biased picture or attempted to report a premeditated position. In recent years the UK government has been accused of spin, with a resulting loss of credibility. The accounting profession recognises that it is extremely important that financial statements should remain credible as they are often the basis for investors' decisions. Lack of credibility could have an adverse effect on investment. Investors want the information to be objective, and adherence to the historical cost rule is one of the ways the accountants use to safeguard objectivity. For example, by reporting non-current assets at the cost actually paid, the accountant avoids the subjective judgement involved when assets are valued. We have seen, though, that there are numerous occasions when the accounting process requires subjective judgements to be made. Some such occasions are as follows:

- determining depreciation, when the useful economic life of non-current assets is estimated;
- making allowance for doubtful debts, when the recoverability of the debt is assessed;
- accruing for unpaid bills, when estimates have to be made because actual amounts are as yet unknown;
- determining the net realisable value of inventory.

19.9.8 Completeness

Completeness is required for information to be reliable subject to consideration of materiality and cost. The omission of information can cause the information presented to be biased or even false, e.g. not disclosing that there are likely to be environmental liabilities.

19.9.9 Prudence

Prudence is the exercise of a degree of caution when conditions are uncertain, particularly in respect of estimates that may have to be made when accounting. The aim is to ensure that income and assets are not overstated and expense and liabilities are not understated. The uncertainties might be of a recurring nature, such as providing for doubtful debts, when too low an estimate would result in the income and assets being overstated. The uncertainties could also be of an infrequent nature, such as the expected outcome of a legal dispute. In the latter case, although liabilities should not be understated, it is not the place of prudence to provide for the worst outcome. For example, if a liability is estimated to be finalised at a figure between £6,000 and £10,000 with the likelihood that it will finally be agreed at £8,500. Prudence is not providing for the maximum liability of £10,000 but for the most likely amount of £8,500.

19.9.10 Substance over form

This requires the substance of a transaction to be reported rather than in accordance with its legal form. For example, if X sells a load of timber to Y for £60,000 subject to an agreement that X has the option to buy it back at an agreed price (say £60,000 plus interest at a specified rate for the period until it is bought back), the transaction is not really a sale but a financing one to borrow that amount and should be accounted for accordingly.

Activity 19.10 Identification of the defining accounting convention

You are now familiar with a number of accounting concepts. Identify which among them would be relevant when deciding on:

(a) the value at which inventory is reported on the Statement of financial position;

(b) setting up an Allowance for doubtful debts;

(c) writing off depreciation of non-current assets;

(d) whether to capitalise advertising expenses intended to enhance future sales.

19.10 The elements of financial statements

As we have seen in Chapter 4 the Framework[1] identifies five elements, three of which constitute the Statement of financial position: These three are:

1. **Assets**. These are resources controlled by an entity as a result of past transactions or events and from which future economic benefits are expected to flow.
2. **Liabilities**. These are present obligations of an entity arising from a past transaction or event the settlement of which is expected to result in an outflow of resources embodying economic benefits.
3. **Equity (ownership)**. This is the residual interest in the assets of an entity after deducting all its liabilities.

Two remaining elements identify the performance of the business in the Statement of income. These are:

1. **Income**. The increase in economic benefits during the accounting period in the form of inflows or enhancement of assets or decreases of liabilities that result in increases in equity. Contributions from equity participants are not income.
2. **Expense**. The decrease in economic benefits during the accounting period in the form of outflows or depletions of assets or incurrence of liabilities that result in decreases in equity. Distributions to equity participants are not expenses.

19.11 Recognition of an element in a financial statement

19.11.1 What does recognition mean?

According to the *Framework*[1] 'recognition' consists of:

(a) identifying an item as an asset, liability, equity, income or expense;
(b) depiction of that item in a financial statement in both words and monetary amount;
(c) inclusion of the monetary amount in the totals of the appropriate financial statement.

Identification is not the same as recognition. For example, a repair garage may identify the cost of a screwdriver as an expense, but will not recognise it in so far as that amount is not depicted separately (in words and amounts) in the Statement of income. Similarly, in the USA, where reporting assets at current value is not permitted, the current value of a freehold property may be identified and perhaps communicated to the stakeholders as a note in the financial statements. But the value would not be recognised because it would not be included in the totals of the Statement of financial position.

19.11.2 When should an element be recognised?

Provided the amount involved is material, an item satisfying the definition of any of the five elements will qualify for recognition only if:

(a) it is probable that future economic benefits associated with it will flow to or from the entity, and
(b) the cost or value of that item can be measured reliably.

19.11.3 Recognition of an element is obligatory

If an item meets the definition of an element and qualifies for recognition, it is obligatory that it should be included either in the Statement of income or Statement of financial position. If an item meets the definition of an element but does not qualify for recognition it should be disclosed as a note.

Summary

- There is a range of different stakeholders who have a legitimate interest in financial reports.
- These stakeholders have different areas of interest in a business entity.
- Financial statements are prepared assuming separate entity, going concern, money measurement and stable value of money.
- Financial statements are prepared adopting working rules of time interval, accruals and matching, realisation, historical cost, valuation and non-aggregation.
- Unless capital is maintained, drawing out by the owner of the whole profit would represent in part a repayment of capital invested in the business.
- To report a true and fair view the accounting information included in financial statements should possess qualitative characteristics identified as materiality, relevance, reliability, comparability, understandability, objectivity, completeness, prudence and substance over form.
- The key elements constituting financial statements are assets, liabilities, equity, income and expense.
- An item which meets the definition of an element and qualifies for recognition should be recognised in the financial statements.

References

1. Interest in seeking answers to these questions arose when the accounting profession launched its quest for a conceptual framework. The current position in this study is contained in the *Framework for the Preparation and Presentation of Financial Statements* (hereafter referred to as the *Framework*) issued by the International Accounting Standards Board in April 2001.
2. Companies Act 2006, section 830, London, The Stationery Office.
3. Companies Act 2006, section 393, London, The Stationery Office.
4. The diagrammatic presentation is taken from *Statement of Principles of Financial Reporting* (1999), London, Accounting Standards Board.

Suggested answers to activities

19.1 Limitations of financial statements

Traditional financial statements are intended to serve two main purposes. The first is as a vehicle for discharging stewardship. The second is as a basis for making informed economic decisions. On both counts the financial statements are inadequate for the following reasons:

(i) The financial statements are only capable of reporting the financial effects of transactions and events. These statements do not communicate non-financial effects (such as staff morale, quality of product lines), equally valuable for assessment of performance and position.

(ii) The information contained in financial statements is largely historical and fails to reflect future possibilities that could enhance or impair the entity's performance and financial position and is, therefore, of inadequate significance for decision making.

(iii) Since the natural operating cycle of an entity does not always coincide with its accounting periods, the financial statements relating to the accounting periods have necessarily to be prepared on the basis of:

- allocating continuous operations to discrete accounting periods;
- dealing with uncertainties remaining at the end of each period by making assumptions and estimates and these introduce an element of conjecture, subjectivity and tentativeness to the performance.

19.2 Economic decisions based on information in financial reports

(i) Whether to hold or sell their shares.

(ii) Whether to reappoint or replace the management (i.e. directors).

19.3 Areas of stakeholder interest

The authors suggest that the importance of the different areas to each group of stakeholders can be ranked as Very, Highly or Potentially Important as stated below:

Stakeholders	Stewardship	Profitability	Liquidity	Solvency	National goal	Employee welfare
1. Investors	Very	Very	Highly	Potentially	Potentially	Potentially
2. Lenders	Potentially	Highly	Very	Potentially	Potentially	Potentially
3. Suppliers	Potentially	Highly	Very	Potentially	Potentially	Potentially
4. Employees	Potentially	Highly	Highly	Potentially	Potentially	Very

19.4 The going concern assumption

(i) Assets are recognised for inclusion in a Statement of financial position on the basis that the entity will remain ongoing. For example, the prepaid portion of rent is recognised as an asset on the assumption that the entity will remain ongoing and continue to occupy the premises.

(ii) Liabilities are recognised on the basis that the entity will remain in operation. For example, if the entity ceases business and employees lose their jobs, the compensation it may have to pay its employees is not accounted for unless such cessation of business is under contemplation.

(iii) Assets are valued on the premise that the entity will continue to operate and on the present scale. For example, assume that machinery of a specialised nature acquired for £500,000 and written down to £250,000 has a realisable value of only £50,000. The lower realisable value is ignored so long as disposal of the machinery is unlikely and the written-down value of the machinery is recoverable from its use. Similarly, the amount realisable on inventory and recoverable from customers is likely to be lower in a forced realisation on a business ceasing and is not taken into account when preparing annual financial statements.

(iv) Liabilities are accounted at the amount that will have to be paid if the business remains ongoing. Any penalties that may arise from settling a loan earlier than the agreed date are ignored.

(v) In a Statement of financial position, assets are classified as non-current and current in accordance with whether they are intended to be realised or used within the next accounting period. Such a classification is valid only on the going concern assumption. In the event of closure of business all assets are for realisation and would fall within a single category. Similarly the classification of liabilities as current and non-current depends on the intended period of repayment, if the business remains ongoing. In the event of winding up, the whole classification has to be altered to identify preferential creditors, secured creditors and unsecured ones.

19.5 Business information which money cannot measure

(a) Significant business information of interest to those who have a claim for information cannot be accounted for because it is not measurable in terms of money. Such information includes the following:

(i) the quality and competence of the entity's employees;
(ii) the morale among the staff, their motivation and threat of industrial action;
(iii) the quality of the entity's assets and how well they are maintained;
(iv) the competitive edge the entity has over its rivals in such forms as reputation, location, brand names and past history.

(b) Such information, which cannot be measured in terms of money, is communicated by being narrated in financial statements as footnotes or in management or directors' reports.

19.6 Alternative to historical cost accounting

The reluctance to substitute current values for historical cost arises from several factors including the following:

(i) The value of an asset or a transaction is subjective and, therefore, could vary according to the thinking and mood of the person doing the valuation.

(ii) Value could mean different things. For example, value in use is different from market value. Value in use would vary according to the intended use to which the item is to be put. Market value could itself refer to the value at which the item could be disposed of (realisable value) and the value at which the item could be replaced (the replacement value).

(iii) The value cannot be verified (for example during an audit) and that may affect the credibility of the information provided in accounts.

19.7 Realisation rule inhibits performance reporting

Applying the realisation rule, Tessa is able to report a profit because she realised by sale her investments. Vanessa, on the other hand, cannot account for the holding gain until she realises that gain, and perhaps more, by selling the investments on a future date. Although Vanessa's decision is perhaps wiser, her performance in terms of profit reported is poorer. However, as we will learn at a higher level, the accounting profession is seeking to relax the realisation rule relating to investments. For example, investments in quoted shares, if irrevocably designated at the time of acquisition as held at fair value through profit and loss, are required to be reported on every Statement of financial position at their market value on the date of reporting and the holding gain or loss arising in that connection to be included in the Statement of income.

Statements of financial position

	Tessa	Vanessa
	£'000	£'000
Investments	–	£50,000
Cash and bank	£60,000	–
	£60,000	£50,000
Capital	£50,000	£50,000
Profit	£10,000	0
	£60,000	£50,000

19.8 IASB'S underlying assumptions

(a) The underlying assumptions are (i) accruals, (ii) going concern.

(b) This is because, unless informed otherwise, all stakeholders are expected to assume that transactions and events have been accounted for on an accruals basis and that financial statements have been prepared on the assumption that the entity is a going concern.

19.9 Conflict between qualities of information

The following provides some instances of conflict between relevance of information and reliability of information:

(i) In order to report the financial performance and position of an entity, information on all its assets and liability would be relevant. Yet one (or more) of these elements may have to be left out of financial statements because of uncertainty as to its existence or measurement.

(ii) Waiting for uncertainties to be resolved would imperil the timeliness of information because out-of-date information would be irrelevant for decision making.

(iii) Reliability of information demands neutrality as well as prudence, and these two may be mutually conflicting. Neutrality is freedom from deliberate and systematic bias whereas prudence requires a deliberate effort at conservatism when reporting performance.

To sort out such conflicts it has been suggested that:

(i) In the event of conflict between relevance and reliability, financial statements should use the most relevant of whichever information is reliable.

(ii) The tension between neutrality and prudence should be resolved by finding a balance that ensures that deliberate and systematic understatement of assets or gains and overstatement of liabilities or losses does not occur.

19.10 Identification of the defining accounting concept

Inventory valuation	Time interval	Prudence	Non-aggregation	Consistency
Bad debts allowance	Prudence	Neutrality	Going concern	
Depreciation expense	Prudence	Neutrality	Going concern	Consistency
Advertising expense	Prudence	Neutrality		

Multiple choice questions

Stakeholders and their interests

19.1 Admittedly the primary interest of shareholders of a company will be the discharge of stewardship by the directors and the profitability of their business. Nevertheless they will also be watchful of the company's liquidity levels for the following reasons:

(i) Liquidity problems will result in failure to take advantage of profit-making opportunities

(ii) Faced with liquidity problems the company may not pay dividends

(iii) Low liquidity may result in resignation of company directors

(iv) If liquidity is low the company may not be able to pay its creditors in time

Which of the above statements are correct?

a	All four	
b	i & ii	
c	i, ii & iv	
d	ii, iii & iv	

19.2 Profitability of a company is one of the main interests of its shareholders because:

(i) Higher profit results in reporting higher earnings per share and hence better prices for shares
(ii) Higher profit could result in bigger amounts being paid as dividends
(iii) Losses will, in time, erode the capital base and threaten the existence
(iv) It is of greater prestige to be shareholders in a profitable company

Which of the above statements are correct?

a	All four	
b	i, ii & iii	
c	i, ii & iv	
d	ii, iii & iv	

19.3 Which of the following statements is incorrect?

(a) The financial statements are intended only for the use of shareholders and investors
(b) Employees of a business will have an interest in profitability and liquidity levels as well
(c) Banks will be averse to lending to a loss-making company even it is currently very liquid
(d) When considering granting credit facilities special-purpose financial statements may be called for

Accounting concepts

19.4 Accounting concepts must be defined clearly and well understood by both those who prepare financial statements and those who use the information therein for decision making for the following reasons:

(i) The information in financial statements then becomes more meaningful
(ii) It would assist accountants to account for unusual transactions
(iii) It would assist standard-makers to be consistent in their pronouncements
(iv) It would improve comparability of financial statements

Which of the above statements are correct?

a	All four	
b	i & ii	
c	i, ii & iii	
d	ii, iii & iv	

19.5 When accounting for transactions and preparing financial statements certain assumptions are made and a number of working rules are complied with. Which of the following would you regard as assumptions rather than working rules?

(i) Accruals	(ii) Money measurement	(iii) Separate entity
(iv) Historical cost	(v) Going concern	(vi) Non-aggregation
(vii) Prudence	(viii) Stable value of money	(ix) Consistency

a	i, ii, iii	
b	ii, iii, v, viii	
c	i, v, viii, ix	
d	iii, v, viii, ix	

19.6 Which of the following statements is incorrect?

(a) The non-aggregation rule is applied when comparing cost and net realisable value of inventory
(b) Non-current assets are depreciated to comply with the matching concept
(c) Comparability of financial statements is impaired unless the consistency concept is applied
(d) A transaction is accounted according to its legal form rather than its commercial substance

19.7 Which accounting concept needs to take precedence when accounting for the cost of advertising which is expected to significantly enhance the sales in future years?

(a) Consistency concept
(b) Matching concept
(c) Prudence concept
(d) Neutrality concept

19.8 Which of the following statements is the most appropriate explanation of the prudence concept?

(a) Income should not be accounted for until realised in cash

(b) Faced with uncertainty an accountant should exercise a degree of caution

(c) It is better to understate profit rather than to overstate it

(d) It is better to account for expenses even if there is uncertainty on how much is payable

19.9 In times of rising prices accounting on the basis of the historical cost concept would tend to:

(a) Inflate profit and inflate assets

(b) Understate profit and understate assets

(c) Inflate profits and understate assets

(d) Understate profit and inflate assets

19.10 The prudence concept is the compelling reason for which of the following accounting treatments:

(a) Reporting as an asset the unsold portion of goods purchased for sale

(b) Accounting for the personal expenses of the proprietor met by the business as drawings

(c) Setting up an allowance for receivables not expected to be recovered

(d) Accounting for sales though a portion of them is not received by the balance sheet date

19.11 In the financial statements issued by large companies like Imperial Chemical Industries (ICI) the amounts stated are rounded off to the nearest million pounds. The reason for this is:

(a) The materiality concept

(b) To keep details secret from rival companies

(c) To show how big their company is

(d) Because this is currently fashionable

19.12 An item of information or amount is not separately reported in a financial statement, on account of materiality, if:

(a) It accounts for less than 5% of the balance sheet total

(b) It would not be significant for economic decisions made by stakeholders

(c) It is less than one million pounds

(d) Its reporting will assist competitors

19.13 Though income is usually accounted for on an accruals concept, dividends proposed by an entity in which shares are held are not accounted for until received. The accounting convention used is:

(a) Prudence and consistency

(b) Consistency and going concern

(c) Realisation and prudence

(d) Prudence and realisation

19.14 The expenses relating to the proprietor and his household should be treated as drawings rather than as business expenses on the basis of which of the following accounting concepts?

(a) Matching concept

(b) Prudence concept

(c) Separate entity concept

(d) Substance over form concept

19.15 Identify three of the following accounting concepts as justification for depreciating non-current assets:

(i) Realisation (ii) Matching (iii) Neutrality
(iv) Substance over form (v) Prudence (vi) Going concern
(vii) Time interval (viii) Consistency (ix) Separate entity

a	i, ii, iii	
b	ii, iv, v	
c	ii, v, vi	
d	iv, vii, ix	

19.16 To be reliable financial statements must be neutral. This means that when accounting and reporting one has to be objective – avoiding subjective judgement. However, subjective judgement (based on past experience) is necessary in which of the following areas?

(i) When estimating the useful economic life of non-current assets
(ii) When assessing recoverability of trade receivables
(iii) When assessing inflow of future economic benefits
(iv) Estimating the extent of obligation to pay when invoice is awaited

a	i only	
b	i and ii	
c	i, ii and iii	
d	i, ii, iii and iv	

19.17 Faced with uncertainty there is a need to exercise prudence. Which of the following would be excessive use of prudence?

(a) Non-recoverability of trade receivables is accounted for based on past experience
(b) Depreciation is accounted for estimating the useful economic life of non-current assets
(c) Future repairs to non-current assets are accounted for at the point the asset is acquired
(d) Accrued expenses are accounted for though the related invoices are yet to be received

19.18 Insisting that financial statements should be a faithful representation of transactions and events during an accounting period, an accountant refuses to present the financial statements until invoices relating to all expenses are received. Which of the following desirable qualities may be sacrificed?

(a) Prudence
(b) Timeliness
(c) Reliability
(d) Neutrality

19.19 A non-current asset, acquired for £240,000 and depreciated by £90,000, is reported in the Statement of financial position at the written-down value of £150,000, although, being an item specially manufactured for the business, its realisable value is expected to be only £95,000. Which accounting concept is followed?

(a) Prudence
(b) Money measurement
(c) Going concern
(d) Substance over form

19.20 £580 paid for a laptop computer is written off as an expense rather than capitalised because the business does not capitalise items that cost less than £1,000. This is an application of which concept?

(a) Prudence
(b) Money measurement
(c) Going concern
(d) Materiality

19.21 For identifying the value at which inventory is reported on the Statement of financial position the cost should be compared with the net realisable value of each group of interchangeable (fungible) items. This is necessary because of:

(a) Prudence concept
(b) Non-aggregation rule
(c) Going concern concept
(d) Realisation concept

19.22 How does the use of the historical cost concept understate assets and overstate profit in times of rising prices?

(i) The assets may be reported in terms of pound sterling of a lower value
(ii) Liabilities may be reported in terms of pound sterling of a higher value
(iii) Depreciation/cost of sales in the Statement of income fail to reflect current value
(iv) Non-current assets may be reported in terms of currency with a higher value

a	i only	
b	i and ii	
c	ii and iii	
d	iii and iv	

19.23 Stella's Confectionery has systematically cultivated good customer relationships both by showing courtesy and by sending Christmas gifts. She feels that the goodwill she has built up is worth £100,000. Which accounting concept prevents her from reporting goodwill as an asset in her Statement of financial position?

(a) Prudence
(b) Money measurement
(c) Separate entity
(d) Going concern

19.24 A supermarket uses the FIFO cost-flow assumption when determining the cost of inventory remaining unsold by the year-end. Why is it essential that it should continue with the same practice?

(a) This is the practice adopted by everyone in a similar trade
(b) So that its performance and position in the year may be compared with those of previous years
(c) Otherwise its financial statements would become meaningless
(d) So that the cost of any shoplifting by customers could be identified

Capital maintenance

19.25 Capital maintenance means that:

(a) All assets of the business are maintained in an excellent state of repair
(b) The money capital at the end of the accounting period is the same as at the beginning
(c) The owner has not taken home any of the business assets
(d) The non-current assets of the business are maintained in an excellent state of repair

Qualitative characteristics of information in financial statements

19.26 The Framework issued by the IASB suggests that to show a true and fair view the information in financial statements should:

(a) Comply with Accounting Standards and possess suggested qualitative characteristics
(b) Be an accurate and full record of transactions within each accounting period
(c) Not be so drawn that it could mislead users
(d) Be prepared on a consistent basis from year to year

19.27 Which of the following statements is incorrect in relation to financial statements?

(a) The information included in it should be relevant and reliable
(b) It should convey information in a consistent and understandable way
(c) When identifying information for inclusion in it subjectivity is not permitted
(d) An amount/item may not be reported separately unless it is material for decision making

19.28 Which of the following statements is incorrect in relation to financial statements?

(a) A non-current asset should not be reported at a value higher than what it can be sold for
(b) A liability should be reported only if there is a present obligation to pay
(c) Expenses should be included whether it has been paid for or are yet to be paid for
(d) Assets should be reported only if it is within control and future economic benefit is expected

19.29 Besides identifying materiality as the threshold quality, the Framework issued by IASB identifies four others as primary qualitative characteristics that make financial statements useful. Which are these?

(i) Substance over form (ii) Relevance (iii) Prudence
(iv) Faithful representation (v) Comparability (vi) Timeliness
(vii) Reliability (viii) Neutrality (ix) Consistency
(x) Understandability (xi) Completeness

a	i, ii, iii, iv	
b	ii, vii, ix, x	
c	iv, v, vii, xi	
d	ii, v, vii, x	

19.30 Which of the following qualitative characteristics of information included in financial statements have been identified in the IASB's Framework as desirable for promoting reliability:

(i) Faithful representation (ii) Timeliness (iii) Materiality
(iv) Comparability (v) Prudence (vi) Neutrality
(vii) Substance over form (viii) Relevance (ix) Understandability
(x) Completeness

a	i, v, vi, ix, x	
b	ii, iv, v, viii	
c	i, ii, vi, viii	
d	i, v, vi, vii, x	

Elements of financial statements

19.31 In terms of the definition of an asset stated in IASB's Framework which of the following would you identify as an asset of a business engaged in intercontinental transport of goods?

(i) Lease of premises for five years from the beginning of this year
(ii) A significant amount paid for television advertising
(iii) A heavy goods truck intended to be acquired after the year-end
(iv) Amount due from a customer in respect of transport work already carried out

a	i and iv	
b	i and ii	
c	i, ii and iii	
d	i, ii and iv	

19.32 Which of the following would be your justification for treating as an asset the amount due from a customer in respect of transport work already carried out?

(i) The customer is within our control because he relies on us for more work

(ii) The amount receivable is within our control because we fix the credit terms

(iii) The amount receivable represents a future economic benefit expected

(iv) The amount receivable arises from (past) work already carried out

a	i only	
b	i and ii	
c	ii, iii & iv	
d	i, ii & iv	

19.33 The IASB's Framework defines a liability as:

(a) Amounts a business may have to pay after the balance sheet date

(b) Obligations to pay which may arise depending on some future events

(c) Unpaid portion of expenses incurred in the current accounting period

(d) Present obligations arising from past events which will result in outflow of economic benefit

19.34 The IASB's Framework defines equity interest as:

(a) Amount of capital introduced by the owner of the business

(b) Opening capital + profit – drawings

(c) Residual interest in the assets of an entity after deducting its liabilities

(d) What a business owes its owner or owners

Answers to multiple choice questions

19.1: c 19.2: b 19.3: a 19.4: a 19.5: b 19.6: d 19.7: c 19.8: b 19.9: c 19.10: c 19.11: a 19.12: b 19.13: d 19.14: c 19.15: c 19.16: d 19.17: c 19.18: b 19.19: c 19.20: d 19.21: b 19.22: d 19.23: b 19.24: b 19.25: b 19.26: a 19.27: c 19.28: a 19.29: d 19.30: d 19.31: a 19.32: c 19.33: d 19.34: c

Progressive questions

PQ 19.1 The accruals and matching assumption

Susan Pizzy, a young graduate operating as a dealer in computer software, requests your help to finalise the accounts of her shop for the year ended 31 December 2011. After you have completed the task, she writes to you making the following points:

(i) The total price paid for software in the year should be regarded as expense. There is no point showing the cost of the unsold portion as an asset in the Statement of financial position.

(ii) She had deliberately avoided paying the last half year's rent and the last quarter's bills for gas and electricity hoping that there would be a corresponding improvement in profit in the first year.

(iii) The amount of £36,000 she had received upfront on subletting a portion of her shop for three years, at £1,000 per month, should all have been treated as her income for the current year because she has no intention of repaying any portion of it even if the tenant were to leave early.

Required: Draft your response to the points made by Susan.

PQ 19.2 The governing accounting concept

When preparing their financial statements of a sole trader's business for the year ended 31 December 2011, the following accounting adjustments were made:

(i) £16,500 due from a customer was written off as irrecoverable.

(ii) 20% of the cost of vehicles was written off as depreciation.

(iii) An item of inventory costing £6,000 was written down to its realisable value of £4,500.

(iv) School fees paid for the proprietor's son were debited to the Drawings account.

(v) £2,500 paid for a photocopying machine was written off (instead of being capitalised).

(vi) Insurance paid for the period after the reporting date was transferred to a Prepayments account.

(vii) Cost of inventory in hand at the year-end was determined, as usual, on a first in first out basis.

(viii) A dividend proposed for the year in respect of shares held in a limited company was not accounted for as income because it had not been received.

Required: Identify the main accounting concepts on the basis of which the above adjustments were made.

PQ 19.3 Conflict among accounting concepts

In the recent past accountants have shown an interest in identifying the concepts which underlie the techniques they use when accounting for transactions. They acknowledge that some among the accounting concepts are fundamental ones but observe also that occasionally there is a conflict between concepts.

Required:

(a) Illustrate with a transaction a conflict between the following concepts:

(i) The matching working rule and the materiality convention
(ii) The materiality convention and the objectivity convention
(iii) The matching working rule and the prudence convention
(iv) The separate entity assumption and the substance over form convention.

(b) Explain how you would resolve the conflict, pointing out whether your judgement will be swayed because one of the concepts in conflict is identified as a fundamental one.

PQ 19.4 Accounting concepts and treatment of transactions (ACCA)

(a) Explain clearly the following accounting terms in a manner which an intelligent non-accountant could understand in the context of a profit-oriented organisation:

(i) expense
(ii) prudence
(iii) objectivity and
(iv) matching.

(b) Your client has received the following invoice, and has come to you for advice:

	£
From: Marketing Services plc	
Agreed monthly fees for general advice – three months to 31 Dec. at £1,000 per month	3,000
Supply of a photocopier on 1.10.2010 with 5-year guarantee for use by marketing dept	10,000
Deposit paid by us on your behalf for television advertising time in February 2011	5,000
Advertising in newspaper from 1 November to 30 November 2010	50,000

Required: Write a letter to your client suggesting, for each of the four items in the invoice, how each item is likely to affect the expenses figure in the accounting year ended 31 December 2010. You should explain your suggestions and justify them by reference to accounting conventions.

Test questions

Test 19.1 The Framework

The Framework for the preparation and presentation of financial statements adopted by IASB in April 2001 attempts to establish a conceptual framework for the accounting and reporting functions.

(a) Who would benefit from such a conceptual framework?

(b) What have been identified as underlying assumptions?

(c) What have been identified as the qualitative characteristics that information in financial statements should possess?

Test 19.2 Accounting concepts in relation to accounting for inventory

In relation to measuring and accounting for inventory, explain how each of the following accounting concepts would apply:

(a) Going concern
(b) Accruals and matching
(c) Consistency
(d) Prudence
(e) Materiality
(f) Valuation rules
(g) Non-aggregation rule
(h) Substance over form

Test 19.3 Information needs of a bank

In support of its application for a £60 million loan, Presage plc submitted its Statement of financial position and Statements of cash flows for the preceding five years. The financier has called also for:

(i) the Statement of income for the same period;

(ii) the break-up value of the company's freehold premises and machinery;

(iii) the corporate plan, the management budgets and cash flow forecasts for the next year.

The managing director of Presage is reluctant to provide this information, being of the opinion that:

(i) the Statement of income should be of no concern to a financier because the loan together with interest is payable irrespective of the company's performance;

(ii) break-up values are irrelevant because the company is expected to remain in operational existence for a long time;

(iii) corporate plans, management budgets and cash flow forecasts contain sensitive information, are prepared only for internal use and should not be disclosed.

Required: Advise the managing director.

Test 19.4 Relevance of concepts to year-end adjustments

Norwich Tanners and Curriers (NTC) extracted its year-end Trial Balance as shown on the right.

You are informed as follows:

(i) Inventory is ascertained on 5 July 2011 at £752,000. During the five days after 30 June purchases were £154,000 and sales (made at cost plus a third) were £180,000. The inventory results include at £9,000 the cost of spares bought for repairing machinery.

(ii) Machinery and vehicles are depreciated at 5% and 20% per annum respectively using the reducing balance method.

(iii) Insurance includes £16,000 paid for the year ending on 30 September 2011.

(iv) 6% Loan notes, issued on 1 October 2010, are redeemable at par on 30 September 2014.

(v) Salary £32,000, advertising £18,000 and rent £12,000 remain unpaid by the year-end.

(vi) £4,000 of trade receivable should be written off and the allowance adjusted to 5% of receivable.

(vii) Amount reported as taxation is the amount by which tax paid on profit of the previous year exceeded the amount provided for. Current year tax, at 20%, is estimated at £44,000. On 30 June 2011, the tax base was £75,000 lower than the corresponding written-down value of assets.

(viii) On 30 June 2011 the Directors of NTC declared a dividend of 3p per share.

Trial Balance as at 30 June 2011

	£'000	£'000
Machinery at cost	880	–
Depreciation – machinery	–	380
Motor vehicles at cost	520	–
Depreciation – vehicles	–	200
Inventory – 1 July 2010	826	–
Salaries	268	–
Insurance	24	–
Telephone and postage	12	–
Sales	–	5,712
Purchases	4,086	–
Advertising	164	–
Motor vehicle maintenance	28	–
Machinery maintenance	46	–
Receivable and payables	584	398
6% Loan notes	–	200
Rent	36	–
Allowance for doubtful debts	–	25
Share capital – shares of 50p	–	500
Share premium account	–	50
Interest on 6% Loan notes	6	–
Taxation	3	–
Bank overdraft	–	60
Cash in hand and at bank	16	–
Deferred tax	–	18
Other admin expenses	298	–
Retained earnings	–	254
	7,797	7,797

Required:

(a) Prepare a Statement of income with the Statement of changes in equity for the year ended 30 June 2011 and the Statement of financial position as at that date.

(b) With regard to the adjustments that had to be made in respect of information provided as (i) to (vii), explain the need for these adjustments on the basis of generally accepted accounting concepts.

Chapter 20

Revenue recognition

By the end of this chapter

You should learn:

- About the point and the amount at which income may be accounted for

20.1 What is revenue recognition?

IAS 18 *Revenue*[1] defines revenue as 'The gross inflow of economic benefits during the period arising in the course of the ordinary activities of an entity'.

Therefore, depending on the nature of business, revenue could refer to the main earnings of a business, ranging from sales, through fees, commission, interest, dividends to royalties. The focus of this chapter is to identify (a) the point and (b) the amount at which the revenue can be recognised for purposes of accounting, i.e. for reporting in the Statement of income.

We need to be clear that revenue we are dealing with is the gross inflow, as distinguished from the net inflow which the *Framework*[2] identifies as 'income' and for the identification of which it adopts a Statement of financial position approach (see Activity 20.1).

Activity 20.1 Statement of financial position approach to measuring income

The assets and liabilities of a business were £300,000 and £80,000, respectively, at the commencement of an accounting period and £390,000 and £50,000, respectively, a year later. During the year the owner of the business introduced £50,000 as additional capital.

Required: What is the income for the year?

20.2 Problems with revenue recognition

Problems arise with revenue recognition mainly because of abandoning the venture concept in favour of the time interval rule.

20.2.1 The venture concept

Every business has its own revenue-earning cycle. For example, for a farmer, the cycle would be the time between getting the field ready and reaping the harvest, which might be three to five months, depending on the crop. A bridge construction, on the other hand, may take several years to complete. If the venture concept had been adopted, the farmer would prepare his accounts after the crop is harvested and the bridge builder after the bridge is constructed. Then, at the point of accounting:

- all transactions relating to the venture would have been completed;
- all uncertainties relating to the venture would have been resolved.

20.2.2 The time interval rule

At the present day, however, stakeholders prefer to have accounting information at regular intervals and with greater frequency. Consequently we have rejected the venture concept, replacing it with the time interval rule. The effect of this rule is that the accounting period rarely coincides with the revenue-earning cycle. As a result there could be incomplete transactions as well as unresolved uncertainties at the point of reporting. This gives rise to many problems including the following.

1. *The problem of recognising income when the production process is incomplete.* When the income-generating activity (say production of goods) cuts across more than one accounting period, there is a problem of deciding how much of the income is to be regarded as earned in each period. There are two possible solutions:
   - To recognise a part of the total income in proportion to the efforts made in each period. For example, let us assume that an entity is engaged in building a house which is expected to take more than a year. It estimates the cost at £150,000 and selling price is agreed at £200,000, expecting a profit of £50,000. If it spends £75,000 during the first accounting period, it may recognise half the sale price (£100,000) as income and report a profit in that period of £25,000.
   - An alternative solution might be to delay recognition of the income until the income-generating activity is fully completed so that (when the house is sold) there would be a resolution of significant uncertainties such as those relating to measurement of the accomplishment and receipt of the proceeds.
2. *The problem of measuring income when the sale process is incomplete* because a portion of inventory remains unsold. To illustrate, let us consider the problem faced by a trader who finds that he cannot sell all of the goods that he had purchased within the accounting period. Let us assume that a business purchased 300 logs of fine ebony at £200 per log. Within the accounting period, it sold 200 logs at £300 each. Demand is buoyant and it is reasonably certain that the remainder can be sold at the same price. The whole venture is expected to yield a profit of £100 per log on 300 logs = £30,000. The problem is how much of that profit may be recognised within the current accounting period. There are two possible solutions:
   - The normal solution would be to recognise the profit only in respect of the logs sold within the period – ignoring those relating to the logs in hand until earned upon sale.
   - Another solution is to recognise within a period also at least a part of the profit relating to unsold logs, perhaps on the premise that these logs improved in value during the period because of the impact of time on the logs.

One opting for the normal solution has still to confront the problem of determining the precise point at which the sale takes place. This is because the movement of goods/services does not always coincide in timescale with the movement of title (ownership) and the proceeds. It is also possible that terms and covenants may be built into the transaction making it completely different in commercial reality from what it appears to be on the face of it or in legal form.

3. *The problem of recognising income when there are outstanding commitments.* The accounting recognition of an income received in the period may have to be deferred to a future period, at least partially, because a portion of income may relate to efforts yet to be made and expenses yet to be incurred. This applies, for example, to:
   - products sold with a promise of after-care or with a maintenance contract;
   - subscriptions received in advance for periodicals yet to be produced.

20.3 Relevance of accounting concepts to revenue recognition

The approach to be adopted for revenue recognition should be founded on the accepted accounting concepts (Chapter 19) including the following:

- **Money measurement.** To be accountable the income should be measurable in terms of money.
- **Accruals.** If one were to abandon the accruals rule, opting instead to account for income on the basis of receipts, most problems involved in revenue recognition would be overcome. It is the commitment to recognising income on the basis of accomplishments (rather than cash inflow) which makes it necessary to determine the precise point at which and the manner in which the accomplishments are measured for the purpose of accounting.
- **Realisation.** If revenue is recognised for purposes of identifying the amount available for distribution to investors, then it follows that it should be realised either in the form of cash or another asset capable of being easily converted into cash.
- **Prudence.** The prudence convention is paramount for determining the point of revenue recognition. Prudence demands that revenue should not be recognised in respect of incomplete transactions until all major uncertainties involved are substantially resolved or are capable of reliable measurement.
- **Objectivity.** Objectivity is important for safeguarding credibility of accounting information. For the purpose of maintaining objectivity, accounting is usually transaction-based, so that the amount to be recognised is established by an arm's length market transaction.
- **Consistency.** Consistency in applying criteria to revenue recognition is crucial if there is to be a reliable comparison of financial performance over time. For example, where the income-earning process progresses through distinct stages and it is possible to recognise revenue, with equal justification, at more than one of these stages, what is crucial is whether the practice that has been adopted for revenue recognition remains consistent from period to period.
- **Substance over form.** What might appear to be a sale legally following the normal invoicing procedures may be subject to contract terms which allow the seller to continue to enjoy substantial rewards and risks as if ownership remained with the seller. For

example, when faced with a cash flow problem, a business dealing in the sale of ebony logs may sell its holding of logs but reserve to itself the option to buy it back at a price which is less than the market price. In these circumstances, what appears legally to be a sale would not be one because it is not unconditional. If the market price of the logs improves the business will exercise the option to buy them back and reap the rewards of selling them for a higher price.

20.4 Traditional approaches to revenue recognition

The accounting profession has traditionally adopted three alternative approaches to revenue recognition. These are:

- the critical event approach (also known as the transactions approach);
- the accretion approach;
- the revenue allocation approach.

20.5 The critical event approach or transactions approach

The income-earning process may involve a cycle of some or all of nine related stages as shown below (though not necessarily in that sequence):

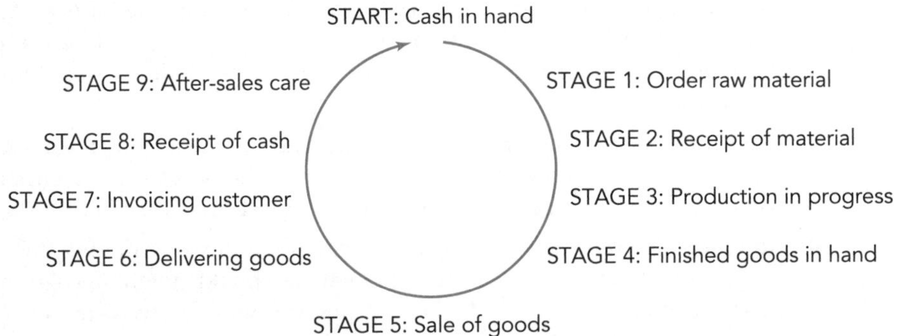

The critical event approach assumes that at a particular stage in this cycle there is a critical point which makes it acceptable to recognise revenue. The criteria applied under this approach to identify such a stage are that:

- The income should have been substantially earned at the stage selected.
- Any uncertainty remaining at that stage should be capable of estimation with sufficient accuracy so that it could be taken into account when measuring the revenue.

For identifying that stage several factors are taken into account, including the following:

- the terms of the agreement between the parties;
- the custom of trade and practices followed in the type of business;
- the provisions in the applicable law as well as case law.

Let us now consider each of the above stages to assess which among them might be the one most appropriate as the critical event which triggers revenue recognition.

Stage 1: Placing an order with a supplier to acquire materials. This stage is unlikely to trigger revenue recognition because significant uncertainties such as those listed in the box on the right will remain. The situation may be different if the purchase of raw material is specifically to meet a firm order because in that situation the buyer would have been found and the sale price agreed. But other uncertainties identified as 1, 2 and 5 on the list would still remain.

1. Completion of production.
2. How much will it cost?
3. Can a buyer be found?
4. What is the selling price?
5. Collection of the sale proceeds?

Stage 2: Receipt of materials from the supplier. The business will now hold inventory in its warehouse and the related transactions would have been accounted for. However, unless based on a firm order, all five uncertainties listed above would remain substantially unresolved.

Stage 3: Production is in progress. While the production process is still ongoing, all five uncertainties would remain. However, where the production is to meet a firm order, uncertainties identified as 3 and 4 are resolved. In such circumstances and where the production process cuts across more than one accounting period, as in the case of long-term contracts, Accounting Standards[3] permit revenue recognition as each stage of production is completed.

Stage 4: Production process completed. If the business is producing finished goods to hold in its warehouse as inventory to meet customer orders as they arise, uncertainties identified as 3, 4 and 5 would still remain. Therefore there cannot be any revenue recognition. On the other hand, in a transaction in which the greatest uncertainty concerns production, the completion of production could be the critical event triggering the revenue recognition. By that stage the uncertainties as to whether the goods could be produced and at what cost will have been resolved. If the further uncertainties regarding whether a buyer can be found and if the selling price is achievable can also be resolved then revenue may be recognised. Such a situation would apply, for example, when:

- production is against a firm order;
- the product might be a mined precious metal the sale of which is virtually certain at a price fixed in the international market;
- the products are periodicals produced in respect of subscriptions, which have been received in advance.

Stage 5: The sale of goods. This stage is commonly regarded as the crucial stage for revenue recognition for most trading transactions. This is because selling resolves the most crucial of a trader's uncertainties, which are whether a buyer can be found and the price at which the item can be sold. The uncertainties that do remain at this stage (such as whether the sales may be rescinded and goods returned and whether the proceeds will be received) are usually capable of reasonable estimation. This would not be the case, however, where the sale contract permits the buyer to rescind the contract within a stipulated period or where the contract includes commitment to onerous after-sales care. A problem with revenue recognition at this stage is the identification of the precise point when the sale is completed. The Sale of Goods Act 1979 provides that the ownership of goods passes from the seller to the buyer when all of the conditions stated in the box on the right are met. IAS 18[1] points out that in most retail sales the revenue is recognised at the point legal title passes to the buyer. Usually, delivery and invoicing of goods are not crucial to revenue recognition. However, the Sale of Goods Act reserves to the buyer the right to reject the goods until the buyer has had a reasonable time to inspect the goods to check whether they are the correct items and are in good condition.

1. A contract of sale is made.
2. Goods are physically capable of immediate delivery.
3. This position is notified to the buyer.

Stage 6: The delivery of the goods. The common practice in the UK is to recognise revenue at the point of delivering the goods to customers. This is also the position approved in the USA.[4] In real life, delivering the goods to the custody of the customer is accepted as the cut-off point at which the sale may *prudently* be regarded as having taken place. Some uncertainties do remain with regard to collection of the sales proceeds and the cost of after-sales services, but these are usually capable of reasonable estimation on the basis of past experience.

Stage 7: Raising an invoice for a credit sale. In the UK this is regarded as a mere routine procedure to confirm to the customer the terms of the sale and is usually not considered a critical event for revenue recognition. Outside the UK, however, this stage is commonly regarded as the revenue-recognition stage in most trading transactions.

Stage 8: Receiving sale proceeds. Unless the debt is time barred and cannot be legally enforced, a business could resort to legal debt collection if necessary. The collection of proceeds could, however, replace stage 6 as the critical event triggering revenue recognition in cases such as:

- where sales are made to overseas customers, particularly in countries with exchange restrictions;
- where considerations of professional etiquette prevent pursuit through legal process of bills for services.

Stage 9: After-sales care. The costs involved in after-sales care could well be substantial (in cases such as the sale of vehicles and in respect of rectification work arising from civil engineering contracts). Yet revenue recognition is usually not delayed until this stage because the costs which could arise are capable of measurement on the basis of past experience and can therefore be taken account of when recognising revenue. For example, if the agreed contract price is £200,000 for constructing a residence, and the past experience is that on average £3,000 is needed for rectification work, £197,000 would be recognised as revenue at the point the earning process is regarded as completed.

20.6 The accretion approach

Instead of awaiting a critical event to trigger revenue recognition, the accretion approach allows revenue to be recognised as the value of the product improves either on the basis of continuing production process or the passage of time. This approach is not consistent with the transactions approach adopted in historical cost accounting because there is no objective and verifiable arm's length transaction with a third party. This approach to revenue recognition is accepted accounting practice in three specific areas as follows.

1. **Where income is earned by permitting others the use of one's asset.** Depending on the terms of the contract and the established custom of trade, income is recognised on a time basis to the extent that time enhances the claim against the other party. This would be the case with regard to interest earned on loans, rent earned on premises let out and royalty earned on a patent or a copyright assigned to others. The recognition of income would be permitted provided any remaining uncertainties (such as the collectibility of the dues) are capable of reliable estimation.
2. **Where income recognised is on long-term contracts.** On long-term contracts it is usual to recognise revenue as progress is made with the efforts.[3]
3. **Where income arises from natural growth or ageing.** Some products improve in value because of the passage of time. This is the case with timber, spirits and wine, which mature with age. It would also be the case with growing crops and livestock. The accretion approach to recognising income is adopted in these cases provided the following conditions are met:
   - The product should have a verifiable market value at different stages of its growth.
   - There should not remain any significant uncertainty other than those that can be reliably measured.
   - The revenue recognition is for the purpose of reporting the earnings and not for the purpose of distributing the amount earned because the distribution has to await the realisation of the earning.

20.7 Revenue allocation approach

This is a combination of the other two approaches. For example, an entity adopting the critical event approach to revenue recognition, if confronted with substantial uncertainty (say with regard to onerous after-sales service or the possibility that the sale may be rescinded) at the stage it usually recognises revenue, would adopt one of two solutions as follows:

(a) adhere to the critical event approach, making the best possible estimation of the uncertainty;

(b) adopt the revenue allocation approach, allocating appropriate portions of revenue between, for instance, the sales activity and the after-sales activity.

20.8 Requirements of IAS 18[1] *Revenue Recognition*

20.8.1 When is revenue recognised?

Revenue is recognised only when both of the following conditions are met:

(a) It is probable that future economic benefits will flow in.

(b) The economic benefit can be measured reliably.

20.8.2 At what value is revenue recognised?

Revenue is measured at the fair value of consideration received or receivable. When goods or services are exchanged or swapped and the items involved are similar in nature and value, such an exchange is not recognised as a transaction and nor is revenue recognised. If items exchanged are dissimilar, revenue is recognised at the fair value of goods or services received.

(a) **Income from sale of goods is recognised** when all of the following conditions are satisfied:
   (i) Significant risks and reward of ownership are transferred to the customer.
   (ii) The seller does not retain control of the goods sold nor any management involvement with it.
   (iii) The amount of income generated can be measured reliably.
   (iv) The inflow of economic benefits from the sale is probable.
   (v) The costs incurred or to be incurred in respect of the sale can be reliably measured.

(b) **Income from rendering of services is recognised** by reference to the stage of completion of the services (this is known as *the percentage of completion method*) provided the outcome can be reliably estimated, i.e.
   (i) Income can be measured reliably.
   (ii) Inflow of economic benefits is probable.
   (iii) The stage of completion can be measured reliably.
   (iv) Costs incurred and yet to be incurred to complete the activity can be reliably measured.

(c) **Income from interests, royalties and dividends** is recognised if the amount can be reliably measured and inflow of economic benefits is probable, as follows:

   Interest: on time proportion basis taking into account effective yield on the asset.
   Royalties: on an accruals basis in accordance with the substance of the agreement.
   Dividends: when the right to receive payment is established (i.e. dividend is declared).

Summary

- Problems of revenue recognition arise because of the need to comply with the time interval rule.
- When recognising income it is essential to comply with the concepts of money measurement, accruals, realisation, prudence, objectivity, consistency and substance over form.
- The traditional approaches to revenue recognition are the critical event approach, the accretion approach and the revenue allocation approach.
- The revenue is recognised only when it can be reliably measured and inflow of economic benefits from it is probable.

References

1. IAS 18 *Revenue*, revised 1998, effective 1.1.2001, London, International Accounting Standards Board.
2. *Framework for the Preparation and Presentation of Financial Statements* (1989), London, International Accounting Standards Board.
3. IAS 11 *Construction Contracts*, revised 1993, effective 1.1.1995, London, International Accounting Standards Board.
4. FASB 48 *Revenue Recognition when Right of Return Exists*, 1981, Norwalk, CT, Financial Accounting Standards Board.

Suggested answers to activities

20.1 Statement of financial position approach to measuring income

As at	Start	End
Assets	£300,000	£390,000
Liability	(£80,000)	(£50,000)
Equity	£220,000	£340,000

Increase in equity during accounting period	£120,000
Less: Capital contribution by the owner	(£50,000)
Income (net of expenses in the period)	£70,000

Multiple choice questions

Revenue recognition

20.1 Which of the following statements are correct?

(i) Revenue recognition is the determination of the point and the amount at which income is accounted for

(ii) Income should not be accounted for unless inflow of economic benefit is probable and the amount thereof may be estimated reliably

(iii) Income should not be accounted for unless it is received in cash

(iv) A sale made subject to the customer right to return within a week should not be recognised as income until that week is over

a	i and ii	
b	i, ii and iv	
c	i, ii and iii	
d	i, ii, iii and iv	

20.2 Which of the following statements are correct?

(i) Problems of revenue recognition would not have arisen if accounting applied the venture concept or recognised earnings only upon receipt in cash

(ii) The sale of an item with a warranty to restore it to workable condition up to a year after sale may be recognised as income if the commitment involved can be measured

(iii) No income is recognised unless its amount is established objectively

(iv) Exchange of items of similar nature and value is neither recognised as a transaction nor is income thereon recognised

a	i only	
b	i and ii	
c	i, ii and iii	
d	i, ii, iii and iv	

20.3 Which of the following statements are correct in respect of a business which produces goods to be held as inventory, ready for sale?

(i) Sales income should not be recognised until a buyer is found and price is agreed on

(ii) Sales income should not be recognised if the buyer is in another country and receipt of the amount depends on whether the buyer receives exchange clearance from government

(iii) Sales income should be recognised only when proceeds are received

(iv) Whether the sale is recognised at point of sale, delivery or invoicing depends on what its practice has been in the past

a	i only	
b	i, ii and iii	
c	i, ii and iv	
d	i, ii, iii and iv	

20.4 It is usual for a retail shop to recognise revenue when:

(a) The customer pays for the goods sold ☐

(b) The goods for sale have arrived from the supplier ☐

(c) The goods have been delivered to the customer's premises ☐

(d) The customer becomes legally obliged to pay for the goods ☐

20.5 A trader sells computer hardware with a warranty that he is responsible for any repair within a year of sale. He may recognise the sales income at the point of sale because:

(a) That is usually the practice among such traders ☐

(b) It is unlikely that repairs will become necessary within the first year ☐

(c) There is a possibility of not undertaking the repairs, blaming the customer for wrong usage ☐

(d) From experience the trader can quantify the cost of such repairs and account for it separately ☐

20.6 Rachel manufactures surgical gloves. Upon receiving an order from a hospital for supplying them with their requirements for three years ending on 31 December 2012, she raised an invoice for £15,000 and has accounted for it by crediting the Sales account and debiting the Receivables account. For preparing the financial statements in respect of the year ended 31 December 2010 the adjusting entries required are:

(a) Debit Sales account and credit Cash account with £10,000 ☐

(b) Debit Sales account and credit Deferred income account with £10,000 ☐

(c) Debit Sales Account and credit Receivables account with £10,000 ☐

(d) Debit Receivables account and credit Deferred income account with £10,000 ☐

General

20.7 The most appropriate definition of an imprest system of petty cash control is that it is a system where:

(a) An assistant is appointed to help with the work of the cashier ☐

(b) The amount available for spending by petty cashier is left to the discretion of the cashier ☐

(c) The petty cashier is allowed to make payments during the cashier's absence ☐

(d) The cashier checks the amount spent at regular intervals and reimburses the exact amount ☐

20.8 With regard to accounting concepts which of the following statements are correct?

(i) The realisation concept requires that income should not be accounted for until it is received in cash

(ii) Accounting should reflect commercial substance rather than legal form

(iii) Whenever faced with uncertainty prudence should prevail

(iv) For promoting comparability of financial statements consistency should take precedence over concepts such as prudence and accruals

a	ii, iii and iv	
b	i, iii and iv	
c	i, ii and iv	
d	i, ii, iii and iv	

Answers to multiple choice questions

20.1: b 20.2: d 20.3: c 20.4: d 20.5: d 20.6: c 20.7: d 20.8: a

Progressive questions

PQ 20.1 The critical event approach

Ajit commenced business on 1.1.2012 producing designer drawing room suites, selling them to approved retailers on one month credit, at £1,250 per suite. His activities during the first year are tabulated on the right. MV is the net amount realisable at each stage of completion of a suite.

	Stage reached by 31 December 2012	Units	Unit cost	Unit MV
1	Acquisition of raw materials	320	£225	£225
2	Construction/assembly of carcass	290	£540	£675
3	Completion of upholstery	260	£680	£920
4	Lacquer coating, polishing, finishing	240	£750	£1,250
5	Sale of the finished product	200	£750	£1,250
6	Delivery of the finished product	190	£750	£1,250
7	Invoicing of units delivered	185	£750	£1,250
8	Receipt of the sale proceeds	145	£750	£1,250

Ajit informs you that:

(i) Customers have yet to pay for 40 units because they were delivered in December 2012.

(ii) Five units delivered on 31.12.2012 were not invoiced until the next day.

(iii) Because of a transport breakdown there was a delay in delivering ten units sold on 31 December.

(iv) Forty units completed by 31.12.2012 were sold within the next three days.

Ajit claims to have earned £128,850 in the year and submits his calculations as shown on the right.

	Profit	Total
190 suites delivered by 31.12.2012	£500	£95,000
10 more suites delivered next day	£500	£5,000
40 more suites completed in current year	£500	£20,000
20 more suites completed to stage 3	£240	£4,800
30 more suites completed to stage 2	£135	£4,050
		£128,850

Required:

(a) Would you agree with Ajit?

(b) In what circumstances could Ajit recognise revenue relating to incomplete or unsold goods?

PQ 20.2 Approaches to revenue recognition (ACCA)

(a) What do you understand by the term revenue recognition?

(b) Briefly outline a policy on revenue recognition for each of the following:

(i) magazine subscription received by a publisher;

(ii) the sale of cars on credit terms;

(iii) work in progress on a long-term contract.

PQ 20.3 Recognising revenue at different stages (ACCA)

A firm produces a standard product. The stages of production and sale of the product are as follows:

Stage	A	B	C	D	E	F	G	H
Activity	Raw material	WIP–1	WIP–2	Finished goods	For sale	Sale agreed	Delivered	Paid for
Costs to date	£100	£120	£150	£170	£170	£170	£180	£180
NRV	£80	£130	£190	£300	£300	£300	£300	£300

NRV = Net realisable value

Required:

(a) What general rules do accountants apply when deciding when to recognise revenue on any transaction?

(b) Apply this rule to the above situation. State and explain the stage at which you think revenue will be recognised.

(c) How much would the gross profit on a unit of this product be? Why?

(d) Suggest arguments in favour of delaying the recognition of revenue until stage H.

(e) Suggest arguments in favour of recognising revenue at appropriate successive amounts at stages B, C and D.

Test questions

Test 20.1 A case study

As a financial consultant, your advice is sought on whether and to what extent revenue may be recognised in each of the following independent circumstances:

(i) Your client A publishes medical journals. At the beginning of his first year's trading he received £15,000 in advance being a three-year subscription for the journal. The business is now preparing its accounts at the end of the first year.

(ii) Your client B accepted an order for 5,000 tons of sugar and received payment in full of £90,000. He has placed an order for sugar to satisfy this customer but the sugar was not in stock at the year-end.

(iii) Your client C received £150,000 for granting a franchise to another company, allowing them to deal exclusively in the products of C within a defined area for five years.

(iv) Your client D, a mail order company, dispatches goods to its customers on approval, on terms that the goods may be returned, without obligation, within two weeks of delivery. On the last day of the year, goods with a sales value of £214,600 remained with customers within the approval period.

(v) Your client E sold a machine to a customer, on three months' credit, stating on the invoice, in small print, that the title to the goods remains with E until the goods are paid for. The goods are still to be paid for by the year-end.

(vi) Your client F, a company owning tea estates in Sri Lanka, reports that as at the year-end it holds a stock of 3,250 tons of pinkpechoe highland tea, which realised £297,400 in the following week's London Tea Auctions. The expenses of realisation amounted to £6,000.

Required: Advise your clients, giving reasons to support your advice.

PART E

ACCOUNTING FOR NON-CURRENT ASSETS, LIABILITIES AND PROVISIONS

Chapter 21

Accounting for tangible non-current assets

By the end of this chapter

You should learn:

- How to identify an asset and non-current asset
- About items that may be included within cost of an asset
- The need to capitalise borrowing cost
- When subsequent expenses may be capitalised
- The need to depreciate non-current assets

You should be able to:

- Account for the acquisition of non-current assets at cost
- Account for self-constructed non-current assets

21.1 Identification of an asset

An **asset** is defined in the *Framework*[1] as a resource which meets the following three criteria:

1. *The resource should be controlled* by the enterprise, so that it could have access to its benefits and the ability to deny or restrain others' access. It is the control (and not physical custody or legal ownership) that is crucial to asset recognition.
2. *The control should have resulted from past transactions or events.* The transaction could be a payment or a contract to make a payment. For example, we regard trade receivables as an asset because we expect to receive payments on the basis of a past transaction, i.e. the sale. The event could be one (such as an accident causing damage to the property) creating a claim against another party.
3. *Future economic benefits should be expected* to flow from the resource. Future means after the completion of the current accounting period. The economic benefit may take the form of an ability to generate an inflow of cash (e.g. a coffee-making machine in a coffee shop) or reduce an outflow (e.g. a security system installed to avoid having to employ security guards). The economic benefits could include the ability to use the property, sell or exchange the property or exploit its value, for example by pledging it as security for borrowing.

Despite meeting all of the above three criteria many businesses opt to regard a resource as an expense (rather than as an asset) if it is not regarded as sufficiently material. For example, a vehicle-repairing garage which paid £5 to buy a screwdriver may treat it as an expense rather than as an asset.

Each organisation sets its own accounting policy for the capitalisation level. For example, the following is an extract from the University of Abertay Dundee 2006 Annual Report: 'Equipment, furniture and coherent packages of equipment costing £10,000 or more have been capitalised and depreciation charged in accordance with agreed rates.'

Activity 21.1 Asset recognition criteria

Would you classify the following as assets?

(i) A property leased for ten years.

(ii) An amount paid for a machine which has yet to be manufactured.

(iii) An amount receivable from a customer for goods sold.

(iv) Prepaid rent.

21.2 Identification of tangible non-current assets

IAS 16[2] refers to tangible non-current assets as property, plant and equipment (PPE) and defines them as those assets which:

1. have a physical substance (i.e. exist physically) – otherwise they would be intangible assets;
2. are held for use in any of the following:
   (i) the production or supply of goods or services,
   (ii) rental to others, or
   (iii) administrative purposes;
3. are expected to be used during more than one accounting period.

Activity 21.2 Property, plant and equipment

Would you classify the following as PPE?

(i) A standby machine intended to maintain rather than enhance production capacity.

(ii) Premises which are used to store goods rather than for producing goods.

(iii) Residential quarters built to provide accommodation for office staff.

(iv) Machinery owned by the business but leased out to others.

The types of PPE will vary according to the nature of the business, e.g. retailers might have retail premises, computer equipment, warehouses and delivery vehicles as their main types of PPE; water companies might have reservoirs, pipelines and pumping stations; and building contractors might have a land bank and heavy machinery.

21.3 Recognition of property, plant and equipment in accounts

Even if a resource qualifies for recognition as a PPE, it may not be so recognised (i.e. recorded in the ledger and reported on the Statement of financial position) unless the following asset recognition criteria are all met:

(a) The risks and rewards associated with the asset are with the business.

(b) The flow of future economic benefits, after the period-end, is either certain or at least probable.

(c) The cost of the asset (or where reported on the valuation model, its market value) can be reliably measured.

Risks and rewards: the rewards associated with PPE are their custody, continuous use and claim on whatever benefits they generate. The risks are the costs of repairs, maintenance, insurance and any loss that may arise from excess capacity or obsolescence.

The cost of the asset can be reliably established by the market transaction, if it is an acquired one, or by the amounts incurred on material, labour and other inputs, if it is a self-constructed one. A reliable establishment of current value, needed if the asset is to be accounted on the valuation model, would be more difficult, unless there is an active market for assets of that type.

21.4 Measurement of PPE on the cost model

IAS 16 requires that when assets identifiable as PPE are accounted on the cost model, the cost should be comprised of all the expenses as stated below:

- those directly attributable (see box on the right) to bring the asset to the location from which it is to be used and the condition in which it becomes suitable for its intended use;
- incremental costs that could have been avoided if the asset had not been acquired or constructed;
- estimated cost of dismantling or removing the asset when its use ceases and for restorimg the site.

1. Purchase price
2. Import duty, non-refundable purchase tax
3. Site preparation and clearing costs
4. Initial delivery and handling charges
5. Installation costs
6. Professional fees, e.g. architects/engineers

Directly attributable costs: the inclusion of the directly attributable costs within the asset's cost should cease when substantially all activities that are necessary to get the asset ready for use are complete, even if the asset has not yet been brought into use. It means that the cost of relocating the asset, after its use had commenced, cannot be capitalised. Start-up and pre-production costs are also excluded unless necessary to bring the asset to working condition. The principle is that capitalisation should stop once the asset is ready for the use intended by the management. It follows that expenses such as those listed on the right cannot be included within the cost of an asset.

- Cost of opening a new facility
- Cost of introducing or promoting a new product
- Cost of conducting business in a new location
- Cost of administration and staff training
- Loss because the asset operates below capacity
- Initial operating loss until demand builds up
- Cost of re-locating the asset
- Cost of re-organising the business activites

When identifying the cost of the asset care should be taken to remove from it (a) any related grants, (b) any wastage and unrelated costs and (c) where the asset is a self-constructed one, any internal profit. If there should be any incidental earnings, e.g. from using a land as a car park until the construction begins, such earnings need to be separately accounted for as income. Such earnings cannot be offset from cost.

Dismantling cost is also capitalised. For example, if a company prospecting for oil incurred £5 million on constructing the oil rig, and is expected to incur one million more when the oil rig is dismantled after five years when the well runs dry, it should capitalise £5 million as well as the present value of one million. The present value is one million discounted for five years by the interest rate applicable to the company. The reason for discounting the present value is because that amount need not be paid until after five years. If, at any time after commencement of exploitation, the company learns that because of new legislation it will have to spend £2 million more on restoring the site and cleaning up the environment, the present value of that additional obligation (not even known when it commenced using the asset) should also be capitalised on the day it becomes aware of that liability.

Accounting for non-current assets on the valuation model has been dealt with in Chapter 8.

Activity 21.3 Initial measurement of PPE at cost

Identify the cost (to be capitalised) of the following items related to acquisition of PPE:

(a) Selma Ltd paid £480,000 for a property, spent £15,000 on demolishing a dilapidated building on it and £5,500 on clearing the site. £5,400 was paid as legal expenses related to the transfer of title. £1,900 was realised on selling the bricks, timber and material salvaged from demolition.

(b) For constructing its office premises on the property in (a) above, Selma Ltd paid £3,500,000 to the contractor, £500,000 to the architect, £1,500 for planning permission and £2,500 as legal expenses. £50,000 of the architect's fee was for a design that was discarded when the original design was altered by Selma Ltd.

(c) A cattle ranch paid £12,000 for a used heavy goods lorry and £4,000 to fit a larger body for transporting cattle and a further £3,000 to make the vehicle roadworthy. In addition, insurance cost and road tax for the year amounted to £340 and £250, respectively.

(d) A steel rolling mill paid £180,000 for a machine, £1,500 for delivery to the factory and £4,500 for having it installed. Start-up costs, including material wastage during the start-up period, amounted to £3,000.

21.5 Accounting for an asset acquired in exchange for another

When accounts are prepared on an historical cost basis, the historical cost of an asset acquired in exchange for another (trade-in) is the current market value of the asset that was surrendered. For illustration let us assume that X plc surrenders land in exchange for a machine from Y plc. If we assume that X plc reported the land at £500 while Y plc reported the machine at its depreciated cost of £450 and if the current value of these assets are the same as their carrying value, X plc will report the machine at £500.

If, on the day of the exchange, the market value of the land is £600, the historical cost of the machine for X plc would be £600 and the difference between the carrying value of the land (£500) and its market value (£600) is accounted for as the gain on disposal of land. However, there are two exceptions as follows:

1. *If the exchange lacks commercial substance* (as it would when such an exchange took place between members of a group of companies) then the historical cost of the machine for X plc would be £500.
2. *If the market value of one of the assets in exchange can be measured more reliably,* for example if the market value of the machine could be established more reliably (than that of the land) at £480, then the historical cost of the machine to X plc would be £480. This means that X plc would have made a loss of £20 on the disposal of land.

21.6 Accounting for subsequent expenses

We have studied that expenses incurred after the asset is ready for use (referred to as subsequent expenses) cannot be capitalised. Exceptionally, however, such subsequent expenses may be capitalised if they meet the capitalisation criteria, i.e. (a) future economic benefits are expected to flow and (b) related costs can be reliably identified. Accordingly, the following subsequent expenses should be capitalised:

(a) any such expense which is expected to enhance significantly beyond the currently assessed levels either the value of the asset, the value of its output, its operating performance or lowers its operating costs; or

(b) the cost of an overhaul that significantly improves the economic life of the asset; or

(c) the cost of replacing a component which has a significantly different economic life, after the cost of the component replaced has been written off (see paragraph 21.11).

Activity 21.4 Capitalisation of subsequent expenses

Your advice is sought as to how the following payments should be dealt with when preparing financial statements for the year ended 31 December 2012:

(i) £1,200 paid for replacing a vehicle's crankshaft when it became necessary following an accident.

(ii) £14,500 paid for an additional thermostat fitted to the cold storage room for the purpose of improving the freezing capacity by 150%.

(iii) £12,000 paid for replacing a lining on a furnace. The furnace, installed four years earlier at a cost of £96,000, is expected to remain in economic use for at least 20 years provided its lining is replaced every four years.

(iv) £7,500 paid for overhauling and restoring to a roadworthy condition a pick-up truck acquired at a cost of £24,000 and fully depreciated by 30 September 2012.

(v) £24,000 paid for installing a new production process resulting in significant cost savings.

21.7 Capitalisation of borrowing costs

21.7.1 What are borrowing costs?

Borrowing costs are expenses incurred to raise finance for buying or constructing PPE.

21.7.2 Borrowing cost should be capitalised

The borrowing cost should be capitalised if it relates to a 'qualifying asset' defined as any asset that takes a substantial amount of time to get ready for use. This could mean that loan interest relating to an acquired asset cannot be capitalised if the process of acquiring does not take substantial time. Note that until the recent amendment to IAS 23,[3] companies were permitted a choice to either capitalise or expense borrowing costs relating to PPE.

21.7.3 Capitalisation rules

These have been prescribed in IAS 23 as follows:

(a) *The amount of the borrowing costs capitalised should be what was actually incurred.* This is saying that notional costs (that would have been incurred if the business had borrowed instead of using its own funds) cannot be capitalised.

(b) *The interest capitalised should be the amount related to the capitalisation period* which:

- commences on either the date from which the borrowing costs were in fact incurred or the date on which construction activity started, whichever is later;
- ends when substantially all work necessary (bar minor modifications) to get the asset ready for intended use is complete; and
- excludes any extended period when construction activity was suspended.

For example, let us assume that the construction started on 1 February, an 8% loan of £500,000 was raised on 1 March to finance the work, construction activity was suspended during the month of July and the construction was completed by 30 September at a cost of £450,000. The construction activity lasted eight months, but the capitalisation period is only six months. This is because no interest cost was actually incurred in February and activity had been suspended for a month in July. The amount of borrowing cost to be capitalised would, therefore, be £450,000 × 8% for 6/12 months = £18,000. The interest incurred in July would be treated as an expense of £3,000 in the Statement of income.

(c) *If the borrowing is not specific to the construction activity the capitalisation rate* should be the weighted average cost of various borrowings. For illustration let us assume that X plc incurred £700,000 on a construction activity which was spread over eight months, and it has in issue, thoughout the year, £300,000 6% Loan notes and £600,000 9% Loan notes. The interest cost for the year (working 1) would be £72,000 on a total borrowing of £900,000 (£300,000 + £600,000). The capitalisation rate (weighted average borrowing costs) amounts to (working 2) 8%. The amount of borrowing cost to be capitalised would be £28,000 (working 3).

Working (1)	
Total interest cost	
6% of £300,000	£18,000
9% of £600,000	£54,000
Total interest	£72,000

Working (2)
The capitalisation rate
$\frac{\text{Interest } £72{,}000}{\text{Borrowing } £900{,}000} \times 100 = 8\%$

Working (3)
Interest capitalised
8% of £700,000 × 8 months = £28,000

(d) *The company should disclose* (i) the amount capitalised in the accounting period and (ii) the capitalisation rate.

Activity 21.5 Capitalisation of interest when the borrowing is specific to the asset

Sawa plc commenced construction of its head offices on 1 March 2012. Construction was completed by 1 December at a cost of £324,000. Because of local flooding, construction work was suspended for a month in May. The construction is financed by a bank loan carrying interest at 14% per annum, obtained on 1 April 2012.

Required: At what cost should the building be accounted for in the Statement of financial position as at 31 December 2012? Ignore depreciation of building for the year.

21.8 Depreciation of non-current assets

We are already familiar (Chapter 7) with the concept of depreciation, alternative methods of measuring it and how it is accounted for. It is time to define depreciation, consider and weigh the need for it and study the rules relating to it as stated in IAS 16.

21.8.1 Definition of depreciation

Depreciation is the allocation of the depreciable amount of a tangible non-current asset to each accounting period within its estimated useful life[4] in a systematic manner that takes account of the pattern of consumption of economic benefits flowing from it.

The depreciable amount is the cost (or valuation) of the asset less its anticipated residual amount. The residual amount is the estimated amount currently receivable (i.e. without considering factors that might affect the amount that may be realised when the asset is eventually disposed of) from the disposal of the asset at the end of its economic life. The Standard[2] differentiates useful life from the economic life of the asset. The estimate of useful life is not based on the technical specification of the manufacturer but is the period the entity expects to make use of the asset based on its past experience with similar assets.

Depreciation is known as *amortisation* when the cost of intangible assets, e.g. the cost of a trademark, is allocated to each accounting period and as *depletion* when the same is done with the cost of natural resources, e.g. a coal mine.

21.8.2 Factors that cause depreciation of non-current assets

For a non-current asset (such as a car) the normal reason for the consumption of economic benefits is usage, often referred to as wear and tear. The extent of physical wear and tear arising from use would depend on factors such as hours and shifts worked and the quality of care and maintenance. There could be other factors as well causing a reduction in the useful life, and these include:

(a) economic obsolescence, i.e. where the use of the asset is no longer economical, because the output is no more in demand;

(b) technological obsolescence such as that arising from improvements in production methods;

(c) legal and other limitations on the use of the asset, e.g. a fixed expiry date on leases.

21.9 Why non-current assets should be depreciated

We saw that for current assets the amounts reported in the Statement of financial position should not exceed their net realisable value. In the case of non-current assets the approach is different in that the assets are not being held for resale but for use within the business. They are reported in the books of account initially at cost and, after its use has commenced, on every Statement of financial position, at their depreciated cost even if their net realisable value is lower. This is because we prepare financial statements on the going concern assumption (Chapter 19) that the business will continue in operation and, therefore, there is no danger of having to dispose of the asset at the lower realisable value.

But the non-current assets, unless they have infinite useful life (as in the case of land), should be depreciated in each of the accounting periods in which they are used, for the following reasons:

1. **Statutory requirements.** Company law[5] as well as Accounting Standards[2] require the depreciable amount of every non-current asset with a finite life to be allocated on a systematic basis over its useful life.
2. **The prudence concept.** All non-current assets (other than land) have a finite life, on completion of which the economic benefits from the asset would cease to flow. Prudence demands that this fact should be recognised by writing off in each accounting period a proportion of the cost of the asset to represent the amount of the economic benefit consumed during that period.
3. **The matching concept.** To determine the profit, the income earned in a period is matched with all expense incurred in the earning process. If an expense is omitted, the profit for the period is overstated. For illustration, let us assume that Mickey and Minney each earned £30,000 during the year from driving minicabs,that Mickey used his own car acquired for £20,000 and expected to have a useful life of four years and that Minney hired a car for £6,000 per year. Let us also assume that their other expenses amounted to £10,000. If Mickey did not depreciate his car, he would report a profit of £20,000 whereas Minney would report only £14,000. Mickey's profit is overstated because it fails to take into account the expense of using his own car. As Mickey's car will not remain in use forever, an appropriate proportion of the cost of his car should be recognised as an expense and matched with the income he earned during the year.
4. **To present a fair view.** Unless non-current assets are depreciated and the depreciation expense matched with income, the report of financial performance within the accounting period (in the Statement of income) and the financial position at the end of the period (in the Statement of financial position) will both fail to present a fair view – the profit will be exaggerated because it fails to take into account the consumption of

non-current assets during the period and the Statement of financial position will overstate the non-current assets by not reducing their cost by the amount consumed. If the accounts do not give a fair view then they reduce their *relevance* for investors who might be misled into thinking that the profits available for drawings and dividends could be maintained at the current level without introducing more capital, i.e. not realising that their capital is being reduced.

5. **Capital maintenance.** If we continue with the Mickey and Minney illustration, we can see that, if Mickey did not depreciate his car and withdrew for living expenses all of the profit (reported at £20,000), by the end of the fourth year (when the car has to be replaced) he would have to introduce fresh capital for the replacement. However, had he depreciated over the four years, at the end of the fourth year he would have maintained his capital at the amount he introduced originally to buy the car. There is often a misconception that the depreciation charged will always be available at the end of the asset's life in the form of cash and available to buy a replacement. This could be true if the business ensures that annually an amount equal to the depreciation charge is retained in the form of cash.

Let us observe (see below) how, by depreciating the car annually, Mickey would retain an equal amount of resources within the business, so that repeated over four years he would have retained sufficient resources to replace the car, if replacement is possible at the original cost. Assuming that Mickey depreciates his car at £5,000 per year the cash would build up as follows:

	Year 1	Year 2	Year 3	Year 4
	£	£	£	£
Earnings (received in cash)	30,000	30,000	30,000	30,000
Expenses (paid for in cash)	(10,000)	(10,000)	(10,000)	(10,000)
Cash available (at the bank)	20,000	20,000	20,000	20,000
Drawings by Mickey (limited to the profit)	(15,000)	(15,000)	(15,000)	(15,000)
Cash retained at bank each year	5,000	5,000	5,000	5,000
Cumulative amount at the bank	5,000	10,000	15,000	20,000

If, because of inflation, the prices of cars have gone higher, Mickey may possibly have to replace it with a smaller car. That is why it is said that depreciation maintains money capital (i.e. £20,000) but not the real capital (i.e. the capacity of the business to operate at the same level).

21.10 The case for depreciating buildings

Buildings differ from other non-current assets in that their economic life is significantly longer. They do not, however, have an infinite life. Therefore the cost of buildings should be depreciated. Even so, many hotels, banks and building societies have resisted the requirement to depreciate buildings on grounds such as:

1 **Difficulty of identifying the cost of the building** separately from that of land because they were acquired together many years ago. The difficulty, however, is not real, because the Royal Institution of Chartered Surveyors has sufficient records which help in identifying the cost of buildings.

2 **Determination of economic life is a difficult exercise** in the case of buildings and more particularly in the cases of dams and reservoirs, airport terminals and runways. This difficulty cannot though be an excuse for not depreciating. What needs to be done is to estimate the economic life on the basis of past experience and keep the estimate under review at regular intervals. For example, the British Airport Authority have been depreciating their airport terminals and runways, estimating the useful life as 40 years; and when preparing their financial statements in 1990, revised the estimate of useful life to 100 years. Similarly, Cable and Wireless have been depreciating their analogue cables, estimating the useful life as 15 years; but in 1993, to be ready for the changeover to digital television by the millennium, they revised the estimate of remaining useful life to seven years.

3 **Immateriality of the amount.** It has been argued that the economic life of buildings, if they are well maintained, may tend towards infinity or is at least so long that the annual charge for depreciation would be immaterial. Although, admittedly, exceptionally good maintenance could extend the economic life and correspondingly reduce depreciation, it cannot be a justification for not depreciating. The annual depreciation, taken by itself, might be small but when accumulated over many years it could result in a significant amount.

4 **Depreciation amounts to a double charge on profits** when the high cost of maintenance is also taken into account. This argument misses the point that the cost of maintenance (like the cost of servicing a vehicle) is part of the recurrent expense whilst the depreciation is an allocation to each accounting period of an appropriate portion of the cost of the asset. It is conceded, however, that high maintenance cost, by extending the asset's economic life, will lower the depreciation charge.

5 **Buildings have no depreciable cost** because their residual value tends to appreciate with time. Admittedly, the ageing process tends to add value to certain assets like period buildings, timber and wine. The Trusthouse Forte (taken over by Granada since 1997) report refers to such improvement when it identifies improvements in value other than those attributable to inflation. The question, however, is whether such improvement in market value, which would be irrelevant when accounts are prepared on a going concern basis (because the asset is not intended to be sold), should be permitted to mask the depreciable cost of an asset. Remember that IAS 16 specifically requires depreciation to be written off even if the fair value of an asset is more than the carrying value.[6]

The need for depreciating buildings continues to be a bone of contention in the UK. A survey conducted in the 1990s found that almost a third of listed companies in the UK – ranging from banks, building societies, insurance companies, to supermarkets, hotels and public utilities – were not depreciating their buildings, despite the requirements for it in company law as well as the Accounting Standards. The Financial Reporting Review Panel (FRRP) appointed in 1991 with responsibility to monitor compliance with company law and accounting standards was able to require SEP Industrial holdings to depreciate their buildings, but excused Trusthouse Forte from having to do the same.

Activity 21.6 Focus on the absence of a depreciable cost

(a) A vintner buys two casks of wine at £50 each. One he sells for £75, and the other, remaining in hand, has a market value of £80. Is it acceptable for him to capitalise (i.e. to report as an asset in the Statement of financial position) the unsold cask at £80 and to report the cost of the one sold at £20, i.e. after removing £80 from purchases of £100?

(b) The Trusthouse Forte group explains their failure to depreciate buildings as follows:

   (i) Their buildings are maintained in a continual state of sound repair by making renovations and building extensions.
   (ii) The life of the building is so long that annual depreciation becomes immaterial.
   (iii) The residual values of buildings after adjusting for the impact of inflation are so high that there is no depreciable cost.

Required: Would you accept these as justifiable reasons for not depreciating buildings?

21.11 The component approach to depreciation and capitalisation

IAS 16 requires a component approach to be adopted for purposes of depreciation as well as for capitalising subsequent expenses relating to PPE. The component approach needs to be adopted when:

(a) A part (a component) included within any asset reported as PPE has a cost that is significant in relation to the cost of the whole asset.[7]

(b) The component's useful life and the pattern of consumption of the component are significantly different from other components of that asset.

When such components exist, then the component approach needs to be taken when:

(i) **Accounting for depreciation**. For example, a furnace acquired for £80,000 may have a useful life of say ten years; whereas it may need to be relined every two years because the lining's useful life is only two years. This means each component needs to be depreciated on the basis of its own useful life.

(ii) **Capitalising the cost of replacement** of the lining after the cost of the original one is written off in two years.

Activity 21.7 Depreciation on the component approach

On 1 January 2012 Falkirk plc moved into its new premises acquired at a cost of £500,000 and wishes to depreciate it using the straight-line method. Its structural engineer reports as stated on the right.

Required: Calculate the depreciation to be written off in the year ending 31.12.2012.

Components	Cost	Useful life
Physical structure	£340,000	50 years
Roof	£120,000	20 years
Plumbing	£18,000	15 years
Electrics	£12,000	10 years
Air conditioning	£10,000	5 years
	£500,000	

Activity 21.8 Capitalisation of subsequent expenses on the component approach

Dunkirk plc acquired a plane on 1 January 2012 for £6 million. It has been advised that the plane has a useful life of ten years, but its seats and galleys will require replacement every two years at a cost of £500,000.

Required:

(a) What will be the depreciation written off in the year ended 31 December 2012?

(b) Explain how you propose to account for the replacement of seats and galleys.

21.12 Depreciation of infrastructure assets by renewal accounting

The word infrastructure refers to basic facilities in a country such as its roads, railway, canals, dams, telecommunication network, underground pipe network and so on. When we refer to infrastructure assets we refer to those owned by a business. Renewal accounting is the term used to describe the practice of offsetting against profit the cost of replacements rather than the depreciation of original cost.

For example, in order to remain effective in their professional practice, solicitors need to maintain an up-to-date library which involves having to replace existing volumes with newer editions. In these circumstances it is usual accounting practice for solicitors to report their library at initial cost and to write off the cost of replacements in lieu of depreciation. Cinemas and theatres use renewal accounting when accounting for seats in their auditorium; and so do hotels when they account for crockery and cutlery.

In the UK, renewal accounting has been used when public utilities account for infrastructure assets. This is because companies like Thames Water plc and Severn Trent plc have a statutory responsibility to maintain in perpetuity their infrastructure assets (such as the network of mains, raw water storage reservoirs and sludge pipe lines). The Accounting Standard in the UK, while permitting the renewal cost to be substituted for depreciation, requires that the cost to be written off in each accounting period is not what the company actually incurred (because that figure would be within the discretion of the management), but the renewal cost that should have been incurred in the period in accordance with an asset management plan independently certified.

The requirements of FRS 15[8] (UK) are as follows:

1. The infrastructure asset is a system or network that as a whole is intended to be maintained at a specified level of service potential by continuing replacement and refurbishment of its components.
2. The level of annual expenditure required to maintain the operating capacity of the infrastructure asset should be calculated from an asset management plan that is certified by a person who is appropriately qualified and independent.
3. Any identifiable major components within the infrastructure asset with a determinable finite life should be depreciated over that economic life.

When using renewal accounting, the actual cost incurred on renewal in the year is capitalised while the amount of renewal cost that should have been incurred in the year, as certified professionally, is written off, in lieu of depreciation. For example, if the infrastructure asset was reported on 1 January 2012 at £214 million and £48 million was incurred in 2012 on renewals, whereas £72 million should have been incurred according to the certified asset management plan, then the business needs to:

1. capitalise the actual cost incurred on the renewal £48m;
2. write off, in lieu of depreciation, the amount (£72m) that should have been incurred;
3. report the asset in the Statement of financial position at £190m (see the ledger account on the right).

Infrastructure asset account

	£m		£m
Balance b/d	214	Depreciation	72
Cash a/c	48	Balance c/d	190
	262		262
Balance b/d	190		

The aim is to prevent any possible manipulation of reported performance by removing from the discretion of the business the amount it writes off as depreciation.

21.13 Requirements of IAS 16[2] regarding depreciation

The main requirements of IAS 16 include the following:

1. The depreciable cost of PPE (including buildings) should be allocated to each accounting period on a systematic basis over its useful life.
2. Each component of the asset that is significant in relation to total cost must be depreciated separately. This becomes crucial if the estimate of economic life of a component is significantly different from the remainder of the asset.
3. Depreciation is written off even if the asset's realisable value exceeds the carrying amount.
4. Land and buildings are separable assets and are dealt with separately for accounting purposes, even when they are acquired together. An increase in the value of land on which the building stands does not affect the determination of the useful life of the building.
5. Depreciation begins when the asset is available for use (not when its use begins) and continues even if the asset is idle until the asset is de-recognised (i.e. removed from accounting records).
6. No depreciation method is prescribed, though the straight-line method, the diminishing balance method and the units of production method are mentioned. The requirements are that:
   - the method used should reflect the pattern in which the asset's economic benefits are consumed;
   - the method of depreciation should be consistently applied from period to period unless there is a change in the expected pattern of economic benefits from the asset.
7. The depreciation charge for the period should be recognised as expense (stated in the Statement of income) unless it is included in the carrying amount of another asset.
8. On each reporting date there should be a review of:
   (i) the residual value of the asset;
   (ii) the estimated economic life of the asset; and
   (iii) the depreciation method being used.

9. PPE is de-recognised (i.e. removed from the ledger account) upon its disposal or when the asset is withdrawn from use and no future economic benefits are expected from its use or disposal.
10. See box on the right for the disclosures that are required with regard to PPE.

Disclosures required
1 Basis of measurement
2 Method of depreciation
3 Economic life or depreciation rate
4 Cost (or value) of asset
5 Accumulated depreciation
6 Any allowance for impairment
7 Reconciliation of movement
8 Any restriction on title to asset
9 Expense in the year to construct
10 Commitment to acquire PPE

Activity 21.9 Review of depreciation method and estimate of useful life

(i) When its airport terminals and runways were constructed at a cost of £476 million, an Airport Authority estimated the economic life at 40 years and depreciated them from 1 January 1997, the date of commencement of use, using the straight-line method. In a review that took place on 1 January 2012 the estimate of economic life is revised to 100 years.

(ii) A machine acquired for £160,000 on 1 July 2010 is depreciated at 25% per annum using the reducing balance method. As from 1 January 2012 the management decides that the straight-line method, assuming remaining economic life of three years, would better reflect the pattern of consumption of economic benefits from the machine.

Required: What is the total depreciation to be written off in the year ending on 31 December 2012 for the airport terminals and the machine?

Summary

- Tangible non-current assets are described in International Accounting Standards as property, plant and equipment (PPE).
- To be identified as PPE the asset:
  (i) should have physical substance;
  (ii) should be used for production/supply of goods, or let out to others or for administrative purposes; and
  (iii) be available for use after the current accounting period.
- To recognise something as a non-current asset in the Statement of financial position:
  (i) the risks and rewards relating to it should be with the entity;
  (ii) there should be sufficient certainty of economic benefits flowing from it after the accounting period; and
  (iii) the cost/value of the asset should be capable of reliable measurement.
- Non-current assets are initially measured at cost. Costs include all expenses directly attributable to placing them in the location and condition for use, up to the point they are ready for use.
- The cost of non-current assets should include borrowing costs, if they relate to qualifying assets (i.e those that take a substantial amount of time to get ready for use).

- Except where (like land) it has infinite life, all non-current assets (including buildings) should be depreciated in a systematic manner, the method reflecting the pattern of consumption of economic benefits.
- Infrastructure assets are depreciated on a renewal accounting system provided the amount written off, in lieu of depreciation, is independently determined, based on a certified asset management plan.
- At the end of each accounting period the depreciation method, estimates of the economic life and residual value of non-current assets should be reviewed and necessary accounting adjustments made prospectively.

References

1. *Framework for the Preparation and Presentation of Financial Statements* (1989), London, International Accounting Standards Board.
2. IAS 16 *Property, Plant and Equipment*, revised 2003, effective 1.1.2005, London, International Accounting Standards Board.
3. IAS 23 *Borrowing Costs*, revised 2003, effective 1.1.2005, London, International Accounting Standards Board.
4. IAS 16 in para 44 explains that useful life depends on the asset's expected usefulness and points out that it can be shorter than the asset's economic life.
5. Companies Act (2006), London, The Stationery Office.
6. IAS 16 in para 52.
7. IAS 16 in para 43.
8. UK FRS 15 *Accounting for Tangible Fixed Assets*, February 1999, London, Accounting Standards Board.

Suggested answers to activities

21.1 Asset recognition criteria

(i) In the case of leasehold property, the asset is the control, if that has been established, of access to the property and the economic benefits expected to flow from it after the accounting period.

(ii) A machine yet to be produced is an asset because, upon payment, the access to future economic benefits from the machine is established.

(iii) A trade receivable is an asset because the sale establishes control of the legally enforceable right to the future economic benefits in the form of cash flow expected from the customer.

(iv) Prepaid rent is an asset because the payment made establishes the future right to occupy the premises and be entitled to the economic benefits flowing from it.

21.2 Property, plant and equipment

(i) A standby machine is classified as PPE because it is held for use in production and will be used for more than one accounting period. Whether it maintains or enhances earning capacity is not relevant.

(ii) Property for storage (warehouse) is PPE because it is held on a continuing basis for supply of goods.

(iii) Residential quarters are PPE because they are held for administrative purposes on a continuing basis.

(iv) Machinery leased out to others is PPE because it is held for rental to others on a continuing basis.

21.3 Initial measurement of PPE

(a) Land:

Property cost	£480,000[a]
Demolishing cost	£15,000[a]
Site clearing expense	£5,500[a]
Legal expenses	£5,400[a]
Less: Salvage sale	(£1,900)[b]
	£504,000

(b) Building:

Contractors' cost	£3,500,000[a]
Architect's fees	£450,000[a]
Planning permission costs	£1,500[a]
Legal fees	£2,500[a]
	£3,954,000

(c) Motor vehicles – lorry:

Cost of buying	£12,000[a]
Cost of enhancement	£4,000[c]
Roadworthiness	£3,000[a]
	£19,000

(d) Machinery – steel rolling mill:

Cost of buying	£180,000[a]
Cost of delivery to site	£1,500[c]
Installation costs	£4,500[a]
	£186,000

Notes:
(a) Cost of acquisition, including all expenses until the asset is in the condition and in the location for intended use, should be capitalised.
(b) Amount earned from salvaging is not an incidental earning, but a reduction in the cost of demolishing the old building and is, therefore, reduced from the cost of that activity.
(c) The cost of building a larger body, though a subsequent expense, meets the capitalisation criteria and is capitalised.
(d) Costs expensed (because they fail to meet the capitalisation criteria) are £50,000 waste and expenses on insurance and road tax.
(e) Starting-up cost cannot be capitalised except when it is regarded as essential for placing the asset in a condition in which it can be used.

21.4 Capitalisation of subsequent expenses

(i) £1,200 paid for the crankshaft is written off as repairs and maintenance because the expenditure is incurred for restoring (rather than enhancing) the vehicle to its previously assessed levels of performance.

(ii) £14,500 paid for the additional thermostat is capitalised (added to the cost of the cold storage room) because it enhances the performance of the room to newly required levels.

(iii) From the time of acquisition the cost of the lining (£12,000) is depreciated over four years; while the cost of the furnace (£84,000) is depreciated over 20 years. Therefore, the cost of the new replacement lining (£12,000) is capitalised and reported as an addition to the cost of the furnace because it replaces an asset component treated separately for depreciation, after the cost of the original lining is fully written off.

(iv) £7,500 for overhauling and restoring the roadworthiness of the pick-up truck is capitalised (added to the cost of motor vehicle) because it restores the economic benefits, which have been written off by way of depreciation.

(v) £24,000 incurred on the production process results in significant cost reductions. It is capitalised.

21.5 Capitalisation of borrowing costs

Interest capitalised is 14% of £324,000 for seven months because the loan was obtained a month after construction began and no construction work was undertaken during one month.

Office premises account

Cash a/c	£324,000		
Interest	£26,400		
	£350,460		

21.6 Focus on the absence of a depreciable cost

(a) In the case of the vintner, the application of unrealised gain of £30 on the cask yet remaining in hand to reduce the cost of the cask sold is not acceptable for the following reasons:

(i) Accounting is transactions-based. Profit can be recognised only when goods are sold. The gain on the unsold cask will not be objectively established until that is also sold.

(ii) The profit is the difference between the sale price of the cask and the amount paid to purchase that cask. The cost of casks in hand remains £50 irrespective of other events.

One could well ask if it would be fair for a stonemason owning a stock of marble, from which he used a few pieces every year, to use the unrealised gains expected from the marble remaining unused to reduce the cost of that used.

(b) The reasons advanced by Trusthouse for not depreciating buildings appear suspect because:

(i) The avoidance of depreciation of buildings by pointing to the high cost of maintenance is not far removed from endeavours to avoid depreciation of machinery by pointing to superlative maintenance.

(ii) Although, admittedly, because of very long economic lives, annual depreciation could be immaterial, over the long years of economic life the amount would accumulate to very significant amounts.

(iii) The buildings are not intended for disposal. Therefore, appreciation in value of buildings is not relevant for the determination of depreciable cost; just as in the case of the appreciation in value of the unsold cask of wine and unused marble.

(iv) IAS 16 has specifically stated that increases in fair value to levels higher than the carrying value of an asset should not justify failure to depreciate that asset.

21.7 Depreciation on the component approach

On the component approach the depreciation for the year will be £17,200 (see calculation on the right).

Component	Cost	Useful life	Depreciation
Physical structure	£340,000	50 years	£6,800
Roofing	£120,000	20 years	£6,000
Plumbing	£18,000	15 years	£1,200
Electrics	£12,000	10 years	£1,200
Air conditioning	£10,000	5 years	£2,000
	£500,000		£17,200

21.8 Capitalisation of subsequent expenses on the component approach

(a) Depreciation in 2012 is £800,000 (see calculation on component approach). The cost of the plane excluding the cost of the seats and galley was £5,500,000.

(b) In two years, the cost of the seats and galley would be fully written off and then, in the third year, the cost of their replacement (expected to be again £500,000) will be capitalised.

Components	Cost	Life	Depreciation
The airplane	£5,500,000	10 years	£550,000
Seats and galleys	£500,000	2 years	£250,000
			£800,000

21.9 Review of depreciation method, estimate of useful life and residual value

Depreciation of airport terminals and runways:

Until 1.1.2012 the asset has been in use for 15 years.

Written-down value on 1.1.2012
= £476,000 × 25/40 years = £297,500

On the revised economic life 85 years of use remain.

Annual depreciation = £297,500/85 years = £3,500

Depreciation of machine:

In 2010: 25% of £160,000 × 6/12 = £20,000

In 2011: 25% of £160,000 – £20,000 = £35,000

In 2012: £160,000 – 20,000 – 35,000 = £105,000
£105,000/3 years = £35,000

Multiple choice questions

Assets and non-current assets

21.1 Which of the following attributes are essential for a resource to be recognised as an asset?

(i) It must be owned by the entity and remain in its custody

(ii) It must be within the entity's control

(iii) Its control should have been established by a past transaction or event

(iv) There must be reasonable assurance of flow of future economic benefits

a	ii and iii	
b	i, ii, iii	
c	i, ii, iii & iv	
d	ii, iii & iv	

21.2 Even when a resource has all the attributes necessary for recognition as an asset, a business has a policy of treating the resource as an expense unless it costs £1,000 or more. This is an example of complying with which accounting concept?

(a) Prudence concept

(b) Materiality concept

(c) Substance over form concept

(d) Relevance concept

21.3 Which of the following transactions results in the acquisition of an asset?

(a) £45,000 spent on providing computer training for all members of the staff

(b) £4,500 paid on a contract to service all business vehicles during the current year

(c) £78,500 due from customers in respect of sales

(d) £2,400 paid for repairing a vehicle which met with an accident

21.4 A new business paid £128,000 (5% of its first year's turnover) to an agent on an advertising contract in the hope that it will generate sales over the next few years. Identify one of the following reasons as the most pertinent one for not reporting the whole amount as an asset at the end of the first year:

(a) It is not the common practice in business of this nature

(b) Advertising is not an asset because it does not have physical substance (it is intangible)

(c) The payment does not give the business control over its customers' behaviour

(d) There is no reasonable assurance that economic benefit in the form of sales will flow from it

21.5 In addition to £98,400 already paid in 2012, the advertising agent has sent an invoice for a further amount of £61,800. £45,000 of the invoice is for a television campaign commencing January 2013. Which of the following amounts will you report as an asset at the year-end 31 December 2012?

(a) £61,800 remaining unpaid for advertising

(b) £160,200 the total advertising cost expected to improve the sales in future years

(c) £98,400 because that is the portion already paid for generating future income

(d) £45,000 included in the invoice for a television campaign to commence in January 2013

Non-current assets

21.6 Which of the following is not a necessary attribute of a tangible non-current asset?

(a) Physical existence
(b) Possibility of selling in the open market without selling the whole business
(c) Continuing use after the end of current accounting period
(d) Use for production/supply, or administrative purpose or for letting to others

21.7 Which of the following costs relating to acquisition of a machine cannot be included in its cost?

(a) Cost of reinforcing the factory floor and fitting shatterproof glass to factory windows
(b) Cost of building a concrete pedestal with iron girders to which the machine is harnessed
(c) Cost of material unavoidably wasted during the running-in period
(d) Cost of relocating the machine when senior staff complained of noise pollution

21.8 Which of the following relating to construction of office premises cannot be included in its cost?

(a) Legal expenses and stamp duty incurred in checking on and transferring the title to the property
(b) Fees paid to the architect for preparing the plans and quantity surveyor for the bill of quantity
(c) Relocation expenses paid to the former tenant to obtain vacant possession of the premises
(d) Cost of material and labour on a portion demolished because it did not conform with planning

Borrowing costs

21.9 Which of the following would you regard as the threshold criteria when deciding whether or not to capitalise any part of borrowing costs?

(a) Is the asset financed by the borrowing an acquired one or self-constructed one?
(b) Is it the policy of the business to capitalise borrowing costs?
(c) Is the asset a qualifying asset in that it took a substantial time to bring it to intended use?
(d) Is it common practice for competitors to capitalise borrowing costs?

21.10 To finance the construction of its office premises a mortgage loan of £4,000,000 was raised on 1 February 2012, at 9% interest per annum. The property was acquired on 15 February for £1,500,000. The construction commenced on 1 March and was completed by 30 October at a total cost of £2,800,000. The premises were not occupied until 1 December. How much of the mortgage interest incurred in 2012 should be capitalised?

a	£387,000	
b	£252,000	
c	£168,000	
d	£360,000	

Capitalisation of subsequent expenses

21.11 Which of the following statements is correct? It is permitted to add to the cost of the corresponding asset the cost incurred for:

(i) Restoring to working condition a factory gutted by fire
(ii) Replacing a roof, treated separately for depreciation, on completion of its life
(iii) Overhauling a building used as a warehouse for intended use as office premises
(iv) Redecoration of the building in preparation for silver jubilee celebrations

a	i only	
b	i and ii	
c	ii and iii	
d	ii and iv	

Depreciation

21.12 Which of the following statements is correct?

(a) Normally land need not be depreciated

(b) Difficulty of estimating economic life is a valid reason for not depreciating airline terminals

(c) In view of long life depreciation of buildings is immaterial and could therefore be ignored

(d) If residual value of building, adjusted for inflation, is more than its cost there is no depreciable cost and, therefore, there is no need to depreciate

21.13 On 6 January 2011 £580,000 was paid for a property. The amount includes £20,000 for a building located in the property but in a state of disrepair. The building was refurbished at a cost of £30,000 and is used as a store. The expectation is that the building could remain in use for ten years. In the meantime, because of an urban revival programme the property's value is estimated at £800,000 as at 31 December 2011. Assuming the use of the straight-line method, the amount of depreciation in 2011 should be:

a	None	
b	£2,000	
c	£5,000	
d	£58,000	

21.14 Identify whether each of the following statements is true or false by placing a tick in column X if true and column Y if false:

	X	Y
(a) By depreciation an entity sets aside cash resources which will be readily available to pay for replacement of assets in use		
(b) Depreciation is no more than an allocation of depreciable cost in a systematic manner over the estimated economic life of the asset		
(c) Factors to be considered when determining the depreciation charge are:		
(i) The cost of the asset		
(ii) The residual value (also known as scrap value or salvage value)		
(iii) The method of depreciation in use		
(iv) The amount at which the asset is insured		
(v) Expenses to keep the asset in a working condition		

21.15 Place a tick in the appropriate grid to identify whether each of the following statements is more suited as reference to the straight-line method (X) or reducing balance method (Y):

	X	Y
(a) Once computed the annual depreciation of an asset remains constant from year to year		
(b) The depreciation expense fails to reflect the fall in market value of the asset		
(c) Its virtue is the simplicity of calculating the amount		
(d) The annual expense tends to remain constant when depreciation is taken together with repairs		
(e) Conveys a wrong impression that depreciation is a function of time rather than use		
(f) Progressively declining depreciation expense probably reflects reducing earning power of asset		
(g) Depreciation calculation may become complicated when enhancement costs are capitalised		
(h) The method is known also as the accelerated depreciation method		
(i) Asset tends to cost more with the asset's age when depreciation is taken together with repairs		
(j) Unless deliberately removed the asset is not eliminated from accounts by depreciation process		

21.16 A manufacturer acquired a machine for £50,000 on 1 January 2012 and estimates the economic life as four years and scrap value as £10,000. Calculate the depreciation expense in the first year, if the depreciation method used is:

(a) The straight-line method

(b) The reducing balance method at 40% per annum of reducing balance

(c) The sum of the years' digits method

	X		Y		Z	
(a)	£18,000		£12,500		£10,000	
(b)	£20,000		£16,000		£25,000	
(c)	£20,000		£10,000		£16,000	

21.17 A company operating a minicab service depreciates its vehicles over four years using the sum of the year's digits method. Its vehicles were all acquired on 1 March 2011 for £180,000, except a minibus acquired for £60,000 on 1 April 2012. What is the depreciation charge for the year ended 31 December 2012?

a	£68,000	
b	£72,000	
c	£75,000	
d	£96,000	

21.18 A freight hauler acquired a truck for £90,000 on 1 January 2010 and another for £70,000 on 30 June 2011. He estimates the economic life of each truck at four years and scrap value as 10% of cost. Calculate the depreciation charge for the year ended 31 December 2012, if the depreciation method used is:

(a) The straight-line method

(b) The reducing balance method at 40% per annum of reducing balance

(c) The sum of the years' digits method

	X		Y		Z	
(a)	£28,125		£36,000		£40,000	
(b)	£44,900		£29,760		£31,824	
(c)	£38,250		£35,100		£30,150	

21.19 In keeping with IAS 16 requirement that each component that is significant in relation to the total should be treated separately, the total cost of self-constructed office premises has been broken down as stated on the left. The policy is to depreciate assets with a finite life using the straight-line method and assuming that scrap value is not material. Calculate the depreciation written off in a year.

Item	Cost	Life
Land	£2,000,000	Infinite
Building	£2,800,000	50 years
Roofing	£800,000	25 years
Plumbing	£240,000	20 years
Lighting	£180,000	10 years

a	£120,400	
b	£80,400	
c	£153,143	
d	£118,000	

Review of depreciation method, scrap value and estimate of economic life

21.20 A machine acquired on 1.1.2004 for £320,000 is being depreciated using the straight-line method, assuming 20 years economic life and a scrap value of £20,000. Calculate the depreciation to be written off in the year ended 31 December 2012, if a review undertaken on 1 January 2012 reveals the need for each of the changes listed below:

(a) The depreciation method is changed to the sum of the years' digits

(b) Scrap value is revised to £120,000

(c) Estimate of economic life is revised from 20 years to 40 years

	X		Y		Z	
(a)	£30,769		£32,308		£27,692	
(b)	£10,000		£6,667		£16,667	
(c)	£4,500		£7,500		£5,625	

Renewal accounting of infrastructure asset

21.21 A business engaged in providing water supply to a community has incurred £280,000 on laying a network of underground pipes. During the current year it incurred £18,000 on replacing a few lines. In accordance with an asset management plan drawn up by an independent expert it should be spending £35,000 per year. Under the renewal accounting approved by FRS 15 the network should be reported at the year-end at:

a	£280,000	
b	£298,000	
c	£263,000	
d	£297,000	

Impairment review

21.22 A machine acquired for £480,000 on 1 January 2006 and depreciated using the straight-line method, assuming 20 years' life and 10% scrap value, was damaged in an accident on 1 January 2012. Though it was restored to working order at a cost of £20,000, it is expected to be operational for four years more and the present value of the income it is expected to generate is only £84,000. The machine, being of a specialised nature, cannot be sold for more than £10,000. What is the amount to be written off as impairment as at 1 January 2012 and as depreciation for the year ended 31 December 2012?

	Impairment	Depreciation	
a	£266,400	£21,000	
b	£256,499	£23,500	
c	£286,400	£21,000	
d	£266,400	£23,500	

Answers to multiple choice questions

21.1: d 21.2: b 21.3: c 21.4: d 21.5: d 21.6: b 21.7: d 21.8: d 21.9: c 21.10: c 21.11: c 21.12: a 21.13: c 21.14a: y 21.14b: x 21.14ci: x 21.14cii: x 21.14ciii: x 21.14civ: y 21.14cv: y 21.15a: x 21.15b: x 21.15c: y 21.15d: y 21.15e: x 21.15f: y 21.15g: x 21.15h: y 21.15i: x 21.15j: y 21.16a: z 21.16b: y 21.16c: z 21.17: c 21.18a: y 21.18b: z 21.18c: x 21.19: d 21.20a: z 21.20b: y 21.20c: z 21.21: c 21.22: a

Progressive questions

PQ 21.1 Distinguishing an asset from an expense (ACCA)

Do you regard each of the following as an asset of a business for accounting purposes? Explain your answer:

(a) a screwdriver bought in 2012;

(b) a machine hired by the business;

(c) good reputation of the business with its customers.

PQ 21.2 Identification of the cost of assets (ACCA)

Sema plc, a company in the heavy engineering industry, carried out an expansion programme in the 2012 financial year, in order to meet a permanent increase in contracts. The company selected a suitable site and commissioned a survey and valuation report, for which the fee was £1,500. On the basis of the report the site was acquired for £90,000. Solicitors' fees for drawing up the contract and conveyancing were £3,000. Fees of £8,700 were paid to the architects for preparing the building plans and overseeing the building work. This was carried out partly by the company's own workforce (at a wages cost of £11,600), using company building materials (cost £6,800) and partly by subcontractors who charged £69,400, of which £4,700 related to demolition of an existing building on the same site.

The completed building housed two hydraulic presses. The cost of press A was £97,000 (ex works) payable in a single lump sum two months after installation. Sema was given a trade discount of 10% and a cash discount for prompt payment of 2%. Hire of a transporter to collect the press and convey it to the new building was £2,900. Installation costs were £2,310 including hire of lifting gear, £1,400. Press B would have cost £105,800 (delivered) if it had been paid for in one lump sum. However, Sema opted to pay three equal annual instalments of £40,000 starting on the date of acquisition. Installation costs were £2,550 including hire of lifting gear £1,750.

Required:

(a) Using such of the above information as is relevant write up the Premises account and Plant account.
(b) State with reasons which of the above information was excluded from the accounts you wrote up.

PQ 21.3 The case of an intercontinental transport company

A business engaged in intercontinental transport of heavy goods makes the following payments during its financial year ended 30.9.20X0:

Payments relating to the property:

(i) £585,500 to acquire the freehold of a garage site.
(ii) £25,000 as compensation to the previous owner of the garage for his personal relocation expenses.
(iii) £2,500 as stamp duty, £300 as land registry fees, and £2,500 as solicitor's conveyancing fees for transfer of the title to the garage.
(iv) £14,500 for constructing a security fence around the property's perimeter.
(v) £145,500 for structural changes to the building, £17,800 for fitting shatterproof window glass, £400 for fixing electric bulbs of higher wattage and £12,600 for redecorating.
(vi) £37,400 in legal fees defending a decision to restrict the right of way of neighbours across the property.
(vii) £126,200 for constructing a compound for parking containers.
(viii) £35,500 for entertaining business contacts on moving into the property.

Payments relating to machinery:

(i) £214,500 on ordering machinery, from Japan, for servicing trucks.
(ii) £12,400 for freight and insurance and £46,500 for duty when the machinery arrived from Japan.
(iii) £12,600 for reinforcing the garage floor and £8,800 for constructing a base for the machine.
(iv) £1,200 for lubricating the machine and £1,100 for test runs.
(v) £21,400 for relocating the machine following a complaint by senior management of noise pollution.

Required:

(a) State the criteria you would use to identify the payments to be treated as part of the cost of assets.
(b) Determine, with explanation, the value at which you would report the assets.

PQ 21.4 Costs incurred subsequent to commencement of asset usage

A business manufacturing machine tools entered into the following transactions in the year ending 30 June 2012:

(a) £246,500 was paid for computerising the design of machine tools.

(b) Machinery used for producing tools had been purchased for £465,000 in 2010 and had been expected to have a useful economic life of 10 years. However, modifications costing £125,000 were made on 1 July 2011 to meet changing customer needs and as a result sales revenue is expected to improve by 50%.

(c) Conveyor belts were installed at a cost of £85,000 when the company commenced business in 2009 and had an expected useful economic life of five years. They were repaired in January 2012 at a cost of £6,000 for damage arising from vandalism.

(d) £25,000 spent in April 2012 on the refurbishment of the conveyor belts already referred to substantially extended their useful life by three years.

Required: Explain, with reasons, how you would account for each of the payments reported above.

Test questions

Test 21.1 Identification of an asset from an expense

(a) Explain why you would regard the following accounting treatments to be incorrect:

- (i) £14,200 paid during the year for the monthly servicing of machinery was capitalised.
- (ii) When the motor in a machine ceased because an electrical fault burnt the armature, £7,500 paid for replacing the dynamo was capitalised.
- (iii) In relation to the acquisition of a property, £12,500 paid as stamp duty fees and £10,000 paid to the solicitor for conveyancing were posted to the Property maintenance account.
- (iv) £120,000 paid for a set of computer terminals was posted to the Stationery account.

(b) Identify the effect of each of the above errors, which occurred during the year ended 31 December 2012, on the profit which has been reported as £1.246 million and net assets at the year-end reported as £4.985 million. (Ignore the effect of depreciation.)

Test 21.2 Capitalisation of borrowing costs

Exeter plc acquired land for £400,000 and related expenses on conveyancing and stamp duty amounted to £50,000. The construction of the company headquarters commenced on 1 February 2012, and with an interruption of a month, because of heavy rain, was completed by 31 October 2012, at a cost of £650,000, though the company did not move into the premises till 1 December of the same year. Financing of the construction was intended to be partly from issuing a loan note, but the 8% Loan notes of £500,000 could not be issued until 1 April 2012. Exeter plc does not depreciate land and depreciates buildings at 20% per annum on cost.

Required: Explain with reasons the amount at which the land and building will be reported on the company's Statement of financial position on 31 December 2012.

Test 21.3 Acquisition of an aircraft with airworthy clearance

An airline commenced business on 1 April 2010, and on the same day acquired a single aircraft for £3 million. However, it had to pay £240,000 for a major inspection without which the aviation authorities would not permit flight clearance. The inspection and clearance need to be repeated at 18-month intervals and would cost the same amount. During the year to 31 March 2011, insurance and regular maintenance of the aircraft cost £184,000 and £218,000 respectively. The aircraft is expected to remain in use for twenty years and the depreciation is to be on the straight-line method.

Required: At what value will be aircraft be reported on the Statement of financial position of the airline on 31 March 2011?

Chapter 22

Accounting for intangible assets and government grants

By the end of this chapter

You should learn:

- What an intangible asset is
- When an intangible asset may be accounted for
- That internally generated goodwill and other intangibles have normally to be expensed
- That grants shall be accounted for on an accruals basis using either the deferral method or the offset method

You should be able to:

- Account for intangible assets
- Account for amortisation and impairment of intangible assets
- Account for and report government grants in cash and in kind using either method

22.1 What is an intangible asset?

The main characteristic of an intangible asset is that it has no physical substance, i.e. it cannot be seen or touched but its existence can be perceived by its revenue-earning capacity. We include in this category only non-current assets provided they are non-monetary, i.e. trade receivables, though without physical substance, are not referred to as an intangible asset. A common example of intangible assets is goodwill but there are many other intangible assets as well and we will refer to these before we take up goodwill for discussion.

22.2 Intangible assets other than goodwill

22.2.1 The asset should be identifiable

Some examples of intangibles (other than goodwill) are listed overleaf. To be capitalised such intangible assets should be identifiable and should meet capitalisation criteria.

- Brand names (Sony, Hoover, Dyson) and associated trade marks
- Patents and copyrights
- Import quotas, airport landing rights
- Licence to operate TV/radio station
- Franchises
- A new process or technical knowledge

When is an asset identifiable?

An asset is regarded as identifiable when:[1]

either it is *separable* i.e. it can be sold, assigned or transferred without selling the whole business;

or it arises from a legal or contractual right regardless of whether the asset is separable.

It is this identifiability that distinguishes other intangibles from goodwill.

22.2.2 What are the capitalisation criteria?

If an intangible is identifiable, it still cannot be recognised as an asset unless it meets three capitalisation criteria:

1. It should be controlled, i.e. the entity should have the power to obtain future economic benefits flowing from it and to restrict others' access to it. For example, in the case of patents, franchises and licences the control stems from the ability to enforce the control in a court of law.
2. The flow of future economic benefits should be at least probable. The future benefit could take the form of revenue from sales, cost savings or other benefits arising from it. When an intangible is one that has been acquired the flow of future benefit could be assumed because unless there is assurance of benefit a payment would not have been made for it. If an asset's useful life can be measured then there is a presumption that future economic benefits are expected.
3. The cost or value of the asset should be capable of reliable measurement. Again when an asset is an acquired one, or when there is an active market in that asset, a reliable estimate of cost is possible.

Let us consider whether the identifiability requirement as well as the capitalisation criteria would be met in each of following scenarios in which a business may acquire an intangible:

(a) **Where the intangible asset is one separately acquired**. Where an intangible has been purchased it is reasonable to presume that (a) control is obtained, (b) commensurate future benefit is expected and (c) the cost is reliably established by a market transaction. Therefore, intangibles of this type are reported as assets.

(b) **Where the intangible is acquired as part of a business combination**. If an intangible asset (other than goodwill) is acquired as part of a business combination, the relevant standard[2] requires the asset to be recognised at its fair value. Ideally the fair value should be a price quoted in an active market. If there is no active market, the fair value of the intangible is the amount the acquirer would have paid for it in an arm's length transaction.

If an intangible asset acquired as part of a business combination is regarded as one with a finite life, there is a rebuttable presumption that the fair value of that intangible asset can be measured reliably.[3] The existence of a reliably measurable fair value creates the presumption that the asset is identifiable and it meets all three capitalisation criteria. Therefore, such intangibles are capitalised by the acquirer company, separately from goodwill, even if the intangible is not reported in the books of the business acquired.

However, if fair value cannot be reliably established, then the intangibles are regarded as subsumed within goodwill.[4]

(c) **Government-granted intangibles.** Examples of these are airport landing rights, licences to operate radio or television and import quotas. Such intangibles may be acquired by a business free of charge or for a nominal amount. Provided the capitalisation criteria are met, such intangibles may be capitalised either at their fair value or at a nominal amount plus any further expenses incurred to prepare the asset for intended use. Once capitalised such government-granted intangibles should be amortised over their estimated useful lives, which cannot exceed the period for which such rights are granted, but may be shorter depending on the period over which the asset is expected to be used. If the rights are conveyed for a limited term that can be renewed, the useful life should include the renewal periods only if there is evidence to support renewal without incurrence of significant costs.

(d) **Internally generated intangibles.** The normal rule is that, except in the case of development cost (see paragraph 22.5), internally generated intangibles cannot be capitalised because it is difficult to establish (a) whether and when it could be regarded as identifiable, (b) whether flow of future economic benefits is probable and (c) a reliable estimate of its cost because it is often difficult to distinguish between costs incurred directly on the intangible and those incurred for maintaining or enhancing internally generated goodwill or on day-to-day operations. The capitalisation of intangibles listed below, when internally generated, is expressly prohibited by IAS 38.[4]

- Brands
- Publishing titles
- Customer lists
- Mastheads

Activity 22.1 Whether capitalisation of intangibles is permitted

Sasha Whitmore is the new owner of a catering establishment acquired on 1 July 2011, from Sunshine Caterers (SS). She seeks your advice on whether she could report the following resources as assets in her financial statements:

(a) She obtained from SS a list of customers who have remained regulars for over a decade and their total custom has usually been worth in excess of £12 million per year.

(b) Catering contracts to local hospitals, awarded to SS by the National Health Trust and reported in the books of SS at £500, have been transferred to Sasha. It is not certain whether Sasha will be in a position to sell, assign or transfer these contracts, if necessity arises, nor whether the contracts will be renewed when the current awards expire on 30 June 2015.

(c) A logo and the brand name used by SS are very well known and are a significant reason for winning catering contracts. Neither the logo nor the brand name had been reported in the books of SS. Sasha feels that the brand name should have a market appeal for at least 20 more years and that, in the circumstances, she would have been willing to pay £400,000 to take over the logo together with its brand name.

(d) As a way of cultivating customer loyalty Sasha sent lavish Christmas hampers to all the customers in the list referred to in (a) above, at a cost of £540,000.

(e) The staff at SS are privy to a secret process which kept food warm over several hours without loss of flavour or taste. Since the SS staff are continuing in her employ, Sasha is of the opionion that a value of £200,000 can be placed on this secret process.

Required: How would you advise Sasha?

22.3 Accounting for intangibles other than goodwill

22.3.1 At what amount is an intangible asset accounted for?

Initially, intangible assets are measured at cost. Recognition of cost ceases when the asset is ready for its intended use. Any costs written off before the intangible asset met the capitalisation criteria cannot be capitalised. Thereafter, intangible assets may be reported on the valuation model, provided the fair value is determined by reference to an active market and the revaluation is made with such regularity as at the date of each Statement of financial position that the carrying value does not differ from its fair value on that date.

22.3.2 Does the intangible asset need to be amortised?

The answer depends on whether, at acquisition, the useful life of the asset is regarded as indefinite (not necessarily infinite) or finite:

(a) If the useful life of the intangible is assessed as indefinite, i.e. based on an analysis of all relevant factors, it is assessed that there is no foreseeable limit to the period over which net cash inflow may be expected from the asset, then the asset should not be amortised, but it should be impairment tested annually.[5]

(b) If the useful life of the intangible is assessed as finite, it shall be amortised in each accounting period, allocating the cost in a systematic manner, over its estimated useful life.

22.3.3 Disclosures required in the financial statements

In respect of intangible assets the following disclosures are required to be made in the financial statements:

1. a statement of movements during the accounting period in such assets and in the corresponding accumulated amortisation;
2. whether life is indefinite and, if finite, the estimate of useful life or amortisation rate used;
3. the amounts written off as expense and as amortisation relating to intangible assets.

22.4 Accounting for goodwill

The goodwill is the difference between the value of a whole business, as a going concern, and the aggregate of individual fair values that may be assigned to its identifiable assets and liabilities. It may be purchased or internally generated.

22.4.1 Purchased goodwill

The term purchased goodwill refers to what has been acquired through a transaction with third parties (see Chapter 13). It is defined in the Standard[2] as the payment made by the acquirer of a business in anticipation of future economic benefits from assets that are not individually identified and separately recognised. The Standard requires that purchased goodwill should be:

- recognised as an asset, initially at cost;
- not amortised; and
- reported on every Statement of financial position at cost less amounts written off as impairment.

Note that:

(i) If company A pays £500 to acquire company B, and at the date of acquisition the fair value of net assets of company B is £450, the difference of £50 is the cost of purchased goodwill.

(ii) The fair value of company B's assets should include all its identifiable assets that meet the capitalisation criteria even if any of them is not recorded by that company.

(iii) Unlike tangible non-current assets that are depreciated, goodwill is not amortised in each accounting period.

(iv) An impairment review (see Chapter 8) needs to be carried out annually to check whether, for some reason, there has been a fall in the value of goodwill.

22.4.2 Internally generated goodwill

This is an expression used when a business could, if so desired, be sold for an amount that is greater than the fair value of its net assets – having created the increase in value through its own efforts. This is referred to also as 'home-grown goodwill'. Unlike purchased goodwill, it has not arisen from a transaction with parties outside the business. Such internally generated goodwill should not be recognised as an asset (except in a partnership) because:

(a) it is not separable;

(b) the probability of flow of economic benefit (say in the form of customer attachment) is not assured;

(c) its cost cannot be reliably measured because it is not always possible to identify the activity that generates customer attachment and attribute a cost to that activity.

22.5 Research and development costs

22.5.1 Research phase costs shall be expensed

The Standard requires that all expenses incurred on pure research in furtherance of knowledge and applied research efforts to achieve a specific result should be expensed, because it would not be possible to demonstrate that future economic benefits would flow.

22.5.2 Development phase costs shall be capitalised

Costs incurred in the development phase are required to be (compulsorily) capitalised, provided all six of the following conditions are met:

1. Technical feasibility is established – the asset will be available for sale or for use.
2. The management intends (i.e. is committed) to complete what is under development.
3. The entity is able to complete the development.
4. Flow of future economic benefits can be established, i.e. demonstrate ability to sell or to use it.
5. Availability of resources to complete – technical, financial and other resources.
6. The cost of the development can be reliably measured.

What this means is that, before it is capitalised, it is necessary to establish the amount of the development cost as well as the recoverability of that cost. Remember that what is identified as development costs is usually the cost of producing prototypes to obtain assurance on technical feasibility and market acceptability, before commercial production commences.

There are three points relating to development costs that should be remembered:

1. Having capitalised the costs incurred during the development phase, the entity is obliged to commence amortising that cost as soon as commercial exploitation of it begins, over the expected economic life of that intangible asset, i.e. over the period during which the benefits are expected to flow.
2. The cost of any assets, e.g. equipment acquired for assisting with research efforts, should be capitalised and depreciated under the usual rules stated in respect of Property, plant and equipment (Chapter 21).
3. Where research is carried out on the basis of a contract with a third party and the costs incurred can be fully recovered from that party, the costs incurred even in the research phase can be recognised as an asset – though not as an intangible asset, but as work in progress reported as a current assets.

It is worth noting that the Accounting Standards in the USA require development costs to be expensed and the Standards in the UK[6] permit a choice between capitalising and expensing. IAS 38, on the other hand, requires obligatory capitalisation, if all six of the conditions are fully met. Let us inquire into the merits and demerits of each of these positions.

22.6 The case against capitalising development costs

The case for expensing development costs can be made as follows:

1. Development costs need to be expensed because unless there is an assurance of future economic benefits they would not qualify for recognition as an asset.
2. Expenses on research and development, like advertising, are no more than expenses necessary to maintain the market position of any business. For example, the market position commanded by Sony television may be in peril if a rival model develops a television capable of responding to oral command.
3. Research and development costs would not always qualify for recognition as an asset because there is no assurance of future economic benefit. Empirical evidence gathered in the USA in the 1970s revealed that only a small percentage of research projects prove technically feasible, only a small percentage of such technically feasible projects prove commercially viable and only a small percentage of such commercially viable projects are

finally implemented. The findings of that survey were that only 2% of new product ideas and 15% of product development projects were commercially successful. Given such poor correlation between the research projects and the economic benefits yielded by them, there is insufficient justification for recognising the cost of these projects as assets.

4. Capitalising the development costs could imperil a company's liquidity if it makes decisions on such matters as dividend distribution without considering the cash flow implications of the amounts tied up in development projects. Rolls-Royce found itself in such a situation in the 1960s. This is why there is a requirement in company law[7] that distributable profit should be identified after deducting from profit identified by a company any development costs capitalised by it.
5. Many companies prefer to expense development costs both for maintaining the secrecy of their efforts in this area and because capitalisation would unfavourably affect a number of accounting ratios such as ROCE (Chapter 12).

22.7 The case for capitalising development costs

The capitalisation of development cost is advocated on the following grounds:

1. Capitalisation of development costs is necessary for properly matching revenue earned with related expenses. The Society of British Aerospace Companies[8] pointed out that it takes at least five years to design and develop a new model of aircraft and after development the aircraft continues to sell for about ten years and its spares continue to sell many years more. In these circumstances, unless the cost of developments is deferred (reported as an asset in the meantime) to be matched with the benefits when they arise perhaps decades later, the following consequences would ensue:
   - The income arising in those future years would not be properly matched with expenses incurred to earn it. As a result the performance in the period of development would be understated and those when the benefits are reaped overstated.
   - There would be an understatement of the company's resources on its Statement of financial position because of its failure to report as an asset resources capable of yielding future benefits.
2. The capitalisation of development cost is necessary also if the Statement of financial position and the Statement of income are to show a true and fair view. Expensing development costs in the year in which these are incurred would understate the capital employed by the company. This was one reason why Rolls-Royce lobbied hard for permission to defer its development costs because the defence contracts it was seeking worked on the basis of reimbursement of cost plus a profit margin which was calculated at a percentage of the capital employed in the company.
3. Insistence that development costs must be written off in the periods in which they are incurred could discourage development efforts, because expensing development costs would lower profit levels, depress earnings per share and diminish the stature of the company in the investment market.
4. It would appear to be an anomaly to insist that a company should write off the cost of its own development efforts and to permit it to report as an asset the total cost of acquiring an asset developed by a third party at a price which includes that party's cost of developing it.

Activity 22.2 Why such a hype on the accounting treatment of research and development (R&D) cost?

What a company spends on its research and development activities is no different from what is spent on other areas such as salaries and advertising. Why is there such a hype and importance attached to the accounting treatment of costs in this area?

Activity 22.3 Capitalising the development cost

Able plc, a pharmaceutical company, was searching for a medication capable of reducing the level of LDL cholesterol in the bloodstream. On 1 January 2009 it paid £360,000 to acquire equipment for carrying out research. During 2009 £146,000 was incurred on researching the medication and in 2010 £98,000 on developing the prototype of the successfully identified medication. £21,000 of the development cost was incurred prior to 1 March 2010 when the project met the asset recognition criteria. Further development costs of £121,000 were incurred on this project in 2011. The product launched in January 2012 with the expectation that its market will continue for not less than five years with revenue covering the total cost almost threefold. The research equipment is expected to have a useful life of five years and would usually be depreciated using the straight-line method.

Required: At what value will the project assets be reported on the company's Statement of financial position as at 31 December 2012?

Clue: Depreciation of equipment is included in the development cost from the day it met the asset recognition criteria.

Activity 22.4 Amortisation and impairment of development cost

In addition to the information provided in Activity 22.3, you are informed that, besides depreciation of equipment, further development costs of £36,000 were incurred in 2012 by Able plc on the same project up to the date of launch of the medication on 30 April 2012. The commercial viability of the product is estimated to be five years.

Required:

(a) Show how these transactions will be reported on the Statement of income for the year ended 31 December 2012 and the Statement of financial position as at that date.

(b) On 1 January 2013 it was learnt that because of an alternative product launched by a rival, the recoverable amount of the product launched by Able is estimated at £200,000 on this date and the commercial life of the product two years from that date. How will these developments be reported on Able plc's financial statements in the year ended 31 December 2013?

(c) By January 2014, the rival product was discredited and on that basis, the recoverable amount from Able plc's product was revised to £160,000 and the useful life expected to last until the end of December 2017. How will the development cost feature in the Statement of income for the year ended 31 December 2014 and the Statement of financial position as at that date?

Activity 22.5 Research activity carried out on behalf of third parties

Pharma plc, engaged in the production of pharmaceutical drugs, has been contracted by the World Health Organisation (WHO) to search for an immediate remedy for the common cold. Under this contract WHO will reimburse Pharma the full cost incurred by them on research as well as development of the drug, irrespective of its success. During the year ended 30 June 2012, Pharma has incurred £348,000 on this effort with very limited success.

Required: Explain how this cost should be treated when Pharma plc prepares its financial statements for the year ended 30 June 2012.

22.8 Government grants – alternative approaches to accounting

A *government grant* is any form of assistance, in money or in other forms, received by an entity from the government (including its agencies and similar bodies whether local, national or international). It may be received by the entity usually because it has complied with specified conditions (e.g. providing employment to the disabled) or as an inducement to secure future compliance. The aim of providing the assistance is usually to induce the entity to pursue a course of action that may be socially and economically desirable. For example a grant may be given as an inducement for the entity to locate its activities in a particular area, either to create more employment or to achieve a balanced growth. Or the grant may be intended to nurture small industrial projects or to encourage modernisation of industrial machinery for the purpose of restoring competitive edge. Any government assistance, if it can be measured in money terms, needs to be properly accounted for so that:

(a) the impact of that assistance on the performance and position of the entity may be reported;

(b) it becomes possible to make comparisons with prior periods and with other entities.

There are two alternative approaches to accounting for government grant: the capital approach and the income approach.

22.8.1 The capital approach

This is where the amount received as grant is reported on the Statement of financial position as part of the reserves. Those advocating this approach claim that:

- The grant, when related to an asset, is usually a way of financing the asset.
- It would be inappropriate to regard the grant as income because it is often not earned but represents an incentive to take a course of action.

22.8.2 The income approach

This is where the grant is reported as an income and included in the Statement of income, either immediately upon receipt or in suitable instalments. The case for taking this approach to accounting is made is as follows:

- Grants are usually not gratuitous. They need to be earned by compliance with specified conditions that would involve a cost and hence there is a need to match these costs with appropriate portions of the grant.
- Since taxes are regarded as expenses, it is logical to treat as income any grant which is an extension of the fiscal policy of the government.
- It is not logical to add grants directly to capital because they do not represent funds provided by the owners.

The Accounting Standard[9] upholds the income approach.

22.9 Asset-related government grants

Where the government grant takes the form of transfer of an asset (e.g. land) or assistance to acquire an asset, the Standard[9] requires the accounting to be on the income approach, adopting either the *deferral method* or the *offset method*.

(a) **The deferral method of accounting.** This method requires that the grant should be recorded as a deferred income, and in each accounting period, a portion of the grant should be treated as income on a systematic and rational basis over the life of the related asset. One way of doing this is to transfer to the Statement of income in each accounting period a portion of the deferred income according to how depreciation on the related asset is measured. For example, if the asset is depreciated at 10% of cost, then treat as income for that period 10% of the related grant, the remainder being reported as a liability in the Statement of financial position; and any portion of the grant expected to be treated as income in the next accounting period as a current liability and the remainder as non-current.

For illustration let us assume that a charity received a government grant of £25,000 to buy a vehicle and that it acquired the vehicle for £40,000, opting to depreciate it at 20% of cost. If the charity's choice is the deferral method for accounting for the grant, its Statement of income would report £8,000 as depreciation expense and £5,000 as income from grant; while its Statement of financial position at the year-end will report £15,000 of the grant as a non-current liability and £5,000 as a current liability.

(b) **The offset method of accounting.** This alternative method deducts the grant, when received, from the cost of the related asset, so that the net cost is the amount that is depreciated in each period. If we use the same charity for illustration, assuming this time the charity's choice is the offset method, it would offset the grant from the cost of the vehicle, so that the net cost of the vehicle (£40,000 less £25,000) will be depreciated, reporting a depreciation expense of £3,000 in the Statement of income, while the vehicle will be stated on the Statement of financial position at £12,000.

The International Accounting Standard permits a choice of either of the two methods, pointing out that irrespective of the method chosen by the charity, its reported performance would remain identical because the net expense included in the Statement of income would be £3,000. However, each of the two methods has its detractors.

Problems with the deferral method

- The grant could relate to an asset (e.g. land) which is not depreciated. IAS 20 suggests that the land may have been received as a grant which requires compliance with certain conditions and, in that case, the grant may be treated as income in the periods when costs are incurred to meet the specified conditions. This situation is met with by most public utilities. Public utilities like Thames Water do not depreciate their infrastructure assets such as underground pipes and yet receive grants towards their effort. The grant would be conditional on incurring specific expenses (such as on maintenance of the infrastructure assets at specific levels of performance). Accordingly the grant is regarded as income in each period in a way that matches the corresponding costs.
- When the grant is reported on the deferral method, the remainder of the amount not treated as income in the period needs to be reported as a liability. This would not comply with the accepted definition of a liability because, in the case of a grant, there is no present obligation to transfer the economic benefit.[10] To illustrate let us assume that X plc receives a grant of £10 million on condition that its activities are located in Cardiff, with a proviso that if it leaves Cardiff within ten years, a proportion of the grant should be refunded. If in the first year it treats 10% of the grant as income, it needs to report the remainder (£900,000) as a liability, though it has no obligation to pay it back. Of course it is obliged to refund the grant if it leaves Cardiff, but as at the end of the first year the obligating event (leaving Cardiff) has not occurred and, therefore, the obligation is not a present obligation as at the date of reporting.

Problem with offset method

The legal opinion obtained by the Consultative Committee of Accountancy Bodies in the UK is that the adoption of the offset method breaches the requirements of company law in two places: (a) company law requires non-current assets to be reported at purchase price or production costs; (b) company law states that there shall be no offset of an asset against a liability or an income from an expense. This prompted the Accounting Standard on government grants in the UK[11] to advise that the offset method is not available to companies. Nevertheless most public untilities in the UK (including Thames Water plc, Severn Trent plc) are continuing to adopt the offset method when accounting for grants and capital contributions from the government as an offset from the costs incurred by them on infrastructure assets. Other companies (e.g. Courtaulds) also adopt the offset method.

Activity 22.6 Reporting an asset-related grant on deferral method

Winterblues is a charity providing warm food and soup to the homeless and destitute. It prepares financial statements annually on 31 December. On 1 April 2011 it received from its local borough a grant of £60,000 for a vehicle which it acquired on the same date for £80,000. It would usually depreciate vehicles of this class using the straight-line method and assuming an economic life of five years.

Required: Set out the extracts of the charity's Statement of income for 2011 and the Statement of financial position as at the year-end, reporting on the deferral method.

Activity 22.7 Reporting an asset-related grant on the offset method

Accepting the circumstances as reported in Activity 22.6, but assuming that Winterblues uses the offset method for reporting grants, set out related extracts in the Statement of income for 2011 and the Statement of financial position as at the year-end.

22.10 Income-related government grants

22.10.1 Examples of income-related grants

An entity may receive a grant which is not related to any asset, in any one or more of the following circumstances:

(a) As an inducement to incur certain expenses, e.g. clean up the effluence before it drains out into the public waterways or engage in charitable activities, or provide relief to those less fortunate.

(b) For provision of financial relief to an entity particularly when its continuity is at peril – as happened in 2009 with many high street banks and with Rolls-Royce in the early 1960s.

22.10.2 The accounting requirements for income-related grants

These are as follows:

(a) The grant should be recognised as income of the period to which it relates (accruals basis). Recognising the grant as income, on a receipts basis, would not be acceptable unless there is no basis for recognising the grant as income other than in the period in which it is received.

(b) Recognise the grant as income on a systematic and rational basis over the periods necessary to match it with related costs.

(c) A grant received as compensation for expenses or losses already incurred or for the purpose of giving financial support to an entity (involving no future costs) should be recognised as income in the period in which the grant becomes receivable.

(d) The income-related grant may be presented in the Statement of income in one of two ways:

  (i) separately as an income under a general heading such as 'other income'; or
  (ii) as a deduction when reporting the related expense.

Both methods are acceptable so long as it assists with proper understanding of the situation.

22.11 Other requirements on accounting for grants

1. **Non-cash grants.** When a grant is received in kind (rather than cash), say in the form of land or other resources, it may be accounted for at the fair value (market value) of what is received or at a nominal amount.
2. **Conditions for receiving a grant.** Grants are not to be accounted for unless there is reasonable assurance that (a) the entity will comply with the conditions attaching to the grant; and (b) the grant will be received.
3. **Disclosures required.** There shall be a disclosure of:
   (a) the accounting policy relating to accounting for grant, including whether the method used for accounting is the deferral or the offset;
   (b) the nature and extent of government assistance accounted for;
   (c) other assistance from which the entity has benefited;
   (d) unfulfilled conditions relating to grants that have been recognised.

Summary

- Intangible assets (other than goodwill) can only be included in the Statement of financial position if they are (a) identifiable and (b) meet in full all three capitalisation criteria.
- Internally generated goodwill and other intangibles are required to be expensed.
- When acquired as part of a business that has been acquired (known as a business combination) goodwill is capitalised.
- When acquired as part of a business combination other intangible assets are also capitalised provided their fair value can be reliably established.
- Intangible assets acquired separately are capitalised at cost.
- Development cost must be capitalised if it meets six specified criteria.
- Government grants are accounted for on the income approach, normally on an accruals basis, using either the deferral method or the offset method.

References

1. IAS 38, *Intangible Assets*, revised 2004, effective 1.4.2004, London, International Accounting Standards Board.
2. IFRS 3, *Business Combinations*, 2004, London, International Accounting Standards Board.
3. IAS 38, *Intangible Assets*, paragraph 35.
4. IAS 38, *Intangible Assets*, paragraph 68.
5. IAS 38, *Intangible Assets*, paragraph 63.
6. SSAP 13 (1977) *Accounting for Research and Development*, London, Accounting Standards Board.
7. Companies Act 2006 section 844, London, The Stationery Office.
8. In a letter dated 15 August 1975 addressed to the Technical Director of the Institute of Chartered Accountants (E&W) protesting against the requirement in their ED14 that all development costs should be expensed.
9. IAS 20, *Accounting for Government Grants and Disclosure of Government Assistance*, revised 1983, effective 1.1.1984, London, International Accounting Standards Board.
10. *Framework for the Preparation and Presentation of Financial Statements*, 1989, London, International Accounting Standards Board.
11. SSAP 4, *The Accounting Treatment of Government Grants*, 1974, London, Accounting Standards Board.
12. The information on R&D expenses, during the year ended 31 May 1994, of some international companies was obtained from a scoreboard, prepared by Company-Reporting (Edinburgh Consultancy) for the Department of Trade and Industry and published in the *Financial Times*.

Suggested answers to activities

22.1 Whether capitalisation of intangibles is permitted

All of the resources referred to by Sasha are intangible assets (no physical substance) and other than goodwill. What needs to be considered on deciding whether these can be capitalised are (i) whether they are identifiable and (ii) whether they meet the capitalisation criteria.

(a) The list of customers is not identifiable because it cannot be sold, assigned or transferred without selling the whole business as a going concern. Besides, Sasha would not have control over future custom nor will she be assured that future economic benefit will flow from that list. Sasha has no way of having control over or protecting the loyalty of the customers on the list. Hence this resource cannot be capitalised.

(b) The catering contracts to hospitals are government-granted intangibles. They are identifiable assets, although they may not be separable (i.e. to sell, assign or transfer), because they arise from a contract. They meet the capitalisation criteria because the economic benefits from the contracts are within Sasha's control, future economic benefit in the form of regular earnings is assured, and the cost may be reliably established as the amount that Sasha would have been willing to pay for them as a separate acquisition. Therefore, the contracts, though recorded at a nominal value as an asset in the books of SS, can be capitalised in the books of Sasha, at the amount she would be willing to pay to acquire them separately. However, in the absence of an assurance that the contract will be renewed, any value placed on the asset should be amortised over the four years remaining on the current contract.

(c) The logo and the associated brand is an identifiable asset because it is separable – it is possible to sell, assign or transfer it, without disposing of the whole business as a going concern, although, to be economically effective, it would normally be acquired as part of a whole business. For example, the acquisition of the brand name 'St Michael' may not be effective unless acquired with the whole business of Marks and Spencer. Besides it satisfies the capitalisation criteria because the brand would be within Sasha's control (may have been registered), and it has a proven track record of generating income. IAS 38 states that if an intangible asset acquired as part of a business combination has a finite life (Sasha estimates the life of the brand as 20 years) there is a rebuttable presumption that the fair value of that asset can be reliably estimated. There is then a case for reporting the brand name at £400,000 – the amount Sasha would have been willing to pay to acquire it separately.

(d) The amount paid for cultivating customer loyalty cannot be capitalised because it would not establish control over the custom, there would be no assurance that it would generate sales and, more importantly, it would be impossible to identify whether the cost incurred is for generating future cash flows or maintaining the existing custom.

(e) The secret process the SS staff are privy to, no doubt capable of generating cash flows, cannot be capitalised. Admittedly the technical knowledge of a secret process does give assurance of future economic benefit in the form of improvement in sales. But what is lacking is control over the future economic benefit, unless the secret knowledge is protected say by patenting the process.

22.2 Why such hype on the accounting treatment of R&D cost?

The commercial and economic environment today is so intensely competitive and the consuming public so fastidious that no business can hope to survive, let alone thrive, unless they make substantial investment in research and development activities. Shown on the right[12] are some examples of the amounts of outlay some international companies have been making on such activities in one year. The level of investment on this activity is regarded as so crucial to survival that irrespective of whether the related cost is capitalised or expensed, the investors wish to know the outlay on such activity. Accordingly, it is a requirement of company law in the UK that information on costs incurred on research and development, irrespective of whether they are expensed or capitalised, should be communicated within the directors' report of every company. IAS 38 too requires disclosure of such information as part of financial statements.

Research and development expenses of some multinational companies

	£'m	% of sales
General Motors, USA	4,076	4.36%
Daimler-Benz, Germany	3,520	9.25%
Ford Motor, USA	3,394	4.63%
Hitachi, Japan	3,035	6.65%
Siemens, Germany	2,996	9.43%
Glaxo, UK	739	15.00%
SmithKline Beecham, UK	575	9.33%
Zeneca, UK	490	11.00%
Wellcome, UK	325	15.90%

The outlay on these activities is so significant that the financial position and the performance reported in the financial statements will be correspondingly affected by whether the accounting policy of the company is to capitalise or expense their outlay on these activities. If the costs on R&D are expensed, the peformance reported in terms of profit will be lower and correspondingly the EPS will be lesser; whereas the ROCE will be better. If the R&D costs are capitalised, the company would report more as their capital employed and that would affect their ROCE, though their profit and EPS would tend to be better.

22.3 Capitalising development cost

Statement of financial position as at 31 December 2012		
	£'000	£'000
Non-current assets:		
Equipment at cost	360	
Accumulated depreciation[a]	(288)	72
Development cost[c]	330	
Amortisation[d]	(66)	264

(a) Equipment is capitalised and depreciated at 20% per annum for four years to 31.12.2012 £288

(b) Expenses on research phase (£146) and on development until March 2010 are expensed.

(c) Development cost is capitalised as follows:

2010: £98,000 – £21,000
2011:

Depn: 2010: £72,000 × 10/12
2011:

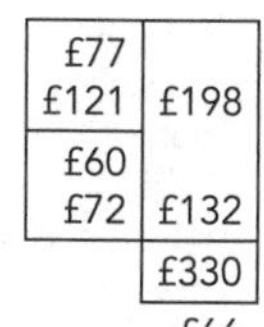
£77
£121 £198
£60
£72 £132
£330

(d) Amortisation: £330,000/5 yrs £66

22.4 Amortisation and impairment of development cost

Statement of income for year ended 31 December			
	2012	2013	2014
	£'000	£'000	£'000
Depn of equipment	(48)[a]	(72)	–
Amortisation	(52)[c]	(100)	(40)
Impairment dev. cost	–	(138)[d]	–
Impairment reversal	–	–	60[f]

(a) Depn of equipment in 2012: 72 less 24 capitalised

(b) Dev. cost: (198 + 36) + depn (132 + 24) = £390,000

(c) Amortisation in 2012: 20% of 390 for 8 mths = £52,000

(d) Impairment in 2013: Cost 390 – Ac. amort. 52 = £338,000

Less recoverable amount £200,000 = £138,000

(e) Acc. Amortisation by 31.12.2013: £52 + £100 = £152,000

(f) Reversal of impairment as at 1.1.2014: Cost £390 – Ac. amort. (£152) – impairment £138 – Recoverable £160

Statement of financial position as at 31 December						
	2012		2013		2014	
	£'000	£'000	£'000	£'000	£'000	£'000
Equipment	360		360		360	
Acc. depreciation	(288)	72	(360)	–	(360)	–
Development cost[b]	390		390		390	
Amortisation	(52)	338	(152)		(192)	
Impairment			(138)	100	(78)	120

22.5 Research activity carried out on behalf of third parties

The transactions in this question are not governed by IAS 38. The costs involved in this transaction are fully recoverable from a client. Hence there need not be any distinction between whether the costs relate to the research or development phase of the drug. The total cost of £348,000 should be reported as a current asset on the year-end Statement of financial position, described as work in progress until the time it is invoiced to WHO when it will be reported as receivables.

22.6 Reporting an asset-related grant on the deferral method

Notes:
(a) Depreciation of vehicle: 20% of £80,000 for 9 months.
(b) Grant treated as income: 20% of £60,000 for 9/12 mths = £9,000.
(c) Reporting of the deferred portion of the grant: as current liability the amount that will be treated as income next year and remainder as non-current liability.

Statement of income for year ended 31.12.11	
	£'000
Depreciation[a]	12
Government grant[b]	9

Statement of financial position as at 31 December 2011	
	£'000
Non-current assets:	
Motor vehicle at cost	80
Accumulated depreciation[a]	(12)
	68
Non-current liabilities:	
Deferred income – grant[c]	39
Current liabilities:	
Deferred income – grant	12

22.7 Reporting an asset-related grant on the offset method

Notes:
(a) The cost of the vehicle is reported net of the grant.
(b) Depreciation: 20% of £20,000 for nine months = £3,000.

Statement of income to 31.12.2011	
	£'000
Depreciation[b]	3

Statement of financial position as at 31.12.2011	
	£'000
Motor vehicle[a]	20
Accumulated depreciation[b]	(3)
	17

Multiple choice questions

The concept – intangibles including goodwill and research and development cost

22.1 Which of the assets named below is not an intangible asset?

(a) Brand name ☐
(b) Inventory ☐
(c) Goodwill ☐
(d) Patent ☐

22.2 Which of the following statements relating to intangible assets is/are correct?

(a) Research on market potential, prior to launching a product, can be capitalised
(b) Applied research, calculated to achieve a stated aim, can be capitalised
(c) An asset should never be capitalised if it has no physical existence
(d) A resource, though intangible, may be capitalised if it qualifies to be capitalised, if it is identifiable and meets the capitalisation criteria

w	a only	
x	a & d	
y	b & c	
z	d only	

22.3 Which of the following qualities should an asset possess for it to qualify for recognition as an asset?

(a) It should have physical existence
(b) It should be within the entity's control
(c) It should always be separable, i.e. realisable without selling the whole business
(d) There should be a probability of future economic benefit from it

w	a & b	
x	c & d	
y	b & c	
z	b & d	

22.4 Which of the intangibles named below is the only one which may be capitalised, at least initially, though (i) it is not separable, (ii) there is no active market in it and (iii) flow of economic benefit from it is not probable?

(a) Home-grown goodwill
(b) Separately acquired brand
(c) Goodwill acquired with a business
(d) Government-granted intangible

22.5 A company paid £10 million to acquire a reputed brand name. Although there is no active market in that asset it is permitted to report the brand name as an asset for which two of the following reasons?

(a) It was so very expensive to acquire
(b) Its cost has been established by a market transaction
(c) It is a name of such high market reputation
(d) Future economic benefits from it are probable because otherwise it would not have been acquired at such a cost

w	a & b	
x	b & d	
y	b & c	
z	a & d	

22.6 Which of the following intangibles are prohibited from being recognised as an asset?

(a) Home-grown goodwill
(b) Separately acquired intangibles
(c) Internally generated intangibles
(d) Goodwill acquired as part of an ongoing business

w	a & b	
x	c & d	
y	a & c	
z	b & d	

22.7 For which of the following reasons is the recognition as an asset of an internally generated intangible prohibited?

(a) Because there may not be an active market for that asset
(b) Because its cost is usually relatively insignificant
(c) Because it is difficult to reliably identify the related costs
(d) Because it is difficult to establish the probability of flow of economic benefits

w	a & b	
x	c & d	
y	b & c	
z	b & d	

22.8 Which of the following are essential for recognising an intangible asset (other than goodwill) when a business is acquired as a going concern?

(a) There is a probability that future economic benefits would arise from it
(b) It should have been reported as an asset by the business acquired
(c) Its value should have been stated on the agreement for buying the business
(d) There should be a reliable basis for valuing it

w	a & d	
x	c & d	
y	b & c	
z	b & d	

22.9 Expenses on which of those listed below should be capitalised?

(a) Pure research

(b) Applied research

(c) Development cost

(d) Applied research and development cost

22.10 A company is searching for a white board marker the writings of which, instead of being rubbed off, may be blown out when lecturers breathe on them from a distance. Which of the following expenses incurred by the company qualifies to be classified as development cost?

(a) Mixing chemicals to study how they react to human breath

(b) Advertising the product to study whether there is a market for it

(c) Buying equipment and chemicals for use on this project

(d) Production of sample markers to be distributed free to learn of customer reaction

22.11 Which of the following need to be established before development costs are capitalised?

(a) A customer should have ordered the development of the product

(b) The cost of the product should be reliably identified

(c) The business should have all necessary resources to complete the project

(d) The business should be committed to completing the development

w	a, c & d	
x	b, c & d	
y	b & c	
z	a, b & d	

22.12 If a development projects meets with all the conditions stipulated in IAS 38, the requirement of the standard is that the costs of that project:

(a) shall be fully written off as expense

(b) shall be fully capitalised

(c) may be capitalised depending on company's policy

(d) may be partly capitalised and partly expensed

22.13 Which of the following are valid reasons for capitalising development costs?

(a) For properly matching the cost of a development with benefits arising therefrom

(b) To ensure that resources available for generating income are fully reported

(c) Otherwise there will be reluctance to develop new projects

(d) Otherwise there would be an anomaly between a developed asset and purchased one

w	a, c & d	
x	b, c & d	
y	All four	
z	a, b & d	

22.14 Which of the following are reasons for writing off research and development costs as expenses?

(a) Poor co-relation between costs and delayed flow of economic benefit

(b) It may not always be probable that there will be a flow of future economic benefit

(c) To keep the cost of development a secret from rival companies

(d) Otherwise the liquidity of the company could be at peril

w	a, c & d	
x	b, c & d	
y	All four	
z	a, b & d	

22.15 The cost of goodwill purchased as part of an acquisition of an ongoing business shall:

(a) Never be amortised, but there shall be an annual impairment review
(b) Be amortised over 20 years
(c) Be amortised over 40 years
(d) Be written off immediately after the acquisition

22.16 Intangible assets, other than goodwill, acquired as part of an ongoing business or acquired separately:

(a) Should be never amortised
(b) Should be amortised systematically over their estimated useful life
(c) Should be written off over not more than five years
(d) Should be reviewed for impairment if their useful life is regarded as indefinite

w	a, c & d	
x	b & d	
y	b & c	
z	a, b & d	

22.17 Which of the following statements with regard to accounting for goodwill and other intangibles is not correct?

(a) Impairment written off in respect of an intangible can be corrected when circumstances change
(b) The cost of an intangible asset with an indefinite life must be regularly reviewed
(c) Amortisation is the name given to depreciation of an intangible asset
(d) An amount expensed can be added back to cost when the intangible meets asset recognition criteria

Concept – government grant

22.18 Which of the following is not a government grant?

(a) Cost-free land allocated to build a staff health care centre
(b) A cost-free licence received from a local borough to operate a taxi service
(c) Compensation received from a property developer to gain access to land
(d) An amount received towards the cost of cleaning factory effluence before draining it into a nearby river

22.19 Which of the following would be the justification for accounting for government grants on the 'income approach' rather than the 'capital approach'?

(a) If tax paid to government is an expense then grant received from them is an income
(b) Grant is earned by complying with what the grant-giving authority instructs
(c) Grant cannot be regarded as part of the capital invested by the owner
(d) Grant needs to be matched with related expenses

w	a, c & d	
x	b, c & d	
y	All four	
z	a, b & d	

22.20 Government grants should normally be accounted on an accruals basis. Which of the following grants received would you account on a receipts basis?

(a) Received by a charity to operate one of its identified activities
(b) Received in the form of land for a business to relocate to a deprived area
(c) Received to make good past losses to keep the business from closure
(d) Received to enhance the literacy and communication skills of staff

22.21 IAS 20 permits the reporting of government grant either on the deferral method or on the offset method. As accountant of a limited company which of the following reasons will prompt you to opt for the deferral method rather than the offset method?

(a) Under the offset method the asset will not be reported at its real cost

(b) Under the offset method the company's profit will be understated

(c) On the offset method the depreciation expense is netted against income from grant

(d) The deferral method would identify the liability that needs to be refunded if the terms of the grant are not complied with

w	c & d	
x	b, c & d	
y	All four	
z	a & c	

22.22 With regard to government grants and accounting for them which of the following statements is inaccurate?

(a) Assistance in cash or kind received from government or others is known as a government grant

(b) A government grant should preferably be accounted for on an accruals basis

(c) When a grant is not in cash the grant should always be accounted for at a nominal value

(d) The asset-related grant may be reported either on the deferral method or offset method

Answers to multiple choice questions
22.1: b 22.2: z 22.3: z 22.4: c 22.5: x 22.6: y 22.7: x 22.8: w 22.9: c 22.10: d 22.11: x 22.12: b 22.13: y 22.14: z 22.15: a 22.16: x 22.17: d 22.18: c 22.19: y 22.20: c 22.21: z 22.22: c

Progressive questions

PQ 22.1 Accounting for intangibles

Explain the circumstances in which you would capitalise the cost of:

1. A reputed brand name acquired as part of a business combination and expected to have a useful life of at least 20 years
2. Acquiring a patent for manufacturing a product that has significant market potential
3. Regular gifts given and parties conducted to maintain customer loyalty
4. Research to improve the customer satisfaction with products of the company

PQ 22.2 Accounting for research and development costs (ACCA 1)

Lion is a company producing medicinal drugs. At 1 October 2010 the following balances existed in the records:

- Deferred development expenditure £1,200,000. See details in the box on the right.
- Equipment used in research £300,000 (cost £500,000, depreciation to date £200,000).

> Project Q: £800,000. This is the balance remaining of expenditure totalling £ one million on a completed project which is being amortised on the straight line basis over 10 years.
>
> Project R: £400,000. This is the accumulated costs to 30 September 2010 of developing a new drug. The project was completed in July 2011 and sales of the drug are expected to begin in January 2012.

During the year ended 30 September 2011 the following costs were incurred:

Project R: Costs to complete £250,000.
Project S: (a research project) £140,000.

Purchase of testing equipment for use in the research department £180,000.

Estimated useful life of equipment is five years, and full depreciation is charged in the year of acquisition.

Required:

(a) Calculate the figures to be included in Lion's Statement of income for the year ended 30 September 2011, the Statement of financial position as at that date, and state the headings under which they will appear.

(b) Prepare disclosure notes required by IAS 38 Intangible assets (note on accounting policy is not required).

PQ 22.3 Costs in research phase and development phases

Statement of financial position as at 30 June 2012	
	£'000
Non-current assets	2,050
Development costs	980
Current assets	824
	3,854
	£'000
Share capital	4,000
Retained loss	(452)
	3,548
Current liabilties	306
	3,854

Jason, Jim and Jones are the only shareholders of a private limited company, operating under the name Triple Jay Computers Ltd. They are manufacturers and dealers in both computer hardware and software. Their draft Statement of financial position, as at the end of the first year's operations, is shown on the left.

The company has incurred considerable costs on research and development activities and strongly advocates that the total cost of these activities should be reported as an asset. Their main concern is that if these costs are expensed they would be reporting an even worse performance.

Particulars of the amount reported as R&D costs are as follows:

1. Market research to target products to particular customer groups and specific needs	£128,400
2. Research to keep product quality in line with market expectation	£75,450
3. Ongoing operational research to improve durability and performance of hardware	£256,250
4. Experimental work to observe the impact of environmental changes on microchips	£36,400
5. Search for computer hardware capable of responding to oral command	£128,650
6. (a) Search for hardware capable of operating 2,000 leagues under the seabed	£194,950
(b) Construction of prototypes of above mentioned hardware	£48,000
7. Cost of quality tests that all products are subjected to prior to delivery to customers	£78,800
8. Costs of corrective and remedial action to products during the guarantee period	£33,100
	£980,000

Required:

(a) Advise the company on how the costs reported by them as R&D should be treated in accounts.

(b) Re-draft the Statement of financial position in compliance with your advice.

PQ 22.4 Accounting for grants

Salvage Society was registered as a charity on 1 January 2011 when some retired persons in Wimbledon contributed £72,200 for the purpose. The amount was placed in a bank and recorded as an Accumulated fund. The following is a summary of the activities in the year ended 31 December 2011:

1. On 1 January it acquired its own premises for £420,000, receiving 75% of the amount as a grant from the London Borough of Merton. The Society attributes a third of the cost to land and proposes to depreciate the cost of the building at 2% p.a. using the straight-line method.

2. The London Borough of Merton has agreed also to support the activities of the Society, making an annual grant of £25,000. A cheque for that amount, received on 7 May 2011, was in respect of the Borough's financial year ending on 31 March 2012.
3. Donations and charitable contributions received during the year amount to £69,800; while the Society's expenses are summarised on the right.

Staff salary	£10,000
On provision of meals to homeless	£21,520
Expenses on charitable activities	£41,660
Administrative expenses	£9,440

4. Salary is paid to the Administrative Secretary, appointed on 1 March 2011 at a salary of £1,000 per month. The Department of Social Welfare has agreed to bear 80% of the salary. A cheque for £9,600 was received from the Department in November 2011.
5. During the year the Society has provided 26,250 meals to homeless persons. Hunger Relief, another registered charity, has agreed to share this cost, at 50p per meal provided, and a cheque for £11,250 was received in December 2011.

Required: Prepare
(a) the Statement of income of the Society for the year ending 31 December 2011, including in its Accumulated fund any surplus arising from its activities in the year;
(b) the Statement of financial position as at that date.

Test questions

Test 22.1 The capitalisation criteria for costs on the development phase

The year-end Trial Balance of Cavalier plc, as at 30 June 2012, reports Development costs at an amount of £780,000. The break-down of this amount is as shown on the right.

	Notes	£'000	£'000
Project 312	(a)		225
Project 339:			
Balance b/f	(b)	312	
Expenses in 2011	(c)	78	390
Project 346			
Bank	(d)	45	
Equipment	(e)	120	165
			780

You are informed as follows:

(a) The commercial exploitation of Project 312 commenced on 1 July 2010. The cost of this project is being amortised over ten years using the straight-line method.
(b) The Project 339 fully met the capitalisation criteria on 1 July 2011 and commercial exploitation of the project is expected to commence by 2014.
(c) The costs relating to Project 339, which had been written off before the project met the capitalisation criteria, have now been capitalised.
(d) Project 346 is a new one, on which £45,000 has been incurred exploring the technical feasibility as well as the market potential. Cavalier has all the resources as well as the commitment to complete this project.
(e) £120,000 is the cost of equipment acquired for Project 346 on 1 January 2012. The equipment is expected to have a useful life of four years, no scrap value and is usually depreciated using the straight-line method.

Required: Advise Cavalier plc on how it should treat the above information when preparing the financial statements for the year ended 30 June 2012.

Test 22.2 Accounting for intangibles

Alpha plc paid £900,000 to acquire the whole of the equity in Beta plc on 31 December 2011, when the net assets of Beta plc were reported as shown on the right. As at the date of acquisition:

	£'000
Ordinary shares of £1	400
Share premium account	80
Retained earnings	220

(a) Beta plc reports at £80,000 development costs which fail to meet the capitalisation criteria of the Alpha group.

(b) Certain brand names owned by Beta, but not reported in their books, are, in the opinion of Alpha's directors, worth £90,000 and are expected to have a useful life of ten more years.

(c) The staff with Beta are in possession of knowledge of certain manufacturing processes which could be exploited to good advantage for generating substantial profit. Prior to acquisition, the directors of Alpha were willing to pay £100,000 to acquire that knowledge.

Required: Identify the amount Alpha paid to acquire the goodwill in Beta, explaining your treatment of items stated as (a), (b) and (c).

Chapter 23

Liability, provision, contingency and post reporting-date events

By the end of this chapter

You should learn:

- When a liability may be referred to as a provision
- Of the need to standardise accounting for provisions
- What a contingency is and that contingency is not accounted for, but disclosed, unless remote

You should be able to:

- Identify a liability and determine when it should be recognised in the books of account
- Identify events after the reporting period and those which affect information on financial statements and others which need to be disclosed

23.1 What is a liability?

A liability is an obligation to transfer economic benefit. The obligation may be satisfied in a number of ways, for example by payment, the transfer of an asset such as land or providing a service. Not all liabilities are recognised, however, in the financial statements as there is a requirement in IAS37[1] that an obligation to transfer economic benefit should be recognised and accounted for as a liability only when it meets all four of the following conditions, which we shall refer to as liability recognition criteria:

1. It should be *a present obligation to transfer economic benefits*. The emphasis is on the word present, i.e. the obligation should already exist on the date of reporting. The obligation need not necessarily be a legal one such as the amount legally payable when goods have been purchased. The obligation may also be a constructive one. A constructive obligation is one which arises either from an established pattern of past practice or from anything that created a valid expectation in the minds of third parties that the entity will meet the obligation (e.g. like Richard Branson's promise to pay three billion USD to fight global warming).

   An example of a commonly met constructive obligation is some manufacturers' willingness to remedy free of charge any manufacturing defects, even when these arise outside the warranty period.

2. The obligation should *arise from a past transaction or event*. For example, the act of purchasing is the transaction that gives rise to the obligation to pay the supplier. An accident on work premises, giving rise to an obligation to compensate the injured party, is an event triggering the obligation. The transaction or event giving rise to the obligation is known as the obligating event, and the requirement is that the event should have happened prior to the reporting date. This is why final dividends proposed by the directors of a company do not qualify for recognition as a liability because the obligating event is the resolution of shareholders which would not take place until many weeks after the date of the Statement of financial position.
3. The obligation to transfer should be at least *probable (if not certain)*. The word probable means that 'it is more likely than not that a present obligation exists on the reporting date'. The crucial test to establish whether the present obligation exists is that there should be no realistic alternative to settling the amount owed.
4. It should be possible to make a *reliable estimate of the amount* of the obligation. The estimation could be on the basis of a contract, an invoice, an agreement, past experience or expert advice.

Activity 23.1 Recognition as a liability

When you were interviewed on 7 May 2011 for the position of head of the accounts department you learnt that those who held the position before you were sent for induction to the parent company in the United States at a cost of £20,000. You assumed duties on 1 June 2011 and your employment contract stipulates your salary at £84,000 per annum with a year-end bonus, on satisfactory completion of each year's service, calculated at 25% of your earnings in that year.

Required: Explain how much should be accounted for as a liability in the year ended 30 June 2011 and set out, in the form of a journal entry, how the liability should be accounted for.

23.2 Referring to a liability as a provision

A liability is referred to as a *provision* only when there is uncertainty as regards its *timing and amount*.[2] Hence, to be accounted for as a provision the amount involved should:

(a) qualify to be identified as a liability, i.e. meet all four criteria stated in 23.1, and

(b) there should be uncertainty as to the *timing* of the payment or its *amount* or both.

The insistence that to be identified as a provision the obligation should first qualify for recognition as a liability is mainly to prevent manipulation of profit. One form of manipulation is what accountants refer to as attempts at *income smoothing*. Income smoothing is a deliberate effort to report smooth trends in earnings from year to year, by setting up provisions (say for intended company reorganisation or asset refurbishment) in a period when earnings are higher and releasing the provision to improve earnings in periods when the earnings are lower.

To be referred to as a provision, rather than as payables or accruals, there has to be an uncertainty as regards when the obligation has to be met or the amount at which it has to be met or both. It is important to note that the uncertainty cannot relate to *whether* there will be a payment because then the item would fail to satisfy one of the liability recognition criteria. Similarly, unless the amount is measurable with *some degree of reliability* the item fails a liability recognition criterion.

The problem of uncertainty as to amount is resolved by accounting for the *best estimate* of the amount at which the entity could settle the obligation on the reporting date. In assessing that amount the entity uses management's judgement, past experience and, if necessary, expert opinion. However, it is necessary to take into account *all the uncertainty* surrounding the amount. Future events that may affect the amount required to settle the obligation should also be taken into account where there is sufficient objective evidence that such events will occur. For example, if the obligation under consideration is one to remedy manufacturing defects in products sold, due consideration should be given to the possibility that the defect may not be remedied at the very first attempt.

Activity 23.2 The question of whether there is a present obligation

A supermarket receives a claim for £50,000 from a customer in respect of injuries suffered when the shopping trolley dragged him down the travelator. The claim is contested at court. The brakes on the trolley were found to be defective. The supermarket's defence is that there is a constantly repeated announcement to hold on to the hand-railings while using the travelator and, if it had been heeded, the customer's injuries would have been minimal. The legal opinion is that damages awarded could vary between £500 and £4,000 depending on the court's opinion on the extent of blame to be attached to the supermarket.

Required: What is your opinion on whether there is a present obligation arising from a past event?

Activity 23.3 Account as a liability or a provision?

Michael Orwell is a farmer carrying out field trials of genetically modified corn. One of his neighbours, an organic farmer, has obtained a court order

(i) restraining Michael from sowing more GM seeds and

(ii) awarding damages to be assessed when Michael harvests his crop.

The damages would be the difference in selling price between organically certified corn and non-certified corn. The amount will not be known for certain until the harvest in the summer but the best estimate, based on acreage and the expected market prices, is £3,000.

Required:

(a) Bearing in mind that £3,000 is the best estimate of damages payable, explain why the liability should be accounted for and whether it should be described as a provision.

(b) Set out the journal entry accounting for the liability.

Activity 23.4 Provision cannot be set up unless there is a liability

Prentice Printers commenced business on 1 July 2010, acquiring the printing machine on that day for £480,000. The useful life of the machine is estimated at ten years and the total cost of repair and maintenance during the whole life estimated at £120,000. Accordingly, in the financial statements for the year ended 30 June 2011, they have depreciated the machine by £48,000 and have, in addition, set up a provision for machine maintenance of £12,000, being a tenth of the total anticipated cost. The actual cost of maintenance that year was £3,200 which was offset against the provision.

Required: Comment on the correctness of this accounting for provision.

23.3 Accounting for provisions

23.3.1 Provision = a liability + uncertainty

In addition to qualifying for recognition as a liability there has to be uncertainty with regard to either timing or amount or both. An example is the provision for staff pension. On the basis of the employment contract there is definitely an obligation to pay and the obligating event is the performance of service by the employee. There is uncertainty, however, on what the amount would be (because it may depend on length of service and salary at the point of retirement) and also, probably, on when it will be payable (on reaching the usual retirement age or earlier occurrence of a disability).

Activity 23.5 Provision cannot be set up unless there is uncertainty

When preparing the financial statements for the year ended 31 December 2011, Camilus Plc has accounted for

(a) a provision for amounts payable to a supplier because as at the date of reporting the supplier's invoice has not been received;

(b) a provision for office cleaning in the month ended 31 December 2011;

(c) a provision for fitting air-conditioning ducts intended to take place in 2012;

(d) a provision for audit fees of £150,000, because the amount of audit fees payable would not be known until the auditor's invoice is received, after his work is completed.

Required: Comment on the correctness of the accounting for provisions.

23.3.2 Provisions should not be exaggerated

The amount accounted for as the provision should be the best estimate at the reporting date of the amount necessary to settle the obligation or to transfer it to a third party. When measuring the amount of the provision, risks and uncertainties should be taken into account; but taking care not to create excessive provisions to deliberately overstate the liability and understate the profits.

23.3.3 No provision where liability can be prevented by the entity's future actions

For example, if an entity has caused environmental damage prior to the reporting date, a provision will be set up if there is an obligation to pay a penalty. But the entity cannot set up a provision for environmental damages that may be caused after the reporting date because it could, by its own action, prevent the damages.

Activity 23.6 Provision cannot be set up if the obligation can be avoided

City Builders (CB) is engaged in a major civil engineering contract which includes a penalty clause that requires payment of damages if the completion of the contract is delayed. Though as at 31 December 2011 (the reporting date) the contract is progressing well, CB fears that as the contract work progresses it may not be able to avoid the obligation to pay the penalty. Accordingly, when preparing the financial Statements for 2011 CB has set up a provision for penalty amounting to £12 million.

Required: Comment on whether the provision has been set up correctly.

23.3.4 Provision is set up at the best estimate considering probabilities

Where there is a present obligation arising from past transactions or events, but the amount of the obligation is uncertain because it depends on future events which could fall anywhere within a range, the best amount to be accounted for as a provision is identified by giving appropriate weights to each of the possible outcomes.

Activity 23.7 Where the uncertain amount of the obligation needs to be estimated

Gabriels' Bakery is guilty of supplying stale bread to some of its retailers and, as at 31 December 2011, expects to receive claims for compensation. All customers are expected to claim back the amount at which they were invoiced and some expected to claim also compensation for loss of earnings at 10% of the invoiced amount. With a view to maintaining relationships Gabriels would not contest the claims. The position has been summarised as follows:

Retailer groups	Amount of sales	Percentage expected to claim back the sale price	Percentage expected to claim compensation
A	£450,000	100	–
B	£300,000	100	60
C	£250,000	100	40

Required: Explain how the amounts claimed should be treated when preparing the financial statements for the year ended 31 December 2011.

23.3.5 The amount of the provision cannot be reduced by expected gains from related asset

For example, when a manufacturer undertakes to replace defective goods with new ones, within the warranty period, it would have to account for the obligation to replace, estimating the uncertain cost of such replacements. It is possible that the goods replaced could be sold after the defects have been remedied. This possibility as well as the anticipated gains on the sale of the ones replaced cannot be taken into account when identifying the amount set up as provision for warranty.

23.3.6 Accounting for any related recovery

Where all or a part of the obligation, accounted for as a provision, is expected to be reimbursed by a third party (e.g. the obligation to replace defective items sold arose because of defects in the materials purchased to manufacture these items), the amount of the expected reimbursement should reduce the loss accounted for when and only when the reimbursement is virtually certain to be received. In this situation the reimbursement expected should be reported separately, as an asset, in the Statement of financial position.

23.3.7 The amount should be the discounted present value of the obligation

Where the effect of time value of money is material, i.e. where the obligation is to be met say after more than one year, the amount at which the provision should be set up is the amount payable discounted by the applicable rate of interest. For example, if an oil rig constructed at a cost of £50 million needs to be dismantled in five years when the oil well runs dry and if the cost of dismantling the rig is estimated at £5 million, payable five years from now, and the applicable interest rate is 5% per annum, the amount of the provision should be calculated at £3,917,631 (£5,000 × 100/105^5).

23.3.8 A provision can be applied only for the intended purpose

This requirement would guard against another form of manipulation of accounts usually referred to colloquially as *'big bath accounting'*. A situation in which this happens is when a new chief executive wishes to create an accounting environment in which he could keep reporting steadily improving earnings levels, by setting up provisions (often unnecessarily) in the period when he assumed office and using the provision to offset expenses in subsequent periods so that improved earnings can be reported in these periods. Big bath accounting is known to have occurred also when a company acquires another (business combinations), when the acquirer sets up provisions for intended reorganisation of the acquired company or, even worse, sets up a provision for future operating losses – practices that are now prohibited.[3]

23.3.9 Provision for onerous contracts

An onerous contract is one in which the unavoidable costs of meeting the obligations under a contract exceed the economic benefits expected to arise from it. For example, let us assume that an entity has leased office premises, for ten years, at an annual rent of £20,000 payable in arrears, with a condition that if the lease agreement is cancelled prior to completion of the full term the entity has to pay a significant penalty. If the entity has moved away from the leased premises and, as at the reporting date, three years of the lease period remain, the entity is involved in an onerous contract, under which it has an obligation to pay a cancellation penalty or continue to pay £20,000 in each of the three years following the reporting date. Although the settlement of the obligation is after the reporting date, the obligation is a present one on the reporting date because the obligating event is the signing of the lease agreement and that has already taken place. Accordingly the entity needs to account for a liability (not a provision). However, the amount at which the liability should be accounted for would be uncertain, if the lease is transferrable. In that event the amount of the obligation the entity should bear would depend on whether the premises can be sublet and how much can be earned from subletting. In the circumstances the entity has to set up a provision, estimating the loss expected to arise from the onerous contract.

23.3.9 Annual review of the provision

The amount accounted for as a provision should be reviewed at every reporting date and (a) adjusted by increasing or decreasing it to reflect the current best estimates; and (b) reversed when no longer needed.

23.3.10 Disclosures

The disclosures are required in respect of the provisions:

- Movements in the provision during the year, identifying
  - any amount released as no longer required and
  - amount of interest that unwound in the year.

- A description of the nature and when cash outflow is expected.
- An indication of uncertainties (on timing/amount).
- Any expected reimbursements.

23.4 What is a contingent liability?

The word contingency suggests uncertainty, but in this case it is in relation to the obligation rather the timing or amount of the obligation. A contingent liability is *one where the occurrence of the obligation is itself uncertain, being dependent on occurrence of other future event or events*, outside the control of the entity. The Accounting Standard[2] identifies two different categories of contingent liabilities. These are:

(a) A *possible obligation* that arises from a past event but the existence of the obligation will be confirmed only by the occurrence of one or more uncertain future events not wholly within the entity's control.

(b) A *present obligation* failing to meet in full the liability recognition criteria because either the transfer of future economic benefits is less than probable or the amount of the obligation cannot be measured with sufficient reliability.

Some areas in which contingent liabilities usually arise are as follows:

- Unsettled legal claims by customers, employees or others on matters including those stated in the box on the right.
- Arbitration and other pending labour awards.
- Obligations under product warranties/guarantees.
- Bills of exchange with recourse, if discounted.
- Pension liability not provided for in the accounts.
- Performance guarantees given to or on behalf of subsidiaries or others.
- Liabilities arising from regulations – say one prohibiting release of toxic chemicals.

■ Faulty goods
■ Breach of contract
■ Violation of copy rights
■ Injury to health or welfare
■ Environmental pollution
■ Breach of regulations

23.5 Accounting for contingent liabilities

The accounting requirement[2] is that contingent liabilities should *not* be accounted for (by inclusion in the ledgers or financial statements) as long as the conditions that necessitated their classification as a contingent liability (rather than an actual one) remain. However, the users of the financial statements will need to be aware of the existence of such contingent claims. Hence it is required that:

- Contingent liabilities should be disclosed (as notes to financial statements) unless the prospect of a transfer of economic benefit is remote.
- The disclosure should be made irrespective of whether or not the amount involved can be estimated reliably.

23.6 Demarcating liabilities, provisions and contingent liabilities

The following table illustrates how obligations of an entity should be treated when accounting:

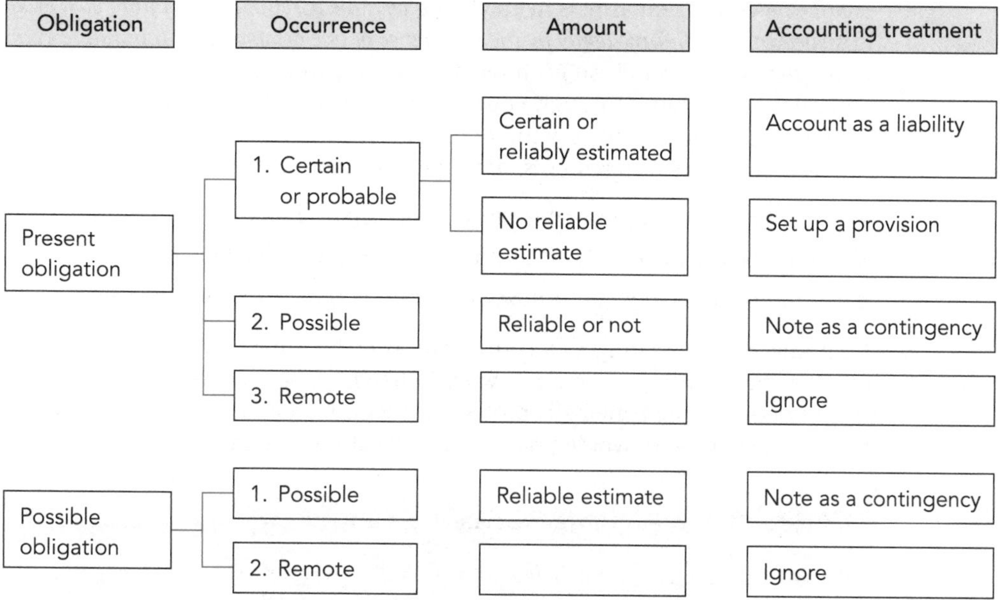

23.7 Thresholds on whether occurrence is probable, possible or remote

	Range
Virtually certain	> 95%
Probable	50 to 95%
Possible	5 to 50%
Remote	< 5%

A contingent liability is accounted for in the financial statements, disclosed as a note to the financial statements or ignored depending on the entity's opinion as to whether or not the transfer of future economic benefit to settle the obligation is virtually certain, probable, possible or remote. In the absence of any official guidance on the area, the authors suggest the ranges stated on the right. What is important is not the accuracy of the suggested ranges so much as the adoption of a uniform approach to identification of these thresholds, so that information users are not misled when comparing financial performance over time and of different companies.

Activity 23.8 Is the obligation probable, possible or remote?

A building contractor received a claim for £1 million on behalf of one of his workers paralysed with head injuries suffered when scaffolding at a building site collapsed. The insurance refused to meet the claim on the premise that the worker was not wearing a protective helmet at the time of the accident. At the time of preparing the financial statements, as at 30 June 2012, the legal opinion of the solicitors was that damages of between £400,000 and £750,000 may be awarded against the company depending on whether the paralysis is temporary or permanent. The medical opinion is that there is a 25% chance that the paralysis will be permanent. State with reasons whether the contractor should account for any liability or provision or merely disclose a contingent liability.

23.8 Contingent assets

For the sake of completeness we will also consider the treatment of contingent assets in this chapter. A contingent asset is defined[2] as *a possible asset that arises from past events and whose existence will be confirmed only by the occurrence of one or more uncertain future events not wholly within the entity's control*. An example of a contingent asset is a claim (say for compensation) a business is pursuing through courts, where the outcome, depending as it would on the court's award, remains uncertain.

The accounting requirements[2] are that contingent assets:

- Should never be accounted for in the financial statements.
- Should be disclosed only when the inflow of economic benefit is *probable*.
- Should be ignored when inflow of benefits is *either possible or remote*.

If an uncertainty relating to a contingent asset no longer exists, then, of course, the asset ceases to be a contingent one and would, therefore, be accounted for as normal. Where the inflow of economic benefits is probable, the note should describe the asset, the nature of the contingency and, where practicable, indicate the financial effects.

Activity 23.9 A contingent asset

Metalworks manufacturers of safety helmets had to write off £120,000 being the cost of helmets which had to be destroyed because they failed the safety test. Metalworks has filed a court action claiming £90,000 from the new suppliers of raw material on the premise that defective material supply was responsible for the loss. The suppliers are contesting the claim. The legal advice is that there is around a 20 to 40% chance of success for the claim.

Required: Should Metalworks account for the claim as an asset at £90,000?

23.9 Events after the reporting period

There would inevitably be a time gap (usually of many weeks) between the last day of the accounting period (say 31 December 2011) and the date on which the financial statements are approved (say 31 March 2012). The *Events after the reporting period* are those events, both favourable and unfavourable, that occur between (a) the reporting date and (b) the date on which financial statements are authorised for issue by the owners (or in the case of a company by the board of directors). The Accounting Standard[3] requires that when financial statements are prepared, *material* events after the reporting period must be reviewed, for the purpose of identifying those that are referred to as (a) adjusting events and (b) others referred to as non-adjusting events.

23.9.1 Adjusting events

The name 'adjusting events' is given in the Accounting Standard to anything that has come to light after completion of the reporting period which requires adjustment to the information reported on the financial statements. These are of two types:

1. **Those that assist in identifying the position** to be reported on the Statement of financial position. These events, though occurring after the reporting date, provide evidence of conditions that existed on the reporting date which, had they been known at that date, would have been included in the financial statements. When information on such events becomes available the financial statements are adjusted, e.g. information may be obtained after the reporting date that a trade receivable is not recoverable because the customer has been adjudicated bankrupt. In the light of this information the amount receivable needs to be reported, not as an asset on the Statement of financial position, but as an expense in the Statement of income.

   Under the time interval rule, we have seen that when preparing financial statements an entity may confront many uncertainties and has to make a number of estimates. Events that happen after the reporting period allow the entity to have the benefit of hindsight and may clarify or resolve some of those uncertainties. For example the information received on the basis of events after the reporting period may clarify:

   - the recoverability or otherwise of trade receivables;
   - the net realisable value of inventory to ascertain whether it is lower than cost;
   - a court decision resolving a claim by or against the entity;
   - the occurrence of a material fraud or error;
   - the cost of an asset or service received within the accounting period.

2. **Those that invalidate the assumption of going concern** on the basis of which the financial statements are prepared. We have learnt (Chapter 19) that the financial statements are prepared on the assumption that the business will remain a going concern, i.e. in operational existence at current levels of operation for the foreseeable future. It is on the basis of this assumption, for example, that we report non-current assets at their depreciated cost even if their realisable value is lower. If, however, events after the reporting period cast doubts on the going concern status of the entity, then it would be necessary to re-state the information on the Statement of financial position, i.e. the non-current assets would be reported at their net realisable value. Examples of events that could cast doubt on the going concern status of an entity are the loss of a major market or a significant line of business, denial of a significant line of credit, loss of key personnel and crystallisation at a significant amount of a contingent liability.

23.9.2 Non-adjusting events

Non-adjusting events after the reporting period are events which are *not* indicative of conditions that *existed* on the reporting date but are of major significance to users of financial statements when making their assessment of future profitability or liquidity of the entity. Such events are required, therefore, to be disclosed as notes because their non-disclosure would affect the ability of those who use the financial statements to make informed decision. The nature of the event as well as an estimate of the financial effects are required to be disclosed in respect of non-adjusting events such as:

- major acquisition/disposal of a new business or a new line of activity;
- significant changes in physical capacity or performing ability of the business;
- loss of major resources, production facilities, financing;
- major business combinations or restructuring of business;
- major changes in finance such as from a share issue or obtaining loans;
- changes in interest rates, tax liability, exchange rates, political and economic conditions.

In addition, the Standard[2] requires the disclosure also of (a) the date on which the financial statements were authorised for issue and (b) who authorised the issue.

Activity 23.10 Events after reporting period

Karen Retail's draft Statement of financial position, shown below on the right, was approved by the board of directors for release to shareholders on 4 March 2012. Following events took place between 1 January 2012 and 4 March.

(a) The shopfittings were newly installed by Simon Smith whose original estimate was £800. Simon was paid money from time to time as work progressed. The style and nature of fittings were also amended. The fittings were completed by 30 December 2011 but the final bill from Simon, showing the total cost as £960, did not arrive till 19 January.

(b) It was only on 7 January that it was realised that inventory costing £20 was damaged by November 2011 rains. These goods had to be discarded.

(c) On 1 March 2012 a cheque for £35 was received from a customer whose debt had been written off already.

(d) The adjoining shop premises were also leased from 1 March 2012 and this doubles the retailing capacity.

Required: Taking account of the events after the reporting period re-draft the Statement of financial position as at 31 December 2011.

Statement of financial position as at 31 December 2011

	£	£
New shopfittings at cost		800
Motor vehicles at cost	240	
Accumulated depreciation	(108)	132
Current assets:		
Inventory	412	
Trade receivables	214	
Cash and bank	28	654
		1,586
	£	**£**
Capital	800	
Profit for the year	267	1,067
Current liabilities:		
Trade payables	296	
Owed to Simon Smith	184	
Accrued expenses	39	519
		1,586

Summary

- IAS 37 requires a distinction to be maintained when identifying and accounting for liabilities, provisions and contingencies.
- A liability is a present obligation (legal or constructive) to transfer economic benefit. However, to account for it as a liability it should meet four liability recognition criteria:
  1. it should be a present obligation;
  2. the obligating event should have already happened;
  3. the transfer of economic benefits should be certain or at least probable; and
  4. the amount should be capable of reliable estimation.
- A provision is (a) a liability and (b) with uncertainties relating to the timing, amount or both.
- There are strict requirements relating to accounting for provisions.
- A contingent liability is either (a) a possible liability the occurrence of which depends on one of more future events outside the entity's control, or (b) a present liability which fails the liability recognition criteria either because its occurrence is less than probable or it cannot be reliably estimated.

- A contingent liability should not be accounted for; it must be reported as a note, unless its occurrence is remote.
- A contingent asset is one the existence of which depends on one or more future events outside the entity's control.
- A contingent asset should never be accounted for; it must be disclosed in a note if its occurrence is probable.
- Events after the reporting period are of two types: (a) adjusting events if they establish the position on the reporting date or invalidate the going concern assumption, and (b) non-adjusting events when they need to be disclosed because their non-disclosure would affect the ability of financial statement users to make informed decisions.

References

1. *Framework for the Preparation and Presentation of Financial Statements*, London, International Accounting Standards Board.
2. IAS 37 *Provisions, Contingent Liabilities and Contingent Assets*, issued in 1998, London, International Accounting Standards Board.
3. IFRS 3 *Business Combinations*, 2003, London, International Accounting Standards Board.
4. IAS 10 *Events After the Reporting Period*, revised in December 2003, London, International Accounting Standards Board.

Suggested answers to activities

23.1 Recognition as a liability

A liability definitely exists because all four of the following criteria have been met:

1. As regards induction in the USA there is a constructive obligation (on the basis of discussion at the interview) creating an expectation that it is part of the package. As regards the salary (£84,000 p.a.) and bonus (25% of the salary) there is a legal obligation (based on the contract of employment).
2. The present obligation arises from a past event. The obligating event triggering the obligation is the assumption of duties on 1 June 2011.
3. The obligation to pay is certain. The employer has no realistic alternative. Even if the employer can avoid future obligation (e.g. salary payable for the period after 1 July 2011) by taking a course of action (e.g. dismissal) it cannot avoid the obligation to pay June 2011 salary. As regards the bonus payable upon satisfactory completion of a full year's service, theoretically the employer can avoid it (by dismissal), but on a balance of probability it is unlikely to happen.
4. The amount of the liability can be measured reliably, on the basis of the employment contract with regard to salary (£7,000) and bonus (£1,750) and on the basis of past experience (£20,000) in respect of induction in the USA.

Dr Salaries account	£8,750	
Dr Staff induction	£20,000	–
Cr Salary accrued	–	£7,000
Cr Bonus payable	–	£1,750
Cr Staff induction	–	£20,000

Being accounting for staff costs

23.2 The question of whether there is a present obligation

The obligating event that triggers the obligation is the accident, provided the blame is assigned, at least in part, to the supermarket. Since the matter of assigning the blame remains unresolved, the existence of the obligation is in doubt. IAS 37 suggests that in such a situation the existence will have to be decided on, taking account of all available evidence. Since at least part of the blame (for defective brakes on the trolley) is likely to be assigned to the supermarket, it is more likely than not that an obligation does exist. The legal opinion is able to reliably estimate the damage within a stated range. Hence a liability definitely exists. The liability will have to be accounted for at the best estimate within that range.

23.3 Account as a liability or a provision?

The liability definitely exists because (a) based on the court order there is an obligation to pay, (b) the obligating (past) event triggering the obligation is the cultivation of GM crop, (c) the obligation is certain because there is no realistic alternative, and (d) the amount can be reliably estimated, as it has been, at £3,000. However, there remains an uncertainty as regards the amount because that will depend on (i) the crop harvested by Michael and (ii) the difference in prices at that time between GM crop and organic crop. Michael has no previous experience of this and the best estimate cannot be more than a conjecture. Hence Michael should account for the expense at £3,000, but report the liability as a provision to clarify that the amount remains uncertain.

Dr Compensation payable	£3,000	–
Cr Provision for compensation	–	£3,000
Being compensation payable with regard to GM crop		

23.4 When accounting for a provision is prohibited

The accounting for the provision is wrong and is one prohibited by the Accounting Standard. The actual cost of maintenance during the year ended 30 June 2011, if it remains unpaid, qualifies to be recognised as a liability, as it meets all four of the liability recognition criteria. On the other hand, making a provision for future repairs is not permitted because no liability exists on the reporting date for the following reasons: (a) there is no present obligation to transfer economic benefit – such an obligation would arise only when the need to repair arises, (b) the obligating event is the need to repair and since it has not arisen there is no past event triggering the obligation, (c) the obligation is neither certain nor probable because, though a need to repair is bound to arise sooner or later, the printer could avoid having to repair by replacing the machine with a new one.

23.5 Provision cannot be set up unless there is uncertainty

All four of the provisions have been wrongly set up for the following reasons:

(a) The supplier's invoice: this is a liability because the amount to pay is legally enforceable. The obligating event is making of the purchase which has already happened and therefore the obligation exists on the reporting date. The settlement is certain because otherwise future purchases cannot be made. The amount can be reliably established either from the invoice received in the post reporting period or by communicating with the supplier. In the absence of any uncertainty as regards amount or timing (it needs to be paid within agreed credit period) the liability cannot be referred to as a provision.

(b) This again is a liability. It is a present obligation because the obligating event (which has already happened) is the cleaning done in December 2011. The settlement of the obligation is legally enforceable because there would be a contract with the cleaner and the amount is reliably ascertainable from the contract. Again, in the absence of uncertainty the obligation cannot be referred to as a provision.

(c) As at the reporting date (31 December 2011) there is no obligation to pay for the air-conditioning ducts which are not in place until 2012. Hence there is no liability to be reported as at the reporting date.

(d) Audit fees qualify to be identified as a liability, although the obligating event (carrying out of the audit function) has not taken place as at the reporting date, because an audit is legally obligatory and relates to the year 2011. The settlement of that obligation is also certain because case law has established that otherwise the auditor would have a lien on the books and vouchers of the company. The amount cannot, of course, be certain until an invoice is received from the auditor, probably taking into account the time it takes to carry out the audit. But the extent of uncertainty is not regarded as sufficient to identify the liability as a provision because, based on past experience, it should be possible to estimate the amount reliably.

23.6 Provision cannot be set up if the obligation can be avoided

IAS 37 prohibits setting up of a provision if the liability can be avoided by the entity's action. There is no liability for penalty as at the reporting date (31 December 2011) and the liability which could arise in 2012 may be avoided, e.g. by employing more workers or ensuring that non-availability of supplies does not hold up work.

23.7 Where the uncertain amount of the obligation needs to be estimated

There is definitely a liability to pay compensation. The obligating event (supplying stale bread) has already occurred and, therefore, there is a present obligation, as at the reporting date (31 December 2011), to settle the obligation. The settlement of the obligation is certain because Gabriels' Bakery wishes to maintain relationships. There is, however, an uncertainty as to the amount of the liability. Therefore a provision should be set up for the best amount at which the obligation is expected to be settled, at £1,028,000 (see working on the right), and accounted for as:

Group	Invoice	Earnings	Repayable
A	£450,000 × 100%	–	£450,000
B	£300,000 × 100%	60% of £30,000	£318,000
C	£250,000 × 100%	40% of £25,000	£260,000
Provision for compensation			£1,028,000

Dr Sales account £1,000,000

Dr Compensation for damages £28,000 (expense, to be reported after identifying gross profit)

Cr Provision for compensation payable £1,028,000.

23.8 Is the obligation probable, possible or remote?

The obligating event is the accident met with by the worker on the company premises and while on legitimate company work. The worker has sustained serious injuries and, therefore, a transfer of economic benefits (i.e. a cash payment) appears probable, if not certain. The amount, though capable of reliable estimation on the basis of past experience, remains uncertain. Therefore, a provision should be made for the estimate of £400,000. The possibility that further amounts up to £200,000 may become payable (if the paralysis is permanent) should be disclosed in a note to the accounts as a contingent liability.

23.9 A contingent asset

The claim for £90,000 is not an asset because (until the supplier admits the claim) there is as yet no expectation of receiving future economic benefit. Whether the claim will succeed depends on the decision of the courts and, hence, it is a contingent asset. The legal opinion is that the chance of success is 20% to 40%, placing it within the range we may regard as possible. Hence the contingent asset cannot even be disclosed as a note because it is only if the chance of success is probable that existence of a contingent asset can be disclosed.

23.10 Events after the reporting period

Statement of financial position as at 31 December 2011

	£	£
New shopfittings at cost		960
Motor vehicles at cost	240	
Accumulated depreciation	(108)	132
Current assets:		
Inventory	392	
Trade receivables	249	
Cash and bank	28	669
		1,761

	£	£
Capital	800	
Profit for the year	282	1,082
Current liabilities:		
Trade payables	296	
Owed to Simon Smith	344	
Accrued expenses	39	679
		1,761

(a) Shopfittings have cost £160 more and the amount payable to Simon Smith should also be increased by this amount.

(b) Events after the reporting date establish that the inventory in hand on 31 December 2011 was £20 lower.

(c) Events after the reporting date (receipt of the cheque) establish that the value of receivables existing as at 31 December 2011 was £35 more.

(d) The improvement to retailing capacity, being significant (doubles retailing capacity), should be disclosed as a note because it is a non-adjusting post reporting-date event.

Profit reported for the year ended 31 December 2011 increases by the debt recovery (£35) and decreases by the loss of inventory (£20).

Multiple choice questions

Recognising a liability and a provision

23.1 Which of the following is not essential for recognition as a liability?

(a) There should be a present obligation to transfer economic benefit ☐

(b) The obligation to transfer economic benefit should be certain ☐

(c) The obligating event triggering the obligation should have already happened ☐

(d) It should be possible to make a reliable estimate of the amount ☐

23.2 Which of the following statements is correct?

(a) There is no need to account for a liability if the amount is not known for certain ☐

(b) When an asset is acquired a provision will need to be made for all repairs needed during its use ☐

(c) The amount of audit fees remaining unpaid may be referred to as a provision ☐

(d) A liability with uncertainty regarding either its timing or amount may be called a provision ☐

23.3 Which of the following statements is incorrect?

(a) Damages awarded by court against the business may be ignored because it will be appealed

(b) A liability is a present obligation, arising from past transaction, which probably has to be paid

(c) A liability has to be accounted for at the best reliable estimate even if the amount is not certain

(d) If the occurrence of the obligation is in doubt there is no need to account for the liability

23.4 Which of the following requirements in IAS 37 are calculated to ensure that provisions are not created and used to either understate or overstate the performance and net assets of a business?

(i) A provision cannot be made for anticipated future losses

(ii) A provision is defined as a liability with uncertainty in timing or amount

(iii) A provision cannot be used for any purpose other than what it was intended for

(iv) The need for and amount of provision shall be reviewed on every reporting date

a	i & ii only	
b	i, ii & iii	
c	ii, iii & iv	
d	All four	

23.5 Alan Smith received summons dated 7 March for an interview, attended the interview on 28 March, received the appointment letter dated 11 April and assumed duties on 15 April. Which of those listed on right is the obligating event triggering recognition of liability by the employer?

a	Summoning for the interview on 7 March	
b	Attendance at interview on 28 March	
c	Receipt of the letter of appointment – 11 April	
d	Assumption of duties on 15 April	

23.6 A fashion designer received a claim for £100,000 as damages because some wedding garments were not delivered in time for a wedding. The designer admits the delay but disputes the amount of the claim, pointing out that alternative wedding garments cost no more than £18,000. How would you advise the designer to treat the claim when finalising the financial statement for the year?

a	Ignore the claim	
b	Account for a liability of £100,000	
c	Account for a liability of £18,000	
d	Account for the best estimate as liability	

23.7 On 7 May 2012 Adler Printers signed a contract with Boon plc for £12 million. In terms of this contract Boon plc is required to supply 40,000 reams per year of high-quality printing paper for three years from 1 July 2012. By 31 December Boon has supplied 16,000 reams and has sent an invoice for £4 million. Adler has made no payment to Boon. How and at what amount should Adler Printers show the amount owed to Boon as at 31 December 2012?

a	£4 million as a liability	
b	£12 million as a liability	
c	£1.6 million as a liability	
d	£1.6 million as a provision	

23.8 A manufacturer of audio equipment offers a warrant to remedy manufacturing defects, at no cost to the customer, if identified within six months of sale, but customarily has extended this facility for up to nine months. During the year to 31 December 2012 the sales, made evenly through the year, amounted to £24 million. Past experience has been that around 5% of items sold return for remedial treatment and remedial work costs, on average, 3% of sale price. How should the manufacturer report its obligation for remedying manufacturing defects as at 31 December 2012?

a	£27,000 as a liability	
b	£18,000 as a liability	
c	£27,000 as a provision	
d	£18,000 as a provision	

23.9 Radon plc is facing a claim for £500,000 from a customer, in respect of a fire the cause of which has been traced to a defective electric circuit in a refrigerator sold by Radon. The legal opinion is that the claim will succeed; but Radon will be able to reclaim 75% of the amount from Fallon who supplied the circuit-breakers which malfunctioned. How should Radon report this on its Statement of financial position?

a	£125,000 as a liability	
b	£500,000 as a liability and £375,000 as asset	
c	£125,000 as a provision	
d	£500,000 as provision and £375,000 as asset	

23.10 A builder finds that, on account of the negligence of his workmen, he has to replace the bathroom suite in a residence still under construction. The replacement is expected to cost £15,000; but it is anticipated that the damaged suite may fetch around £1000. At what amount should the builder account for his obligation to replace the bathroom suite on his year-end Statement of financial position?

a	£14,000 as a provision	
b	£14,000 as a liability	
c	£15,000 as a liability	
d	£15,000 as a liability and £1,000 as an asset	

Liability, provision and contingent liability

23.11 Which of the following statements is correct?

(a) A contingent liability may be accounted for if its occurrence is certain

(b) A contingent liability should always be disclosed in a note

(c) A contingent liability should be disclosed as a note, unless its occurrence is remote

(d) A contingent liability may always be ignored

23.12 Which of the following should be disclosed as a note to financial statements as a contingent liability?

(a) A customer's claim that is unlikely to succeed

(b) A customer's claim which, according to legal opinion, has a 75% chance of success

(c) Liquidated damages awarded against a company by a court, for wrongful dismissal of an employee

(d) A customer's claim for injuries suffered on company premises with 5% chance of success

Post reporting-date events

23.13 The following is a list of events that took place between the date of the Statement of financial position (30.6.2012) and the date it was approved for sending to shareholders. Place a tick in the appropriate grid (x) if the event is an adjusting event (y) if it is a non-adjusting event.

	x	y
(a) The exchange rate with the country of the main supplier has become very unfavourable		
(b) A cheque was received from a customer whose debt has already been written off		
(c) In a reorganisation the company has abandoned a line of activity yielding 20% of its profit		
(d) Received information of an accident that destroyed a company vehicle in May 2012		
(e) Received claim for compensation from an employee wrongly dismissed in April 2012		
(f) Company raised capital by issuing shares at a premium		
(g) Inventory reported at cost is found to be defective and cannot be sold		
(h) Court awarded substantial damages to a customer whose claim was not expected to succeed		

Answers to multiple choice questions

23.1: b 23.2: d 23.3: a 23.4: d 23.5: d 23.6: d 23.7: c 23.8: a 23.9: b 23.10: c 23.11: c 23.12: b 23.13a: y 23.13b: x 23.13c: y 23.13d: x 23.13e: x 23.13f: y 23.13g: x 23.13 h: x

Progressive questions

PQ 23.1 Accounting for liabilities, provisions and contingencies (ACCA amended)

(a) How does IAS 37, *Provisions, Contingent Liabilities and Contingent Assets*, distinguish the identification and accounting for a liability, a provision and a contingent liability?

(b) State with reason how you would account for the following items:

(i) The directors of a company have discovered a painting in a cupboard and have sent it to an auction house, who have confirmed that it should sell for £1 million in the following month's auction.

(ii) A claim has been made against the company for injury suffered by a pedestrian in connection with building work by the company. Legal advisers are of the view that the company will probably have to pay damages of £200,000 but that a claim can be made against the building subcontractors for £100,000.

(iii) The manufacturer of a snooker table has received a letter from a professional snooker player, who was defeated in the final of a major snooker competition, threatening to sue the manufacturer for £1 million, being his estimate of his loss of earnings through failing to win the competition, on the grounds that the table was not level.

PQ 23.2 Whether accrued liability, provision and contingent liability

The financial statements of Casserole plc, in respect of the year ending on 31 December 2011, are to be adopted by their board at a meeting scheduled for 7 May 2012. By a letter dated 15 April 2012 your advice is sought on how to account for the following transactions and events:

(a) Casserole plc has cancelled, with effect from 30.9.2011, a franchise it had granted to Pan Ltd in the Isle of Wight. Pan Ltd has filed action claiming liquidated damages in a sum of £300,000 and further punitive damages at £400,000. The legal opinion is that because Casserole plc did not have sufficient grounds for premature termination of franchise, it will be liable for the liquidated damages, and the award of any punitive damages depends on the attitude the court adopts.

(b) On 4 March 2012 Casserole plc received a claim for £250,000, in addition to £50,000 paid as compensation on terminating the services of a branch manager with effect from 30.11.2011. Because there were several instances of provable managerial inadequacies, the chance of the claim being enforced against the company is estimated at less than 5%.

(c) A batch of goods sold in November/December 2011 has proved defective. Customers have as a result made claims for repayment as follows:

Claims received by 31.12.2011	£180,000
Claims received by 14.4.2012	£90,000
Further claims expected to be received	£30,000

These goods had been sold at cost plus 25%, but have no value upon return. Casserole plc considers that it is possible to make a counter-claim against the supplier from whom they had acquired the goods.

(d) The company is currently subject to an investigation by the Director General of Fair Trading in respect of possible contravention of orders made by Restrictive Practices Court. Though the charges are strenuously contested and Casserole plc is doing its utmost to vindicate its trading practices, the legal advisers are unable to foresee the outcome. In the event the findings are adverse, damages awarded against the company may range from £100,000 to almost ten times that amount. The company is averse to admitting to such an investigation because of the damage it may cause to its reputation and is unwilling to account for any claim which may arise because that could amount to an admission of guilt.

Required: In respect of each of the above claims, clarify whether the obligation to transfer future economic benefit should be accounted for either as liability or as a provision or disclosed in a note to the accounts as a contingent liability.

PQ 23.3 Accounting for contingent liabilities and assets (ACCA – amended)

Your managing director is having a polite disagreement with the auditors on the subject of accounting for contingencies. It appears that your firm is involved in four unrelated legal cases, P, Q, R and S. In case P the firm is suing for £10,000, in case Q the firm is suing for £20,000, in case R the firm is being sued for £30,000 and in case S the firm is being sued for £40,000. The firm has been advised by its lawyers that the chances of the firm winning each case is as stated on the right.

Case	% of likely success
P	8
Q	92
R	8
S	92

Required: Write a memorandum to the managing director which:

(a) explains why IAS 37 is relevant to these situations;
(b) states the required accounting treatment for each of the four cases in the accounts for the year;
(c) gives journal entries for any necessary adjustments in the double-entry records;
(d) suggests the contents of any notes to published accounts as required by IAS 37.

PQ 23.4 Post reporting-date event

Robin Dale Ltd, a wholesalers, prepared his draft Statement of financial position as shown on the right. Following events occurred prior to the approval of the financial statements by the Directors of the company on 4 August 2012:

(a) Inventory reported at £826,000 includes £30,000, the cost of certain items which were shop-soiled and which can be sold for only £21,000 after being reconditioned at a cost of £3,000. The shop-soiling was detected only on 3 July 2012.
(b) Collin Dare from whom £50,000 was receivable was adjudicated bankrupt on 17 July 2012. In a letter dated 24 July the trustee in bankruptcy has warned Robin Dale Ltd not to expect more than 10p in £1.
(c) Investments reported as a current asset on the Statement of financial position includes at £54,000 the cost of 90,000 ordinary shares of £1 each. These shares had been quoted at 80p each on 30 June 2012, but were sold for £48,000 two weeks later.

Statement of financial position as at 30 June 2012

	Cost	Accumulated depreciation	£'000
Non-current assets	364	(112)	252
Current assets:			
Inventory		826	
Trade receivables		468	
Investments		112	
Cash and bank		34	1,440
			1,692
			£'000
Capital			1,000
Profit for the year			110
			1,110
Trade payable			582
			1,692

Required:

(a) Advise Robin Dale Ltd on how these events after reporting date should be treated when accounts are finalised for the year ended 30 June 2012.
(b) On the basis that your advice is accepted prepare a revised Statement of financial position as at 30 June 2012 along with any notes.

PQ 23.5 Again post reporting-date event (CIMA)

D plc is a large paper-manufacturing company. The company's finance director is working on the published accounts for the year ended 31 March 2012. The chief accountant has prepared the following list of problems which will have to be resolved before the statements are finalised.

(a) A fire broke out in the company's Westown factory on 4 April 2012. This has destroyed the factory's administration block. Many of the costs incurred as a result of this fire are uninsured.

(b) A major customer went into liquidation on 27 April 2012. The customer's balance on 31 March remains unpaid. The receiver has intimated that unsecured creditors will receive very little compensation, if any.

(c) One of the company's employees was injured during the year. He had been operating a piece of machinery which had been known to have a faulty guard. The company's lawyers have advised that the employee has a very strong case, but will be unable to estimate likely financial damages until further medical evidence becomes available.

(d) One of the company's customers is claiming compensation for losses sustained as a result of a delayed delivery. The customer has ordered a batch of cut sheets with the intention of producing leaflets to promote a special offer. There was a delay in supplying the paper and leaflets could not be prepared in time. The company's lawyers have advised that there was no special agreement to supply the goods in time for this promotion and, furthermore, that it would be almost impossible to attribute the failure of the special offer to the delay in the supply of paper.

Required: Explain how each of the above matters should be dealt with in the published accounts for the year ended 31 March 2012. Assume that the amounts involved are material.

Test questions

Test 23.1 Identification and accounting for liabilities

Sylvia carries on business as a baker trading as The French Confection. When finalising the accounts of The French Confection for the year ending on 31 March 2012, she seeks your advice on whether she should account for the following claims on her resources (i.e. record them in the ledgers and report them in the Statement of income and/or Statement of financial position):

(a) She is planning to acquire a new convector oven for £7,500 on 1 April 2012.

(b) She hired the services of a pastry cook in September 2011 on the understanding that the chef would be trained in oriental cuisine and this training is expected to cost £9,000.

(c) She acquired a kitchen grinder for £12,000 on 1.7.2011, intending to use it for five years. The manufacturers advised her that its motor would require replacement annually at a cost of £500.

(d) The Public Health Inspector notified her on 1 March 2012 that The French Confection was required to pay a penalty of £1,000 for a minor breach of health and safety laws.

(e) One of her regular customers, a reputable restaurant, complained on 10 March 2012 that a consignment of pastries, invoiced to the restaurant at £14,000, was not fresh. To defend her reputation as a supplier of fresh pastries Sylvia's policy usually is to make a refund of 125% of the value of any defective products.

Required: Explain how each transaction/event stated as (a) to (e) should be accounted for and reported in the Statement of income for the year ended 31 March 2012 and the Statement of financial position as at that date.

Test 23.2 Accounting for provisions

A building contractor seeks your advice on how the following claims should be treated when finalising accounts for the year ended 31 December 2012:

(a) When the scaffolding at a building site collapsed, a worker sustained head injuries and was paralysed. In the opinion of the company solicitors, damages of around £400,000 may be awarded. The insurance company refuses to meet the claim on the premise that the worker concerned was not wearing a protective helmet at the time of the accident.

(b) The contractor's practice is to take responsibility for all remedial work relating to any construction work for three years from the date of completion. In respect of a building handed over in December 2011, a provision of £40,000 for remedial action was made when the accounts were prepared for the year ending 31.12.2011. Remedial actions on that building during 2012 have already cost £28,000. Investigations into major cracks on the building reveal the need for underpinning and that may cost £30,000 more and perhaps a further £5,000 in the event of any price escalation.

(c) A worker has filed legal action claiming £100,000 on the basis that his ailments arose from the vibration of working with angle grinders. He has produced medical opinion to support this claim. It may be possible to come to an out-of-court settlement at an amount of around £50,000. The insurance company is prepared to admit this claim at £40,000.

(d) A customer has claimed £25,000 as the cost of luxury bath suites damaged because of negligence of the contractor's workers. Negligence of the workers has been established. The contractor will be able to realise £10,000 by disposing of the damaged bath suites.

Required: Advise the contractor for items (a) to (d) above.

Test 23.3 Liability: provision or contingent liability?

Warren Industries manufactures and retails domestic appliances. The business had prepared draft accounts by 21.2.2012 and seeks your advice on how they should account for the following claims in the accounts for the year ended 31.12.2011:

(a) The audit fees for the year ended 31.12.2011 (£15,000 in the preceding year) remain to be negotiated.

(b) Holiday pay (usually ranging between £60,000 and £72,000) is yet to be calculated and accounted for.

(c) A claim for damages, at £40,000, is received from a customer on 7.3.2012 in respect of injuries sustained within the company premises on 29.11.2011. The legal advisers are of opinion that the company will be held liable for an amount probably of around £20,000 because of its failure to display a 'wet floor' sign.

(d) The domestic appliances are sold under warranty by which the company undertakes to either remedy at no cost to the customer or to replace an appliance, should any manufacturing defects become apparent within six months of the date of sale. As at 31.12.2011, £6,240,000 of sales are within the warranty period.

    (i) The company's experience in previous years has been that 80% of the appliances sold had no defect, 15% had minor defects and about 5% required replacement.

    (ii) Based on this experience it estimated that if minor defects are detected in all appliances sold, it would cost £400,000 to rectify. If major defects are detected in all appliances sold it would cost £5.2 million to replace the appliances.

(e) On 18 February 2012 the company received notification that a customer has filed action against the company claiming £1 million on the premise that an electrical fault in the appliance sold by the company was responsible for the electrocution of his wife. The company solicitors are of the opinion that the claim is unlikely to succeed because the company's appliances are produced strictly in accordance with British Standards and are rigorously tested prior to delivery.

Required: Advise the company on the accounting treatment, identifying whether each claim should be accounted for as an accrued liability or a provision. State clearly how each satisfies the criteria for recognition as an accrual or provision.

Test 23.4 Events after the reporting period

Sophie Peters produces ladies' designer wear. Her order-books are full and she counts among her customers many leading retailers in the city. Her problem, however, is that despite working three shifts a day, and stretching her capacity to the limits, she is unable meet the orders on time. She requires £180,000 to enhance production capacity and £200,000 more to clear her liabilities. She has prepared her draft Statement of financial position as shown on the right. She reports her post reporting-date events which occurred prior to the approval of her financial statements as follows:

(a) On 11 April 2012 she raised £380,000 from a bank at 6% per annum interest, pledging machinery as collateral.

(b) Additional machinery, acquired for £180,000 on 15 April, improved her production capacity by 25%.

(c) On 3 April she received back from one of her retailers goods sold for £40,000 on 27 March. These goods were found to have been significantly damaged because of defective packing. The damaged goods have no sale value.

Required: Advise Sophie on how each of the events after the reporting period would affect what she includes in or adds as disclosure notes to her Statement of financial position as at 31 March 2012.

Statement of financial position as at 31 March 2012

	£'000	£'000
Non-current assets:		640
Machinery		(280)
Current assets:		360
Inventory		
Trade receivable	116	
Cash and bank	248	
	6	370
		730

	£'000
Capital	120
Profit for the year	58
	178
Trade payable	468
Salary accrued	42
Rent accrued	24
Advertising accrued	18
	730

Suggested answers to progressive questions

Chapter 1 The need for accounting

PQ 1 The effect of transactions on the Statement of financial position

Transactions	1	2	3	4	5	6
Assets:	£	£	£	£	£	£
Cash	300,000	200,000[a]	250,000[b]	175,000[c]	250,000[d]	242,000[f]
Premises		100,000	100,000	100,000	100,000	100,000
Inventory				75,000	45,000[e]	45,000
	300,000	300,000	350,000	350,000	395,000	387,000
Capital/Liability:						
Capital	300,000	300,000	300,000	300,000	300,000	300,000
Profit	–	–	–	–	45,000	37,000[g]
Bank loan	–	–	50,000	50,000	50,000	50,000
	300,000	300,000	350,000	350,000	395,000	387,000

(a) £300,000 – £100,000 = £200,000
(b) £200,000 + £50,000 = £250,000
(c) £250,000 – £75,000 = £175,000
(d) £175,000 + £75,000 = £250,000
(e) £75,000 – £30,000 = £45,000
(f) £250,000 – £8,000 = £242,000
(g) £45,000 – £8,000 = £37,000

PQ 1.2 The effect of transactions on the Statement of financial position

Transactions	1	2	3	4	5	6
Assets:	£	£	£	£	£	£
Cash	480,000	320,000[a]	200,000[b]	320,000[c]	400,000[f]	387,000[g]
Vehicles		160,000	160,000	160,000	160,000	160,000
Inventory			120,000	72,000[d]	72,000[e]	72,000
	480,000	480,000	480,000	552,000	632,000	619,000
Capital/Liability:						
Capital	480,000	480,000	480,000	480,000	480,000	480,000
Profit	–	–	–	72,000	72,000	59,000[h]
Bank loan	–	–	–	–	80,000	80,000
	480,000	480,000	480,000	552,000	632,000	619,000

(a) £480,000 – £160,000 = £320,000
(b) £320,000 – £120,000 = £200,000
(c) £200,000 + £120,000 = £320,000
(d) £120,000 – £48,000 = £72,000
(e) £120,000 – £48,000 = £72,000
(f) £320,000 + £80,000 = £400,000
(g) £400,000 – £13,000 = £387,000
(h) £72,000 – £13,000 = £59,000

Chapter 2 Controlling and accounting for cash

PQ 2.1 Control over cash

(a) Cash-based businesses:
Window cleaners, Hairdressers, Manicurists, Laundry, Newsagent, Dentists

(b) Important to write up the Cash account:
- To monitor receipts and payments
- To ensure availability when cash is needed
- To prevent theft (defalcation)

(c) To control cash, besides writing up Cash account:
- Cash surplus to immediate needs be left with bank
- Ensure custody is with trustworthy employee
- Insist on vouchers for every receipt/payment
- Physical cash count on random basis

PQ 2.2 Sorting out the side

In (x): b, d   Out (y): a, c, e   None (z): f

PQ 2.3 Writing up the Cash account

Cash account

Date	Particulars	Amount	Date	Particulars	Amount
2010		£	2010		£
1.1	Capital	15,000	2.1	Purchases	300
2.1	Sales	450	2.1	Rent	1,500
7.1	Sales	250	2.1	Stationery	90
			3.1	Purchases	150
			4.1	Stationery	60
			5.1	Motor vehicle	1,500
			6.1	Vehicle expenses	225
			6.1	Drawings	450
			7.1	Vehicle expenses	40
					4,315
				Balance c/d	11,385
		15,700	7.1		15,700
8.1	Balance b/d	11,385			

PQ 2.4 Writing up the Cash account and Bank account

Cash account

Date	V	Particulars	F	Amount	Date	V	Particulars	F	Amount
2010				£	2010				£
2.4		Sales		1,200	3.4		Office cleaning		140
3.4		Sales		1,800	5.4		Drawings		250
4.4		Sales		2,500	5.4		Wages		300
5.4		Sales		3,400	5.4		Bank		7,800
					5.4		Balance c/d		410
				8,900					8,900
6.4		Balance b/d		410					

Bank account

Date	V	Particulars	F	Amount	Date	V	Chq	Particulars	F	Amount
2010				£	2010					£
1.4		Capital		12,000	1.4		01	Rent		3,000
5.1		Cash		7,800	1.4		02	Shop fittings		1,200
					1.4		03	Purchases		2,400
					2.4		04	Advertising		240
					3.4		05	Purchases		1,800
					4.4		06	Electricity		270
					4.4		08	Advertising		124
					5.4		09	Telephone		115
					5.4		–	Balance c/d		10,651
				19,800						19,800
6.1		Balance b/d		10,651						

PQ 2.5 Writing up the Cash account and Bank account

Cash Book

Date	V	Particulars	F	Cash	Bank	Date	V	Chq.No	Particulars	F	Cash	Bank
2010				£	£	2010					£	£
1.4	Rec.01	Capital		12,000	–	1.4	PV01	–	Bank		12,000	–
1.4	PV01	Cash		–	12,000	1.4	PV02	001	Rent		–	3,000
2.4	CSM01	Sales		1,200	–	1.4	PV03	002	Fittings		–	1,200
3.4	CSM02	Sales		1,800	–	1.4	PV04	003	Purchases		–	2,400
4.4	CSM03	Sales		2,500	–	2.4	PV05	004	Advertising		–	240
5.4	CSM04	Sales		3,400	–	3.4	PV06	–	Cleaning		140	–
5.4	PV13	Cash		–	7,800	3.4	PV07	005	Purchases		–	1,800
						4.4	PV08	006	Electricity		–	270
						4.4	PV09	007	Advertising		–	124
						5.4	PV10	008	Telephone		–	115
						5.4	PV11	–	Drawings		250	–
						5.4	PV12	–	Wages		300	–
						5.4	PV13	–	Bank		7,800	–
											20,490	9,149
						5.4	–	–	Balance c/d		410	10,651
				20,900	19,800						20,900	19,800
6.4	–	Balance b/d		410	10,651							

PQ 2.6 Balancing the Cash account

(a) To check the accuracy he balances the Cash account, usually at the end of every business day.

(b) No; notwithstanding a balanced Cash account there is no assurance that the Cash account is a full and accurate record of all cash transactions, if the Cashier decides to misappropriate and attempts to cover up by:

- not entering the amount received in the Cash account;
- creating fictitious vouchers or altering vouchers.

(c) The cash in hand is £1220.25 less than what the amount should have been. Possible reasons could include:

(i) Entered in Cash Book more than amount received.
(ii) An amount paid was more than what was entered.
(iii) A customer was paid in excess as 'change'.
(iv) Arithmetic mistake made when balancing Cash Book.

Chapter 3 The double-entry accounting system

PQ 3.1 Double-entry system of accounting

(a) The double-entry system is a system of accounting in which every transaction is accounted for by a matching pair of debit and credit entries.

(b) Two entries are required so that when the total of amounts entered on each side are equal, it provides an assurance that every amount entered has been analysed.

PQ 3.2 The Cash account entry and the ledger account entry

1	Dr Cash account	Cr Capital account
2	Dr Furniture account	Cr Cash account
3	Dr Purchases account	Cr Cash account
4	Dr Advertising account	Cr Cash account
5	Dr Cash account	Cr Sales account
6	Dr Cash account	Cr Baxter Loan a/c
7	Dr Rent account	Cr Cash account
8	Dr Stationery account	Cr Cash account
9	Dr Motor vehicle a/c	Cr Cash account
10	Dr Vehicle maintenance account	Cr Cash account
11	Dr Baxter Loan account	Cr Cash account
12	Dr Vehicle maintenance account	Cr Cash account

PQ 3.3 Identify the account and the side to which the entry is made

	Cash a/c	Ledger account	Side
1	Dr	Capital account	Cr
2	Cr	Furniture account	Dr
3	Cr	Advertising account	Dr
4	Cr	Purchases account	Dr
5	Cr	Stationery account	Dr
6	Cr	Motor vehicle account	Dr
7	Cr	Furniture account	Dr
8	Cr	Motor vehicle account	Dr
9	Cr	Motor vehicle maintenance	Dr
10	Cr	Motor vehicle maintenance	Dr
11	Cr	Stationery	Dr
12	Cr	Drawings	Dr
13	Dr	Sales	Cr
14	Cr	Motor vehicle maintenance	Dr
15	Cr	Telephone	Dr

PQ 3.4 Postings from the Cash account

Trial Balance as at 9 January 2010		
	£	£
Capital account	–	15,000
Purchases account	450	–
Rent account	1,500	–
Stationery account	150	–
Motor vehicles a/c	1,500	–
MV maintenance a/c	265	–
Sales account	–	700
Drawings account	450	–
Cash account	11,385	–
	15,700	15,700

PQ 3.5 Posting from the Cash account and the Bank account

Trial Balance as at 5 April 2010		
	£	£
Capital account	–	12,000
Cleaning account	140	–
Sales account	–	8,900
Drawings account	250	–
Wages account	300	–
Rent account	3,000	–
Furniture account	1,200	–
Advertising account	364	–
Purchases account	4,200	–
Electricity account	270	–
Telephone account	115	–
Cash account	410	–
Bank account	10,651	–
	20,900	20,900

PQ 3.6 A ledger account and its balance

Credit balances in the Capital account, Sales account and in the Loan owed to a Mr Rich account.
Debit balances in all the rest.

PQ 3.7 Preparation of a Trial Balance when one balance is omitted

Trial Balance as at 31.3.2010		
	£	£
Cash account	2,500	–
Purchases account	170,500	–
Sales account	–	295,900
Rent account	18,000	–
Audit fees account	1,200	–
Motor vehicles account	60,000	–
Loan to cashier account	5,000	–
Machinery account	7,000	–
Furniture account	24,000	–
Bank loan account	–	3,000
Stationery account	400	–
Salaries account	21,600	–
Advertising account	4,200	–
Sales commission account	9,200	–
Telephone account	300	–
Capital account (answer)		25,000
	323,900	323,900

PQ 3.8 Posting from the Cash account

Trial Balance as at 11 November 2010		
	£	£
Capital account	–	15,000
Rent account	1,000	–
Stationery account	45	–
Office equipment account	3,000	–
Motor vehicle account	2,500	–
Motor vehicle maintenance a/c	185	–
Purchases account	5,040	–
Sales account	–	7,000
Advertising account	200	–
Wages account	550	–
Cash account	9,480	–
	22,000	22,000

PQ 3.9 Accounting under the double-entry system

(a)

Cash Book

Date	V	Particulars	F	Cash	Bank	Date	V	Chq	Particulars	F	Cash	Bank
2010				£	£	2010					£	£
3.1	Rec.1	Capital a/c		10,000	–	3.1	PV01	–	Bank a/c		9,500	–
3.1	PV01	Cash a/c		–	9,500	3.1	PV02	01	Furniture		–	800
3.1	CSM01	Sales a/c		2,100	–	3.1	PV03	02	Purchases		–	1,800
4.1	Rec. 02	Sylvia loan a/c		1,000	–	3.1	PV04	–	Cleaning		40	–
4.1	CSM02	Sales a/c		1,840	–	3.1	PV05	03	Advertising		–	240
5.1	CSM03	Sales a/c		1,850	–	4.1	PV06	04	Purchases a/c		–	1,450
5.1	PV11	Cash a/c		–	5,840	4.1	PV07	05	Furniture		–	1,600
6.1	CSM04	Sales a/c		1,250	–	5.1	PV08	–	Cleaning		50	–
7.1	CSM05	Sales a/c		2,480	–	5.1	PV09	06	Purchases		–	2,240
						5.1	PV10	07	Advertising a/c		–	420
						5.1	PV11	–	Bank a/c		5,840	–
						6.1	PV12	–	Cleaning a/c		40	–
						6.1	PV13	08	Purchases a/c		–	1,800
						7.1	PV14	09	Advertising a/c		–	280
											15,470	10,630
						7.1	–	–	Balance c/d		5,050	4,710
				20,520	15,340						20,520	15,340
8.1	–	Balance b/d		5,050	4,710							

(b)

Trial Balance as at 7.1.2010			
		£	£
Furniture	800 + 1,600	2,400	–
Capital		–	10,000
Purchases		7,290	–
Cleaning	40 + 50 + 40	130	–
Sales		–	9,520
Advertising	240 + 420 + 280	940	–
Sylvia Loan		–	1,000
Bank a/c		4,710	–
Cash a/c		5,050	–
		20,520	20,520

Workings:
Purchases: 1,800 + 1,450 + 2,240 + 1,800 = £7,290
Sales: 2,100 + 1,840 + 1,850 + 1,250 + 2,480 = £9,520

(c) See the third point in paragraph 3.9 of Chapter 3

Chapter 4 The Statement of financial position and Statement of income

PQ 4.1 Effect of an entry on an account

Account	Increase	Decrease
Capital account	Cr	Dr
Staff salary account	Dr	Cr
Motor vehicles account	Dr	Cr
Sales account	Cr	Dr
Loan from Sally account	Cr	Dr

PQ 4.2 Preparation of a Trial Balance and identification of class

Trial Balance as at 30.6.2010			
	£	£	
Cash a/c	8,476	–	Asset
Capital a/c	–	5,000	Equity
Furniture a/c	330	–	Asset
Purchases a/c	8,400	–	Expense
Sales a/c	–	12,600	Income
Loan from Jim	–	1,200	Liability
Advertising a/c	355	–	Expense
Stationery a/c	55	–	Expense
Staff welfare a/c	40	–	Expense
Office equipment a/c	300	–	Asset
Telephone a/c	49	–	Expense
Salaries a/c	780	–	Expense
Postage a/c	15	–	Expense
	18,800	18,800	

Statement of income year ended 30 June 2010		
	£	£
Sales		12,600
Purchases		(8,400)
Gross profit		4,200
Advertising	355	
Stationery	55	
Staff welfare	40	
Telephone	49	
Salaries	780	
Postage	15	(1,294)
Net profit		2,906

Statement of financial position as at 30 June 2010	
	£
Non-current assets:	
Furniture	330
Office equipment	300
Current asset:	
Cash	8,476
	9,106
	£
Capital	5,000
Profit for the year	2,906
	7,906
Loan from Jim	1,200
	9,106

PQ 4.3 Sorting out the side of the balance in an account

Trial Balance as at 31.12.2010

	£	£	
Capital	–	50,000	Equity
Salaries	12,160	–	Expense
Furniture	24,500	–	Asset
Penny Loan	–	10,000	Liability
Motor vehicle	36,000	–	Asset
Telephone	3,440	–	Expense
Sales	–	269,600	Income
Advertising	11,220	–	Expense
Staff welfare	3,230	–	Expense
Cash	18,450	–	Asset
Purchases	208,600	–	Expense
Rent	12,000	–	Expense
	329,600	329,600	

Statement of income year ended 31.12.2010

	£	£
Sales		269,600
Purchases		(208,600)
Gross profit		61,000
Salaries	12,160	
Telephone	3,440	
Advertising	11,220	
Staff welfare	3,230	
Rent	12,000	(42,050)
Net profit		18,950

Statement of financial position as at 31.12.2010

	£
Non-current assets:	
Furniture	24,500
Motor vehicles	36,000
Current assets:	
Cash	18,450
	78,950
	£
Capital	50,000
Profit for the year	18,950
	68,950
Loan from Penny	10,000
	78,950

PQ 4.4 Trial Balance extracted wrongly

Cash account reports an asset; while Stationery account, Salaries account, Advertising account and Vehicle maintenance account report expenses. Hence the balance on each of these accounts would be on the debit side.

Trial Balance as at 31.12.2010

	Dr £	Cr £
Motor vehicle	7,200	–
Stationery	145	–
Capital	–	4,000
Cash	538	–
Purchases	4,215	–
Sales	–	6,948
Joe's Loan	–	3,500
Rent	400	–
Salaries	800	–
Advertising	528	–
Vehicle mainten.	412	–
Interest	210	–
	14,448	14,448

Statement of income year ended 31.12.2010

	£
Sales revenue	6,948
Purchases	(4,215)
Gross profit	2,733
Stationery	(145)
Rent	(400)
Salaries	(800)
Advertising	(528)
Vehicle mainten.	(412)
Interest	(210)
Profit for the year	238

Statement of financial position as at 31.12.2010

	£
Motor vehicle	7,200
Cash	538
	7,738
	£
Capital	4,000
Profit for the year	238
	4,238
Joe's Loan	3,500
	7,738

PQ 4.5 When a business operates at a loss

Trial Balance as at 31.3.2010

	£	£
Sales	–	86,000
Purchases	62,500	–
Cash	1,495	–
Interest	900	–
Salaries	14,250	–
Rent	3,000	–
Stationery	240	–
Motor vehicles	12,000	–
Vehicle mainten.	1,075	–
Bank loan	–	5,000
Postage	105	–
Staff welfare	325	–
Advertising	4,200	–
Office expense	165	–
Furniture	8,000	–
Bank	7,245	–
Capital	–	25,000
Audit fees	500	–
	116,000	116,000

Statement of income year ended 31.3.2010

	£	£
Sales		86,000
Purchases		(62,500)
Gross profit		23,500
Salaries	14,250	
Rent	3,000	
Vehicle maint.	1,075	
Postage	105	
Staff welfare	325	
Advertising	4,200	
Office expense	165	
Audit fees	500	
Stationery	240	
Interest	900	(24,760)
Loss for the year		(1,260)

Statement of fin. position as at 31.3.2010

	£	£
Non-current assets:		
Furniture		8,000
Motor vehicles		12,000
Current assets:		
Bank	7,245	
Cash	1,495	8,740
		28,740
	£	£
Capital	25,000	
Loss for the year	(1,260)	23,740
Current liabilities:		
Bank loan		5,000
		28,740

Just as profit increases the owner's equity (capital) in the business, loss decreases it.

PQ 4.6 Preparing financial statements

Statement of income for the year ended 31.12.2010

	£'000
Sales	299
Purchases	(148)
Gross profit	151
Telephone	(10)
Rent	(12)
Advertising	(14)
Stationery	(6)
Salaries	(46)
Profit	63

Statement of financial position as at 31 December 2010

	£'000
Non-current assets:	
Furniture	120
Current assets:	
Cash and bank	23
	143
	£'000
Capital	80
Profit	63
	143

Chapter 5 Accounting for credit transactions

PQ 5.1 Writing up the Sales Day Book

Trial Balance as at 1.1.2010	£	£
Capital	–	20,000
Furniture	8,000	–
Expenses	800	–
Purchases	4,600	–
Sales[a]	–	5,795
John Lyon	450	–
Duncan Brown	725	–
Liza Lester	975	–
Ron Dyer	845	–
Cash[b]	9,400	–
	25,795	25,795

Statement of income for one day 1.1.2010	£
Sales	5,795
Purchases	(4,600)
Gross profit	1,195
Expenses	(800)
Net profit	395

Statement of financial position as at 1.1.2010	£	£
Non-current assets:		
Furniture		8,000
Current assets:		
Trade receivables:		
John Lyon	450	
Duncan Brown	725	
Liza Lester	975	
Ron Dyer	845	
	2,995	
Cash	9,400	12,395
		20,395

	£
Capital	20,000
Profit	395
	20,395

Workings:
(a) Sales: 2,800 + (450 + 725 + 975 + 845) = £5,795
(b) Cash: 20,000 + 2,800 – 8,000 – 800 – 4,600 = £9,400

PQ 5.2 Books of prime entry

(a) Payment for purchase	CB	(g) Purchase return	PRDB
(b) Credit purchase	PDB	(h) Repayment of loan	CB
(c) Payment for vehicle	CB	(i) Credit sale	SDB
(d) Receipt of loan	CB	(j) Return of credit sale	SRDB
(e) Cash sales	CB	(k) Acquisition of asset	None
(f) Repayment on return	CB		

PQ 5.3 The ledgers

(a) Electricity a/c	NL	(f) Suppliers' a/c	PL
(b) Machinery a/c	GL	(g) Cash a/c	CB
(c) Customers' a/c	RL	(h) Capital a/c	GL
(d) Sales a/c	NL	(i) Bad debts a/c	NL
(e) Salaries a/c	NL	(j) Depreciation a/c	NL

PQ 5.4 Prime entry for sales and returns inwards

Trial Balance as at 31.1.2010	£	£
S. Ally a/c[a]	21,100	
Peter Gill a/c[b]	8,300	
Jane Butt a/c[c]	14,400	
Bob Smith a/c[d]	3,200	
Sally John a/c	5,400	
Sales a/c[e]	–	56,400
Returns inwards a/c[f]	4,000	
	56,400	56,400

Notes:
(a) Ally: 14,500 + 2,600 + 6,200 – 2,200 = £21,100
(b) Gill: 6,800 + 2,900 – 1,400 = £8,300
(c) Butt: 11,200 + 3,200 = £14,400
(d) Smith: 3,600 – 400 = £3,200
(e) Sales: 14,500 + 6,800 + 3,600 + 11,200 + 6,200 + 5,400 + 3,200 + 2,600 + 2,900 = £56,400
(f) Returns: 1,400 + 2,200 + 400 = £4,000

PQ 5.5 Prime entry, posting and extraction of a Trial Balance

Trial Balance as at 8.4.2010	£	£
Capital a/c	–	10,000
Furniture a/c	4,000	–
Rent a/c	300	–
Drawings a/c	200	–
Cash a/c[a]	5,080	–
Purchases a/c[b]	7,485	–
Purchase retn[c]	–	350
Sales a/c[d]	–	10,270
Returns inwards[e]	470	–
City Stores[f]	–	3,525
Global Ltd[g]	–	1,435
Advertising[h]	400	–
Hugh Soft[i]	3,540	–
Mary Bold[j]	1,715	–
Shelly Gray[k]	2,390	–
	25,580	25,580

Notes:
(a) Cash: 10,000 + 845 + 565 + 745 – 4,000 – 300 – 280 – 120 – 200 – 2,175 = £5,080
(b) Purchases: 1,480 + 2,175 + 1,645 + 2,185 = £7,485
(c) Purchase return: 140 + 210 = £350
(d) Sales: (credit 1,150 + 825 + 855 + 1,865 + 1,775 + 1,565 + 825) + (cash 845 + 565) = £10,270
(e) Sales returns: 85 + 30 + 210 + 145 = £470
(f) City Stores: 1,480 + 2,185 – 140 = £3,525
(g) Global Ltd: 2,175 + 1,645 – 210 – 2,175 = £1,435
(h) Advertising: 280 + 120 = £400
(i) Hugh Soft: 1,150 + 1,775 + 825 – 210 = £3,540
(j) Mary Bold: 825 + 1,865 – 85 – 145 – 745 = £1,715
(k) Shelly Gray: 855 + 1,565 – 30 = £2,390

PQ 5.6 How returns and drawings are treated in financial statements

(a) Drawings a/c, Purchase returns a/c and Sales returns a/c balances are offset from the balance in their corresponding main account.

(b)

Statement of income period ended 30 June 2010	£	£
Sales	10,270	
Less: Sales returns	(470)	9,800
Purchases	7,485	
Less: returns	(350)	(7,135)
Gross profit		2,665
Rent	300	
Advertising	400	(700)
Net profit		1,965

Statement of fin. position as at 30.6.2010	£	£
Non-current assets:		
Furniture		4,000
Current assets:		
Trade receivables:		
Hugh Soft	3,540	
Mary Bold	2,460	
Shelly Gray	2,390	8,390
Cash in hand		6,510
		18,900

	£	£
Capital	10,000	
Net profit	1,965	
Less: Drawings	(200)	11,765
Current liabilities:		
Trade payables:		
City Stores	3,525	
Global Ltd	3,610	7,135
		18,900

PQ 5.7 Books of account of a continuing business

Statement of income period ended 15.4.2010	£	£
Sales[a]		10,110
Purchases[b]		(8,425)
Gross profit		1,685
Rent	300	
Advertising[c]	500	(800)
Net Profit		885

Statement of fin. position as at 15.4.2010	£	£
Non-current assets:		
Furniture		4,000
Current assets:		
Trade receivables:		
Hugh Soft[d]	6,925	
Mary Bold[e]	4,720	
Shelly Gray[f]	4,465	16,110
Bank balance[g]		3,480
Cash in hand[h]		760
		24,350

	£	£
Capital b/f	11,765	
Net profit	885	
Drawings	(250)	12,400
Current liabilities:		
Trade payables:		
City Stores[i]	6,560	
Global Ltd[j]	5,390	11,950
		24,350

Notes:

(a) Sales: 1,825 + 1,550 + 1,285 + 1,125 + 975 + 725 + 845 + 835 + 945 = £10,110
(b) Purchases: 3,250 + 1,200 + 1,835 + 2,140 = £8,425
(c) Advertising: 275 + 225 = £500
(d) Hugh: 3,540 + 1,825 + 725 + 835 = £6,925
(e) Mary: 2,460 + 1,285 + 975 = £4,720
(f) Shelly: 2,390 + 1,550 + 1,125 + 845 + 945 – 2,390 = £4,465
(g) Bank: 5,500 + 2,390 – 3,610 – 275 – 300 – 225 = £3,480
(h) Cash: 6,510 – 5,500 – 250 = £760
(i) City Stores: 3,525 + 1,200 + 1,835 = £6,560
(j) Global Ltd: 3,610 + 3,250 + 2,140 – 3,610 = £5,390

Chapter 6 Inventories, profit margin and gross profit ratio

PQ 6.1 The effect of ignoring closing inventory

Statement of income year ended 31.12.2010

	£'000	£'000
Sales		640
Purchases	516	
Inventory	(112)	(404)
Gross profit		236
Expenses		(94)
Net profit		142

Statement of financial position as at 31 December 2010

	£'000	£'000
Non-current-assets		240
Current assets:		
Inventory	112	
Loan to staff	15	
Cash and bank	75	202
		442
		£'000
Capital		300
Net profit		142
		442

PQ 6.2 Consistent profit margin as a check on accounting

(a)

	£'000	£'000	£'000
Sales		5,840	
Less: Returns inwards		(124)	5,716
Opening inventory		324	
Purchases	4,620		
Returns outwards	(76)	4,544	
		4,868	
Closing inventory		(581)[c]	(4,287)[b]
Gross profit			1,429[a]

Notes:

(a) A profit margin of one-third converts to a gross profit ratio of one-fourth. Hence, the gross profit for the year, at one-fourth of £5,716, should be £1,429.

(b) Gross profit (£1,429) taken off sales reveals that the cost of goods sold should be £4,287.

(c) Opening inventory (£324) plus purchases (£4,544) less cost of sales (£4,287) identifies that the closing inventory should have been £581 and not £546.

(b) Reasons why the actual closing inventory (£546) is lower than what it should be may be any one or more of the following:

(i) Error in counting, or finding the cost of inventory in hand on 31.12.2010.

(ii) Sales have been understated either because of defalcation of sales proceeds or because of errors such as under-charging customers.

(iii) Failure to account for disposal of goods other than by way of sales – e.g. those removed by proprietor for personal use, those issued free and goods lost perhaps because of shop-lifting by customers or misappropriation by employees.

PQ 6.3 A purchase invoice yet to be accounted for

Statement of income year ended 31.12.2010

	£	£
Sales		563,200
Inventory	146,800	
Purchases[a]	440,700	
Carriage in[b]	11,400	
Inventory	(242,600)	
Drawings[c]	(450)	(355,850)
Gross profit		207,350
Expenses[b]	18,000	
Salary	24,800	(42,800)
Net profit		164,550

Statement of financial position as at 31.12.2010

	£	£
Non-current assets		180,000
Current assets:		
Inventory	242,600	
Trade receivables	98,500	
Cash and bank	11,700	352,800
		532,800
	£	£
Capital	300,000	
Net profit	164,550	
Drawings[c]	(18,450)	446,100
Current liabilities:		
Trade payables[a]		86,700
		532,800

Notes:

(a) Invoice, not recorded in the book of prime entry, should be included in the purchases and in trade payables.

(b) Carriage inwards is part of the cost of goods purchased for sale.

(c) The cost of goods removed by the proprietor should be removed from the cost of goods sold and included in the amount drawn by the proprietor.

PQ 6.4 Identifying the inventory included in a Trial Balance

(a)

Trial Balance as at 31.12.2010		
	£'000	£'000
Non-current assets	910	–
Sales	–	4,845
Salaries & wages	288	–
Rent	150	–
Returns inwards	125	–
Advertising	54	–
Drawing[a]	160	–
Inventory 31.12.	592	–
Trade receivables	495	–
Trade payables	–	326
Other expenses	165	–
Cash and bank	14	–
Capital	–	800
Cost of sales[b]	3,018	–
	5,971	5,971

(b)

Trial Balance as at 31.12.2010		
	£'000	£'000
Non-current assets	910	–
Gross profit[c]	–	1,702
Salaries & wages	288	–
Rent	150	–
Advertising	54	–
Drawings[a]	160	–
Inventory 31.12.	592	–
Trade receivables	495	–
Trade payables	–	326
Other expenses	165	–
Cash and bank	14	–
Capital	–	800
	2,828	2,828

(c)

Statement of income year ended 31.12.2010		
	£'000	£'000
Gross profit		1,702
Salaries & wages	288	
Rent	150	
Advertising	54	
Other expenses	165	(657)
Net profit		1,045

Statement of financial position as at 31 Dec. 2010		
	£'000	£'000
Non-current assets		910
Current assets:		
Inventory	592	
Trade receivables	495	
Cash and bank	14	1,101
		2,011
	£'000	£'000
Capital	800	
Net profit	1,045	
Drawings[a]	(160)	1,685
Current liabilities:		
Trade payables		326
		2,011

Notes:

(a) Drawings including the goods removed = 148 + 12 = £160,000

(b) Cost of sales: 412 + 3,248 + 112 – 54 – 12 – 592 – 96 = £3,018,000

(c) Gross profit: (4,845 – 125) – 3,018 = £1,702,000

(d) Usually the inventory in the Trial Balance is the 'opening' inventory. Exceptionally, if the Trial Balance is one extracted from the books after the cost of sales has been ascertained (as in answer (a)) or after the gross profit has been identified (as in answer (b)), then the inventory stated in the Trial Balance would be the 'closing' inventory.

PQ 6.5 The need to revise the value of closing inventory

Statement of income year ended 31.12.2010			
	£'000	£'000	£'000
Sales		4,845	
Returns		(125)	4,720
Inventory 1.1.		412	
Purchases	3,248		
Returns	(96)	3,152	
Carriage in		112	
Advertising		(54)	
Drawings[c]		(12)	
Inventory 31.12[a]		(548)	(3,062)
Gross profit			1,658
Inventory loss[b]		6	
Salaries & wages		288	
Rent		150	
Advertising		54	
Other expenses		165	(663)
Net profit			995

Statement of financial position as at 31.12.2010		
	£'000	£'000
Non-current assets		910
Current assets:		
Inventory[b]	542	
Trade receivables	495	
Cash & bank	14	1,051
		1,961
	£'000	£'000
Capital	800	
Net profit	995	
Drawings[c]	(160)	1,635
Current liabilities:		
Trade payables		326
		1,961

Notes:

(a) Error in valuing inventory:

480 items were valued at £100	£48,000
Correct value: 480 × £100/12	£4,000
Value of inventory inflated by	£44,000
Hence correct value: 592 – 44	£548,000

(b) NRV of defective garments: 28 – 3 = £25
Cost of 400 @ £40 = £16,000
NRV: 400 @ £25 = £10,000
Fall in value of defective garments = £6,000
Inventory reported as asset should be at: 548,000 – 6,000 = £542,000

(c) Drawings: 148,000 + 12,000 = £160,000

PQ 6.6 Possible reasons for a fall in gross profit ratio

(a) A business dealing in many lines may suffer a fall in the gross profit ratio, even while its sales rise, if there is a change in sales mix, i.e. reduced sale of more profitable lines and increased sale of less profitable lines.

(b) A deliberate policy of reducing profit margin with a view to improving sales or seeking a better share of the market.

(c) Error in counting/valuing year-end inventory, e.g. omitting to count goods with customers on approval, goods in bonded warehouse.

(d) Failure to properly match Purchases, Sales with opening and closing inventory.

(e) Fraud: defalcation of sales proceeds, inflation of purchases (when goods were not received), shop-lifting by customers etc.

PQ 6.7 Identifying inventory on basis of GP ratio (GCSE Edexcel)

Statement of income	Break		Brunch	
	£	£	£	£
Sales		40.00		13.50
Purchases	38.40		12.96	
Less: Inventory	(5.44)		(1.80)	
Loss of goods	(0.96)	(32.00)	(0.36)	(10.80)
Gross profit		8.00		2.70
Loss of inventory		(0.96)		(0.36)
Net profit		7.04		2.34

Sales:

Break: 200 @ 20p each	£40.00
Brunch: 90 @ 15p each	£13.50

Purchases:

Break: 5 × 48 @ 16p	£38.40
Brunch 3 × 36 @ 12p	£12.96

Units lost:	Break	Brunch
Purchased	240	108
Sold	(200)	(90)
In stock	(34)	(15)
Lost	6	3

PQ 6.8 A trader takes inventory after the year-end date

	£	£
Cost of inventory on 6 April 2011		216,400
(a) Purchases between 1.4.2011 & 6.4.2011		(48,400)
Sales between 1.4.2011 & 6.4.2011	74,100	
Sales returns between 1.4. & 6.4.	(2,100)	
Sales not delivered	(6,000)	
Profit at one-third of sale price	(22,000)	44,000
(b) Carry forward error (156,500 as 165,500)		(9,000)
(c) Goods in bonded warehouse		164,400
Expense inventory (1,600 + 2,800)		(4,400)
(d) Goods on approval	5,400	
Returned before 6 April	(1,800)	
Profit at one-third of sale price	(1,200)	2,400
Inventory to be removed from cost of sales		365,400
(e) Shop-soiled goods at cost	14,400	
Net realisable value (12,000 less 5%)	(11,400)	(3,000)
Inventory to be reported on S of FP		362,400

PQ 6.9 A manufacturer's inventory taken after the year-end

	£	£
Cost of inventory – 5 July 2011		865,200
(a) Furniture rollers 1,200 @ £20	24,000	
Actual cost: 1,200 @ £20/12	(2,000)	(22,000)
(b) Sales between 1.7. & 5.7.	144,000	
Sales not delivered	(48,000)	
	96,000	
Profit: £96,000 × 1/4	(24,000)	72,000
(c) Purchases between 1.7 & 5.7	200,000	
Yet to be received to hand	(150,000)	(50,000)
(d) Purchases pre 30.6 yet to be received		75,000
(e) Value of hinges – ignore – not for sale		–
(f) Office shelves: 400 @ £300	120,000	
NRV 400 @ £225	(90,000)	(30,000)
(g) Dining suite at cost	4,800	
NRV: £6,000 – £1,500	(4,500)	(300)
Cost of inventory on S of FP		809,900

PQ 6.10 Physical count taken after the year-end

	£	£
Inventory as at 31 May 2011		87,612
(c) Over-added inventory sheet		(126)
Under-added inventory sheet		72
(d) Delayed invoice omitted from inventory sheet		2,010
(e) Carry forward error (1,234 as 1,243)		(9)
(f) Goods yet to arrive		638
(g) Generators yet to be purchased		(347)
(h) Samples wrongly included in inventory		(63)
(i) Goods with customers (602 – 418)		(184)
(j) Goods on approval yet to be purchased		(267)
(a) Deteriorated goods at cost	570	
At NRV (800 – 120)	(680)	No loss
(b) Damaged goods at cost	200	
At NRV (110 – 40)	(70)	(130)
Cost of inventory to appear on S of FP		89,207

PQ 6.11 Using GP ratio to identify misappropriation

(a) Cost of inventory on 30 April 20x5

	Dept. A		Dept. B		Dept. C	
	£	£	£	£	£	£
Inventory as at 3.5.20X5		3,700		8,100		21,600
Sales	420		250		1,500	
Less: Returns		–		–	(300)	
	420		250		1,200	
Less: Profit margin[a]	(120)	300	(50)	200	(600)	600
Purchases		–		(1,500)		–
Purchases returns		270		–		800
Actual inventory on 30.4.		4,270		6,800		23,000

(b) Statement of income

	Dept. A		Dept. B		Dept. C	
	£	£	£	£	£	£
Sales		18,725		11,750		147,000
Inventory 1.4.	4,200		7,800		22,500	
Purchases	14,200		8,400		74,000	
	18,400		16,200		96,500	
Inventory 30.4.[b]	(5,025)	(13,375)	(6,800)	(9,400)	(23,000)	(73,500)
Gross profit[a]		5,350		2,350		73,500

There is a problem in Dept. A because inventory should be £5,025; whereas it is £4,270.

Notes:
(a) Gross profit is found by applying the respective profit margin to each department's sales.
(b) Closing inventory in each department is the balancing figure.

PQ 6.12 Delayed inventory count

		£	£
Results of inventory count on 6 January 2011			412,850
Less: Purchases after year-end – invoiced		74,800	
Less: received after 6 January		800	(74,000)
Less: Purchases before the year-end – invoiced received after 6 January			(12,400)
Add: Sales after year-end – invoiced	128,400		
Less: returned before the count	42,000		
	86,400	86,400	
Less: Profit	[86,400/5] =	(17,280)	69,120
Add Goods with customers – returnable		40,000	
Less: Profit	[40,000/5] =	(8,000)	32,000
Less: Overcast inventory sheet		94,800 – 84,800	(10,000)
Less: Incorrect pricing	[(48 × 15) – (48/12 × 15)] =	720 – 60	(660)
Less: Consumable inventory		3,000 + 4,000	(7,000)
Less: Reduction to NRV	(18 × 900) =	16,200	
	(18 × (400 – 50)) =	6,300	(9,900)
Inventory as at 31 December 2010			400,010

PQ 6.13 Cost-flow assumption – FIFO, LIFO and AVCO

(a) FIFO basis of cost-flow assumption – on periodic basis

Date	Receipts			Issues			Balance	
	Qty	Price	Value £	Qty	Price	Value £	Qty	Value £
1.1	Balance b/f						50	1,500
8.1	–	–	–	30	£30.00	900	20	600
10.1	100	£30.00	3,000	–	–	–	120	3,600
12.1	–	–	–	30	£30.00	900	90	2,700
15.1	–	–	–	50	£30.00	1,500	40	1,200
21.1	120	£30.50	3,660	–	–	–	160	4,860
23.1	–	–	–	30	£30.00	900	130	3,960
28.1	–	–	–	60	–	1,825[a]	70	2,135
1.2	–	–	–	20	£30.50	610	50	1,525
5.2	–	–	–	30	£30.50	915	20	610
14.2	150	£31.00	4,650	–	–	–	170	5,260
20.2	–	–	–	40	–	1,230[b]	130	4,030
23.2	–	–	–	60	£31.00	1,860	70	2,170
1.3	–	–	–	30	£31.00	930	40	1,240
4.3	120	£31.50	3,780	–	–	–	160	5,020
10.3	–	–	–	50	–	1,555[c]	110	3,465
14.3	–	–	–	30	£31.50	945	80	2,520
19.3	–	–	–	40	£31.50	1,260	40	1,260
23.3	100	£32.00	3,200	–	–	–	140	4,460
27.3	–	–	–	60	–	1,900[d]	80	2,560
30.3	–	–	–	60	£32.00	1,920	20	640

Notes:

(a) Issue on 28.1:

10 @ £30 =	£300	
50 @ £30.50	£1,525	£1,825

(b) Issue on 20.2:

20 @ £30.50	£610	
20 @ £31.00	£620	£1,230

(c) Issue on 10.3:

40 @ £31.00	£1,240	
10 @ £31.50	£315	£1,555

(d) Issue on 27.3:

40 @ £31.50	£1,260	
20 @ £32.00	£640	£1,900

LIFO basis of cost-flow assumption – on periodic basis

Date	Receipts			Issue			Balance	
	Qty	Price	Value £	Qty	Price	Value £	Qty	Value £
1.1	Balance b/f						50	1,500
8.1	–	–	–	30	£30.00	900	20	600
10.1	100	£30.00	3,000	–	–	–	120	3,600
12.1	–	–	–	30	£30.00	900	90	2,700
15.1	–	–	–	50	£30.00	1,500	40	1,200
21.1	120	£30.50	3,660	–	–	–	160	4,860
23.1	–	–	–	30	£30.50	915	130	3,945
28.1	–	–	–	60	£30.50	1,830	70	2,115
1.2	–	–	–	20	£30.50	610	50	1,505
5.2	–	–	–	30	–	905[a]	20	600
14.2	150	£31.00	4,650	–	–	–	170	5,250
20.2	–	–	–	40	£31.00	1,240	130	4,010
23.2	–	–	–	60	£31.00	1,860	70	2,150
1.3	–	–	–	30	£31.00	930	40	1,220
4.3	120	£31.50	3,780	–	–	–	160	5,000
10.3	–	–	–	50	£31.50	1,575	110	3,425
14.3	–	–	–	30	£31.50	945	80	2,480
19.3	–	–	–	40	£31.50	1,260	40	1,220
23.3	100	£32.00	3,200	–	–	–	140	4,420
27.3	–	–	–	60	£32.00	1,920	80	2,500
30.3	–	–	–	60	–	1,900[b]	20	600

Notes:

(a) Issue on 5.2:

10 @ £30.50	£305	
20 @ £30.00	£600	£905

(b) Issue on 30.3:

40 @ £32	£1,280	
20 @ £31.00	£620	£1,900

Average cost basis of cost-flow assumption – on periodic method

Date	Receipts			Issue			Balance	
	Qty	Price	Value £	Qty	Price	Value £	Qty	Value £
1.1	Balance b/f						50	1,500.00
8.1	–	–	–	30	£30.00	900.00	20	600.00
10.1	100	£30.00	3,000	–	–	–	120	3,600.00
12.1	–	–	–	30	£30.00	900.00	90	2,700.00
15.1	–	–	–	50	£30.00	1,500.00	40	1,200.00
21.1	120	£30.50	3,660	–	–	–	160	4,860.00
23.1	–	–	–	30	£30.25	907.50	130	3,952.50
28.1	–	–	–	60	£30.25	1,815.00	70	2,137.50
1.2	–	–	–	20	£30.25	605.00	50	1,532.50
5.2	–	–	–	30	£30.25	907.50	20	625.00
14.2	150	£31.00	4,650	–	–	–	170	5,275.00
20.2	–	–	–	40	£30.50	1,220.00	130	4,055.00
23.2	–	–	–	60	£30.50	1,830.00	70	2,225.00
1.3	–	–	–	30	£30.50	915.00	40	1,310.00
4.3	120	£31.50	3,780	–	–	–	160	5,090.00
10.3	–	–	–	50	£30.75	1,537.50	110	3,552.50
14.3	–	–	–	30	£30.75	922.50	80	2,630.00
19.3	–	–	–	40	£30.75	1,230.00	40	1,400.00
23.3	100	£32.00	3,200	–	–	–	140	4,600.00
27.3	–	–	–	60	£31.00	1,860.00	80	2,740.00
30.3	–	–	–	60	£31.00	1,860.00	20	880.00

(b) Cost-flow assumptions acceptable to IAS 2 are:

1. FIFO
2. Weighted average cost method

(c)

	FIFO basis		AVCO basis	
Sales[a]		£31,000		£31,000
Inventory	£1,500		£1,500	
Purchases	£17,890		£17,890	
	£19,390		£19,390	
Inventory	(£640)	(£18,750)	(£880)	(£18,510)
Gross profit		£12,250		£12,490

Note:

(a) 620 units sold at £50 each = £310,000

Chapter 7 Accruals, prepayments, depreciation and bad debts

PQ 7.1 The impact of every transaction on account balances

Activities	Transaction
One to two	Credit purchase £3,000
Two to three	Credit sale for £8,000 of goods costing £5,000
Three to four	£4,800 collected from Trade receivables
Four to five	£2,000 paid to payables
Five to six	£200 expense paid
Six to seven	£300 expense accrued
Seven to eight	£500 w/off as depreciation
Eight to nine	£100 drawings

PQ 7.2 Period-end adjustments

Statement of income	£
Cost of sales	200,000
Stationery	3,000
Rent	12,000
Salaries	25,000
Depreciation	3,600

Statement of financial position as at 31 December 2010	£
Vehicle	18,000
Acc. depreciation	(3,600)
	14,400
Current assets:	
Inventory	14,500
Unused stationery	600
Prepaid rent	3,000

	£
Current liabilities:	
Salary accrued	2,200

PQ 7.3 Payments in advance and in arrears

(a)

Rent account (when paid in advance)

		£			£
1.1.	Balance b/f[a]	2,000	31.12.	Income Statement	24,000
1.2.	Cash a/c	6,000			
1.5.	Cash a/c	6,000			
1.8.	Cash a/c	6,000			
1.11.	Cash a/c	6,000	31.12.	Bal. c/d	2,000
		26,000			26,000
1.1.	Balance b/d	2,000			

(b)

Rent account (when paid in arrears)

		£			£
31.1.	Cash a/c	6,000	1.1.	Bal. B/d[b]	4,000
30.4.	Cash a/c	6,000			
31.7.	Cash a/c	6,000	31.12.	Income Statement	24,000
31.1.	Cash a/c	6,000			
31.12.	Balance c/d	4,000			
		28,000			28,000
			1.1.	Bal. B/d	4,000

Notes:

(a) When £6,000 was paid in advance on 1.11.2009, that amount would include £2,000 paid in advance for January 2010.

(b) Rent for November & December 2009, at £2,000 per month, will remain unpaid as at 1 January 2010.

PQ 7.4 Relations between payments and expense in a continuing business

(a) Vehicle maintenance	£25 accruals
(b) Insurance	£625 expense
(c) Salaries	£2,545 payments
(d) Rates	£355 payments
(e) Telephone	£370 expense

PQ 7.5 Relations between payments and expense in a continuing business

(a) Rent	£400 asset
(b) Fuel	£700 expense
(c) Equipment	£1,600 expense & £6,400 asset
(d) Motor vehicle	£2,000 expense & £6,000 asset
(e) Salaries	£6,900 expense
(f) Insurance	£1,300 payment
(g) Telephone	£360 payment

PQ 7.6 Accounting for expenses on an accruals basis

Rent account

		£			£
11.7.	Cash	600	1.6.	Bal. b/d	400
14.11.	Cash	800	31.5.	Income Statement	2,400
16.3.	Cash	800			
31.5.	Bal. c/d[a]	600			
		2,800			2,800
				Bal. b/d	600

Insurance account

		£			£
1.6.	Balance b/f	360	31.5.	Inc. statement	1,160
24.9.	Cash	1,200	31.5.	Balance c/d[b]	400
		1,560			1,560
		400			

Rates account

		£			£
1.6.	Balance b/f	350	31.5.	Inc. Statem.	1,450
3.10.	Cash	700			
8.4.	Cash	800	31.5.	Balance c/d[c]	400
		1,850			1,850
	Balance b/d	400			

Notes:

(a) Two months' rent were in arrears on 1.5.2009. Out of twelve months in current year, rent has been paid for 11 months only leaving three months' rent in arrears.

(b) £1,200 as insurance covers a full year up to four months after the Statement of financial position date: £1,200 × 4/12 = £400 prepaid.

(c) £800 paid as rates covers six months out of which three months are after Statement of fin. position date: £800 × 3/6 = £400 prepaid.

PQ 7.7 Accounting for renting a photocopy machine (ICSA)

City Equipment account

		£			£
1.5.	Balance b/f	8,000	1.5.	Balance b/f	1,245
30.6.	Cash	5,000	30.4.	Income Statement[b]	34,312
30.9.	Cash	5,000			
31.12.	Cash	5,000			
1.1.	Cash-rent	15,000			
31.3.	Cash	5,000			
30.4.	Bal. c/d[c]	2,557	30.4.	Bal. c/d[a]	10,000
		45,557			45,557
	Balance b/d	10,000		Balance b/d	2,557

Notes:

(a) £15,000 paid as rent covers a year which is eight months into next year: £15,000 × 8/12 = 10,000.

(b) Expense for the year consists of:

Rent – eight months to December 2009	8,000
Rent – four months from Jan. to April 2010	5,000
Copy charges: 710,400 × 3p each	21,312
	34,312

(c) £2,557 owed as copy charges is the balancing figure.

PQ 7.8 Accounting for income on an accrual basis: 1

(a) Commission earnings	£550 income
(b) Interest receivable	£200 asset
(c) Rent receivable	£1,550 income
(d) Commission receivable	£1,230 income
(e) Interest receivable	£300 asset
(f) Rent receivable	£7,000 receipt

PQ 7.9 Accounting for income on accrual basis: 2

Rent receivable account

		£			£
31.12.	Income statement	8,000	x	Cash	6,000
			31.12.	Balance c/d	2,000
		8,000			8,000
1.1.	Balance b/d	2,000	y	Cash	12,000
31.12.	Income statement	8,000			
31.12.	Balance c/d	2,000			
		12,000			12,000
				Balance b/d	2,000

PQ 7.10 Bad debt recoveries

(a) The amount received from Maggie, a debt written off already, should not be credited to the Trade receivables a/c. It should be treated as an income and included in the Statement of income, described as 'bad debt recoveries'.

(b) **Allowance for doubtful debts account**

	£		£
Bad debt w/off	8,400	Balance b/f[a]	7,460
Balance c/d[c]	8,800	Income Statement	9,740
	17,200		17,200
		Balance b/d	8,800

Notes:

(a) Balance b/f is 4% of £186,500

(b) Trade receivables balance c/d down at year end:
186,500 + 528,400 – 8,400 – 19,200 – (471,600 – 4,300) = £220,000

(c) Balance c/f is 4% of £220,000 = £8,800

PQ 7.11 Allowance for doubtful debts over several accounting periods

Allowance for doubtful debts account

		£			£
2010	Bad debt w/off	18,400	2010	Balance b/f[a]	17,275
2010	Balance c/d	20,625	2010	Inc. Statement	21,750
		39,025			39,025
2011	Bad debt w/off	11,800	2011	Balance b/d[a]	20,625
2011	Balance c/d	18,420	2011	Inc. Statement	9,595
		30,220			30,220
2012	Bad debt w/off	17,650	2012	Balance b/d[a]	18,420
2012	Balance c/d	27,425	2012	Inc. Statement	26,655
		45,075			45,075
2013	Bad debt w/off	14,400	2013	Balance b/d[a]	27,425
2013	Balance c/d	25,640	2013	Inc. Statement	12,615
		40,040			40,040
			2014	Balance b/d[a]	25,640

Note:

(a) Balance of allowance c/d at the end of each year is 5% of trade receivables outstanding on the respective dates.

PQ 7.12 Annual adjustment of allowance for doubtful debts

Allowance for doubtful debts account

		£			£
			2009	Balance b/f	2,400
2009	Balance c/d	4,250	2009	Statement of income	1,850
		4,250			4,250
2010	Bad debts w/off	4,000	2010	Balance b/d	4,250
2010	Balance c/d	5,750	2010	Statement of income	5,500
		9,750			9,750
2011	Bad debts w/off	1,500	2011	Balance b/d	5,750
	Statement of income	215			
	Balance c/d	4,035			
		5,750			
			2012	Balance b/d	5,750
					4,035

Allowances as at 31.12	2009	2010	2011
30 to 45 days	3% of 45,000 = £1,350	3% of 75,000 = £2,250	3% of 64,500 = £1,935
46 to 60 days	5% of 28,000 = £1,400	5% of 30,000 = £1,500	5% of 22,000 = £1,100
60 + days	10% of 15,000 = £1,500	10% of 20,000 = £2,000	10% of 10,000 = £1,000

A bad debt is a receivable which is eliminated from the books because it is not regarded as recoverable and that amount is offset from the allowance set up for the purpose; doubtful debts are those doubtful of recovery, but writing them off from the books would be premature.

PQ 7.13 Receivables and allowances over successive years (ACCA adapted)

Trade receivables account

		£			£
2010	Balance	10,000	2010	Returns	1,000
	Sales	100,000		Cash	90,000
				Bad debt	500
				Discount	400
				Balance c/d	18,100
		110,000			110,000
2011	Balance b/d	18,100	2011	Returns[b]	1,800
	Sales[b]	90,000		Cash	95,000
				Payables	3,000
				Bad debts	1,500
				Discount	500
				Balance c/d	6,300
		108,100			108,100
2012	Balance b/d	6,300			

Allowance for doubtful debts account

		£			£
2010			2010	Bal. B/d	400
	Bad debt	500		Income Statement	1,195
	Bal. c/d[a]	1,095			
		1,595			1,595
2011	Bad debt	1,500	2011	Bal. b/d	1,095
	Balance c/d[c]	315		Income Statement	720
		1,815			1,815
			2012	Bal. b/d	315

Notes:

(a) 5% of (18,100 – 200) = 895 + 200 = £1,095

(b) 90% of sales & returns

(c) 5% of 6,300 = £315

PQ 7.14 Trial Balances extracted on same date at different stages of accounting

Trial Balances as at 31 December 2010

Trial balance (1)

	£'000	£'000
Capital a/c	–	100
Furniture a/c	10	–
Motor vehicle a/c	20	–
Sales a/c	–	492
Postage a/c	1	–
Sales commission a/c	4	–
Staff welfare a/c	3	–
Salaries & wages a/c	48	–
Lighting/heating a/c	2	–
Rent a/c	15	–
Advertising a/c	9	–
Cash a/c	10	–
Trade receivables a/c	34	–
Purchases a/c	465	–
Trade payables a/c	–	29
	621	621

Trial balance (2)

	£'000	£'000
Capital a/c	–	100
Furniture a/c	10	–
Motor vehicle a/c	20	–
Sales a/c	–	492
Postage a/c	1	–
Sales commission a/c	4	–
Staff welfare a/c	3	–
Salaries & wages a/c	48	–
Lighting/heating a/c	2	–
Rent a/c	15	–
Advertising a/c	9	–
Cash a/c	10	–
Trade receivables a/c	34	–
Cost of sales[a]	387	–
Closing inventory[a]	78	–
Trade payables a/c	–	29
	621	621

Trial Balance (3)

	£'000	£'000
Capital a/c	–	100
Furniture a/c	10	–
Motor vehicle a/c	20	–
Sales a/c	–	492
Postage a/c	1	–
Sales commission a/c	4	–
Staff welfare a/c	3	–
Salaries & wages a/c[d]	52	–
Lighting/heating a/c[e]	3	–
Rent a/c[f]	12	–
Advertising a/c	9	–
Cash a/c	10	–
Trade receivables a/c	34	–
Cost of sales	387	–
Closing inventory	78	–
Trade payables a/c	–	29
Depreciation – furniture[b]	2	–
Accum. depn. furniture[b]	–	2
Depreciation – vehicle[c]	4	–
Accum. depn. Vehicle[c]	–	4
Salaries accrued[d]	–	4
Lighting accrued[e]	–	1
Prepaid rent a/c[f]	3	–
	632	632

Trial Balance (4)

Statement of income year ended 31.12.2010	£'000
Sales	492
Cost of sales	(387)
Gross profit	105
Salaries	(52)
Staff welfare	(3)
Lighting/heat	(3)
Postage	(1)
Depreciation – Furniture	(2)
Rent	(12)
Depreciation – Vehicle	(4)
Sales commission	(4)
Advertising	(9)
Net profit	15

Statement of financial position as at 31 December 2010	£'000
Furniture 10 (2)	8
Vehicle 20 (4)	16
Inventory	78
Receivables	34
Prepaid rent	3
Cash	10
	149
	£'000
Capital	100
Net profit	15
	115
Payables	29
Salary accrued	4
Lighting accrued	1
	149

Notes:

(a) Closing inventory is transferred to an asset a/c from Purchases.

(b) Furniture is depreciated at 20% of cost: 20% of £10,000 = £2,000.

(c) Vehicles too are depreciated at 20% of cost: 20% of £20,000 = £4,000.

(d) Salaries is increased by the amount remaining unpaid, reported as a liability.

(e) Similarly, lighting is increased by the amount remaining unpaid.

(f) Amount of rent paid in advance for next year is transferred to an asset a/c.

PQ 7.15 A basic question from Trial Balance to Statement of financial position sheet

Statement of income year ended 31.12.2010

	£	£
Sales	532,750	
Returns	(7,250)	525,500
Inventory	52,500	
Purchases	326,850	
Inventory	(72,400)	(306,950)
Gross profit		218,550
Salaries[a]	61,700	
Rent[b]	24,000	
Depn – vehicle[c]	30,000	
Depn – furniture[d]	2,400	
Other expenses	22,680	
Bad debts[e]	7,420	(148,200)
Net profit		70,350

Notes:

(a) Salary: 48,540 + 13,160
(b) Rent: 18,000 + 6,000
(c) Vehicle: 20% of 150,000
(d) Furniture: 5% of 48,000
(e) Bad debt: 4,400 + 3,020
(f) 80,000 + 30,000
(g) 16,800 + 2.400

Statement of fin. position 1.12.2010

		£	£
Non-current assets:			
Motor vehicle		150,000	
Accumulated depreciation[f]		(110,000)	40,000
Furniture		48,000	
Accumulated depreciation[g]		(19,200)	28,800
Current assets:			
Inventory		72,400	
Trade receivables	60,400		
Allowance for dd	(3,020)	57,380	
Cash and bank		5,180	134,960
			203,760
		£	£
Capital		80,000	
Net profit		70,350	150,350
Current liabilities:			
Trade payables		34,250	
Accrued salary		13,160	
Accrued rent		6,000	53,410
			203,760

PQ 7.16 Another Trial Balance to Statement of financial position question

Statement of income year ended 30 June 2010

	£'000	£'000
Sales		590
Inventory	42	
Purchases	348	
Carriage inwards	14	
Inventory	(72)	(332)
Gross profit		258
Salary[a]	90	
Stationery	12	
Depn – furniture[b]	4	
Rent[c]	24	
Postage	7	
Business rates	12	
Telephone	9	
Depn – vehicle	6	
Bad debt[d]	7	(171)
Interest[e]		(6)
Net Profit		81

Workings:

(a) Salary: 78 + 12 = £90
(b) Furniture depn: 10% of £40 = £4
(c) Rent: 40 – £4 prepaid – 12 drawings
(d) Bad debts: 5 + 2 = £7
(e) Vehicle depn: 50 – 10 scrap @ 20% for nine months = £6
(f) Interest: 12% of 60 for 10 months = £6
£3 of this was paid already and remainder is reported as a liability.

Statement of financial position as at 30.6.2010

	£'000	£'000	£'000
Non-current assets:			
Furniture	40	(4)	36
Motor vehicle	50	(6)	44
Current assets:			
Inventory		72	
Receivables	40		
Allowance[d]	(2)	38	
Prepayment[c]		4	
Cash/bank		67	181
			261
		£'000	£'000
Capital		90	
Net profit		81	
Drawings[c]		(12)	159
Non-current liabilities:			
Loan from Brown			60
Current liabilities:			
Trade payables		27	
Salary accrued[a]		12	
Interest accrued[f]		3	42
			261

PQ 7.17 Preparing a business forecast

	2010		2011		2012	
	£'000	£'000	£'000	£'000	£'000	£'000
Sales		320,000		630,000		900,000
Inventory	–		60,000		105,000	
Purchases	300,000		525,000		800,000	
Inventory	(60,000)	240,000	(105,000)	480,000	(200,000)	705,000
Gross profit		80,000		150,000		195,000
Expenses		(32,000)		(56,000)		(72,000)
Depreciation		(2,000)		(2,000)		(2,000)
Net profit		46,000		92,000		121,000

Notes:
8,000 × £40 = £320,000
10,000 @ £30 = £300,000
10,000 – 8,000 @ £30 = £60,000
8,000 @ £4 = £32,000
£10,000 cost of plant/5 yrs = £2,000
14,000 @ £45 = £630,000
15,000 @ £35 = £525,000
3,000 @ £35 = £105,000
14,000 @ £4 = £56,000
18,000 @ £50 = £900,000
20,000 @ £40 = £800,000

Chapter 8 Disposal, revaluation and impairment of non-current assets

PQ 8.1 A basic question involving disposal of a non-current asset

Sale proceeds of warehouse		£240,000
Cost of warehouse	£180,000	
Structural alterations	£30,000	
Accumulated depreciation	(£22,500)	(£187,500)
Gain on disposal		£52,500

Acc. depn: 2/3 of 180,000 + 30,000/50 years × 7.5 years = £22,500

PQ 8.2 Depreciation using the straight-line method and accounting for disposal

(a)

	£
Accumulated depreciation to 31.3.2010	
AC504: 20% of 320,000 for 3.25 years	208,000
DL201: 20% of 480,000 for 1.25 years	120,000
FN378: 20% of £520,000 for 1/2 year	52,000
	380,000

(b)

Statement of income year ended 31.3.2011	£
Gain on disposal[a]	84,000
Depreciation[b]	276,000

Statement of financial position as at 31 March 2011	£'000
Machinery[c]	1,600
Accumulated Depreciation[d]	(432)

(a) Gain on disposal: £180,000 – 320,000 – (208,000 + 16,000 depreciation) = £84,000
(b) Depreciation: 20% of £320,000 for 3 months + of £480,000 and £520,000 for full year and of £600,000 for six months = £276,000
(c) Machinery: £1,320,000 + £600,000 acquisition – £320,000 disposal = £1,600,000
(d) Accum. depreciation: £380,000 + £276,000 – (208,000 + 16,000 on disposal) = £432,000

PQ 8.3 Depreciation on the reducing balance method and accounting for disposal

(a) Accumulated depreciation on 1.1.2010: £540,000 – £296,400 = £243,600
(b) Depreciation on machine sold:

	£	£
Cost of the machine	60,000	
2009: 40% of 60,000 for 6 months	(12,000)	12,000
Wdv on 31.12.2009	48,000	
2010: 40% of 48,000 for full year	(19,200)	19,200
Wdv on 31.12.2010	28,800	31,200
2011: 40% of 28,800 for six months	(5,760)	5,760
	23,040	36,960

(c) Depreciation on machine scrapped:

	£	£
Cost of the machine	40,000	
2008: 40% of 40,000	(16,000)	16,000
Wdv on 31.12.2008	24,000	
2009: 40% of 24,000	(9,600)	9,600
Wdv on 31.12.2009	14,400	25,600
2010: 40% of 14,400	(5,760)	5,760
Wdv on 31.12.2010	8,640	31,360
2011: 40% of 8,640 × 9 months	(2,592)	2,592
Wdv on 1.10.2011	6,048	33,952

(d) Depreciation on remaining machinery:

	£	£
Cost of all machinery – 1.1.2011	540,000	
Cost of the machine sold	(60,000)	
Cost of machine scrapped	(40,000)	440,000
Acc. depn. on all – 1.1.2011	243,600	
Acc. depn. on machine scrapped	(31,360)	
Acc. depn. on machine sold	(31,200)	(181,040)
WDV on remaining machine on 1.1.2011		258,960
Deprn: @ 40% on 258,960		103,584

(e) Depreciation for the year 2011:

	£
Depreciation on machine sold	5,760
Depreciation on machine scrapped	2,592
Depreciation on remaining machines	103,584
On new machine: 40% of 90,000 × 4 mths	12,000
Total depreciation in the year	123,936

(f)

	£
Disposal: proceeds	26,200
Wdv	(23,040)
Gain on disposal	3,160

(g)

Machine scrapped: Loss of wdv	6,048

Statement of income year ended 31.12.2011	
	£
Depreciation[e]	(123,936)
Gain on disposal	3,160
Loss by scrappage	(6,048)

Statement of movement of non-current assets	
	Machinery
	£
Balance b/f	540,000
Acquisition	90,000
Disposal	(100,000)
Balance c/f	530,000
Accumulated depreciation	£
Balance b/f	243,600
Depreciation	123,936
Disposal	(70,912)
Balance c/f	296,624
Wdv 31.12.2011	233,376
Wdv 31.12.2010	296,400

PQ 8.4 How depreciation features on financial statements

Movement of non-current assets					
	Land	Buildings	Vehicles	Machines	Total
	£'000	£'000	£'000	£'000	£'000
Balance b/f	800	1,600	760	1,200	4,360
Acquisitions	–	–	–	400	400
Disposal	–	–	–128	–	–128
Balance c/f	800	1,600	632	1,600	4,632
Accumulated depreciation					
Balance b/f	–	448	240	600	1,288
Depreciation	–	32	130	65	227
Disposal	–	–	–44	–	–44
Balance c/f	–	480	326	665	1,471
WDV-30.9.2011	800	1,120	306	935	3,161
WDV-30.9.2010	800	1,152	520	600	3,072

Notes:

(a) Cost split in the ratio 1:2

(b) Vehicle balance b/f had been increased by £40 because of the wrong credit.

(c) The cost of machine acquired is separated

(d) Depn on building: 2% of 1,600 = **32**

(e) Depn on vehicles;
One sold: 25% of (128 – 16) **28**
Others: 25% of (760 – 128) – (240 – 16) **102** **130**

(f) Accum.depn on vehicle sold: 16 + 28 = **44**

(g) Depreciation on machines: Continuing: 5% of 1,200 **60**
New: 5% of 400 for three months **5** **65**

(h) Loss on disposal of vehicle:
WDV at disposal: 128 – 44 **84** **40** **44**

Sale proceeds	40
WDV on date of sale: 128 – 44	(84)
	(4)

PQ 8.5 How depreciation, disposal and revaluation feature on financial statements

Statement of income-year ended 30.6.2011	£'000
Depreciation of buildings[a]	48
Depreciation of furniture[b]	140
Amortisation of brand name[c]	240
Loss on disposal of furniture[d]	280

As reserves:	£'000
Gain on revaluation of land and building	1,620

Statement of financial position as at 30 June 2011	Cost	Depn	£'000
Non-current assests:			
Land and buildings at valuation			4,500
Furniture	800	(460)	340
Brand name	720	(240)	480

(a) Depn – building: 2% of 2/3 of 3,600 = £48
(b) Depreciation of furniture: 20% of 800 for 9 months + 20% of 800 for full year = £140
(c) Amortisation of brand: 720 × 5/15 = £240
(d) Disposal loss: 800 – 280 ac. depreciation – 240 proceeds = £280

Revaluation reserve:
3,600 cost – (672 + 48 ac. depreciation) – 4,500 fair value = £1,620

Chapter 9 Accounting for limited companies

PQ 9.1 Allotment of shares

Application and allotment account

	£		£
Cash – refund	400,000	Cash – application	2,400,000
Share capital[a]	8,000,000	Cash – allotment	6,960,450
Share premium	1,000,000	Balance c/d	39,550
	9,400,000		9,400,000
Balance b/d	39,550		

Ordinary share capital account

			£
		Applic & allotment a/c[a]	8,000,000

Share premium account

			£
		Applic & allotment a/c	1,000,000

Note:
(a) Called-up capital is par value (£1) less call still to be made (20p). At any point of time the Share capital account records the called-up value (80p each) of the number of shares in issue (10 million).

Statement of financial position as at 31.12.2010	£
Capital and reserves:	
Ordinary shares of £1, 80p called	8,000,000
Share premium account	1,000,000
As asset:	
Call up capital not received	39,550

PQ 9.2 Financial statements for internal use – a trading company

Statement of income year ended 30 June 2011

	£	£
Sales revenue		4,428,200
Inventory	428,620	
Purchases	3,936,500	
Inventory	(512,450)	
Sales promotion	(18,400)	(3,834,270)
Gross profit		593,930
Distribution costs:		
Sales promotion	18,400	
Depn – vehicle	29,700	
Telephone . . .	3,688	
Salaries/wages	40,830	
Advertising	24,400	
Sales commission	32,600	(149,618)
Administrative expenses:		
Salaries/wages	95,270	
Telephone . . .	14,752	
Audit fees	6,000	
Depn – building	11,200	
Rent	24,000	(151,222)
Interest		(32,000)
Profit before taxation		261,090
Taxation		(112,000)
Profit after tax		149,090

Statement of changes in equity:

Retained earnings b/f	348,780
Profit after tax	149,090
Dividend paid	(12,000)
Retained earnings c/f	485,870

Statement of financial position as at 30 June 2011

Non-current assets:	Cost	Acc. Depn	£
Land & buildings	840,000	(146,650)	693,350
Motor vehicles	180,000	(110,700)	69,300
Current assets:			
Inventory		512,450	
Trade receivables		562,400	
Prepaid rent		6,000	
Cash and bank		12,550	1,093,400
			1,856,050
		£	£
Capital & reserves:			
Ordinary shares of 50p each		300,000	
Share premium account		30,000	
Retained earnings		485,870	815,870
Non-current liabilities:			
8% Debentures			400,000
Current liabilities:			
Trade payables		494,640	
Taxation		112,000	
Interest accrued		16,000	
Salaries accrued		11,540	
Audit fees accrued		6,000	640,180
			1,856,050

PQ 9.3 Financial statements for internal use – a manufacturing company

(a) Statement of income year ended 31 March 2011

	£'000	£'000
Sales revenue		3,282
Returns inwards		(44)
		3,238
Inventory – 1.4.2010	212	
Purchases	2,385	
Carriage inwards	21	
Depreciation – machinery	140	
Rent	20	
Inventory – 31.3.2011	(398)	
Cost of goods sold		(2,380)
Gross profit		858
Distribution costs:		
Depreciation – vehicles	99	
Bad debts	28	
Advertising	74	(201)
Administrative expenses:		
Rent	40	
Salaries & wages	316	
Administrative expenses	194	(550)
Operating profit		107
Dividend received		51
Interest paid		(4)
Profit before taxation		154
Taxation		(38)
Profit after taxation		116

Note: Dividend proposed £120,000.

Statement of changes in equity

	£'000
Balance b/f	176
Profit after tax	116
Dividend paid	(30)
Balance c/f	262

(b) Statement of fin. position as at 31 March 2011

	£'000	£'000	£'000
Non-current assets:			
Machinery	2,800	(560)	2,240
Motor vehicles	920	(479)	441
Investments			340
			3,021
Current assets:			
Inventory		398	
Trade receivables	960		
Allowance for d. debts	(48)	912	
Cash & bank balance		11	1,321
			4,342
		£'000	£'000
Equity & reserves:			
Ordinary shares of 50p each		3,000	
Share premium account		600	
Accumulated profit		262	3,862
Current liabilities:			
Trade payables		398	
Accrued expenses		12	
Taxation		29	
Bank overdraft		41	480
			4,342

Workings:

1. Bad debts: 12 + 16 = 32
2. Allowance for doubtful debts: 32 + 16 = 28
3. Taxation expense: 29 + 9 under-provision = 38
4. Depreciation on vehicles:

Old vehicles: 20% of (920 – 60 new – 380 ac.dep =	96
New vehicle: 20% of 60 for 3 months =	3
	99

PQ 9.4 Financial statements for internal use (CIMA amended)

Statement of income for year ended 31 March 2011

	£	£	£
Sales revenue		249,760	
Less: Returns		(12,900)	236,860
Inventory		74,000	
Purchases	134,630		
Less: Returns	(4,875)	129,755	
Depreciation – plant[a]		24,000	
Inventory		(124,875)	(102,880)
Gross profit			133,980
Distribution costs:			
Distribution exp.[b]		4,200	
Depreciation – vehicle[c]		3,800	(8,000)
Administrative expenses:			
Admin expenses[d]		10,650	
Depreciation – building[e]		2,000	(12,650)
Disposal of vehicle[f]			(1,000)
Discount received			1,850
Discount allowed			(3,200)
Profit before taxation			110,980
Taxation			(19,000)
Profit after taxation			91,980
Retained earnings b/f			69,695
Retained earnings c/f			161,675

Statement of fin. position as at 31.3.2011

	£	£	£
Non-current assets:			
Land	–	–	60,000
Buildings	50,000	-22,000	28,000
Plant/machine	120,000	-98,000	22,000
Motor vehicle	18,000	-12,600	5,400
			115,400
Current assets:			
Inventory		124,875	
Trade receivables		122,500	
Prepayments[h]		20,000	
Cash and bank		3,500	270,875
			386,275

	£	£
Capital & reserves:		
Ordinary shares of £1 each		100,000
Retained earnings c/f		161,675
		261,675
Current liabilities:		
Trade payables	99,800	
Accrued expenses[g]	9,800	
Taxation	15,000	124,600
		386,275

Notes:

(a) 20% of 120,000
(b) 6,900 + 5,300 – 8,000 = 4,200
(c) 25% of (32,000 – 14,000) less (16,800 – 8,000) = 3,800
(d) 22,150 + 4,500 – 12,000 = 14,650
(e) 4% of 50,000
(f) 14,000 – 8,000 – 5,000 = 1,000
(g) 4,500 + 5,300
(h) Prepayments 12 + 8 = 20

PQ 9.5 Financial statements for publication (from ACCA, CAT 6 amended)

(a)

Statement of financial position as at 31 May 2011

	$'000	$'000	$'000
Non-current assets:			
Land			345
Building	1,040	(212)	828
Plant	1,200	(600)	600
Goodwill[b]			68
			1,841
Current assets:			
Inventory		560	
Trade receivables[c]		660	
Bank		147	1,367
			3,208

	$'000	$'000
Capital and reserves:		
Share capital £1		1,080
Share premium account		40
General reserve		70
Retained earnings		238
		1,428
Non-current liabilities:		
10% Loan notes		580
Current liabilities:		
Trade payables	1,030	
Accruals	100	
Taxation	70	1,200
		3,208

Statement of income year ended 31 May 2011

	$'000
Sales revenue	3,485
Cost of sales	(2,715)
Gross profit	770
Distribution costs	(163)
Admin. Expenses	(321)
Operating profit	286
Interest	(58)
Profit before tax	228
Taxation	(70)
Profit after tax	158

Workings:

	Cost of sale	Distrib. cost	Admin exp.
	$'000	$'000	$'000
Inventory	515	–	–
Purchases	2,170	–	–
Returns inward	(17)	–	–
Salaries/wages	146	73	73
Depn – plant	200	–	–
Depn – building	13	26	13
Goodwill	–	–	17
Heating & light	108	54	108
Carriage inward	105	–	–
Bad debt	–	10	–
Discount	–	–	70
Discount	–	–	(80)
Admin. expense	–	–	60
Acquired	35	–	–
Directors	–	–	60
Inventory	(560)		
	2,715	163	321

Statement of changes in equity	Share capital	Share premium	General reserve	Retained earnings	Total
Balance b/f	800	200	35	115	1,150
Acquisition of business	100	20	–	–	120
Bonus issue	180	(180)	–	–	–
Transfer	–	–	35	(35)	–
Profit after tax	–	–	–	158	158
Balance c/f	1,080	40	70	238	1,428

(a) Sales: 3,500 – returns 15 = 3,485
(b) Goodwill: 85 – 17 impairment = 68
(c) Receivables: 700 – 40 allowance = 660

(b) Goodwill, acquired as part of an on going business, is capitalised. Such goodwill need not be amortised; but annually an impairment test should be made and any loss written off immediately.

PQ 9.6 Financial statements for publication (ACCA amended)

(a)

Statement of financial position as at 31 December 2011	£'000	£'000	£'000
Non-current assets:			
Land & buildings at valuation[a]			2,430
Plant & machine	1,500	(900)	600
Goodwill			180
Current assets:			
Inventory		1,950	
Receivables[b]		1,340	
Bank balance		200	3,490
			6,700
		£'000	£'000
Capital and reserves:			
Ordinary shares of £1			400
10% Preference shares			600
Revaluation reserve[c]			350
Share premium			180
Retained earnings			2,232
			3,762
Non-current liabilities:			
5% Loan notes		1,000	
Deferred taxation		28	1,028
Current liabilities:			
Trade payables		1,750	
Taxation		105	
Interest accrued[d]		25	
Preference dividend[e]		30	1,910
			6,700

Statement of income for year ended 31.12.2011	£'000
Sales revenue	8,900
Cost of sales	(4,503)
Gross profit	4,397
Distribution costs	(934)
Admin. Expense	(1,442)
Goodwill impair.	(120)
Operating profit	1,901
Interest[d]	(50)
Profit before tax	1,851
Taxation	(93)
Profit after tax	1,758
Pref. dividend[e]	(60)
Retained profit	1,698

Changes in equity	
Acc. Profit b/f	550
Retained profit	1,698
Dividend paid	(16)
Acc. Profit c/f	2,232

	Cost of sale £'000	Distr cost £'000	Adm. exp. £'000
Inventory	2,124	–	–
Purchases	4,329	–	–
Depn. machinery	–	225	75
Depn. – building	–	128	192
Bad debt: 25 + 50 – 15	–	60	–
Rates/insurance	–	175	175
Admin. expenses	–	–	850
Directors' emolument	–	–	150
Distribution expenses	–	346	–
Inventory	(1,950)	–	–
	4,503	934	1,442

Notes:

(a)

Land & buildings		4,800
Acc. depreciation	1,750	
Depreciation in 2011	320	(2,070)
Loss on revaluation		(300)
As on S of FP		2,430

(b)

Receivables: 1,500 – 25 + 15	1,490
Allowance: 100 + 50	(150)
	1,340

(c) Revaluation reserve (650 – 300 revaluation loss offset); = £350,000

(d) Interest: 5% of 1,000 = £50,000 less paid £25,000 = £25,000 accrued

(e) Preference dividend needs to be accounted for because they have priority over ordinary dividend which has been paid.

(b) Consumer's claim, under legal dispute, does not qualify to be accounted for as a liability because (i) its occurrence is not probable and (ii) the amount cannot be reliably estimated. It needs to be disclosed as a Note, unless its occurrence is remote.

PQ 9.7 Financial statements for publication – advanced

Statement of comprehensive income for the year-ended 31.12.2011	£'000
Sales revenue[a]	3,260
Cost of sales[b]	(1,687)
Gross profit	1,573
Distribution cost[c]	(160)
Administrative expenses[d]	(327)
Operating profit	1,086
Dividend income	15
Preference dividend[e]	(12)
Profit before taxation	1,089
Taxation[f]	(191)
Profit after tax	898
Comprehensive income:	
Prior period adjustment[g]	(360)
Total comprehensive income	538

Statement of financial position as at 31 December 2011	Cost	Ac.dep	£'000
Non current assets:			
Land & buildings	2,400	(396)	2,004
Plant and machinery	960	(420)	540
Motor vehicles	240	(138)	102
Trade investments			96
Current assets:			
Inventory		370	
Trade receivables		494	
Prepayments		3	
Cash and bank		23	890
			3,632
		£'000	£'000
Equity and reserves			
Ordinary shares of £1		1,200	
Share premium account		240	
Retained earnings		1,182	2,622
Non-current liabilities:			
6% Redeemable pref.shares		200	
Deferred tax		24	224
Current liabilities:			
Trade payables		492	
Accrued expenses		43	
Taxation		179	
Preference dividend		12	
Dividend declared		60	786
			3,632

Statement of changes in equity

	Share capital	Share premium	Retained earnings	Total £'000
Balance b/f	800	400	704	1,904
Bonus issue	200[i]	(200)	–	–
Share issue for cash	200	40	–	240
Prior period adjustment	–	–	(360)[h]	(360)
Profit for the year	–	–	898	898
Dividend declared	–	–	(60)	(60)
Balance c/f	1,200	240	1,182	2,622

Notes:

(a) Sales: 3,284 – 24 = £3,260

	Cost of Sales[b]	Distrib cost[c]	Admin. expense[d]
Functional grouping of expenses	£	£	£
Inventory	312	–	–
Purchases	1,594	–	–
Depn: P&M	60	–	–
Depn: building	27	9	–
Depn. Vehicles	–	42	–
Salaries & wages	80	16	64
Rent	–	–	24
Bad debts	–	23	–
Advertising	–	54	–
Inventory – closing	–386	16	–
Directors' emolum.	–	–	60
Audit fees	–	–	10
Telephone	–	–	45
Other admin exp.	–	–	124
	1,687	160	327

(e) Preference dividend, being of redeemable variety, is reported as a finance cost, before taxation.

(f) Taxation: under provision 9 + 179 current tax + 3 def.tax = 191

(g) Any gain/loss reported within reserves, but recognised in the current year. Is reported as part of comprehensive income.

(h) Back-log depreciation of building, arising from a change of policy, is treated as a prior-period adjustment.

(i) Bonus shares: 25/125 of 1,200 – new issue of 200 = 200 shares.

Chapter 10 Incomplete records

PQ 10.1 Three scenarios when financial statements can or cannot be prepared

Scenario (a):

Statement of affairs as at 31.12.2011	2010	2011
	£	£
Non-current assets	240,000	284,000
Inventory	112,400	138,200
Receivables	136,800	164,600
Cash/Bank	12,600	15,400
Payables	(62,500)	(77,800)
Capital	439,300	524,400

Estimation of profit:
£524,400 – £439,300 = £85,100

Scenario (b):

Profit above	£85,100
Drawings: £200 × 52 weeks	£10,400
Estimated profit	£95,500

Scenario (c):

Statement of income year ended 31.12.2011	£	£
Sales[a]		661,100
Inventory	112,400	
Purchases[b]	486,200	
Inventory	(138,200)	(460,400)
Gross profit		200,700
Rent	24,000	
Salary	48,800	
Expenses	16,400	
Depreciation	16,000	(105,200)
Net profit		95,500

Statement of fin. position as at 31.12.2011	£	£
Non-current assets[c]		284,000
Current assets:		
Inventories	138,200	
Trade receivables	164,600	
Cash and bank[d]	15,400	318,200
		602,200
		£
Capital	439,300	
Net profit	95,500	
Drawings	(10,400)	524,400
Current liabilities:		
Trade payables		77,800
		602,200

Notes:

(a) 633,300 + 164,600 – 136,800

(b) 62,500 + 486,200 – 77,800

(c) 240,000 + 60,000 – 284,000

(d) 12,600 + 633,300 – 60,000 – 10,400 – 24,000 – 48,800 – 16,400 – 470,900

PQ 10.2 A basic question on incomplete records

(a)

Statement of affairs as at 1.1.2011

	£
Non-current assets	96,400
Acc. depn	(24,600)
	71,800
Inventory	235,500
Receivables	43,200
Bank	2,160
Payables	(97,200)
Capital	255,460

(b)

Statement of income year ended 31.12.2011

	£	£
Sales[a]		2,163,600
Inventory	235,500	
Purchases[b]	1,744,200	
Inventory	(252,800)	(1,726,900)
Gross profit		436,700
Salary	180,000	
Expenses	154,800	
Depreciation	7,800	(342,600)
Net profit		94,100

Statement of fin. position as at 31.12.2011

	£	£	£
Non-current assets	112,800	(32,400)	80,400
Current assets:			
Inventory		252,800	
Trade receivables		46,800	
Cash and bank[c]		39,360	338,960
			419,360

	£	£
Capital	255,460	
Profit	94,100	
Drawings	(40,000)	309,560
Current liabilities:		
Trade payables		109,800
		419,360

Notes:

(a) Sales: 2,160,000 + 46,800 – 43,200 = £2,163,600
(b) Purchases 1,731,600 + 109,800 – 97,200 = £1,744,200
(c) Cash/bank: 2,160 + 2,160,000 – 40,000 – 1,731,600 – 180,000 – 154,800 – 16,400 = £39,360

PQ 10.3 Incomplete records with goods taken by sole trader

Statement of affairs as at 30.4.2010

	£
Fixtures	1,200
Inventory	4,350
Receivables	3,800
Rent prepaid	300
Bank	1,200
Payables	(3,320)
Accrued exp.	(620)
Capital	6,910

Statement of income for year ended 30.4.2011

	£	£
Sales[a]		85,180
Inventory	4,350	
Purchases[b]	50,530	
Inventory	(6,200)	(48,680)
Gross profit		36,500
Rent[c]	3,800	
Expenses[d]	12,930	
Depreciation[e]	450	(17,180)
Net profit		19,320

Statement of fin. position as at 30.4.2011

	£	£
Fixtures		1,500
Current assets:		
Inventory	6,200	
Receivables	5,860	
Prepaid rent	500	
Cash and bank[f]	2,350	14,910
		16,410

		£
Capital	6,910	
Profit	19,320	
Drawings	(15,000)	11,230
Current liabilities:		
Trade payables	4,250	
Accrued expense	930	5,180
		16,410

Notes:

(a) Sales: 63,120 + 5,860 – 3,800 = £65,180 + cash sale £20,000
(b) Purchases: 49,600 + 4,250 – 3,320 = £50,530
(c) Rent: 300 + 4,000 – 500 = £3,800
(d) Expenses: 12,620 + 930 – 620 = £12,930
(e) Depreciation: 1,200 + 750 – 1,500 = £450 depreciation
(f) Cash/bank: 1,200 + 63,120 + 20,000 – 49,600 – 12,620 – 4,000 – 15,000 – 750 = £2,350

PQ 10.4 Involving cash and bank transactions

CASH BOOK

	Cash	Bank		Cash	Bank
Balance	300	12,800	Payables a/c	12,800	144,400
Cash	–	204,450	Rent a/c	–	10,000
Receivables	229,410	–	Salaries a/c	–	22,000
			Cleaning a/c	720	1,500
			Vehicle a/c	–	18,000
			Misc. exps	940	2,850
Balance	–	2,010	Drawings	10,400	–
			Bank a/c	204,450	–
			Balance c/d	400	18,500
	229,710	217,250		229,710	217,250

Statement of income year ended 31.12.2011

	£	£
Sales[a]		256,410
Inventory	112,000	
Purchases[b]	174,500	
Inventory	(142,800)	(143,700)
Gross profit		112,710
Rent	10,000	
Salary	22,000	
Office cleaning	2,220	
Miscellaneous	3,790	
Depreciation[c]	37,800	(75,810)
Profit		36,900

Statement of financial position as at 31.12.2011

	£	£
Non-current assets[d]	198,000	
Accum. depreciation[e]	(109,800)	88,200
Current assets:		
Inventory	142,800	
Receivables	48,400	
Bank	18,500	
Cash	400	210,100
		298,300

	£	£
Capital on 1.1.2010	222,000	
Profit for the year	36,900	
Drawings	(10,400)	248,500
Payables		49,800
		298,300

Notes:

(a) 229,410 + 48,400 – 21,400 = £256,410
(b) 12,800 + 144,400 + 49,800 – 32,500 = £174,500
(c) 20% of 180,000 + 20% of 18,000 for six months = £37,800
(d) 180,000 + 18,000 = £198,000
(e) 72,000 + 37,800 = £109,800

PQ 10.5 Cost of goods taken by owner (ACCA 1.1 amended)

Statement of income for the year ended 30 Sept. 2011		
	£	£
Sales[a]		604,200
Inventory	38,000	
Purchases[b]	431,300	
Inventory	(46,000)	
Drawings[c]	(20,500)	(402,800)
Gross profit		201,400
Expenses[d]		(94,000)
Profit for the year		107,400

Notes:

(a) Sales: 519,400 + 79,000 + 125,000 – 119,200 = £604,200

(b) Purchases: 408,100 + 14,200 + 77,100 – 68,100 = 431,300

(c) Drawings: If goods are sold at cost plus 50%, the gross profit will be a third of sales: hence gross profit in the year, at one-third of sales (1/3rd of 604,200) = 201,400. Hence the difference is the cost of goods taken for personal use by Bob.

(d) Expenses: 89,400 + 4,100 + 4,600 + 2,400 – 3,900 – 2,600 = 94,000

Cash Book

	Cash	Bank		Cash	Bank
Balance b/f	300	20,500	Bank – deposited	12,900	–
Cash – deposited	–	12,900	Payables	14,200	408,100
Receivables – takings	519,400	79,000	Expenses	4,100	89,400
			Drawings	47,900	30,000
			Balance c/d	200	25,300
	79,300	552,800		79,300	552,800
Balance b/d	200	25,300			

PQ 10.6 Adopt the crossword puzzle mentality

CLUE: Balance the Statement of financial position to ascertain the loss for the year as £60,400; then proceed up the Statement of income to find a gross profit of £222,500. Sales amount is found by multiplying the gross profit by three – because the question states that the sale price is fixed at cost plus 50% (i.e. one-third of sale).

Non-current assets account

	£'000		£'000
Balance	240		
Bank[a]	60	Balance c/d	300
	300		300
Balance	300		

Accumulated depreciation a/c

	£'000		£'000
		Balance b/f	48
Balance c/d	73.5	Depreciation	25.5
	73.5		73.5
		Balance b/d	73.5

Expenses account

	£'000		£'000
Pre-payment	6	Balance	12.6
Bank[a]	246.2	Income	
Balance c/d	17.8	statement	257.4
	270		270

Trade receivables account

	£'000		£'000
Balance b/f	48.2	Bank[a]	651.3
Sales[b]	667.5	Balance c/d	64.4
	715.7		715.7
Balance b/d	64.4		

Trade payables account

	£'000		£'000
Bank[a]	307.7	Balance	185.2
Balance c/d	212.6	Purchase[b]	335.1
	720.3		720.3
		Balance b/d	212.6

Bank account	
	£
Balance	38,600
Receivables	651,300
N.C.Asset	(60,000)
Drawings	(20,800)
Expenses	(246,200)
Purchases	(307,700)
Balance	55,200

Statement of income year ended 31.12.2011		
	£	£
Sales		667,500
Inventory	426,400	
Purchases	335,100	
Inventory	(316,500)	(445,000)
Gross profit		222,500
Depreciation		(25,500)
Expenses		(257,400)
Net loss		(60,400)

Statement of fin. position as at 31.12.2011		
	£	£
Non current assets	300,000	
Accum. depreciation	(73,500)	226,500
Current assets:		
Inventory	316,500	
Trade receivables	64,400	
Bank	55,200	436,100
		662,600
		£
Capital	513,400	
Loss for the year	(60,400)	
Drawings	(20,800)	432,200
Current liabilities:		
Trade payables	212,600	
Accrued expenses	17,800	230,400
		662,600

Chapter 11 Statements of cash flows

PQ 11.1 Statements of cash flow on both direct and indirect methods

(a)

Statements of cash flow year ended 31.3.2012	£'000	£'000
Cash flow from operating activities:		
Operating profit	103	
Depreciation[a]	80	
Inventory increase	(72)	
Receivables decrease	26	
Payable decrease	(33)	104
Interest paid		(12)
Dividend paid[c]		(30)
Tax paid[b]		(42)
Net cash generated		20
Cash flow from investing activities:		
Non-current assets		(160)
Cash flow from financing activities:		
Share capital[d]	150	
Share premium[e]	35	
Loan note redemption[f]	(65)	120
Net cash outflow		(20)
Cash & cash equivalent – 31.3.2010		12
Cash & cash equivalent – 31.3.2011		(8)

Notes:

(a) Depreciation £320,000 – £240,000 = £80,000

(b) Only last year's tax of £42,000 is paid.

(c) Dividend paid is the balancing figure in the Statement of retained earnings shown on the right.

Movement of equity	£'000
Retained earnings b/f	74
Profit after tax	46
Dividend paid	(30)
Retained earnings c/f	90

(d) Share capital: £600,000 – £750,000

(e) Share premium account

	£'000		£'000
Debenture redemption premium	15	Balance b/f	100
Balance c/d	120	Cash	35
	135		135
		Balance b/d	120

(f) Debenture redemption account

	£'000		£'000
Cash a/c	65	Balance b/f	200
Balance c/d	150		
	215		215
		Balance b/d	150

(b)

Statements of cash flow year ended 31.3.2012	£'000	£'000
Cash flow from operating activities:		
Sales[a]	866	
Purchases[b]	(653)	
Expenses[d]	(109)	104
Interest paid		(12)
Dividend paid		(30)
Tax paid		(42)
		20
Cash flow from investing activities:		
Non-current assets acquired		(160)
Cash flow from financing activity:		
Share capital	150	
Share premium a/c	20	
Redemption of loan	(50)	120
Net cash outflow		(20)
Cash & cash equivalent – 31.3.2010		12
Cash & cash equivalent – 31.3.2011		(8)

Notes:

(a) Trade receivables account:

	£'000		£'000
Balance b/f	438	Cash	866
Sales	840	Balance c/d	412
	1,278		1,278
Balance b/d	412		

(b) Trade payables account:

	£'000		£'000
Cash	653	Balance b/f	298
Balance c/d	265	Purchases	620
	918		918
		Balance b/d	265

(c) Cost of sales:

	£'000
Inventory	324
Purchases	620
Inventory at end	(396)
Cost of sales	548

(d) Statement of income:

Sales	840
Cost of sales[c]	(548)
Gross profit	292
Depreciation	(80)
Other op. expenses	(109)
Operating profit	103

PQ 11.2 A basic question – either method (CIMA amended)

Statement of cash flows year ended 30.9.2011	£'000	£'000
Operating activities:		
Profit before tax	2,486	
Interest	14	
Disposal loss[a]	230	2,730
Depreciation[b]		290
Inventory increase		(200)
Receivables increase		(50)
Payables increase		80
		2,850
Taxation[c]		(760)
Interest		(14)
Dividend paid[d]		(660)
		1,416
Investing activities:		
Non-current assets	(1,900)	
Asset disposal	80	(1,820)
Financing activities:		
Share issue[e]	384	
Loan redemption	(200)	184
Cash outflow in the year		(220)
Cash as at 30 Sept. 2011		300
Cash as at 30 Sept. 2012		80

Notes:

(a) Disposal loss: 310,000 – 80,000 (proceeds) = £230,000

(b) Depreciation: (6,800,000 + 1,900,000) – (310,000 + 8,100,000) = £290,000

(c) Tax paid: (595,000 + 800,000) – 635,000 = £760,000

(d) Dividend paid: (360,000 + 700,000) – 400,000 = £660,000

(e) Share capital: 1,000,000 – 1,100,000 = £100,000
Share premium: 225,000 – 509,000 = £284,000

PQ 11.3 A basic question – on the indirect method (CAT 6 – June 2005 amended)

Statement of cash flows year ended 31.5.2011		
	£'000	£'000
Operating activities:		
Profit before tax	1,052	
Disposal loss	20	
Operating profit	1,072	
Depreciation	700	
Inventory increase	(80)	
Receivables increase	(130)	
Payables decrease	85	1,647
Interest paid		(10)
Tax paid		(145)
Dividend paid		(270)
		1,222
Investing activities:		
Non-current assets	(2,800)	
Disposal of asset	180	(2,620)
Financing activities:		
Issue of shares	1,280	
Redemption of loan	(110)	1,170
Cash outflow in the year		(228)
Cash & cash equi. – 31.5.2010		170
Cash & cash equi. – 31.5.2011		(58)

Comment on the change in financial position:

- Net cash outflow of £228,000 leaves the company with an overdraft of £58,000.
- Operating cash flow (£1,072) is adequate to meet the year-end current liability of £688. The cash flow ratio (1,072/688 × 100) of 156% is satisfactory.
- Cash generated by operating activity is sufficient to meet commitments such as interest (£10), tax (£145) and dividend (£270) leaving an amount of £1,222 free cash.
- Significant cash outflow has been on investing activity and this improves the asset base as well as the earning capacity.
- Company is financing its investment activities by equity issue and is also replacing loan capital by equity, improving its gearing position as well as its market stature.

PQ 11.4 On indirect method involving revaluation (ACCA 1.1 amended)

Statement of cash flows year ended 31.12.2011		
	£'000	£'000
Operating activities:		
Operating profit	2,650	
Disposal gain[a]	(150)	
Depreciation[b]	1,250	
Inventory decrease	400	
Receivables increase	(900)	
Payables increase	500	3,750
Interest paid		(300)
Tax paid[c]		(600)
Dividend paid		(750)
		2,100
Investing activities:		
Non-current assets[d]	(3,300)	
Asset disposal	500	(2,800)
Financing activities:		
10% Loan note		1,000
Cash flow in the year		300
Cash on 31 Dec. 2010		100
Cash on 31 Dec. 2011		400

(a) 800 – (450 + 500) = 150
(b) (450 + 5,600) – 4,800 = £1,250
(c) Payment of last year's tax
(d) 8,000 + 500 (revaluation) – 800 disposal – 11,000

PQ 11.5 Interpretation of information in the Statement of cash flows

(a) Depreciation is not a source of cash. It is an operating expense, deducted when determining operating profit, but an expense which would not involve a cash outflow in the current year. The cash outflow would have been in the year the related asset was acquired. Depreciation is added back to operating profit to identify the amount by which cash flow would have improved because of the operating activities in the current year, provided there is no change in all working capital items such as inventory, receivables and payables.

(b) Upon disposal of an asset at a loss, cash flow improves only by the amount of the proceeds on disposal. The disposal loss has no impact whatever on the cash position. If the operating profit had been identified after deducting the disposal loss, there arises a need to add back the loss for the same reason that we add back depreciation – both of these do not involve a cash outflow.

(c) The first impression is that liquidity has worsened with a cash outflow and a bank overdraft at the year-end. However, there has been a significant cash inflow from operating activities, which when compared with the year-end current liability, produces a cash flow ratio of 202.5% (632/312 × 100) which is very satisfactory. Even after paying interest, tax and dividend, there is an amount of £537,000 available as free cash, available for working capital management and investment activities. Though more cash resources have been tied up in inventory and receivables, there may be sound reasons for this such as, for example, increasing inventory holdings either preparing for a sales push or to tide over supply problems. The asset base of the company has improved with investing activities amounting to £350,000. Financing has been well managed, with equity replacing loans leading to an improvement in gearing.

PQ 11.6 Cash flow involving revaluation, deferred tax as well as a bonus issue

Statement of cash flows year ended 30.6.2012		
	£'000	£'000
Operating activities:		
Operating profit	473	
Depreciation[a]	170	
Operating cash flow	643	
Working capital management:		
Inventory increase	(114)	
Receivables increase	(62)	
Payables decrease	(79)	
	388	
Interest paid	(18)	
Dividend paid	(50)	
Tax paid[b]	(59)	261
Investing activities:		
Non-current assets[c]	(262)	
Disposal of asset	12	(250)
Financing activities:		
Share capital[d]	398	
Share premium[e]	10	
Loan note repaid	(360)	48
Cash inflow in the year		59
Cash & cash equivalent 30.6.2011		(23)
Cash & cash equivalent 30.6.2012		36

(a)	£'000
Depn. equipment	40
Depn. buildings	50
Amortisation – brand	32
Disposal loss (70 – 10 – 12)	48
	170

(b)	£'000
Tax: b/f	118
Charge in the year	84
Balance c/f	–143
Cash outflow	59

(c)	£'000
Non-current assets:	
Balance b/f	800
Disposal	–70
Impairment	–32
Balance c/f	–960
Cash outflow	262

(d)	£'000
Share capital 30.6.2011	1,000
Bonus issue	200
Share capital 30.6.2012	(1,600)
New issue for cash	400
Expenses of issue	(2)
	398

(e)	£'000
Share premium:	
Balance b/f	240
Bonus issue	–200
Expenses w/off	–2
Balance c/f	–48
Cash inflow	10

Chapter 12 Accounting ratios and interpretation of financial statements

PQ 12.1 A basic interpretation of financial statements

Profitability:

(a) Return on capital employed:

$$\frac{25 + 9}{200} \times 100 = 17\%$$

(b) Return on equity:

$$\frac{25}{125} \times 100 = 20\%$$

Liquidity:

(a) Current ratio:

$$\frac{100}{50} = 2 \text{ times}$$

(b) Liquidity ratio:

$$\frac{37{,}500}{50{,}000} = 0.75 \text{ times}$$

Operational efficiency:

(a) Total asset turnover:

$$\frac{625}{200} = 3.125 \text{ times}$$

(b) Stock turnover:

$$\frac{425}{(54.5 + 62.5)/2} = 7.3 \text{ times}$$

- Without more information on market rates of returns, industrial averages and performance in prior years, it is not possible to say whether 17% ROCE and 20% return on equity are satisfactory. However, 17% ROCE makes affordable the payment of 12% p.a. on loan capital.
- Liquidity appears satisfactory because the current ratio of 2 is what is generally expected. That the liquidity ratio is less than one may be of some concern. The degree of concern depends, however, on such matters as the ready realisability of stock, whether bank accommodation is readily available and so on.
- Operational efficiency of the business again cannot be assessed purely on the basis of a total asset turnover of three and stock turnover in excess of seven, unless additional information is available on industrial averages and past performance.

PQ 12.2 Return on capital employed

(a)	£10,000	£800	£200	£5,000	10%	2	20%
(b)	£15,000	£1,600	£200	£8,000	12%	1.875	22.5%
(c)	£10,000	£300	£200	£2,500	5%	4	20%
(d)	£20,000	£800	£200	£5,000	5%	4	20%
(e)	£40,000	£3,800	£200	£10,000	10%	4	40%
(f)	£20,000	£300	£200	£5,000	2.5%	4	10%

PQ 12.3 Profitability – inter-firm comparison (CAT amended)

(a)

Accounting ratios	Aber	Cromby
Gross profit ratio	20%	30%
ROCE	11.8%	6.3%
EPS	9.2 c	4 c

Comments:

1. Cromby's GP ratio is better. Reasons could be that Cromby caters to customers with fastidious taste, for whom quality of service is more important than price, or that Aber's purchases are from more expensive sources or that Aber is unable to negotiate trade discounts at levels that Cromby is able to.
2. ROCE for Aber is double that of Cromby and yet the return of 11.8% would not justify its borrowing at 20% (i.e. finance cost of 15/Loan notes of 75 × 100). Comparably better ROCE (on a turnover of half that of Cromby) may indicate that Aber is keeping a tight lid on expenses. It could also suggest that Aber is under-capitalised (i.e., its asset base is not adequate to sustain its level of activity). On the other hand, Cromby's cost of capital, including the cost of overdraft, is (at 13%) lower than that of Aber's. Yet borrowing at 13% is not justified when it earns only 6.3%. There is a possibility that Cromby is over-capitalised (e.g. showrooms may be better fitted out to cater for customers with fastidious taste). It is also possible that Cromby is reporting its assets on the valuation model whereas Aber is reporting on the cost model.
3. Limitations of ratio analysis:
   - Ratios calculated for different businesses, even those engaged in the same line of activity, may not always be comparable because (a) the assets may have been acquired in different time periods when the inflation levels of that period will affect the reported values, (b) the accounting policies adopted could be not the same and (c) the trading practices may not be identical.
   - In the absence of a norm (what is the best ratio in the circumstances) the ratios are meaningless and their usefulness depends on the ability of those who use them as comparators (with what was in the previous year or what they were expected to be) to interpret them for taking corrective action.

PQ 12.4 Liquidity and performance on inter-temporal comparison (ACCA amended)

(a)

Accounting ratios	2011	2012
(i) Current ratio	2.3	1.65
(ii) Quick ratio	1.05	0.81
(iii) Inventory turnover ratio	104 days	109 days
(iv) Trade receivable days	59 days	69 days
(v) Trade payable days	72 days	98 days

(b) Comments:

(i) Lower current ratio (20%) may indicate liquidity problem.
(ii) Increased receivable days may be part of sales promotion measures which pushed up sales by 23%.
(iii) The type of business may be one that requires large inventory holding; but inventory management has worsened in the year.
(iv) Such high payable days may fall foul of credit terms permitted by suppliers.

PQ 12.5 Stock market ratios (CAT 6 amended)

(a)

Accounting ratios	Tresven	Hilladay
Dividend per share	20 c	10 c
Dividend cover	1.1 times	5 times
Earnings per share	22 c	20 c
Price earning ratio	6.7 times	13.4 times
Earnings yield	14.7%	15%
Interest cover	254 times	100 times

(b) Comments:

- Tresven, though earning marginally better than Hilladay, pays double the dividend.
- The low dividend cover suggests that, when faced with lower profit levels, it cannot sustain its dividend levels.
- Despite the high levels of dividends, the PE ratio reflects that the investors have greater confidence in Hilladay; such confidence would, in due course, translate into even higher share prices, yielding capital gain to those holding Hilladay shares,
- Earnings yield of both companies is broadly comparable.
- Interest cover for both companies is significantly high. What this means is that their current profit levels are more than adequate to meet their interest commitments. Given the level of cover Tresven should have no difficulty raising more loan capital.

PQ 12.6 Interpretation from an investor's focus

General Comment:

The business is still at an early stage. It is not unusual for a business at this stage to be unprofitable.

- Sales in the second year have improved by 40% in comparison with the first and, therefore, a projected increase is plausible, but should be substantiated by detailed forecasts, based on valid and sustainable assumptions.
- Gross profit ratio in the second year has fallen by 10%. This may be because of deliberate reduction in sale prices as a calculated measure to boost sales. Whether further reductions are contemplated to improve sales should be inquired into.

Year to 31.3	2010	2011
Gross Profit ratio	40%	35.7%

- Fixed overheads: Whether the increase of £2,800 in fixed overheads arose wholly from the rent for enlarged premises should be established.
- Variable overheads: In proportion to the increase in sales, the variable overheads in the second year should have been £19,600 whereas it was £24,500. This could be because the rate of sales commission and the extent of advertising may have been increased for stimulating sales. Whether the expenses will remain at current levels or require increase needs to be investigated.
- Net profit to sales ratio in the first year was 8%. If the higher rental payment in the second is ignored, the ratio in the second would have been 2%.
- During the second year, as compared with the first:
  - Total asset turnover improved by 35%
  - Non-current asset turnover improved by 36%
  - Working capital turnover improved by 51%
  - Inventory turnover improved by 45%
  - Trade receivables turnover improved by 3% and
  - Trade payables turnover reduced (favourable) by 36%.

Year to 31.3	2010	2011
Total asset turnover	1.1	1.5
Non Current asset turnover	1.4	1.9
Working capital turnover	5.3	8
Inventory turnover	7.6	11
Trade Receivables turnover	7.2	7.4
Trade Payable turnover	15	9.6

The apparent improvements in these ratios, however, arose because of inadequate liquidity. For example, Trade payables on 31.3.2011 and Inventory levels on that date are likely to have been substantially bigger if the business has the resources or was able to obtain extended credit facility from suppliers.

Profitability:

- Return on capital employed in year one was 9% and in year two, if additional rent is not taken into account, is 3%. To bring payables within the suppliers' credit period and to pay off the bank overdraft, William requires at least £6,000 as a loan from his mother by 1.4.2011.

  At best the ROCE in the year to 31.3.2012 (see working on right) will be (4,250 + 600/71,900 × 100 =) 6.75%.

Projection – Year to 31.3.2012		
		£
Sales	as anticipated	150,000
Cost of sales		(96,450)
Gross profit	35.7% as in year 2	53,550
Fixed O/H	as in year 2	(11,200)
Variable O/H	25% – year 2 levels	(37,500)
Interest	8% p.a. on £6,000	(600)
Profit anticipated (hopefully)		4,250

- Return on equity will be (4,250/64,400 × 100 =) 6.6%.

Liquidity:

William admits that liquidity of the business is strained. Ratios need not be calculated.

- Though current levels of earning are substantially lower than what could be earned from employment, William may prefer the freedom and challenge of developing his own business.
- He must, however, work out his prospects by preparing three to five years' forecasts.
- He could ask for assistance from the Small Business section of his bank and from the Department of Trade and Industry.
- His mother should take comfort from her son's ability to pay her interest at rates she can earn elsewhere and that the interest cover is expected to be (£4,250 + £600/£600 =) more than eight times.

PQ 12.7 Preparing financial statements from accounting ratios

Statement of income year to 31.5.2011	
	£
Sales	50,000[d]
Cost of sales	(28,750)[h]
Gross profit	21,250
Expenses	(12,500)[i]
Depreciation	(1,500)[a]
Profit	7,250

Statement of financial position as at 31.5.2011		
	£	£
Non-current assets		15,000[a]
Less: Depreciation		(1,500)[a]
		13,500
Current assets:		
Inventory	5,750[g]	
Receivables	6,250[e]	
Cash/bank	22,500[f]	34,500
		48,000[c]
		£
Capital		20,750[j]
Profit for the year		7,250
Drawings		(3,000)
Current liabilities:		25,000
Trade payables		23,000
		48,000

(a) Depreciation (at 10% of cost) = £1,500;
Non-current assets
£1,500 × 100/10 = £15,000;
Wdv: £15,000 – £1,500 = £13,500

(b) Current asset ratio 1.5
Working capital: £11,500
Current assets: £11,500 × 3 = £34,500
Current liabilities: £11,500 × 2 = £23,000

(c) Total assets: Non-current assets (£13,500)
Plus Working capital £11,500 = £25,000
Plus £23,000 = £48,000

(d) Net asset turnover: 2
Sales = £25,000 × 2 = £50,000

(e) Receivables turnover: 8 times; Receivables = £50,000/8 = £6,250

(f) Acid test ratio: 1.25; Current liabilities = (b) £23,000
Liquid assets: £23,000 × 1.25 = £28,750
Cash = Liquid assets (£28,750) – Trade receivables (£6,250) = £22,500

(g) Current assets are £34,500 (b) and Liquid assets are £28,750 (f) Inventory: Current assets (£34,500) – Liquid assets (£28,750) = £5,750

(h) Inventory turnover ratio is 5; Cost of sales = £5,750 × 5 = £28,750

(i) General expenses: 25% of sales: £50,000/4 = £12,500

(j) Capital employed (£25,000) + Drawings (£3,000) less Profit (£7,250) = Opening capital

Chapter 13 Consolidation of financial statements

PQ 13.1 Fully owned subsidiary incorporated by the parent

Consolidated Statement of fin. position as at 31 December 2012		
		£
Non-current assets	400 + 120	520
Current assets	150 + 60	210
		730

		£
Ordinary shares[a]		400
Share premium[b]		80
Consolidated reserves	220 + 30	50
		730

Notes:

(a) Only the parent's share capital and premium are reported on the group S of FP.

(b) Parent's investment is cancelled against the subsidiary's share capital and share premium.

PQ 13.2 Fully owned subsidiary acquired immediately upon incorporation

Consolidated Statement of financial position as at 31 December 2012			
		£	£
Non-current assets	840 + 90		930
Goodwill[c]			30
Investments	(240 – 180) + 20		80
Current assets:			
Inventory	280 + 80	360	
Trade receivables[d]	(310 – 72) + 112	350	
Cash and bank	20 + 18	38	748
			1,788

		£
Ordinary shares of £1 each		800
Share premium account		160
Consol. accumulated profit	515 + 55	570
		1,530
Current liabilities:		
Trade payables[d]	215 + (115 – 72)	258
		1,788

Notes:

(c) is the premium paid to buy whole of the subsidiary.

(d) inter-company debt of 72 is cancelled.

PQ 13.3 Consolidation involving items in transit and unrealised profit

Consolidated Statement of fin. position as at 31.12.2012			
		£'000	£'000
Non-current assets:			
Tangible at cost	960 + 420	1,380	
Acc. depreciation	240 + 160	(400)	980
Goodwill			45
Investments	(430 – 405) + 30		55
Current assets:			
Inventory	484 + 188 + 48 – 30	690	
Trade receivables	(319 – 48 – 24 – 40) + 296	503	
Cash and bank	17 + 16 + 24	57	1,250
			2,330

		£'000	£'000
Equity and reserves:			
Ordinary shares of £1 each		800	
Share premium account		80	
Consolidated accumulated profit		580	1,460
Current liabilities:			
Trade payables	494 + (312 – 40)	766	
Taxation	75 + 29	104	870
			2,330

Notes:

(a) Cost of control:

Parent's investment	405
Subsidiary's:	
Share capital	(300)
Share premium	(60)
Goodwill	45

(b) Consolidated accumulated profit

Parent's profit	521
Subsidiary's profit	89
Unrealised profit	(30)
	580

(c)

Subsidiary's inventory	72
Goods in transit	48
Unrealised: 25% of	120

PQ 13.4 Consolidation involving pre-acquisition profit and fair valuation

Consolidated Statement of fin. position as at 31 Dec. 2012

		£'000	£'000
Non-current assets:			
Tangible assets at cost	740 + 520	1,260	
Accumulated depreciation	210 + 180	(390)	870
Goodwill	40 – 10		30
Investments at cost	(920 – 820) + (80 + 40)		220
Current assets:			
Inventory	428 + 312 + 42 – 40	742	
Trade receivables	(516 – 42 – 30 – 42) + 475	877	
Cash and bank	24 + 13 + 30	67	1,686
			2,806

		£'000	£'000
Equity and reserves:			
Ordinary shares of £1 each		1,200	
Share premium account		60	
Consolidated accumulated profit		642	1,902
Current liabilities:			
Trade payables	398 + (259 – 42)	615	
Taxation	148 + 21	169	
Dividend declared		120	904
			2,806

Notes:

(a) Cost of control:

Parent's investment	820
Subsidiary's:	
Share capital	(600)
Share premium	(60)
Fair valuation	(40)
Pre-acquisition profit	(80)
Goodwill	40

(b) Consolidated profit:

Balance b/f	492
Dividend-subsidiary	60
Sub's profit (220 – 80)	140
Unrealised profit	(40)
Goodwill impaired	(10)
	642

(c)

Inventory with sub	118
Goods in transit	42
Unrealised: 1/4th of	160

PQ 13.5 Partly owned subsidiary

Consolidated Statement of fin. position as at 31.3.2012

		£'000	£'000
Non-current assets:			
Land at cost	400 + (100 + 360)		860
Other tangible assets	770 + 450		1,170
Goodwill			48
Investments	(780 – 760) + 60		80
Current assets:			
Inventory	544 + 240 + 16 – 12	788	
Trade receivables	(386 – 16 – 8 – 18) + 198	542	
Cash and bank	42 + 15 + 8	65	1,395
			3,553

		£'000	£'000
Equity and reserves:			
Ordinary shares of 50p each		1,600	
Share premium account		160	
Consolidated accumulated profit		759	2,519
Non-control interest	368 + 1/3 of 120		408
Current liabilities:			
Trade payables	349 + (194 – 18)	525	
Taxation	72 + 29	101	626
			3,553

Cost of control

Investment	760
NCI: 400 shares @ 92p	368
Share capital	(600)
Share premium	(30)
Fair valuation gain	(360)
Pre-acquisition profit of sub.	(90)
Goodwill	48

Consolidated accum. profit:	
Parent's profit	691
2/3 of sub's post-acqui. profit	80
Unrealised profit	(12)
	759

PQ 13.6 Consolidation of Statement of financial position (CAT 6)

(a)

Goodwill	£'000
Parent's investment	660
NCI's 120 shares @130	156
Sub's Share capital	(600)
Fair valuation	(70)
Pre-acqui. Profit	(95)
Goodwill	51

(b)

Consolidated Statement of financial position as at 31.10.2012

			£'000
Non-current assets:			
Land & buildings	315 + (278 + 70 fair value)		663
Plant	285 + 220		505
Goodwill			51
Current assets:			
Inventory	357 + 252 – 12 unrealised	597	
Trade receivables	(525 – 25 inter-co) + 126	626	
Bank	158 + 30	188	1,411
			2,630

			£'000
Equity and reserves:			
Ordinary shares of £1		1,500	
Consol. reserves	580 + 80% of (215 – 95) – 12	664	2,164
Non-controlling interest	156 + 20% of (215 – 95)		180
Current liabilities:			
Trade payables	220 + (91 – 25)		286
			2,630

(c) When preparing group accounts the parent and the subsidiary, though legally two separate entities, are regarded as a single economic entity. Therefore:

(i) Unless inter-company debts are cancelled the same item is double-counted, i.e. reported as an asset and its mirror image as a liability.

(ii) Any inter-company trading should also be cancelled for the same reason (an entity cannot sell to itself) and any profit on sale by one within the entity to another (unless earned by passing it on to a third party) should be eliminated (because an entity cannot earn profit against itself).

PQ 13.7 Consolidation of Statement of income

Consolidation schedule

	Parent	Subsid.	Adjust	Consol.
	£'000	£'000	£'000	£'000
Sales revenue	1,760	1,180	(360)	2,580
Cost of sales	(942)	(756)	360	(1,338)
Unrealised profit	(12)[a]	–	–	(12)
Gross profit	806	424	–	1,230
Expenses	(482)	(275)	–	(757)
Profit before tax	324	149	–	473
Taxation	(72)	(29)	–	(101)
Profit after tax	252	120	–	372
Non-contr. interest	–	(40)[b]	–	(40)
Goup profit	252	80	–	332

Statement of changes in equity:

Balance b/f	501	16[c]	–	517
Group profit	252	80	–	332
Dividend paid	(90)[d]	–	–	(90)
Balance c/d	663	136	–	759[e]

Notes:

(a) Unrealised: 32 + 16 × 1/4 = 12

(b) NCI; A third of £120 = £40

(c) Two-thirds of the subsidiary's post-acquisition profit: 2/3 of 114 – 90 = 16

(d) Only the dividend paid by the parent.

(e) This amount must be the same as the amount shown as consolidated accum. profit in the answer to PQ 13.5.

PQ 13.8 Consolidation of Statements of income (CAT 6)

(a) Goodwill:

Investment		3,500
NCI's shares: 1 million @ 1.10		1,100
Sub's Share capital	4,000	
Sub's pre-acquisition profit	200	(4,200)
Goodwill on acquisition		400

(b)

Consolidation schedule				
	Parent	Sub	Adjust	Consol
	£'000	£'000	£'000	£'000
Sales revenue	6,400	2,600	(200)	8,800
Cost of sales	(3,700)	(1,450)	200	(4,950)
Unrealised profit	(54)	–	–	(54)
Gross profit	2,646	1,150	–	3,796
Distribution cost	(1,100)	(490)	–	(1,590)
Admin. expenses	(700)	(320)	–	(1,020)
Goodwill impaired	–	(70)[a]	–	(70)
Profit before tax	846	270	–	1,116
Taxation	(400)	(90)	–	(490)
Profit after tax	446	180	–	626
Non-contr. interest	–	(45)	–	(45)
Group profit	446	135	–	581

Note:

(a) Goodwill impairment in the current year £70 (300 – 230) is shown as an offset from the subsidiary's column so that the NCI too will suffer their portion of the loss.

(c) To be accounted for as an associate, the investee
  (a) should not be a subsidiary or a joint venture;
  (b) the investor should have in it:
    (i) participating interest (i.e 20% or more votes);
    (ii) significant influence (i.e. ability to influence its operating and financing policy) . This may be inferred if the investor has representation on the investee's board or its policy-making committees, or the investee depends on the investor for material transactions, key personnel, technical know-how.

PQ 13.9 Consolidation of Statements of financial position and Statement of income (CAT 6)

(a) Cost of control

	£'000	£'000
Parent's investment		28,000
NCI: 28,000 × 30/70		12,000
Sub's Share capital	30,000	
Gen. reserve	500	
Accum. profit	1,500	(32,000)
Goodwill at acquisition		8,000

(b)

Consolidation schedule				
	Black	Bury	Adjust	Consol
	£'000	£'000	£'000	£'000
Sales	245,000	95,000	(16,800)	323,200
Cost of sales	(140,000)	(52,000)	16,800	(175,200)
Unrealised	(1,440)	–	–	(1,440)
Gross profit	103,560	43,000	–	146,560
Distrib. cost	(12,000)	(10,000)	–	(22,000)
Admin. exp.	(55,000)	(13,000)	–	(68,000)
Goodwill	–	(1,000)[c]	–	(1,000)
Profit bef.tax	36,560	19,000	–	55,560
Taxation	(13,250)	(5,000)	–	(18,250)
Profit aft.tax	23,310	14,000	–	37,310
NCI	–	(4,200)	–	(4,200)
Group profit	23,310	9,800	–	33,110

(c)

Consolidated Statement of financial position as at 31 October 2010			
		£'000	£'000
Non-current assets:			
Property, plant	110,000 + 40,000		150,000
Goodwill			5,000
Current assets:			
Inventory	9,360 + 3,890 – 1,440	11,810	
Receivables	14,640 + 6,280 – 1,500 – 7,000 div		
	3,500 + 2,570	12,420	
Bank		6,070	30,300
			185,300

		$'000	$'000
Capital and reserves:			
Share capital			100,000
General reserve	9,200 + (70% of 1,000 – 500)		9,550
Consolidated accumulated profit[a]			29,206
Non-controlling interest			13,584
			152,340
Current liabilities:			
Trade payables	9,000 + 2,460 – 1,500	9,960	
Dividend to non-controlling interest		3,000	
Dividend declared		20,000	32,960
			185,300

Notes:

(a) Consolidated profit: 27,300 – 1,440 (unrealised) + 70% of (9,280 – 1,500) (pre-acquisition profit) – (goodwill 2,100) = £29,206,000

(b) NCI: 12,000 + 30% of (1,000 – 500) + 30% of (9,280 – 1,500) – Goodwill impairment 30% of 3,000 = £13,584,000

(c) Goodwill impairment in the current year £1m (6m – 5m) is deducted from subsidiary's column so that NCI too would suffer their share.

PQ 13.10 Consolidated Statements of income and financial position – advanced

Consolidation schedule

	Major	Minor	Adjust	Consol
	£'000	£'000	£'000	£'000
Sales revenue	2,654	1,280	(180)	3,754
Cost of sales	(1,894)	(947)[c]	180	(2,661)
Unrealised profit	–	(15)	–	(15)
Gross profit	760	318	–	1,078
Operating expenses	(413)	(186)	–	(599)
Operating profit	347	132	–	479
Goodwill impairment	–	(40)	–	(40)
Interest income	8	–	(8)	–
Interest expense	–	(12)	8	(4)
	355	80	–	435
Taxation	(115)	(20)	–	(135)
Profit before tax	240	60	–	300
Non-controlling interest	–	(12)	–	(12)
Group profit	240	48	–	288

Consolidated statement of changes in equity

	Major	Minor	Adjust	Consol
	£'000	£'000	£'000	£'000
Balance b/f	383	8[d]	–	391
Group profit for year	240	48	–	288
Dividend declared	(60)	–	–	(60)
Balance c/f	563	56	–	619

Consolidated Statement of financial position as at 31 March 2012

			£'000
Non-current assets:			
Property, plant	760 + (450 + 150 fair valuation – 10 depreciation)		1,350
Goodwill	240[a] – 40[a] impairment		200
Investments	(710 – 680 – 100 Loan notes) + 25		55
Current assets:			
Inventory	372 + 228 + 20 transit – 15 unrealised	805	
Receivables	(395 – 8 interest) + (154 – 90 inter-company)	451	
Cash/bank	38 + 28 + 5 transit	71	1,127
			2,732

			£'000
Equity and reserves:			
Ordinary shares of £1 each		1,200	
Consolidated retained earnings	563 + 20 div + 68 subsidiary's[b] – 32 goodwill[a]	619	1,819
Non-controlling interest	(100 shares @ 1.45) + 17 profit[b] – 8 goodwill[a]		154
Non-current liabilities:			
8% Loan notes			50
Current liabilities:			
Trade payables	(390 + 20 transit + 5 cash – 90 inter-co) + 132	457	
Accrued expenses	35 + (14 – 8 interest)	41	
Taxation	127 + 19	146	
Dividend to non-controlling interest		5	
Dividend declared		60	709
			2,732

(a) Goodwill:

		£'000
Investment by Major		680
FV of NCI (100 @ 1.45)		145
Minor's:		
Share capital	500	
FV – PPE	150	
FV – investments	(5)	
Pre-acquisition loss	(60)	(585)
Goodwill at acquisition		240
Goodwill at FV on 31.3.2012		(200)
Impairment of goodwill		40

(b) Minor's retained earnings

	£'000
As reported	50
Pre-acquisition loss	60
Post acquisit. profit	110
Unrealised profit	(15)
Depreciation (£5 x 2)	(10)
Adjusted profit	85
NCI's share: 20%	(17)
Group's share	68

(c) Minor's cost of sales

	£'000
As reported	942
Depreciation (extra)	5
Adjusted	947

(d) Minor's balance b/f

	£'000
As reported	(45)
Pre-acquisition loss	60
Post-acquin. profit b/f	15
Depreciation – extra	(5)
Adjusted profit	10

Group share: 80% of 10 = 8

Chapter 14 Accounting for partnerships

PQ 14.1 Partnership appropriation with no agreement

(a)

Capital accounts

	A	B	C		A	B	C
					£	£	£
				Balance b/f	200,000	200,000	100,000

(b)

Current accounts

	A	B	C		A	B	C
	£	£	£		£	£	£
Goods removed	20,000	–	–	Rent account	–	12,000	–
Drawings	24,000	18,000	12,000	Profit share	5,000	5,000	5,000
				Balance c/d	39,000	1,000	7,000
	44,000	18,000	12,000		44,000	18,000	12,000
Balance b/d	39,000	1,000	7,000				

(c)

Statement of income year ended 31.12.2012

	£'000	£'000
Sales		748
Less: Returns inwards		(32)
		716
Inventory – 1.1.2012	112	
Purchases	497	
Carriage inwards	12	
Goods removed by A	(20)	
Inventory – 31.12.2012	(152)	
Cost of goods sold		(449)
Gross profit		267
Distribution costs:		
Depreciation of vehicle	48	
Bad debts	18	
Advertising	18	(84)
Administrative expenses:		
Rent	36	
Depreciation of furniture	28	
Salaries	104	(168)
Net profit for the year		15
Partners –		
A	5	
B	5	
C	5	(15)

(d)

Statement of financial position as at 31.12.2012

	£'000	£'000	£'000
Non-current assets:			
Furniture	280	(140)	140
Motor vehicles	240	(120)	120
Current assets:			
Inventory		152	
Trade receivables	200		
Less: Allowance	(10)	190	
Cash and bank balance		24	366
			626
		£'000	£'000
Capital a/c			
A		200	
B		200	
C		100	500
Current a/c			
A		39 Dr	
B		1 Dr	
C		7 Dr	(47)
			453
Current liabilities:			
Trade payables		165	
Salary accrued		8	173
			626

PQ 14.2 Partnership appropriation when there is an agreement

(a)

Current accounts

	X	Y	Z		X	Y	Z
	£	£	£		£	£	£
Balance b/f	13,100			Balance b/f	–	9,000	8,000
Salaries a/c	–	15,000	10,000	Rent a/c	–	2,000	–
Interest – drawings	–	450	100	Salary	6,000	–	–
				Interest on loan	–	–	2,500
				Interest on capital	15,000	15,000	10,000
Balance c/d	114,200	81,417	45,833	Profit share	106,300	70,867	35,433
	127,300	96,867	55,933		127,300	96,867	55,933
				Balance b/d	114,200	81,417	45,833

(b)

Statement of income year ended 31 March 2012

		£	£
Sales			1,822,250
Inventory – 1.4.2011		198,000	
Purchases		1,245,000	
Inventory – 31.3.2012		(248,000)	(1,195,000)
Gross profit			627,250
Distribution costs:			
Bad debts		6,300	
Depreciation – vehicles		30,000	
Advertising		18,600	(54,900)
Administrative expenses:			
Rent		12,000	
Loss by shop-soiling		14,000	
Salary		72,000	
Depreciation of buildings		7,600	
Depreciation of furniture		21,000	
Sundry expenses		28,200	
Administrative expenses:		127,000	(281,800)
Discount allowed			(2,500)
Profit for the year			288,050
Salary to partner			(36,000)
Interest on capital:	X	15,000	
	Y	15,000	
	Z	10,000	(40,000)
Interest on drawings:	Y	450	
	Z	100	550
Profit share:	X	106,300	
	Y	70,867	
	Z	35,433	(212,600)

(c)

Statement of financial position as at 31.3.2012

		£	£	£
Non-current assets:				
Land & buildings		580,000	(37,600)	542,400
Furniture		210,000	(69,000)	141,000
Motor vehicles		150,000	(102,000)	48,000
Current assets:				731,400
Inventory			234,000	
Trade receivables		260,000		
Allowance for d. debts		(10,400)	249,600	483,600
				1,215,000
			£	£
Capital account:	X		300,000	
	Y		300,000	
	Z		200,000	800,000
Current account:	X		114,200	
	Y		81,417	
	Z		45,833	241,450
Non-current liabilities:				
Loan from Z				50,000
Current liabilities:				
Trade payables			121,400	
Bank overdraft			2,150	123,550
				1,215,000

Workings: interest on drawings:
Y: £15,000 @ 4% for 9 months = £450
Z: £10,000 @ 4% for 3 months = £100

PQ 14.3 Appropriation with a partner admission (ACCA)

Actual appropriation

Profit	£34,000
Interest:	
Checke	(£2,500)
Tikk	(£1,500)
Profit:	
Checke	(£18,000)
Tikk	(£12,000)

Projected appropriation

Profit + Senior's salary	£48,000
Salary – Senior	(£7,000)
Interest:	
Checke	(£2,500)
Tikk	(£1,500)
Senior	(£1,000)
Profit share:	
Checke	(£18,000)
Tikk	(£12,000)
Senior	(£6,000)

PQ 14.4 Sharing profits with a new partner

Statement of income (extract) year ended 30 June 2012

	6 months to 31.12	6 months to 30.6.
Profit (150 + 30 rent) apportioned	90,000	90,000
Rent to Carton	(30,000)	(6,000)
Partnership profit	60,000	84,000
Salary to Sydney	–	(12,000)
Interest on capital – Sydney	–	(13,200)
– Carton	–	(4,800)
Profit share – Sydney	(60,000)	(32,400)
– Carton	–	(21,600)

Partners' Capital accounts

	Sydney	Carton
Balance b/f	400,000	–
Goodwill – old ratio	100,000	–
Capital introduced	–	200,000
Goodwill written off	(60,000)	(40,000)
Capital as from 1.1.2012	440,000	160,000

Interest is due at 6% on capital balances for six months.

PQ 14.5 Formation of a new partnership (CAT 6)

(a)(i)

Capital a/c – A Little

	£'000		£'000
		Balance b/f	160
		Reval.-freehold	10
Transferred	205	Goodwill	35

Capital a/c – B. Sutton

	£'000		£'000
Reval. plant	15	Balance b/f	79
Transferred	89	Goodwill	25

Workings:
In the books of the partnership:

Capital accounts

	Little	Sutton		Little	Sutton
	£'000	£'000		£'000	£'000
Goodwill written off	40	20	Net assets	205	89
Balance c/d	165	69			
	205	89		205	89
			Balance b/d	165	69

(a)(ii)

Statement of fin. pos. as at 1.6.2012

	£'000	£'000
Non-current assets:		
Freehold property		120
Plant & equipment		80
Current assets:		
Inventory	27	
Receivables	18	
Cash and bank	23	68
		268

	£'000	£'000
Capital:		
Little	165	
Sutton	69	234
Trade payables		34
		268

(b) Advantages:

- Pooling together more resources (capital), varied skills, business contacts.
- The work load is shared.
- Business risks are taken together.

Disadvantages:

- Two persons having to work together, reacting to each other.
- Having to agree on work loads, sharing of profits, limiting drawings.
- Each person can, by own action, bind the other and commit to unlimited liability.

Note: Each party's goodwill is credited to his Capital account. As a result, when the books of the partnership are opened the goodwill would appear at (35 + 25) £60. This is written off in the ratio in which the partners agree to share profits and losses.

PQ 14.6 Admission of a new partner in the year and retirement of another

Appropriations – 4 months to	1.5.2010	1.9.2010	31.12.2010
	£	£	£
Profit for the period[a]	172	172	86[b]
Salary to Beta	(12)	(12)	(12)
Interest on capital – Alpha	(10)	(11)	–
Beta	(6)	(6)	(5)
Gamma	–	(7)	(5)
Profit – residual	144	136	64
Shared: Alpha	(96)	68	–
Beta	(48)	34	(32)
Gamma	–	34	(32)

	Alpha	Beta	Gamma
	£	£	£
Capital accounts			
1.1. Balance	500	300	–
1.5. Goodwill adjustment:			
Credit in old ratio	160	80	–
Debit in new ratio	(120)	(60)	(60)
Capital introduced	–	–	400
Capital balance	540	320	340
1.9. Goodwill adjustment			
Credit in old ratio	150	75	75
Debit in new ratio	–	(150)	(150)
Capital balance	690	245	265

Statement of financial position as at 31 Dec. 2010

	£'000	£'000
Land and buildings		860
Furniture		280
Inventory	214	
Receivables	484	
Bank	145	843
		1,983
	£'000	£'000
Capital accounts:		
Beta	245	
Gamma	265	510
Current accounts:		
Beta	137	
Gamma	78	215
Alpha – Loan	860	
Interest	86	946
Payables		312
		1,983

(a)

Partnership profit	£'000
Sales	1,500
Expenses:	
Cost of sales	(624)
Operating expense	(222)
Deprn-furniture	(40)
Deprn-building	(14)
Salary	(36)
Advertising	(48)
Profit	516
Profit for each period:	
£516/3	172
But in third period:	
Profit =	172
Interest to Alpha	(86)
	86

Partner's Current accounts	Alpha	Beta	Gamma
Partnership profit	172	172	86
Salary to Beta	(12)	(12)	(12)
First period to 1.5.2010:			
Interest on capital:	10	6	–
Share of profit	96	48	–
Second period to 1.9.2010:			
Interest on capital:	11	6	7
Profit share	68	34	34
Third period to end of the year			
Interest on capital:	–	5	5
Share of profit	–	32	32
Drawings	(15)	(30)	–
Balance c/f	170	137	78

Alpha's Loan: 690 + 170 = 860 + 86 interest = £946

PQ 14.7 Piecemeal dissolution of a partnership (ACCA)

(a)

Realisation account

	£	£		£	£
Land & buildings	350,000		Cash Book:		
Acc. depreciation	(50,000)	300,000	Land & building	380,000	
Plant & mach	220,000		Machinery	88,000	
Acc. depreciation	(104,100)	115,900	Motor vehicle	38,000	
Motor vehicles	98,500		Receivables	68,400	574,400
Acc. depreciation	(39,900)	58,600	Capital accounts:		
Inventory		110,600	Beta – vehicle		9,000
Trade receivables		89,400	Gamma – vehicle		14,000
Interest – Delta[b]		1,000	Gamma – inventory		120,000
Expenses		2,400	Gamma – receivable		20,000
Gain on realisation:[c]			Payables[a]		3,400
Alpha Capital	31,450				
Beta Capital	18,870				
Gamma Capital	12,580	62,900			
		740,800			740,800

Notes:

(a)

	£
Payables:	118,400
Cash Book – payment	(115,000)
Discount received	3,400

(b) Interest to Delta:
10% of 40,000 for 3 months = £1,000

(c) Gain on partnership dissolution shared among the three partners in their profit-sharing ratio.

(b)

Cash Book

	£			£	£
Balance b/f	12,600	Payables			115,000
Realisation a/c	574,400	Delta	40,000 + 1,000		41,000
Gamma Capital	35,220	Expenses			2,400
		Alpha Capital		265,050	
		Beta Capital		198,770	463,820
	622,220				622,220

(c)

Capital accounts

	Alpha	Beta	Gamma		Alpha	Beta	Gamma
Realisation a/c:	£	£	£		£	£	£
Motor vehicle	–	9,000	14,000	Balance b/f	233,600	188,900	106,200
Inventory	–	–	120,000	Realisation gain	31,450	18,870	12,580
Receivables	–	–	20,000	Cash Book	–	–	35,220
	265,050	198,770	–				
Cash Book	265,050	207,770	154,000		265,050	207,770	154,000

PQ 14.8 Disposal of a partnership as a going concern

(a) Closure of the partnership books:

Realisation account

	£'000		£'000
Property, plant	740	Investment – gain	15
Acc. depreciation	280	Trade payable	328
	460	LSB-consideration	1,080
Inventory	482		
Trade receivables	320		
Cash and bank	8		
Expenses	3		
Gain on dissolution:			
Lock	75		
Stock	50		
Barrel	25		
	1,423		1,423

LSB Ltd account

	£'000		£'000
Realisation	1,080	Investments:	
		Shares	960
		Loan Notes	100
		Cash Book	20
	1,080		1,080

Cash Book

	£'000		£'000
Balance b/f	8	Realisation	8
LSB Ltd	20	Expenses	3
Lock	64	Stock	22
		Barrel	59
	92		92

Partners' Capital accounts

	Lock	Stock	Barrel		Lock	Stock	Barrel
	£	£	£		£	£	£
Current accounts	–	8	6	Balance b/f	500	300	200
Investments taken over	95	–	–	Current account	4	–	–
LSB – shares allotted	480	320	160	Bank overdraft	32	–	–
LSB – Loan notes	100	–	–	Gain on realisation	75	50	25
Cash Book	–	22	59	Cash	64	–	–
	675	350	225		675	350	225

(b) In the books of LSB Ltd:

Purchase of business account

	£'000		£'000
Allowance for dd	16	Goodwill[a]	14
Trade payables	328	Property, plant	600
		Inventory	482
		Tr. receivables	320
Balance c/d	1,080	Cash Book	8
	1,424		1,424
		Balance b/d	1,080
Ordinary shares	800		
Share premium	160		
6% Loan Notes	100		
Cash Book	20		
	1,080		1,080

Statement of financial position as at 31 March 2012

	£'000	£'000	£'000
Property, plant			600
Goodwill			14
Inventory		482	
Trade receivables	320		
Allowance	(16)	304	786
			1,400
		£'000	£'000
Equity and reserves:			
Ordinary shares £1		800	
Share premium account		160	960
Non-current liability:			
6% Loan notes			100
Current liabilities:			
Trade payables		328	
Bank overdraft[b]		12	340
			1,400

(a) Balancing amount.
(b) £8 taken over – £20 paid.

PQ 14.9 Conversion of a partnership to a limited company

To convert the books of the partnership to those of the new company four steps are necessary:

Step (1) The balances in the capital and current accounts of the partners are closed by transfer to a Purchase of business account.

Step (2) Adjust for any asset (e.g. investment) or liability (e.g. overdraft) retained by the partners by transferring them to the Purchase of business account.

Step (3) Account for any changes in value. For example, the Property, plant with a carrying value of £460,000 is being taken over by the company at a value of £600,000. To account for the asset at the new fair value, the balance in the Accumulated depreciation account is transferred to the asset account and then the balance in the asset account is increased by £140,000, crediting that amount to the Purchase of business account. Similarly, goodwill paid for at £14,000 is recorded debiting the Goodwill account and crediting the Purchase of business account. By now the the Purchase of business a/c (see below) would record the purchase consideration owed to the partners.

Purchases of Business account

		£'000			£'000
Current – Stock	S1	8	Capital – Lock	S1	500
Current – barrel	S1	6	Capital – Stock	S1	300
Investments	S2	80	Capital – Barrel	S1	200
Allowance for dd	S2	16	Current – Lock	S1	4
			Bank Overdraft	S2	32
			Property, plant	S3	140
Balance c/d		1,080	Goodwill	S3	14
		1,190			1,190
Share capital	S4	800	Balance b/d		1,080
Share premium	S4	160			
6% Loan Notes	S4	100			
Cash Book	S4	20			
		1,080			1,080

Step (4) Account for the discharge of the purchase consideration by accounting for the allotment of shares, issue of loan notes and payment of cash.

Annotations (S1, S2 and so on) used in the answer identify each of these four steps.

PQ 14.10 Another conversion of a partnership to a limited company

Purchase of business account

	£'000		£'000
Current a/c – Berty	180	Capital a/c – Andrew	600
Current a/c – Clive	60	Capital a/c – Berty	500
Allowance[b]	9	Capital a/c – Clive	400
Balance c/d	1,501	Current a/c – Andrew	100
		Property – fair value[a]	150
	1,750		1,750
Share capital	1,000	Balance b/d	1,501
Share premium	500	Goodwill[c]	19
Cash	20		
	1,520		1,520

Statement of financial position as at 1 July 2012

	£'000	£'000	£'000
Goodwill			19
Property			550
Furniture			180
Motor vehicles			168
Current assets:			
Inventory		396	
Receivables	480		
Allowance for d.debts	(24)[b]	456	
Cash/bank[c]		15	867
			1,784

	£'000	£'000
Equity and reserves:		
Share capital of £1	1,000	
Share premium a/c	500	1,500
Current liabilities:		
Trade payables		284
		1,784

Notes:

(a) Fair valuation of property: 550 – 400 = £150

(b) Increase in allowance for d. debts: 24 – 15 = £9

(c) Cash taken over 35 less cash paid to partners 20 = £15

Chapter 15 Bank account and bank reconciliation

PQ 15.1 A basic question on the three-column Cash Book

(a)

Cash Book

Particulars	Disc	Cash	Bank	Particulars	Disc	Cash	Bank
	£	£	£		£	£	£
Balance b/f	–	50	–	Balance b/f	–	–	100
Sales a/c	–	500	–	Wages	–	100	–
Cash a/c	–	–	370	Bank	–	370	–
Q's a/c	10	–	[a]190	P's a/c	30	–	[b]270
Q's a/c	4	–	[a]96	Wages	–	–	100
				Bk charge	–	–	30
				Balance c/d	–	80	156
	14	550	656		30	550	656
Balance b/d	–	80	156				

(c)

Trial Balance as at 31 January XX

	£	£
Capital a/c	–	300
Non-current assets	350	–
P's a/c	–	100
Purchases a/c	400	–
Sales a/c[c]	–	800
Wages a/c[d]	200	–
Discount allowed	14	–
Discount received	–	30
Bank charges	30	–
Cash a/c	80	–
Bank a/c	156	–
	1,230	1,230

Notes:

(a) 200 × 90/100 = £190 & 100 × 96/100 = £96

(b) 300 × 90/100 = £270 (c) Sales: 500 + 300 = £800

(d) Wages: 100 + 100 = £200

PQ 15.2 Two-column Cash Book

Cash Book

Date	V	Particulars	F	Cash	Bank	Date	V	Chq	Particulars	F	Cash	Bank
2012				£	£	2012					£	£
16.5	?	Balance b/f		425	15,200	16.5	?	–	Stationery a/c		24	–
16.5	?	Sales a/c		345	–	16.5	?	54	Purchases a/c		–	2,400
17.5	?	Peter's a/c		–	1,250	16.5	?	–	Advertising a/c		65	–
17.5	?	Sales a/c		840	–	17.5	?	55	Rent a/c		–	1,500
17.5	?	Rick's a/c		–	1,600	17.5	?	56	Rocco a/c		–	5,800
17.5	?	Cash a/c	C	–	1,121	17.5	?	–	Bank a/c	C	1,121	–
18.5	?	Bank loan a/c		–	10,000	18.5	?	57	Motor vehicles a/c		–	22,500
18.5	?	Sales a/c		980	–	18.5	?	–	Bank a/c	C	1,000	–
18.5	?	Brown's a/c		–	1,500	18.5	?	58	Advertising a/c		–	450
18.5	?	Cash a/c	C	–	1,000	18.5	?	59	Black's a/c		–	1,650
19.5	?	Sales a/c		450	–	18.5	?	–	Vehicle maintenance		45	–
19.5	?	Tim's a/c		–	2,800	20.5	?	–	Cash a/c	C	–	500
20.5	?	Bank a/c	C	500	–	20.5	?	–	Brown's a/c		–	1,500
20.5	?	Pat's a/c		–	850	20.5	?	–	Wages a/c		850	–
20.5	?	Morris' a/c		–	1,800	20.5	?	–	Staff welfare a/c		42	–
20.5	?	Sales a/c		–	245	20.5	?	–	Bank charges a/c		–	30
						20.5	?	60	Advertising a/c		–	240
						20.5	?	–	Rates a/c		–	225
						20.5	–	–	Balance c/d		393	571
				3,540	37,366						3,540	37,366
21.5	–	Balance b/d		393	571							

PQ 15.3 Amending the Cash Book and preparing a bank reconciliation (ACCA)

Bank account

	£		£
Balance b/f	3,856	Not banked	50
Error in CB	100	Dishonoured	48
		Interest	10
		Balance c/d	3,848
	3,956		3,956
Balance b/d	3,848		

Bank reconciliation statement as at 30.6.2012

	£
Actual balance at bank	3,848
Add: cheques not presented	218
wrong credit by the bank	95
Balance as reported on bank statement	4,161

PQ 15.4 A bank reconciliation with an overdraft

Bank account

	£		£
Bank charges	14	Balance b/f	5,240
		Trade subscription	30
		Business rates	240
Balance c/d	10,296	Carry forward error	4,800
	10,310		10,310
		Balance b/d	10,296

Bank reconciliation as at 14.9.2012	£
Actual overdraft as bank	(10,296)
Deposits yet to be cleared	(11,600)
Cheques yet to be presented to the bank	18,250
Overdraft as reported on the bank statement	(3,646)

PQ 15.5 Reconciliation with a missing item

Bank account

	£		£
Jerry Ross	14,750	Balance b/f	10,240
M. Pitman	2,400	Bank charges	15
		Balance c/d	6,895
	17,150		17,150
Balance b/d	6,895		

Bank reconciliation as at 30 September 2012	£
Balance as per bank statement	5,680
Deposits awaiting clearance	4,800
Cheques yet to be presented	(3,585)
Actual balance at bank as per Cash Book	6,895

PQ 15.6 A simple true-to-life question

Bank account (in Cash Book)

	£		£
Balance b/f	7,593	Gas (DD)	145
		Bank charges	32
		Balance c/d	7,416
	7,593		7,593

Bank reconciliation as at 6 September	£
Balance per bank statement	5,062
Cheques yet to be presented[a]	(4,346)
Deposits not cleared[b]	6,700
Bank balance per cash book	7,416

Notes:

(a) Cheques not presented:

Electricity	46
Sarah & Co	110
Ulster	4,190

(b) Deposits not cleared

1,200
3,200
900
1,400

PQ 15.7 Tracing items for a bank reconciliation statement

(a) Items outstanding as at 20 May:

(i) Cheques not presented:

Chq 55 for rent	£1,500
Chq 58 for advertising	£450
Chq 59 to Black	£1,650
Chq 60 for advertising	£240
	£3,840

(ii) Cheques awaiting clearance:

Deposits made on 20 May	£3,650

(b)

Bank reconciliation statement as at 20 May	£
Balance as per bank statement	986
Deposits awaiting clearance	3,650
Cheques yet to be presented for payment	(3,840)
Bank balance as per Cash Book	796

PQ 15.8 Bank reconciliation statements as at two dates

Bank reconciliation as at 21 January 2012	
	£
O/D as per bank statement	(150)
Cheques not presented[b]	(1,840)
Deposits not cleared[a]	3,250
Bank balance as per CB	1,260

Bank reconciliation as at 26 January 2012	
	£
Bal. as per Bank statement	9,315
Deposits not cleared[c]	1,840
Cheques not presented[d]	(12,320)
o/d as per Cash Book	(1,165)

Bank account

	£		£
Dividend	1,500	Balance b/f	2,210
		Rates s/o	400
Balance c/d	1,165	Bk charges	55
	2,665		2,665
		Balance b/d	1,165

Notes:

(a) Deposit prior to 21.1 realised on 21.1. = £3,250

(b) Cheques drawn prior to 21.1. Presented after 21.1: = chq 24 for £220 and chq 25 for 1,620 = £1,840

(c) Deposits prior to 26.6 awaiting clearance: Deposits on 26.1 of £1,840.

(d) Cheques awaiting clearance on 26.1: Chq 27 for 1,360, chq 30 for 760, chq 32 for 1,500, chq 33 for 750, chq 34 for 650, chq 36 for 5,460, chq 37 for 1,280 and chq 38 for 560 = £12,320.

PQ 15.9 Focus on discounts allowed and received

Purchases ledger:

Alpha account

		£			£
2.5	Returns	1,800	1.5	Balance b/f	214,600
4.5	Bank	214,600	1.5	Purchases	16,400
			3.5	Purchases	16,400
5.5	Balance	37,500	4.5	Purchases	6,500
		253,900			253,900
				Balance b/d	37,500

Beta account

		£			£
1.5	Returns	6,500	1.5	Balance b/f	346,500
2.5	Discount[a]	3,200			
2.5	Bank a/c	336,800			
		346,500			346,500
3.5	Returns	1,500	3.5	Discount[b]	150
			5.5	Balance c/d	1,350
		1,500			1,500
	Balance b/d	1,350			

Gamma account

		£			£
5.5	Discount[c]	2,370	1.5	Balance b/f	126,400
5.5	Bank a/c	163,330	1.5	Purchases	15,600
			3.5	Purchases	11,200
			4.5	Purchases	12,500
		165,700			165,700

Sales ledger

Peter's account

		£			£
1.5	Balance b/f	139,800	5.5	Discount[d]	5,439
2.5	Sales a/c	17,500	5.5	Bank a/c	159,261
4.5	Sales a/c	7,400			
5.5	Sales a/c	11,200	5.5	Balance c/d	11,200
	Balance b/d	175,900			175,900
	Balance b/d	11,200			

Paul's account

		£			£
1.5	Balance b/f	69,300			
2.5	Sales a/c	22,200			
3.5	Sales a/c	8,200			
4.5	Sales a/c	8,600			
		108,300			

James' account

		£			£
1.5	Balance b/f	49,200	1.5	Bank a/c	47,474
3.5	Sales a/c	13,600	1.5	Discount[e]	1,726
5.5	Sales a/c	26,400			40,000
		89,200	5.5	Balance c/d	89,200
	Balance b/d	40,000			

John's account

		£			£
1.5	Balance b/f	136,800	2.5	Bank a/c	149,796
2.5	Sales a/c	18,000	2.5	Discount[f]	5,004
4.5	Sales a/c	4,500	5.5	Balance c/d	4,500
		159,300			159,300
	Balance b/d	4,500			

Mark's account

		£			£
1.5	Balance b/f	16,600	2.5	Returns	1,200
1.5	Sales a/c	6,000	2.5	Bank a/c	20,578
5.5	Bank a/c	20,578	2.5	Discount[g]	822
5.5	Journal[h]	822	5.5	Balance c/d	21,400
		44,000			44,000
	Balance b/d	21,400			

Nominal ledger:

Purchases account

		£			
5.5	P. Day Bk	78,600			

Purchases returns account

					£
			5.5	P. Ret. D.B.	9,800

Sales account

					£
			5.5	Sales D.B.	143,600

Sales returns account

		£			
5.5	S. Ret. D.B.	1,200			

Discount allowed account

		£			£
5.5	Cash Book	12,991	5.5	Journal[h]	822

Discount received account

		£			£
5.5	Journal[b]	150	5.5	Cash Book	5,570

Notes:

(a) 10% of 38,500 less return 6,500 = £3,200

(b) 10% discount received is reversed upon return of goods.

(c) 10% of (11,200 + 12,500 Only) = £2,370

(d) 5% of 17,500 + 7,400 + 3% of 139,800 = £5,439

(e) 3% of £36,700 + 5% of £12,500 = £1,726

(f) 5% of £18,000 + 3% of £136,800 = £5,004

(g) 3% of £12,400 + 5% of (£4,200 + £6,000 − £1,200)

(h) Upon dishonour of cheque, the discount allowed is reversed.

PQ 15.10 Petty cash system (AAT)

Petty Cash Book

Receipts		Payments			Analysis				
Date	Amount	Date	Particulars	Amount	Cleaning	V. Expense	Postage	Stationery	Travelling
2012	£	2012		£	£	£	£	£	£
1.5	[a]300	2.5	Postage	18	–	–	18	–	–
		3.5	Travelling	12	–	–	–	–	12
		4.5	Cleaning	15	15	–	–	–	–
		7.5	Petrol	22	–	22	–	–	–
		8.5	Travelling	25	–	–	–	–	25
		9.5	Stationery	17	–	–	–	17	–
		11.5	Cleaning	18	18	–	–	–	–
		14.5	Postage	5	–	–	5	–	–
		15.5	Travelling	8	–	–	–	–	8
		18.5	Stationery	9	–	–	–	9	–
		19.5	Cleaning	23	23	–	–	–	–
		20.5	Postage	13	–	–	13	–	–
		24.5	Servicing car	43	–	43	–	–	–
		26.5	Petrol	18	–	18	–	–	–
		27.5	Cleaning	21	21	–	–	–	–
		29.5	Postage	5	–	–	5	–	–
		30.5	Petrol	14	–	14	–	–	–
				286	77	97	41	26	45 [b]
			Balance c/d	14	*GL7*	*GL11*	*GL9*	*GL14*	*GL29* [c]
	300			300					
1.6	14								
1.6	[a]286								

Let us assume that the Petty Cash Book is treated as one of the main books of accounts – i.e. part of the double-entry system.

(a) Both amounts identified as [a] are posted from the main Cash Book.
(b) The total of each analysis column is posted to the appropriate expense account in the Nominal ledger.
(c) Stated as [c] is the folio number of the respective accounts in the Nominal ledger, written into the Petty Cash Book by the petty cashier after completing the posting.

Chapter 16 The Journal and correction of errors

PQ 16.1 Opening the books of a retail outlet

Sundries	Dr		
To Sundries			
Furniture account		£36,000	–
Motor vehicles account		£24,000	–
Inventory account		£48,000	–
Bank Loan account		–	£12,000
Capital account			£96,000
Being assets and liabilities introduced as part of capital			

PQ 16.2 Journal entries to account for transactions

Sundries	Dr		
To Bob Salmon		–	£18,000
Motor vehicles a/c		£15,000	–
Bad debts a/c		£3,000	–
Being vehicle acquired in settlement of debt			
Sundries	Dr		
To Vehicle repairs		–	£6,000
Repairs recoverable		£1,200	–
Salaries a/c		£4,800	
Being recovery of vehicle repair			
Sundries	Dr		
To Motor vehicles		–	£28,000
Drawings a/c		£15,000	–
Accumulated depreciation a/c		£13,000	–
Being vehicle taken over by proprietor			

PQ 16.3 Trial Balance difference placed in Suspense account

		Dr	Cr
(a) Suspense account	Dr	£1,200	–
To Purchases a/c		–	£1,200
Being correction of error			
(b) Lal Jason a/c	Dr	£800	–
To Suspense a/c		–	£800
Being correction of error			
(c) Return inwards a/c	Dr	£1,700	–
To Suspense a/c		–	£1,700
Being correction of error			
(d) Stationery a/c	Dr	£120	–
To Office Equipment		–	£120
Being correction of error			
(e) Rent a/c	Dr	£3,600	–
To Suspense a/c		–	£3,600
Being correction of error			
(f) Suspense a/c	Dr	£270	–
To Advertising a/c		–	£270
Being correction of error			
(g) Suspense a/c	Dr	£6,000	–
To Mike Shane a/c		–	£6,000
Being correction of error			
(h) Suspense a/c	Dr	£8,400	–
To Return outwards a/c		–	£4,200
Return inwards a/c		–	£4,200
Being correction of error		£8,400	–
(i) Joe Roger's account	Dr	£6,250	–
To Jill Rogers		–	£265
Sales a/c			£3,600
Susspense a/c			£2,385
Being correction of error			
(j) Rent account	Dr	£12,000	–
To Suspense a/c		–	£12,000
Being correction of errors			

Suspense account

	£		£
Balance b/f	4,615	Journal (b)	800
Journal (a)	1,200	Journal (c)	1,700
Journal (f)	270	Journal (e)	3,600
Journal (g)	6,000	Journal (i)	2,385
Journal (h)	8,400	Journal (j)	12,000
	20,485		20,485

PQ 16.4 Clearing the amount placed in suspense (ACCA)

		Dr	Cr
(i) Trade receivables a/c	Dr	£87	–
To Suspense a/c		–	£87
Being correction of error			
(ii) Machinery a/c	Dr	£1,200	–
To Repairs a/c		–	£1,200
Being correction of error			
(iv) Suspense a/c	Dr	£360	–
To Sales a/c		–	£360
Being correction of error			
(v) Supplier's a/c	Dr	£358	–
To Suspense a/c		–	£358
Being correction of error			
(vi) Electricity a/c	Dr	£152	–
To Electricity accrued		–	£152
Being correction of error			

Suspense account

	£		£
Balance (difference)	1,536	Journal i	87
Journal iv	360	Cash Book	720
		Journal v	358
		Cash Book	731
	1,896		1,896

Note:
Errors (iii) and (vii) would be corrected by entries in the Cash Book, which is itself a book of prime entry. Hence no journal entry is needed to correct these two errors.

PQ 16.5 Clearing the suspense to prepare financial statements (University of Oxford)

		Dr	Cr
(i) Office equipment a/c	Dr	£1,500	–
To Purchases a/c		–	£1,500
Being correction of error			
(ii) Purchases a/c	Dr	£800	–
To Trade payables a/c		–	£800
Being correction of error			
(iii) Sundry expenses a/c	Dr	£200	–
To Suspense a/c		–	£200
Being correction of error			
(iv) Suspense a/c	Dr	£1,000	–
To Purchase returns a/c		–	£1,000
Being correction of error			
(v) Suspense a/c	Dr	£500	–
To Trade receivables a/c		–	£500
Being correction of error			
(vi) Sales returns a/c	Dr	£3,200	–
To Suspense a/c		–	£3,200
Being correction of error			
(vii) Trade payables a/c	Dr	£1,300	–
To Suspense a/c		–	£1,300
Being correction of error			

Statement of income year ended 31.3.2012

	£	£
Sales[a]		44,000
Inventory	1,800	
Purchases[b]	9,900	
Inventory	(2,400)	(9,300)
Gross profit		34,700
Expenses[c]	6,400	
Depn. equip.	300	
Depn. vehicle	400	(7,100)
Net profit		27,600

(a) Sales: 47,200 – 3,200
(b) Purch: 11,600 – 1,500 + 800 – 1,000 = £9,900
(c) Sundry exp: 6,200 + 200
(d) Receivables: 3,600 – 500
(e) Payable: 2,000 – 1,300 + 800

Suspense account

Balance b/f	3,200	Journal iii	200
Journal iv	1,000	Journal vi	3,200
Journal v	500	Journal vii	1,300
	4,700		4,700

Statement of financial position as at 31.3.2012

	£	£	£
Premises			28,000
Off. equip	1,500	(300)	1,200
M. vehicle	4,300	(3,000)	1,300
Current assets:			
Inventory		2,400	
Trade receivables[d]		3,100	
Cash and bank		400	5,900
			36,400

	£	£
Capital	7,300	
Net profit	27,600	34,900
Current liabilities:		
Trade payables[e]		1,500
		36,400

PQ 16.6 Profit identified without correcting errors (CIMA)

(i) Trade receivables	Dr	£300	–
To Trade payable		–	£300
Being correction of error			
(ii) Heating & lighting	Dr	£300	–
To Suspense a/c		–	£300
Being correction of error			
(iii) G. Gordon's a/c	Dr	£800	–
To G. Goldman's a/c		–	£800
Being correction of error			
(iv) Insurance a/c	Dr	£1,000	–
To Suspense a/c		–	£500
Being correction of error			
(v) Purchases returns a/c	Dr	£700	–
To Suspense a/c		–	£700
Being correction of error			

	£
Profit as reported in the question	9,750
Heating & lighting	(300)
Purchases returns (reduced)	(700)
Revised profit for the year	8,750

Statement of fin. position as at 31.3.2012

	£	£	£
Non-current assets:			
Land & buildings	10,000	(2,000)	8,000
Plant	12,000	(3,000)	9,000
Current assets:			
Inventories		2,500	
Receivables[a]		1,800	
Prepaid rent		400	
Prepaid insurance		500	
Cash and bank		8,250	13,450
			30,450
		£	£
Capital		19,400	
Profit for the year		8,750	28,150
Current liabilities:			
Trade payables[b]		2,000	
Wages accrued		300	2,300
			30,450

Notes:
(a) Receivables: 1,500 + 300 = £1,800
(b) Payable: 1,700 + 300 = £2,000

Journal entry iv:
Usually the pair of entries in the journal should be equal. But the situation in this case is peculiar. In the Insurance a/c prepayment (which should be debit) of £500 has been brought down as a credit. To rectify that the Insurance a/c needs to be debited with £1,000. The only error in the Trial Balance, however, is that the debit balance in the Insurance a/c has been left out. As a result imbalance in the Trial Balance would be a debit shortfall of £500 which would be part of the amount placed in suspense.

PQ 16.7 Financial statements prepared without clearing suspense (AAT)

i) Shop fittings a/c	Dr	£60	–
To Suspense a/c		–	£60
Being correction of error			
ii) Suspense a/c	Dr	£6	–
To Trade payables a/c		–	£6
Being correction of error			
iii) Bank charges a/c	Dr	£21	–
To Suspense a/c		–	£21
Being correction of error			
iv) Suspense a/c	Dr	£54	–
To Trade receivables a/c		–	£54
Being correction of error			
v) Suspense a/c	Dr	£30	–
To Trade receivables a/c		–	£30
Being correction of error			

Suspense account

	£		£
Journal ii	6	Balance b/f	9
Journal iv	54	Journal i	60
Journal v	30	Journal iii	21
	90		90

S of FP as at 31 March 2012

	£	£	£
Non-current assets:			
Shop fittings[a]	1,560	(300)	1,260
Delivery van	3,200	(800)	2,400
Current assets:			
Inventory		2,917	
Trade receivables[b]		2,070	
Cash and bank		1,223	6,210
			9,870
		£	£
Capital 1.4.2011		7,500	
Profit for the year[c]		5,476	
Drawings		(5,000)	7,976
Current liabilities:			
Trade payables[d]			1,894
			9,870

Notes:
(a) Shop fitting: 1,500 + 60
(b) Receivables: 2,154 – 54 – 30
(c) Profit: 5,497 – 21
(d) Payable: 1,888 + 6

	£
Profit for the year	
As reported in the question	5,497
Bank charges	(21)
	5,476

PQ 16.8 Suspense account cleared after preparing financial statements

(a) Trade payables Dr		£34	–
To Suspense a/c		–	£34
Being correction of error			
(b) Suspense a/c Dr		£18	–
To Net Profit		–	£18
Being correction of error			
(c) Trade payables Dr		£58	–
To Suspense a/c		–	£58
Being correction of error			
(d) No journal entry			
(e) Drawings a/c Dr		£14	–
To Net profit		–	£14
Being correction of error			

Statement of fin. position – 31.12.2012

	£'000	£'000	£'000
Non-current assets	640	(280)	360
Current assets:			
Inventory		546	
Trade receivables		396	
Cash and bank		54	996
			1,356
		£'000	£'000
Capital		750	
Net profit		230	
Drawings[a]		(64)	916
Current liabilities:			
Trade payables[b]		406	
Accrued expenses		34	440
			1,356

Suspense account

	£'000		£'000
Balance	74	Journal a	34
Journal b	18	Journal c	58
	92		92

	Gross profit	Net profit
	£'000	£'000
As reported	758	198
Advertising	–	18
Carriage	(48)	–
Goods drawn	14	14
	724	230

Notes:
(a) Drawings: 50 + 14 = 64
(b) Payables: 498 – 34 – 58 = 406

Chapter 17 Control accounts

PQ 17.1 Trade receivables control and Trade payables control accounts

Trade payables control a/c

	£		£
Balance b/f	9,400	Balance b/f	225,700
Purchase returns	11,500	Purchases	264,600
Discount recd	9,450		
Cash Book	198,500		
Receiv. control	15,500		
Balance c/d	257,450	Balance c/d	11,500
	501,800		501,800
Balance b/d	11,500	Balance b/d	257,450

Trade receivables control account

	£		£
Balance b/f	348,250	Balance b/f	16,200
Sales	412,200	Sales returns	26,450
Discount – reversal	350	Disc. allowed	15,950
Dishonoured cheque	6,650	Cash Book	368,500
Collection expenses	150	Bad debts	3,800
Interest charge	225		
Balance c/d	17,200	Payable control	15,500
		Balance c/d	338,625
	785,025		785,025
Balance b/d	338,625	Balance b/d	17,200

PQ 17.2 Wrongly prepared Control account and reconciliation (London Examinations)

Trade receivable ledger control account

	£		£
Opening balance b/f	45,230	Opening balances b/f	260
Sales invoices	175,320	Cash/cheques	189,630
		Credit notes	450
		Bad debts written off	2,300
		Payable control – contra	180
Balance c/d	150	Balance c/d	27,880
	220,700		220,700
Balance b/d	27,880	Balance b/d	150

Reconciliation

	£
Balance	27,480
Add: Sophie	490
	27,970
Less credits added	240
Cr. balances netted	27,730
Add: credit c/f	150
Debit balances b/d	27,880

PQ 17.3 Errors affecting the Trade payables ledger control account (ACCA)

Corrections to Trade payables	£
(a) An invoice wrongly entered	198
(b) Cash discount not accounted for	(100)
(c) Purchases posted to wrong side	500
(d) Contra offset not entered	(400)
(e) Credit note accounted as an invoice	(120)

PQ 17.4 Reconciliation of Payables control balance with individual balances

	Control	Individual
	£	£
As reported in the question	326,200	333,600
(a) Wrong listing of debit	–	(1,700)
(b) Credit note not accounted for	(3,600)	(3,600)
(c) Contra offset posted wrongly	(16,400)	–
(d) Overcast Return outwards	3,000	–
(e) Payments not posted[a]	–	(19,100)
Correct amount of payables	309,200	309,200

Note:
a) Balancing amount.

PQ 17.5 Trade receivables control and reconciliation (ACCA)

	Control	Individual
	£	£
Balances as reported	54,358.37	54,468.59
1. Debt collection fees	–	108.81
Bad debts written off	–	(474.16)
2. Sales Day Book over-cast	(500.00)	–
3. Sales Returns DB over-cast	(10.00)	–
4. Credit balance taken as debit	–	(673.46)
5. Contra on wrong side	–	(757.64)
6. Debit balance listed wrongly	–	(27.27)
7. Dishonoured cheque	–	1,203.50
Correct receivables	53,848.37	53,848.37

PQ 17.6 Trade receivables control and reconciliation (CAT amended)

Sales Ledger Control account

	£		£
Balance b/f	39,982	Discount	9
Posting error	178	Credit note	240
		Bank a/c	325
		Balance c/d	39,586
	40,160		40,160
Balance b/d	39,586		

	£
Sum of the list of balances as stated	39,614
Invoice left out from individual a/c	288
Discount not accounted for	(9)
Credit note wrongly treated as invoice	(240)
Addition error	27
Listing a credit balance as a debit	(94)
Corrected sum of the individual a/c	39,586

£39,586 is reported as a current asset.

PQ 17.7 Reconciliation of Control account balance with sum of individual balances

	Control a/c	Sum – list
	£	£
Balances as reported in the question	330,600	322,800
(a) A sale of £12,400 posted as £21,400	–	(9,000)
(b) Overcast of the Sales Day Book	(1,600)	–
(c) Wrong accounting of dishonour	–	13,600
(d) Listing a credit balance as a debit	–	(5,600)
(e) Discount allowed – under-added	(600)	–
(f) Delivery expenses wrongly debited	(160)	(160)
(g) Bad debt not written off	(2,600)	–
(h) Casting error in customer's account	–	3,000
(i) Debt collection expenses	650	650
(j) Recovery from bad debt written off	7,200	–
(k) Recovery by offset contra	(8,200)	–
(l) Settlement discount not accounted	(225)	(225)
Actual trade receivables on S of FP	325,065	325,065

PQ 17.8 Control accounts with a Suspense account (ACCA)

(a) Suspense a/c	Dr	£4,000	–
Being correction of error[a]			
(b) Purchase ledger control	Dr	£3,600	–
To Suspense a/c		–	£3,600
Being correction of error			
(c) Trade receivables a/c	Dr	£500	–
To Sales a/c		–	£500
Being correction of error			
(d) Suspense a/c	Dr	£13,600	–
To Partner's Current a/c		–	£13,600
Being correction of error			

Suspense account

	£		£
Journal (a)	4,000	Balance b/f	14,000
Journal (d)	13,600	Journal (b)	3,600
	17,600		17,600

Note:

(a) The error is not in the ledger accounts. In the ledger, the Discount allowed account has a debit balance of £3,000 as it should and, similarly, the Discount received account has a credit balance. By switching the sides when listing these accounts in the Trial Balance, a credit shortfall of £4,000 was created and that placed in suspense. All that needs to be done is to remove that credit from the Suspense a/c.

PQ 17.9 Correction of errors and suspense account (ACCA)

Trial Balance as at 30.6.2012

	£	£
Allowance for doubtful debt	–	200
Bank overdraft	–	1,654
Capital a/c	–	4,591
Trade receivables/payables	2,983	1,637
Discount received	–	252
Discount allowed	733	–
Drawings	1,200	–
Office furniture	2,155	–
General expenses	829	–
Purchases	10,923	–
Returns inwards	330	–
Rent and rates	314	–
Salaries	2,520	–
Sales	–	16,882
Inventory	2,418	–
Accumulated depreciation	–	364
Suspense account	1,175	–
	25,580	25,580

1. Trade payables	Dr	£20	–
To Suspense a/c		–	£20
Being correction of error			
2. Furniture a/c	Dr	£173	–
To General expenses		–	£173
Being correction of error			
3. Purchases a/c	Dr	£370	–
To Suspense a/c		–	£370
Being correction of error			
4. Sales ledger control	Dr	£450	–
To Suspense a/c		–	£450
Being correction of error			
5. Capital a/c	Dr	£300	–
To Suspense a/c		–	£300
Being correction of error			
6. Sales a/c	Dr	£86	–
To Sales ledger cont.		–	£86
Being correction of error			
7. Discount allowed a/c	Dr	£35	–
To Suspense a/c		–	£35
Being correction of error			

Suspense account	
Dr balance	1,175
Cr Journal 1	(£20)
Cr Journal 3	(£370)
Cr Journal 4	(£450)
Cr Journal 5	(£300)
Cr Journal 7	(£35)

Chapter 18 Accounting for Sales tax (VAT) and payroll

PQ 18.1 Accounting for sales and sales returns with VAT – basic

(a) The entry on 27/2 records a sales return.
(b) Credit sales are deemed to be realised because the income, not received in cash, is in the form of an asset the cash realisation of which is certain.
(c)

ANG Ltd	£6,815	–
John Stores	£3,290	–
ML Ltd	£470	–
Sales	–	£9,000
VAT a/c	–	£1,575

(d) Allowance is a reduction of an asset (trade receivable) where the reduction in value is foreseen, but it would be premature to write off the asset's value.

PQ 18.2 Accounting for purchases with VAT – basic (CCEA)

The Purchases Day Book

20x6	Voucher	Customer	Folio	£	Purchases	VAT
1.4		Robert & Co	PL x	141	120	21
4.4		Robert & Co	PL x	470	400	70
				611	520	91
					NL21	NL78

Purchases account

	£'000		NL21
Purch Day Bk	520		

VAT Account

	£'000		NL78
	91		

PQ 18.3 Accounting for transactions with VAT (CIMA)

VAT account

	£		£
Purchases	4,725	Balance b/f	3,250
Expenses	420	Sales	14,875
		Purch. returns	525
Balance c/d	15,072	Bank	1,567
	20,217		20,217
		Balance b/d	15,072

Bank account

	£		£
Purch. retns	3,525	Balance b/f	6,250
VAT	1,567	M. Vehicles	9,400
Receivables	125,000	Admin exp.	2,820
		Payables	42,000
		Balance c/d	69,622
	130,092		130,092
Balance b/d	69,622		

PQ 18.4 Financial statements of a trader not familiar with VAT accounting

Statement of income year ended 30.6.2012

	£	£
Sales[a]		86,240
Inventory	8,840	
Purchases[b]	57,600	
Inventory	(14,800)	(51,640)
Gross profit		34,600
Expenses[c]	17,085	
Depn. furniture[d]	1,046	
Entertainment	440	
Depn. vehicle[e]	6,350	
Bad debt[f]	1,200	(26,121)
Profit for the year		8,479

Statement of financial position – 30.6.2012

	£	£	£
Non-current assets:			
Furniture	19,200	(5,786)	13,414
Vehicles	51,000	(13,850)	37,150
Current assets:			
Inventory		14,800	
Receivables		5,730	
VAT recoverable[g]		800	
Cash and bank		815	22,145
			72,709

	£	£
Capital	60,000	
Profit for the year	8,479	68,479
Current liabilities:		
Trade payables	4,230	
VAT payable[g]	200	4,430
		72,709

Notes:
(a) Sales: 101,332 × 100/117.5
(b) Purchases: 67,680 × 100/117.5
(c) Depreciation – furniture:

10% of (11,200 – 4,740)	£646
10% of 8,000 for 6 months	£400

(d) Expenses: 20,075 × 100/117.5
(e) Depreciation on vehicles:

20% of (27,500 – 7,500) =	£4,000
20% of 23,500 × 6 months	£2,350

(f)

Bad debts: written on	£1,410
VAT recoverable	(£210)

(g)

VAT on sales	£15,092
VAT on purchases	(£10,080)
VAT on furniture	(£1,400)
VAT on bad debts	(£210)
VAT on expenses	(£2,990)
VAT paid	(£212)
VAT recoverable	£200

PQ 18.5 Payroll accounting (CIMA)

(a)

Salaries and wages account

	£		£
Bank a/c – net pay	34,000	Journal (see below)	56,700
PAYE – deducted from employees	16,500		
NIC – deducted from employees	2,900		
NIC – employer's contribution	3,300		
Total expense	56,700		56,700

Journal entries:

Dr. Customers' accounts	£41,500	
Dr. Non-current assets	£10,500	
Dr. Administration expenses	£4,700	
Cr Salaries and wages a/c		£56,700
Being allocation of salaries and wages		

Workings

	£	£
Customers' accounts		
Normal: 8,180 × £5	40,900	
Overtime: 80 × £7/50	600	41,500
Non-current assets:		
Normal: 1.350 × £5	6,750	
Overtime: 500 × £7/50	3,750	10,500
Non-productive hours: 940 × £5		4,700
		56,700

(b) The costs incurred building in-house non-current assets result in an asset appearing in the Statement of financial position. It is important that costs are not capitalised unfairly avoiding the cost being expensed. However, IAS16 requires the cost of own labour to be capitalised.

PQ 18.6 Accounting for pay-sheet recoveries and National Insurance

Statement of income for the year ended 31.3.2012

	£'000
Sales	4,990
Cost of sales	(3,642)
Gross profit	1,348
Salaries[a]	(385)
Admin. expenses	(486)
Distribution cost	(263)
Net profit	214

Statement of financial position as at 31.3.2012

	£'000	£'000
Non-current assets:	660	
Acc. depreciation	(238)	422
Current assets:		
Inventory	614	
Receivables	512	
Staff loan	18	
Cash and bank	23	1,167
		1,589

	£'000	£'000
Capital	900	
Profit	214	1,114
Current liabilities:		
Trade payables	468	
National Insurance	7	475
		1,589

Notes:

(a)

	£
Salaries: paid	320
Loan recovery	2
NI employee[b]	28
NI employer[c]	35
	385

(b) NI Employee = (320 + 2) × 8/92 = £28

(c) NI Employer = 10% of 320 + 2 + 28 = £35

PQ 18.7 Involves VAT and payroll

(a)

Three-column Cash Book

Date	V	Particulars	F	Disc.	Cash	Bank	Date	V	Chq	Particulars	F	Disc.	Cash	Bank
14.9		A. Barton		20	–	380	1.9		–	Balance b/d		–	–	347
8.9		C. Dodd		30	–	1,170	10.9		?	Swinburn		60	–	1,140
22.9		C. Dodd		–	–	799	15.9		?	VAT		–	–	832
25.9		G. Gray		–	–	170	17.9		?	P. Taylor		20	–	380
							20.9		?	Motor vehicle		–	–	11,515
30.9		Balance				13,695	30.9		–	Wages (net)[a]		–	–	2,000
				50		16,214						80		16,214
							1.1			Balance b/d				13,695

Note:

(a) Net wages paid

Gross wages	£2,500
PAYE	(£300)
NI deducted	(£200)
Net wages	£2,000

(b)

A. Barton account

		£			£
1.9	Balance b/d	400	3.9	Sales retn DB	47
3.9	Sales DB	188	4.9	Cash Book	380
			4.9	CB – discount	20
			30.9	Balance c/d	141
		588			588
1.10	Balance b/d	141			

C. Dodd's account

		£			£
1.9	Balance b/d	1,200	8.9	Sales return DB	141
8.9	Sales DB	940	8.9	Cash Book	1,170
12.9	Sales DB	423	8.9	CB – discount	30
			22.9	Cash Book	799
			30.9	Balance c/d	423
		2,563			2,563
1.10	Balance b/d				

F. Gray's account

		£			£
1.9	Balance b/d	340	25.9	Cash Book	170
			25.9	Bad debts	170
		340			340

Allowance for doubtful debts account

		£			£
25.9	F. Gray	170	1.9	Balance b/f	450
?	Bad debts	240	30.9	Income state.	857
30.9	Balance c/d	897			
		1,307			1,307

Calculation of allowance for doubtful debts needed:

30 to 60 days: £7,500 – £200 contra = £7,300 @ 5% =	£365
60 to 90 days: £3,600 @ 10%	£360
Over 90 days: £1,100 – £240 written off = £860 @ 20%	£172
	£897

PQ 18.8 Revising the Statement of financial position (ACCA)

Workings

	Retained	Payables	Inventory	Bank	Stationery	Prepayments	Fixtures
In question	9,000	7,100	9,500	4,900			24,000
(i) Sale or return		(4,000)	(4,000)				
(ii) Unpresented cheques	(160)			(400)		240	
(iii) Inventory	7,555		7,555				
(iv) Stationery treated as non-current					1,000		(1,000)
(v) See Note a							
(vi) Discount received not recorded	340	(340)					
Amounts used in the answer	16,735	2,760	13,055	4,500	1,000	240	23,000

Statement of financial position as at 31 March 2012

	£'000	£'000	£'000
Non-current assets:			
Freehold property	20,000	(3,000)	17,000
Fixtures and Fittings	23,000	(9,000)	14,000
Current assets:			
Inventory		13,055	
Trade receivables		7,700	
Prepayments		240	
Stationery		1,000	
Bank balance		4,500	26,495
			57,495

	£'000	£'000
Equity and reserves:		
Ordinary shares of £1	30,000	
Share premium a/c	5,000	
Retained earnings	16,735	51,735
Current liabilities:		
Trade payables	2,760	
Dividend declared	3,000	5,760
		57,495

Notes:

	£'000	£'000
Results of inventory count 6 April		9,500
Less: Purchases after year-end	4,700	
Less: Returns	(180)	(4,520)
Add: Sales after year-end	16,000	
Less: Returns	(300)	
Less: Profit margin @ 25% GP ratio	(3,925)	11,775
Under-casting in inventory sheets		300
Inventory sheets undercast		17,055
Less: Goods with us on sale or return basis		(4,000)
Closing inventory – 31 March		13,055

PQ 18.9 Correction of errors involving the Suspense account (CIMA)

(a) Journal				(b)
(i) Suspense a/c	Dr	£492	–	Profit improves by £492
To Sales returns a/c		–	£246	
Sales a/c		–	£246	
Being correction of posting sales to debit of Sales returns a/c				
(ii) Suspense a/c	Dr	£45	–	No impact on profit
To Trade receivables		–	£45	
Being correction of a sale for £1,249 posted as £1,294				
(iii) No journal entry required				Profit reduces by £37
(iv) VAT a/c	Dr	£45	–	Profit improves by £45
To Purchases a/c		–	£45	
Being accounting for recovery of VAT				
(v) Payables a/c	Dr	£258	–	No impact on profit
To Receivables a/c		–	£258	
Being correction of accounting for offset by contra				
(vi) Business rates a/c	Dr	£2,250	–	Profit reduced by £2,250
To Accrued expenses a/c		–	£2,250	
Being accounting for accruals				
(vii) Carriage inwards a/c	Dr	£52	–	No impact on profit
To Carriage outwards a/c		–	£52	
Being correction of error of Commission				
(viii) Bad debts a/c	Dr	£40	–	Profit reduced by £40
To Trade receivables a/c		–	£40	
Being write off of a trade receivable				
(ix) Sundries	Dr			Profit improves by £5,250 difference between van expense and loss on disposal
To Sundries				
Motor vehicle a/c		£4,050	–	
Loss on vehicle disposal		£150	–	
Suspense a/c		£5,400	–	
Motor van expenses a/c		–	£5,400	
Supplier of vehicle a/c		–	£4,200	
Being correction for erroneous accounting on trade-in				

Chapter 19 Conceptual framework of accounting

PQ 19.1 The accruals and matching rule

(a) *Reporting unsold purchases as an asset:*
- To match the sales income with the cost of goods that have in fact been sold, the cost of those not sold needs to be removed.
- The goods remaining unsold would be an asset, to be so reported on the Statement of financial position because they are within the control of the entity, as a result of past transaction (i.e. purchase) and are expected to bring future economic benefit next year when they are sold. More importantly the cost of the goods remaining unsold needs to be matched with the income from selling these goods in the next accounting period.

(b) *Accounting for expenses remaining unpaid:*
The accruals concept requires that the results of performance within an accounting period should be determined by comparing accomplishments in the period (whether matched by cash inflows or not) with the efforts made for the purpose as measured by expenses (whether paid for or not). Hence unpaid expenses (on rent, electricity and gas) have to be accounted for.

(c) *Deferral of income yet to be earned*
Under the accruals rule, income is recognised only to the extent earned within the period. Though £36,000 is received in the period, only a third of it, relating to the current period, is earned by the reporting date. The remainder is, therefore, accounted for as a deferred income and stated on the Statement of financial position along with liabilities, though there is no intention to repay.

PQ 19.2 The governing accounting concept

(i) Prudence concept
(ii) Prudence concept/matching (accruals concept)
(iii) Prudence concept/Non-aggregation concept
(iv) Separate entity concept
(v) Materiality concept
(vi) Matching/accruals concept
(vii) Consistency concept
(viii) Realisation and prudence

PQ 19.3 Conflict among accounting concepts

(a) *Instances of conflicts between concepts:*
- *Where the matching concept conflicts with the materiality concept*
An office stapler costing £4 is written off as part of stationery in the year it was bought, based on the materiality threshold test. Theoretically, because it would remain useful over several years, an appropriate portion of its cost should have been deferred to these years, in accordance with the matching rule. In practice, of course, this would not happen.
- *Where the materiality concept conflicts with the objectivity concept*
The materiality threshold amount is a subjective decision. When ICI decides to round off each item in its financial statements to the nearest million pounds, it makes a subjective decision that amounts less than a million are not material to it; whereas it is material to most other companies. Similarly an item of office equipment costing say £1,000 may be material to and therefore capitalised by one entity and written off by another.
- *Where the matching concept conflicts with the prudence concept*
The matching concept requires that the cost of developing a product which is expected to be marketed in a future year should be capitalised – reported as an asset in the year the cost is incurred and written off as expenditure in the years when the product generates sales income. The prudence convention, however, requires the cost to be immediately written off because the product's ability to generate income would be a reality only when it happens and should not be anticipated until then.
- *Where the entity concept conflicts with substance over form concept*
If a house belonging to entity 'A' is leased to entity 'B', the separate entity concept requires that the house should appear as an asset on A's Statement of financial position; whereas the substance over form concept requires that the house should appear as an asset in B's Statement of financial position as well.

(b) Resolving the conflict of concepts: When two or more concepts are at conflict, the concept chosen is the one that fairly reports the substance of the transaction or event. For example, the decision to write off as expense an office stapler costing £4 is based on the materiality test, in preference to the matching or accruals concept, although the latter is the fundamental concept.

PQ 19.4 Accounting concepts and treatment of transactions (ACCA)

(a) (i) *Expense*: is an outflow of business resource which cannot be recognised as an asset either because it is not expected to yield economic benefits after the period-end or its cost is immaterial.
(ii) *Prudence*: is the exercise of caution when confronted with conditions of uncertainty so that income and assets are not overstated and expense and liability are not understated.
(iii) *Objectivity*: (meaning neutrality) means freedom from bias when accounting and reporting financial information so that the information could be relied on for decision making.
(iv) *Matching or accruals*: is the accounting concept that requires the performance and efforts made in each accounting period should be properly matched for identifying the results of that accounting period, accounting for each in accordance with when it occurred rather than when the resulting cash inflow or outflow occurred.

(b) The Board of directors
.... (name of the client)

Dear Sirs,

Re: accounting for the invoice dated xxxxx from Marketing Services plc

Our advice is as follows:

(i) The monthly fees for general advice (£3,000) should be expensed as the services relate to three months ending by the period-end.

(ii) The colour photocopier supplied on 1.10.2010 has a guaranteed life of five years. Of that period only three months fall within the current accounting period. The remainder of the cost is expected to yield future economic benefit for four years and nine months after the period-end. Therefore, that portion (£10,000 × 57/60 = £9,500) should be reported as an asset (capitalised).

(iii) The cost (£5,000) for services yet to be provided should not be accounted for at all because the corresponding liability is yet to arise.

(iv) £50,000 is on an advertising campaign already completed by the period-end. Therefore the liability should be recognised as a current liability. The benefit of that cost cannot be recognised as an asset, even if some benefit may be expected in the future, because there is no assurance of such benefit flowing in. On the basis of prudence, the cost should be written off as an expense.

Please don't hesitate to contact us if you have any further queries.

Chapter 20 Revenue recognition

PQ 20.1 The critical event approach

(a) *Ajit's claim of earning a profit of £128,850 for the year is unacceptable because:*
Ajit should account for his income using the critical event approach. Normally, the critical event in a trading business like his is the sale of furniture. Section 18 of the Sale of Goods Act 1979 does not require delivery of goods as essential for recognising a sale. Yet, if Ajit wishes to abide by the practice common among traders in the UK, he should recognise sale only at the point of delivery. Accordingly his profit for the year would be £500 per suite on 190 suites delivered = £95,000. At the point the sale is made, all major uncertainties (such those in respect of saleability and the amount it can be sold for) are resolved and further uncertainties remaining (recoverability and after-sales care) are capable of being reliably estimated.

(b) *Revenue recognition on unsold goods is not permitted because:*

- The accretion approach to revenue recognition is not available for application to trading transactions.
- Prudence concept would deter any income being recognised until the major uncertainty on finding a buyer is resolved (notwithstanding the fact that, for his products, the prospects are excellent).

Exceptionally, however, Ajit could recognise profit on the units yet to be sold, in the following circumstances:

- If his product qualifies for recognition as a construction contract (i.e. contract specifically negotiated for the construction of an asset) and its outcome can be reliably estimated, then under IAS 11 the revenue and profit can be recognised on the percentage of completion method, by reference to the stage of completion by the date of the Statement of financial position.
- If Ajit's production is based on a firm order: If goods are produced to order, the critical event triggering the revenue recognition is the completion of production. Hence, if Ajit produces his units only on the basis of firm orders to produce these units, the uncertainties in respect of saleability and the sale price would be resolved at the point of receiving the order – so that income may be recognised at the point the production is completed, but prior to sale, delivery or invoicing. Income on the 50 units yet to be completed cannot be recognised.

PQ 20.2 Approaches to revenue recognition (ACCA)

(a) The term 'revenue recognition' identifies the point and the amount at which revenue (income) is recognised and accounted for.

(b) A policy on revenue recognition could be:
   (i) magazine subscription received by a publisher, the point at which production of magazine is completed;
   (ii) the sale of cars on credit terms, the delivery of the car to the customer;
   (iii) work in progress on a construction contract, the completion of each stage of the contract.

PQ 20.3 Recognising revenue at different stages (ACCA)

(a) The general rule accountants apply is to recognise revenue on the transactions approach, at that critical point of the earning cycle when (i) the income may be regarded substantially as earned and (ii) any remaining uncertainties can be estimated with sufficient degree of accuracy so that they could be taken into account when measuring the revenue.

(b) In the situation stated in the question revenue could justifiably be recognised at stage F because by then most uncertainties (such as whether goods can be produced, at what cost, whether a buyer can be found and at what price) would all have been resolved and remaining uncertainties (on the cost of delivery, whether the debt can be recovered and the cost of any after-sales care) can be estimated fairly accurately on the basis of past experience.

(c) The gross profit of a unit (at stage F) is £130 (i.e. difference between the sale price and the cost to place the item sold in the location and in the condition in which it was sold). £10 the cost of delivery (carriage outwards) is not part of the cost of sales.

(d) Revenue recognition may be delayed until stage H, if recovery of the sale price is significantly in doubt, as it would be in the case with export sales to countries with exchange control restrictions.

(e) Arguments in favour of recognising revenue at appropriate successive amounts at stages B, C and D could be made where (i) the production is against an already received order, (ii) the net realisable value at each of these stages can be reliably established and (iii) the costs to be incurred in the remaining stages can be estimated accurately.

Chapter 21 Accounting for tangible non-current assets

PQ 21.1 Distinguishing an asset from an expense (ACCA)

(a) A screwdriver does appear to qualify for recognition as an asset because (i) it is resource within the control of the business, (ii) the control has been acquired from a past transaction i.e. either paid or promised to pay and (iii) there is an expectation of future economic benefits either by creating cash inflow (e.g. producing items for sale) or by reducing cash outflow (e.g. not having to pay outsiders for repair). However, because the cost involved (£15) is immaterial it would rather be expensed.

(b) A machine hired by the business would qualify to be an asset if the terms of the hire bestows on the business most of the rewards of owning the business (such as uninterrupted use for most of its economic life and entitlement to substantially all of what the machine produces) as well as the related risks (such as having to bear the cost of repair, maintenance, insurance, obsolescence and idle capacity).

(c) A good reputation of the business with its customers may apparently meet all three criteria for asset recognition, but is not recognised nor reported as an asset because (i) the expectation of future benefit in the form of continued custom may not be assured and (ii) its cost or current value cannot be reliably established.

PQ 21.2 Identification of the cost of assets (ACCA)

(a)

Premises account

	£
Valuation fees[a]	1,500
Acquisition[a]	90,000
Solicitor's fees[a]	3,000
Architect's fees[a]	8,700
Wages cost[a]	11,600
Materials[a]	6,800
Subcontractors[b]	69,400
	191,000

Plant account

	£
Press A: Cost[a]	87,300
Transport[a]	2,900
Installation[c]	2,310
Press B: Cost[a]	105,800
Installation[c]	2,550
	200,860

(b) Expenses excluded from the cost are:
(i) Cash discount on Press B, this being an amount earned by early payment.
(ii) Similarly interest (£120,000–105,800) paid for delaying the payment on Press B.

Notes:
(a) All expenses in placing the asset in the location and the condition for use are included in its cost.
(b) The cost of putting the premises in a condition for use needed demolition work.
(c) The cost of hiring the lifting gear is part of the cost of installing the plant.

PQ 21.3 The case of an intercontinental transport company

(a) The criterion for capitalising is whether the cost is for a resource which qualifies (i.e. meets the three criteria) for recognition as an asset. Otherwise they should be expensed.

(b) The asset accounts will appear as follows:

Freehold land & buildings a/c

	£
Cash bk – price of property	585,500[a]
Cash bk – compensation	25,000[b]
Cash bk – stamp fees	2,500[c]
Cash bk – registration fees	300[c]
Cash bk – conveyancing	2,500[c]
Cash bk – boundary wall	14,500[c]
Cash bk – structural change	145,500[d]
Cash bk – shatterproof glass	17,800[d]
Cash bk – challenge to title	37,400[e]
Cash bk – parking compound	126,200[d]
	957,200

Plant and machinery a/c

	£
Cash bk – cost of machine	214,500[a]
Cash bk – freight/insurance	12,400[f]
Cash bk – duty	46,500[f]
Cash bk – re-inforcing floor	12,600[d]
Cash bk – iron pedestal	8,800[d]
Cash bk – test runs	1,100[g]
	295,900

Notes:
(a) The cost of acquiring the asset (both freehold and machinery) is capitalised because acquisition is the past transaction placing the resource within control and creating an expectation of future economic benefits for many years.
(b) Compensation for previous owner's re-location is essential for placing the property in a condition in which it can be used. Therefore it is capitalised.
(c) Costs of securing the title to the property, building the security fence to deny others access to the property, and cost of conveyancing are all essential costs incurred to place the property in a condition in which it can be used.
(d) Costs of structural alteration, installation of shatter-proof glass, reinforcing the floor and building a pedestal are necessary for placing the assets in a condition in which they can be used.
(e) Cost of defending the title, as part of the buying process, is capitalised because until the title is legally established the property is not in a condition for use.
(f) Freight, insurance and duty are costs incurred to bring machinery to the location of intended use.
(g) Cost of test runs is capitalised only on the assumption that this expense is an essential prerequisite for placing the machine in a condition for use.
(h) On the other hand, recurrent expenses (such as on colour washing, replacing bulbs, lubrication machinery) are expensed; and so is the cost of the moving-in celebration and re-location after commencing the use of the asset.

PQ 21.4 Costs incurred subsequent to commencement of asset usage

(a) Cost of computerising the designing of machine tools (£246,500) should be capitalised because the cost obviously has been incurred in anticipation of future economic benefits in the form of significant improvements to cash flows arising from the speed and precision designing of machine tools.
(b) The cost of modifications to the machinery, to meet changes in customer needs, is capitalised because it is expected to enhance the sale revenue (by 50%) substantially beyond the earlier assessed levels.
(c) The cost of repairing damage from vandalism should be written off because it would merely restore the performance of the asset to previously assessed levels.
(d) The refurbishment cost may be capitalised because it is a major overhaul that significantly extends the duration of economic life and hence the economic benefits from the conveyor belts which have been consumed and the cost of the refurbishment should be written off in the accounting periods over its remaining useful economic life.

Chapter 22 Accounting for intangible assets and government grants

PQ 22.1 Accounting for intangibles

To be reported as an intangible asset the resources need to be 'identifiable' and for recognition as an asset they must meet all three of the capitalisation criteria, these being (a) within the entity's control, (b) future economic benefits are at least probable and (c) reliable estimation of cost or value.

(a) *Brand name acquired as part of a business combination*: This should be capitalised because firstly it is identifiable since it can be sold, transferred or assigned without selling the whole business and secondly, it satisfies all three asset recognition criteria – namely, it will remain within control of the acquirer, is expected to bring future economic benefit (it is stated in the Standard that flow of benefit is a rebuttable presumption when the asset has a finite life) and it is assumed the cost is either established in an open market (a reputed brand name) or is what would have been paid for it, had it been acquired separately.
(b) *The patented manufacturing process*: This too should be capitalised because it is a separately acquired intangible. Firstly it is identifiable – as its acquisition is based on a contract with the patent owner; and secondly, it meets with all three of the asset recognition criteria. It is within control because the patented right can be legally enforced; future economic benefits are expected to flow both because it is said to have significant market potential and because if there were no future benefit flow it would not have been acquired; and the cost is reliably identified at the amount paid for the acquisition.
(c) *Gifts and parties to maintain customer loyalty*: This cannot be capitalised because firstly it is not an identifiable asset and secondly it does not measure up to the capitalisation criteria because (a) there is no way of controlling customer loyalty, (b) it is difficult to establish whether flow of future economic benefits is probable and (c) a reliable estimate of its cost cannot be established because it is difficult to distinguish costs incurred to build up customer attachment from costs of other activities.
(d) *Cost of research to improve customer satisfaction*: This cannot be capitalised because this is an expense incurred in the research phase (as distinguished from the development phase) and therefore capitalisation is not permitted by the Standard. Like any other home-grown intangibles, it too cannot be capitalised mainly because there is no way of establishing that economic benefit will flow from it.

PQ 22.2 Accounting for research and development costs (ACCA 1)

(a) Calculation:

	Q	R	Total
	£'000	£'000	£'000
Balance b/f	1,000	400	1,400
Acc. amortisation	(200)	–	(200)
Cash	–	250	250
Amortisation[a]	(100)	–	(100)
	700	650	1,350

Equipment:

	£
Balance b/f	300
Cash	180
Depn.[b]	(136)
WDV	344

Include in cost of sales

	£'000
Research cost[c]	140
Amortisation	100
Depn – equip.	136
	376

Notes:
(a) 10% of £1,000 = £100
(b) 20% of (500 + 180)
(c) Project S is still a research project and hence is expensed.

(b) Disclosures:

Movement of development cost	Cost	Amortis.	WDV
	£'000	£'000	£'000
Balance b/f	1,400	(200)	1,200
Additions	250	–	250
Amortisation in year to 30.9.2011	–	(100)	(100)

Notes: Total development costs expensed in the year, within cost of sales, is £376,000.

PQ 22.3 Costs in research phase and development phases

(a) Advice:
1. The costs on all items mentioned from 1 to 5 have to be written off because it is the requirement of IAS38 that all expenses on the research phase should be written off because it would not be possible to demonstrate that future economic benefits will flow.

2. The cost of searching for a computer hardware capable of operating 2,000 leagues under the seabed is also an expense within the research phase which should also be written off. However, the cost of producing the prototypes should be capitalised, because it is a cost incurred in the development phase, provided the six conditions stated in IAS 38, to establish the cost and the recoverability of £48,000 incurred, are all complied with.
3. £78,800 incurred on quality testing the products prior to delivery and £33,100 on corrective and remedial actions on products sold, during the warranty period, are part of the recurrent operational expenses which have to be written off.

Statement of financial position as at 30 June 2012

	£'000
Non current assets	2,050
Development costs	48
Current assets	824
	2,922
	£'000
Share capital	4,000
Retained loss	(1,384)
	2,616
Current liabilities	306
	2,922

(b) The Statement of financial position based on the advice is shown above.

PQ 22.4 Accounting for grants

Statement of income year ended 31.12.2011

	£	£
Donations & contributions		69,800
Asset-related grant[a]	25,000	6,300
Income-related grant	(6,250)	
Deferred income[b]		18,750
Depreciation – premises[a]		(5,600)
Staff salary[c]	10,000	
Amount recovered[c]	(8,000)	(2,000)
Cost of free meals	21,520	
Expenses shared[d]	(13,125)	(8,395)
Administrative expenses		(9,440)
Charitable activities		(41,660)
Surplus in the year		27,755

Statement of financial position as at 31 December 2011

	£	£	£
Freehold premises	420,000	(5,600)	414,400
Due from Hunger Relief[d]			1,875
Balance at bank			230
			416,505
		£	£
Accumulated fund b/f		72,200	
Surplus for the year		27,755	99,955
Deferred income:			
Capital grant[a]		308,700	
Revenue grant[b]		6,250	
Salary refund[c]		1,600	316,550
			416,505

Notes:

(a) Asset-related grant is accounted on the deferral method, treating 2% as income, in line with the depreciation policy on the related asset (315,000 × 2/100).

(b) Income-related grant is from the Borough's financial year ending on 31 March 2012. Only 75% of that period corresponds with the Society's accounting period. Accordingly 25% of the grant is deferred.

(c) Salary is payable for ten months @ £1,000 p.m. 80% of that amount, received as refund, is matched with the expense and the remainder reported as a deferred income.

(d) In keeping with the agreement relating to free meals £1,875 recoverable from Hunger Relief is reported as an asset.

Chapter 23 Liability, provision, contingency and post reporting-date events

PQ 23.1 Accounting for liabilities, provisions and contingencies (ACCA amended)

(a) IAS 37 requires that to be identified as a provision the obligation should first qualify for recognition as a liability (meet all four liability recognition criteria) and then there should be uncertainty relating to amount or timing or both. To be identified as a contingent asset or liability there needs to be uncertainty as regards the existence of the asset/liability. Whether future economic benefits will flow in (in the case of assets) or flow out (in the case of liabilities) should depend on one or more future events which are outside the control of the entity.

(b) Accounting for the specific items mentioned:
   (i) The auction room has confirmed that the painting will be sold for £1 million. Yet it is prudent to treat the benefit to be received as 'probable' and disclose the contingent asset as a Note. It could be accounted for as an asset when the sale has been made.
   (ii) Expert opinion from legal advisers is that the pedestrian's claim for £200,000 will succeed. The obligation to pay has arisen from a past obligating event, there is no alternative and the amount has been reliably estimated. Therefore, the claim should be accounted for as a liability. The counter-claim for £100,000 from the subcontractor remains a possibility (can). It is a contingent asset which needs to be disclosed.
   (iii) The defeated snooker player's claim for the lost winnings of £1 million, blaming the defeat on the snooker table being not level, is speculative. Its chance of success seems remote. The claim may be ignored.

PQ 23.2 Whether accrued liability, provision and contingent liability

(a) *Premature cancellation of franchise*: The obligating event is the cancellation of franchise, which took place on 30.9.2011. Hence as at 31.12.2011 there is an obligation to transfer economic benefit in the future, arising from a past event, and, in accordance with legal opinion, the transfer of economic benefit is probable. A reliable estimate of the amount is made for liquidated damages at £300,000. Taking into account the element of uncertainty in the amount, a provision is made for £300,000 rather than account for it as accrued liability. Because the obligation to pay any punitive damages is yet to be confirmed by an uncertain event (court's verdict) the claim for punitive damages is reported as a contingent liability.

(b) *Damages for wrongful dismissal*: Because the company apparently is justified in doing what it did, the obligating event is not the dismissal on 30 November 2011, but the court's confirmation of the obligation to pay further damages. It seems remote (5%) that the court will uphold the claim. Therefore the claim is ignored.

(c) *The claims relating to defects in goods sold*: The claims in respect of a defective batch of goods convert the sales income into a liability. Accordingly, the Sales account is debited with £300,000 and the Claims for refund account credited. The obligating event is the sale of defective goods; the obligation to make refunds appears certain and the amount is measured with reliability. Since a counter-claim against the supplier is only a possibility, the claim, though actively pursued, cannot be either accounted for or disclosed in a Note. The cost of these goods (£300,000 × 100/125 = £240,000) is transferred from Cost of goods sold (trading account) to a loss on defective goods account (Statement of income).

(d) *Claims from regulatory authority*: Sentiments (such as the protection of image or reputation) and potential consequences cannot sway the need to account accurately to convey a true and fair view of the entity's performance and position. Notwithstanding the entity's confidence in its defences, it is unlikely that investigations would have commenced without a basis. But this is a possible obligation, the outcome of which is to be confirmed by uncertain events, and it is not possible to make a reliable estimate of the amount of future economic benefits, which may have to be transferred. In the circumstances the entity should disclose the position in a Note.

PQ 23.3 Accounting for contingent liability and assets (ACCA – amended)

(a) IAS 37 is relevant because each of these cases concerns a liability, contingent liability or contingent asset.

(b) The accounting treatment suggested is as follows:

CASE P: Our claim for £10,000 is a contingent asset; with 8% chance of success it should be ignored.

CASE Q: Our claim for £20,000, another contingent asset, should be disclosed because success is probable (92%).

CASE R: £30,000 claim against us is a contingent liability. With 8% chance of success, it is disclosed as possible.

CASE S: £40,000 claim against us, with 92% chance of success, needs to be recognised as a liability: but the amount being in doubt, the liability should be identified as a provision.

(c) Journal entry needed:

Compensation a/c	Dr	£40,000	–
To Provision for compensation		–	£40,000
Being accounting for a claim			

(d) Notes (for disclosure):

(i) A claim by the company for a compensation of £20,000 is awaiting resolution by courts.

(ii) A claim for £30,000 compensation from the company awaits legal resolution.

PQ 23.4 Post reporting-date event

(a) The shop-soiling of inventory, though discovered in the period after the date of the Statement financial position, occurred prior to period-end. It is an adjusting event which reduces the inventory and the profit.

(b) The receiver's letter confirms that as at the reporting date the receivables are worth only 10% of value reported.

(c) Investments had a market value on the reporting date of (90,000 @ .80p =) £72,000. Hence it is not an adjusting event. However, the loss should be disclosed in a Note, if material.

Statement of financial position as at 30 June 2012			
	£	£	£
Non-current assets	364	(112)	252
Current assets:			
Inventory (826 – 12)		814	
Receivables (468 – 45)		423	
Investments		112	
Cash and bank		34	1,383
			1,635
		£	£
Capital		1,000	
Profit (110 – 12 – 45)		53	1,053
Current liabilities:			
Trade payables			582
			1,635

PQ 23.5 Again post reporting-date event

(a) This is a non-adjusting post reporting-date event, which requires disclosure because it affects profitability and liquidity.

(b) The event after the reporting date confirms that there is no asset as at the reporting date. It is, therefore, an adjusting event.

(c) Employee's claim is probably going to be successful. All criteria for recognition as a liability are met, except that it is not possible to estimate the amount. Disclose.

(d) The claim may be ignored in view of the legal opinion that it is unlikely to succeed.

Index